Lecture Notes in Computer Science   10289

Commenced Publication in 1973
Founding and Former Series Editors:
Gerhard Goos, Juris Hartmanis, and Jan van Leeuwen

More information about this series at http://www.springer.com/series/7409

Aaron Marcus · Wentao Wang (Eds.)

Design, User Experience, and Usability

Designing Pleasurable Experiences

6th International Conference, DUXU 2017
Held as Part of HCI International 2017
Vancouver, BC, Canada, July 9–14, 2017
Proceedings, Part II

 Springer

Editors
Aaron Marcus
Aaron Marcus and Associates, Inc.
Berkeley, CA
USA

Wentao Wang
Baidu, Inc.
Beijing
China

ISSN 0302-9743   ISSN 1611-3349   (electronic)
Lecture Notes in Computer Science
ISBN 978-3-319-58636-6   ISBN 978-3-319-58637-3   (eBook)
DOI 10.1007/978-3-319-58637-3

Library of Congress Control Number: 2017939729

LNCS Sublibrary: SL3 – Information Systems and Applications, incl. Internet/Web, and HCI

Printed on acid-free paper

This Springer imprint is published by Springer Nature
The registered company is Springer International Publishing AG
The registered company address is: Gewerbestrasse 11, 6330 Cham, Switzerland

Editors
Aaron Marcus
Aaron Marcus and Associates, Inc.
Berkeley, CA
USA

Wentao Wang
Baidu, Inc.
Beijing
China

ISSN 0302-9743   ISSN 1611-3349   (electronic)
Lecture Notes in Computer Science
ISBN 978-3-319-58636-6   ISBN 978-3-319-58637-3   (eBook)
DOI 10.1007/978-3-319-58637-3

Library of Congress Control Number: 2017939729

LNCS Sublibrary: SL3 – Information Systems and Applications, incl. Internet/Web, and HCI

Printed on acid-free paper

This Springer imprint is published by Springer Nature
The registered company is Springer International Publishing AG
The registered company address is: Gewerbestrasse 11, 6330 Cham, Switzerland

Aaron Marcus · Wentao Wang (Eds.)

Design, User Experience, and Usability

Designing Pleasurable Experiences

6th International Conference, DUXU 2017
Held as Part of HCI International 2017
Vancouver, BC, Canada, July 9–14, 2017
Proceedings, Part II

 Springer

Foreword

The 19th International Conference on Human–Computer Interaction, HCI International 2017, was held in Vancouver, Canada, during July 9–14, 2017. The event incorporated the 15 conferences/thematic areas listed on the following page.

A total of 4,340 individuals from academia, research institutes, industry, and governmental agencies from 70 countries submitted contributions, and 1,228 papers have been included in the proceedings. These papers address the latest research and development efforts and highlight the human aspects of design and use of computing systems. The papers thoroughly cover the entire field of human–computer interaction, addressing major advances in knowledge and effective use of computers in a variety of application areas. The volumes constituting the full set of the conference proceedings are listed on the following pages.

I would like to thank the program board chairs and the members of the program boards of all thematic areas and affiliated conferences for their contribution to the highest scientific quality and the overall success of the HCI International 2017 conference.

This conference would not have been possible without the continuous and unwavering support and advice of the founder, Conference General Chair Emeritus and Conference Scientific Advisor Prof. Gavriel Salvendy. For his outstanding efforts, I would like to express my appreciation to the communications chair and editor of *HCI International News*, Dr. Abbas Moallem.

April 2017   Constantine Stephanidis

HCI International 2017 Thematic Areas and Affiliated Conferences

Thematic areas:

- Human–Computer Interaction (HCI 2017)
- Human Interface and the Management of Information (HIMI 2017)

Affiliated conferences:

- 17th International Conference on Engineering Psychology and Cognitive Ergonomics (EPCE 2017)
- 11th International Conference on Universal Access in Human–Computer Interaction (UAHCI 2017)
- 9th International Conference on Virtual, Augmented and Mixed Reality (VAMR 2017)
- 9th International Conference on Cross-Cultural Design (CCD 2017)
- 9th International Conference on Social Computing and Social Media (SCSM 2017)
- 11th International Conference on Augmented Cognition (AC 2017)
- 8th International Conference on Digital Human Modeling and Applications in Health, Safety, Ergonomics and Risk Management (DHM 2017)
- 6th International Conference on Design, User Experience and Usability (DUXU 2017)
- 5th International Conference on Distributed, Ambient and Pervasive Interactions (DAPI 2017)
- 5th International Conference on Human Aspects of Information Security, Privacy and Trust (HAS 2017)
- 4th International Conference on HCI in Business, Government and Organizations (HCIBGO 2017)
- 4th International Conference on Learning and Collaboration Technologies (LCT 2017)
- Third International Conference on Human Aspects of IT for the Aged Population (ITAP 2017)

Conference Proceedings Volumes Full List

1. LNCS 10271, Human–Computer Interaction: User Interface Design, Development and Multimodality (Part I), edited by Masaaki Kurosu
2. LNCS 10272 Human–Computer Interaction: Interaction Contexts (Part II), edited by Masaaki Kurosu
3. LNCS 10273, Human Interface and the Management of Information: Information, Knowledge and Interaction Design (Part I), edited by Sakae Yamamoto
4. LNCS 10274, Human Interface and the Management of Information: Supporting Learning, Decision-Making and Collaboration (Part II), edited by Sakae Yamamoto
5. LNAI 10275, Engineering Psychology and Cognitive Ergonomics: Performance, Emotion and Situation Awareness (Part I), edited by Don Harris
6. LNAI 10276, Engineering Psychology and Cognitive Ergonomics: Cognition and Design (Part II), edited by Don Harris
7. LNCS 10277, Universal Access in Human–Computer Interaction: Design and Development Approaches and Methods (Part I), edited by Margherita Antona and Constantine Stephanidis
8. LNCS 10278, Universal Access in Human–Computer Interaction: Designing Novel Interactions (Part II), edited by Margherita Antona and Constantine Stephanidis
9. LNCS 10279, Universal Access in Human–Computer Interaction: Human and Technological Environments (Part III), edited by Margherita Antona and Constantine Stephanidis
10. LNCS 10280, Virtual, Augmented and Mixed Reality, edited by Stephanie Lackey and Jessie Y.C. Chen
11. LNCS 10281, Cross-Cultural Design, edited by Pei-Luen Patrick Rau
12. LNCS 10282, Social Computing and Social Media: Human Behavior (Part I), edited by Gabriele Meiselwitz
13. LNCS 10283, Social Computing and Social Media: Applications and Analytics (Part II), edited by Gabriele Meiselwitz
14. LNAI 10284, Augmented Cognition: Neurocognition and Machine Learning (Part I), edited by Dylan D. Schmorrow and Cali M. Fidopiastis
15. LNAI 10285, Augmented Cognition: Enhancing Cognition and Behavior in Complex Human Environments (Part II), edited by Dylan D. Schmorrow and Cali M. Fidopiastis
16. LNCS 10286, Digital Human Modeling and Applications in Health, Safety, Ergonomics and Risk Management: Ergonomics and Design (Part I), edited by Vincent G. Duffy
17. LNCS 10287, Digital Human Modeling and Applications in Health, Safety, Ergonomics and Risk Management: Health and Safety (Part II), edited by Vincent G. Duffy
18. LNCS 10288, Design, User Experience, and Usability: Theory, Methodology and Management (Part I), edited by Aaron Marcus and Wentao Wang

Design, User Experience and Usability

Program Board Chair(s): **Aaron Marcus, USA, and Wentao Wang, P.R. China**

- Sisira Adikari, Australia
- Claire Ancient, UK
- Jan Brejcha, Czech Republic
- Hashim Iqbal Chunpir, Germany
- Silvia de los Rios Perez, Spain
- Marc Fabri, UK
- Patricia Flanagan, Australia
- Nouf Khashman, Qatar
- Tom MacTavish, USA
- Judith A. Moldenhauer, USA
- Francisco Rebelo, Portugal
- Kerem Rizvanoglu, Turkey
- Christine Riedmann-Streitz, Germany
- Patricia Search, USA
- Carla Galvão Spinillo, Brazil
- Marcelo Márcio Soares, Brazil
- Virginia Tiradentes Souto, Brazil

The full list with the Program Board Chairs and the members of the Program Boards of all thematic areas and affiliated conferences is available online at:

http://www.hci.international/board-members-2017.php

HCI International 2018

The 20th International Conference on Human–Computer Interaction, HCI International 2018, will be held jointly with the affiliated conferences in Las Vegas, NV, USA, at Caesars Palace, July 15–20, 2018. It will cover a broad spectrum of themes related to human–computer interaction, including theoretical issues, methods, tools, processes, and case studies in HCI design, as well as novel interaction techniques, interfaces, and applications. The proceedings will be published by Springer. More information is available on the conference website: http://2018.hci.international/.

General Chair
Prof. Constantine Stephanidis
University of Crete and ICS-FORTH
Heraklion, Crete, Greece
E-mail: general_chair@hcii2018.org

http://2018.hci.international/

Contents – Part II

Mobile DUXU

Designing the Playing Experience

Designing the Virtual, Augmented and Tangible Experience

Wearables and Fashion Technology

Contents – Part III

DUXU for Children and Young Users

DUXU for Art, Culture, Tourism and Environment

DUXU Practice and Case Studies

Contents – Part I

Aesthetics and Perception in Design

User Experience Evaluation Methods and Tools

User Centered Design in the Software Development Lifecycle

DUXU Education and Training

Persuasive and Emotional Design

Mix and Match: Designing an Installation for Music Festivals Aiming to Increase Social Sustainability

Vlad-Doru Epure, Beatrix Ivicsics, István Kovács, Louise Skjoldborg Lessel,
Nikolaj Schlüter Nielsen, Jakob Ranum, and Evangelia Triantafyllou[✉]

Department of Architecture Design and Media Technology, Aalborg University,
Copenhagen, Denmark
{vepure15,bivics15,ikovac15,llesse15,nsni15,
jranum15}@student.aau.dk, evt@create.aau.dk

Abstract. This paper presents the design of Mix and Match, a music installation intended for music festivals that utilizes the users' musical preference in order to create a collaborative experience that would also present the upcoming artists in the music scene. The design aimed at increasing social sustainability in music festivals, i.e. bridging social capital, while accounting for different user identities. This resulted in an inclusion of music of different genres that would be explored by all audiences. In conjunction with the festival liminoid structures, the collaborative aspect of the installation became a centerpiece of the design, as interaction between people, who have never met before, becomes common at music festivals.

Keywords: Interactive · Installation · Music festivals · Social sustainability · Interactive sound

1   Introduction

This paper presents the design of Mix and Match, a music installation intended for music festivals that utilizes the users' musical preference in order to create a collaborative experience that would also present the upcoming artists in the music scene. The design aimed at increasing social sustainability in music festivals, i.e. bridging social capital, while accounting for different users' identities. This resulted in an inclusion of music of different genres that could be explored by diverse audiences. In conjunction with the festival's liminoid structures [13], the collaborative aspect of the installation became a centerpiece of the design, as interaction between people, who have never met before, becomes common at music festivals.

In the following sections, we first develop a theoretical framework for exploring and designing interactive installations for music festivals and we review approaches on creating such installations. Then, we present our own design and implementation of such an installation, Mix and Match, which was the result of considering different prototypes. We evaluated Mix and Match by conducting observations and a survey with 24 participants separated in six groups. The evaluation was designed to address the effectiveness, efficiency, safety, utility, learnability and memorability of the installation. We conclude this paper with a discussion of the evaluation results and perspectives for future work.

© Springer International Publishing AG 2017
A. Marcus and W. Wang (Eds.): DUXU 2017, Part II, LNCS 10289, pp. 3–17, 2017.
DOI: 10.1007/978-3-319-58637-3_1

2   Theoretical Framework

Festivals can be difficult environments to design for, as there are special social practices that apply and need to be understood. Moufakkir andPernecky [8] suggest three practice-based perspectives that are often observed on the festival attendees' value creation. These social practices include:

- Bonding practices: deepening bonds with friends and family as a motivational factor for attending.
- Communing practices: experiencing the festival as "time out of time", that is, a special place with different social constructs and communal experiences, separated from normality.
- Belonging practices: long-lasting communities of interests, where festival attendees identify themselves with particular social worlds and celebrate a shared social identity for example as, "a music fan, rugby follower or opera enthusiast".

Being aware of these practices should have an influence on the way an installation for a festival is designed and the way its users are understood. These three practice-based perspectives can be also used to map out the design space of a festival, and to try to understand the social space of an installation.

2.1   Liminoid Environments and Communal Experiences

According to Moufakkir and Pernecky [8], festivals take place in liminoid environments as defined by Turner [13]. Liminoid environments are "(…) temporal fringe spaces where usual, everyday social conventions may be temporarily suspended or reversed" [8]. This could have consequences for the behavior of the festival attendees, their personal boundaries and, in the end, the barriers for interaction with installations. The "time out of time" liminoid structures, "(…) can help to create very strong, if only temporary, social links among complete strangers, termed "communitas" [8], as well as bring together disparate groups of people through communal consumption experiences. An interactive installation could provide such a communal consumption experience and thereby contribute to social sustainability.

The temporary social links that arise at festivals between complete strangers is an interesting subject of investigation for an installation, where bonding practices between strangers could be in play. The theory mainly describes bonding practices as occurring between friends and families, but perhaps by focusing on the collaborative aspect in an installation, it is possible to create these temporary social links between both groups of friends and strangers and thus assist the bonding practices at the festival site.

In communitas, hierarchies and social class become less important factors in the interaction between people; it is about equality, contact and spontaneity [13]. This is a part of the belonging practices, where attendees get together at the festival to celebrate their shared tastes, regardless of who they are outside of the festival space. In this way, music is able to bring together people, who might not meet otherwise.

2.2   Social Capital and Social Identity

An important trend at festivals is the accumulation of social capital among festivalgoers. Identity and social status is no longer about what you own, instead it is about what you do or seek to do. "It is our accomplishments and talents and wider interests that have become the new form of currency by which degrees of personal success can be measured, (…) and which we mention over dinner or post on our social networks" [15]. According to Yeoman [15], the next decade will be defined strongly by our ability to accumulate social capital. Social capital also plays a role for people attending a festival, as doing so will increase their social capital among peers, who believe that this is a festival worth attending.

There are several definitions of social capital. The theory of social capital defined by Putnam emphasizes "network, norms and social trust with cooperation and collaboration producing mutual benefits for individuals, including a sense of well-being" [11]. This means that social capital is associated with the structure of relationships and the interaction between individuals.

Social capital is therefore an interesting concept when designing installation, because it relates to the negotiation of trust and collaboration between possible diverse groups using the installation simultaneously. We assume that social capital is exchanged when two festival attendees accept each other's music taste, so it is important to understand the various kinds of social capital that could be at play in a collaborative installation at a music festival. Wikis [14] studied social capital at music festivals in general using Putnam's theory about bonding- and bridging social capital. Bonding social capital describes the bond between people with homogenous demographic backgrounds and values, while bridging social capital describes an individual's or group's inclusion of other people or groups with diverse demographic backgrounds and values. Wilks examined three different types of music festivals and the empirical data showed that bonding social capital has a significant importance for the music festival experience. She also found that bridging social capital is not an influential component of a festival, which deviates from the theory about festivals being a liminoid environment.

Social identity is another important aspect that relates to how the festival attendees interact with each other and consequently how the festival community is structured [1]. Social identity is, "(…) the total sum of social identifications used by a person to define him or herself and others" [12], where social identification is the structure of social categorization. Social categorization identifies people by describing who they are and who they are not [12]. When relating this to the festival environment, it can be used to describe the person's preferences and taste, such as which genres of music they like and which genres they do not like.

2.3   Festivals as a Setting for New Experiences

Music festivals can be the setting for new experiences, since they present "the new" in various ways. It could be for instance the presentation of an upcoming band or artist, a new installation or activity or new information, to name a few. Experiences can be described as transformations of the self. Jantzen and Rasmussen describe a way of understanding experiences in relation to the construction of identity [7]. According to them, an experience consists of: (a) an expectation pre-experience, (b) the experience, defined as a "break" in the everyday routine, and (c) the stories told about the experience, in which the meaning of the experience is constructed. The stories told about experiences become a part of one's identity.

An important part of an experience is the expectations set for the experience. It is important that an experience lives up to the expectations to be satisfactory, that it goes beyond them to be extraordinary, and, most importantly, that it does not fail in terms of the promised experience [7]. In this regard, a product with flaws can trigger a feeling of failure for the user because they may believe that the product's flaws are a result of their own lack of ability in using the product.

Despite the open-minded and playful atmosphere of a festival, it is therefore important to understand that designing an installation for such a space means understanding the expectations of the festival attendees in order to give them a feeling of being competent when using the installation. This also means that a positive experience will create positive stories about it and thus increase the popularity of the installation. It is also important to consider the experience of the interactive installation as part of the festival space and the stories that the participants should tell about it afterwards. Should the story be one of personal capabilities, social negotiations or openness to trying new things? The designer of an interactive installation for a music festival should therefore seek to offer a new experience, which its users will value, and to frame it in such a way, so the users can easily understand it and engage with it.

3 Background

In the field of sound installations, there have been different approaches focusing on bringing audiences together. SwingScape is an installation presented at Roskilde Festival, Denmark in 2010 [3]. The installation comprised of a constantly interactive environment in an urban space, which was socially engaging and motivated people to be physically active in a playful way. The SwingScape consisted of eight swings equipped with accelerometer sensors capturing their motion. In this installation, festival attendees were able to create different sounds, while sitting on a swing. It was also possible for them to interact with other people sitting on their own swings. Each swing controlled different aspects of the total soundscape, so for optimal results constant communication among users was required. When the swings were moving, visual feedback was given that changed according to the user-interaction in order to provide an instant perception of one's effect on the installation.

MidiBall is an interface designed for concert audiences [6]. It has a simple interface in the form of agiant ball, designed to bounce between the audience at large concerts. As people hit the ball, they trigger sounds and visual effects that are integrated in the concert. This instantly creates a bond between the band and the audience. MidiBall is a nice example of a successfully integrated experience in an event that has no participation barriers.

Illutron designed an interactive art installation consisting of six oil drums with sensors for Skanderborg festival, Denmark in 2015 [5]. By interacting with the drums, visitors had immediate individual feedback via different LED strings mounted on poles. Furthermore, when the participants managed to solve the puzzle of drumming the correct beat, they received collective feedback in the form of a giant fire cannon going off and the drums turning red. This art installation provided visual feedback on many levels and urged visitors to cooperate.

Augmented Groove uses human gestures for moving vinyl disks in order to control the modulation and mixing of music [9]. Users are wearing a virtual reality headset that has a camera and a video display, which overlays animations on the vinyl disks. The purpose of the interface is to create a collaborative DJ interface that bridges the gap between experienced musicians and novices.

Iamascope is another sound installation that has visual effects as part of the experience [2]. Iamascope is actually an interactive kaleidoscope that creates video and audio feedback. The system uses a camera in order to capture the user and creates a kaleidoscopic image. The user's movements control the music and provoke changes to the image displayed. The complex musical process consists of ten active zones in the interaction space mapped to sound like a guitar. The guitar chords change periodically according to pre-composed melodies.

Based on our investigation of the relevant theoretical background and other sound installations, we concluded on a set of design requirements for Mix and Match. The installation should be a communal consumption experience, designed as a tool for connecting different social identities and categorizations that are present at music festivals. It should create temporary social links between strangers (bridging social capital) and encourage collaboration between them. Moreover, it should implement a tool for the negotiation of music taste (social identity) and have a high transparency with a short learning curve for the users to feel competent. Finally, mistakes in the interaction should be easy to recover from and the users should be able to explore the capabilities of the system on their own, without having an overwhelming amount of choices.

4   Methods

During the design and implementation of Mix and Match, we followed the "Research Through Design" approach, in which "…designers produce novel artefacts in an attempt to make the right thing: a product that transforms the world from its current state to a preferred state" [16]. The preferred state for the installation is described by the aforementioned design requirements in the previous section.

According to this approach, design is treated as a research discipline that produces knowledge, rather than being simply a practice of making. This HCI research method proposes a set of four criteria for evaluating a design research contribution [16]:

- Process: the process is thoroughly documented and good rationale is presented for the choice of methods
- Invention: there is a novel contribution that advances the current state of the art
- Relevance: making an impact to change the world to a preferred state

- Extensibility: the ability to build on the resulting outcomes; either employing the process in a future design problem, or understanding and leveraging the knowledge created by the resulting artifacts.

The outcome of the "Research Through Design" approach can be a design artefact, called an exemplar, which can lay the groundwork for discussing future designs, as an exemplar provides concrete embodiments of theory and technical opportunities.

The process of our design was iterative, exploring the possibilities of the technology that could be used to create a collaborative music experience. It also focused on prototyping and testing the usability and technical limitations of different prototypes. Houde and Hill [4] provided an excellent framework for defining, discussing and creating prototypes (Fig. 1).

- Role prototypes are built to investigate questions of what an artifact could do for a user. "They describe the functionality that a user might benefit from, with little attention to how the artifact would look and feel, or how it could be made to actually work" [4].
- Look and feel prototypes "(…) are built primarily to explore and demonstrate options for the experience of an artifact. They simulate what it would be like to look at and interact with (…)" [4].
- Implementation prototypes are built to answer technical questions about how a future artifact might actually be made to work. "They are used to discover methods by which adequate specifications for the final artifact can be achieved" [4].

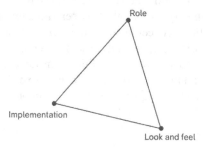

Fig. 1. Prototypes are placed on the model according to their purpose (figure taken from [4])

In the following, we use this framework for presenting the prototypes that we created through the design process.

5   Design and Implementation

The design of Mix and Match evolved around the idea of developing an installation, where users could affect a soundscape through some form of collaboration, preferably by creating sound together. The Mix and Match installation consists of an interactive area where trigger zones containing sound loops with drums, guitars, vocals etc. from different songs can be activated by users. These trigger zones are controlled by a computer and are triggered according to the users' placement in the interactive area, making it possible to create unique remixes of songs. The loops are synced and constantly playing, but are muted when not triggered by a user.

During the design process, we followed an iterative approach for building several prototypes with the purpose of clarifying how users interact with the interface. Initially, we built two prototypes: one focused on the implementation of sound in the installation (referred to as implementation prototype) and the other focused on the look, feel and perception of the overall concept (referred to as the "look and feel" prototype). Figure 2 shows the purpose of the two prototypes represented on the Houde and Hill's model [4].

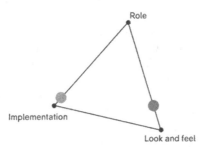

Fig. 2. The purpose of the implementation prototype (orange) and the "look and feel" prototype (green) on the model proposed by Houde and Hill (Color figure online)

The "look and feel" prototype was tested with actual users in order to develop a final and improved design. Since this prototype was not fully implemented, we followed the Wizard of Oz method for testing, where a human controls aspects of the system to make it appear functional to the user [10]. A four by four grid made with tape covering approximately four square meters was laid out on the floor and in the test participants were asked to try the installation without any introductory instructions given to them. Whenever a user stepped into one of the trigger zones, one of observers pressed a corresponding button. Six groups of four people participated in this test (one group at a time) and explored the installation while we were observing their behavior. At the end of the observation, we conducted a group interview on the participants' understanding of the installation, their opinion on the overall idea, and their feedback for further development.

The results of this test were predominantly homogeneous. The attitude towards the concept was very positive, the participants found the installation easy to understand and most of them could see it working well at a music festival. Our observations revealed also the following findings that we used for building the final design.

Some participants tried to step out of the grid or stand on the lines between two tracks to avoid triggering any sounds, while others tried to find complete songs or patterns in the placement of the tracks. Interacting with the prototype was sometimes too challenging for four people, because the feedback of who was triggering which track was not clear enough. Moreover, some participants tried to see if it was possible to trigger several tracks at the same time and others tried to go back and forth between the tracks very quickly, to test the responsiveness of the installation. Many participants looked down at their feet to ensure that they were within the trigger zones, and most of them spent a great deal of time discussing the location of certain tracks trying to memorize where each track was located.

Regarding the social behavior, most groups expressed positive opinions on how participants are required to work as a team to interact with the installation. Moreover, in most of the cases there was at least one person who took a leader role and tried to guide the interaction of the group with the installation. One of the groups explicitly expressed that the installation was "very social", while another suggested that the installation would be more entertaining to use in larger groups of people. Finally, there was a group, which expressed the desire to build up a dance routine to match their interaction with the installation.

An implementation prototype was built at this stage of the design process to investigate the optimal way of handling the sound loops. Since the main functionality of the installation was decided to be making users capable of mixing many different audio tracks, the slightest latency issues could cause confusion to the users. Therefore, the focus of the prototype was testing whether the game engine Unity could be a reliable software to handle the audio for the installation. For evaluating this, we conducted and thoroughly documented a technical test of the implementation prototype. During this test, one of the authors muted and unmuted tracks randomly while carefully listening to the output using headphones. No bugs or latency issues occurred during the test. This led us to conclude that Unity was a suitable software for mixing several audio channels and could be used as a part of this installation.

The final design was based on the same concept and many of the same ideas used in the initial prototypes. The data gathered from the two prototype tests combined with the aforementioned design requirements have been used in the process of developing an improved design that is depicted in Fig. 3.

For implementing the final design, we used a USB camera, a computer running TSPS (a software for detecting where the users are located in the interactive area) and Unity, and a set of speakers. The camera was set up above the interactive area facing towards the ground while streaming video that is processed by TSPS, which then sent the users' location to Unity. A plug-in for Unity was used that implements a receiver that translates TSPS data to actual coordinates, and places it in a scene. Within the scene, colliders were placed and each one of them had a different sound loop attached to it. When a detected user is within the area of a collider, the attached loop is played on the speakers. The loop is muted when no users are detected within the collider.

The installation had four different loops (bass, vocals, guitar, drums) from four different songs. All the sound loops were synced to 110 BPM because this worked well as an average tempo, and they were tuned to the key of G#, so nothing would sound misplaced.

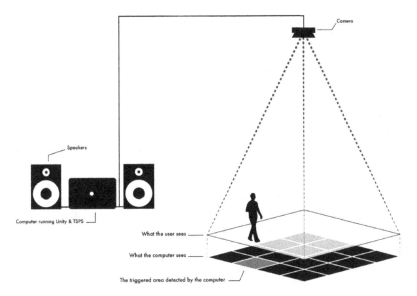

Fig. 3. The final design - illustration of what the computer sees compared to what the users see

6   Evaluation

In order to evaluate the usability of the Mix and Match installation, we conducted observations and a survey with 24 participants separated in six groups. The evaluation was designed to address the effectiveness, efficiency, safety, utility, learnability and memorability of the installation, as defined in [10]. During the evaluation, we tried two different layouts for the music tracks in the interactive area: a structured grid (where each row contains loops from the same song and each column contains loops from the same instrument type) in comparison to a random placement of the different loops in the interactive area.

The observations were conducted as an AB/BA test, where half of the participating groups tested the structured layout first, and then tested the random layout, while the other half first tested the random and then the structured layout. For the usability part, the participants had to complete a series of tasks, which were based on behavior we observed at the initial "look and feel" prototype test. The aim of the tasks was to get the users to move around as much as possible in the installation and to be diverse enough in order to observe as many types of collaborative behavior as possible. The tasks included in the usability test were the following:

1. Firstly, we asked the participants to try the installation without providing any instructions to them. This task aimed at testing the learnability of the installation.
2. Then, we asked them to create a mix, which they thought sounded nice. This task investigated their collaboration and the effectiveness of the installation to facilitate social interaction.

3. Since this installation contained parts of different songs, we asked the participants if they could recreate a song from an artist. This task focused on user understanding of the interface and its learnability.
4. Then, we asked the participants to pick their least favorite sound, because we wanted to explore their way of collaborating and the efficiency of the installation in supporting them to do the task.
5. As the final test before changing the layout of the interface, we asked the participants if they were able to recreate the mix they previously thought sounded nice (task 2). This task tested the memorability of the interface in regards to whether there is sufficient support to help the users remember how to carry out tasks.
6. Finally, we rearranged the tracks on the interactive area and asked the participants to recreate the same song from the same artist as they had done for task 3. This task was included to let the users compare the usability of the two layouts (structured grid vs. random) as well as to observe the learnability of the interface in relation to the change.

After completing these tasks, each participant filled out a questionnaire with 29 questions in total, where they indicated to which degree they agreed to various parameters for each task. These parameters included whether they had a clear understanding of how to interact with the interface, as well as how easy it was to collaborate with the other participants. The questionnaire also asked the participants to compare the two layouts for which was most logical, most fun to explore and easiest to use.

For the utility goal of providing the right kind of functionality, we included the following question in the questionnaire: "In your opinion, does the installation need more functionality? And if so what do you think could improve it?", as well as a series of questions about how users perceived the two layouts. Finally, for the safety goal, we observed errors occurring in the software during the test, as well as what the users perceived as mistakes while interacting, and how they recovered from them.

In the following, we comment on the most prominent results of the evaluation.

6.1 Preferences Regarding the Two Layouts

As it was previously mentioned, we tested the installation with two different layouts: one where the sounds are placed randomly in the grid and one where the sounds from the same artist are lying on the same line. Half of the groups were exposed to the random layout first, followed by the structured layout – we refer to these groups as the AB groups. The other half of the groups were exposed to the structured layout first, followed by the random layout – these are referred to as the BA groups. We chose this test setting because the participants were asked to carry out more tasks with the layout they were first exposed to, so this could insert a bias in their layout preference. Before presenting the results on preferences between the two layouts, it is important to note that the first AB group only tried the first layout, as problems occurred with the second layout. Therefore, this group is not included in the results that compare the two layouts.

Most groups reported that the structured layout was the easiest to use, but they found that the random layout was more fun to explore (Fig. 4). This indicates that the random is more exploratory, while the structured makes it easier for the participants accomplish specific tasks in the installation (create something they like). This was actually our hypothesis for this comparison.

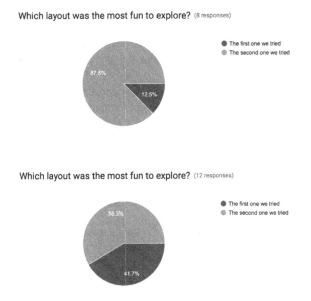

Fig. 4. Answers to the question "Which layout was the most fun to explore" AB groups on top, BA groups below

A possible explanation to why the participants found the random layout more fun, could be that the random placements of the tracks made it more difficult to predict where the different sounds were placed, thus more time was spent exploring the installation. This also means that it required more mental effort to remember the placement of the different tracks, which reminds of a memory game. In the structured layout, participants could faster figure out where the tracks were placed and this could lead to users getting bored quickly. Once we figured out the structure, the fun decreased, as one group explained.

Based on our observations, we concluded that the different layouts support two different kinds of collaborative behavior. While both facilitated a lot of pointing and negotiation about where to stand, only the structured layout made the users move in a coordinated manner. For instance, in the structured layout participants stood in one line and moved collectively through the installation while remaining in line. The interface with the random layout did not dictate such behavior. In the random layout, the participants mainly walked around and explored the installation. The collaboration thus focused more on remembering the positions of tracks in this case. This observation made us conclude that placing the tracks in different patterns is an interesting point for further explorations for installation, since finding patterns could become an important way of interacting collaboratively.

6.2 Collaboration for Recreating the Mix that Sounded Nice

The last task that the participants performed in terms of collaboration was to re-create the mix they thought sounded nice in task 3. It was apparent from the observational data that most groups found this task difficult regardless of the layout in the installation. To solve this task, the participants seemed to recall primarily their own physical location, and secondarily, the position of the others relative to their own. This brought a lot of discussion about who was where, what did not sound right, and what the mix in task 3 sounded like.

When the participants believed they had recreated the mix of task 3, an observer noted their positions in the grid. The positions of the participating groups in task 3 and 5 are shown in Fig. 5. As it is apparent from Fig. 5, only the participants in groups number 2, 4 and 5 recreated the exact same mix as in task 3. We chose not to compare the results between the structured and random layout, since they relate more to the group's individual ways of collaborating on the task and much less on the layout.

Grid layout   **Random layout**

Create track   **Re-create track**   **Create track**   **Re-create track**

Group 1

1			
	2		4
		3	

Group 1

1			4
	2	3	

Group 2

	1		
2		4	
		3	

Group 2

	1		
3		2	
		4	

Group 3

			3
1		2	
		4	

Group 3

1			4
2			
		3	

Group 4

	12	34	

Group 4

	12	34	

Group 5

1	2	3	4

Group 5

3	1	2	4

Group 6

	1		
2		3	4

Group 6

			4
3			1
	2		

Fig. 5. Positions of the participants in each group during task 3 and task 5.

Group 1 completed the task almost correctly. They mostly relied on how they had placed themselves relative to each other. Therefore, the pattern is similar, but the sounds they were triggering were not the same. The group did not seem to notice that the resulting sound had changed.

Group 2 completed the task without failure. Three of them remembered perfectly where their position had been previously and they knew which individual track was missing from the song, so they easily figured out the last position they had to trigger.

Group 3 got two out of the four positions correct. Two of the group members remembered which sounds they triggered before but they switched their previous positions. These two were trying to help the others finding their previous positions.

Group 4 relied entirely on their placement in relation to the white line around the installation and got the task right.

Group 5 performed the task correctly since they had chosen the sounds of the same artist in task 3. Since they were using the installation with the structured layout, it was easy for them to recreate the same mix.

Group 6 got two out of four positions correct. This group was the most unsure about their previous positions and actually they completely switched around their positions.

6.3 Other Observations

During the initial prototype test, a visible grid was present on the floor, while during the final evaluation only the frame of the interactive area was visible. By comparing the observations on the users' collaborative behavior during the initial prototype test and the final usability test, we concluded that the presence of a visible grid on the floor that indicates each interactive zone made users look very often on the floor. When this visible grid was absent, users looked more at each other. We consider this finding important, since our intention was to create an interface, which lets the users bond over their choices and music taste by discussing it collaboratively.

Our observations also suggest that the Mix and Max can be viewed as a communal consumption experience, where participants are trying to create something together. Though the installation was not designed as a game, the manner in which the participants behaved when they used it was playful, and it reminded us of the kind of behavior that maybe seen in a liminoid space. Additionally, the participants reported that they enjoyed the experience, and we observed that they were eager to explore the interface of the installation. Because of this focus on playing, we assume that users of this installation may de-emphasize their individual tastes in music when collaborating. This assumption should be explored and validated in a future study.

7 Discussion and Conclusion

This paper presented the design of Mix and Match, a music installation intended for music festivals that utilizes the users' musical preference in order to create a collaborative experience that could also present upcoming artists in the music scene. An iterative approach towards building different prototypes was taken in order to clarify how users interact with the interface. The results yielded by the tests provided valuable information towards understanding the users - the test subjects immediately familiarized themselves with the interaction and explored the tracks in the installation. Then, they attempted to create new music or recreate existing songs from the loops provided. The users enjoyed the collaborative aspect as they quickly started cooperating in order to succeed in the creative process. When interacting, leaders emerged that started coordinating the participants in order to achieve their own creative goals. This was observed less in the tests where participants were assigned tasks by the evaluators. No explanation was found for this phenomenon, but it should be explored in future tests.

The design process revolved around making the installation a collaborative exploration that would evolve into collective creation when interacting with the installation. This required a focus on lowering the interaction barrier without reducing interaction times, which has been achieved through removing any pre-requisites from the users, they simply had to move around inside the installation in order to interact. Furthermore, the installation rewarded collaborative use, as multiple users activated multiple tracks at the same time with more interesting and complex melodies being composed. Future designs will feature accompanying visual effects to further augment the experience. Care will be taken that the effects do not impair the collaboration, by making users overly focused on the visual effects instead of each other.

The prototype was evaluated by a usability test, which revealed that placing the tracks randomly in the installation makes for a more exploratory experience, whereas structuring the tracks in straight lines makes the installation easier to learn and use. Moreover, track placement also affects the way the participants are able to interact in the installation, since coordinated collective movement happens only in the structured layout. The evaluation proved that Mix and Match has achieved the goal of engaging users in collaborative creation. However, the detection was not accurate enough for the installation to be displayed at a musical festival yet. We conclude this paper with further technical developments in order to improve this installation. The implementation has proven to be riddled with technical difficulties, as the featured detection system was extremely dependent on the environment. This implied the need for controlled lighting conditions, cancelling the shadows and maintaining color contrast between the users and the background. These requirements severely add to the difficulty for an easy integration within a festival space, but despite these, the prototype worked well as a proof of concept and allowed us to examine the design concepts in real scenarios. Due to the small sample size of this evaluation, results and conclusions can not be seen as definitive but merely indications and tendencies. However, these are valid directions that future development of the installation should take into consideration.

References

1. Arcodia, C., Whitford, M.: Festival attendance and the development of social capital. J. Conv. Event Tour. **8**, 1–18 (2007)
2. Fels, S., Mase, K.: Iamascope: a graphical musical instrument. Comput. Graph. **23**, 277–286 (1999)
3. Grønbæk, K., Kortbek, K.J., Møller, C., Nielsen, J., Stenfeldt, L.: Designing playful interactive installations for urban environments – the swingscape experience. In: Nijholt, A., Romão, T., Reidsma, D. (eds.) ACE 2012. LNCS, vol. 7624, pp. 230–245. Springer, Heidelberg (2012). doi:10.1007/978-3-642-34292-9_16
4. Houde, S., Hill, C.: What do prototypes prototype. In: Helander, M., Landauer, T., Prabhu, P. (eds.) Handbook of Human-Computer Interaction, vol. 2, pp. 367–381. Elsevier, Amsterdam (1997)
5. Illutron: http://Illutron.Dk/Skanderborg-Festival-2015. 25 January 2017
6. Jacobson, L., Blaine, T., Pacheco, C.: Time for Technojuju. New Media Mag., **18** (1993)

7. Jantzen, C., Rasmussen, T.A.: Er oplevelsesøkonomi gammel vin på nye flasker?. In: Oplevelsesøkonomi, pp. 21–47. Aalborg Universitetsforlag (2007)
8. Moufakkir, O., Pernecky, T.: Ideological, Social and Cultural Aspects of Events. CABI, Wallingford (2014)
9. Poupyrev, I., Berry, R., Billinghurst, M. et al.: Augmented reality interface for electronic music performance. In: Proceedings of HCI, pp. 805–808 (2001)
10. Preece, J., Rogers, Y., Sharp, H., et al.: Human-Computer Interaction. Addison-Wesley Longman Ltd., Essex (1994)
11. Putnam, R.D.: Bowling alone: America's declining social capital. J. Democr. **6**, 65–78 (1995)
12. Tajfel, H.: Social Identity and Intergroup Relations. Cambridge University Press, Cambridge (2010)
13. Turner, V.: The Ritual Process: Structure and Anti-Structure. Transaction Publishers, Piscataway (1995)
14. Wilks, L.: Bridging and bonding: social capital at music festivals. J. Policy Res. Tour. Leisure Events **3**, 281–297 (2011)
15. Yeoman, I.: A futurist's thoughts on consumer trends shaping future festivals and events. Int. J. Event Festiv. Manage. **4**, 249–260 (2013)
16. Zimmerman, J., Forlizzi, J., Evenson, S.: Research through design as a method for interaction design research. In: HCI, pp. 493–502 (2007)

Explore the Categories on Different Emotional Branding Experience for Optimising the Brand Design Process

Amic G. Ho[⊠]

The Open University of Hong Kong, Hong Kong SAR, China
amicgh@gmail.com

Abstract. Recognised the importance of design impressions, design scholars noticed that there are some trends among the brands awareness on consumer attitudes toward their designs outcomes include products and services. More and more customer services were developed for enhancing the relationships with consumers through social networks, integrated mobile and location-based technologies. Some scholars investigate the theories of psychology and sociology to understand the message procedures of consumers and how it would influence the feeling associated with the brand. So, how would this influence the consumer's expectation of brand experience? How this change would influence the emotional brand building and how would it influence the brand building procedures?

This research study aimed to review the different cases of the development of emotional branding experience and categorised them into four types of brands providing emotional experience to the customers: personalities-driven emotional brand, appeal-driven emotional brand, sensory-driven emotional brand, navigation-driven emotional brand. These new branding strategies providing satisfied consumer's expectation on brand experience were investigated. A field experiment was adopted to examine the methods. The branding process and the design outcomes were compared and provided how would the specify brand building process. It helped to optimise the branding design process to facilitate them to create the most effective emotional brand experience to the consumers. This study is the preliminary discussion on the new development of the emotional branding by integrated the studies of design, psychology and business and how would the brand strengthen the emotional attachment with the consumer.

Keywords: Emotional attachment · Branding · Communication design · Consumers

1 Introduction

In the commercial world, the most valuable brands are those able to build a strong emotional connection with the consumers. In certain ways, the brand would like to build the emotional attachment with the consumer as 'the best friends forever'. As in life, it is not an easy task to build a friendship in marketing. This relationship is formed by constant connections and engagement those provide memorable experiences. In early years, most studies explored the methods and techniques to bonding emotion to brands. Some scholars investigate the theories of psychology and sociology to understand the

© Springer International Publishing AG 2017
A. Marcus and W. Wang (Eds.): DUXU 2017, Part II, LNCS 10289, pp. 18–34, 2017.
DOI: 10.1007/978-3-319-58637-3_2

message procedures of consumers and how it would influence the feeling associated with the brand. Under the influence of digital technologies, channels for cement the relationships between brands and consumers are flourishing. People often need fast, two-way interaction to achieve emotional satisfaction. When safety and comfort of the design outcomes have been achieved, emphasis the design attributes were shifted toward to provide the purposes on decoration, emotion, and symbolic (Crilly et al. 2004). A successful design outcome must achieve the consumers' emotional needs beside utility and quality (McLoone et al. 2012). Incorporating 'feeling' into design outcomes with emotional design experiences is the trend of design after the twenty-first century. The design outcomes took the role which connected designers and consumers; at the same times, design outcomes influence consumers with the recognised creativity of designer's (Lin and Chang 2004). So, how would this influence the consumer's expectation on brand experience? How this change would influence the emotional brand building and how would it influenced the brand building procedures? This study investigated how branding strategies newly developed to satisfy the consumer's expectation on brand experience, and how would the specify brand building process would provide to creative in order to facilitate them to create the most effective emotional brand experience to the consumers.

After recognised the importance of design outcomes impressions, design scholars observed that there are changes of consumer attitudes toward brands. A marketing scholar, Roberts studied how brands attracted growing interest (Roberts 2004). One of his followers, Martin (2005) asserted that design should be no longer work as a part of brand strategy; instead, design outcomes shaped customer perceptions. Branding represented certain of meaning through its signs. Companies used brand identities (images, logos and insignia) to deliver messages (such as a concept of lifestyle) and create familiarity with a design outcome. Brand concept would be more abstracted and spiritual. It is the summary of consumer's emotional response for design outcomes (Wang et al. 2008). It reflects consumers' 'mood', 'knowledge', 'attitudes', and 'behaviours'. Therefore, emotional characteristics of design outcomes and emotion of brand are crucial. A brand portrays a personality which attaches certain specific values and symbols in order to create the relationship between consumers and a brand. More and more studies explored the methods and techniques to bonding emotion to brands. Based on the studies those conducted by the pioneer, designers investigated the opinions consumer on the interactions between emotional design outcomes and brand emotion. They explored the contribution of emotion in the process of brand building and design outcomes through emotion and subjective evaluations.

2 The Development of Emotion Bonding to Brands

Before understanding how emotion bonding to brands, it is essential to understanding how emotion connected with visual communication. Scholars have found that emotions considerably influence individuals' interpretation of their experiences (Zettl 2002; Beaudry and Pinsonneault 2010) Audiences respond to design through cognition. The emotional elements of design should be taken into account when considering the usability of design outcomes. Being applied in visual communication, visual design elements may affect audience emotions. It means that the functions of visual communication design—informing, persuading, and influencing—work with emotion to provide an experience to the audience. These findings are not only relevant to optimizing designs for ease of use, but for invoking emotional experiences such as happiness, involvement, trust, and satisfaction in users. Most research concerning emotion has been conducted while users were using products. Few studies have considered the user experience of visual communication because users' emotional responses and reactions while consuming visual communication designs are too subtle to be easily measured or identified. However, emotion plays an important role in the examination of information and communication technology systems (Kim et al. 2003; Sun and Zhang 2006). Emotional responses and the reactions of audiences can be regarded as indicators of the usability of visual communication designs. These responses provide insights for further explorations of how to optimise visual communication design for audience needs. The main aspect to consider is how design elicits audience emotion, which mostly works within the persuasion process after the audience has been informed.

2.1 Emotion in Visual Communication

Before investigating how emotion is delivered by the elements of visual communication, it is necessary to understand how emotion influences the functions of visual communication design. After an audience obtains information, the process of influencing them through persuasion begins. Perloff (2010) proposed that persuasion is a process of communication requiring strong and clear messages to be delivered from one party to another. It involves a multitude of elements beyond words, such as aesthetics, interactions, and functions. Through persuasion, audience attitudes should be strengthened as it worked as a periodically reminder of the desired experience about the brand.

2.2 Elaboration Likelihood Model

According to the knowledge on how attitudes and behaviours can be shaped by persuasion, Petty and Cacioppo (1986) proposed the elaboration likelihood model (Fig. 1) for explaining the approaches of messages and how to maximise the influence of design outcomes on audience attitudes and behaviours.

The study proposed that when an individual receives information, it is elaborated at varying levels. "Elaboration" refers to the level of effort applied with regard to evaluation, memory, and judgment (Petty and Cacioppo 1986). When people receive persuasive messages, they elaborate at two levels, namely central and peripheral route processing. The central route refers to the focus on the message during information processing; audiences pay more attention to strong, qualified messages. Attitudes that are shaped or developed in central route processing tend to endure and be resistant to counterarguments. By contrast, peripheral route processing is trickier to recognise. Audiences pay less attention to messages when they are being affected by other factors, such as visual appeal, the origin of the source, or presentation. Thus, the attitudes shaped or developed are less enduring and are easily influenced by counterarguments, requiring

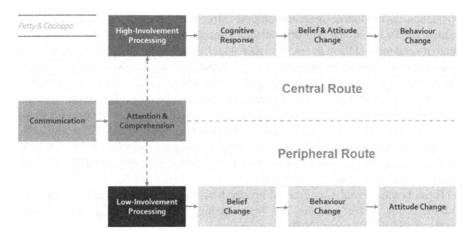

Fig. 1. The model of elaboration likelihood (Petty and Cacioppo 1986)

continual reinforcement. In this model, central route processing leads audiences to greater elaboration than peripheral route processing because the structure and content of messages are closely judged. However, audiences are also affected by message characteristics such as the strength, credibility, and relevance of the information. Audiences may be influenced if these other factors are effective, and this would simultaneously render the overall persuasive attempt more enduring and resilient to counterarguments.

2.3 Persuasion and Motivation

Designers must be aware of the negative side of the persuasion that accompanies messaging and design. Distractions can undermine designers' persuasive techniques. Pop-ups, long loading times, or processes that are too complicated can annoy audiences and detract from relevant information. Such distractions, whether physical or intangible, are found throughout the elaboration process. Two paths of thinking support further investigations of how emotion functions in visual communication design. There are three elements to persuade audiences effectively according to the analysis presented in (Petty and Cacioppo 1986): (1) "Message" refers to "what's being said, marketing efforts, content, and copy;" (2) "Design" refers to "visual hierarchy, navigation, and layout;" and (3) "Delivery" refers to "load time, user experience, rewards, and bells and whistles". These elements provide designers with ways to understand the target audience, including what kind of information motivates them. This supports developing a list of questions to understand the values of audiences concerning their "fears, hopes, and dreams" and the "current challenges designers face in persuading them."

Designers can also review previous research on persuasion to improve the effectiveness of their designs. Emotional branding is an approach which proposed consumer-centred, relational, and storytelling in the process of brand communication. It aims to build up in-depth and affective connections among consumers for brands. (Roberts 2004) Senses and emotions are the main channels involved to form an in-depth, long-lasting and emotional connection to the brand. In other words, brand transcends material satisfaction during the design consumption (Morrison and Crane 2007; Rahinel and Redden 2013). Emotional concerns attached brands able to enhance the potential of creativity and most of them are more sustainable (Lynch and De Chernatony 2004). The most obvious method of building an emotional brand is connecting the brand with certain ideological associations. It was found that brand or design outcome worked best with it reflected the consumers' needs those based on the demographic information from the substantial research, sufficient knowledge on the consumers' values or concepts those able to stimulate their emotional responses and connect to the brand. These values or concepts can be delivered into through graphics and language adopted by the brand. To illustrate this technique, Walt Disney World Ads is the example, which bonded the family values and essence of childhood.

Those brands obtain strong brand loyalty from the consumers as they understand customers' favourable attitudes and repurchasing behaviours (Wang et al. 2008). Bergkvist and Bech-Larsen (2010) proposed the understanding, emotional attachment and passion towards a brand were grouped as brand love as result. This brand love is the foundation for developing brand loyalty and active engagement. In other words, brand love is formed by positive emotional responses those generating brand loyalty. Park et al. (1986) pointed out that brand loyalty creates symbol and experience with all these elements and shapes consumer awareness. Carroll and Ahuvia (2006) revealed that the 'consumers love' is an emotion attributed to a particular brand. Themes and Symbols were used by some brands to create meaning for a consumer. Hence, 'theme' would be the big idea presented throughout advertisement; 'symbol' is the representative of the theme. Symbol represents the promise provided by the brand and consumers agree with this promise. He used the advertising of cosmetic products and services (i.e. design outcomes) as the example. He descripted that the cosmetic manufacturers sell hope instead of the products. Consumers buy vitality instead of oranges; and buy prestige instead of a car (Packard 1957). Bernay and Howard (1955) has similar concept with Packard, he analysed how the themes of influenced the effectiveness of the advertising in his book, The Engineering of Consent. He found that successful themes able to enhance the motivations of human. This motivation was built on the consumers' subconscious desires for achieving certain goals. Bernays listed out the factors those are possible to drive motivation under the support of the ideological values or personal experience. Sometimes, they work with symbolism. Designers these factors in order to generate the theme for a specific point of view based on the brand concept. Bernays suggested that symbols (i.e. design elements) may represent various themes at the same period. He proposed 'Hello Kitty' as the example, a kitten (Hello Kitty) represents experience of 'playfulness and comfort'. In other words, symbols (includes the styles of design, design elements) provide a promise for consumer satisfaction which associated with the brand concept. Packard highlighted eight potential needs those are most effective on motivating consumers to make purchasing decisions. The eight potential needs (Packard 1957) are: 'Emotional security', 'Reassurance of worth', 'Ego-gratification', 'Creative outlets', 'Love objects', 'Sense of power', 'Sense of roots' and 'Immorality'. These needs are attached with affective (i.e. emotion) in a subconscious approach and work as the foundation of emotional branding. They inspired designers to generated a self-fulfilling prophesy for satisfying the needs of consumer needs. At the same time, the linkage of design outcomes and emotion was investigated. Yen (2005) and her team explored the relationships of brand and emotional responses stimulated by design outcomes through conducting a consumer-emotion survey. They found that the design outcomes provided by emotional-brands have emotional design characteristics, particularly about beauty. According to their study, emotional design characteristics influence the presentation of the consumers' desired on emotion aspects, included repurchasing, recommending to others, attachment with the products, pleasing experience in the purchasing process. Also, most of the design outcomes under those emotional-brand with features like simple shapes, pure colours, and natural textures. These features involved various concerns from design, fashion and psychologist studies. The findings of Yen's study supported the future development of emotional design. The methods of eliciting the emotional reaction were explored. Yen proposed music playing as one of the example of the building up emotional attachment by the brands. He suggested that music playing simultaneously and created enjoyment for enjoying the design outcomes. This example works best to evoke emotion. It created a connection to the design outcomes and the sadness or happiness (possible or negative emotion) of consumer's. It is essential in life. Hence, it is an example of emotional branding.

After integrating the perspectives of previous studies, there are various techniques were investigated for achieving emotional response of consumers to a brand. However, influenced by the development of new media, the interactions between consumers and brands are more frequency. The information procedures are more complicated. Consumers have more channels to get the promotional message about the brands (Davis 2010). The emotional attachment of the brands could not be built through single media but multimedia with a clear approach (Whyte 1997). The brand communication through multimedia, involved many touch points to connect consumers included its technology platforms, their vendor market, their services and applications. Behind the variety touch points, how would the brand build up the bonding between brands and consumers (i.e. how to sense, reason, and feel)? According to Whyte (1997), we understand that people often need fast, two-way interaction to achieve emotional satisfaction, (some scholars described as in achieving empathy.)

One of the effective methods is inviting consumers to share and co-create the branded content. This can be done by encouraging consumers' input, for example, photos, Tweets, videos, etc. from consumers (Richard 2004). Also, the brands cooperate with content providers such as publishers, entertainment companies, etc. to offer exclusive experiences. Richard emphasised the effort of customer services and supporting the activities those engaged consumers on improving brand's capability on blending successful engagements (i.e. 'fans') in social networking. They later can be grouped as communities of members (i.e. 'followers') or even will to process direct interaction (i.e. 'consumers') and relationships (i.e. 'super fans') with the brand. Richard summarised several key trends:

- Brand strategies being developed based on integrated mobile and location-based marketing,
- Social networks such as Facebook and Twitter driving the executions of customer service,

- Branded membership concepts and reward programs would extend the brand as a big consumer brands
- Real-time personalising will be ensuring to increase the connections to the consumers.

How the creative team would build the emotional satisfaction under this new trend? If the different touch point or approaches were set, how would the creative team manipulate the design procedures? In order to have a more in-depth knowledge on how the emotional branding build up the bonding between brands and consumers, there is a need to categories the types of emotional branding according to the approaches that the brands adopted to build the bonding with the consumers. Afterwards, the specific design procedures of each category would be identified in order to provide the hints to build emotional bonding with consumers.

3 The New Perspective on the Types of Emotional Branding: 4 Types of Emotional Branding

3.1 Personalities-Driven Emotional Brand

The original business concept is developed to satisfy the specific emotional needs of the consumers. The positioning, vision and mission, etc. are set to interpret the ideology of the brands. This type of emotional branding emphasised the importance of the positioning of the brands. According to Abbing and Gessel (2008), branding drives the sustainable growth of the business. This type of brands explores how innovative design outcomes leading the brand to achieve their promise by providing 'meaningful manifestations', 'interactions and experiences'. These build up the bridge in between the business and consumers for a relatively durable relationship. They also releveled that design management work out the important role in connecting branding and innovative design outcomes by providing the consumers with storytelling to facilitate this relationship started from the mission and vision of the business. A concept first started in Japan, The Home Maid Café is a brand which is a typical example. It targeted the niche market of the cosplay lovers. In order to satisfy the emotional needs of the consumers those suffered from the huge living pressure. The brand concept of maid café indeed is simple. It's a café for consumers enjoying drinks and snacks. The café was decorated as the Princess Peach. As described by Abbing and Gessel (2008), the waitresses in the café dressed up like a French Maid, with lace. They appear with a lot of cute pose throughout the meal. The consumers are treated as if they are a 'master' and the waitresses (i.e. the maid) are their servants. Once consumers entering the café, the waitress say 'okaerinasaimase goshujin sama' which means 'welcome home master' with a high-pitched voice… (When the waitress serves consumer a drink,) she will do some magic tricks when they delivering the dishes to make it more attractive. Their tricks include magic words, special poses and clapping. They also invite consumers' participation by repeating after them. The consumers would reject the social pressure those exerted on them by their society to work hard and have a productive career, also, provide the consumers a space for refusing to grow up.

Based on the featured methods for this type of brand to drive deeper consumer engagement, the specify brand building process (Fig. 2) would be proposed as the followings:

- Screening the social needs
- Target consumers' extraction
- Branding Story Development

  - Screening the social needs
  - Target consumers' extraction
  - Branding Story Development

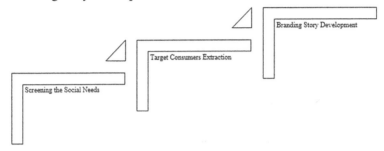

Fig. 2. Specify brand building process for personalities-driven emotional brand

3.2 Appeal-Driven Emotional Brand

The emotional bonding is developed through a unique brand identity. This unique style of the brand identity presents the personality of the brand to hit the consumers' heart. This type of emotional branding was developed base on the exploration on how emotional design characteristics influence the emotional responses and reactions include repurchasing, recommendation, attachment and passion of consumers. For example, the logo of H&M is detonated by two red letters 'H' and 'M', both are in red, with a '&' sign in between them. The small space between two letters, 'H' and 'M', are equal; both left side of the two letters are thinner than their right sides. They are in rounded forms yet straight, slant toward the right. Thicker line and thinner lines appears to be asymmetry of the letters. This logo presented as an artistic symbol. Consumer described their points of view about the logo: 'initials', 'handwriting style', 'pop art painting', 'simple and fashionable', 'affordable luxury',' rebellious', 'humanity', 'peace, neutrality, love'.

Based on the featured methods for this type of brand to drive deeper consumer engagement, the specify brand building process (Fig. 3) would be proposed as the followings:

- Mood fitting
- Visualise
- Systematise
- Execution
- Identity Management

- Mood fitting
- Visualise
- Systematise
- Execution
- Identity Management

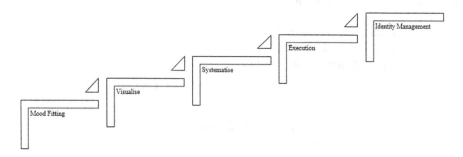

Fig. 3. Specify brand building process for appeal-driven emotional brand

3.3   Sensory-Driven Emotional Brand

The emotional bonding with consumers was built by the senses. The physical touch of the designs or the environment where the services those are designed for satisfying the consumers' emotional needs. The design outcomes (include design and services) of an emotional brand involves attractiveness, beauty, and creativity characteristics. Sensory-driven emotional brand emphasised the emotion al interaction within the consumption process. This type of brand delighted the design and service up-to-standard in order to get the leading role in the industry.

Starbuck, brand by 'bringing people together', is the example to explain how a brand create connections with consumers through sensory. Frist, from the 'free Wi-Fi service' to 'the music played instore', 'the large tables with room for groups and meetings' all set up and installation of the stores are designed to encourage the inter-actions between customers. Sweet (2008) described how its business is happening and people are sharing, 'Go into any Starbucks…Everything in there is about connection, discovery, inspiration and creation.' The interior design was embodied a trendy style decoration which is comfortable: The café uses loft style, bright spaces with inspired furniture. Also, in order to create the contemporary respite, fabrics are adopted. The setting separates a corner from the fast-paced culturally world.

Based on the featured methods for this type of brand to drive deeper consumer engagement, the specify brand building process (Fig. 4) would be proposed as the followings:

- User experience and interaction map
- Material allocation
- Prototype testing
- User feedback analysis
- Design modification

- User experience and interaction map
- Material allocation
- Prototype testing
- User feedback analysis
- Design modification

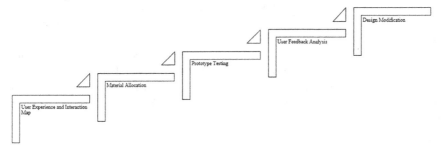

Fig. 4. Specify brand building process for sensory-driven emotional brand

3.4   Navigation-Driven Emotional Brand

This type of brand would be easily found in social media, like Facebook, a consistency would be found. It emphasised the relationships in-between content, audience and engagement. The emotional bonding is built by the leading paths that provide by brand to the consumers. By well planning advertising campaigns and media plans, the emotional feature of the brand would provide great impact to the consumers' heart. In order to provide an integrated and long-term content solution for the brands, designer have to adopt alternative perspectives in the process of sourcing, curating, publishing, and managing content actively. These methods were similar to the activities proposed by Sweet (2008):

- Directly communicating with the consumers by using text, email, apps for providing in-time surprise and updated information
- Encouraging the social interactions among the consumers for increasing viral promotion.
- Obtaining more 'status-oriented rewards' those included the recognition from the publics by taking the roles of trend leader, specialist, etc.
- Launching services in right locations during campaigns for generating the brand engagement which provide the experiences and sales in the real connections.
- Increasing the replying speed and viral uptake towards the consumers by adopting creative ideas those reflecting the brand's authenticity.

Took reference from the experience of the flagship brands those are success in social media. The conversations with consumers are key channels to engage fans. These channels enable the brand to truly connect with its followers and consumers thus build a relationship which 'leading long-term brand development', 'heading to the value for the company' as the result. LEGO Club Magazine is one of the best examples to illustrate the concept of navigation-driven emotional brand. In the 1980s to 1990s, there was a tremendous threat to LEGO from the field of competing construction toys. The company understood it had to build a powerful brand. It adopted integrated marketing approach to go up against the other construction toys competitors. Contributed by the incredible branding and emotional-attached marketing efforts through LEGO Club Magazine, LEGO is customised for subscribers with specified market and age. The LEGO Club Magazine allows kids to obtain emotional content which relevant to them in funny and creative approaches. The LEGO Club which worked as 'one of the biggest and most popular children's member clubs in the world, extended its offering, to improve its magazine (i.e. the design outcome) with more cartoon (called LEGO bricks in action) from the version of 2011. These stories with better integration of customer photos.

Based on the featured methods for this type of brand to drive deeper consumer engagement, the specify brand building process (Fig. 5) would be proposed as the followings:

- Media and communication strategy development
- Message and Communication path organisation
- Production management
- Procurement management
- Message distribution
- Sustainability management in Brand Communication

- Media and communication strategy development
- Message and Communication path organisation
- Production management
- Procurement management
- Message distribution
- Sustainability management in Brand Communication

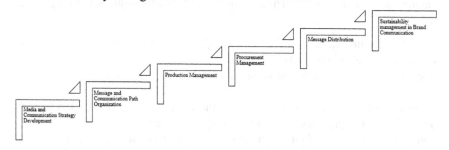

Fig. 5.   Specify brand building process for navigation-driven emotional brand

4   A Field Experiment on the Effectiveness of Emotional Branding Experience Optimising the Brand Design Process

A field experiment was adopted to examine the methods. Fifteen brand designers were invited to participate in the experiment. They were divided into two groups, group A followed the proposed brand design process and the group B did not follow. Each designer randomly chose a brand project and recorded their process of the brand design. The branding process and the design outcomes were compared. The resulted reflected how would the specify brand building process would provide to creative. It helped to optimise the branding design process in order to facilitate them to create the most effective emotional brand experience to the consumers. This study is the preliminary discussion on the new development of the emotional branding by integrated the studies of design, psychology, socialist, marketing and business and how would the brand strengthen the emotional attachment with the consumer.

4.1 Research Process

There were two parts of the study were conducted; stage 1 was the field observations. It aimed to observe the manipulating of branding process with or without emotional branding strategies. Ten designers for the field observation and fifty consumers for the assessment of communication design, through an interview, were invited to participate in this study. The field observation was under video-recording. The ten designers were separated into two groups, Design Team A and Design Team B. Design Team A got a lecture on the manipulation of emotion extraction system in information retrieval. The skills of emotion recognising and recording emotional changes during the design research were taught. Design Team B worked without any information about emotion extraction system in information retrieval. In stage 1, every designer was asked to set up the consumers' portfolio after their research. In stage 2, the brand experience consumed by consumers was recorded. The feedbacks of consumers were analysed and discovered whether the professionals' design would prove better design experience to the consumers. Some questions about the designers' feedback in design research process were asked in stage 1 as the following:

- Please set up the consumers' portfolio.
- Which element you obtain in your research is the most insightful to your design?

Also, in order to collect the feedback of consumers in stage 2, some questions about the user experience were asked in the assessment of branding experience. The questions were listed in the following:

- On a scale of 1–100, how close was the design can provide you with the best assistance in your branding experience?
- On a scale of 1–100, how close was the consumers' portfolio successfully described your situation?
- Here are some keywords (the keywords were exerted from the stage 1 answer of designers in question 2) about your branding experience. Which of them you think it is mostly related to your branding experience?
- On a scale of 1–100, how much do you agree that the following kinds of design element are able to provide you design experience of the brand?

4.2 Research Result

The fifty invited consumers consumed the ten design outcomes and provided the score one by one (100 marks as the highest and 1 mark as the lowest). The score obtained by Design Team A was higher than Design Team B on the satisfaction of consumers (shown in Fig. 6). The consumers' portfolio developed by Design Team A got a higher level of appreciation than the Design Team B (shown in Fig. 7). Compared the keywords those were exerted from the stage 1 answer of designers in question 2 and the keywords selected by consumers in the question 3 of stages 2. The keywords selected by the designers in Design Team A more than Design Team B. The comparison of the percentage of accuracy was shown in Fig. 8. There are some highlights feedbacks provided by the consumers. They pointed out that the design solutions which supported by the emotional branding strategies were much more creative. The presentations of visual, audio elements were much more able to satisfy their needs. The field observation on the design process of the design teams also showed that the Team A which adopted emotional branding strategies is much more effective for them to generate creative branding design.

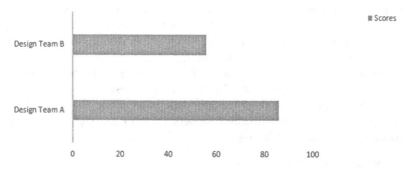

Fig. 6. The average scores of the consumers' satisfaction

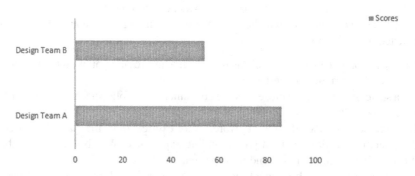

Fig. 7. The level of appreciation of consumers' portfolio

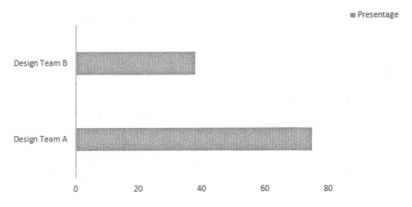

Fig. 8. The designers' recognition on consumers' need

5   Discussion on the Findings

According to the finding from question 3, it was found that the feedback of participants examined the investigation on the relationship between design elements and emotion. They recosnised that the colour, shape and typography as the tools to provide brand experience to the consumers (shown in Fig. 9). The Design is a process of continuous improvement in which every new interaction involves a new learning curve. The research in (Ho and Siu 2012), which focused on emotion and design, provides valuable insight into how various aspects of design connect with audiences, particularly regarding perception and emotion. There is a science to designing engaging content. Colors, shapes, typefaces, and space create interactions and associations, and a skilled designer can use each of these design elements effectively. The key lies in understanding the

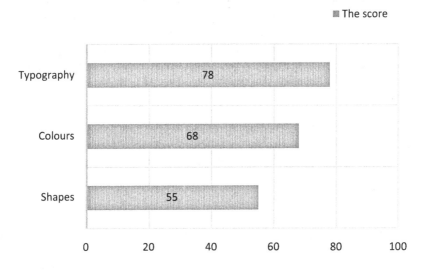

Fig. 9. The levels of recognition on design element can provide design experience of the brand

emotions of a particular audience and introducing to them the appropriate characteristics of a brand thus audiences have distinct perceptions.

5.1 Informed Use of Shapes

Shape, as a portion of two-dimensional space, it has special meanings, it also worked as the foundational components of the grammar of visual thinking. Circular graphics convey positive emotions, and tend to connote community, friendship, love, and unity. Rings are the universal symbol of relationships and are associated with marriage and partnership, depicting strength and resolution. Curves are associated with femininity, suggesting flexibility, adaptability, and compliance. Straight-edged shapes imply stability and consistency in a more concrete sense and can also be used to indicate balance. Triangles are regarded as the symbols of authority and rational; at the same time, they are found in religious firms. Vertical lines represent power, toleration, and hostility while horizontal lines represent cooperative, stable and silent. Deliberate asymmetric spaces can make designs livelier. The default space between characters and design elements can also convey meaning or tone.

5.2 The Language of Colors

Color is a subjective element in design. The reactions it stimulates in one audience may differ considerably from those evoked in other audiences. This may be due to cultural background, personal preference, and numerous other factors. Designers should seek to understand the diverse effects of colors on a variety of people.

5.3 The Emotion of Typefaces

Fonts tell distinct stories. Typography plays a crucial role in developing a strong identity and a solid first impression, because a design can set the mood with typography. Serifs create a sense of authority, tradition, respect, and grandeur, whereas clean sans serif fonts invoke the modern, objective, stable, and universal. The style and appearance of text signals to readers what to expect. A well-considered typeface combined with quality images in an advertisement or other instance of visual communication can have a considerable impact on an audience. Emotion influences an audience's feelings towards the message delivered, and this emotion can be influenced by the design elements of visual communication. Designers must therefore consider how design can influence the emotions of an audience, so that they can affect audiences' feelings through visual communication design by organizing the feelings stimulated by design elements.

6 Conclusion

Based on the above analysis on the development of emotional design and how it is influenced by new media, the changes of consumer's communication are understood. As the brands need to keep up-to-day with the consumers in order to keep the close relationship with the consumers, their methods to provide emotional experience to the consumers were changed. In this study, the featured communication way of four types of emotional branding was analysed and the corresponding brand development procedures were suggested. This is the preliminary discussion on the new development of the emotional branding by integrated the studies of design, psychology, socialist, marketing and business and how would the brand strengthen the emotional attachment with the consumer. Further research on how the emotional attachment influence their purchasing decision making is necessary.

References

Abbing, E.R., Gessel, C.: Brand-driven innovation. design. Manage. Rev. **19**(3), 51–58 (2008). doi:10.1111/j.1948-7169.2008.tb00129.x

Beaudry, A., Pinsonneault, A.: The other side of acceptance: studying the direct and indirect effects of emotions on information technology use. MIS Q. **34**(4), 689–710 (2010). doi:10.2307/249688

Bergkvist, L., Bech-Larsen, T.: Two studies of consequences and actionable antecedents of brand love. J. Brand Manage. **17**(7), 504–518 (2010). doi:10.1057/bm.2010.6

Bernays, E.L., Howard, W.C.: The Engineering of Consent. University of Oklahoma, Norman (1955)

Carroll, B.A., Ahuvia, A.C.: Some antecedents and outcomes of brand love. Mark. Lett. **17**(2), 79–89 (2006). doi:10.1007/s11002-006-4219-2

Crilly, N., Moultrie, J., Clarkson, P.J.: Seeing things: consumer response to the visual domain in product design. Des. Stud. **25**(6), 547–577 (2004). doi:10.1016/j.destud.2004.03.001

Ho, A.G., Siu, K.W.M.: Emotion design, emotional design, emotionalise design: a review on their relationships from a new perspective. Des. J. **15**(1), 9–32 (2012). doi:10.2752/175630612X13192035508462

Hui, Y.Y., Po, H.L., Lin, R.: Emotional product design and perceived brand emotion. Int. J. Adv. Psychol. (IJAP) **3**(2), 59 (2014). doi:10.14355/ijap.2014.0302.05

Kim, M.K., Park, M.C., Jeong, D.H.: The effects of customer satisfaction and switching barrier on customer loyalty in Korean mobile telecommunication services. Telecommun. Policy **28**(2), 145–159 (2004). doi:10.1016/j.telpol.2003.12.003

Kim, J., Lee, J., Choi, D.: Designing emotionally evocative homepages: an empirical study of the quantitative relations between design factors and emotional dimensions. Int. J. Hum.-Comput. Interact. Stud. **59**, 899–940 (2003). doi:10.1016/j.ijhcs.2003.06.002

Lin, R., Chang, C.L.: A study of consumer perception in innovative product. In: International Conference, Australia, November 17–21 (2004)

Lynch, J., De Chernatony, L.: The power of emotion: brand communication in business-to-business markets. J. Brand Manage. **11**(5), 403–419 (2004). doi:10.1057/palgrave.bm.2540185

McLoone, H., Jacobson, M., Goonetilleke, R.S., Kleiss, J., Liu, Y.L., Schütte, S.: Product design and emotion: frameworks, methods, and case studies. In: Proceedings of the Human Factors and Ergonomics Society Annual Meeting (2012). doi:10.1007/978-3-319-20907-4_11

Morrison, S., Crane, F.G.: Building the service brand by creating and managing an emotional brand experience. J. Brand Manage. **14**(5), 410–421 (2007). doi:10.1057/palgrave.bm.2550080

Park, C.W., Jaworski, B.J., MacInnis, D.J.: Strategic brand concept-image management. J. Market. **50**(4), 135–145 (1986). doi:10.2307/1251291

Perloff, R.M.: The Dynamics of Persuasion: Communication and Attitudes in the 21st Century. Routledge (2010). doi:10.1080/10810730500228987

Petty, R.E., Cacioppo, J.T.: The elaboration likelihood model of persuasion, 129–170 (1986). doi: 10.1007/978-1-4612-4964-1_1

Rahinel, R., Redden, J.P.: Brands as product coordinators: matching brands make joint consumption experiences more enjoyable. J. Consum. Res. **39**(6), 1290–1299 (2013). doi: 10.1086/668525

Roberts, K.: Lovemarks: The Future Beyond Brands. Powerhouse Books, New York (2004)

Sun, H., Zhang, P.: The role of moderating factors in user technology acceptance. Int. J. Hum.-Comput. Stud. (IJHCS) **64**(2), 53–78 (2006). doi:10.1016/j.ijhcs.2005.04.013

Wang, H.X., Chen, J., Hu, Y.C.: The consistency of product design and brand image. In: IEEE 10th International Conference, pp. 1142–1144 (2008). doi:10.1109/CAIDCD.2008.4730764

Zettl, H.: Essentials of application lied media aesthetics. In: Dorai, C., Venkatesh, S. (eds.) Media Computing: Computational Media Aesthetics. Kluwer Academic, Boston (2002). doi: 10.1109/93.959093

Guiding Human Behavior Through Alternate Reality Experience

Fumiko Ishizawa and Tatsuo Nakajima[✉]

Department of Computer Science and Engineering, Waseda University, Tokyo, Japan
{f.ishizawa,tatsuo}@dcl.cs.waseda.ac.jp

Abstract. This paper discusses design strategies that can be used to refine the meaning of real space, with the goal of guiding human behavior. In our approach, user experience felt by refining the real space's meaning through fictionality is *alternate reality experience*. The alternate reality experience is typically achieved through modifying our eye-sights, and makes our world interactive by influencing human attitude and behavior implicitly through virtual reality technologies. Incorporating fictionality influences the user's behavior and helps them to overcome their daily social issues. We present our experiences with conducting a participatory design workshop in which participants designed services that enhance real spaces using fictional occurrences. Based on our experience conducting the workshop, enhancing real spaces allows people to guide human behavior by showing the consequences of current behavior as possible ideal futures and by presenting a narrative indicating why behavior changes are necessary and how they become possible.

Keywords: Human behavior · Virtual reality · Head-mount display

1 Introduction

Our society is facing various fundamental social problems, including challenges to environmental sustainability and human well-being. Without altering human behavior, it will be essentially impossible to overcome these problems [7, 31]. Researchers have been working to develop persuasive technologies that guide human behavior through computing approaches [15, 24]. Recently, advanced wearable technologies have allowed us to change our vision and to see non-existing things and occurrences in real spaces or to replace some of the actual things that exist in these spaces [9, 28]. In particular, a light-weight head-mounted display can present an eye-level view on a display, but the view can be modified through virtual reality technologies, and thus the meaning of the real space can be changed. In our approach, user experience felt by refining the real space's meaning through fictionality is *alternate reality experience*. The alternate reality experience is typically achieved through modifying our eye-sights, and makes our world interactive by influencing human attitude and behavior implicitly through virtual reality technologies.

Despite advances in this technology, its possibilities have not been well discussed. In particular, to encourage people to reflect deeply on how their current behavior affects

© Springer International Publishing AG 2017
A. Marcus and W. Wang (Eds.): DUXU 2017, Part II, LNCS 10289, pp. 35–47, 2017.
DOI: 10.1007/978-3-319-58637-3_3

their futures – and to get them to change undesirable behaviors – we need a better way to show them different possible futures [9, 22, 23]. In this paper, we conducted a participatory design workshop where participants developed persuasive services to overcome social problems. In these services, people wear head-mounted displays to show modified eye-level views that enhance the meaning of real spaces using fictional events. One important lesson learned is the importance of balancing fiction and reality when designing and representing persuasive and effective possible futures as consequences of current behaviors. Additionally, narratives showing why behavior changes are necessary and how behavior can be changed are both useful and essential for encouraging behavior changes.

This paper is organized as follows. In Sect. 2, we present related work to the proposed idea in this paper. Section 3 shows the enhancement of the meaning of the real space, and Sect. 4 shows an overview of *Alternative Reality*. In Sect. 5, we present how to conduct our participatory design workshop, and in Sect. 6, we describe some lessons learned from the workshop. Finally, Section concludes the paper.

2   Related Work

Altering human behavior through technology has been seen as a promising way to break undesirable daily habits, and some researchers have attempted to develop design frameworks for designing persuasive services [24].

Most recently, digital marketing practitioners have adopted an approach known as *gamification*. Using *badges* and *leaderboards* is a typical approach to achieving gamification. Several studies have discussed systematic gamification designs [3, 5]. In traditional gamification, a set of game mechanics is widely adopted for motivating human behavior; however, incorporating game mechanics into the real world is not easy. Thus, simple mechanics such as badges, leaderboards and points are typically used.

Guiding people's attitudes and behaviors is an important design issue when trying to address various fundamental social issues such as sustainability, health and happiness [7, 31]. Enhancing the semiotic meaning of real space through incorporated fictionality is a powerful technique that can alter people's attitudes and behaviors [20]. As shown in [29], procedural rhetoric is a promising theoretical foundation for increasing persuasiveness by making the enhanced real space meaningful.

There are several existing case studies that use augmented reality technologies to enhance the meaning of real space to influence people's behavior. For example, in [27], the authors propose a service for implicitly influencing the satisfaction people experience while drinking a beverage and for controlling beverage consumption by creating a volume perception illusion using augmented reality technologies. The system proposed in [16] aims to create a method of modifying perceptions of satiety and controlling nutritional intake by changing the apparent size of food using augmented reality technologies.

Augmented reality techniques can be used to enhance existing artifacts [1, 18]. For example, [32] describes several augmented reality games that are enhanced versions of traditional physical games. Specifically, *Augmented Go* [10] demonstrates a promising approach to maintaining the advantages of the physicality of the board game while adding virtuality. *Virtual Aquarium* [15] shows a virtual fish tank in which the movement of the fish reflects a user's tooth-brushing behavior. *Enhanced TCG* [28] enhances our real world by replacing a real-world component with a fictional component for changing the semiotic meaning of the real world.

There are several ways to incorporate fictionality into the real world [19]. One typical approach is to use live action role playing (LARP) [14] or alternative reality games (ARG) [12]. During LARP, players play fictional roles based on a pervasive role-playing concept [11, 13] and a game master to control the gap between fiction and reality. ARG adopts a concept named transmedia storytelling [20], using multiple media to incorporate fictional stories into the real world. These approaches are promising, but the approach requires a rigorous plan that requires a long time to reduce the gap between fiction and reality. Augmented reality and virtual reality technologies offer another possibility to incorporate fictionality into the real world. For example, in [16, 27, 28], by using head-mounted displays, a user immersively changes the meaning of the real world to alter his or her attitude and behavior. The magic circle is defined as the boundary between the real world and the virtual world [17]. If a user is not aware of a magic circle between the worlds, the user cannot notice that the virtual world is not real. Therefore, he/she feels that the virtual scenes actually happen in the real world. The most important issue in realizing immersion blurs the magic circle.

When attempting to solve serious social problems such as sustainability issues, health issues, and happiness [7, 31], guiding people's attitudes and behaviors is an important design issue. Enhancing the semiotic meaning of the real world through incorporated virtuality is a powerful technique for altering people's attitudes and behaviors [21]. As shown in [29], procedural rhetoric is a promising theoretical foundation to increase persuasiveness by making the enhanced real world meaningful.

In [4], Dunne and Raby use design to offer new forms of expression for complex and critical issues; these forms of expression are grounded in the most abstract, speculative and future-focused considerations. Critical questions about emerging technology in everyday situations have presented preferable futures as opposed to predicting the future. They call this design approach *Speculative Design*. The approach taken in *Alternative Reality* can be considered an example of *Speculative Design* because the aim is to investigate whether a user feels as though he/she is watching a future scene when the scene uses only components that exist in the real world.

Our approach is also similar to the *Substitutional Reality* (SR) system [30]. In the SR system, people's reality is manipulated by allowing them to experience live scenes in which they are physically present and recorded scenes that were recorded and modified in advance without losing a user's reality. Our approach is more general than the SR system because *Alternative Reality* can use CG images generated by VR techniques not only recorded images.

Several previous investigations used a 3D model composed from real scenes. For example, in [2], a user interacts with the 3D model of a building to learn routes inside the building. The user can learn the real routes in the real town in the virtual world.

3   Enhancing the Meaning of the Real Space

In this study, we focus on the following five lenses in discussing the enhancement of the meanings of real places, as shown in Fig. 1. Each lens becomes a design frame that can be used to consider how to enhance the meaning of real spaces, with the goal of influencing people's behavior from the frame's point of view.

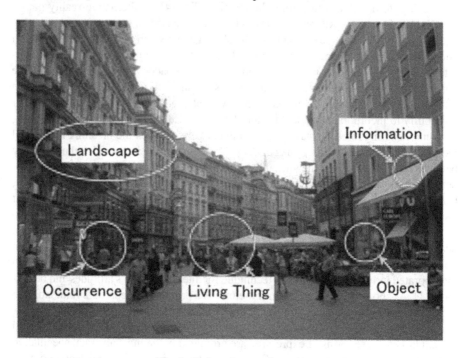

Fig. 1.   Enhancing a real space

Living Things are typically humans or animals. *Objects* are typically static things that appear in real spaces such as bicycles in Fig. 1. *Landscapes* are the backgrounds in real spaces. In particular, we consider the meanings of sets of objects (like buildings in the street, as shown in Fig. 1). *Occurrences* are events that happen in real spaces, such as the street performances in the figure. In Fig. 1, a sign in the street is typical *information*. These five lenses were used in the workshop to structurally discuss how each service enhances the meaning of real spaces.

In existing approaches to enhancing real spaces, *Objects* or *Landscapes* are typically enhanced. Additionally, *Information* is explicitly superimposed on the real space to help people make better decisions. On the other hand, typical VR applications offer fictional *Occurrences* to create impressive environments, and people tend to remember them better than they remember real *Occurrences*. Additionally, for effective behavior changes, the presence of empathetic *Living Things,* such as friends, pets or beautiful flowers, is essential [15].

4   Alternative Reality

Alternative Reality makes it possible to connect the real world with the virtual world from a single temporal perspective [8]. The worlds can also be seamlessly integrated because the virtual world consists of real landscapes, objects and persons. This means that it may be possible to enhance the real world by presenting fictional occurrences along with real events, and thus people experience an enhanced hybrid world in the real world rather than in a fictional world (as in a movie). Incorporating fictionality into real space strongly influences human attitudes and behavior. Thus, this approach can be used to guide people towards a more desirable lifestyle.

In *Alternative Reality*, a user watches a sequence of scenes on an HMD. As shown in Fig. 2, the sequence consists of several scenes. Some scenes are captured from contemporary scenes in the real world (Real Scenes in Fig. 2). The scenes are recorded by a 360-degree camera and shown on the HMD in real-time. However, some scenes in the sequence are not real scenes; such scenes may actually be constructed through VR techniques and are fictional (Virtual Scenes in Fig. 2). Additionally, the virtual scenes may include several events that do not occur in the contemporary real world. Typically, these scenes are constructed using 3D models of real persons, objects and landscapes in advance, but some real persons who are not actually present may appear. One of the important requirements of *Alternative Reality* is that the user feels that these real and

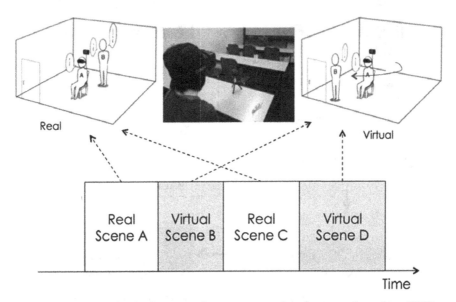

There are two persons in the room. One person watches the room through an HMD. Real scene A is a movie that captures the present room. Virtual scene B is a movie that captured the room in advance. The person who wears an HMD watches the virtual scenes and he/she can feel that the other person is in front of him/her. However, in the present real world, the person is actually behind him/her.

Fig. 2.   An example based on alternative reality

virtual scenes are continuous and, thus, is not aware of the boundary between the two scenes. Therefore, he/she feels that the virtual scenes are actually happening in the real world. The most important issue in achieving this immersion is blurring the boundary between fiction and reality.

The use of an HMD provides a better *immersion* experience by showing a video stream that captures the real world and replacing some real components with fictional components. Additionally, the interactivity with real space offers *agency,* and the user believes that he/she autonomously chooses his/her activities by him/herself.

One typical way of enhancing the meaning of a real space based on *Alternative Reality* presents possible futures in the present real space so as to guide people's behavior. This may be effective because the possible futures clearly show the consequences of the user's current behavior, and behavior changes are encouraged if the possible futures are not desirable. As shown in [8], we have developed two case studies, named *Interactive Improbable Object* (shown in Fig. 3) and *Fictional Future* (shown in Fig. 4) to demonstrate the feasibility of *Alternative Reality*.

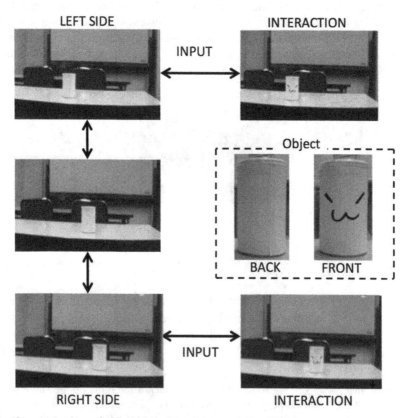

"Interactive Improbable Objects" is a case study in which a moving object with which a user can interact behaves in an improbable way.

Fig. 3. Some scenes in interactive improbable object

"Fictional Future" is a case study containing both present and possible future occurrences

Fig. 4. Some scenes in fictional future

5   Experiences Conducting a Workshop

In the workshop, each group created one or more digitally enhanced speculative images, depicting possible aspects of services based on the *Alternative Reality* concept. These services aim to make people reflect deeply on how their current behavior affects their futures and to give them opportunities to change their undesirable behavior. We discussed an effective way of guiding human behavior by integrating fictionality into real space based on *Alternative Reality*. Incorporating fictionality into real space has the potential to guide our behavior by naturally presenting the goals and effects of our behavior as possible futures. We analyze and propose what types of services make fictionality effective and what pitfalls and benefits *Alternative Reality* offers when naturally integrating persuasive fictionality. These discussions enable us to extract useful insights in order to develop services that will use AR technologies to encourage better human lifestyles in the future.

In the workshop, five groups (with three people in each group) discussed design issues in the following two stages. In the first stage, each group suggested a couple of proposals for services that used the *Alternative Reality* concept to guide human behavior. This discussion allowed us to determine what types of services could use *Alternative Reality* effectively. Then, each group discussed alternative approaches to implementing the proposed services – without *Alternative Reality* – and presented the benefits and potential pitfalls of these alternative approaches. These discussions made clear the types of services that could use *Alternative Reality* effectively.

Most of the services proposed in the workshop that aimed to guide human behavior were based on a narrative, such as reminding someone of something, cleaning a room, or looking at one's poor physical condition. For example, in the service based on looking at one's poor physical condition, a user looks through an HMD and sees his/her body shape growing gradually fat if he/she continues bad eating habits. However, showing the future effect of a bad habit is limited in its power to persuade people; it is important to show people – through the narrative – how to change their habits and why they should do so [15]. In contrast, there are a few suggestions that do not use the narrative, such as instructing someone in the correct way to use a machine or changing the color of a food.

Services that include a narrative can naturally deliver messages that persuade people. For example, in typical movies, people are persuaded by narrators or actors simply by watching the movie [6]. Based on the five lenses described above, enhancing a real space with fictional occurrences is difficult to achieve through traditional AR technologies because most AR technologies focus on the enhancement of objects and landscapes in the real space, or just show information superimposed on the real space. On the other hand, incorporating a narrative into the real space is not difficult because fictional occurrences instigated by a friend (a living thing) and inserted in virtual scenes can be easily realized through *Alternative Reality*. Thus, in the human behavior change services proposed in the workshop, the use of *Alternative Reality* is more appropriate than the use of traditional AR technologies.

In the second stage of the workshop, each group selected one service from those suggested in the previous stage and discussed the design of the service in detail.

We selected the following two services because they highlighted how to use a narrative as a central mechanism to persuade people to change their behavior.

The first service is a reminder service, as shown in Fig. 5. When a user is likely to leave an umbrella on a train or a bag in a cafe, his/her view inserts a virtual scene of a fictional occurrence where an authentic person reminds the user to remember the umbrella or bag before leaving instead of alarming him/her about not forgetting it. The user believes that the authentic person teaches him/her to be more careful about not forgetting the item. Using a narrative is essential to make the user behave more carefully

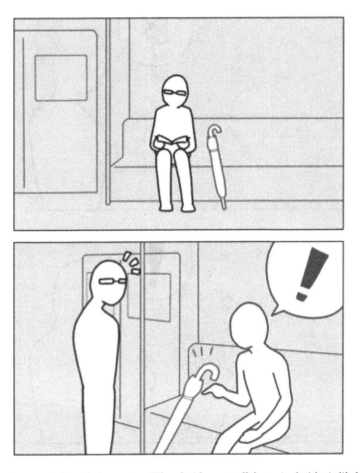

A user is on a train with the service. When he/she gets off the train, he/she is likely to leave an umbrella. The realistic authentic human automatically generated by the service talks him/her to make him/her be more careful for his/her belongings as a reminder before getting off the train in a virtual scene. It makes him/her be more careful not to forget them because the authentic human's appearance seems his/her ideal possible future appearance.

Fig. 5. An illustration of a reminder system to make a user more careful.

because the narrative easily presents why behavior changes are necessary and how to change one's behavior. In contrast, the user treats an alarm as a single occurrence and changes his/her behavior only temporally, rather than for the long term.

The second service trains people to express opinions that they usually hesitate to discuss, as shown in Fig. 6. Using this service makes users more able to offer helpful opinions in a positive way and helps avoid misunderstandings. The narrative, which involves empathetic friends, lowers the hurdles to sharing opinions. When the user is

A user has colleagues who do not work together seriously. He/she wants to offer them opinions, but the shy user usually hesitates to discuss. Then, the service allows him/her to train to express his/her opinions that may be sometimes negative to the colleagues and to avoid the misunderstanding with other colleagues. The service presents some virtual scenes that the user's opinions help his/her colleagues well as possible futures, therefore, the user believes that his/her behavior will have good influences on the colleagues' futures.

Fig. 6. An illustration of a training system to give opinions that are usually hesitated to say.

not busy, a virtual scene shows an occurrence where a friend asks for his/her opinion on a person whom they met a little earlier. Practicing giving his/her opinion about someone he/she met earlier lowers the hurdle to sharing opinions of others, and the user's habit – perhaps caused by his/her shyness – can be changed.

6   Lessens Learned

The results of the workshop suggest that services using the *Alternative Reality* concept allow people to guide human behavior by, first, showing the fictional effects of behavior as possible ideal futures and, second, by presenting narratives indicating why behavior changes are necessary and how they are possible. Narratives can be easily incorporated through virtual occurrences that are one of the five lenses presented earlier in this paper. The five lenses are a useful set of tools for analyzing the reality of the enhanced real space. Each lens becomes a frame through which to analyze the reality of the enhanced elements in the real space one by one.

When using traditional AR technologies, if the enhanced real space does not offer exaggerated effects, people may not be aware of the enhanced meanings of the real space. If using *Alternative Reality*, as shown above, it is possible to incorporate fictional occurrences by inserting them in a virtual scene. This approach shows the merits of adopting *Alternative Reality* when designing services that aim to change human behavior. Fictional occurrences can easily include a narrative and naturally present persuasive messages via a friend's voice. Although the approach is ambient, the effect of the voice is strong enough to make the user aware of the meanings of the possible futures, and the user's agency is increased because communicating with a friend is interactive without compromising the immersion effect of the real space. This approach also increases the possibility of enhancing human intrinsic motivation, which is essential for long-term behavior changes [15].

We still need to investigate alternative ways of guiding human behavior. As shown above, reality is an important design resource for designing effective methods of behavior change, but it is a fact that a narrative alone may not be effective at persuading people. For example, people are sometimes stubborn and do not listen to their friends' voices. The fictional effect, which makes people marvel, is also an important design resource for human behavior change [11]. Based on the insights discussed in design fiction, the *suspension of disbelief* is an essential design strategy for designing believable fictionality [26]. This strategy is different from traditional approaches to maintaining the reality of incorporated fictionality in real space. Investigating how to design believable fictionality that still makes users marvel is one important future direction in our research.

One potential pitfall is that the current approach may cause some miscommunication between the user and his/her friends because inserted occurrences with these friends are fictional. Thus, the friend may not know about the fictional occurrences. Consequently, asking about these fictional occurrences may cause some potential misunderstandings. Additionally, the friend's personality should be consistent with that of the virtual friend who appears in the services. If not, the fictional occurrences may lose their sense of reality and reduce the effectiveness of behavior changes. Maintaining consistency between fiction and reality is also one of our important future directions.

7 Conclusion

The paper discussed how to enhance the meaning of real spaces in order to overcome social problems through behavior changes. We presented some lessons learned that we extracted from our experiences conducting a participatory design workshop where participants designed persuasive services that enhanced real space.

References

1. Azuma, R.T.: A survey of augmented reality. Presence **6**(4), 355–385 (1997)
2. Bailey, J.H., Knerr, B.W., Witmer, B.G.: Virtual Spaces and real world places: transfer of route knowledge. Int. J. Hum. Comput. Stud. **45**(4), 413–428 (1996)
3. Deterding, S., Dixon, D., Khaled, R., Nacke, N.: From game design elements to gamefulness: defining "Ramification". In: Proceedings of the 15th International Academic MindTrek Conference: Envisioning Future Media Environments (2011)
4. Dunne, A., Raby, F.: Speculative Everything: Design, Fiction, and Social Dreaming. MIT Press, Cambridge (2013)
5. Huotari, K., Hamari, J.: Defining gamification – a service marketing perspective. In: Proceedings of the 16th International Academic Mindtrek Conference, pp. 17–22 (2012)
6. Igartua, J.-J., Barrios, I.: Changing real-world beliefs with controversial movies: processes and mechanisms of narrative persuasion. J. Commun. **62**, 514–531 (2012)
7. Institute of Government: MINDSPACE: Influencing Behavior through Public Policy. Cabinet Office (2010)
8. Ishizawa, F., Nakajima, T.: Alternative reality: an augmented daily urban world inserting virtual scenes temporally. In: García, Carmelo R., Caballero-Gil, P., Burmester, M., Quesada-Arencibia, A. (eds.) UCAmI 2016. LNCS, vol. 10069, pp. 353–364. Springer, Cham (2016). doi:10.1007/978-3-319-48746-5_36
9. Ishizawa, F., Sakamoto, M., Nakajima, T.: Analyzing two case studies for enhancing the meaning of the real space. In: Proceedings of the 9th Nordic Conference on Human-Computer Interaction (2016)
10. Iwata, T., Yamabe, T., Nakajima, T.: Augmented reality go: extending traditional game play with interactive self-learning support. In: Proceedings of the 17th IEEE Conference on Embedded and Real-time Computing Systems and Applications, pp. 105–114 (2011)
11. Ludden, G.D.S., Schifferstein, H.N.J., Hekkert, P.: Surprise as a design strategy. Des. Issues **24**(2), 28–38 (2008)
12. McGonigal, J.: Reality Is Broken: Why Games Make Us Better and How They Can Change the World. Penguin Press, New York (2011)
13. Montola, M.: Tangible pleasures of pervasive role-playing. In: Proceedings of International Conference on DiGRA 2007 (2007)
14. Montola, M., Stemros, J., Waern, A.: Pervasive Games - Theory and Design. Morgan Kaufmann, New York (2009)
15. Nakajima, T., Lehdonvirta, V.: Designing motivation in persuasive ambient mirrors. Pers. Ubiquit. Comput. **17**(1), 107–126 (2013)

16. Narumi, T., Ban, Y., Kajinami, T., Tanikawa, T., Hirose, M.: Augmented perception of satiety: controlling food consumption by changing apparent size of food with augmented reality. In: Proceedings of the Conference on Human Factors in Computing Systems (2012)
17. Nieuwdorp, E.: The pervasive interface: tracing the magic circle. In: Proceedings of DiGRA 2005 Conference: Changing Views – Worlds in Play (2005)
18. Rolland, J., Biocca, F., Hamza-Lup, F., Yanggang, H., Martins, R.: Development of head-mounted projection displays for distributed, collaborative, augmented reality applications. Presence Teleoperators Virtual Environ. **14**(5), 528–549 (2005)
19. Sakamoto, M., Nakajima, T.: Gamifying intelligent daily environments through introducing fictionality. Int. J. Hybrid Inf. Technol. **7**(4), 259–276 (2014)
20. Sakamoto, M., Nakajima, T.: Incorporating fictionality into the real world with transmedia storytelling. In: Marcus, A. (ed.) DUXU 2015. LNCS, vol. 9186, pp. 654–665. Springer, Cham (2015). doi:10.1007/978-3-319-20886-2_61
21. Sakamoto, M., Nakajima, T., Alexandrova, T.: Enhancing values through virtuality for intelligent artifacts that influence human attitude and behavior. Multimedia Tools Appl. **74**(24), 11537–11568 (2015)
22. Sakamoto, M., Nakajima, T.: In search of the right design abstraction for designing persuasive affordance towards a flourished society. In: Proceeding of the 9th International Conference on Design and Semantics of Form and Movement (2015)
23. Sakamoto, M., Nakajima, T., Akioka, S.: Gamifying collective human behavior with gameful digital rhetoric. Multimedia Tools and Applications (2016). doi:10.1007/s11042-016-3665-y
24. Spagnolli, A., Chittaro, L., Gamberini, L.: Interactive persuasive systems: a perspective on theory and evaluation. Int. J. Hum. Comput. Interact. **32**(3), 177–189 (2016)
25. von Stackelberg, P., Jones, R.E.: Tales of Our tomorrows: transmedia storytelling and communicating about the future. J. Future Stud. **18**(3), 57–76 (2014)
26. Sterling, B.: Design fiction. Interactions **16**(3), 20–24 (2009)
27. Suzuki, E., Narumi, T., Sakurai, S., Tanikawa, T., Hirose, M.: Illusion cup: interactive controlling of beverage consumption based on an illusion of volume perception. In: Proceedings of the 5th Augmented Human International Conference (2014)
28. Takahashi, M., Irie, K., Sakamoto, M., Nakajima, T.: Incorporating fictionality into the real space: a case of enhanced TCG. In: Proceedings of the 2015 ACM International JoinConference on Pervasive and Ubiquitous Computing and Proceedings of the 2015 ACM International Symposium on Wearable Computers (2015)
29. Treanor, M., Schweizer, B., Bogost, I., Mateas, M.: Proceduralist readings: how to find meaning in games with graphical logics. In: Proceedings of Foundations of Digital Games. (2011)
30. Wakisama, S., Fujii, N., Suzuki, K.: Substitutional reality system: a novel experimental platform for experiencing alternative reality. Scientific Reports (2012). doi:10.1038/srep00459
31. Wolfe, A.K., Malone, E.L., Heerwagen, J., Dion, J.: Behavioral change and building performance: strategies for significant, persistent, and measurable institutional change. US Department of Energy (2014)
32. Yamabe, T., Nakajima, T.: Playful training with augmented reality games: case studies toward reality-oriented system design. Multimedia Tools Appl. **62**(1), 259–286 (2013)

A Quality Table-Based Method for Sentiment Expression Word Identification in Japanese

Shujiro Miyakawa[✉], Fumiaki Saitoh, and Syohei Ishizu

Aoyama Gakuin University, 5-10-1 Fuchinobe, Sagamihara 252-5258, Japan
c5616185@aoyama.jp, {saitoh,Ishizu}@ise.aoyama.ac.jp

Abstract. Identifying and summarizing opinions from online reviews is a valuable and challenging task and aspect-level sentiment analysis is a research-based approach to this task. Sentiment expression word identification is important sentiment identification task since many unique expression words appear in each entity domain and it is confirmed that text data from the internet has many collateral expressions. Generally, syntax-based model is applied to sentiment expression word identification method. Syntax-based model can consider low frequency word; however, we need to consider many syntax relations and that may be not practical. Therefore, it is difficult to identify sentiment expression words with syntax-based model. This paper proposes quality table-based method for sentiment expression word identification. The method identifies sentiment expression words with supervised learning. The training set is created with both seed expression-aspect and word-aspect deployment based on characteristic of quality table's relation. This paper proposes a non-syntax and relation-based model in order to solve syntax-based models' problems. This paper carries out an experimental test, demonstrates how many unique SEWs are extracted, and verifies the coverage of SEW with annotated text.

Keywords: Aspect-level sentiment analysis · Sentiment identification · Customer review · Quality table · Supervised learning

1 Introduction

With the growth of the Internet and social networking services like Twitter and Facebook, people can easily transmit evaluations, opinions, emotions, and impressions regarding products or services offered. Many companies collect and utilize such consumer review text data as effective information for product development and marketing. Therefore, identifying and summarizing opinions from online reviews is a valuable and challenging task. Sentiment analysis (SA) or opinion mining is a research-based approach to this task. SA can be divided into three research domains: document-level, sentence-level, and aspect-level. This paper specializes in aspect-level SA. Generally, aspect-level SA has three processes: sentiment identification, sentiment classification, and aggregation. Figure 1 illustrates the representative aspect-level SA processes. In the first process, both sentiment expression word (SEW) and aspect is identified. Some surveys focus partly on SEWs or aspects. In the second

© Springer International Publishing AG 2017
A. Marcus and W. Wang (Eds.): DUXU 2017, Part II, LNCS 10289, pp. 48–59, 2017.
DOI: 10.1007/978-3-319-58637-3_4

process, SEWs and aspects are classified with sentiment values (e.g. positive or negative). In the third process, the sentiment values are aggregated for each aspect to provide a brief overview. This paper focuses on sentiment identification.

Fig. 1. Aspect-level sentiment analysis process

As mentioned above, both SEWs and aspects are identified in the first process. Because aspect detection is a primary task of sentiment identification, many aspect detection methods have been proposed. However, SEW identification is also an important task. In many cases SEW is identified with a sentiment dictionary. Sentiment dictionary has a huge set of expression words. Also, sentiment values of aspects can be scored using sentiment values of SEWs that are obtained from sentiment dictionaries. However, it is reported that SEWs have many types of word expressions in each entity domain. Therefore, most sentiment identification or classification methods are dependent upon sentiment dictionaries; some SEWs cannot be extracted with a sentiment dictionary because SEWs have many types of word expressions; and sentiment identification and classification methods may have low performance. Therefore, SEW identification is important task and many syntax-based models are applied to the task. Syntax-based model can consider low frequency word; however, we need to consider many syntax relations and that may be not practical. Therefore, it is difficult to identify SEWs with syntax-based model.

This paper proposes a method for SEW identification and tries to identify unique SEWs that do not exist in sentiment dictionaries. This paper shows when given word sets that are likely to be SEWs, SEWs can be identified from the word sets efficiently, and unique SEWs can be extracted effectively with supervised learning. The method applies supervised learning in order to obtain SEWs more efficiently. Data sets for supervised learning are created based on the characteristics of a quality table (QT). A QT is a binary table used in quality function deployment methodology. The characteristics of a QT give each word features; a supervised learning classifier learns the words' features. The features are obtained with point mutual information (PMI). In supervised classification, there a case where the data set is unbalanced data. Therefore, synthetic minority over-sampling technique (SMOTE) algorithm, the algorithm for unbalanced data, is applied in this paper. This paper proposes a non-syntax and relation-based model in order to solve syntax-based models' problems. This paper carries out an experimental test, demonstrates how many unique SEWs are extracted, and verifies the coverage of SEW with annotated text.

2 Related Work

Many aspect-level SA methods have been developed for both English and Japanese. In both languages, the same three processes are employed. In this section, we discuss some related works in English and Japanese. In addition, we found out the difference point between related works and this paper.

Aspect-level SA in English presents three challenging tasks: aspect detection, sentiment analysis, and joint aspect detection and sentiment analysis. Aspect detection is identifying some aspects of products or services from target entity text data. Two types of model are frequently used for aspect detection: frequency-based and syntax-based. Frequency-based models consider high frequency single nouns or compound nouns as aspects. This straightforward method is powerful, and many approaches apply this method. This method clearly does not consider low frequency words; however, low frequency words are valuable aspects for customers and for companies. High frequency words are also likely to be mistaken as aspects. Therefore, a method that can also consider low frequency words as aspects is needed. To address this problem, a method of statistically determining a threshold value has been proposed. Syntax-based models analyze the syntactic relationships in sentences and identifying words that fit the syntactic relationship as aspects. The simplest syntactic relationship is dependence (e.g. given a sentence "wonderful design", where expression word "wonderful" is an adjective modifying the aspect "design"). The strength of the syntax-based model is that low frequency words can be extracted as aspects. However, text data transmitted by Internet users, such as customer reviews, have many collateral word expressions that do not apply to syntactic relations. Therefore, in order to achieve better results, it is necessary to consider many syntax relations. In addition to the two model methods mentioned above, a method using supervised learning and unsupervised learning has also been proposed. In Japanese, SEW identification is also an important task. Similarly, aspect detection is mostly frequency-based and syntax-based and the same problems appear. Many syntax-based models, such as anaphoric analysis and dependency-based, are proposed in Japanese aspect-level SA. Japanese, in particular, has more word expressions than English does at same one's meaning, which means we can express the meaning "good" with various words in Japanese. Text from the internet is hard to analyze syntactically. Therefore, it is difficult to identify SEWs with a syntax-based model.

Sentiment analysis involves inferring sentiment values of each aspect according to pre-defined sentiment values such as "positive" or "negative" and classifying aspects. In sentiment analysis, dictionary-based models and supervised learning are frequently applied. Dictionary-based models infer sentiment values with dictionaries of prepared SEWs and sentiment values. In some cases, the dictionary may be created directly from the corpus others are created in advance—open source dictionaries. Open source dictionaries have greater numbers of set of pairs of SEWs and sentiment values; however, some SEW sentiment values which don't exist in the open source dictionary cannot be taken in consideration. As customer reviews have various SEWs for each entity, it is required to construct a sentiment dictionary for each entity, and methods to create a sentiment dictionary directly from customer reviews are actively proposed. Sentiment value estimation methods include estimation using association with SEW (such as SO-Score) and inferring directly from customer reviews with supervised learning.

In summary, both sentiment identification and sentiment classification processes depend on sentiment dictionaries; however, text from the Internet using a syntax-based model makes it difficult to identify and classify aspects since expressions frequently appear that are not included in the sentiment dictionary.

This paper proposes a quality table-based method for SEW identification. This paper proposes a non-syntax and relation-based method in order to solve both frequency-based and syntax-based models' problems.

3   Technics and Method

3.1   Quality Table

The QT is a binary table representing the relationship between the required qualities: the customer's demands for the product or service, and the characteristics of the product, which are aspects of the product or service. QT is used in the quality function development methodology. The required quality can be translated to the characteristics of the product with the QT. In other words, the voice of the customer can be converted into the voice of the engineer, therefore product design reflecting the customers' requests can be performed.

This research focuses on the characteristics of the QT, representing the relationship between each required quality and each characteristic of the product. Required qualities are described as feature vectors that consist of relationships between each characteristic and its qualities. Required quality can be featured by a relationship with each characteristic of the product. Words may be featured by a relationship with each aspect. Featuring words with each aspect makes it obvious that certain words are likely to be SEWs and some words are less likely to be; some are extracted as SEW and the others are not. This research proposes a QT-based method for SEW identification. This paper discusses only sentiment identification. However, application for sentiment classification and aggregation is expected since QT-based methods preserve relationships between each SEW and its aspect. Therefore, conventional sentiment analysis methods (e.g. SO-score) and statistical methods (e.g. principal component analysis), for aggregation, are expected to be applied.

3.2   SMOTE Algorithm

One challenge in classification is classes with a significantly smaller number of samples than that of other classes. Such data sets are called unbalanced data. Solving such classification problems with general supervised learning approaches may be impossible. Many algorithms to solve these problems have been proposed. In this research, the number of seed expressions as positive class is even smaller than that of words as unlabeled classes. Therefore, classification in this research has unbalanced data, and synthetic minority over-sampling technique (SMOTE) is applied to solve the problem.

SMOTE (Chawla et al. 2002) is a well-known algorithm to fight that problem. Over-sampling of the minority class and under-sampling of the majority class are carried out with SMOTE algorithm. Figure 2 shows the image of SMOTE algorithm. The number of minority samples are increased and that of majority samples are decreased, we can obtain balanced data from unbalanced data with SMOTE algorithm. SMOTE will increase the minority samples by artificially creating and decrease majority samples by randomly under-sampling. For each point of minority sample, we randomly select points between the k-nearest neighbor and add it to minority samples.

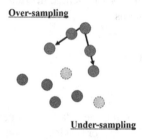

Fig. 2. SMOTE algorithm

3.3   Pointwise Mutual Information

Pointwise mutual information (PMI), or point mutual information, is a measure of association. PMI between two words, $word_1$ and $word_2$, is defined as follows (Church and Hanks 1989):

$$PMI(word_1, word_2) = \log_2 \left(\frac{p(word_1 \& word_2)}{p(word_1)p(word_2)} \right)$$

Here, $p(word_1 \& word_2)$ is the probability that $word_1$ and $word_2$ co-occur. If the words are statistically independent, the probability that they co-occur is given by $p(word_1)p(word_2)$. The ration between $p(word_1 \& word_2)$ and $p(word_1)p(word_2)$ is a measure of the degree of statistically dependence between the words. The relation in QT is given with PMI. When given words set, $\{word_1 \cdots word_n\}$, and aspects set, $\{aspect_1 \cdots aspect_m\}$, PMI_{ij} is defined as follows:

$$PMI_{ij} = PMI(word_i, aspect_j) = \log_2 \left(\frac{p(word_i \& aspect_j)}{p(word_i)p(aspect_j)} \right) \left(\begin{array}{l} i = 1, \ldots, n \\ j = 1, \ldots, m \end{array} \right)$$

PMI_{ij} is a measure of association between $word_i$ and $aspect_j$. A $word_1$ can be characterized with PMI_{1j} for each $aspect_j$. As the same way, seed expression can be characterized with PMI. And a classifier learns the seed expression's features and classify words into certain words which have similar feature with seed expression or not. The certain words can be expected to be SEW and that is the main purpose of this QT-based method.

3.4 Proposed Method

In this section, a QT-based method for SWE identification is described. Before the method is performed, preprocessing is done as shown Fig. 3.

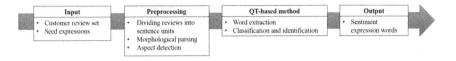

Input	Preprocessing	QT-based method	Output
• Customer review set • Seed expressions	• Dividing reviews into sentence units • Morphological parsing • Aspect detection	• Word extraction • Classification and identification	• Sentiment expression words

Fig. 3. Constitution of this paper

Input data are customer reviews set and seed expressions. A seed expression is often used as a clue to identify the SEWs in the sentiment identification process. There are commonly four seed expressions used ["良い" (good), "最高" (satisfied), "悪い" (bad), "不満" (dissatisfied)]. In this research, we also use the four seed expressions mentioned above.

Preprocessing consists of three processes: dividing reviews into sentence units, morphological parsing, aspect detection. Consumer review sentences were divided into sentence units in accordance with end-of-sentence punctuation, such as ".", "!", and "?". And morphological parsing is performed to determine the morphemes from which a given word is constructed. Then Aspect detection is performed. Frequency-based aspect identification model has powerful performance however low frequency word cannot be considered. And syntax-based model can also cover low frequency words however a lots of syntax relations required to be considered. This paper focuses on the co-occurrence relationship with seed expressions. Co-occurrence relation means that two words co-occur in the same sentence. In the frequency-based model, there is a problem that high frequency words are erroneously extracted as aspects and a problem that low frequency words cannot be taken into account. By considering the co-occurrence relation, it is possible to delete a weakly related word even at a high frequency, and to leave a strongly related word even at a low frequency. Therefore, aspects are extracted based on co-occurrence relation. Co-occurrence relation is generated with PMI measure. PMI measure of each single noun and compound noun is calculated, and the PMI threshold is statistically determined, only single or compound nouns that exceed the threshold are extracted. However, since it is considered that all words obtained with PMI do not hold as aspects, it is necessary to select certain aspects from the extracted words.

Selection is carried out with comparing characteristics of the product. Characteristics of the product can be categorized into seven elements as shown Table 1. Accordance with the seven elements, aspects are extracted. Then the method is applied, we identify the expressions of sentiment. A number of syntax-based models are applied to SEW identification methods however syntactic-based model methods need to use many syntactic relations in order to produce powerful results. This paper proposes a QT-based method for SEW identification. QT-based method has two processes: words extraction and classification. Figure 4 describes processes of the method.

Table 1. Seven elements of characteristic of the product

Physical element	Appearance characteristic, Mechanical properties,...
Functional element	Efficiency, Safety,...
Human element	Image, Rarity,...
Time element	Environmental resistance, Persistence,...
Economic element	Advantage, Compatibility,...
Productive element	Workability, Yield,...
Market element	Timeliness, Life cycle,...

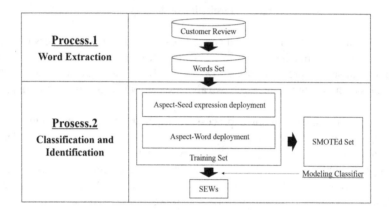

Fig. 4. Processes of the QT-based method

Words which can be SEW are extracted in word extraction process. Obviously the SEW consists of single words or compound words. Word extraction is generally done based on part of speech (POS). In Japanese text, the high frequency POS of the single SEW are adjective, noun, verb and adverb. However, the combination of POS in compound SEW cannot be determined since the patterns of the combination are too excessive. In this paper, annotation for customer reviews is performed, and accordance with the result of annotation, POS patterns of both single and compound SEW are determined and we obtain words set in this process.

Classification and identification process, supervised learning classification is used to obtain SEW from the words set. Training set of supervised learning is created with based on relationship of quality table. Initially, the relationship between each aspect and seed expressions is generated with PMI measure and then seed expression-aspect deployment is created. Next as the same way, the relation between each word from the words set and aspect is generated by PMI measure, and words-aspect deployment is created. Seed expression-aspect deployment and words-aspect deployment are combined as data set for supervised learning. Table 2 illustrates training set for classification. The purpose of using supervised learning is to classify words set into two classes, "positive" or unlabeled. Therefore, the classification target is words set. Feature of the target is PMI measure with each aspect. Learn the features of the seed expressions and find certain words with similar features with seed expressions from the words set. Here, the number of samples of seed expressions and that of words set can be biased.

That is, it is considered that the number of data set of class "positive" is extremely small as compared with that of unlabeled class. Therefore, this data set can be regarded as unbalanced data. In this paper, SMOTE algorithm is applied to the unbalanced data. Lastly, words classified as class "positive" from the words set are extracted as SEW. Also, add the extracted SEWs to the seed expressions and repeat the classification and identification process several times to obtain more SEWs. Then the result of classification is evaluated with precision. In the experimental test, we compare the number of SEWs obtained from the words set with that of SEWs from sentiment dictionary. Then in verification test, precision and recall rate are calculated and verify the coverage of annotated SEWs.

Table 2. Training set for supervised classification

		Aspects			Class
		Aspect$_1$	$\cdots$	Aspect$_k$	
Seed expressions	Seed$_1$	PMI$_{11}$	$\cdots$	PMI$_{1k}$	"Positive"
	$\vdots$	$\vdots$	$\cdots$	$\vdots$	"Positive"
	Seed$_n$	PMI$_{n1}$	$\cdots$	PMI$_{nk}$	"Positive"
Words	Word$_1$	PMI$_{11}$	$\cdots$	PMI$_{1k}$	
	$\vdots$	$\vdots$	$\cdots$	$\vdots$	
	Word$_m$	PMI$_{m1}$	$\cdots$	PMI$_{mk}$	

4   Results

In accordance with the method, experiment is performed for Japanese language text. The experiment result was evaluated for effectiveness and how new SEWs that do not exist in open source sentiment dictionary can be extracted, by comparing the SEWs in the experiment result with a pre-identified one in the open source sentiment dictionary. 450 customer reviews are for experiment and 113 ones for verification from RAKUTEN market review, the electronic commerce service in Japan. Seed expressions are these following four words, ["良い" (good), "最高" (satisfied), "悪い" (bad), "不満" (dissatisfied)]. R, the software environment for statistical computing, was used for all processes.

4.1   Pre-experiment

Aspects and sentiment expression words annotation was performed for a verification review set. They were annotated as one pair. Aspects and SEWs obtained totaled 223 sets. Then 110 unique annotated aspects were obtained. In the 110 aspects, 95 aspects consisted of single noun or compound nouns. Most of the annotated aspects consisted of single nouns or compound nouns. That result is the same as conventional aspect annotation. Next, 113 unique SEWs were obtained. Table 3 shows the result of SEW annotation.

Table 3. Result of SEW annotation

	Single word				Compound words			
Index	80				Double Word			Others
					33			9
POS	N	Adj	V	Adv	V + Adj	N + V	Others	-
Frequence	32	35	20	3	8	6	19	

As shown in Table 3, a single word is more likely to appear than compound words as SEWs. This research revealed that single word SEWs consist of nouns, adjectives, verbs, or adverbs as SEWs. That result was similar to another researcher's annotation in Japanese. Compound words have various POS patterns, many types of POS patterns appear at low frequency. A frequently POS pattern in compound words is "Verb + Adjective"(e.g. "傷付きやすい"(easily hurt)) and "Noun + Verb"(e.g. "つる つるする"(slippery)). It is observed that more than triple word combination, POS patterns are very uneven. Therefore, this paper focuses on single and double words.

4.2   Experiment

In preprocessing process, 450 customer reviews are divided into 1602 sentence units and morphological parsing is carried out with RMeCab. Then aspects detection is performed. At first 3208 single nouns and compound nouns are extracted. Then they are screened out with threshold of PMI measure and eliminated into 329 words. 98 aspects are obtained accordance with the elements of characteristic of the product.

Here, the method is applied to 450 customer reviews. At first process, 965 words are extracted from the customer reviews. Then at second process, training set is created with both the 965 words as unlabeled samples and 4 seed expressions as positive sample. The features were generated with PMI measure. And support vector machine was used as classifier and modeled with SMOTEd set. Evaluation of the model is performed with cross-validation test for SMOTEd set as shown Table 4. SEWs were obtained from unlabeled samples classified into false positive (FP) domain as positive one. Obtained SEWs in each repetition of classification are described in Table 4. 34 Single SEWs and 30 double SEWs, totally 64 SEWs are extracted. The highest FP-precision (SEW/FP) value is 50.0% at 5th repeatation, conversely worst is 21.0% at 3th repeatarion. Average is 36.8%.

Table 4. Number of SEWs extracted from 450 reviews

Repetition	Cross-validation test	FP	SEW	SEW/FP
1st	95.3%	83	35	42.2%
2nd	98.6%	28	7	25.0%
⋮	⋮	⋮	⋮	⋮
6th	98.7%	17	6	35.3%
Total	-	174	64	-
Average	-	29.0	10.7	36.8%

It was confirmed that mis-typing words, such as "使い安い"(easy to operate), and unique expressions on compact digital camera review, such as "サスガキャノン"(Canon is great as expected) and "フォーカスする"(focus on), can be extracted.

4.3 Evaluation of Experiment

Japanese open resource sentiment dictionary was obtained from web site of Okazaki laboratory which opens declinable sentiment words [10]. Declinable word is general term of the declinable POS, in Japanese, that means verbs and adjectives. This paper aims to compare the result of experiment with the sentiment dictionary and turn out how many unique SEWs which isn't from the sentiment dictionary can be obtained. The sentiment dictionary has 5280 declinable SEWs. Then, in 34 single SEWs, the number of total declinable SEWs is 8, and it was confirmed that of unique declinable SEWs which isn't included in the sentiment dictionary is 4. The ratio between the number of unique declinable SEWs and that of total declinable SEWs is 50%. It is revealed that the number of SEWs which cannot be obtained with dictionary-based model is 4 in case of declinable words.

4.4 Verification of Coverage

Coverage of annotated SEWs are verified with 113 customer reviews accordance with the method. As the same with experiment, preprocessing is carried out. 333 sentence units are obtained and same 98 aspects is used for verification. Total number of annotated SEWs is 113, the number of annotated single SEWs is 80 and that of annotated compound SEWs is 33. However the method cannot consider all 33 annotated compound SEWs since only both POS patterns, "verb + ajective"and "noun + verb", are designed. That fact can be confirmed in Table 2. Therefore, the verification is restricted with case where the number of annotated SEWs is 94. Then the method is applied to the customer reviews and classification was repeated 6 times as the same with experiment. Table 5 illustrates the final result of verification with precision, recall and F-measure.

Table 5. Prediction table

		True	
		Positive	Negative
Prediction	Positive	46	101
	Negative	48	476

Precision = 31.3%, Recall = 48.9%, F-measure = 38.2%

Totally 46 annotated SEWs were extracted correctly and 48 ones were missed. 101 words were misclassified as SEW and 476 words were classified as non-SEW correctly.

5   Discussion

It is confirmed the precision of the method in verification is 31.3%. Two problems which causes the low precision are assumed, and here we discuss the two problems. First problem is considered that process of dividing reviews into sentence units in preprocessing doesn't not works well. The processes is got involved in the stage where the training set is created, therefore if the process doesn't work well, classification doesn't work well and precision becomes lower. Dividing reviews is performed accordance with end-of-sentence punctuation however there is a case where customer review ends without end-of-sentence punctuation is observed. That case was confirmed in 563 customer reviews, 44 ones don't include end-of-sentence punctuation. Therefore, reviews weren't splitted correctly, and PMI measure wasn't calculated correctly because of that. Verification and improving of accuracy of dividing reviews is required.

Considering noun word in word extraction process may be the second problem. In the process, single nouns were considered as they are likely to be SEWs. However, it was confirmed that not only single noun SEWs were extracted but also many single noun aspects were done. As shown in Table 5, 101 words are misclassified into false positive domain and 20 aspects were observed in that false positive domain. Excluding the 20 aspects, precision becomes higher at 36.2%.

6   Conclusion and Future Work

This paper proposes a quality table-method for SEW identification. It is revealed that the method extracted SEWs which includes mis-typing and unique ones with precision at 36.8%. And the result of SEWs has effective SEWs which isn't included in sentiment dictionary. The coverage of the method was verified with recall at 48.9% and precision at 31.3%.

A half of annotated SEWs were missed and many words were misextracted as SEW with the method, therefore improving both precision and recall is future work. The explanation of that problem is considered the process of dividing reviews into sentence units. It can be expected that improving the process make the precision higher. And the SEWs-aspects deployment will be obtained and it may be helpful for sentiment classification and aggregation. Utilizing the deployment can be expected.

Acknowledgments. In this research, we used Rakuten market review data provided by Rakuten Inc. and the National Institute of Informatics. The authors would like to thank them.

References

1. Kobayashi, N., Inui, K., Matsumoto, Y., Tateishi, K.: Collecting evaluative expressions for opinion extraction. J. Nat. Lang. Process. **12**(3), 203–222 (2005). (in Japanese)
2. Schoten, K., Fransincar, F.: Survey on aspect-level sentiment analysis. IEEE Trans. Knowl. Data Eng. **28**(3), 813–830 (2015)

3. Tsytsarau, M., Plpanas, T.: Survey on mining subjective data on the web. Data Min. Knowl. Disc. **24**(3), 478–514 (2012)
4. Zagibalov, T., Carroll, J.: Automatic seed word selection for unsupervised sentiment classification of Chinese text. In: COLING 2008 Proceedings of the 22nd International Conference on Computational Linguistics, vol. 1, pp. 1073–1080 (2008)
5. Medhat, W., Hassan, A., Korashy, H.: Sentiment analysis algorithms and applications: a survey. Ain Shams Eng. J. **5**(4), 1093–1113 (2014)
6. Turney, P.D., Littman, M.L.: Unsupervised learning of semantic orientation from a hundred-billion-word corpus. Technical report NRC Technical Report ERB-1094, Institute for Information Technology, Nation Research Council Canada (2002)
7. Chawla, N.V., Bowyer, K.W., Hall, L.O., Kegelmeyer, W.P.: SMOTE: synthetic minority over-sampling technique. J. Artif. Intell. Res. **16**, 321–357 (2002)
8. Inui, T., Okumura, M.: A survey of sentiment analysis. J. Nat. Lang. Process. **13**(3), 201–241 (2006)
9. Nasukawa, T., Kanayama, H.: Acquisition of sentiment lexicon by using context coherence. IPSJ Natural Language Processing, 2004-NL-162, pp. 109–116 (2004). (in Japanese)
10. Japanese Sentiment Polarity Dictionary, 10 February 2017. http://www.cl.ecei. tohoku.ac.jp/index.php?Open%20Resources%2FJapanese%20Sentiment%20Polarity%20 Dictionary. (in Japanese)

EcoTrips

Leveraging Co-benefits and Metaphorical Metrics in a Mobile App to Promote Walking and Biking for Short Trips

Hannah Park[✉], Angela Sanguinetti, and Gabriel Castillo Cortes

Consumer Energy Interfaces Lab, University of California, Davis, USA
{hnpark,asanguinetti,gcastillo}@ucdavis.edu

Abstract. There is an overreliance on personal vehicle travel for short trips in the United States. This paper describes a mobile application, called EcoTrips, that promotes walking and biking for short trips by tracking users' travel behavior and providing a variety of feedback. EcoTrips conveys environmental impacts of travel behavior, and also leverages a variety of co-benefits of green travel by providing feedback related to fitness, finances, and time management. Feedback is conveyed in conventional as well as metaphorical metrics to make the data more comprehensible and meaningful. EcoTrips is unique among similar apps in that it provides a very high degree of flexibility for users to tailor the metrics that are displayed. It is also unique in that it is both the subject of HCI research and publicly available in English and in the United States. In a small pilot field study, participants reported some increase in awareness of the impacts of their travel behavior, and some small changes in their travel mode choices. Participants also highlighted the importance of maximizing the personalization of data. Given the expanding landscape and prevalence of pervasive and personal mobile and wearable technologies, HCI researchers should continue to develop eco-feedback and trip planning technologies to promote green travel modes for short trips.

Keywords: Eco-feedback · Green transportation · Travel modes · Mobile app

1 Introduction

There is an overreliance on private vehicles in the United States [2]. Rails-to-Trails Conservancy [30] estimated that half of all car trips in the US could be biked in 20 min and one quarter of all car trips could be walked in 20 min. They also estimated that there are 60 billion car trips of one mile length or less every year in the US.

Various environmental, social, and economic issues have been attributed to this overreliance on the private automobile [17]. In particular, the resultant vehicle emissions have immense implications for climate change. Extrapolating from the estimate of 60 billion one-mile car trips per year, and assuming an average of 411 g of carbon dioxide (CO_2) emissions per mile [12], these short trips can account for approximately 24,660,000 metric tons of CO_2 emissions in the US every year. Therefore, promoting

© Springer International Publishing AG 2017
A. Marcus and W. Wang (Eds.): DUXU 2017, Part II, LNCS 10289, pp. 60–76, 2017.
DOI: 10.1007/978-3-319-58637-3_5

walking and biking for local trips instead of personal vehicle transport could lead to substantial reductions in CO_2 emissions. For example, a bicycle commuter who rides five miles to work four days a week could save 100 gallons of gasoline and 2,000 lb of CO_2 emissions per year [17].

Improving facilities and infrastructure to increase access, convenience, and safety for walking and biking are crucial to enable greener transportation mode choices (e.g., [27]. However, structural supports alone may be insufficient to create and sustain behavior change [16]. Travel mode choices are also influenced by complex individual learning histories and social norms; they are habitual and may be resistant to change despite changes in the physical transportation infrastructure [4, 40].

Promising behavioral strategies to influence travel mode choices include the use of eco-feedback technologies, i.e., those that "provide feedback on individual or group behaviors with a goal of reducing environmental impact" [14, p. 1]. One behavioral theory particularly relevant to eco-feedback is Schwartz's Norm Activation Model [27, 36], which contends that altruistic (including pro-environmental) behavior is motivated by moral norms, which are promoted by the awareness of the consequences of one's behavior for others (or the environment). Eco-feedback aims to increase awareness of such behavioral consequences.

The recent phenomena of personal data tracking devices like the Fitbit and the game Pokémon GO are examples of the potentially powerful impact of leveraging mobile applications (apps) and wearable technology for health, fitness, and entertainment related to travel behavior [3, 28]. These services emphasize fitness and fun, respectively, and may increase non-vehicular travel, but they do not explicitly discourage driving. The present research details the creation and testing of an eco-feedback mobile app called EcoTrips, designed to promote walking and biking, and discourage driving, for short trips (3 miles one way or less). First, we review relevant HCI eco-feedback research and similar apps.

2 Review of Green Travel Eco-Feedback Apps

HCI researchers have developed mobile apps to promote physical activity [6] and reduce private vehicle use by providing users feedback on their behavior. Moreover, some transportation-focused eco-feedback apps leverage fitness and economic co-benefits to promote green travel behavior [13, 19]. Including information regarding co-benefits is important because motivators for pro-environmental behavior vary, including by culture [10], and presumed universal incentives, like money, are not always effective [5, 9]. Another strategy in green travel apps has been to include trip planning functionalities via information on public transportation and route alternatives, which also serves as an added benefit to users [20, 35]. EcoTrips is an example of the former–providing eco-feedback along with information regarding co-benefits of green travel behavior. See Table 1 for a list of relevant apps.

UbiGreen [13] was the first example of this type of eco-feedback app. It promoted walking, biking, and carpooling via two different interface designs, each involving a linear sequence of images. One was a growing tree and the other a polar bear scene; as the user's green transportation increased, the tree grew progressively or the environment around the polar bear became richer. The app also provided information about possible economic and health co-benefits via icons at the bottom of interface; e.g., a piggy bank icon would light up when economic benefits were achieved via green travel modes. In a field test, authors found that the nature imagery helped users connect emotionally with the data, but they also wanted numerical data to gain a more accurate understanding of their performance.

The tree and polar bear in UbiGreen are examples of iconic representations [21], as opposed to indexical (numbers and graphs), and empathetic gauges [29]. Research suggests that these types of data visualizations can motivate users by creating an emotional connection to the data in eco-feedback interfaces [8, 21, 23, 29]. On the other hand, indexical, or scientific data visualizations support learning and retrospection [21, 29].

Another similar project, Quantified Traveler [19], included a smartphone app to track travel data and a companion eco-feedback website. Like UbiGreen, Quantified Traveler provided information about co-benefits of greener travel modes relevant to a variety of user motivations, i.e., finances, fitness, and time management. Specifically, it provided numeric feedback and graphs reflecting travel time, cost, Calories burned, and CO_2 emissions. Quantified Traveler also provided comparison data for the average American, the average resident of the San Francisco Bay Area, and the average of other subjects in the study.

None of the apps that have been the focus of HCI research are currently publicly available in English, or in the United States; however, there are several publicly available apps with similar goals and strategies (Table 1). For example, CommuteGreener [43] is a trip planning app with the primary advertised goal of helping users avoid traffic congestion. It also provides textual and numeric feedback related to values of environment, finances, and fitness, including CO_2 emissions, travel cost, and Calories burned. Emissions information is also provided in terms of "trees saved" and Calories burned in terms of hamburgers.

Froehlich et al. [15] discussed how metaphorical metrics, like trees saved or hamburgers in CommuteGreener, can be more understandable than abstract, scientific terms, and also more emotionally evocative. Thus, metaphorical metrics represent another kind of "empathetic linking", similar to empathetic gauges. Petersen et al. [29] defined empathetic linking in the context of eco-feedback as "the packaging of information in a form that emotionally or experientially connects consumption decisions to feelings and concern for social and ecological communities" (p. 83). Furthermore, metaphorical metrics and empathetic linking more generally represent a potentially powerful way of increasing awareness of behavioral consequences per the Norm Activation Model of pro-environmental behavior [34].

Table 1. Green travel eco-feedback apps

App name	Values	Conventional metrics	Metaphorical metrics	Subject of HCI research	Publicly available
UbiGreen	Environment	–	–	X	–
	Finances	–	–		
	Fitness	–	–		
Quantified traveler	Environment	X	–	X	–
	Finances	X	–		
	Fitness	X	–		
	Time management	X	–		
Peacox	Environment	X	–	X	–
	Time management	X	–		
MatkaHupi	Environment	X	–	X	–
CityMapper	Environment	X	–	–	X
	Finances	X	–		
	Fitness	X	–		
	Time management	X	–		
CarbonDiem	Environment	X	–	–	X
TripGo	Environment	X	–	–	X
	Finances	X	–		
	Time management	X	–		
CommuteGreener	Environment	X	X	–	X
	Finances	X	–		
	Fitness	X	X		
EcoTrips	Environment	X	X	X	X
	Finances	X	X		
	Fitness	X	X		
	Time Management	X	–		

3   EcoTrips

EcoTrips is a mobile app that promotes walking or biking for short trips (3 miles one-way or less) by raising awareness of personal and environmental impacts of travel behavior. It provides a variety of information to appeal to different value orientations [25, 37]. Within different information categories (fuel consumption, environmental impact, and Calories), EcoTrips supplies numeric data in terms of conventional and metaphorical metrics, paired with illustrative icons as in UbiGreen [15], in order to deliver detailed information and evoke emotional response, thus supporting both understanding of and emotional connection to environmental consequences of travel behavior.

In addition to providing information tailored to users' values, Petersen et al. [29] suggest making it easy for users to select the information they want. In EcoTrips, the user can select which metrics to display (or not). In this way, EcoTrips provides a high degree of flexibility for tailoring information compared to previous similar apps.

3.1 Development

EcoTrips is an Android mobile app. It uses Moves API to track travel mode and trip data. Data collected by the Moves API are based on users' location. Inferences are made by the Moves API about travel mode, i.e., whether the user is most likely walking, biking, or traveling by vehicle.

The EcoTrips back end retrieves Moves data and summarizes it to create the raw data for visualizations in EcoTrips. The synchronization of data between EcoTrips backend and the Moves API is controlled by EcoTrips usage; while actively used, the app sends an update request to the server to trigger updating every two hours. This update can also be forced by the user with the refresh button at the top of the app screen.

Calculations shown on the app are done on the server side to save battery and response time while using the application. The downside to this approach is that every time the user makes a change to configurable data in the settings, e.g., user's body weight or personal vehicle fuel economy, the app has to sync with the server to recalculate the feedback data. This process is done automatically, but there is a slight delay.

EcoTrips back end is a useful resource for data analytics. Data stored anonymously in the server can be pulled in reports without compromising the identity of users. Although not developed yet, it is easily feasible to create a report tool using the back end infrastructure.

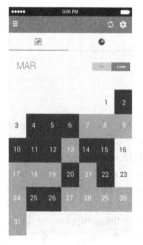

Fig. 1. Calendar screen

Fig. 2. Statistics screen A

Fig. 3. Statistics screen B

3.2 Design

The app consists of two main screens: the Calendar Screen illustrates predominate daily travel mode and the Statistics Screen presents numeric feedback via conventional and metaphorical metrics paired with illustrative icons. In the Calendar Screen (Fig. 1), days are color-coded according to predominate travel mode (vehicle, walking, or biking), defined as the travel mode with the longest total travel time. A toggle button on the top right allows the user to view data for either all their trips or only their short trips (3 miles one way or less). This feature was intended to avoid discouraging users who have an unavoidable long distance commute and to promote a focus on short trips.

The Statistics Screen (Figs. 2 and 3) conveys costs and benefits of travel behavior in terms of a variety of metrics, including Calories burned, CO_2 emissions, CO_2 emissions saved by biking and walking instead of driving, fuel usage, distance traveled, and travel time. These metrics represent a mix of values in order to motivate users with different value orientations. Specifically, Calories, fuel cost, and travel time appeal to person-centered values, whereas CO_2 emissions and CO_2 savings appeal to environmental values.

Calories burned, CO_2 savings, CO_2 emissions, and fuel usage are not only expressed in scientific terms (i.e., Calories, pounds of CO_2, and gallons of gas), but also in two additional units that attempt to make the information more concrete, relatable, and/or emotional/visceral. For example, Calories burned can be displayed in terms of Calories, as well as the equivalent amounts of grams of butter and minutes of jogging. Fuel consumption can be displayed in terms of gallons of gas, and also monetary cost and tons of dinosaur (i.e., prehistoric plant and animal material converted into oil over time by pressure and heat). The latter is intended to elicit an emotional response and help the user connect their behavior to the ultimate source of fuel (Figs. 4 and 5).

Fig. 4. About EcoTrips, page 1   **Fig. 5.** About EcoTrips, page 2

Carbon emissions and savings are particularly abstract and therefore important to convey in meaningful terms [18, 26]. EcoTrips calculates and displays CO_2 emissions from vehicle travel in pounds as well as the equivalent in seconds of erupting volcano, as a more visceral metaphorical metric, and monetary cost (i.e., if one were to purchase carbon credits). CO_2 savings from walking/biking rather than driving is also presented in pounds, as well as the estimated number of trees that would offset (i.e., absorb) that same amount of CO_2 in one year, and monetary savings in terms of cost of carbon credits. Carbon credit markets have become popular and growing considerably [22] among some consumers, as evidenced by the variety of brands/systems (e.g., MyClimate, The Conservation Fund, TerraPass and Carbonfund.org); a carbon credit is a certificate representing the reduction of one metric ton, or 2,205 lbs, of carbon dioxide emissions. Carbon credits worth $278 million (USD) were purchased in voluntary carbon markets in 2015 which is increased 10% compared to 2014 [42].

Calculations employed for the above metrics are listed in Table 2. We used a variety of sources to build these equations, including Dr. Bill Haskell's Compendium of Physical Activities (CPA; [1]) for calculating metrics related to Calories burned when traveling by foot, by bike, and by vehicle. Users' weight was also used to calculate Calories metrics. A default of 137 lbs (the average weight of an adult human according to Walpole et al. [39] was used if not otherwise specified.

To calculate fuel consumption and cost, EcoTrips uses a default fuel economy of 25 mpg, which is the average for a 2015 model-year vehicle according to the U.S. Environmental Protection Agency [12]. Fuel cost is set at $2.33/gallon based on current fuel cost according to the US Energy Information Administration [11]. Tons of dinosaur (technically, prehistoric material) required per gallon of gas was estimated at 98, based on a study at University of Utah [7].

Fig. 6. Settings page 1

Fig. 7. Settings page 2

For CO_2 emissions and savings calculations, we relied on an estimate by the Environmental Protection Agency (EPA) that one gallon of gas consumed corresponds to 19.4 lbs of CO_2 emissions. We translated CO_2 emissions in pounds into seconds of volcano eruption based on data regarding Yellowstone National Park's Mud Volcano which produces about 176,300 tons of CO_2 per year [41], an average of 11 lbs of CO_2 per second. We used Terrapass carbon credit system to convert pounds of CO_2 emitted and saved into dollar amounts; at the time of our calculations the price for 1,000 lbs of CO_2 was $5.95. To translate CO_2 savings into trees EcoTrips uses an estimate from McAliney [24] that one mature tree absorbs 48 lb of CO_2 per year.

A Settings Screen (Figs. 6 and 7) allows users to select (and deselect) metrics to personalize the Statistics Screen. Users can also enter their body weight (lbs) and personal vehicle fuel economy (mpg) for more accurate calculations of Calories burned, fuel usage, and carbon emissions and savings. The functionality to specify personal vehicle fuel economy was added after our field study.

Table 2. Calculations for EcoTrips metrics

Metric category	Metric	Equation
Calories burned	Calories	(1) Foot = [1.587 × User's weight(lbs)] + [walking time (min) ÷ 60] (2) Bike = [3.08 × User's weight(lbs)] + [biking time (min) ÷ 60] (3) Vehicle = [0.59 × User's weight(lbs)] + [driving time(min) ÷ 60] (4) Total Calories burned(Cal) = (1) + (2) + (3)
	Grams of butter	$\dfrac{\text{Total Calories burned(Cal)}}{7.14}$
	Minutes of jogging	$\dfrac{\text{Total Calories burned(Cal)}}{\text{User's weight} \times 3.17} \times 60$
CO_2 emitted	Pounds	$19.4 \times \dfrac{\text{Driving distance(miles)}}{\text{Vehicle fuel economy(mpg)}}$
	Seconds of volcano	$\dfrac{CO_2 \text{ emissions(lbs)}}{11}$
	Dollars	$\dfrac{CO_2 \text{ emissions(lbs)}}{100,0} \times 5.95$
CO_2 saved	Pounds	$19.4 \times \dfrac{\text{Biking} + \text{walking distance}}{\text{Vehicle fuel economy(mpg)}}$
	Adult trees / year	$\dfrac{CO_2 \text{ saved (lbs)}}{48}$
	Dollars	$\dfrac{CO_2 \text{ saved (lbs)}}{1000} \times 5.95$
Fuel used	Gallons	$\dfrac{\text{Driving distance}}{\text{Vehicle fuel economy (mpg)}}$
	Dollars	Fuel usage(gal) × 2.33
	Tons of dinosaur	Fuel usage(gal) × 98

4 Field Study Methodology

We conducted a pilot field study with a beta version of EcoTrips in May 2015. Participants were recruited at University of California, Davis, via department email lists. To be eligible, participants had to be the owner of the vehicle and Android smartphone (EcoTrips only runs on Android OS). Each participant received a $10 gift card at the end of the study.

4.1 Procedure

Prior to using EcoTrips, participants completed a survey regarding their travel behavior, motivations for and barriers to walking/biking for short trips, and environmental attitudes. Immediately after this initial survey, participants were guided through the process of downloading the Moves app. Baseline data on participants' travel behavior (mode and trip frequency, duration, and distance) were collected via Moves for at least one week, then participants downloaded EcoTrips and were instructed to use it for at least one week. Participants were then asked to complete another survey to assess changes in travel behavior, awareness of consequences of mode choices, and environmental attitudes. We also compared travel behavior data while using EcoTrips to baseline levels.

4.2 Participants

Eleven participants completed the study. Eight were students and three were faculty. Six were female and five were male. Age ranged from 18 to 44 ($M = 26$; $SD = 8.18$).

Six participants indicated that they considered themselves environmentalists, yet only one participant indicated it was most important to them to 'minimize environmental impact' when choosing a transportation mode for short trips (less than 3 miles one way). Four participants indicated it was most important to 'minimize costs', three selected 'minimize travel time', three selected 'maximize physical activity', and none selected 'maximize scenic beauty and/or contact with nature'. This confirms the importance of emphasizing person-centered co-benefits of green travel behavior.

Biking is an extremely common travel mode for both students and faculty on UC Davis campus, so we expected the potential for shifting from personal vehicle travel to walking or biking would be limited. For example, in the initial survey most participants reported that they 'frequently' (5) or 'always' (1) tried to minimize how much they drive (5 said 'occasionally'; none said 'rarely' or 'never'). When asked if they were willing to commit to walking or biking instead of driving for trips less than 3 miles one way, most (7) responded 'yes', 2 responded 'I already do this all the time', 1 'no', and 1 'not sure'.

Given these sample characteristics, we were less interested in behavior change and more interested in the impact of EcoTrips on participants' awareness of their travel behavior and its consequences, and their environmental attitudes, as well as their reactions to the design and content of the app. We included several open-ended questions in the final survey concerning what, if any, changes in attitudes or behaviors participants noticed while using the app, and what, if anything, they learned from it.

5   Field Study Results

We analyzed travel behavior for seven days of baseline tracked by the Moves app, and seven days after EcoTrips installation (i.e., the testing period); both baseline and testing periods included five weekdays and two weekend days. Upon data analysis, it was noted that one participant did not use EcoTrips and one participant only had three days of baseline data. Data from the former was excluded from all analyses; data from the latter was excluded from quantitative analysis of travel behavior only. Descriptive, but not inferential, statistics are presented for both travel behavior and survey data due to the small sample size. Responses to open-ended survey questions were analyzed qualitatively by coding according to emergent themes.

5.1   Travel Behavior

As suspected, our sample was already driving relatively infrequently for short trips (3 mi or less) before using EcoTrips (Table 3). In fact, five participants took no short driving trips during the baseline week. Quantitative travel data showed no salient or consistent difference in number of short driving trips or associated distance.

Table 3. Number and distance of short driving trips for each participant during baseline week and testing week.

Participant		1	2	3	4	5	6	7	8	9
Number of short driving trips	Baseline	0	8	1	0	1	0	0	0	1
	Testing	0	5	6	0	0	0	1	0	6
Distance of short driving trips (miles)	Baseline	0	6.36	2.79	0	0.25	0	0	0	0.42
	Testing	0	3.08	6.06	0	0	0	1.69	0	5.15

In the final survey, after using EcoTrips, a minority of participants reported that their behavior had changed. In particular, two participants reported walking more (i.e., "I tried to walk more when I could"; "I have walked more for trips under 3 miles"); one participant reported biking more; and one participant reported driving less, crediting raised awareness from the statistics on the app (i.e., "I did drive a little less after seeing the figures").

5.2   Awareness of Consequences

Participants were asked about their level of knowledge concerning consequences of their driving before and after using EcoTrips (Table 4). Before using EcoTrips, participants reported being very knowledgeable about both the amount of gas their driving consumes and money they spend on gas; after EcoTrips, there was no increase in these variables, and in fact a decrease in median awareness of gas used. Participants' median response for awareness of carbon emissions from their driving was "No idea". Unfortunately, they did not demonstrate an increase in awareness of emissions after using EcoTrips by this measure.

Table 4. Median awareness of consequences of personal vehicle travel behavior before and after using EcoTrips. Question text: How knowledgeable are you about the following characteristics of your travel?

	Gas used	Money spent on gas	CO_2
Before EcoTrips	Very Knowledgeable	Very Knowledgeable	No idea
After EcoTrips	Somewhat Knowledgeable	Very Knowledgeable	No idea

Open-ended survey responses, on the other hand, revealed some increase in awareness of emissions:

The information about pounds of CO_2 saved and used was interesting, I hadn't thought about my transportation in that way before.

I already knew biking was better overall, but seeing the numbers reinforced my feelings.

I do like that it makes aware of the emission I'm causing.

Some participants seemed to gain awareness of their short trips in particular, in alignment with the objectives of EcoTrips.

...every little bit counts.

... other times I drove I realized it was really unnecessary. I can easily bike or take the bus.

It made me more aware of the short trips.

I'm now more aware of the shorter distances I drive, and how they would be bikeable if I made the effort.

5.3   Environmental Attitudes

As a brief measure of environmental attitudes, we used the inclusion of nature in self scale [33] in both the pre- and post-EcoTrips surveys (Fig. 8). This scale measures how an individual includes nature within her or his cognitive representation of self. The results indicated that five participants did not change their reported perceptions of connectedness after using EcoTrips, four participants reported an increased level of connectedness, and one reported a decreased level of connectedness (Table 5).

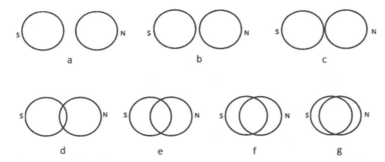

Fig. 8. The Inclusion of Nature in Self Scale. Question text: Which image above best describes your relationship with nature? In other words, how interconnected are you with the natural environment? (S = Self; N = Nature)

Table 5. Inclusion of Nature in Self before and after using EcoTrips

Participant	1	2	3	4	5	6	7	8	9	10
Before EcoTrips	f	d	e	d	d	f	d	d	f	e
After EcoTrips	f	d	e	e	e	f	e	e	e	e

6 Opportunities for Improving EcoTrips

A strong theme in open-ended responses in the final survey was participants' desire for more personalized data. Specifically, participants were unsatisfied with the use of average data for vehicle emissions:

C02 emissions depends on the vehicle, so I couldn't take the value given as true.

If I really care about the carbon produced by *my* behavior, it doesn't help me much to instead learn how much carbon I would have produced in the average vehicle.

Some things to note are that some of what is categorized as driving was actually busing through Unitrans' environmentally friendly buses.

7 Discussion and Conclusion

In this paper we described the design and pilot evaluation of EcoTrips, a mobile application that automatically tracks and provides feedback regarding travel behavior. EcoTrips leverages a variety of co-benefits of green travel and uses metaphorical metrics to make emissions and fuel consumption information more comprehensible and meaningful. It is unique among similar apps in that it is both the subject of academic HCI research and publicly available in English in the United States, where there is an overreliance on personal vehicle travel for short trips. In the pilot study of EcoTrips beta version, open-ended survey data revealed some increases in users' awareness of the impacts of their travel behavior and their interdependence with the natural environment.

Limitations of our field study included our unique sample of university students and staff that infrequently drove for short trips (average of 0.17 short driving trips per day per participant during baseline). Our sample's travel data shows they drove on average 27.9 miles per day, which is lower than average American's 29.8 miles per day [38]. We also had a small sample size and short study duration. Furthermore, there were several bugs in the beta version of the app. We hope to conduct a larger, more naturalistic field study with users who download the final version of the app from Google Play Store.

Based on user responses to the app that highlighted the need for more personalized data, we added several functionalities: vehicle fuel economy can now be personalized; users' can also indicate if their predominant motorized travel mode is an electric vehicle or public transportation. These inputs automatically adjust the gas and carbon calculations. We also plan to integrate an API to make fuel prices dynamic. Our goal is to make the app easy to maintain so it can remain publicly available unlike other apps that have been the focus of HCI research but not made (or remained) publicly available.

Past research shows that eco-feedback is more effective when it includes historical comparisons, social comparisons, and goal-setting [29]. Gamification techniques in the context of eco-feedback apps for travel behavior could also be quite effective and warrant further exploration [20]. EcoTrips includes historical comparison via the Calendar Screen. We intended to include unique social comparison and goal-setting features that we designed but lacked the resources to develop. Specifically, a photo-sharing feature would enable users to post and find beautiful or otherwise interesting routes (Figs. 9, 10, and 11). Personal and collaborative goal-setting was envisioned whereby users could set goals in terms of a variety of conventional and metaphorical metrics (Figs. 12 and 13). We hope to include these features in future development phases.

Fig. 9. Most beautiful routes searchable photo-sharing feature (left)

Fig. 10. Beautiful routes photo tagging feature (middle)

Fig. 11. Beautiful routes social media sharing feature (right)

Fig. 12. Goal-setting screen where users can tailor metrics and timelines for personal or shared goals (left)

Fig. 13. Progress-tracking screen for goal-setting system (right)

In conclusion, both physical infrastructural and behavioral strategies to promote non-motorized transportation modes for short trips are needed to achieve multiple associated social goals, including reduced carbon emissions and improved human health. Among behavioral strategies, technologies that enable trip planning and eco-feedback are particularly promising given the expanding landscape and prevalence of pervasive and personal mobile and wearable technologies. Leveraging the co-benefits of green travel behavior in these technologies is particularly important, as is harnessing the growing body of HCI knowledge concerning effective data visualization.

References

1. Ainsworth, B.E., Haskell, W.L., Whitt, M.C., Irwin, M.L., Swartz, A.M., Strath, S.J., Jacobs, D.R.: Compendium of physical activities: an update of activity codes and MET intensities. Med. Sci. Sports Exerc. **32**(9; SUPP/1), S498–S504 (2000)
2. American Association of State Highway and Transportation Officials: Standard Specifications for Transportation Materials and Methods of Sampling and Testing. AASHTO (2013)
3. Althoff, T., White, R.W., Horvitz, E.: Influence of Pokémon Go on Physical Activity: Study and Implications. arXiv preprint arXiv:1610.02085 (2016)
4. Alfonzo, M.A.: To walk or not to walk? The hierarchy of walking needs. Environ. Behav. **37** (6), 808–836 (2005)

5. Bolderdijk, J.W., Steg, L., Geller, E.S., Lehman, P.K., Postmes, T.: Comparing the effectiveness of monetary versus moral motives in environmental campaigning. Nat. Clim. Change 3(4), 413–416 (2013)

6. Consolvo, S., Klasnja, P., McDonald, D.W., Landay, J.A.: Goal-setting considerations for persuasive technologies that encourage physical activity. In: Proceedings of the 4th international Conference on Persuasive Technology, p. 8. ACM, April 2009

7. Dukes, J.S.: Burning buried sunshine: human consumption of ancient solar energy. Clim. Change 61(1–2), 31–44 (2003)

8. Dillahunt, T., Becker, G., Mankoff, J., Kraut, R.: Motivating environmentally sustainable behavior changes with a virtual polar bear. In: Pervasive 2008 Workshop Proceedings, vol. 8, pp. 58–62, May 2008

9. Dietz, T.: Altruism, self-interest, and energy consumption. Proc. Natl. Acad. Sci. 112(6), 1654–1655 (2015)

10. Eom, K., Kim, H.S., Sherman, D.K., Ishii, K.: Cultural variability in the link between environmental concern and support for environmental action. Psychol. Sci. 27(10), 1331–1339 (2016)

11. EIA: Gasoline and Diesel Fuel Update. U.S. Energy Information Administration, 27 Feb 2017. http://www.eia.gov/petroleum/gasdiesel/

12. EPA: Light-Duty Automotive Technology, Carbon Dioxide Emissions, and Fuel Economy Trends: 1975 Through 2016. US Environmental Protection Agency. EPA-420-R-16-010 (2016). Accessed Nov 2016

13. Froehlich, J., Dillahunt, T., Klasnja, P., Mankoff, J., Consolvo, S., Harrison, B., Landay, J. A.: UbiGreen: investigating a mobile tool for tracking and supporting green transportation habits. In: Proceedings of the SIGCHI Conference on Human Factors in Computing Systems, pp. 1043–1052. ACM, April 2009

14. Froehlich, J., Findlater, L., Landay, J.: The design of eco-feedback technology. In: Proceedings of the SIGCHI Conference on Human Factors in Computing Systems, pp. 1999–2008. ACM, April 2010

15. Froehlich, J., Findlater, L., Ostergren, M., Ramanathan, S., Peterson, J., Wragg, I., Larson, E., Fu, F., Bai, M., Patel, S., Landay, J.A.: The design and evaluation of prototype eco-feedback displays for fixture-level water usage data. In: Proceedings of the SIGCHI Conference on Human Factors in Computing Systems, pp. 2367–2376. ACM, May 2012

16. Gatersleben, B., Appleton, K.M.: Contemplating cycling to work: Attitudes and perceptions in different stages of change. Transp. Res. Part A Policy Pract. 41(4), 302–312 (2007)

17. Gotschi, T., Mills, K.: Active Transportation for America: The Case for Increased Federal Investment in Bicycling and Walking. Rails-to-Trails Conservancy, Washington, DC (2008)

18. Holmes, T.G.: Eco-visualization: combining art and technology to reduce energy consumption. In: Proceedings of the 6th ACM SIGCHI Conference on Creativity and Cognition, pp. 153–162. ACM, June 2007

19. Jariyasunant, J., Abou-Zeid, M., Carrel, A., Ekambaram, V., Gaker, D., Sengupta, R., Walker, J.L.: Quantified traveler: travel feedback meets the cloud to change behavior. J. Intell. Transp. Syst. 19(2), 109–124 (2015)

20. Jylhä, A., Nurmi, P., Sirén, M., Hemminki, S., Jacucci, G.: Matkahupi: a persuasive mobile application for sustainable mobility. In: Proceedings of the 2013 ACM Conference on Pervasive and Ubiquitous Computing Adjunct Publication, pp. 227–230. ACM, September 2013

21. Kim, T., Hong, H., Magerko, B.: Designing for persuasion: toward ambient eco-visualization for awareness. In: Ploug, T., Hasle, P., Oinas-Kukkonen, H. (eds.) PERSUASIVE 2010. LNCS, vol. 6137, pp. 106–116. Springer, Heidelberg (2010)

22. Kollmuss, A., Zink, H., Polycarp, C.: Making sense of the voluntary carbon market: a comparison of carbon offset standards. In: WWF Germany, pp. 1–23 (2008)
23. Lin, J.J., Mamykina, L., Lindtner, S., Delajoux, G., Strub, H.B.: Fish'n'Steps: encouraging physical activity with an interactive computer game. In: Dourish, P., Friday, A. (eds.) UbiComp 2006. LNCS, vol. 4206, pp. 261–278. Springer, Heidelberg (2006)
24. McAliney, M.: Arguments for Land Conservation: Documentation and Information Sources for Land Resources Protection. Trust for Public Land, Sacramento (1993)
25. Nordlund, A.M., Garvill, J.: Effects of values, problem awareness, and personal norm on willingness to reduce personal car use. J. Environ. Psychol. **23**(4), 339–347 (2003)
26. Nieman, A.: Concrete vs abstract visualization. In: Hohl, M. (ed.) Proceedings of the ADSVIS 2011: Making Visible the Invisible: Art, Design and Science in Data Visualisation, p. 49. University of Huddersfield, Huddersfield. ISBN 978-1-86218-103-8 (2011)
27. Pucher, J., Dill, J., Handy, S.: Infrastructure, programs, and policies to increase bicycling: an international review. Prev. Med. **50**, S106–S125 (2010)
28. Pina, L.R., Ramirez, E., Griswold, W.G.: Fitbit+: a behavior-based intervention system to reduce sedentary behavior. In: 2012 6th International Conference on Pervasive Computing Technologies for Healthcare (PervasiveHealth), pp. 175–178. IEEE, May 2012
29. Petersen, J.E., Frantz, C., Shammin, R.: Using sociotechnical feedback to engage, educate, motivate and empower environmental thought and action. Solutions **5**(1), 79–87 (2014)
30. Rails-To-Trails Conservency, Pathway to Prosperity (2016). http://magazine.railstotrails.org/resources/magflipbooks/2016_fall/index.html
31. Sorell, M.L.: Transportation choices: can social marketing make a difference? (Doctoral dissertation, Massachusetts Institute of Technology) (2005)
32. Steg, L., Gifford, R.: Sustainable transportation and quality of life. J. Transp. Geogr. **13**(1), 59–69 (2005)
33. Schultz, P.W.: The structure of environmental concern: Concern for self, other people, and the biosphere. J. Environ. Psychol. **21**, 327–339 (2001)
34. Schwartz, S.H.: Awareness of consequences and the influence of moral norms on interpersonal behavior. Sociometry **31**, 355–369 (1968)
35. Schrammel, J., Busch, M., Tscheligi, M.: Peacox-persuasive advisor for CO2-reducing cross-modal trip planning. In: PERSUASIVE (Adjunct Proceedings) (2013)
36. Stern, P.C., Dietz, T., Abel, T.D., Guagnano, G.A., Kalof, L.: A value-belief-norm theory of support for social movements: The case of environmentalism. Hum. Ecol. Rev. **6**(2), 81–97 (1999)
37. Thompson, S.C.G., Barton, M.A.: Ecocentric and anthropocentric attitudes toward the environment. J. Environ. Psychol. **14**(2), 149–157 (1994)
38. Triplett, T., Santos, R., Rosenbloom, S., Tefft, B.: American Driving Survey: 2014–2015 (2016)
39. Walpole, S.C., Prieto-Merino, D., Edwards, P., Cleland, J., Stevens, G., Roberts, I.: The weight of nations: an estimation of adult human biomass. BMC Public Health **12**(1), 439 (2012)
40. Willis, D.P., Manaugh, K., El-Geneidy, A.: Cycling under influence: summarizing the influence of perceptions, attitudes, habits, and social environments on cycling for transportation. Inte. J. Sustain. Transp. **9**(8), 565–579 (2015)
41. Yellowstone Park Emits Tons of Carbon Dioxide, Study Finds, 25 December 1997. http://www.nytimes.com/1997/12/26/us/yellowstone-park-emits-tons-of-carbon-dioxide-study-finds.html. Accessed 29 May 2015
42. World Bank, Ecofys, Vivid Economics: State and Trends of Carbon Pricing 2016. Washington, DC: World Bank. © World Bank (2016). https://openknowledge.worldbank.org/handle/10986/25160. License: CC BY 3.0 IGO

Publicly Available Green Travel Apps

43. CommuteGreener: commutegreener.com
44. TripGo: https://skedgo.com/home/tripgo/
45. CarbonDiem: carbondiem.com
46. CityMapper: citymapper.co
47. EcoTrips: ecotrips.ucdavis.edu

Experience, Usability and Sense of Things

Axel Sande, Adriano Bernardo Renzi[✉], and Silvia Schnaider

Serviço Nacional de Aprendizagem Comercial/Senac-Rio, Rio de Janeiro, Brazil
axel@gabinitedasartes.com, adrianorenzi@gmail.com,
silviaschnaider@gmail.com

Abstract. This research presents the relation of sense of objects with usability and user experience as it is influenced by the context of use, the interaction with apparatuses and the transformation of the perceived value through a narrative of experience. The research analyses subject meaning and significance fators with usability and experience concepts in a pervasive scenario of ecology systems and cross-channel interactions.

Keywords: User experience · Semantics · Usability

1 Introduction: Third Wave of Computing

The important change of traditional design of objects to the idea of interfaces as design artifacts (late 80's and early 90's), had Bonsiepe [1] as one of the first to see interfaces as a communication object, and a "bridge" between humans, the tool and the objective. Resmini and Rosatti [1] point that Bonsiepe was "thinking inside the box of Industrial Design concepts" and, ten years later, with faster microcomputers, inside cellphones, cars, cameras, houses, appliances etc., capable of communicating with other devices, through a diverse technological possibility of connections, it became clear that the "bridge" is beyond interfaces. This perception changes the way of projecting and evaluating projects' results.

According to Renzi and Freitas' Delphi investigation [2], the future scenario of technology and interaction in the next 5-10 years will bring digital devices more present in people's daily tasks, through the use of common objects, integrated environments and wearable devices. Advancing even more in the third wave of computing (many computers to one user), our digital empowerment becomes ubiquitous and integrated by a dynamic ecology, transforming human-computer interactions in human-information interactions. Resmini and Rosatti's [1] manifest presents Pervasive Architecture Information as a concept further than information spatial organization. It is to develop products under informational and structural scope, for open and expansive systems, what Norman [3] calls system thinking:

> "No product is an island. A product is more than a product. Is a set of integrated and cohesive experiences. Think of all stages of a product or service – from initial intentions and it's first use to the need of help, service and maintenance. Make it all as one integrated system. That's Systems thinking".

A. Marcus and W. Wang (Eds.): DUXU 2017, Part II, LNCS 10289, pp. 77–86, 2017.
DOI: 10.1007/978-3-319-58637-3_6

McMullin and Starmar [4] emphasize the necessity of communication through multiple channels in order to push users into an ubiquitous and holistic experience. And we, designers, should embrace a holistic path to transform multiple and separated interactions into one narrative flow. Resmini and Rosatti [1] add: "HOW" is more important than "WHAT" when information architecture is evolving dynamically. The authors, based on the expansions of information architecture, denote some transformations from the traditional information architecture to a pervasive thinking:

1. Information Architecture becomes an ecosystem – When different medias and different contexts are integrated, no artifact is an isolated and singular device. All artifacts become elements of a great ecosystem, with multiple links and interrelations that must be developed as parts of one whole process of experience.
2. Users become intermediaries – they are participants that contribute to the ecosystem and actively produce new content, or edit (add) to something already published, inserting links, comments or critics. The traditional distinction between authors and readers, or producers and consumers, becomes a thin line.
3. Static becomes dynamic – The active role of the intermediaries (users) makes the structure perpetually unfinished, perpetually in change and open to continuous refinement and manipulation
4. Dynamic becomes hybrid – These new architectures embrace new kinds of media. As well as the line between producers and consumers are thinner, the same occurs with different medias. All experiences are bridge or cross-media, embracing a diverse environment.
5. Horizontality prevails over verticality – the correlation of elements is predominant and over rule traditional top-down hierarchies. In an open architecture and always in metamorphoses, hierarchic models are hard to keep and maintain, since users push the system to spontaneity, ephemeral or temporary semantic structures.
6. Product design becomes experience design – when every artifact, by its content, product or service is part of an ecosystem, the focus change from planning individual devices to planning and developing experiences that permeate artifacts in one whole journey.
7. Experiences become cross-media experiences – experiences connect different environments and medias in ubiquitous ecologies, a process that all parts contribute to build one whole experience journey.

2   Making Sense of Objects Through Its Use

The ISO 9241-110/2.15 [5] defines user experience as "a person's perceptions and responses that result from the use and/or anticipated use of a product, system or service". The definition emphasizes that experience occurs before, during and after the direct use of a system. John C. Thomas, PhD, from the IBM J.T. Watson Research Center sees the processes of user experience as narratives. Similarly, Renzi's research [6] presents the user experience of integrated interactions in a cross-channel system as one whole journey, composed by short scenes, where part of the user experience happens outside the system.

Vilém Flusser [7] alerts to the fact that the control the experiences of others is unattainable, since each experience is attached to individual conditions and expectations. For such unique and private sense, an experience can't be generalized. Therefore, design products can be projected to fulfill part of the whole experience, but possibilities of "scenes" of the narrative are multiple and hardly with determined path. For the author [7], designers can only project system structures that potentially generate experiences.

Absorption of information becomes conducted by distinguishing relevant experiences from irrelevant ones. Based on references, needs and expectations of use, each user will instinctively categorize and choose interactions to fulfill their journey of experience. The understanding of users' perception and common journey can help designers project and evaluate results to better make integrated experiences and possibly break paradigms in the concepts of new digital devices, on either industrial products, information systems, architecture or social environments [8]. For Krippendorff [8], the practices of design have to be reformulated by repositioning its focus from functions to the meanings that objects help build relations in society. It is the pursuit of meaning derived from human interactions with objects.

The author, in his article *On the essential contexts of artifacts or on the proposition that design is making sense (of things)* [9], affirms that although conveniently ambiguous, the phrase "Design is making sense" could be read as "design is a sense of creating activity" that can claim perception, experience and esthetics as its fundamental concern, or it can be regarded as "products of design are to be understandable or meaningful to someone", concerned with the subjective meanings of objectively existing objects.

Krippendorf defends that technological structures and the functionalities of systems/objects have to be integrated as background scene to what really matters: the self-identification and the values of significance related to devices inserted in society daily interactions. His concept of understanding artifacts through its use is in accordance to Lockdown's Design with intent [10], where the system/object influence the user behavior as much as the user influence the system/object behavior. Due to this continuous interaction, Lockdown suggests the importance of planning a system to influence positively user behaviors in situations where is important to strategically direct the use of a product, service or system.

When instigated by something new, users' preconception of how it works is based on their closest references, understanding of cultural conventions and similar experiences to build a mental model of its functionality. The better the understanding of its functions to the novelty's real purpose, the better is the product affordance. And each time users interact with a new product, their comprehension of use becomes clearer as they familiarize with the procedures and learn. With the continuous process of learning, users' references change, as do their mental models and perception of functionality.

Alva Nöe [11], a philosophy researcher, points that perception is an activity of thinking, to act from cognitive processes. Not something that happens, but something that is done. Like a blind person understanding his/her surroundings using the tip of his/her cane, the world is perceived through successive interactions over the time. According to Nöe, perception can be mainly conceptual because just someone in possession of appropriate conceptual skills is capable of having a particular experience.

It couldn't look to you as if the ballerina tripped if you didn't know what a ballerina is, or what tripping is, and it couldn't sound to you like a backfire if you didn't know what a backfire is. [...] The fact that there are different standards for concept possession doesn't alter the fact that some perceptual content is framed precisely in terms of what perceivers know about their worlds [11, p. 184]).

Dr. Alok Nahata, from Nutraceuticals, in an interview at Researchgate.net, defines perception as organization, identification and interpretation of sensorial information, with the intent to represent and comprehend the environment. Every perception involves signals, received by the nervous system, resulted from physical stimuli of sensors. However, perception is not a passive receptor of these signs. It can be molded through learning, memory and expectations. The human brain perception system enables people to see the world complete and stable, even when the received information is incomplete or with rapid variations.

Krippendorf [8] argues that Design is to give sense to things. And to understand these meanings, it is important to relate objects to contexts. The thinking of the form has to be based on its use and the symbolic contexts (social, cultural and psychological) involved in the interaction of users with the projected environment. Its intangibility is directly connected to the common language of a society, where digital systems work as means to convey information with multiple perspectives, multiple consumers and multiple editors in dynamic structures.

Frascara [12] points that Design has to influence behavior, attitude and knowledge in an effective and ethical way, moving from just solving problems to identifying them. Designers should be responsible for discovering the user needs and elaborate structures to enable results to change people's lives: "we need to move from interaction design between people and objects to interaction between people". In "People-centered design: complexities and uncertainties", the author suggests the necessity of an interdisciplinary work with Design in order to impact people in different levels and to urge users to act, fulfill needs and satisfy desires.

The generation of meanings through use occurs after the tangible purpose has been conceived, that is, the semantic validation of the experience comes only posteriorly. During the planning of the product and its form, the criteria for the creation of subjective meaning is oriented mostly based on the understanding of affordance and universal values of perception.

Krippendorff is very influenced by Gibson's definitions of affordance and the notion of perception of the world beyond forms of objects and spatial relations, to a broader understanding of interactions possibilities with objects, even when facing human limitations to describe what is perceived. According to Kripendorff, users perceive what they can learn, not necessarily what is disposed for observation. Humans' perceptions are programmed to foment sense and significance to everything, based on own references, conventions and previous experiences.

In a dynamic cross-channel scenario, where users permeate different objects to build a journey and fulfill objectives, each object/device's meaning is directly linked to the context of use and which part of the journey it is integrated. For instance, using the example of Renzi's research [6] on designers using an integrated system to help them manage their studios, the choice of which device to input or edit relevant information regarding project or financial management to the integrated system, were based on levels of privacy of information, location of the user, type of action, urgency and context of management decision. Each one of these parameters influenced the meaning, the significance and the experience of use. In the cited example, it was also acknowledged that parts of the users' experience journey occurred without any digital device.

3 From Using Isolated Devices to a Pervasive Experience

In 1990, Nielsen and Molich [13] developed a set of ten usability principles to be considered when planning a system with a visual interaction interface. The principles are well known as the "ten usability heuristics" and became a base for the usability evaluation technique, well known as heuristic evaluation. A guide anticipated for helping develop systems for single devices with interface. As new apparatus surged over the years, with different sizes of display and different kinds of interaction, other authors presented new perspectives of usability heuristics for new contexts and possibilities: Apted [14], Inostroza [15], Neto and Campos [16].

For the purpose of cross-channel scenarios, where systems are a dynamic ecology, usability heuristics focusing on singular apparatus are not enough to evaluate or guide the whole journey of experience.

As usability covers the easiness of using, effectiveness and learnability with a system using a device, the research on user experience analyses the whole experience of the user with system, the scenario and circumstances in which the user may open the system from different devices interconnected. Using Jarred Spool's lecture [17] (Fig. 1) as an example of comparison between usability and experience, he shows that Six Flags' detailed map is focused on helping users to perform tasks in a pattern of use (people get in the park, choose the closest ride, get in a long line, ride the roller coaster and then choose another ride and re-start the cycle), while in Disney's map is hard to visually understand specific rides, as Disney is more interested to be a place people take their kids for an adventure. An experience.

While activities are distinct things (tasks) that happens (are performed); experience is making sure everything blends and is connected, even afterwards when people leave the park. The concept of the whole Disney experience in building new memories goes far beyond specific isolated tasks. It considers the whole "adventure" that starts even before the arrival at the airport.

The Disney experience goes beyond single rides as it is a dynamic ecology. And as well as the physical exploratory walking with the family creates a narrative, digital devices can be part of the experience in different contexts within different parts of the users' journey. And for each short scene of the experience, different senses and significances can emerge.

Specifically regarding digital experiences for Disney, there are a number of options for download and use, compatible with different devices, and some of these options were purposefully planned for specific lengths of the experience journey. The app "Disneyland Explorer" (Fig. 2), for instance, brings an overview of the park and helps build expectations while making trip plans. The family can see parts of rides as in an interactive picture book

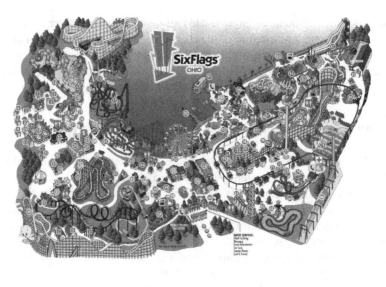

Fig. 1. Map of six flags amusement park and map of disneyworld.

with music, motions and videos. While the app "Wait Times for Disney World" (Fig. 3) focus on the period inside the park as it helps users see the waiting lines and make decisions on where to go first. Users can see many information windows at the same time and have a sense of the overall timelines. Although users might get carried away by the expectation of the adventure and use the app months before the trip, the major probability is to use it while in the park, as the app wouldn't help much outside of it.

Fig. 2. Display example of the app disneyland explorer showing of the park's features for interaction and preview of the rides.

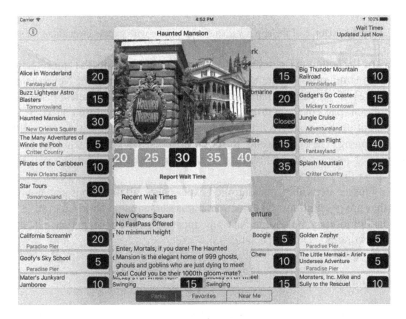

Fig. 3. Display example of the app wait time disneyland showing the waiting time in line for different rides.

The app "My Disney Experience" (Fig. 4) helps users put together the memories of the experience and organize the adventures of the day. The app unifies information regarding scheduled features (Akershus Royal Banquet Hall, dinner reservations, fast pass etc.), waiting times for each ride, shows and all data collected from visitors (users) photo pass (an online collection of all photos of the family taken by Disney photographers). Comparing all three apps, the "My Disney experience" is the most complex and more feasible of use previously and after the family trip, as it can certainly be part of the trip planning and the memories gathering after it.

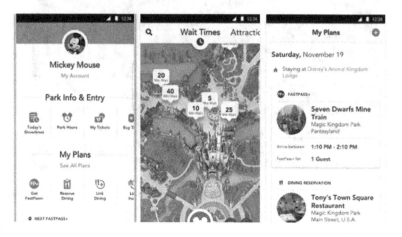

Fig. 4. Display example of the app my disney experience with events throughout the parks

Except by the common Disney brand and their connection with the amusement park, they have no similarities of interaction patterns or visual structure. Nevertheless, all three examples of apps can be part of the Disney experience, as each app seems to be used in different parts of the journey. They can be accessed by different types devices (with different display sizes) in different contexts of use, which can result in different senses of meaning. The expectations, the users and contexts will influence the sense and significance of interactions and objects, as at least one of the examples can be used months earlier the planned trip.

But, as Flusser alerts about uncontrolled experiences, all three apps may not be used at all, as they are possibilities of interaction, but not essential to build a narrative. Many parts of the full journey may not include any apparatus and each experience is attached to individual conditions and expectations.

4   Conclusion

The sense of objects and systems changes with its usage, influenced by different contexts in which it is inserted, by specific scenes of the experience journey and by references and expectations of each user. The perception and analysis of the form is developed through interaction and learning and it changes continuously as perceptions can be molded through memory and expectations, affecting and transforming perceived values within the journey. During the interaction with apparatuses, the experience is induced by perceived meanings of the system use and its contextual significance.

When the evaluation of the formal project outcomes is restricted to usability precepts, there is a risk on focusing too much around data visualization and functionality. In this respect, the emphasis given to the language of form seems to be heavily influenced by a modernist view, linked by the pursuit of neutrality, simplification and based on a so-called "universal common sense". However, such objectives don't fully meet human perceptions because the act of perceiving is based on probing and recognition, and should be defined as a type of subjective and private interpretation, as pointed by Nöe or Flusser. Through the potential malleability of contemporary medias, design projects have the technological capability to foster such subjectivity and individualism.

Findeli and Frascara [18] value the user experience and the empathy process derived from meanings and significances of use. Projects' results are understood and validated through interactions with the system and analyses of users' narrative journey to understand the touch points and possible contexts of use. The mapping of the journey and the moments that could bring a family to instinctively use the system, not necessarily by need, but by empathy or desire of use, derived from the sense of objects and significance of the moment, can help designers, if not to control the users' experiences, to at least contribute to make users enjoy, fall in love with the journey and build narrative memories.

References

1. Resmini, A., Rosatti, L.: Pervasive Information Architecture – Designing Cross-Channel User Experiences. Morgan Kaufmann – inprint of Elsevier. Burlington (2011)
2. Renzi, A.B., Freitas, S.F.: Delphi method to explore future scenario possibilities on technology and HCI. In: Marcus, A. (ed.) DUXU 2015. LNCS, vol. 9186, pp. 644–653. Springer, Cham (2015). doi:10.1007/978-3-319-20886-2_60
3. Norman, D.: Systems thinking: a product is more than the product. Interactions 16(5), 52–54 (2009). http://interactions.acm.org/content/?p=1286
4. Mcmullin, J., Starmer, S.: Leaving flatland: designing services and systems across channels. In: Proceedings of 11th Information Architecture Summit, Phoenix (2010)
5. Vermeeren, A.P.O.S., Law, E.L.C., Roto, V., Obrist, M., Hoonhout, J., Vananen-Vainio-Mattila, K.: User experience evaluation methods: current state and development needs. In: Proceedings: NordiCHI 2010, 16–20 October (2010)
6. Renzi, A.B.: Experiência do ususário: a jornada de Designers nos processos de gestão de suas empresas de pequeno porte utilizando sistema fantasiado em ecossistema de interação cross-channel. Doctorate thesis. 239p. Escola Superior de Desenho Industrial. Rio de Janeiro, Brazil (2016)
7. Flusser, V.: A arte: o belo e o agradável. In: Artefilosofia: Antologias de textos estéticos/ Organização: Gilson Iannini, Douglas Garcia e Romero Freitas. Rio de Janeiro: Civilização Brasileira, pp. 42–46 (2015)
8. Kripendorff, K.: The Semantic Turn: A New Foundation for Design. Taylor & Francis Group, Boca Raton (2006)
9. Kripendorff, K.: On the essential contexts of artifacts or on the proposition that "Design Is Making Sense (Of Things)". Des. Issues 5(2), 9–39 (1989). Spring, The MIT Press
10. Lockton, D., Harrison, D., Staton, N.A.: The design with intent method: a design tool for influencing user behavior. Appl. Ergon. 41(3), 382–392 (2010)

11. Nöe, A.: Action in Perception. The MIT Press, Cambridge (2004)
12. Frascara, J.: Communication Design: Principles, Methods, and Practice. Allworth Press, New York (2004)
13. Nielsen, J.: 10 usability heuristics for interface design (1995). www.nngroup.com/articles/ten-usability-heuristics
14. Apted, T., Collins, A., Kay, J.: Heuristics to support design of new software for interaction at tabletops. In: Computer-Human Interactions, Boston, MA (2009)
15. Inostroza, R., Rusu, C., Roncaglioso, R., Rusu, V.: Usability heuristics for touchscreen-based mobile devices. In: 9th International Conference on Information Technology – IEEE Computer Society. Temuco, Chile (2013)
16. Vilar Neto, E., Campos, F.F.C.: Evaluating the usability on multimodal interfaces: a case study on tablets applications. In: Marcus, A. (ed.) DUXU 2014. LNCS, vol. 8517, pp. 484–495. Springer, Cham (2014). doi:10.1007/978-3-319-07668-3_47
17. Spool, J.: Mobile & UX: Inside the Eye of the Perfect Storm, Interaction South America, Recife (2013)
18. Findeli, A.: Rethinking design education for the 21st century: theoretical, methodological, and ethical discussion. MIT Press J. Winter 17(1), 5–17 (2001)

GreenFLY

Adding Carbon to the Equation in Online Flight Searches

Angela Sanguinetti, Andrew Kwon, Yitong Li, Vishal Chakraborty, Suhaila Sikand,
Otavio Tarelho, Ying Chen, and Nina Amenta[✉]

Consumer Energy Interfaces Lab, University of California, Davis, Davis, USA
{asanguinetti,askwon,ytnli,vch,sksikand,otarelho,
yncchen,abamenta}@ucdavis.edu

Abstract. GreenFLY (greenfly.ucdavis.edu) is an airline flight search website that prominently displays greenhouse gas emissions estimates along with the other important flight information, such as price and times, for each possible flight itinerary. We describe its software components and graphic design principles. Then we present a discrete choice experiment in which we asked participants to choose between itineraries presented in the GreenFLY format. Results suggest that consumers are willing to pay a significant amount for lower-emissions flights in the context of online flight search, especially when lower emissions are combined with fewer layovers.

Keywords: Air travel emissions · Flight carbon calculator · Flight search engine

1 Introduction

Air travel is now estimated to contribute as much as 5% of worldwide greenhouse gas emissions [13]. A single round-trip coach flight from San Francisco to Miami is responsible for about one metric ton of emissions; for comparison, annual greenhouse gas emissions in the United States are about 20 metric tons per person. Therefore, reducing emissions due to air travel is an important goal.

Although generally high relative to other travel modes, emissions for different flight itineraries with the same origin and destination can vary greatly, depending mainly on the number and location of connections/layovers and on the aircraft used [9]. Aircraft emissions are measured in carbon dioxide equivalent, CO_2E, which measures the environmental impact of all greenhouse gasses emitted by giving the corresponding weight of CO_2 only. Different itineraries for the San Francisco-Miami trip can vary by 0.7 tons of CO_2E or more. Taking advantage of these potential savings is an appealing approach to emissions reductions [13].

Specific and relevant information provided at the purchase decision point has been suggested as an effective strategy to help consumers to make environmentally beneficial choices [4]. Online flight searching presents an excellent opportunity for this kind of intervention: someone making an air travel purchase is already carefully examining a website that presents detailed information on many possible itineraries, and choosing a

© Springer International Publishing AG 2017
A. Marcus and W. Wang (Eds.): DUXU 2017, Part II, LNCS 10289, pp. 87–103, 2017.
DOI: 10.1007/978-3-319-58637-3_7

flight based on a variety of factors (e.g., cost, number and length of layovers, airline, airport of departure and arrival, and departure and arrival times). Displaying a CO_2E emissions estimate for each flight would allow the consumer to consider emissions among these other factors.

With greater awareness of the environmental costs of air travel, some consumers might also consider other transportation options, e.g., driving to a slightly farther airport in order to get a direct flight, or driving rather than flying for a family vacation if the distance was not too great. Many consumers making lower-carbon choices would encourage airlines to invest in more efficient aircraft or routing. Increasing public awareness of the environmental costs of air travel would also help inform government regulation and public investment in transportation.

In this paper, we describe the design and development of GreenFLY, a flight search tool that displays CO_2E emissions estimates along with the usual data for different flight itineraries. We describe a discrete choice experiment based on the GreenFLY interface that provides some insight into the potential influence such a tool might have on consumer behavior.

2   Prior Work

Before we describe GreenFLY in detail and present our choice experiment, we review prior relevant work. Specifically, we survey carbon calculators and eco-feedback apps that focus on accounting for carbon in travel behavior and promoting greener travel. Then, we summarize previous economic valuation studies that consider consumer willingness to pay for flight carbon offsets. Finally, we describe past efforts to integrate carbon emissions estimates into the online flight search process.

2.1   Transportation Carbon Calculators and Eco-Feedback Apps

Estimating flight emissions in enough detail to distinguish fairly between specific itineraries requires detailed information about the flight legs, and the more information available the better the estimates (we discuss the information we use below). Detailed carbon calculators have been developed by transportation analytics companies that provide a variety of information to commercial clients on their travel costs and practices. Calculators by TRX (now part of Concor) and Sabre, the travel technology company providing the largest commercial flight search engine, provide very high-quality data but are expensive and not accessible to individual consumers.

Many publicly available personal online carbon calculators provide estimates of the environmental costs of air travel, but not in sufficient detail to compare different flights. Good examples ask users to enter the number of short, long, and extensive flights taken (e.g., UC Berkeley's CoolClimate Network carbon calculator: http://coolclimate.berkeley.edu/calculator) and the origin and destination of flights taken (e.g., Terrapass: https://www.terrapass.com/carbon-footprint-calculator). Layovers are taken into account by the air travel-specific calculators at myclimate (https://co2.myclimate.org/en/portfolios?calculation_id=681294) and the International Civil

Aviation Organization (ICAO; http://www.icao.int/environmental-protection/Carbon-Offset/Pages/default.aspx). None of these freely available calculators take into account aircraft model, which has a substantial impact on emissions.

In addition to carbon calculator websites, there are mobile apps that track transportation behavior and provide eco-feedback [5], including carbon emissions estimates, to promote greener travel. These include some publicly available apps (e.g., Carbon-Diem.com, CommuteGreener.com) and apps created for human-computer interaction research [e.g., 6, 10]. However, these apps have focused mainly on non-motorized (walking, cycling) and motorized ground transportation. An exception is E-Mission [18], a smartphone app that automatically recognizes multiple travel modes, including air, with a companion web interface that provides feedback on carbon emissions (based on averages for each travel mode).

Emissions estimates resulting from these tools can increase users' awareness of the large impact that air travel has on their personal carbon footprints, but they are not geared toward helping consumers proactively reduce their air travel carbon footprint. There are two strategies that enable a more proactive approach. One is the integration of carbon emissions information into online flight search tools, which is the subject of this study. The other is carbon taxes or offsets that the consumer can purchase to compensate for the emissions created by their air travel.

2.2 Economic Valuation of Air Travel Carbon Offsets

There have been a number of studies attempting to quantify air travelers' willingness to pay (WTP) for carbon offsets for their flights [1, 2, 15, 16, 19]. The purchase of carbon offsets is distinct from the goals of GreenFLY and similar tools that integrate emissions information into online flight searching. Carbon offsets provide the consumer with an opportunity to pay for activities that combat climate change in order to offset the carbon they are responsible for producing with their air travel. In contrast, GreenFLY and similar tools provide the consumer with an opportunity to avoid some emissions entirely. To our knowledge, ours is the first study of consumer WTP for carbon in this context. However, previous studies on WTP for carbon offsets are relevant as a point of comparison.

Brouwer et al. [1] recruited 400 air travelers (mostly European) at Amsterdam Schiphol Airport in 2006 to participate in a contingent valuation (CV) study of WTP for carbon offsets. After receiving an explanation of the concept of a carbon tax, participants were asked if, in general, they were will to pay such a tax on their plane ticket. Those who said yes (75%) were then asked if they were willing to pay a specific amount of money for that tax. Using the CV method, if the response was no, the interviewer asked about a second amount that was lower; if the initial response was yes, the interviewer asked about a second amount that was higher. This process continues until an interval is reached between an amount the consumer is willing to pay and an amount they are not willing to pay. Mean WTP for a flight carbon tax was 23.1 Euros (equivalent to 25 Euros per ton of CO_2E).

Similar CV studies were subsequently conducted by Jou and Chen [11], Lu and Shon [15], and MacKerron et al. [16]. MacKerron et al. [16], in 2007, asked 321 UK adults aged 18–34 to imagine flying from New York to London and having the opportunity to purchase a carbon offset for the flight. Mean WTP was GBP £24. Lu and Shon [15] interviewed 1,339 air travelers at Taoyuan International Airport in Taiwan late 2010 to early 2011. They found that passengers flying to China, Northeast Asia, Southeast Asia, and western countries were willing to pay $5, $8.80, $10.80, and $28.60, respectively, to offset their flight carbon emissions (amounting to 1–1.5% of participant flight cost).

Overall, studies have shown that most air travelers say they are willing to pay some amount to offset flight carbon emissions, and often at rates higher than standard carbon offset prices [e.g., 11, 16]. However, as Jou and Chen [11] caution, stated valuation is an easier commitment than actually making the donation. In Brouwer et al. [1], when participants were asked how likely they would be to pay their stated WTP amount if it were a voluntary tax, only 37% percent of North American participants, 47% of European participants, and 50% of Asian participants said they were likely to pay. In Choi and Ritchie [2], most participants agreed that voluntary offset payments must be "a convenient thing to do", and they talked about the importance of the position of the offset option during online booking as well as convenient payment procedures. Providing salient information in a flight search tool about the range of carbon emissions for flight alternatives could be the most convenient strategy, as users could simply purchase a lower emissions flight without any additional donation and payment procedure.

2.3 Integrating CO_2 Estimates into Flight Search Tools

The idea of displaying greenhouse gas emissions estimates during flight search was pioneered, as far as we know, by a company called Brighter Planet, whose main business was carbon accounting for industrial and institutional clients. They developed an air travel emissions calculator, and a plug-in, Careplane, for the major web browsers. Careplane decorated Expedia, Orbitz, Kayak, and a few other flight search sites with emissions estimates during search. Unfortunately, when Brighter Planet went out of business neither their calculator nor the plug-ins were supported, so they no longer give correct results.

Calasi, a later start-up, has a business model in which they market an emissions calculator and information on other flight details, such as in-flight entertainment options, to flight search engine companies. Unfortunately, we are not aware of any flight search sites currently using their emissions data. Calasi also developed a browser plug-in, but again maintenance is a problem.

Flight search is a competitive, low-margin industry. Flight search engines, which provide the data on flight schedules, prices and availability, are expensive, so it is difficult to build a profitable custom flight search site based on a commercial engine. While web plug-ins do not incur the cost of a flight search engine, they are difficult to build and even more difficult to maintain, as both browsers and flight search websites change quickly. In addition, decorating existing flight search pages adds to their clutter instead of providing a sense of clarity and purpose, and plug-ins do not allow for more complex functions (e.g., allowing the user to sort flights by carbon emissions).

3 GreenFLY

GreenFLY is an example of a flight search tool in which emissions estimates are the focus rather than an afterthought. Earlier tools either forced estimates into flight search pages that were not designed to accommodate them, or they were not in the flight search page at all and required users to navigate between multiple interfaces. GreenFLY sorts flight options according to emissions, displays emissions information cleanly and prominently, and provides contextual information for the magnitude of the potential emissions savings.

3.1 Design

GreenFLY's home page and flight search background screen depict clouds rolling through a mountain range to elevate the user as if in flight and suggest cleanliness and nature. The flight search input interface (Fig. 1) resembles a plane ticket on which the user enters origin, destination, flight legs (one-way or round trip), departure/return dates, and cabin (economy, business, etc.).

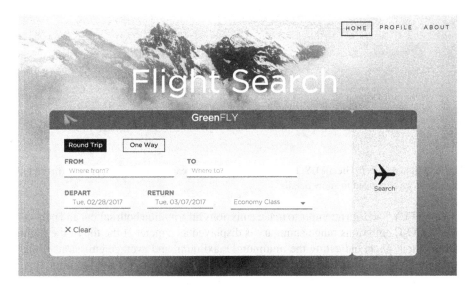

Fig. 1. The query interface for flight search in GreenFLY. The background is meant to suggest cleanliness and nature as well as flight, while the form resembles a ticket.

Once the information is entered, the user clicks the "search" button on the ticket stub and is directed to the flight search results (Fig. 2), which populate the same page, just below the flight search ticket. Continuing with the ticket theme, each flight search result can be expanded to view a ticket for each leg of the trip giving detailed information.

Fig. 2. Flight results in GreenFLY. Emissions estimates appear on the left, and price on the right. Flights can be expanded to show details.

GreenFLY's design attempts to make emissions information both salient and persuasive. A CO_2E emissions range summary is displayed as a meter at the top of the flight search output page, indicating the minimum, maximum, and average emissions of the available flight options. The meter uses a gradient of yellow-orange-red to imply that higher emissions is negative and undesirable. A green dot on the far left of the meter marks the flight option(s) with the lowest emissions. Lowest emissions flight(s) are also labeled as "Your GreenFLY" in green text, with the emissions number also in green text to imply that these are the most positive and desirable flights. To further emphasize the significance of flights with lower emissions, search results appear sorted from least to most emissions by default; the user can also choose to search by price.

Users have the option to add a flight to their personal profile by clicking "Add to Footprint". The profile page (Fig. 3) tracks a user's flight history and three metrics: total CO_2E emissions, kilometers travelled, and number of trips; each statistic is accompanied by an illustrative icon and distinct color. The user can also delete flights from the history, which readjusts the statistics.

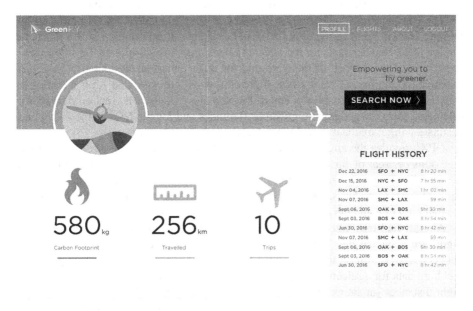

Fig. 3. GreenFLY user profile page. The user can keep track of their flight history and overall carbon footprint.

3.2 Flight Search Engine

GreenFLY uses Google's QPX Express flight search engine API (application program interface) to obtain flight schedule and price information. QPX provides a free interface for low volumes of flight searches (up to 50 per day); but using it for many searches is currently expensive. GreenFLY sends a query containing the origin, destination, class of travel, dates of travel, and trip type (round trip or one-way) to QPX, which returns a list of possible flight itineraries. Using QPX to develop GreenFLY gave us complete control over the presentation of both flight and emissions information.

3.3 Flight Emissions Calculator

GreenFLY's emissions calculator is based on the following formulae:

$$
CO_2E \text{ Emission } [kg/person] = 3.16 \times (\text{Total fuel for journey } [kg] / \# \text{ seats}) \times 1.5 \tag{1}
$$

$$
\text{Total fuel for journey } [kg] = (\text{Aircraft fuel burn rate } [kg/km]) \times (\text{Distance}[km]) \tag{2}
$$

This computation is a simplification of the formula proposed by the International Civil Aviation Organization (ICAO) [7], a UN agency, which was designed for estimating the emissions assignable to an airport from the airport's specific mix of flights.

The constant 3.16^1 in Formula (1) represents the kilograms of CO_2 produced by burning one kilogram of aviation fuel. The constant 1.5 in Formula (2) is a radiative forcing factor that accounts for the effect of releasing emissions high in the atmosphere rather than at the surface of the earth and for other emissions besides CO_2. Various radiative forcing factors are used for flight emissions estimates, and 1.5 is a relatively conservative choice (giving lower emissions estimates). Distance is great-circle distance calculated from the geographic positions (latitudes and longitudes)[2] of the origin and destination input by the user, using the Geodesy package[3].

QPX provides the aircraft model for each flight leg, which can affect the carbon emissions per seat by up to a factor of two [12]; in general, regional jets are less fuel efficient than long-range and medium-range jets, and more modern aircraft are more fuel efficient than older planes. Our emissions estimates use the aircraft model to determine the fuel burn rate and the number of economy class seats on the plane.

Aircraft fuel burn rate is the amount of fuel burnt by an aircraft per kilometer in flight. We collected fuel burn data from a variety of sources. Most of the data were obtained from European Environmental Agency (EEA) [3, Appendix], which provided fuel burn data for a selection of representative aircraft models for a number of specific flight distances (updating an earlier table published by the ICAO [6, page 14]). For distances not provided, we used linear interpolation to estimate fuel burn. Many aircraft not included in the EEA data are mapped to the representative aircraft using tables provided by the ICAO [6, p. 13] and the EEA [3, p. 23]. For aircraft models not provided, we obtained data on the max fuel weight (MFW), maximum range, and capacity for different aircraft models from Jane's Information Group [8]. We estimated fuel burn with the following formula:

$$\text{Fuel burn} \left[\text{kg/km}\right] = \text{MFW}\left[\text{kg}\right] \times \text{Maximum range [km]} \tag{3}$$

This estimate is not as accurate as EEA data, which was based on simulations of flights of various lengths, and takes into consideration the fuel required for taxi, take-off, holding patterns, approaches, and landings. However, matching estimates based on Formula (3) allows us to map unknown aircraft to representative aircraft with similar calculated fuel burns.

The number of seats on a particular aircraft model, in Formula (1) above, varies between airlines, depending on how the aircraft is configured. The standard capacity of most aircraft models was taken from Jane's. Some missing seat number data were obtained from aircraft profiles found on the websites of major airlines.

---

[1] From [6], p. 6.

[2] Available online; we used www.openflights.org/data.html.

[3] The Geodesy repository can be found here: https://github.com/chrisveness/geodesy.

3.4 Software Design

GreenFLY is built on Node.js, supported by a number of JavaScript packages, including Webpack, ES6 and JQuery in the frontend, and Express.js, socket.io, and async on the server side. The main database storing airline, aircrafts, and airports information uses SQLite3. The user registration information is stored in another database using MongoDB.

GreenFLY first takes a user's input including origin, destination, class of travel, dates of travel, and trip type (round trip or one-way), and sends it to the server for query construction. The server then sends the query to QPX to retrieve possible itineraries, as described in Sect. 3.2. After getting back a response from QPX, it parses each itinerary into legs, with each leg containing information about departure airport, arrival airport, departure time, arrival time, aircraft model, price, etc. Then it computes CO_2E emissions for each leg, as described in Sect. 3.3. The parameters needed for computation, namely the number of seats and fuel burn rate for specific aircraft, and the longitude and latitude of airports, are retrieved from the main database. The calculated emissions are then appended to the response received from QPX, and returned to the frontend code in the browser for display.

4 Experiment

We used choice modeling, and in particular a discrete choice experiment, to explore the potential for GreenFLY and similar tools to promote the purchase of greener flights. Choice experiments allow the researcher to examine whether and to what degree specific attributes, or attribute combinations, influence the value of an economic good, i.e., the consumers' willingness to pay (WTP) for those attributes [14]. The general method of a discrete choice experiment is to have research participants choose among options that vary in terms of the attributes of interest.

Discrete choice is a common method in marketing research as it resembles real purchase situations. In our context, asking participants which flight they would choose from visually presented options that vary in terms of cost and number of layovers is a familiar task to anyone who has experience online flight searching. Adding carbon emissions as an attribute, however, is novel to most consumers. We therefore prefaced the experiment by providing participants with some contextual information about air travel carbon emissions.

4.1 Methodology

We designed our discrete choice experiment using Qualtrics survey software and recruited participants via Amazon Mechanical Turk. Participation was restricted to US residents at least 18 years of age (Mechanical Turk provided these filters), with experience purchasing flight tickets and traveling by plane (survey items required participants to confirm they met these inclusion criteria).

Participants were asked where they last traveled to by plane and whether the trip was for business, pleasure, or both. Their responses to those questions were piped into instructions for the later flight choice questions, i.e., "For the next three questions, please imagine you are searching for a flight for an upcoming [business, pleasure, or business and pleasure] trip to [last flight destination]. ... Which flight would you choose given the following options and information?"

We presented the flight itinerary choices using a modified version of our visual design for GreenFLY in order to approximate the experience of using a flight search that emphasized emissions estimates. In addition, it allowed us to give the questions a realistic "look and feel" typical of the flight search task.

Our main research question was: How much more money, if any, are consumers willing to pay to take a flight with less emissions? This issue is complicated, however, by the fact that itineraries with fewer layovers typically have significantly lower emissions, and many consumers will pay more for a flight with fewer layovers, regardless of emissions. Therefore, a second question was: How much do emission reductions encourage consumers to choose a flight with fewer layovers?

To answer these questions, we developed three flight choice scenarios, detailed below, to present to each participant. Each flight choice scenario consisted of three flight options that varied along one or more of the dimensions: cost, carbon emissions, and number of layovers (Table 1). Cost and carbon emissions levels were determined by calculating the average of each for a sample of popular domestic one-way flights, then building levels around that average. Specifically, for cost we used the mean, two standard deviations below and three standard deviations above. For carbon emissions we used the mean, one standard deviation on either side of the mean, and the minimum and maximum values.

Table 1. Attributes varied in our choice experiment.

Cost ($)	480, 459, 438, 417, 396, 375
Carbon emissions (kg CO_2)	231, 274, 381, 488, 595, 634
Number of layovers	Nonstop, 1 layover, or 2 layovers

Flight Choice Scenario 1: Cost and Layovers. The user was asked to choose one of three flight options that varied in terms of cost and number of layovers, which were negatively correlated; e.g., Figure 4. Each flight choice scenario consisted of one nonstop option, one 1 layover option, and one 2 layover option. Participants were randomly assigned to view one of eight possible flight option combinations for this flight choice scenario.

Flight Choice Scenario 2: Cost and Carbon. The user was asked to choose one of three flights that varied in terms of cost and carbon emissions, which were negatively correlated; e.g., Figure 5. Participants were randomly assigned to view one of twenty possible flight option combinations for this flight choice scenario.

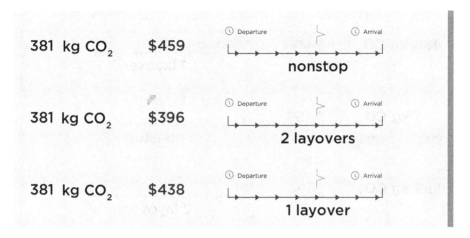

Fig. 4. Example of options presented to respondents in flight choice scenario 1.

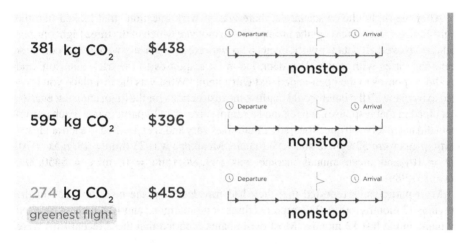

Fig. 5. Examples of options presented to respondents in flight choice scenario 2.

Flight Choice Scenario 3: Cost, Carbon, and Layovers. The user was asked to choose one of three flights that varied in terms of cost, carbon emissions, and number of layovers; carbon emissions was positively correlated with number of layovers and negatively correlated with cost; e.g., Figure 6. Participants were randomly assigned to view one of twenty possible flight option combinations for this flight choice scenario.

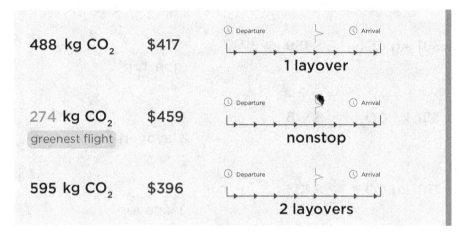

Fig. 6. Example of options presented to respondents in flight choice scenario 3.

After the flight choice scenarios, there was a "trick question" that looked like the flight choice scenarios except the prompt was to indicate which of the three flight options had one layover; all data for participants who answered incorrectly were removed. After removing cases with incomplete data, incorrect responses to the trick question, and invalid responses to the open-ended text entry item, "What was the last place you traveled to by plane?" (the latter would confuse the instructions for the flight choice scenarios that piped in that response), we retained a sample size of 1417 participants. Each participant did not receive all questions, so sample sizes vary and are specified in each analysis. Participants were 52% male and 42% female. Mean age was 33 (min = 18, max = 70, SD = 10) and mean annual income was \$49,096 (min = 0; max = \$450,000, SD = \$37,989).

Most participants reported that they had traveled by plane once or twice in the previous 12 months (60%); 28% reported three or more flights; and 12% had not traveled by plane in the last 12 months. Most participants reported that these recent trips were mostly for pleasure (74%); 11% indicated they were mostly for business, and 15% indicated they were about half and half. Of those who traveled by plane for business (n = 372), 73% indicated that their flight costs were typically covered by work. In terms of their most recent flight, which was used to frame the flight choice selection questions, 78% reported this trip was for pleasure, 12% indicated it was for business, and 10% indicated it was for both business and pleasure. Destinations for most recent flight naturally varied widely, but frequent answers included cities in Florida (236) and California (178), as well as Las Vegas (74) and New York (66).

4.2   Analysis and Results

We computed a conditional logit model for each of the three flight choice scenarios using the *clogistic* function of the *Epi* package in R. This package calculates a model predicting, given the three flight alternatives, the probability that each flight option will be chosen. The probabilities are assigned to each of the three choices using three linked non-linear functions, which take as input a utility score for each of the flight choices. Utility is modeled as a linear function, which the *clogistic* package fits using maximum likelihood. We can think of the linear utility function as describing how the most likely user values each of the factors describing the flight choice. Since cost is one of the factors, it lets us explain other factors in terms of WTP.

The analysis of Question 1, which varied flight options' cost and number of layovers, showed, unsurprisingly, that participants were willing to pay more for flights with fewer layovers. It produced the utility function:

$$U = -1.494 * layovers + -0.0291 * dollars + constant$$

These coefficients, and the model itself, were all highly statistically significant (see Table 2). Note that the coefficients are not standardized and should not be directly compared. This model implies that, when comparing a nonstop flight to a one-layover flight, or a two-layover to a one-layover, the extra layover should cost –1.494 / – 0.0291 = \$51.34 less to be equally desirable to our maximum likelihood consumer. That is, the two flights in Fig. 7 would be roughly equally desirable.

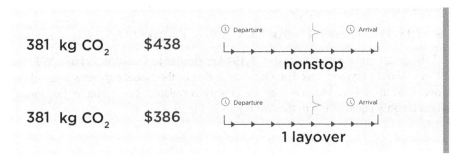

Fig. 7.   Equally desirable flights that differ in cost and number of layovers.

The model for Question 2, which varied flight options' carbon emissions and cost, showed that participants were willing to pay more for lower-carbon flights. It produced the utility function:

$$U = -0.00679 * carbon + -0.03532 * dollars + constant$$

These coefficients, and the model itself, were again all highly statistically significant (Table 2). This model implies that, when comparing flights with varying carbon emissions, our maximum likelihood consumer would be willing to pay –0.00679/– 0.03532 = \$.192 per kg CO_2 spared. This implies a remarkable carbon cost of \$192/ton CO_2. For example, the two flights in Fig. 8 are roughly equally desirable according to the model.

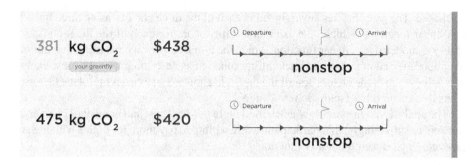

Fig. 8. Equally desirable flights that differ in cost and carbon.

Question 3 varied flight options' cost, layovers, and carbon emissions. Our hypothesis for this question was that including carbon emissions estimates would encourage people to choose flights with fewer layovers, so we designed the question so that carbon emissions are lower for flights with fewer layovers (as they usually are in reality). As a result, the *carbon* and *layover* variables are highly correlated.

Again, our data gave a statistically significant model, with all of it coefficients significant (Table 2):

$$U = -1.15775 * layovers + -0.04908 * dollars + -0.00957 \, kg \, carbon + constant$$

This model gives a carbon cost of $.194/kg, similar to Question 2, but a WTP of $29.76 to avoid a layover, less than Question 1; that is, the model attributes some of the layover cost to carbon, because they are closely correlated. For example, this model assigns roughly equal utility to the two flights in Fig. 9.

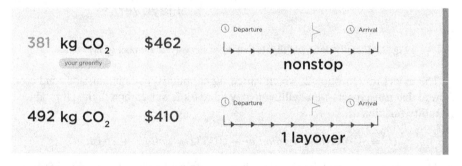

Fig. 9. Equally desirable flights that differ in cost ($52 difference), number of layovers, and carbon (111 kg CO_2 difference).

Thus, assuming the customer is willing to pay $51.34 more for a non stop (the value predicted in Question 1), they also expect to get 111 kg of correlated emissions reductions "for free". But as the emission reductions increase, so does willingness to pay to avoid the layover. For instance, the flights in Fig. 10 also have equal utility.

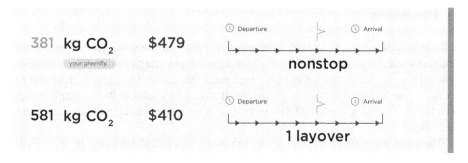

Fig. 10. Equally desirable flights that differ in cost ($69 difference), number of layovers, and carbon (200 kg CO_2 difference).

That is, if the emissions reduction is 200 kg, the model predicts that the customer would pay as much as $68.60 to avoid the layover.

We analyzed this tradeoff in another way, by computing models from the data in Question 3 that just included one factor or the other. We found that a statistically significant model only using the number of layovers and cost implied a WTP of $82.76 to avoid a layover. That is, showing realistic emission reductions raised WTP very significantly from the value of $51.34 that we found when emissions did not vary in Question 1. Similarly, a model computed from Question 3 using only cost and carbon implied a carbon cost of $0.302/kg, significantly greater than the $0.194/kg we saw when number of layovers did not vary in Question 2.

Table 2. Significance of the conditional logistic models for Questions 1-3. The *lrt* statistic is likelihood ratio test and *df* is degrees of freedom.

Question	Regression statistics	Variable	Coefficient (se)	z-statistic	p-value
Question 1 ($N = 1403$)	$lrt = 126$; $df = 2$; $p = 0$	Cost	−0.0291 (0.00325)	−9.06	< .0001
		Layovers	−1.4940 (0.143)	−10.43	<.0001
Question 2 ($N = 1055$)	$lrt = 54.9$; $df = 2$; $p = < .0001$	Cost	−0.03532 (0.00728)	−5.24	< .0001
		Carbon	−0.00679 (0.00171)	−4.25	.00021
Question 3 ($N = 1055$)	$lrt = 296$; $df = 3$; $p = 0$	Cost	−0.04908 (0.00817)	−5.90	< .0001
		Layovers	−1.15775 (0.196)	−5.79	< .0001
		Carbon	−0.00957 (0.00236)	−3.95	.00020

5   Discussion

A flight search tool like GreenFLY requires two parts, a flight search engine and an emissions calculator. As we previously mentioned, flight search engines are expensive to license, so we implemented our own emissions calculator. The biggest challenge in doing so was finding the data. In particular, it would be useful to have complete fuel burn tables, extending the ICAO data to a range of aircraft covering most modern flight itineraries.

There are many other ways in which our emissions calculator could be improved. Some relevant factors that we cannot determine at the time of purchase are the year of aircraft manufacture and the engine (different engines can be installed in the same aircraft model). We might, however, be able to estimate these based on average values for each airline. Number of seats in a given aircraft model varies by airline; we currently use only a single estimate per aircraft regardless of airline. Passenger load (occupancy) and passenger to freight weight ratios can be estimated from historical data, which could be purchased. We plan to open-source our emissions calculator, along with an API, so that other researchers can contribute to its database and algorithms.

Our Mechanical Turk experiment showed that a design like GreenFLY, which displays emissions estimates clearly and with context, very strongly encourages respondents to choose flights with lower greenhouse gas emissions. In the context of flight search with an interface like GreenFLY's, respondents' choices indicated willingness to pay a carbon cost of \$192/ton of CO_2E, almost a factor of ten greater than that seen in other contexts. Showing realistic emissions data and flagging the greenest choice increased the WTP to avoid a layover to \$82.76 from \$51.34, again a very significant change.

While these results show that our existing design does a great job of encouraging emissions reductions, it would be very interesting to study a variety of design factors and see how they affect user behavior. Also, we need to add several features, such as choosing a first-class flight (with corresponding emissions cost), multiple passengers, multi-city flights, and so on, that users expect in a flight search site.

It is also important to verify these results, and any further ideas, in a real flight search application, when respondents are actually spending money. In order to do this, we need to improve GreenFLY. Currently, the user cannot actually purchase flights through GreenFLY; we need to send them to another site to make the actual purchase. Somewhat disturbingly, we find that flights listed as available through QPX are sometimes not available on other search sites. Possibly both of these problems could be solved by switching to another flight search engine (e.g., WeGo). This is a rapidly evolving market and we expect that we should be able to find a good solution in the near future.

This research suggests something like GreenFLY, either as its own niche site or as part of a larger flight search site, would allow consumers to make significant reductions in their personal carbon footprints, help educate the general public on the environmental costs of air travel, and encourage improved aircraft and airline efficiency.

References

1. Brouwer, R., Brander, L., Van Beukering, P.: "A convenient truth": air travel passengers' willingness to pay to offset their CO_2 emissions. Clim. Change **90**(3), 299–313 (2008)
2. Choi, A.S., Ritchie, B.W.: Willingness to pay for flying carbon neutral in Australia: an exploratory study of offsetter profiles. J. Sustain. Tourism **22**(8), 1236–1256 (2014)
3. EMEP/EEA air pollutant emission inventory guidebook, Part B, Section 1.A.3.a, Aviation, and Section 1.A.3.a Aviation Annex (2013)
4. Fogg, B.J.: A behavior model for persuasive design. In: Proceedings of the 4th International Conference on Persuasive Technology - Persuasive 2009 (2009)
5. Froehlich, J., Findlater, L., Landay, J.: The design of eco-feedback technology. In: Proceedings of the SIGCHI Conference on Human Factors in Computing Systems, pp. 1999–2008. ACM, April 2010
6. Froehlich, J., Dillahunt, T., Klasnja, P., Mankoff, J., Consolvo, S., Harrison, B., Landay, J.A.: UbiGreen: investigating a mobile tool for tracking and supporting green transportation habits. In: Proceedings of the SIGCHI Conference on Human Factors in Computing Systems, pp. 1043–1052. ACM, April 2009
7. International Civil Aviation Organisation: ICAO Carbon Emissions Calculator Methodology, 8. USA, May 2015
8. Jackson, P. (ed.): Jane's All the World's Aircrafts. United Kingdom: Jane's Information Group (2013, 2014, 2015)
9. Jardine, C.N.: Calculating the carbon dioxide emissions of flights. Technical report, Environmental Change Institute (2009)
10. Jariyasunant, J., Abou-Zeid, M., Carrel, A., Ekambaram, V., Gaker, D., Sengupta, R., Walker, J.L.: Quantified traveler: travel feedback meets the cloud to change behavior. J. Intell. Transp. Syst. **19**(2), 109–124 (2015)
11. Jou, R.C., Chen, T.Y.: Willingness to pay of air passengers for carbon-offset. Sustainability **7**(3), 3071–3085 (2015)
12. Kwan, I., Rutherford, D., Zeinali, M.: US domestic airline fuel efficiency ranking, white paper, The International Council on Clean Transportation (2014)
13. Lee, D.S., Fahey, D.W., Forster, P.M., Newton, P.J., Wit, R.C.N., Lim, L.L., Sausen, R.: Aviation and global climate change in the 21st century. Atmos. Environ. **43**(22–23), 3520–3537 (2009)
14. Louviere, J.J., Hensher, D.A., Swait, J.D.: Stated Choice Methods: Analysis and Applications. Cambridge University Press, Cambridge (2000)
15. Lu, J.L., Shon, Z.Y.: Exploring airline passengers' willingness to pay for carbon offsets. Transp. Res. Part D Transp. Environ. **17**(2), 124–128 (2012)
16. MacKerron, G.J., Egerton, C., Gaskell, C., Parpia, A., Mourato, S.: Willingness to pay for carbon offset certification and co-benefits among (high-) flying young adults in the UK. Energy Policy **37**(4), 1372–1381 (2009)
17. Schultz, P.W.: The structure of environmental concern: concern for self, other people, and the biosphere. J. Environ. Psychol. **21**(4), 327–339 (2001)
18. Shankari, K., Yin, M., Culler, D., Katz, R.: E-mission: automated transportation emission calculation using smartphones. In: 2015 IEEE International Conference on Pervasive Computing and Communication Workshops (PerCom Workshops), pp. 268–271. IEEE, March 2015
19. van Birgelen, M., Semeijn, J., Behrens, P.: Explaining pro-environment consumer behavior in air travel. J. Air Transp. Manage. **17**(2), 125–128 (2011)

Electric Vehicle Explorer

Educating and Persuading Consumers with an Online Vehicle Energy Cost Calculator

Angela Sanguinetti[✉], Kiernan Salmon, Mike Nicholas, Gil Tal, and Matt Favetti

Consumer Energy Interfaces Lab, University of California, Davis, Davis, USA
{asanguinetti,kmsalmon,mianicholas,gtal,mpfavetti}@ucdavis.edu

Abstract. Most HCI research related to electric vehicle adoption has focused on mitigating barriers related to vehicle range and charging infrastructure, while relatively less attention has been given to helping consumers recognize the benefits of electric vehicles. A significant benefit is reduced energy costs; however, the complexity of comparing gasoline and electricity prices makes it difficult for consumers to quantify. This paper describes and evaluates an online tool called EV Explorer that enables users to compare personalized estimates of annual energy costs for multiple vehicles. We assessed the tool through an online experiment, gauging users' perceptions—before and after using the tool—of their current energy costs, potential savings with electric vehicles, attitude toward electric vehicle charging, and intention to buy or lease an electric vehicle in the future. Statistically significant changes in each of these variables validate the tool as an educational and persuasive strategy to promote electric vehicle adoption.

Keywords: Eco-feedback · Electric vehicles · Vehicle cost calculator

1 Introduction

Vehicle electrification is an important strategy in moving toward a more sustainable transportation future. Replacing gasoline with electricity to power vehicles enables reduced dependence on fossil fuels. Depending on the mix of energy sources used to produce that electricity, electric vehicles can also dramatically reduce climate-altering greenhouse gas emissions.

There are two types of electric vehicles (EVs), also called plug-in electric vehicles (PEVs): (1) battery electric vehicles (BEVs), which are powered exclusively by electricity from rechargeable electric battery packs and have no direct (tailpipe) emissions, and (2) plug-in hybrid electric vehicles (PHEVs), which can run on gas and/or electricity via a rechargeable electric battery and an internal combustion (gas-powered) engine that is smaller relative to those in conventional gas vehicles. Both types of PEVs are more energy efficient and less expensive to operate and maintain compared to conventional gas vehicles and hybrids (HEVS). HEVs require gasoline; they have an internal combustion engine aided by a non-rechargeable electric motor that enables better fuel economy and less emissions compared to similar conventional gas vehicles [1].

© Springer International Publishing AG 2017
A. Marcus and W. Wang (Eds.): DUXU 2017, Part II, LNCS 10289, pp. 104–118, 2017.
DOI: 10.1007/978-3-319-58637-3_8

Barriers to PEV adoption are well-studied; they include relatively higher purchase price and limitations in vehicle range and charging infrastructure [1–3]. These barriers are partly a function of consumers' lack of knowledge and experience with PEVs. For example, Jakobsson et al. [4] found that even prospective buyers of PEVs have very little knowledge regarding range performance, charging infrastructure, and the ability to plug-in at home. The phenomenon of "range anxiety"—fear of being unable to reach one's destination—is in many cases only a perceived barrier, since most drivers' regular commute travel range is lower than the modern electric vehicle's range [2, 3].

HCI research regarding PEV adoption has typically focused on addressing the barriers of range anxiety and lack of knowledge or access to charging infrastructure. For example, Lundström and colleagues [5–8] have developed and tested various interfaces for displaying remaining range to electric vehicle drivers, as well as mobile apps to simulate electrical vehicle range when driving a gas vehicle. Other examples of the latter strategy include BMW's EVolve App and Stanford researchers' Virtual EV Test Drive [9]. These apps are excellent educational tools for prospective PEV buyers, though they require a time commitment of several days or weeks to use properly.

There has been a lack of HCI research focused on conveying the benefits of PEVs to prospective buyers. There is a great need for such a focus given that consumers weigh perceived benefits more heavily than perceived risks when evaluating new technologies [10]. Moreover, increasing perceived benefits can have the effect of lowering perceived risk, likely to reduce cognitive dissonance created by negative aspects of technologies that one considers beneficial [11].

A significant benefit of PEVs can be lower energy costs. However, estimating potential savings is a complex endeavor [1]. Specifically, calculating potential energy savings to be gained with a PEV requires knowledge regarding current gas prices and electricity prices at each place the consumer may charge the vehicle (home, work, and/or public charging stations), as well as fuel economy of the consumer's current vehicle and the electricity consumption per mile of the particular PEV(s) the consumer is considering, all of which vary [12].

Vehicle cost calculators are one strategy to educate consumers about the benefits of PEVs, and perhaps even persuade them to adopt. In general, vehicle cost calculators handle three types of cost information: vehicle purchase, ongoing costs (taxes, insurance, and maintenance), and energy costs (gasoline and electricity). The present research provides an example of a calculator that focuses on energy costs.

There are many other examples of vehicle cost calculators that help users learn about PEV energy costs (Table 1). These calculators vary in terms of a number of features that are potentially important for user experience, education, and persuasion. For example, calculators may display cost information for only one vehicle at a time or multiple vehicles for comparison. The demand on users to input personal data before generating any output also varies, from no required inputs (which minimizes personalization of estimates) to many, which could be fatiguing to a user. The most commonly required input is miles the user drives per day, which, if unknown, may require the user to consult other tools such as mapping programs to estimate driving distance.

Table 1. Vehicle cost calculators that provide energy cost information for PEVs

Tool name[a]	Car comparisons	Required inputs	Destination charger
EV Explorer [18]	4; any type	Home address, destination address	Type, cost, hours parked
Alternative fuels data calculator [19]	8; any type	–	–
Go solar california [20]	2; 1 gas or HEV and 1 PEV	Miles/day	% public charger use, cost
Electric car calculator [21]	2; any type	Miles/weekday, miles/weekend day	–
My plug-in hybrid calculator [22]	–	Miles/day, miles/year, state	Type
PEV calculator (PG&E) [23]	–	Miles/day, zip code	–
PEV calculator (consumers energy) [24]	2; 1 gas or HEV and 1 PEV	–	–
Oncor EV savings calculator [25]	–	–	–
SMUD calculator [26]	2; 1 gas or HEV and 1 of 5 PEVs	–	–

Vehicle cost calculators also vary in terms of optional inputs that allow more tailored estimates of energy costs. For example, most allow the user to modify gas and electricity prices and customize some details about driving distances. Few tools allow the user to specify details regarding charging away from home. Given that 75% of workplace charging is free [13], the ability to specify destination charging costs in particular could increase energy savings estimates for many users, who might then be more persuaded to purchase or lease a PEV.

Finally, these tools vary in terms of the degree of interactivity with the output, i.e., the ease of exploration via modification of inputs. Some tools are highly structured such that the user must begin the entire process again if they wish to explore other inputs. Others allow for easier exploration by including multiple paths to change inputs, displaying results on the same page as inputs, and automatically updating results when inputs are changed.

Although many calculators exist, how they are used, whether they are effective, and which features influence consumer knowledge, attitudes, and intentions to adopt PEVs are not well-studied. Our research explores these questions in the context of one of these tools, called EV Explorer, which was created by members of our research team. EV Explorer utilizes several features that are less common in other existing tools, including a map-based interface for easily calculating commute distances within the site, comparison of up to four vehicles, and ability to customize variables related to charging at commute destination. The application is layered for ease of exploration; the user is only required to enter home address and commute destination address to start comparing energy costs; extensive tailoring can then be done as desired to increase the precision of estimates.

2   Methodology

We first describe the development and user interface design of EV Explorer, then detail the experiment conducted to evaluate its impact on users' knowledge, attitudes, and intention to buy or lease PEVs.

2.1   Website Development and Design

EV Explorer is written entirely in JavaScript. This means all calculations are done in the user's browser, which makes the tool very responsive to use. It uses Node.js [14] to power its webserver and API.

EV Explorer also makes use of several freely available public APIs. The map-driven content is powered by Google Maps [15]; this includes geocoding and route generation in addition to the standard map display. Vehicle information concerning fuel economy and range comes from an API available from the United States (US) Department of Energy Efficiency and Renewable Energy [16]. EV Explorer provides fuel prices relevant to the user by combining fuel price data from the US Energy Information Administration [1] with the user's location from freegeoip [17] based on their IP address. Electricity price was not created dynamically at the time of this study; it was set at $0.14 USD/kWh, which was slightly higher than average electricity price in the US in 2015; it can be customized by the user.

Upon entering the site, EV Explorer prompts the user through two steps. 'Step 1' is to enter a home address (Fig. 1). 'Step 2' is to enter a commuting destination by either typing it in or dragging a marker to the location on the map in the background. Upon completion of these two steps, a stacked bar chart comparison of annual energy costs (distinguishing between electricity and gasoline costs) for four vehicles is presented: one gasoline vehicle, two PHEVs, and one BEV (Fig. 2). A meter at the bottom of the screen shows required range for the user's roundtrip commute compared to total range for the BEV displayed in the cost comparison chart.

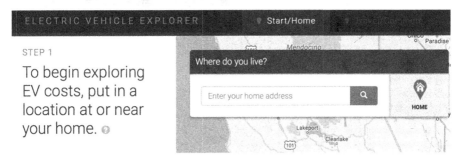

Fig. 1. Step 1: enter home address

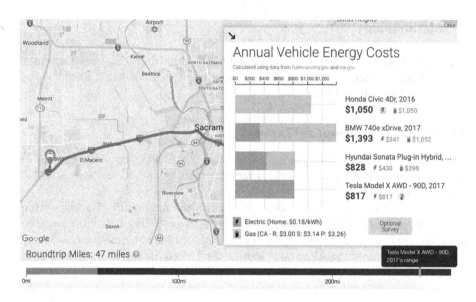

Fig. 2. Main output with annual energy cost comparisons and BEV range information

Travel/Commute Settings ❓

How often do you commute here?

5 times

per

week

☑ Charger at destination?

Charger Type

Level 2 (240 V)

Hours Parked

0

Price to Charge

$ 0

per

hour

☑ Charger at home?

Prices

Currency	USD - US Dollar	
State	California	
Electricity	$ 0.18	/ kWh
Regular	$ 2.9	/ gal
Super	$ 3.03	/ gal
Premium	$ 3.15	/ gal
Diesel	$ 2.97	/ gal
Natural Gas	$ 2.4	/ gal

Cancel   Update

Fig. 3. (Left) Travel/commute settings: commute frequency and charging at destination

Fig. 4. Modifiable energy prices

The user can then explore other features and further customize their annual fuel cost estimates. Specifically, the user can modify the frequency of their commute (default is 5 days per week) and charging opportunities at destination (Fig. 3). Another feature allows the modification of gas and electricity prices (Fig. 4). A feature called 'Car Manager' allows the user to select up to four different vehicles to compare, and allows modification of each vehicle's mileage, range, and time to charge (Fig. 5).

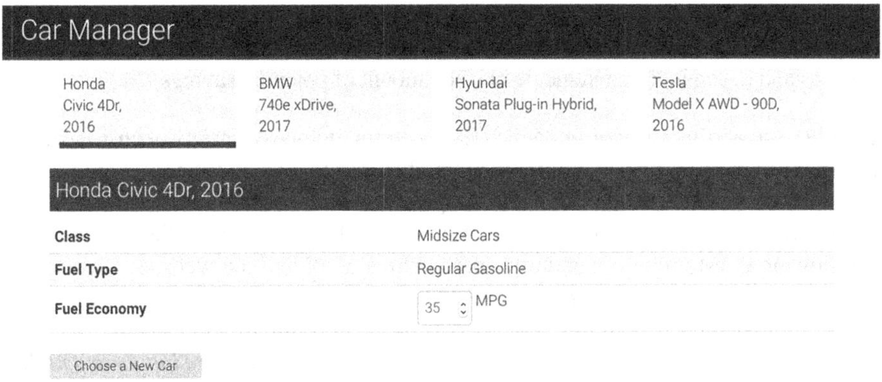

Fig. 5. Car manager: choose a new car and modify vehicle MPG/range/time to charge

2.2 Online Experiment

We conducted an online pretest-posttest experiment to evaluate the impact of EV Explorer on users. We used SurveyMonkey to develop our test instrument and recruited participants via Amazon Mechanical Turk. We asked 108 Mechanical Turk "workers" a series of identical questions before and after visiting EV Explorer via a link embedded in the online survey instrument. Participants were paid $0.65 USD. Average time spent exploring the site and answering questions was approximately 15 min.

At the start of the posttest when participants were asked to answer the same questions they answered in the pretest, there was a prompt noting that the questions were the same and their responses may or may not have changed after using EV Explorer. This design provided a measurement of change in the following variables via corresponding before-and-after questions.

Awareness of Long-term Fueling Costs. Since the focal output of EV Explorer is an estimate of annual fuel costs and users are able to input their current vehicle, we hypothesized that using the tool would increase participants' awareness of their current annual fuels costs. To test this hypothesis, we asked the following question before and after participants' explored the website: *About how much money do you spend on gas and/or electricity to fuel your vehicle(s)? Please enter both a dollar amount and unit of time (e.g., $100/week).*

Knowledge of Potential Savings. Since the focal output of EV Explorer juxtaposes annual energy cost estimates for a gas vehicle, two PHEVs, and a BEV, we hypothesized that using the tool would increase participants' knowledge of potential personal savings with PEVs compared to gas vehicles. To test this hypothesis, we asked the following question before and after participants' explored the website: *Given your driving patterns, how much would/do you save in fueling costs by driving the following vehicle types compared to a gas only vehicle? (Hybrid, Plug-in hybrid electric, Electric; response options: Not sure, No savings, Some Savings, Significant Savings).* We hypothesized that knowledge of savings for PHEVs and BEVs would increase in terms of both (a) fewer "Not sure" responses and (b) an increase in the perceived amount of potential savings.

Attitude Concerning Charging. Since EV Explorer includes a variety of customizable variables for charging infrastructure, we hypothesized that using the tool would result in an increase in participants' understanding of charging requirements and a positive shift in attitudes about the convenience of charging. To test this hypothesis, we asked the following question before and after participants' explored the website: *Given your driving patterns, how (in)convenient are the charging requirements of the following vehicle types compared to fueling a gas only vehicle? (Plug-in hybrid electric, Electric; response options: Not sure, Much more inconvenient, Somewhat more inconvenient, No more or less (in)convenient, Somewhat more convenient, Much more convenient).* Similar to the previous question, greater understanding of charging requirements would be evidenced by fewer "Not sure" responses after using the tool.

Intention to Purchase or Lease. We hypothesized that the above changes in knowledge of potential savings and attitude toward charging as a result of using the tool would lead to an increase in intention to purchase or lease PHEVs and BEVs. To test this hypothesis, we asked the following question before and after participants' explored the website: *How likely are you to buy/lease the following vehicle types in the future? (Gas only, Hybrid, Plug-in hybrid electric, Electric; response options: Very likely, Likely, Neutral, Unlikely, Very unlikely).*

Intervening Variables. In order to help explain any observed changes in knowledge, attitudes, and intentions, and to gain insights for the design of electric vehicle cost calculators, we asked participants which website features they used and what calculations they made while exploring the site (i.e., how much they would spend or save by driving their current vehicle or a different vehicle). In the posttest, participants were encouraged to go back and use features that they may not have noticed independently and they were asked to report whether they noticed the feature or not, thus the results yielded implications for improving the saliency of some features.

We also asked demographic questions to explore relationships between user characteristics and dependent variables. Participants included 63 males, 44 females, and 1 other; average age was 32 ($SD = 10$ years), ranging from 19 to 62. Participants' median household income was $25,000 to $49,999 and their median level of education was a Bachelor's degree. Participants indicated the type(s) of vehicles they drove on a regular basis; 100 out of the 108 participants indicated that they drove a gas vehicle, 8 drove an HEV, 5 drove a PHEV, and 0 drove a BEV.

Data Analysis. We conducted McNemar's or Wilcoxon signed-rank tests to detect paired differences in participants' responses before and after using EV Explorer, for each of our dependent variables. We conducted Mann Whitney U tests to analyze differences in change scores for each dependent variable based on whether or not the participant used each key feature of the website. These tests are appropriate for comparing central tendencies (or proportions) for ordinal variables. To assess our hypothesis that increasing knowledge of savings and knowledge and attitudes regarding charging requirements would increase intention to purchase or lease PEVs, we explored correlations between change scores for these variables. We used an alpha level of .05 to claim significance.

3   Results and Discussion

Results are organized first according to EV Explorer's potential impacts on consumer PEV education and persuasion to adopt. We then examine relationships between consumer knowledge, attitudes, and intentions, followed by an assessment of participant characteristics that influenced user response to EV Explorer. Finally, we consider the influence of specific features of EV Explorer on our outcomes.

3.1   Education

When asked to report personal fuel costs in their own terms, participants framed costs over longer periods of time after using EV Explorer compared to before. Specifically, after using the tool more participants reported fuel costs in terms of years (McNemar's test $p < .031$) and fewer reported fuel costs in terms of weeks (McNemar's test $p = .001$); Table 2. This supports our hypothesis that EV Explorer raised awareness of long-term energy costs.

Table 2. Awareness of long-term fuel costs, savings potential, and charging requirements

		Before EV Explorer	After EV Explorer
Percentage of respondents who reported their fuel cost in terms of each unit of time	1–2 Week(s)	57%	47%[*]
	Month	39%	45%
	Year	1%	7%[*]
Percentage "Not sure" of savings potential with each alternatively-fueled vehicle type	HEV	15%	6%[*]
	PHEV	19%	6%[**]
	BEV	20%	6%[**]
Percentage "Not sure" of (in)convenience of charging	PHEV	13%	10%
	BEV	16%	9%

[*]$p < .05$ [**]$p < .01$

After using EV Explorer, significantly fewer participants reported being "Not sure" about the savings associated with HEVs (McNemar's test $p = .013$), PHEVs (McNemar's test $p < .0001$), and BEVs (McNemar's test $p < .0001$). Similarly, fewer participants reported being "Not sure" about the (in)convenience of charging PHEVs and BEVs, but the differences were not significant. Overall, these findings suggest EV Explorer has an educational function; users learn about their personal long-term fueling costs and potential savings with alternatively-fueled vehicles.

3.2 Persuasion

For participants who had some perception about savings before and after using EV Explorer (i.e., excluding those who were "Not sure"), their estimation of the amount of potential savings significantly increased for each: HEVs ($Z = -3.889, p < .0001$), PHEVs ($Z = -3.812, p < .0001$), and BEVs ($Z = -3.567, p < .0001$); Table 3. For participants who had some perception about the (in)convenience of charging before and after using EV Explorer (i.e., excluding those who were "Not sure"), their attitudes became more positive for BEVs ($Z = -2.010, p = .044$), but not PHEVs ($Z = -0.989, p = .322$); Table 3.

Table 3. Participant attitudes before and after using EV Explorer

		Before EV Explorer		After EV Explorer	
		Median	Mean (SD)	Median	Mean (SD)
Perceived savings (*No savings = 2; Significant savings = 4*)	BEV**	Some savings	3.38 (0.65)	Significant savings	3.63 (.054)
	PHEV**	Some savings	3.28 (0.58)	Significant savings	3.57 (0.55)
	HEV**	Some savings	3.12 (0.46)	Some savings	3.38 (0.55)
Attitude toward charging (*Much more inconvenient = 2; Much more convenient = 6*)	BEV*	Somewhat more inconvenient	3.16 (1.24)	Somewhat more inconvenient	3.40 (1.35)
	PHEV	Somewhat more inconvenient	3.38 (1.25)	Somewhat more inconvenient	3.52 (1.31)
Intention to buy or lease (*Very unlikely = 1; Very likely = 5*)	BEV**	Neutral	2.85 (1.22)	Neutral	3.20 (1.24)
	PHEV**	Neutral	2.91 (1.14)	Neutral	3.31 (1.23)
	HEV*	Likely	3.49 (0.96)	Likely	3.66 (1.02)
	Gas*	Likely	3.79 (1.13)	Likely	3.67 (1.17)

*$p < .05$
**$p < .0001$

Participants reported a significantly greater intention to buy or lease HEVs ($Z = -2.107, p = .035$), PHEVs ($Z = -4.890, p < .0001$), and BEVs ($Z = -4.255, p < .0001$), and a significantly lower intention to buy or lease gasoline vehicles ($Z = -2.408, p = .016$) after using EV Explorer; Table 3. For both PHEVs and BEVs, mean scores in intention to buy or lease crossed over the line of neutrality from the negative side, "Unlikely", before using EV Explorer to the positive side, "Likely", after using EV Explorer, though the median stayed the same ("Neutral"). Overall, these findings suggest EV Explorer has a persuasive function, increasing users' perception of the amount of potential savings with alternatively-fueled vehicles, promoting more favorable attitudes toward BEV charging, and increasing stated intention to purchase or lease alternatively-fueled vehicles (while decreasing intention to purchase or lease gas vehicles).

3.3   Relationships Between Knowledge, Attitude, and Intention

To test our hypothesis that increased knowledge of potential for personal savings with alternatively-fueled vehicles would correspond to increased intention to adopt, we explored correlations between change scores in each variable, for each vehicle type, before-and-after using EV Explorer. In general, we did find that increases in perceived potential energy cost savings were correlated with increased intention to purchase or lease alternatively-fueled vehicles, but not always in a straightforward fashion (see Table 4).

Table 4. Correlations between Change in Intention to Purchase or Lease and each: Change in Perceived Savings, and Change in Attitude toward Charging. Postive correlations are interpreted as an increase in Perceived Savings, or positive shift in Attitude toward Charging, corresponds to an increase in Intention to Purchase or Lease.

| | | Change in Intention to purchase or lease | | | |
		Gas	HEV	PHEV	BEV
Change in perceived savings	HEV	−.75	.233*	.275**	.078
	PHEV	.011	.268*	.173	.030*
	BEV	−.106	.030*	.237*	.056
Change in attitude toward charging	PHEV	N/A	N/A	.127	.143
	BEV	N/A	N/A	.034	.361**

$^*p < .05$ $^{**}p < .01$

Similarly, we explored correlations between changes in attitude toward charging and changes in intention to purchase or lease PEVs pre- and post-EV Explorer. Our hypothesis was that EV Explorer would engender more positive attitudes toward charging by educating consumers about charging requirements, and that this shift would correspond to increased intention to buy or lease PEVs. Our hypothesis was supported for BEVs but not for PHEVs (Table 4).

3.4   Participant Characteristics Related to Outcomes

We explored correlations between demographic variables (sex, age, and income) and change scores in perceived savings, attitude toward charging, and intention to buy or lease each vehicle type. Participant sex did not correlate significantly with any change score. Age correlated negatively with change in attitudes toward BEV charging ($r = -.274, p = .011$) and change in intention to buy or lease BEVs ($r = -.230, p = .017$); Fig. 6. This suggests that younger participants' attitudes and intentions toward BEVs were more malleable compared to older participants; younger participants were more heavily influenced by EV Explorer.

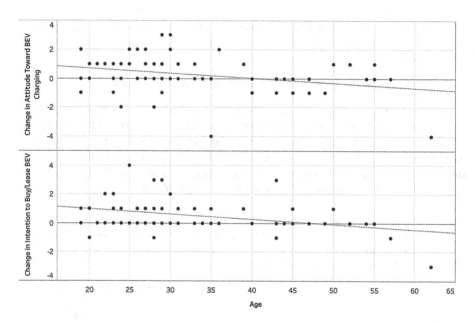

Fig. 6. Negative correlation between age and each: positive shift in attitude toward BEV charging and increase intention to purchase/lease BEV

Household income (participants selected among income ranges rather than speci-fying exact amount) correlated negatively with change in perceived personal savings associated with driving a BEV. That is, participants with lower incomes were more likely to have an increased perception of the significance of personal savings associated with BEVs after using the EV Explorer ($r = -.296$, $p = .006$).

3.5   Use of Website Features and Relationship to Outcomes

Most participants reported that they independently noticed each of the features avail-able on the tool (Table 5). However, only commute frequency and "choose a new car" were both independently noticed *and used* by a majority of participants. Notably, 29% did not independently notice the "choose a new car" feature, but they went back and used it after learning about it from the survey. Similarly, 33% did not initially notice but went back and used the feature allowing them to modify energy prices.

Table 5. Salience and participant utilization of each main EV Explorer feature

		Noticed; used	Did not notice; went back and used	Noticed; did not use	Did not notice; did not use
Commute settings	Commute frequency	71%	8%	19%	1%
	Charging at destination	35%	17%	34%	14%
Car manager	Choose a new car	52%	29%	15%	5%
	Vehicle mileage/ range/time to charge	42%	13%	35%	10%
Energy prices		32%	33%	25%	10%

With the "choose a new car" feature, participants most frequently selected a vehicle they or someone in their household currently drives (52%), followed by a vehicle they are considering getting in the future (44%), a "dream" vehicle (30%), a vehicle they shopped for before deciding on current vehicle (14%), and a vehicle they or someone in their household used to drive (8%). Most commonly selected vehicle types were gas (69%), followed by HEV (37%), BEV (32%), and PHEV (28%). Figure 7 shows a breakdown of vehicle types per category of selected vehicle.

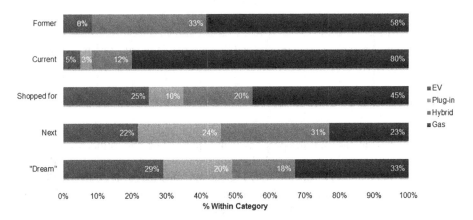

Fig. 7. Types of vehicles participants explored using the car manager feature

Taking advantage of the features allowing modification of commute frequency, information about charging at destination, and energy costs influenced outcomes. In particular, modifying commute frequency was significantly associated with a positive shift in attitude toward charging PHEVs [Mann Whitney $U = 451, p = .025$; Did not use feature: $M(SD) = -.33(.21)$; Used feature: $M(SD) = .21(.10)$]. Modifying information about charging at destination was associated with increased intention to purchase or lease a BEV [Mann Whitney $U = 1129, p = .020$; Did not use feature: $M(SD) = .21(.11)$; Used feature: $M(SD) = .50(.13)$]. Modifying fuel or electricity prices was associated with a positive shift in attitude toward charging PHEVs [Mann Whitney $U = 603.5, p = .003$; Did not use feature: $M(SD) = -.29(.15)$; Used feature: $M(SD) = .31(.11)$] and increased intention to buy or lease an HEV [Mann Whitney $U = 1053$, $p = .044$; Did not use feature: $M(SD) = .03(.10)$; Used feature: $M(SD) = .23(.09)$]. Figure 8 illustrates these significant findings.

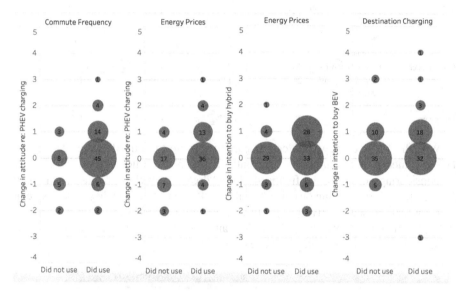

Fig. 8. Relationships between use of features and change scores in attitudes toward charging and intention to purchase/lease

3.6 Limitations and Future Research

There were some drawbacks to the methodology employed. Participant effects, which concern participants guessing the purpose of the study and being influenced by these expectations, are more likely with this kind of within-subjects experimental design. Furthermore, the duration of demonstrated effects on knowledge, attitudes, and intention, and their correlation with actual vehicle purchase decisions, are yet to be investigated. However, this study is the first to validate any impacts of online PEV energy cost calculators and uncover some of the features that make them effective.

Future research should replicate this study using a between-groups design with a much larger sample size. A larger sample size could also reveal more detailed relationships between intervening variables (i.e., demographics and use of features) and outcome variables (knowledge, attitudes, and intention with respect to electric vehicles). A particularly interesting opportunity for future research is to document the behavior of consumers at car dealerships that make this tool available for prospective electric vehicle buyers.

We have modified the design of EV Explorer based on the research findings. For example, we made "choose a new car" and energy price modification features more salient by allowing the user to click on relevant information in the initial bar chart output. In future design iterations of EV Explorer, we plan to incorporate additional commute inputs and information about other vehicle attributes, such as purchase and lease prices and aesthetics (by including images of vehicles), for a more comprehensive tool.

4 Conclusion

EV Explorer and similar tools can help educate consumers about potential energy/cost savings and charging requirements of electric vehicles. These knowledge gains can promote more positive attitudes regarding charging and increased intention to adopt electric vehicles. In our evaluation, these outcomes were more pronounced for users who took advantage of the ability to personalize their energy cost estimates by inputting their commute frequency, details about charging infrastructure at commute destination, and gas and electricity prices, implying that these are important features to consider when designing electric vehicle energy cost calculators. By enabling quick and simple comparison of annual energy costs for conventional gas vehicles and electric vehicles, as well as information about charging requirements based on the user's own commuting context, electric vehicle energy cost calculators like EV Explorer can empower consumers with the knowledge prerequisite to electric vehicle adoption.

References

1. Egbue, O., Long, S.: Barriers to widespread adoption of electric vehicles: an analysis of consumer attitudes and perceptions. Energy Policy **48**, 717–729 (2012). http://dx.doi.org/ 10.1016/j.enpol.2012.06.009
2. Khan, M., Kockelman, K.M.: Predicting the market potential of plug-in electric vehicles using multiday GPS data. Energy Policy **46**, 225–233 (2012). http://dx.doi.org/10.1016/j.enpol. 2012.03.055
3. Tamor, M.A., Milačić, M.: Electric vehicles in multi-vehicle households. Transp. Res. Part C: Emerg. Technol. **56**, 52–60 (2015). http://dx.doi.org/10.1016/j.trc.2015.02.023
4. Jakobsson, N., Gnann, T., Plötz, P., Sprei, F., Karlsson, S.: Are multi-car households better suited for battery electric vehicles? - driving patterns and economics in Sweden and Germany. Transp. Res. Part C Emerg. Technol. **65**, 1–15 (2016). http://dx.doi.org/10.1016/j.trc. 2016.01.018
5. Lundström, A., Bogdan, C., Kis, F., Olsson, I., Fahlén, L.: Enough power to move: dimensions for representing energy availability. In: Proceedings of the 14th International Conference on Human-Computer Interaction with Mobile Devices and Services, pp 201–210. ACM Digital Library (2012). doi:10.1145/2371574.2371605
6. Lundström, A, Bogdan, C.: COPE1-taking control over EV range. In: Adjunct Proceedings of the 4th International Conference on Automotive User Interfaces and Interactive Vehicular Applications, pp. 17–18 (2012)
7. Lundström, A., Hellström, F.: Getting to know electric cars through an app. In: Proceedings of the 7th International Conference on Automotive User Interfaces and Interactive Vehicular Applications, pp. 289–296 (2015). doi:10.1145/2799250.2799272
8. Lundström, A.: Differentiated driving range: exploring a solution to the problems with the "guess-o-meter" in electric cars. In: Proceedings of the 6th International Conference on Automotive User Interfaces and Interactive Vehicular Applications. pp. 1–8 (2014). doi: 10.1145/2667317.2667347

 9. Schewel, L.: Lessons from the virtual Ev test drive. In: Behavior Energy and Climate Change. Stanford University, Palo Alto, CA, 30 November–2 December 2011
10. Starr, C.: Social benefit versus technological risk. Science **165**, 1232–1238 (1969)
11. Alhakami, A.S., Slovic, P.: A psychological study of the inverse relationship between perceived risk and perceived benefit. Risk Anal. **14**(6), 1085–1096 (1994)
12. Kurani, K.: New car buyers' valuation of zero-emission vehicles: California. Contractor: UC Davis. Contract Number: 12–332
13. Nicholas, M.A., Gil, T.: Charging for charging at work: increasing the availability of charging through pricing. In: Institute of Transportation Studies, University of California, Davis, Working Paper UCD-ITS-WP-13-02 (2013)

Data Sources for EV Explorer

14. Node.js Foundation. (n.d.). Node.js. http://nodejs.org. Accessed 24 Sept 2015
15. Google. (n.d.). Google Maps Java Script API. https://developers.google.com/maps/documentation/javascript/. Accessed 24 Sept 2015
16. Energy Information Administration. (n.d.). Open Data. http://www.eia.gov/beta/api/. Accessed 24 Sept 2015
17. Freegoip. (n.d.). freegoip.net. https://freegeoip.net/. Accessed 24 Sept 2015

Electric Vehicle Energy Cost Calculators

18. EV Explorer. http://gis.its.ucdavis.edu/evexplorer/#!/
19. Alternative Fuels Data Calculator. http://www.afdc.energy.gov/calc/#result_a
20. Go Solar California. https://csi.wattplan.com/ev/
21. Electric Car Calculator. https://www.befrugal.com/tools/electric-car-calculator/
22. My Plug-in Hybrid Calculator. http://www.fueleconomy.gov/feg/Find.do?action=phev1Prompt
23. PEV Calculator (PG&E). https://www.pge.com/en/pevcalculator/PEV/index.page
24. PEV Calculator (Consumers Energy). https://www.consumersenergy.com/apps/pev/index.aspx?ekfrm=3751
25. Oncor EV Savings Calculator. http://www.oncor.com/EN/Pages/EV-Savings-Calculator.aspx
26. SMUD Calculator. http://c03.apogee.net/contentplayer/?utilityid=smud&coursetype=misc&id=18862

Beyond Hedonic Enjoyment: Conceptualizing Eudaimonic Motivation for Personal Informatics Technology Usage

Ayoung Suh[1(✉)] and Christy M.K. Cheung[2]

[1] School of Creative Media and Department of Information Systems,
City University of Hong Kong, Kowloon Tong, Hong Kong, SAR
ahysuh@cityu.edu.hk
[2] Department of Finance and Decision Sciences, School of Business,
Hong Kong Baptist University, Kowloon Tong, Hong Kong, SAR
ccheung@hkbu.edu.hk

Abstract. Personal informatics technologies (PITs) have become popular tools that enable people to monitor and track themselves. By providing self-knowledge, PITs increase self-control, foster insight, and promote positive behavioral changes. The pursuit of knowledge about self, excellence, and self-growth is eudaimonic because it makes a person more capable and well informed. Considering the unique technological characteristics, research suggests that eudaimonic motivation should be considered in explaining PIT usage. However, despite increasing scholarly attention being paid to the eudaimonic nature of PITs, a systematic approach to developing a research construct that reflects a PIT user's eudaimonic motivation is lacking in computer-human interaction research. To fill this gap, drawing on the theory of aesthetic experience, we propose a multi-dimensional construct of aesthetic experience to conceptualize eudaimonic motivation for PIT usage. Based on its conceptual definition, we develop the measures to capture the extent of a PIT user's aesthetic experience and empirically examine the construct validity. Compared with widely examined antecedents of technology usage—perceived usefulness, perceived ease of use, and perceived enjoyment—this study shows that a PIT user's aesthetic experience is a key determinant for intention to use. Notably, perceived enjoyment loses its predictive value in favor of aesthetic experience. Our findings suggest that the eudaimonic nature of a PIT should be considered in understanding technology usage.

Keywords: Personal informatics technology · Eudaimonic motivation · Intrinsic motivation · Hedonic enjoyment · Aesthetic experience

1 Introduction

Along with the proliferation of wearable technologies and gamified applications designed for self-tracking and self-monitoring, personal informatics technologies (PITs) have become increasingly popular [15, 17, 25, 38]. People track and analyze data, including mood (MoodScope, https://www.moodscope.com), finances (Mint, http://mint.com),

© Springer International Publishing AG 2017
A. Marcus and W. Wang (Eds.): DUXU 2017, Part II, LNCS 10289, pp. 119–133, 2017.
DOI: 10.1007/978-3-319-58637-3_9

food (MyFitnessPal, https://www.myfitnesspal.com), weight (FitDay, http://www.fitday.com), and physical activity (Garmin, http://www.garmin.com) [13, 31, 36]. These emerging personal tools provide users with a means of exploring and reflecting on information about themselves, thus helping them experience self-improvement [12, 25]. The pursuit of knowledge about self, excellence, and self-growth is eudaimonic because it makes a person more capable and well informed [48, 49]. According to the positive psychology literature [2], self-fulfilling and goal-driven tasks, such as PIT usage, require users to perceive the eudaimonic value rather than the hedonic or instrumental value from technology use [10]. Thus, we argue that eudaimonic motivation should be incorporated into the human-computer interaction (HCI) literature. However, a long-standing tradition in HCI research is to understand information technology usage from two key perspectives: productivity-oriented (utilitarian) motivation and pleasure-oriented (hedonic) motivation. Utilitarian motivation leads users to believe that a given information technology offers external benefits to them, such as task performance, productivity enhancement, prestige, and positive evaluations from others [20, 47]. Hedonic motivation allows users to derive a sense of enjoyment from the use of technology, and it causes a user to become psychologically absorbed while using the technology [22], which leads to a kind of psychological "flow," a sense of merging with the interaction with an information technology [22, 28].

Motivated by the need to incorporate eudaimonic motivation with information technology usage, in this paper, we propose a construct labeled aesthetic experience. This construct derives its theoretical bases from the intrinsic motivation literature. Similar to other intrinsic motivation variables, we posit that aesthetic experience is a key determinant for PIT usage. Given that the construct of aesthetic experience remains new in the HCI literature, we begin by reviewing the concept of AE, highlighting its theoretical foundations in the intrinsic motivation literature. This is followed by arguments justifying the role of aesthetic experience in the technology use model. An operational definition of the multidimensional construct is developed, and the scale development process for the measures of aesthetic experience is presented as well. The role of a user's aesthetic experience is empirically examined by testing a model that explains PIT usage with data collected from around 194 PIT users. The results of this study show that aesthetic experience plays a critical role in explaining an individual's intention to use a PIT. This study contributes to research on information technology usage by introducing the concept of aesthetic experience, extending scholarly attention from pleasure-oriented hedonic motivation to eudaimonic motivation, which allows users to reflect better on their technology usage behaviors. This study also contributes to the industry by offering design guidelines for promoting users' intrinsic motivations for PIT usage.

2   Theoretical Background

PITs are defined as "those that help people collect personally relevant information for the purpose of self-reflection and gaining self-knowledge" [24, p. 558]. PITs afford technological functions for self-tracking and self-monitoring to enable users to observe and record their own actions, thoughts, and emotions [37]. Commercial apps and tools (e.g., Galaxy Gear, iWatch, Nike FuelBand, Garmin VvioFit, and Jawbone Up) are recent examples of the PITs designed for gaining insights and understanding oneself [7, 38]. The primary purpose of PITs is to help users improve self-knowledge by providing a personal history and tools for its review or analysis [26]. Therefore, PITs require prolonged use to reap the benefits from technology usage [17]. However, evidence shows that around half of users stop using the PIT within six months after purchase [35]. Hence, the understanding of what motivates users to continue using PITs is important [41, 50].

2.1   Intrinsic Motivation

An individual experiences eudaimonia when his or her activities are most congruent with deeply held values and are fully engaged [10, 39]; Eudaimonia is characterized by the pursuit of excellence, virtue, and self-realization [3, 49]. Several concepts have been introduced to reflect eudaimonic motivation. Waterman [48] introduced the concept of personal expressiveness (PE) to reflect eudaimonia, arguing, "PE signifies self-realization and is expected to occur specifically in connection with activities affording opportunities for individuals to develop their full potentials, that is, further the development of their skills and talents, advance their life purposes, or both" (p. 680). Waterman [48] showed that measures of hedonic enjoyment and PE were strongly correlated, but were indicative nevertheless of distinct types of experiences. For example, although both PE and hedonic enjoyment measures were associated with positive emotions and self-fulfillment, it was found that PE was more closely related to activities that enabled personal growth and development. While Waterman [48] successfully distinguished hedonic enjoyment from eudaimonic happiness by proposing the concept of PE, his conceptualization of PE mainly focused on one's life outcomes rather than on motivation. Ryff and Keyes [40] identified six distinct aspects of human actualization (eudaimonia): autonomy, personal growth, self-acceptance, life purpose, mastery, and positive relatedness. However, Ryff and Keyes [40] focused on quality of life in terms of well-being rather than motivation. Although these researchers commonly showed when pursuing personal goals, feeling hedonic enjoyment may be disconnected from feeling a sense of self-growth, a concrete conceptualization of eudaimonic motivation has yet to be made.

2.2   Conceptualizing Eudaimonic Motivation

In this study, drawing on the theory of aesthetic experience [11], we propose the concept of aesthetic experience as a manifestation of one's eudaimonic motivation for PIT usage. Aesthetic experience is defined as a self-fulfilling state in which a person feels a sense of meaning and deeply understands the essence of the experienced events [4, 21]. Given that the concept of aesthetic experience reflects a user's sense of self-growth and self-fulfillment while interacting with a technology [5, 29, 33], we conceptualize an individual's aesthetic experience as eudaimonic motivation for PIT usage. Through an extensive literature review [4–6, 14, 21, 42], we identify three dimensions that characterize aesthetic experience: self-expansion, meaningfulness, and active discovery. These three dimensions reflect the overall extent to which a user feels he or she is having an aesthetic experience aesthetic while interacting with a PIT.

3   Modeling Aesthetic Experience as a Determinant for PIT Usage

We build on the technology usage model developed by Van der Heijden [46] that explains information technology usage with a focus on intrinsic motivation. The baseline model has been widely adopted to explain information technology usage for different types of information technologies, including utilitarian, hedonic, and hybrid information technologies [8, 44]. By adding the construct of aesthetic experience as an individual's eudaimonic motivation for PIT usage to the baseline model, we test the validity of the construct of aesthetic experience as another type of intrinsic motivation for information technology usage, as shown in Fig. 1. This model plays an important role in clarifying the nomological network of the construct, aesthetic experience. In this model, perceived enjoyment (PEN) was used to capture hedonic motivation, and aesthetic experience was used to capture an individual's eudaimonic motivation for PIT usage. Because the main objective of this research is to test the validity of the construct (aesthetic experience) and the relationships between variables used in the baseline model have been well established and extensively examined in the previous studies, we develop hypotheses in relation to the focal construct.

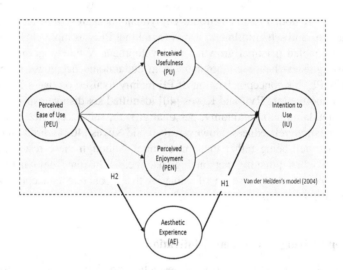

Fig. 1. Research model (the new relationships related to aesthetic experience are highlighted)

PITs enable users to receive immediate and granular feedback about their activities and to track their performance outcomes, which gives them a sense of accomplishment [30]. Previous PIT research has found that PIT users track their activities to determine what goals would be appropriate to pursue or what actions they should take to experience self-improvement [25]. The congruence of human activities with self-growth and deeply held values is a fundamental, first-order goal pursued for its own sake, which is called eudaimonic [39]. On this basis, we posit that eudaimonic motivation is a predictor of PIT usage. According to the theory of aesthetic experience [11], people are more likely to engage continuously with an activity or object when they enter a state of an aesthetic experience—a state of mind in which a user's eudaimonic need for self-progress is fulfilled [21]. Therefore, we infer that aesthetic experience is a valid predictor of one's intention to use.

H1: Aesthetic experience is positively associated with intention to use.

Perceived ease of use is an assessment of the mental effort involved in the use of an information technology [46]. Research has found that perceived ease of use enables users to focus on the interaction with an information technology and not on objectives external to this interaction, regardless of whether the technology is designed for productivity, fun, or both [28]. This has important ramifications for the role of perceived ease of use in predicting the use of PITs. Given that the ultimate goal of a PIT is to make positive behavioral changes by allowing users to reflect upon and extract meaningful insights from the data they collect, user-system interaction is critical [25]. Accordingly, perceived ease of use is a prerequisite to incur AE in the context of PIT usage.

H2: Perceived ease of use is positively associated with aesthetic experience.

4 Scale Development

A systematic and rigorous approach to developing research constructs and validating their measurement instruments are prerequisites to advancing knowledge in relation to technology usage [30, 32]. In this study, we adopt Churchill's [9] approach to develop measures of aesthetic experience. According to Churchill [9], scale development and validation is a longitudinal process that begins with scale construction. The scale is then subjected to a systematic assessment of reliability, validity, and generalizability.

4.1 Domain Specification

As the first step in scale development, we specified the domain of the construct [34]. In this study, we defined aesthetic experience in the use of PITs as the extent to which a user feels his or her needs for a sense of self-expansion, meaningfulness, and active discovery are fulfilled in interactions with a particular PIT.

4.2 Item Generation

As the second step, we generated measurement items for aesthetic experience based on a review of the relevant literature, which resulted in an initial pool of nine items intended to capture the three dimensions of aesthetic experience. Five experienced researchers were invited to evaluate the content validity of each item with respect to our conceptual definitions of the three dimensions of aesthetic experience in the context of PIT usage. They were requested to classify the items into the corresponding dimensions of aesthetic experience. Cohen's kappa and the item placement ratio were assessed to test the validity of the scale. As shown in Table 1, the kappa index for all items was greater than 0.65 [45].

Table 1. Results of card sorting (Kappa coefficient)

		Degree of agreement
Judge	Judge	Kappa
1	2	.862
1	3	.732
1	4	.725
1	5	.100
2	3	.688
2	4	.688
3	4	.701
4	5	.872

4.3   Scale Evaluation

As the third step, we conducted a pilot study by distributing an online questionnaire to 60 PIT users; they were not involved in the previous stages of scale development for review and refinement. Cronbach's alpha was calculated for assessing the validity and reliability of the scale. As shown in Table 2, the scale reliability met conventional standards of internal consistency [19], with a Cronbach's alpha value greater than 0.70.

Table 2. Cronbach's alpha

	Number of items	Cronbach's alpha
Self-expansion	3	.778
Meaningfulness	3	.804
Active discovery	3	.810

5   Full-Scale Field Study

After we refined the scale items based on the participants' feedback in the pilot test, we conducted a full-scale field survey. An online survey company was commissioned for data collection, targeting PIT users with an email invitation soliciting participation in the survey. The PIT users were contacted in an online community in which members share their experiences in using PIT, such as iWatch, Galaxy gear, and Xiaomi smart bands, to track, monitor, and visualize their activity records. To minimize the effects of PIT types, we included users who have used PITs for healthcare and fitness in the survey. We asked participants to write down the name of the PIT they currently use most often and keep the particular PIT in mind while answering the survey questions. The survey ended after 235 valid responses were gathered. After removing 41 responses that contained unanswered items, 194 responses were used for the final analysis. Table 3 summarizes the demographic characteristics of the respondents.

Table 3. Demographic characteristics

Item	Category	Frequency	Ratio (%)
Gender	Male	127	65.5
	Female	67	34.5
	Total	194	100.0
Age	21–30	26	13.4
	31–39	72	37.1
	40–49	66	34.0
	>=50	30	15.5
	Total	194	100.0
Education	High school	17	8.8
	College (2 year)	10	5.2
	College (4 year)	149	76.8
	Graduate	5	2.6
	Above	13	6.7
	Total	194	100.0
Occupation	Student	11	5.7
	Office worker	147	75.8
	Self-employer	11	5.7
	Others	25	12.9
	Total	194	100.0
PIT device used	iWatch	41	44.3
	Galaxy Gear	86	21.1
	Mi Band	44	22.7
	Fitbit	14	7.2
	Others	9	4.6
	Total	194	100.0

5.1 Model Testing

We used the partial least squares (PLS) approach for validating the measurement model and the structural model. Following the two-step analytical approach, we first performed a psychometric assessment of the measurement model, followed by an evaluation of the structural model. This approach allows for more confidence in concluding that the structural relationships are drawn from a set of measurement instruments with desirable psychometric properties [19].

5.1.1 Measurement Model

We tested he measurement model by examining convergent and discriminant validity. Convergent validity refers to the extent to which the items on a scale are theoretically related. We assessed convergent validity using three criteria: (1) composite reliability (CR) should be at least 0.70, (2) the average variance extracted (AVE) should be at least 0.50, and (3) all item loadings should be greater than 0.70 [16]. As shown in Table 4, all the criteria for convergent validity were met, with CR values ranging from 0.710 to 0.921

and AVE values ranging from 0.678 to 0.797. As shown in Table 5, all item loadings are higher than 0.70, except three items for perceived enjoyment (PEN 3, 4, 6) used as reversed items with loading values of less than 0.7. The results imply that the reversed items do not properly reflect the perceived enjoyment construct in the context of PIT usage. Accordingly, we have removed the three reversed items from the final analysis. Because previous studies, such as Lee et al. [23], have used the items (PEN 1, 2, 5) as perceived enjoyment, we do not believe that the exclusion of the three reversed items from perceived enjoyment threatens the validity of the measurement model.

Table 4. The psychometric properties

	AVE	CR	AE	IU	EOU	PEN	PU
AE	0.797	0.921	**0.893**				
IU	0.753	0.902	0.758	**0.868**			
EOU	0.743	0.710	0.317	0.257	**0.862**		
PEN	0.723	0.887	0.770	0.643	0.327	**0.850**	
PU	0.678	0.894	0.756	0.699	0.305	0.698	**0.823**

Note:
(a) The square root of the AVE of each latent construct is given in diagonals
(b) CR: Composite Reliability; AVE: Average Variance Extracted; AE: Aesthetic Experience; IU: Intention to Use; EOU: Perceived Ease of Use; PEN: Perceived Enjoyment; PU: Perceived Usefulness.

Discriminant validity is the degree to which a scale measures the variable it intends to measure. It is indicated by low correlations between the measure of interest and the measures of other constructs [16]. Discriminant validity is demonstrated when the squared root of the average variance extracted for each construct is greater than the correlations among it and all other constructs. In Table 4, the square root of the AVE for each construct is located in the diagonals of the table. The value for each construct was higher than the correlations between it and all other constructs, suggesting sufficient discriminant validity.

5.1.2 Structural Model

Following the confirmation of good psychometric properties in the measurement model, we examined the structural model to assess the explanatory power of the constructs and the significance of the posited paths. By modeling aesthetic experience as a PIT user's eudaimonic motivation, we expected a positive influence on intention to use. We first tested the base-line model, as shown in Fig. 2. The two main factors associated with the model—perceived usefulness (utilitarian motivation) and perceived enjoyment (hedonic motivation)—explained 54% of the variance in intention to use. The results are consistent with those of Van der Heijden [46], except for the path between perceived ease of use and intention to use.

Table 5. Item loadings and reliability

Construct	Item	Loading	t	Cronbach's α
Aesthetic experience	AD	0.938	115.154	0.790
	MEA	0.899	52.763	
	SE	0.838	29.375	
Perceived enjoyment	PEN1	0.885	40.943	0.89
	PEN2	0.854	43.479	
	PEN5	0.810	19.815	
Intention to use	IU1	0.864	45.063	0.836
	IU2	0.875	44.860	
	IU3	0.865	46.519	
Perceived usefulness	PU1	0.849	40.194	0.842
	PU2	0.823	28.753	
	PU3	0.795	26.586	
	PU4	0.826	28.979	
Perceived ease of use	EOU1	0.831	48.613	0.706
	EOU2	0.864	35.432	
	EOU3	0.893	27.568	

To test further the proposed model, we subjected the validated measures for AE to PLS. The results showed that perceived ease of use was positively associated with AE (b = 0.327, p < 0.001), which in turn positively influenced intention to use (b = 0.466, p < 0.001), supporting H1 and H2. Figure 3 presents the results of the PLS analysis for the hypothesis test. The results also show that the positive effect of perceived enjoyment on intention to use was crowded out by AE. Compared to perceived usefulness, AE has a stronger predictive value to explain intention to use (approximately 1.7 times as much).

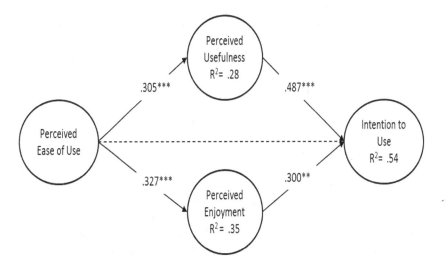

Fig. 2. The baseline model

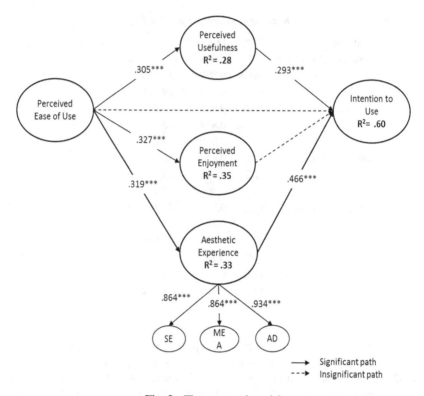

Fig. 3. The structural model

6 Discussion

Motivated by the need to understand how eudaimonic motivation plays a role in explaining PIT usage, this study proposes a multidimensional construct, aesthetic experience, to capture a user's sense of self-growth and self-fulfillment while inter-acting with technologies. The newly developed nine-item scale of aesthetic experience was empirically validated, with sufficient psychometric properties. The construct was also tested in a nomological network in which the aesthetic experience when using a PIT was found to be a critical determinant of intention to use. In other words, the result of this study demonstrates that the eudaimonic motivation for PIT usage is a significant boundary condition for the technology usage model. It is noteworthy that perceived enjoyment lost its predictive value in favor of aesthetic experience.

The implication for further research is that attention should be paid to the important role of eudaimonic motivation. This research demonstrates that if a technology affords users the opportunities to track, monitor, and reflect on their activities and thus help them to experience self-improvement, eudaimonic motivation should be considered an important determinant for intention to use. This finding suggests that progress in technology usage models can be made by focusing on the emerging nature of tech-nology (eudaimonic) in addition to utilitarian and hedonic motivations.

6.1   Implications for Research

This study has advanced our theoretical understanding of information technology usage. In this study, we demonstrated that the eudaimonic motivation is an appropriate exten-sion of current IT usage research. Although there has been a call for an exami-nation of the different types of intrinsic motivation in relation to technology acceptance and use [18, 22], past studies have focused primarily on utilitarian and hedonic motivation [e.g., 1, 46, 51]. The role of eudaimonia motivation has not received much scholarly attention in the field of HCI. This study contributes to the development of motivation theory by conceptualizing eudaimonic motivation and validating its predictive power for PIT usage. Furthermore, by empirically showing that the construct of aesthetic experience can serve as a reliable theoretical concept to explain PIT usage intention, this study complements existing concepts aimed at facilitating technology usage.

6.2   Implications for Practices

As technological developments provide new affordances that facilitate individuals' intrinsic motivation for self-growth and development, the importance of experiences that are intrinsically motivating, i.e., self-fulfilling and self-improving in and of themselves, might dominate as predictors of technology usage. Although the scope of the present study was limited to PITs for personal healthcare and fitness, our model can apply to diverse contexts in which people use technology for self-improvement by tracking, monitoring, and reflecting on their cognitive and physical activities. This study provides insight into work environments because many organizations have incorporated PIT components into their existing information systems to facilitate employees' intrinsic motivation for enterprise technology usage [42, 43]. Information systems developers and managers who wish to implement successfully a new enterprise system need to be cognizant of users' eudaimonic motivation and strive to provide technological functions to support users' needs for self-improvement.

6.3   Limitations and Future Research

Although this study contributes to the HCI literature by proposing the concept of aesthetic experience to conceptualize one's eudaimonic motivation for PIT usage, its predictive power for intention to use may vary depending on the purposes of PITs. We call on researchers to examine our model in different PIT usage contexts to ensure the generalizability of the proposed model. Second, our data were collected from a single source, and all research constructs were measured by respondent perceptions. To alle-viate concern of regarding the common method bias (CMB), objective data on PIT users' actual usage behaviors would provide insight into how intrinsic motivations affect actual technology usage. Finally, we surveyed active members of a PIT community; they may have had a relatively positive experience compared to those not attracted to PITs. Future research could widen the applicability of this study by including data obtained from people who ended their PIT usage due to negative experiences.

7 Conclusion

This study empirically demonstrates that eudaimonic motivation differs from hedonic motivation, as captured by perceived enjoyment, and it has a stronger predictive power than utilitarian motivation for technology usage. Based on the findings of this study, we argue that although utilitarian and hedonic motivations appear meaningful forces for technology usage, people are more likely to use a PIT because of eudaimonic motivation. Hence, we suggest that technological functions that can facilitate one's eudaimonic motivation should be designed and implemented to ensure PIT usage.

Acknowledgement. This research was supported in part by grants No. 6000546 from City University of Hong Kong awarded to the first author.

Appendix A. Measurement Items

Construct	Items	Sources
Self-expansion	1. The PIT increases my ability to accomplish new things 2. The PIT enables me to have a larger perspective on what I am doing 3. The use of PIT results in learning new things	Self-developed
Meaningfulness	1. The PIT makes my activities very important 2. The PIT makes my activities personally meaningful 3. My interaction with the PIT is meaningful	Self-developed
Active discovery	1. The PIT enables me to exercise powers of mind to address challenges 2. The PIT enables me to discover new paths to seek answers or resolution 3. The PIT enables me to be aware of how to proceed to fulfil my purposes	Self-developed
Perceived usefulness	1. The PIT is helpful for my health 2. The PIT helps me better track my health activities 3. The PIT provides useful information for my health 4. The PIT helped me change my health behavior	Adapted from Lowery et al. [28] and Van der Heijden [46]
Perceived ease of use	1. The use of PIT is easy 2. It is easy to learn how to use the PIT 3. It is easy to operate the PIT	Adapted from Lee et al. [23]

(continued)

(continued)

Construct	Items	Sources
Perceived enjoyment	1. The use of the PIT is enjoyable 2. I had fun using the PIT 3. Using the PIT was boring.* 4. The PIT really annoyed me* 5. The PIT experience was pleasurable 6. The PIT left me unsatisfied.*	Adopted from Lowery et al. [28]
Intention to use	1. I would plan on using the PIT in the future 2. I would intend to continue using the PIT in the future 3. I expect my use of it to continue the PIT in the future	Adopted from Lowery et al. [28] and Van der Heijden [46]

* Reversed items

References

1. Agarwal, R., Karahanna, E.: Time flies when you're having fun: cognitive absorption and beliefs about information technology usage. MIS Q. **24**(4), 665–694 (2000)
2. Amabile, T.M.: Within you, without you: the social psychology of creativity, and beyond. Creat. Res. J. **3**(1), 92–98 (1990)
3. Annas, J.: Happiness as achievement. Daedalus **133**(2), 44–51 (2004)
4. Beardsley, M.C.: Aesthetic theory and educational theory. In: Smith, R. (ed.) Aesthetic Concepts and Education, pp. 3–20. University of Illinois Press, Chicago (1970)
5. Beardsley, M.C.: The Aesthetic Point of View: Selected Essays. Cornell University Press, London (1982)
6. Berlyne, D.: Aesthetics and Psychobiology Appleton-Century-Crofts. Appleton-Centry-Crofts, New York (1971)
7. Chamberlain, A., Poole, E., Munson, S., Danis, C., Churchill, E.: Moving beyond e-Health and the quantified self: the role of CSCW in collaboration, community and practice for technologically-supported proactive health and wellbeing. In: Proceedings of the 18th ACM Conference Companion on Computer Supported Cooperative Work and Social Computing, pp. 273–276. ACM, February 2015
8. Cheung, C.M., Chiu, P.-Y., Lee, M.K.: Online social networks: why do students use facebook? Comput. Hum. Behav. **27**(4), 1337–1343 (2011)
9. Churchill Jr., G.A.: A paradigm for developing better measures of marketing constructs. J. Market. Res. **16**, 64–73 (1979)
10. Deterding, S.: Eudaimonic design, or: six invitations to rethink gamification. In: Fuchs, M., Fizek, S., Ruffino, P. (eds.) Niklas Schrape. Lüneburg: Meson press 2014 (2014). Available at SSRN: http://papers.ssrn.com/sol3/Papers.cfm?abstract_id=2466374
11. Dewey, J.: Art as Experience. The Berkeley Publishing Goup, New York (1934)
12. DiClemente, C.C., Marinilli, A.S., Singh, M., Bellino, L.E.: The role of feedback in the process of health behavior change. Am. J. Health Behav. **25**(3), 217–227 (2001)

13. Epstein, D.A., Borning, A., Fogarty, J.: Fine-grained sharing of sensed physical activity: a value sensitive approach. In: Paper Presented at the Proceedings of the 2013 ACM International Joint Conference on Pervasive and Ubiquitous Computing (2013)
14. Fenner, D.E.: Aesthetic experience and aesthetic analysis. J. Aesthet. Educ. **37**(1), 40–53 (2003)
15. Fogg, B.J.: Persuasive technology: using computers to change what we think and do. Ubiquity **5**, 89–120 (2002)
16. Fornell, C., Bookstein, F.L.: Two structural equation models: LISREL and PLS applied to consumer exit-voice theory. J. Market. Res. **19**(4), 440–452 (1982)
17. Fritz, T., Huang, E.M., Murphy, G.C., Zimmermann, T.: Persuasive technology in the real world: a study of long-term use of activity sensing devices for fitness. In: Paper Presented at the Proceedings of the SIGCHI Conference on Human Factors in Computing Systems (2014)
18. Gottschalg, O., Zollo, M.: Interest alignment and competitive advantage. Acad. Manage. Rev. **32**(2), 418–437 (2007)
19. Hair, J.F., Black, W.C., Babin, B.J., Anderson, R.E., Tatham, R.L.: Multivariate Data Analysis, vol. 6. Pearson Prentice Hall, Upper Saddle River (2006)
20. Hsu, C.-L., Lin, J.C.-C.: Acceptance of blog usage: the roles of technology acceptance, social influence and knowledge sharing motivation. Inf. Manage. **45**(1), 65–74 (2008)
21. Jennings, M.: Theory and models for creating engaging and immersive ecommerce websites. In: Paper Presented at the Proceedings of the 2000 ACM SIGCPR Conference on Computer Personnel Research (2000)
22. Ke, W., Tan, C.-H., Sia, C.-L., Wei, K.-K.: Inducing intrinsic motivation to explore the enterprise system: the supremacy of organizational levers. J. Manage. Inf. Syst. **29**(3), 257–290 (2012)
23. Lee, M.K., Cheung, C.M., Chen, Z.: Acceptance of Internet-based learning medium: the role of extrinsic and intrinsic motivation. Inf. Manage. **42**(8), 1095–1104 (2005)
24. Li, I., Dey, A., Forlizzi, J.: A stage-based model of personal informatics systems. In: Proceedings of the SIGCHI Conference on Human Factors in Computing Systems, pp. 557–566. ACM, April 2010
25. Li, I., Dey, A.K., Forlizzi, J.: Understanding my data, myself: supporting self-reflection with ubicomp technologies. In: Paper Presented at the Proceedings of the 13th International Conference on Ubiquitous Computing (2011)
26. Li, I., Dey, A., Forlizzi, J., Höök, K., Medynskiy, Y.: Personal informatics and HCI: design, theory, and social implications. In: CHI 2011 Extended Abstracts on Human Factors in Computing Systems, pp. 2417–2420. ACM (2011)
27. Lindenberg, S., Foss, N.J.: Managing joint production motivation: the role of goal framing and governance mechanisms. Acad. Manage. Rev. **36**(3), 500–525 (2011)
28. Lowry, P.B., Gaskin, J., Twyman, N., Hammer, B., Roberts, T.: Taking 'fun and games' seriously: Proposing the hedonic-motivation system adoption model (HMSAM). J. Assoc. Inf. Syst. **14**(11), 617–671 (2012)
29. McCarthy, J., Wright, P.: Technology as Experience. The MIT Press, Cambridge (2004)
30. McGrath, N., Bayerlein, L.: Engaging online students through the gamification of learning materials: the present and the future (2013)
31. Meyer, J., Simske, S., Siek, K.A., Gurrin, C.G., Hermens, H.: Beyond quantified self: data for wellbeing. In: Paper Presented at the CHI 2014 Extended Abstracts on Human Factors in Computing Systems (2014)
32. Moore, G.C., Benbasat, I.: Development of an instrument to measure the perceptions of adopting an information technology innovation. Inf. Syst. Res. **2**(3), 192–222 (1991)
33. Nardi, B.: My Life as a Night Elf Priest: An Anthropological Account of World of Warcraft. University of Michigan Press, Ann Arbor (2010)

34. Nunnally, J.C., Bernstein, I.H., Berge, J.M.T.: Psychometric Theory, vol. 226. JSTOR, New York (1967)
35. Patel, M.S., Asch, D.A., Volpp, K.G.: Wearable devices as facilitators, not drivers, of health behavior change. JAMA **313**(5), 459–460 (2015)
36. Ploderer, B., Reitberger, W., Oinas-Kukkonen, H., van Gemert-Pijnen, J.: Social interaction and reflection for behaviour change. Pers. Ubiquit. Comput. **18**(7), 1667–1676 (2014)
37. Rapp, A., Cena, F.: Self-monitoring and technology: challenges and open issues in personal informatics. In: Stephanidis, C., Antona, M. (eds.) UAHCI 2014. LNCS, vol. 8516, pp. 613–622. Springer, Cham (2014). doi:10.1007/978-3-319-07509-9_58
38. Rooksby, J., Rost, M., Morrison, A., Chalmers, M.C.: Personal tracking as lived informatics. In: Paper Presented at the Proceedings of the 32nd Annual ACM Conference on Human Factors in Computing Systems, Toronto, Canada (2014)
39. Ryan, R.M., Deci, E.L.: Intrinsic and extrinsic motivations: classic definitions and new directions. Contemp. Educ. Psychol. **25**(1), 54–67 (2000)
40. Ryff, C.D., Keyes, C.L.M.: The structure of psychological well-being revisited. J. Person. Soc. Psychol. **69**(4), 719 (1995)
41. Shin, G., Cheon, E.J., Jarrahi, M.H.: Understanding quantified-selfers' interplay between intrinsic and extrinsic motivation in the use of activity-tracking devices. In: Paper Presented at the iConference 2015 Proceedings (2015)
42. Suh, A.: Applying game design elements in the workplace. In: Paper Presented at the International Conference on Information Systems (ICIS) 2015, Fort Worth, USA (2015a)
43. Suh, A.: Measuring user engagement in an enterprise gamified system. In: Proceedings of CHI Gamification Workshop 2015, Seoul, Korea (2015b)
44. Teo, T.S., Lim, V.K., Lai, R.Y.: Intrinsic and extrinsic motivation in Internet usage. Omega **27**(1), 25–37 (1999)
45. Todd, P., Benbasat, I.: An experimental investigation of the impact of computer based decision aids on decision making strategies. Inf. Syst. Res. **2**(2), 87–115 (1991)
46. Van der Heijden, H.: User acceptance of hedonic information systems. MIS Q. **28**(4), 695–704 (2004)
47. Venkatesh, V., Morris, M.G., Davis, G.B., Davis, F.D.: User acceptance of information technology: toward a unified view. MIS Q. **27**(3), 425–478 (2003)
48. Waterman, A.S.: Two conceptions of happiness: contrasts of personal expressiveness (eudaimonia) and hedonic enjoyment. J. Person. Soc. Psychol. **64**(4), 678 (1993)
49. Waterman, A.S., Schwartz, S.J., Zamboanga, B.L., Ravert, R.D., Williams, M.K., Bede Agocha, V., Brent Donnellan, M.: The questionnaire for eudaimonic well-being: psychometric properties, demographic comparisons, and evidence of validity. J. Posit. Psychol. **5**(1), 41–61 (2010)
50. Wendel, S.: Designing for behavior change: applying psychology and behavioral economics. O'Reilly Media Inc, Sebastopol (2013)
51. Wendy Zhu, W., Morosan, C.: An empirical examination of guests' adoption of interactive mobile technologies in hotels: revisiting cognitive absorption, playfulness, and security. J. Hosp. Tour. Technol. **5**(1), 78–94 (2014)

A Suggestion to Improve User-Friendliness Based on Monitoring Computer User's Emotions

Keum Young Sung[✉]

School of Computer Science and Electronic Engineering,
Handong Global University, Pohang, Republic of Korea
kysung@handong.edu

Abstract. Even with a big progress with computing facilities including notebook PC, tap computers, and smartphones, there is still no consideration at all to deal with users' emotions while they use computing devices. In this study, a primitive idea with some technique is suggested to monitor users' emotional changes while using computing facility. With the help of some physiological signals collected from sensors attached to a mouse or keyboard, the application programs or OS can be made to behave or respond some appropriate actions depending on users' emotional status. Two typical body signals used in this study are finger temperature and skin resistance, which may be measured with a keyboard and a mouse attached with sensors. To respond to user's emotions, an application program should be equipped with some components that are able to analyze user's abrupt emotion changes through input sensors. To fully use affective techniques developed with application software and also operating system, the functionalities dealing with body signals should be included into the programs, and also various sensing techniques for measuring user's temperature and skin resistance should be attached to input devices. The difficulties related to affective UI is to make a general indication of many users' emotions, and to extract particular emotions based on body temperature and skin resistance that are measured with input devices, which is related to the individualization of body signals.

Keywords: Affective computing · Emotion communication · Skin resistance · Skin temperature

1 Introduction

Most application programs and operating systems simply lack considering users' emotions, for example, frustration, anger, confusion, helplessness, and so on, while using the computer systems. Most casual users of application programs or OS, who are using such programs as word processors, spreadsheets, presentation programs, almost all sorts of application programs in every field, and Windows or Linux systems may experience frustration and anger until they are able to use computer systems/programs conveniently, or when they encounter some functionality very undesirable or unfriendly to users. Some users with many complaints often express their raged emotions to the computers by punching or kicking computers.

© Springer International Publishing AG 2017
A. Marcus and W. Wang (Eds.): DUXU 2017, Part II, LNCS 10289, pp. 134–141, 2017.
DOI: 10.1007/978-3-319-58637-3_10

There is a need to improve man-machine interface to make a UI more user-friendly and convenient especially for users who are not skillful or hot-tempered with using some OS or application programs. With the recent trend of affective computing, an emotional communication between computers and users has been suggested, but there has been a very few practically useful UI for this goal. Picard [1] suggested four goals with improved UI for this purpose:

- Reducing user frustration;
- Enabling comfortable communication of user emotion;
- Developing infrastructure and applications to handle affective information; and
- Building tools that help develop social-emotional skill.

Fulfilling the four goals mentioned above, we can increase the level of emotional communication between computing machines and human beings.

When we try to communicate with machine, there are two channels – explicit and implicit channels [2]. The explicit channel is related to characters and languages for communication, and the implicit channel is accomplished by emotions. For complete understanding between a sender and a receiver, there should be both channels, explicit and implicit. The UI technology has been developed centered on a machine using explicit communication channel, e.g., message communication, without considering human emotion.

There are a variety of implicit emotion data as depicted in Fig. 1 [2]. Typical examples include facial expression, body gesture, a movement of head, a direction of eye focus, and voice [3–5], which may express various emotional status, e.g., anger, joy, sorrow, negative or positive emotions. Especially voice delivers delicate change of inner emotions. Body signal represented by electrocardiogram (ECG), change of skin temperature (SKT), Galvanic skin resistance (GSR), photo-plethysmography (PPG) have been used to measure implicit emotions [6–8].

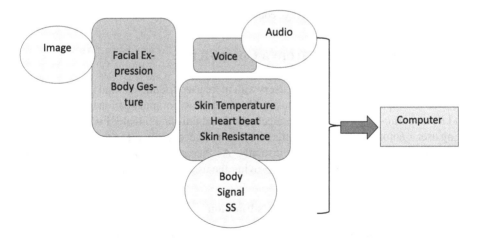

Fig. 1. Means of expressing emotion and body signals being sent to computer

Expression of affection by a computer has many meanings depending on the roles and functions of affective consideration on HCI [9]:

- Recognitions of user's affective expression;
- Adaptation to the user's affective state to generate 'affective' behavior by the machine;
- Modelling of user's affective states; or
- Generation of affective states by the computer's cognitive architecture.

The interpretation of an affective computing may be depicted by Fig. 2, in which an affective computing example provides users with a UI, help functions, guidance functions, and tutoring in perceiving body signals from users.

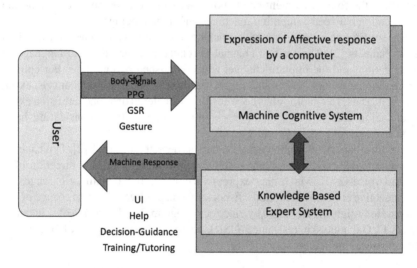

Fig. 2. Affective communication with a machine

2 Emotional Response from a Computer

The UI has been evolved to provide users with more user-friendly or kind interface since a personal computer was first introduced. However, most communication between a user and a computing machine has been mechanical and uni-directional UI without considering user's emotions. Emotional interface does not necessarily mean that the computer should fix or solve user's problem instantly. As Piccard [1] indicated, calming down user's upset mind is quite effective improving the usability of computers.

2.1 Constant Measurement of User's Emotion

For effective emotional communication between a computer user and a computer, the constant measurement of user's emotion by using a mouse and/or keyboard attached with sensor monitoring body signals is suggested in this study. Figure 3 depicts the configuration of the data communication of affective devices. Temperature and skin resistance are measured with sensors attached, and measured signal values are sent to a computer. Body signals are used to check a user's emotion, and a computer may display some friendly messages on the monitor depending on user's changed emotion. All the sensor data may be collected and accumulated to the server for a recording of the change of computer user's emotion change.

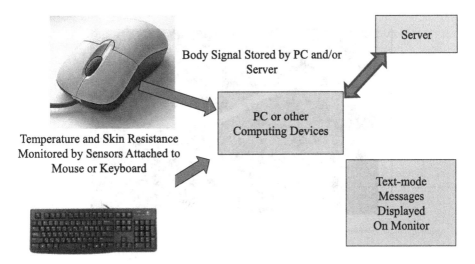

Fig. 3. Monitoring of user's emotional change with a mouse or a keyboard

When specific application program used by a user senses some change of body signals from a user, the application program may display some proper messages that are used to calm down the user's emotion [1]. The program may also play some favorite music of the computer user along with a message. The example messages may be as follows:

Calm down, a little bit more patience makes you an expert;
Why don't you use help service in the menu?;
Could you speak your problem to the microphone?; and
Could you mail your problem to this address, helpdesk@...?

To fully help users for making a continuous use of an application program without frustration, the program should be made with a really useful help or guidance facility. If the help facility can be used with a microphone and a speaker, that would be better. The affective component that deals with users' emotions may include the functionalities of playing users' favorite music or checking users' health status based on some physiological signals.

2.2   Use of a GSR Sensor to Check User's Emotional Change

GSR (Galvanic Skin Response) is used to measure the conductivity of skin. When we feel some strong emotion, the sympathetic nerve get stimulated and sweat glands emit lots of sweat and the resistance of skin is changed.

Using a GSR sensor, Figs. 4 and 5 show a user's change of emotion or mood.

GSR Value

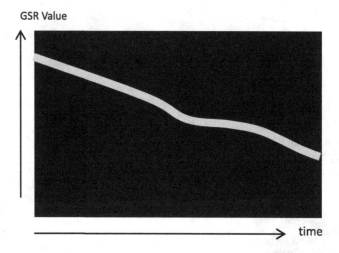

Fig. 4. GSR measurement showing emotional state A

GSR Value

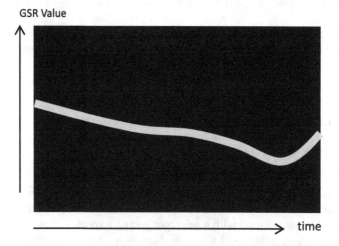

Fig. 5. GSR measurement showing changed emotional state B

Figures 4 and 5 show some change of GSR sensor values depending on the emotional change of users under test. The measurement of emotional signals needs to be standardized for getting generally acceptable emotion state. The GSR sensor is supposed to be attached to the mouse or a keyboard as depicted in Fig. 3. One serious problem is to overcome the effect of noise signals when collecting sensor values from input devices because input devices generates many noise sources such as vibration, impact by hand or fingers, etc.

2.3   Use of Arduino and Smartphone to Simulate Monitoring Body Signal Change

Figure 6 shows the Arduino connection with a temperature sensor and a GSR sensor, which is a prototype before attaching sensors to a mouse or a keyboard. The sensor values are transmitted to a smartphone via a Bluetooth device, HC-06. In this experiment, the Arduino is to be replaced by a mouse or a keyboard, and the smartphone display action is to be implemented by a specific application program or an OS. The dotted line is used to indicate imaginary attachment of sensors to the mouse and the keyboard.

Fig. 6. Arduino connection with temperature and GSR sensors

Figures 7 and 8 show the display of temperature and GSR values transmitted from the Arduino. The set simply shows temperature and GSR values measured by sensors.

Fig. 7. Smartphone showing temperature change transmitted from arduino

Fig. 8. Smartphone showing GSR value change transmitted from arduino

There are many rooms to be improved with the prototype with an Arduino attached with low quality sensors. There is a need to use a temperature sensor that measures the specific narrow range of 35~38 degrees very sensitively. Preparing proper messages depending on sensor values and steep change of sensor values are also in need.

Figure 9 shows the data transmission between a mouse/keyboard and a smartphone, and data storing into a cloud computer. A cloud computer may be replaced by a local server or a notebook PC. Or a smartphone with SQLite may replace the role of a cloud computer in case there is no need to store a large volume of data.

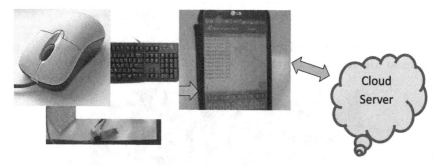

Fig. 9. Communication among mouse, smartphone, and cloud server

3   Conclusions

In this study, a mouse or a keyboard attached with sensors and a prototype with Arduino set have been suggested to make an emotionally user-friendly UI for computer-users who may have some frustration, anger, or other negative emotions while using a computer. Whenever users have any type of complaints, the body data collected with a mouse and/or a keyboard signal the emotional change of users to the OS or a specific application program. The OS or an application program that caused the feeling of frustration or anger may handle properly the emotion of users so that the usability of specific programs may be improved, and also users keep using the computer with emotional composure.

There are many technical difficulties for the realization of suggested ideas as follows:

- Embedding of temperature and skin resistance sensors into the mouse and keyboard;
- The preparation of really helpful and soothing messages from the computer;
- Analysis of body signals for determining a user's emotions; and
- Major modification of popular OS or application programs to communicate with users based on users' emotion.

Currently, the suggested ideas may be difficult to implement considering above difficulties. It is not easy to install some sensitive temperature sensor on a particular location of a mouse and a keyboard. Preparing proper messages for users with complaints needs the combined analysis of temperature and GSR values to accurately know the emotional status of computer users. The support from the makers of OS and application programs to use the API for generating appropriate emotional message based on sensor values is also required. Even with the above mentioned difficulties, the importance of emotional UI is re-emphasized in this study. This study also suggests some idea that may be implemented with widely used input devices, a mouse and a keyboard, to improve emotional UI for comfortable and continuous use of computer systems.

References

1. Picard, R.W.: Affective Computing For HCI
2. Kim, N.S.: And perspectives on emotion recognition technologies. Telecommun. Rev. **19**(5) (2009)
3. Cowie, R., et al.: Emotion recognition in human computer interaction. IEEE Signal Process. Mag. **18**(1), 32–80 (2001)
4. Zeng, Z., Pantic, M., Roisman, G.I., Huang, S.: A survey of affect recognition methods: audio, visual, and spontaneous expressions. IEEE Trans. Pattern Anal. Mach. Intell. **31**(1), 39–58 (2009)
5. Lee, C.M., Narayanan, S.S.: Toward detecting emotions in spoken dialogs. IEEE Trans. Speech Audio Process. **13**(2), 293–303 (2005)
6. Katsis, C.D., Katertsidis, N., Ganiatsas, G., Fotiadis, D.I.: Toward emotion recognition in car-racing drivers: a biosignal processing approach. IEEE Trans. Syst. Man Cybern. Part A **38**(3), 502–512 (2008)
7. DeSilva, L.C., Miyasato, T., Nakatsu, R.: Facial emotion recognition using multi-modal information. In: Proceedings IEEE International Conference on Communication, Signal Process, pp. 397–401 (1997)
8. Cacioppo, J.T., Tassinary, L.G.: Inferring psychological significance from physiological signals. Amer. Psychol. **45**(1), 16–28 (1990)
9. Hudlicka, E.: To feel of not to feel: the role of affect in human-computer interaction. Int. J. Hum.-Comput. Stud. **59**, 1–32 (2003)

EMOVLE: An Interface Design Guide
Through the Design of Emotive Virtual Learning Environments

Angela Villareal-Freire$^{(\boxtimes)}$, Andrés F. Aguirre, and César A. Collazos

Grupo de Investigación y Desarrollo en Ingeniería de Software IDIS,
Universidad del Cauca, Popayán, Colombia
{avillarreal,afaguirre,ccollazo}@unicauca.edu.co

Abstract. There are numerous studies that discuss the importance of developing a good interface design including elements that evoke positive emotions in the user; however little has been said about how to link these elements within the field of Virtual Learning Environments. In this article the development of a guide is proposed, which condenses a set of good practices of interface design coupled with the theories of design for emotions so that not only the developer is facilitated the task of designing for these specific environments, but also will take into account the emotions of learners while designing. This article describes the creation process of the EMOVLE Guide, its application and how it was evaluated from different approaches. In addition it describes one of the guidelines that conforms it.

Keywords: Virtual Learning Environment · Interface design · Emotion · Human-computer interaction · Guidelines

1 Introduction

With the increase of users using the internet, it has been necessary for companies to become interested in aspects of design that capture consumer attention in order to persuade them and generate loyalty with their products [1].

The importance of good design is that it can increase the success of a system and can greatly improve the consumer intention to return to the website, as well as his/her trust and performance [2–6]. On the other hand a bad design can affect negatively and, in the case of commercial pages, can damage the whole corporate image [7–10]. With this goal in mind, for many years emphasis was placed on applying a user-centered design taking into account ergonomic recommendations or golden rules [1,11,12]. These recommendations focused primarily on reducing the cognitive load of users when interacting with a system and performing tasks [1]. In this way human computer interaction was conceived and evaluated under the usability approach and for this reason many of the studies have focused on functionality and usability, leaving aside what users felt when they interact with the system [1,13].

© Springer International Publishing AG 2017
A. Marcus and W. Wang (Eds.): DUXU 2017, Part II, LNCS 10289, pp. 142–161, 2017.
DOI: 10.1007/978-3-319-58637-3_11

Norman and Lockner state that new systems should consider complementing their functionality by injecting fun and pleasure into people's lives as well as conveying feelings through the interface design features; however achieving interfaces that are both intuitive and fun are a challenging task [1,12,14].

In 1991, it began the interest to explore the power of metaphorical and emotional interfaces, since artists and designers have applied metaphors to different systems, objects, and works of art due to it was possible to transmit certain sensations or emotions to viewers that could not be described with only words [15]. In this sense, emotion was identified as a crucial indicator of user preferences and the concept of emotional design took force in its application to the design of everyday objects and by studies that established that the emotional design works better than the usable design; however, despite all the benefits described and the innumerable products successfully developed, these theories of emotional design have not been directly implemented in the educational environments [16,17]. Up to now, incipient research has been found in relation to emotional design applied to graphs and multimedia lessons with the main evidence coming from authors such as Plass and colleagues [18,19]. Other representative studies in this area are described in the research of Angela Villareal, et al. in which are detailed the ideas from Alan Clarke, Daryl Hancock, Um, Plass et al., Dorian Peters between others [20].

Alan Clarke establishes principles for the construction of computer-based learning materials in which includes aspects such as the use of text, color, graphics, multimedia, organization of content and how to arrange the elements on the screen in this type of materials [21].

Um, Plass et al. mentions two methods to induce positive emotions in multimedia learning: through color combinations and through visual forms. For each of these methods, there are guidelines to achieve the goal of promoting positive emotions in the student [22].

Dorian peters establishes 3 categories to design emotion in learning environments: creativity, motivation and commitment. For each of these categories establishes a series of strategies that can be used for the construction of interfaces for learning [23].

Linking emotion design to education or especially, to virtual learning environments (VLE) could not only help students to evoke emotions, but also to reduce the feelings of loneliness and isolation that lead to dropping out the virtual courses.

At this point the EMOVLE Guide (EMOtive Virtual Learning Environment) was consolidated as a tool that would allow developers to have a starting point for designing interfaces for virtual learning environments. The guide was built through a set of guidelines that seek to increase the creativity, motivation and engagement of the learner and these guidelines are supported on techniques that deal with fundamental aspects of design such as typography, color, arrangement of elements on the screen among others.

The aim of this research was achieved through the collection of various studies and the organization of the state of the art of design proposals that consider the affective issue in the construction of interfaces. Subsequently, the studies of Virtual Learning Environments were contemplated from the emotional perspective and were analyzed to determine the limitations to be considered in the developed guide. Finally, a guide was developed that includes the studied principles of emotional design and that considers the limitations detected in the VLEs. Based on the proposed guide, an assessment was made based on two approaches, the first one related to the evaluation that the users made of the guide after having created the interface prototypes, and the second one, according to the comparison of the guidelines used against the EMOVLE Guide to verify whether or not they were implemented correctly. After evaluating the guide, important results were obtained from users who rated the guide as useful, interesting, and a document to be used in later developments. This article mentions the process of building the guide, its application, evaluation and results.

2   EMOVLE Guide Construction

The designed guide is made up of constructs, guidelines and techniques. Techniques are strategies that complement the guidelines and the guidelines help to reach the constructs. The relationship of these three terms is presented in Fig. 1 and the description of each of them is described below.

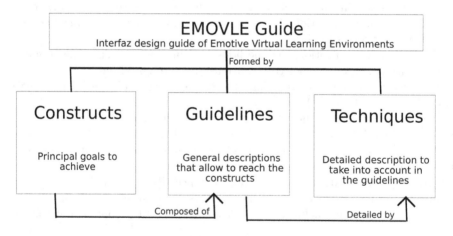

Fig. 1. Elements of the EMOVLE Guide

2.1   Constructs

The constructs were extracted from the classification proposed by Dorian Peters, and correspond to the three aspects to be taken into account for the inclusion of the emotional factor within the interface design of virtual learning environments [23]. According to the author, to evoke emotions in the design, it is necessary to consider 3 key aspects or constructs: creativity, motivation and engagement.

Creativity. Author Susan Winschenk [24] suggests that if a developer wants to design to support creativity, it must be first identified the kind of creativity. In her studies she mentions four types of creativity: deliberate cognitive, deliberate emotional, spontaneous cognitive and spontaneous emotional. Each of the types are described below.

Deliberate cognitive. Require time and a big knowledge. The interfaces should facilitate access and management of these two resources.

Deliberate emotional. In order to promote this kind of creativity, calm should be encouraged. It has to be taken into account not to exaggerate notifications and to limit the distractions.

Spontaneous cognitive. Design must focus on unconscious processing under the theory that problems need to be forgotten to allow the mind to make new connections.

Spontaneous emotional. It is the most difficult type of creativity to design but it should be considered the open space design.

Motivation. People do not always feel motivated to learn all the time. Some authors recommend punishment and reward, but contemporary psychologists and educators have written whole books dedicated to revealing how problematic these approximations can be. The advice given to capture motivation is to ask not how people can be motivated but how the ideal conditions can be created for people to motivate themselves, which leads to two types of motivation: intrinsic motivation and extrinsic motivation.

Engagement. It is the first emotional dimension of learning as instructors require the attention of their learners and seek to maintain this attention during the learning process. Through engagement students will learn better and enjoy more of the experience. The strategies that make up this classification are those that direct visual attention, provide relevance, stimulate curiosity, and provide the right level of challenge.

2.2 Guidelines

The guidelines have been constructed in order to facilitate to the developer the work of designing interfaces of emotive VLEs that promote the positive emotions in the apprentices and make reference to strategies or heuristics that must be implemented in the design of interfaces. Each construct groups a number of guidelines that can be put into practice according to the specific needs. These groups can be seen in Table 1.

Table 1. Guidelines list and the constructs to which they belong

Construct	Guideline	Guideline ID
Creativity	Set a Positive Mood	PM
	Show Personality	SP
	Leverage the Biophilia Effect	BE
	Leverage the Cathedral Space	CS
	Include Delighters	ID
Engagement	Beware of Primal Attention Grabbers	AG
	Use Segmenting and Variety	SV
	Make it Harder	MH
	Make it Easier	ME
	Apply Constraints	AC
	Mix Up the Level of Challenge	MC
	Use Story and Narrative	SN
Motivation	Tap into Intrinsic Motivation	IM
	Embed Learning Into Meaningful Activity	MA
	Use Multimedia	UM
	Support Autonomy by Offering Choices	SA
	Support Self-Expression	SS
	Show and Reward Progress	RP
	Support Social Learning	SL

Table 2. Description of the guidelines template. Structure adapted from the proposal of the W3C

Template element	Description
Number and Name	Number and name of the guideline
Purpose	Background of the guideline
Examples	Application of the guidelines in specific cases
Related resources	Books and materials related to the guidelines
Techniques	Specific procedures that support the guidelines
Glossary	Design-related terms that require a more detailed explanation for understanding and interpretation

To describe each guideline, the World Wide Web Consortium (W3C) guideline description template was used as an international community seeking the unification and development of web standards. Table 2 presents the structure for the description of the guidelines, which corresponds to an adaptation of the template proposed by W3C.

2.3   Techniques

Techniques are basic principles that should be considered when designing any interface and cover general aspects such as color, the layout of the elements on the page, among others.

In these techniques converge the concepts of different recognized authors in the field of user experience, emotional design and usability principles. These studies and the list of the techniques that constitute the guide EMOVLE is presented in Table 3.

These techniques provide basic information, which allows the EMOVLE Guide to be easily extended with other techniques deemed appropriate.

Table 3. List of techniques and related studies

Technique	Related authors
Use of Color (C)	Alan Cooper et al., Nan Jiang, Bonnie Skaalid, Mark Boulton, Robbie Williams
Use of Typography (T)	Alan Cooper et al., Mark Boulton, Robbie Williams
Use of Simplicity (S)	Dan Saffer, Giles Colborne, Bill Scott, Alan Cooper et al., Bonnie Skaalid
Use of Persona (P)	Dan Saffer, Russ Unger, Aarron Walter
Use of Nature in design (N)	William Lidwell
Use of Seduction (D)	Trevor Van Gorp, Aarron Walter, Stephen Anderson, Wilbert Galitz, Bonnie Skaalid
Use of Graphics and multimedia (G)	Wilbert Galitz, Alan Cooper et al., Nan Jiang
Use of Layout of screen elements (L)	Ben Shneiderman, Aarron Walter, William Lidwell, Robert Hoekman, Bill Scott, Jennifer Tidwell

Table 4. Description of the technique template. Structure adapted from the proposal of the W3C

Template element	Description
Number and Name	Number and name of the technique
Description	The technique is described in depth and its application
Applicability	It lists the guidelines where the technique has been applied and aspects related to restrictions of applicability of the technique
Examples	Detailed descriptions of the application of the technique
Resources	Templates and other technical support documentation
Related techniques	Other techniques that support the described technique
Glossary	Design-related terms that require a more detailed explanation for understanding and interpretation are described

To describe each one of them, the structure in Table 4 was proposed based on the W3C description template.

Each technique supports one or more guidelines giving greater detail in the application process and, in turn, one technique can complement others. For example, the guideline *Set a Positive Mood* can be extended by the techniques *Use of Color*, *Use of Typography* and *Use of Simplicity* due to color as typography and simplicity help to reach a good mood on the user. At the same time a technique as *Use of Typography* can be complemented by other technique as the technique *Use of Color* due to one typography with an specific color can give a different message than the same typography with another color. The way in which guidelines and techniques are linked is seen in Table 5 and the relationship between techniques in Table 6.

Table 7 show the description of one guideline and Table 8 presents the description of one of the techniques.

Table 5. Constructs - Guidelines - Techniques relationship

Construct	Guideline	Techniques							
		C	T	S	P	N	D	G	L
Creativity	PM	X	X	X	-	-	-	-	-
	SP	X	X	-	X	-	X	X	-
	BE	X	X	-	-	X	-	-	-
	CS	X	X	X	-	-	-	-	X
	ID	-	-	-	-	-	X	X	-
Engagement	AG	X	X	-	-	-	-	X	-
	SV	-	-	-	-	-	-	X	-
	MH	-	-	X	X	-	X	-	-
	ME	-	-	X	X	-	X	-	-
	AC	-	-	X	-	-	-	-	X
	MC	-	-	-	-	-	X	-	-
	SN	X	X	-	X	-	-	-	-
Motivation	IM	X	X	X	-	-	-	X	-
	MA	-	-	-	-	-	-	X	-
	UM	-	-	-	-	-	X	-	X
	SA	X	X	-	X	-	-	-	X
	SS	-	-	X	-	-	-	-	X
	RP	-	-	X	-	-	X	-	-
	SL	-	-	X	-	-	X	-	-

Table 6. Relationship between techniques

	C	T	S	P	N	D	G	L
C	-	-	-	-	-	-	-	-
T	X	-	-	X	-	-	-	-
S	X	X	-	-	-	-	X	X
P	X	X	X	-	-	-	X	X
N	X	X	-	-	-	-	-	X
D	X	X	-	-	-	-	-	X
G	X	-	-	-	-	-	-	X
L	-	-	X	-	-	X	-	-

Table 7. Guideline: leverage the cathedral space

Number and Name	CRE4 Leverage the cathedral space
Purpose	The height of a roof can help or not to support performance in solving problems. This is known as the cathedral effect. As various authors have explained, high skies promote abstract and creative thinking and low ceilings promote concrete and detail-oriented thinking [25]. It is for this reason that artists prefer spacious spaces and programmers are located in enclosed and dark spaces that help them to focus on detail Although the cathedral effect refers to physical spaces, the interfaces designs may also be spacious and open to possibilities or they can be enriched with features and optimized for detailed work. An example of this is the Mockups application whose interface is extremely simple, free of distractions and spacious in contrast to the Matlab application which has detailed functionalities to support the work
Examples	The application of Balsamiq Mockups (Fig. 2) is an example of a simple, spacious, distraction-free system to support creative thinking
	On the other hand, Fig. 3, shows a screen of the application MatLab where a great amount of components and functionalities are perceived to promote the mentality oriented to the detail
Related resources	Not related
Techniques	Use of Simplicity Use of Color Use of Typography Use of Layout of screen elements
Glossary	Not related

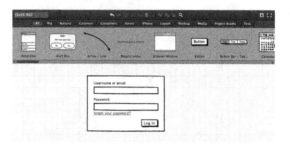

Fig. 2. BalsamiqMockups page

Fig. 3. Matlab screenshot

Table 8. Technique: use of graphics and multimedia

Number and Name	7. Use of Graphics and multimedia
Description	The graphs can be described in one of four categories: of attention, affective, cognitive and compensatory [26, 27]. In this way, the images can attract the attention of the student to the material (graphs of attention) or can promote the enjoyment and affect the emotions and attitudes of the student (affective graphs). Also through the graphics it can be increased understanding or provide information that otherwise can not be taught (cognitive graphs) and finally, the use of compensatory images, involves helping readers by adding keys in the images to decrypt the texts
	On the other hand, the functions of the graphs have been expanded by grouping them into three categories: representational, analog and arbitrary. The representational images allude to the concept that is being discussed, such as photos, drawings and models. Analog graphs are significant because they act as a substitute of the topic being discussed while arbitrary graphs are schematized as drawings that have a logical relationship to the topic as diagrams, charts and flowcharts

(*continued*)

Table 8. (*continued*)

	In this way, several elements need to be considered in order to determine whether or not a graph should be considered. These elements include germaneness, realism, complexity/simplicity, size and cultural factors
	Germaneness: It means that a drawing is not only relevant but essential and can not be removed without impairing comprehension
	Realism: Although people may think that a more realistic drawing is better, in many cases the simplified drawings will give better help as it allows to focus attention on what is needed [28]
	Complexity/Simplicity: The graphics are required to be as simple as possible and complexity should be added only when absolutely required [29]
	Size: Studies have shown that larger figures cause more excitement, are better remembered and are more pleasant than small ones; however, large images contribute to greater download times, so, a balance must be made between the download time and the size so that the user does not feel frustrated in the middle of the wait [29,30]
	Cultural Factors: It is important to keep in mind that the colors used do not offend users according to their cultures. Recommendations can be found when using graphs depending on the cultures in the studies of Horton et al. [31]
	On the other hand, animations should be used when trying to indicate dimensionality, or to illustrate the change over time trying to enrich the graphic representations [32]
	In the case of videos, due to internet restrictions, they are not recommended if they are large. They should only be included in case you want to show movement in a demonstration or at a dance. It is also important to show the size of the video so that the user decides whether or not to wait to see it. Automatic downloads should never be incorporated into the page
	You can use a sound if you want to evoke a specific emotion, if you want to exemplify the sound of something, or can be used in case you are looking to learn another language. If included it must be taken into account that it must be produced with the best quality [30]
	In summary it should always be considered that the user should not take more than a second to move from one page to another nor should it take more than ten seconds for a response from a multimedia file since ten seconds is the limit of people to maintain their attention while waiting [11,32]
Applicability	This technique gives support to the following guidelines: Show personality Include Delighters Beware of primal attention grabbers Using segmenting and variety to sustain attention Tap into intrinsic motivation Use multimedia

(*continued*)

Table 8. (*continued*)

Examples	The lessons on the livemocha.com page, a page specialized in teaching language learning, make correct use of short videos, using them as a strategy to facilitate learning. Figure 4 shows a video to learn the numbers of 1 to 10 Figure 5 shows the use of images as a method to complement the theory. In this case we present a lesson of the use of personas technique in the Interaction Design Foundation [33]
Resources	Not related
Related techniques	Use of color Use of layout of screen elements
Glossary	Not related

Fig. 4. Livemocha example screenshot

Fig. 5. Example of use of graphs in learning

3   Application of the EMOVLE Guide

While the guide is primarily intended for Virtual Learning Environments, it is not exclusive and could be applied to other types of interactive systems. In order to implement the guide, it is necessary first to establish what type of environment is being built, the target audience and define what kind of construct (creativity, engagement, motivation) the system intends to reach in order to delimit the guidelines that will be applied in the design process. Ideally, the greatest number of guidelines should be used, pointing to the three constructs; however depending on the time and the developer resources, only a few could be applied.

Once the guidelines that are to be applied are chosen then it is possible to drill down each one by reading the section of the techniques that are listed in the *Technique* section of each guideline.

4   Development of Non-functional Prototypes

The guidelines and techniques described in the guide have been compiled in order to facilitate the work of the developer and designer when building interfaces of a Virtual Learning Environment. For this reason, users with this profile were chosen to develop non-functional prototypes based on the EMOVLE guide and to evaluate these guidelines according to the experience gained. The detailed information of the sample of participants, the process that was followed to carry out the prototyping activity and the obtained prototypes are described below.

4.1   Selection of Participants

For the sample, 17 students of the seventh semester of the degree of Computer Engineering of the Institución Universitaria Colegio Mayor de Cauca (Colombia) were chosen. They were between 18 and 28 years of age and realized the activity as part of the course of Human Computer Interaction. This profile was chosen since the developed guide is implemented to be used by users knowledgeable in the subject of software development so that it facilitates the work of constructing interfaces of Virtual Learning Environments.

4.2   Prototyping Process

Once the participants were chosen, the activities described in Table 9 were presented. The target audience, the subject of the course and the tool in which the non-functional prototype was developed was the choice of each participant. It is important to clarify that depending on the type of lesson and the target audience some guidelines may or may not be taken into account; however, the more number of guidelines should be put into practice and each of them should be developed according to the EMOVLE guidelines.

After the prototype development, the students answered an evaluation related to the ease of use of the guidelines and their applicability within the interface design process.

Table 9. Description of activities

#	Activity
1	Select the VLE on which the prototype will be developed
2	Determine the components implemented in the prototype
3	Select the prototyping tool
4	Carry out the construction of the prototype
5	Assess the EMOVLE guide using the survey

4.3   Obtained Prototypes

In Figs. 6, 7 and 8 are presented some prototypes obtained by the students. Figure 6 identifies the use of two guidelines: *Use Story and Narrative* and *Support Social Learning*. The first guideline is perceived in the unit that was followed in the interfaces when using elements of a classroom such as books and the fact that all the content of the chat is displayed within a board. The second guideline is shown in the possibility of interacting with other apprentices and sharing comments.

In Fig. 7 another interface proposal is shown, which, like the previous one, makes use of the story and narrative by placing a class board and some back-

Fig. 6. Prototype 1 - Student 1

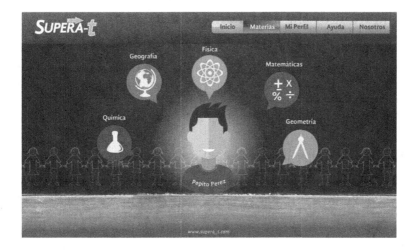

Fig. 7. Prototype 1 - Student 2

Fig. 8. Prototype 1 - Student 3

ground drawings. The proposal of Fig. 7 emphasizes the *Use of Color* and the use of guidelines such as *Beware of Primal Attention Grabbers* through the implementation of a simple interface. Finally in Fig. 8 an interface is shown where the learner can share the videos of the course through the links of social networks which shows the *Support social Learning* guideline and the *Use Multimedia* guideline.

5   Validation of the EMOVLE Guide

The EMOVLE guide was evaluated under two different approaches: the first one, from the students' point of view according to the answers obtained in the evaluation of the guide and the second one, according to the expert point of view validating that each guideline put in practice has been applied correctly. The results of each of the approaches are presented below.

5.1   EMOVLE Guide Evaluation - First Approach

The purpose of the survey was to obtain feedback from the students about the guide in order to determine if it had been useful. In each question the user had to choose a number on a scale of 1 to 5 where 1 corresponded to completely disagree and 5 completely agree. The questions and their results are presented in Table 10.

Table 10. Evaluation results of the EMOVLE guide

Questions	Completely disagree				Completely agree
	5	4	3	2	1
The general structure of the guidelines is appropriate for the needs of the developer?	65%	24%	6%	6%	0%
The general structure of the techniques is appropriate for the needs of the developer?	71%	12%	12%	6%	0%
The terminology included in the guidelines is well defined?	71%	6%	18%	6%	0%
The terminology included in the techniques is well defined?	71%	6%	18%	6%	0%
The guide is not complex?	59%	12%	6%	12%	12%
The guidelines are easy to understand?	59%	24%	12%	6%	0%
The techniques are easy to understand?	59%	18%	18%	6%	0%
The support of a specialized person is not needed to understand the guidelines?	59%	12%	6%	6%	18%
The support of a specialized person is not needed to understand the techniques?	59%	6%	18%	12%	6%
The guidelines do not present inconsistencies?	59%	6%	18%	6%	12%
The techniques do not present inconsistencies?	65%	12%	0%	6%	18%
Most people could use the guide easily?	53%	24%	12%	12%	0%
The examples set out in the guidelines are understandable and easy to apply?	65%	18%	6%	12%	0%
The examples set out in the techniques are understandable and easy to apply?	71%	12%	12%	6%	0%
Is the guide useful?	65%	29%	6%	0%	0%
Is the guide for non-connoisseurs in design?	29%	12%	41%	6%	12%
Is the guide clear?	35%	41%	18%	6%	0%
Is the guide innovative?	35%	35%	24%	0%	6%
Is the guide motivating?	29%	41%	24%	6%	0%
Is the guide short?	6%	6%	29%	24%	35%
Is the guide interesting?	29%	18%	29%	24%	0%

After reviewing the different questions, it is possible to conclude that in general the guide had a good acceptance by the students, since 90% of the questions predominated the highest scores (grades 4 and 5). Also, it can be noted that in questions such as whether to recommend the guide, if it was useful or if it would be used for subsequent interfaces, 100% of the answers were affirmative indicating that the guide met the expectations outlined.

5.2 EMOVLE Guide Evaluation - Second Approach

Once the 16 prototypes were obtained, they were evaluated to ensure that the guidelines were implemented correctly. To this end, each guideline was compared to the document each student sent in which they had to mention how each guideline had been applied in the prototype. The analysis performed is presented in Table 11.

It can be noted that the students were able to implement many of the guidelines and techniques included in the guide. This in turn allows us to consider the applicability of the guide and the possibility of building creative and improved interfaces. It also served to provide students with a starting point in prototyping.

Table 11. Use of the guidelines in the prototypes

Guideline	Percentage of use	Percentage of correct use
PM	13%	100%
SP	7%	0%
BE	7%	100%
CS	7%	100%
ID	7%	100%
IM	33%	40%
UM	0%	0%
UM	67%	90%
SA	40%	67%
SS	47%	57%
RP	7%	100%
SL	60%	44%
AG	40%	83%
SV	73%	72%
MH	33%	60%
ME	93%	57%
AC	40%	67%
MC	33%	80%
SN	40%	50%

6   Conclusions

The emotional design is an interesting area that has obtained results in several technological elements creating loyalty on the users to the products that they acquire. Linking this concept within the Virtual Learning Environments could mean a greater commitment of the trainees to the virtual course in which they are enrolled.

After a detailed review of the bibliography it was noticed that there are no detailed guidelines that point to the creation of Virtual Learning Environments interfaces. Incursing in this aspect can be innovative and is an incipient area of study.

Virtual Learning Environments are systems that have not been explored from an emotional perspective. Much has been said from the vision of usability but still the authors have not ventured to propose guidelines for the creation of emotive interfaces.

If aspects such as emotional design are taken into account when developing Virtual Environments, it is possible to achieve a significant improvement in the way in which the student perceives the system, and therefore, in the way in which he/she receives the information that there is projected.

The principles and theories related of emotional design are versatile enough to be applicable to almost any type of system. This was an advantage when adapting them to be applied to Virtual Learning Environments.

Although the EMOVLE guide was extensive, most of the students stated that it was possible to put it into practice and make use of the recommendations. Within the prototypes obtained were interesting results and creative interfaces, different from each other. This exposes an important aspect in the use of the guide and is that it does not intend to establish an unique interface but is intended to help, refine and maximize individual ideas.

After the implementation of the guidelines, users said that the EMOVLE guide were useful and they would use the guide for later interfaces and would recommend it to other colleagues.

Within the advantages of using the EMOVLE Guide is its practicality and ease of use, since it can be reviewed from general to specific interface design issues and vice versa, in addition, it can be supplemented by other studies and finally it provides specific examples of application. The great difference with other related studies, especially with Dorian Peters' research who established the general structure of the guidelines, is that this guide has been extended and deepened with more authors who provide specific design guidelines and not only focus on what to do but also how to do it. Among the disadvantages is its size, since it contains about 98 sheets which can be a bit cumbersome for some users.

7   Recommendations

Within the recommendations made by the users who developed the prototype, the possibility of trimming the guide was established in order to increase its practicality. It is possible to make a shorter version pointing to specific guidelines.

When developing the interfaces according to the proposed guidelines, it is recommended to take into account the target population and the goal of the Virtual Learning Environment to be developed since not all the guidelines are applicable.

8 Future Work

To integrate the guide to the design of virtual agents, so that not only positive emotions are evoked in students, but if students evoke negative emotions during the learning process, these agents can help mitigate them.

To validate EMOVLE guide in different environments or systems that support the teaching-learning processes to assess their feasibility and versatility.

In order to finish validating the guideline it would be advisable to send it to a network of experts so that they can establish if the construction of this guideline is adequate and if it contains sufficient theoretical support.

Developed prototypes could be evaluated to test if they actually evoke positive emotions.

More detailed techniques could be included in order to obtain a more complete guide to be used by any type of expert.

It is necessary to build a website that supports the guide so that those interested in designing interfaces that evoke positive emotions in students through virtual learning environments, have all the information available about the guidelines and techniques.

Nowadays, the present research is being expanded by applying the EMOVLE Guide to a health environment, specifically for the design of therapeutic systems interfaces for children with attention deficit disorder. This study is part of the doctoral project entitled "EMOINAD Guide: An emotive interface design guide for attention deficit disorder in children".

References

1. Laurier, C., Sordo, M., Serra, J., Herrera, P.: Music mood representations from social tags. In: ISMIR, pp. 381–386 (2014)
2. Kumar, R.L., Smith, M.A., Bannerjee, S.: User interface features influencing overall ease of use and personalization. Inf. Manage. **41**, 289–302 (2004)
3. Nielsen, J.: Designing Web Usability (2001)
4. Palmer, J.: Designing for web site usability. Computer **35**, 102–103 (2002)
5. Wang, Y., Emurian, H.: Trust in e-commerce: consideration of interface design factors. J. Electron. Commer. Organ. **3**, 42 (2005)
6. Zhang, P., Von Dran, G.M.: Satisfiers and dissatisfiers: a two-factor model for website design and evaluation. J. Am. Soc. Inf. Sci. **51**, 1253–1268 (2000)
7. Éthier, J., Hadaya, P., Talbot, J., Cadieux, J.: Interface design and emotions experienced on B2C web sites: empirical testing of a research model. Comput. Hum. Behav. **24**, 2771–2791 (2008)
8. Buschke, L.: The basics of building a great web site. Training Dev. **51**, 46–49 (1997)

9. Liu, S., Tucker, D., Koh, C., Kappelman, L.: Standard user interface in e-commerce sites. Ind. Manage. Data Syst. **103**, 600–610 (2003)
10. Rayport, J.: Best face forward. Harvard Bus. Rev. **82**, 47–59 (2004)
11. Shneiderman, B., Plaisant, C.: Designing The User Interface: Strategies for Effective Human-Computer Interaction. Addison Wesley, Boston (2005)
12. Norman, D.: The Design of Everyday Things. Basic Books, New York (2002)
13. Bastien, J.M. Christian Scapin, D.L.: Ergonomic criteria for the evaluation of human-computer interfaces, p. 79 (1993)
14. Witt, H., Nicola, T., Kenn, H.: Designing a wearable user interface for hands-free interaction in maintenance applications. In: Pervasive Computing and Communications Workshops, pp. 652–655 (2006)
15. Mignonneau, L., Sommerer, C.: Designing emotional, metaphoric, natural and intuitive interfaces for interactive art, edutainment and mobile communications. Comput. Graph. **29**, 837–851 (2005)
16. Chen, Y., Pu, P.: Designing emotion awareness interface for group recommender systems. In: Proceedings of the 2014 International Working Conference on Advanced Visual Interfaces, pp. 347–348. ACM, New York (2014)
17. Laurier, C., Sordo, M., Serra, J., Herrera, P.: Music mood representations from social tags. In: ISMIR, pp. 381–386 (2009)
18. Mayer, R., Estrella, G.: Benefits of emotional design in multimedia instruction. Learn. Instruction **33**, 12–18 (2014)
19. Plass, J., Heidig, S., Hayward, E., Homer, B., Um, E.: Emotional design in multimedia learning: effects of shape and color on affect and learning. Learn. Instruction **29**, 128–140 (2014)
20. Villareal, A.P., Aguirre, A.F., Collazos, C.A.: Propuesta metodológica para la inclusión del aspecto emocional dentro del diseño de interfaces de un entorno virtual de aprendizaje. Revista Colombiana de Computación. pp. 89–99 (2014)
21. Clarke, A.: The Principles of Screen Design for Computer-Based Learning Materials (1994)
22. Um, E., Plass, J.L., Hayward, E.O., Homer, B.D.: Emotional design in multimedia learning. J. Educ. Psychol. **104**, 485 (2012)
23. Peters, D.: Interface Design for Learning: Design Strategies for the Learning Experience. New Riders (Voices that Matter), San Francisco (2014)
24. Weinschenk, S.: The Grid: 100 Things Every Designer Needs to Know About People. Pearson Education, Upper Saddle River (2011)
25. Lidwell, W., Holden, K., ButleR, J.: Universal Principles of Design, Revised and Updated: 125 Ways to Enhance Usability, Influence Perception, Increase Appeal, Make Better Design Decisions, and Teach through Design. Rockport Pub, Beverly (2010)
26. Skaalid, B.: A compilation of guidelines for the design of web pages and sites. Web Design Guidelines. University of Saskatchewan (1998)
27. Levie, W., Lentz, R.: Effects of text illustrations: a review of research. ECTJ **30**, 195–232 (1982)
28. Houseman, J.: If You build it will They come: or, do You have to give a mark for it. In: Association for Media and Technology in Education (1997)
29. Misanchuk, E., Schwier, R., Boling, E.: Visual design for instructional multimedia. In: 1999 Proceedings of World Conference on Educational Media and Technology, p. 1621 (1999)
30. Reeves, B., Nass, C.: The Media Equation: How People Treat Computers, Television, and New Media Like Real People and Places. Computers & Mathematics with Applications (1997)

31. Horton, W.: The Icon Book: Visual Symbols for Computer Systems and Documentation (1994)
32. Nielsen, J.: Guidelines for multimedia on the web. World Wide Web J. **2**, 157–162 (1997)
33. The Interaction Design Foundation. https://www.interaction-design.org/

Auditory User Interface Guideline for Emotional User Experience

Hoon Sik Yoo[1] and Da Young Ju[2(✉)]

[1] Techno and Design Research Center,
Yonsei University, Incheon, South Korea
yoohs@yonsei.ac.kr
[2] Yonsei Institute of Convergence Technology,
Yonsei University, Incheon, South Korea
dyju@yonsei.ac.kr

Abstract. Auditory user interface (AUI) or experience is the most representative domain of the emotional elements with a product that can give a user differentiated experience. Providing information through auditory sense, AUI is a very important element be-cause it renders esthetics, significance, and usefulness to its users, and unity and corporate identity to companies. If there is an AUI guideline to emotions that can be commonly applicable to products, refined user's auditory experiences can be designed and provided based on it. In this respect, the present study has the purpose of developing an AUI guideline that can explain what sounds should be provided by a certain emotional concept of a product. To develop a guideline that can be applied widely, this study carried out an experiment on users, focusing on 'beep' sounds, which are often used for a product. A total of 21 sound samples were created and they were tested in 269 participants. The results demonstrated that emotion is closely related to the number of sounds and chords. More specifically speaking, emotion responded differently to chord types. In future, it is necessary to conduct a study to see the connection between each emotion and product functions agreeable to it as an advanced academic attempt.

Keywords: Auditory user interface · User experience · Emotional design · Guideline development

1 Research Background and Purpose

Challenges are endlessly made to innovate product design. A keen attention is being paid to user's experience using emotional elements as a driving force of innovation. Donald Norman in Interface classified the levels of interaction between users and a product into visceral, behavioral, and reflective level. In visceral level, human uses intuition in determining the experience of using a product. This stage has a very important impact on purchase, use, and sale of a product.

Auditory user interface (AUI) or experience is the most representative domain of the emotional elements with a product that can give a user differentiated experience. Apple's Magic Mouse, for example, installed a very tiny speaker in a mouse in order to give its users a unique experience while scrolling it and it wasn't tiny innovation at all.

© Springer International Publishing AG 2017
A. Marcus and W. Wang (Eds.): DUXU 2017, Part II, LNCS 10289, pp. 162–169, 2017.
DOI: 10.1007/978-3-319-58637-3_12

Providing information through auditory sense, AUI is a very important element because it renders esthetics, significance, and usefulness to its users, and unity and corporate identity to companies. The sound that agree well with the characteristics of a product and one that is good to hear and has esthetic appeal play a role of making users have a positive image on the product that creates such sounds.

Therefore, it is high time we needed a guidance and a system that can help design AUI from emotional point of view. If there is an AUI guideline to emotions that can be commonly applicable to products, refined user's auditory experiences can be designed and provided based on it. In this respect, the present study has the purpose of developing an AUI guideline that can explain what sounds should be provided by a certain emotional concept of a product.

2 Related Work

The UI (User Interface) is classified into five types according to the viewpoint of human sense. This is representative classification according to the senses such as a physical UI (PUI) that can be physically touched, a graphical UI (GUI) that can visually recognize information, an auditory UI (AUI) based on sound information, an olfactory UI (OUI) based on olfactory information, and a gustatory UI (GUI) based on the gustation. The value of using AUI is highlighted to enhance emotional experiences for products and service innovation. The auditory experience provides aesthetic value to the user depending on the mood of the listening sound. In addition, appropriate feedback on operation has a great effect on usability and the auditory sense itself has a new functionality (Fig. 1).

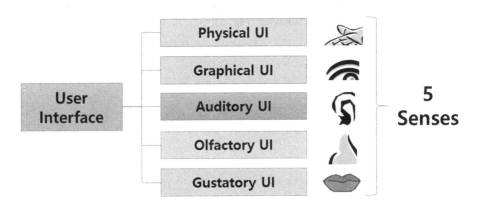

Fig. 1. Classification of the Interfaces to the five senses

The UI (User Interface) is classified into five types according to the viewpoint of human sense. This is representative classification according to the senses such as a physical UI (PUI) that can be physically touched, a graphical UI (GUI) that can visually recognize information.

A representative example of well-designed UX/ UI based on auditory experience is the Korean subway system. The Korean subway provides different sounds to passengers when getting on the inbound or outbound lane. For passengers who have to choose the subway in the same place, these different sounds can improve usability to distinguish information (Fig. 2).

Fig. 2. Scenes on getting on the subway in Korea

An example of a good application of auditory experience to a product is Apple's Magic Mouse. Apple's Magic Mouse has a small built-in speaker that provides feedback sound information on scrolling when the user scrolls. Most users do not even know that a speaker is built in the mouse. However, through this, users can receive more reliable feedback to their behavior (Fig. 3).

Fig. 3. Apple's magic mouse

"Boot up sound" is also an important example of Apple's sound experience. When an Apple computer boots up, a specific sound is output to provide feedback that it has been booted up. This sound is not only an indication of the status of the product but also a representative example of expressing the concept of the product and the identity of the company. In fact, Apple is gradually updating the boot up sound every time a new product is released, and users are taking it as a symbol of Apple (Fig. 4).

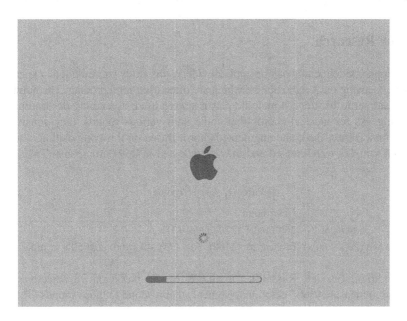

Fig. 4. Apple's MAC OS boot up scene

As shown in the examples above, the auditory experience seems to be a small element, but it has an important effect on product design. As the requirements for systematic AUI design for product design have increased, many researchers have conducted research on this.

Lee (2003) analyzed, as a guideline for designing information, that it is helpful for users to provide different pitch according to the depth of the information to recognize present location, the more the depth is deep, the higher pitch is used and the more depth is low, the more effective it is to use the lower pitch. Lee (2007) and Hwang (2015) also conducted a study, as a guide to the relation between emotions and function, on the ability to provide a higher level of satisfaction to users when a sound with different emotions is provided in accordance with the type of function. According to Lee's study (2007) and Hwang (2015), users prefer the emotion sound close to a high arousal to functions related to on & ascending, and the emotion sound close to a low arousal to functions related to off & descending. In addition, they preferred positive emotions for functions related to inform and preferred negative emotions for functions related to errors. Park (2012) conducted a study that derived guidelines for a specific product such as a washing machine. A detailed sound of each function was extracted to study the tone, intensity, and height of the sound. Kim (2000) conducted a study on guidelines for auditory feedback to improve the usability of portable digital electronic devices in addition to washing machines.

When we look around the existing research, we can see that researches related to information design, functions, usability of washing machine and mobile phone are the main subjects. The purpose of this study is to provide emotional AUI guidelines that can be universally applicable to information devices from a different view point.

3 User Research

To develop a guideline that can be applied widely, this study carried out an experiment on users, focusing on 'beep' sounds, which are often used for a product. The number of sounds was set to be 4 and 4 melodic patterns were used: ascending, descending, and combining. As for musical chords that come with various sounds, they consisted of major, minor, diminished, and augmented chord. Based on this composition, a total of 21 sound samples were created and they were tested in 269 participants (Table 1).

Table 1. Users' Profile

Item	Description
Number of participants	269 (male: 132/female: 137)
Average age (20 s ~ 60 s)	In their 20 s (108), 30 s (73), 40 s (66), and 50 s or order (22)

In addition, Besides, Russell's Circumflex Model based on 28 adjectives were employed to measure users' emotional elements that respond to those sounds (Table 2).

Table 2. Classification of emotion by russell's circumflex model

High Classification Level	Low Classification Level
Negative & high arousal	Frustrated, angry, distressed, tense, annoyed, afraid, alarmed,
Positive & high arousal	Aroused, astonished, excited, delighted, happy
Positive & low arousal	Calm, glad, sleepy, serene, content, at ease, satisfied, relaxed, pleased
Negative & low arousal	Miserable, sad, gloomy, depressed, bored, droopy, tired

4 Result

The emotional responses to the beep sounds showed that the participants experienced such emotion as 'awakened', 'tense', and 'startled' when they consisted of one or two sounds. It is understood that the short and sporadic sound was heard like an alarm to them. For a beep sound that consisted of 3 or more sounds, the respondents showed divided emotional responses by chord type. Major chords gave the participants such emotion as 'satisfied', 'peaceful', 'happy', and 'pleased', regardless of the number of sounds and melodic type while minor chords presented emotions related to 'unlively', 'depressed', 'disheartened', and 'calm'. Diminished and augmented chords can be made with a tone of 3 or more sounds. To diminished scales or chords, they showed

Table 3. Ranks of emotional experience frequency by sound

Sound scale	Melodic type	Chord	First	Second	Third	Fourth	Fifth
1	N/A	N/A	Aroused	Alarmed	Tense	Calm	Annoyed
2	Descending	N/A	Aroused	Tense	Calm	Depressed	Astonished
2	Ascending	N/A	Tense	Astonished	At ease	Aroused	Relaxed
3	Descending	Major	Satisfied	Serene	Relaxed	Calm	At ease
3	Descending	Minor	Depressed	Gloomy	At ease	Frustrated	Tense
3	Ascending	Major	Satisfied	Glad	Calm	At ease	Aroused
3	Ascending	Minor	Calm	Tense	Serene	Relaxed	Depressed
3	Combining	Major	Aroused	At ease	Satisfied	Relaxed	Tense
3	Combining	Minor	Depressed	Frustrated	Calm	Tense	Relaxed
4	Descending	Major	Satisfied	At ease	Aroused	Serene	Droopy
4	Descending	Minor	Droopy	At ease	Depressed	Frustrated	Gloomy
4	Descending	Diminished	Droopy	Tired	Depressed	Gloomy	Frustrated
4	Descending	Augmented	Tired	Depressed	Calm	Annoyed	Tense
4	Ascending	Major	Pleased	Glad	Satisfied	At ease	Content
4	Ascending	Minor	Satisfied	Calm	Glad	Relaxed	Serene
4	Ascending	Diminished	Calm	Depressed	Serene	Droopy	Tense
4	Ascending	Augmented	Aroused	Tense	Satisfied	Alarmed	Calm
4	Combining	Major	Satisfied	Serene	At ease	Relaxed	Calm
4	Combining	Minor	Calm	Relaxed	Tense	At ease	Satisfied
4	Combining	Diminished	Tense	Depressed	Gloomy	Relaxed	Serene
4	Combining	Augmented	Tense	Droopy	At ease	Calm	At ease

Table 4. Ranks of emotional experience frequency comparing male and female

Sound scale	Melodic type	Chord	Sex	First	Second	Third	Fourth	Fifth
1	N/A	N/A	M	Alarmed	Tense	Serene	Depressed	Annoyed
			F	Aroused	Calm	Astonished	Tense	Alarmed
2	Descending	N/A	M	Aroused	Calm	Droopy	Depressed	Excited
			F	Aroused	Tense	Astonished	Calm	Depressed
2	Ascending	N/A	M	Tense	Relaxed	At ease	Serene	Astonished
			F	Astonished	Aroused	At ease	Calm	At ease
3	Descending	Major	M	Satisfied	Relaxed	Aroused	Glad	Tired
			F	Satisfied	Calm	Serene	At ease	Happy
3	Descending	Minor	M	Aroused	Calm	Gloomy	Frustrated	Satisfied
			F	Depressed	Tense	At ease	Gloomy	Frustrated
3	Ascending	Major	M	Satisfied	Pleased	Calm	Aroused	Glad
			F	Glad	At ease	Serene	Satisfied	Aroused
3	Ascending	Minor	M	Relaxed	Glad	Calm	Satisfied	Serene
			F	Calm	Tense	Serene	Depressed	Pleased
3	Combining	Major	M	Content	At ease	Tense	Aroused	Calm
			F	Relaxed	Aroused	Satisfied	At ease	Serene
3	Combining	Minor	M	Calm	Frustrated	Depressed	Annoyed	Happy
			F	Depressed	Droopy	Frustrated	Content	At ease
4	Descending	Major	M	Satisfied	Depressed	Aroused	Tired	Droopy
			F	At ease	Serene	Satisfied	Calm	Astonished
4	Descending	Minor	M	Droopy	Satisfied	Content	Gloomy	Pleased
			F	Droopy	At ease	Calm	Depressed	Sad
4	Descending	Diminished	M	Gloomy	Droopy	Miserable	Depressed	Tense
			F	Tired	Depressed	Droopy	Frustrated	At ease
4	Descending	Augmented	M	Tired	Depressed	Calm	At Ease	Aroused
			F	Depressed	Tired	Annoyed	Tense	Calm
4	Ascending	Major	M	Pleased	Satisfied	Delighted	At Ease	Glad
			F	Glad	Pleased	Content	Excited	At Ease
4	Ascending	Minor	M	Satisfied	Calm	Relaxed	Aroused	Glad
			F	Tense	Satisfied	Calm	Content	Serene
4	Ascending	Diminished	M	Calm	At Ease	Depressed	Annoyed	Afraid
			F	Calm	Serene	Depressed	Tense	Droopy
4	Ascending	Augmented	M	Satisfied	Tense	Aroused	Relaxed	Serene
			F	Aroused	Tense	Alarmed	Satisfied	Frustrated
4	Combining	Major	M	Relaxed	Aroused	At ease	Satisfied	Frustrated
			F	Satisfied	Serene	Calm	At ease	Pleased
4	Combining	Minor	M	Relaxed	Calm	Sleepy	Tired	Gloomy
			F	Calm	Tense	At ease	Satisfied	Depressed
4	Combining	Diminished	M	Gloomy	Tense	Relaxed	Serene	Tired
			F	Droopy	Depressed	Tense	Calm	Annoyed
4	Combining	Augmented	M	Droopy	Tense	At ease	Frustrated	Relaxed
			F	Calm	At ease	Annoyed	Tense	Aroused

emotions related to 'disheartened', 'calm', 'unlively', and 'tense' while they experienced such emotions as 'awakened' and 'tense' as well as 'tired' and 'unlively' from augmented chords (Tables 3 and 4).

5 Conclusion and Future Work

This study conducted evaluation on users' emotions responding to sound type for the purpose of designing AUI. The results demonstrated that emotion is closely related to the number of sounds and chords. More specifically speaking, emotion responded differently to chord types (major, minor, diminished, augmented), so this finding can help making a guideline to sound selection suitable for product concept. In future, it is necessary to conduct a study to see the connection between each emotion and product functions agreeable to it as an advanced academic attempt.

Acknowledgments. This research was supported by the MSIP (Ministry of Science, ICT and Future Planning), Korea, under the "ICT Consilience Creative Program" (IITP-R0346-16-1008) supervised by the IITP (Institute for Information & communications Technology Promotion)

This material is based upon work supported by the Ministry of Trade, Industry & Energy (MOTIE, Korea) under Industrial Technology Innovation Program. No.10060517, 'Development of an user-centered product design support system based on cognitive and affective information'

References

Blattner, M.M., Sumikawa, D.A., Greenberg, R.M.: Ear-cons and icons: their structure and common design principles. Hum.-Comput. Interact. **4**, 11–44 (1991)

Norman, D.: Emotional Design. Basic Books (2005)

Jeon, M., Lee, J.-H.: The ecological AUI (auditory user interface) design and evaluation of user acceptance for various tasks on smartphones. In: Kurosu, M. (ed.) HCI 2013. LNCS, vol. 8007, pp. 49–58. Springer, Heidelberg (2013). doi:10.1007/978-3-642-39330-3_6

Lee, J.H., Jeon, M.H, Kim, M.S.: Auditory displays on the depth of hypertext. In: Proceedings of the 9th International Conference on Auditory Display (ICAD), Boston, MA, 7–9 July (2003)

Lee, J.H., Jeon, M.H.: Developing the design guideline of auditory user interface for domestic appliances. Korean J. Sci. Emot. Sensibility **10**(3), 307–320 (2007)

Hwang, H.J., Ju, D.Y.: Finding favorable textures for haptic display. In: Antona, M., Stephanidis, C. (eds.) UAHCI 2015. LNCS, vol. 9176, pp. 94–102. Springer, Cham (2015). doi:10.1007/978-3-319-20681-3_9

Park, J.Y., Park, S.H.: A study on audio user interface focused on the operating sounds and signal sounds. Des. Convergence Study **11**(6), 87–102 (2012)

Kim, H.S., Park, M.Y.: Design considerations of auditory feedback for enhancing the usability of portable digital electronic products. J. Ergon. Soc. Korea **19**(3), 51–60 (2000)

Reassurance Experience Design
for "Financial Planning Users"

Yang Zhang[✉] and Pengbo Zhu

Baidu, Beijing, P.R. China
zhangyang22@baidu.com

Abstract. In recently years, most people have been more enthusiastic in investing as their income increase. The "internet plus finance" investing way are gradually replacing traditional ways, because of the high threshold and low efficiency of banks. But there always exists concerns of the safety when they choose internet financial products. So it's been a big challenge for internet finance UX designers to keep the convenient and open properties of internet finance products, while in accordance with industry regulations. This article will elaborate the key points of reassurance experience design for "Financial Planning Users", based on the design examples of financial products "Baidu Wallet" and "Baidu Finance".

Keywords: Internet finance · Financial planning users · Reassurance experience design

1 Introduction

In June 2012, the former national leaders first publicly used the concept of Inclusive Finance at the G20 Summit in Mexico. By the Third Plenary Session of the 18th Central Committee of the Communist Party of China in November 2013, Inclusive Finance was formally proposed as a major strategy in comprehensively deepening the reform and perfecting financial market system in China. However, in the design of financial products, the domestic traditional financial industry still screens the small segment of the population to provide services in the latitude of assets or risk, or provide financial services through a series of barriers, such as raising the minimum investment amount and requiring proof of revenue at entity counter. This allows users that are accustomed to the equality and convenience of the internet services to gradually flood into the internet financial products.

In early 2015, the domestic large-scale P2P platform "yizubao" brokeand fled with money. This exposed a series of crisis of internet financial platform. This also caused the users' trust crisis to the internet financial platform. According to the latest report of CNNIC, the number of internet financial users was 78.49 million by the end of June 2015, nearly same as the data of the end of 2014, while internet users fell 0.3% points. The Yu'E Bao's second-quarter scale shrank 97.3 billion Yuan, a decline of 13.7%.

© Springer International Publishing AG 2017
A. Marcus and W. Wang (Eds.): DUXU 2017, Part II, LNCS 10289, pp. 170–177, 2017.
DOI: 10.1007/978-3-319-58637-3_13

CNNIC Internet Finance Planning Users Data Graph [1]

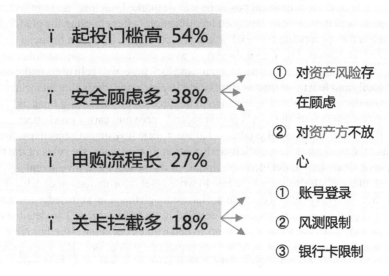

Internet Finance Planning Users Research Conclusion Graph [2]

We can conclude from the data above that Internet financial users begin to focus more on asset security, rather than simply pursuing high profits. In the macro view, this is also the trend of consumption promotion, product competition will ultimately be implemented to a better and safer user experience. Based on this background, Baidu Finance locate the financial products as "Professional and Reassuring ways of Financial Planning" after weighing and research, through which we hope to give users safe and reassuring feelings and experience, and forming the reliance and favor of Baidu financial brand. As a result, customers will ultimately be accustomed to buying Baidu financial products.

2   Design for Internet Finance Assurance Experience

Internet finance users have different education background and finance planning experience, which determines the difference of cognitive ability. So, it's always been a difficult point for internet finance experience design to make a balance between helping them gain the information via online operation and feeling reassurance and convenience by the advantages of internet finance itself.

2.1   The Reassurance Experience Design in the Process of Gaining Information

We found through the survey of financial users that users need to select a trustworthy financial platform before deciding to purchase a financial product. And users used to determine whether the platform is credible by querying whether there are the endorsement and payment guarantee from large financial institutions. Based on this pain point, we retain the obvious "du" element in the logo design of different Baidu finance products. At the same time the prominent positions will be marked, such as "account security risk insurance" and the specially designed identification. After choosing the platform, users will select the appropriate financial products according to their own financial objectives and available assets. So, a clear display of asset classification and asset threshold, for instance, the minimum investment amount and lock time, will help users make decisions more easily and feel more trustworthy. Generally speaking, designing financial products based on the user's psychology change in the process of purchasing financial products will be consistent with the user's psychological curve and earn a good effect.

After selecting financial products that meet their investment objectives, users will conduct the final asset information confirmation. For instance, the rules of the transaction, investigate target, detailed description of the product and investment agreement. At first, many platforms were reluctant to write asset information too detailed. For they think most internet financial users do not have enough financial knowledge to understand these complex rules, agreements and detailed investigate targets. Too detailed content may interfere with users and affect users to make quick decisions. But through research, we found that users do not need a very rapid investment decision when purchasing financial products. On the contrary, they'll try to know more detailed information. They prefer to believe in the financial products with detailed introduction, even if they can't fully understand. User's care about security determines the sensitivity to product information. If we change the perspective to think about this problem, user experience designers can consider how to reduce the cognitive cost of information by graphical interpretation of professional terms and progressive display of information levels, which can improve the reassurance experience during the process of gaining the information, while not boring users with too much information at the same time.

Image Above: Baidu Finance Asset Details page

2.2 The Reassurance Experience Design in the Information Operation

Users need to conduct a lot of information operation in the process of purchasing financial products. For instance, binding bank card, providing authentication and setting password, etc. It needs to provide very private and important personal information for users to complete these operations, at the same time requiring many operating costs. To strengthen the user reassurance experience, we can't pursue high efficiency blindly. This is also the care of user psychology. Therefore, when users need to provide important personal information, clearly informing users where their information will be used and commitment that information will not be leaked in a proper way will make users more willing to complete the information input. This Significantly reduces the probability of user behavior interruptions.

In the process of internet finance planning, there exist some characteristics, comparing with traditional financial products. For instance, the safety card for redemption funds to ensure fund safety and the large payment method to raise purchase amount. As a designer, we should try to make complex functions more understandable to ensure a good user experience, not making them confused. Therefore, in the design of Baidu finance, we applied a lot of graphic education and path guidance to make complex functional operations more intuitive and visible. The purpose is to let users understand the product at the lowest cognitive cost.

Image Above: Safety Card, large payment process education

3 Innovation and Caution of Reassurance Experience of Internet Finance

Anything is a double-edged sword. The internet finance has technical advantages and convenience, comparing with traditional financial industry, which is conducive for the internet financial products to make experience innovation. But there are some problems in the process. For instance, how should we treat the regulations of the traditional financial industry and how to avoid the problems of the internet itself such as security risks. These are what we have to face when making reassurance experience design innovation.

3.1 Respect the Habits of Users, Keep Awe of the Industry Regulations

Internet financial products can improve the experience on the basis of traditional bank financial products. But the internet financial products can't depend on random imagination and innovation without borders. Internet financial products should keep awe of the financial industry itself, and the experience design should respect the user cognition.

Take Baidu Finance design as example: During the purchasing the financial products, users need to be evaluated of the risk tolerance, which requires them to complete a large number of test topics. Initially we considered whether we could omit this process. But we found that without risk testing and notification, users could not form a clear risk perception and judgment, which leads users to choose financial products that exceed their own risk tolerance, resulting in additional economic losses.

Finally, we classify assets at different risk dimensions to avoid this problem. We allow users to ignore the test process for low risk products. For products with a certain risk, the risk must be clearly informed. And users could choose whether to do the test at their own decisions.

3.2 Use Internet Technology to Make Reassurance Experience Innovation

In recent years, hacking, loopholes and other events make users easily to feel worried when using the internet financial products, especially involving payments and being read personal information. Internet financial financing is a new concept for many users. So, users would mistrust the financial products at first. The cost of accessing to information in the internet era is greatly reduced, at the same time users care more about the privacy of personal information.

The experience design of internet finance needs some design methods to help users improve the security experience. From the cognitive perspective, the main factor that effect user's perception is the user's visual perception. And the visual carrier of financial products mainly contains text and image. Firstly, Copy is art. Use clear and effective text language, which makes users feel more professional. Secondly, use elements that make users feel safe and stable in graphic design, which can affect the user's subconscious and make people feel secure. Especially in some professional scenes, extracting elements that represent the industry itself will make users easier to accept, easier to understand the product itself and reduce its use of panic.

As for the application of internet technology, in the acquisition of personal information, the acquisition of key information should be verified. And new technologies should be appropriately used, such as fingerprint, photograph while reading, voice recognition to reduce the operation cost. This way will help users feel the convenience of technology and then feel safe.

With the development of technology, more and more new technologies will emerge, which will bring new opportunities and challenges for the design of internet financial products. Designers should always care the development of new technologies and consider how to use new technologies to bring better user experience to users.

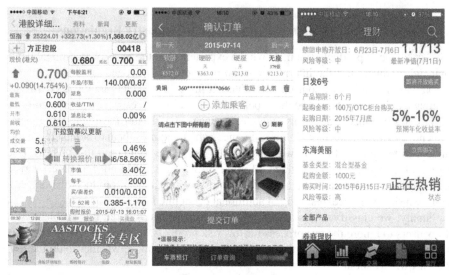

Image Above: apps from the internet

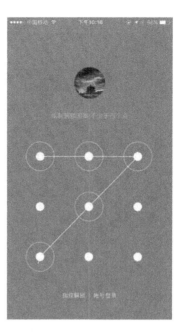

Image Above: Baidu Finance Gesture Fingerprint Password Operation

4   Conclusion

The internet finance reassurance design should strengthen the users' reassurance feeling of platform and brand. In the information presentation and operation, do not over-seek the simplicity and rapid completion of information. We can reduce the user's using and understanding threshold by product design methods. Use internet technology to make reassurance experience innovation in key nodes and processes, while respecting industry norms and users' cognitive habits, and finally help users gain reassurance experience while enjoying the convenience of internet finance planning.

Reference

Date Resource: Chinese finance planning user data of 2015 from CNNIC. 36th Chinese Internet Development Status statistics reports. http://cnnic.cn/hlwfzyj/hlwxzbg/hlwtjbg/201507/P020150723549500667087.pdf

Mobile DUXU

Towards Designing Mobile Banking User Interfaces for Novice Users

Victor Ndako Adama[1], Ibrahim Shehi Shehu[1(✉)], Solomon Adelowo Adepoju[1], and Rasheed Gbenga Jimoh[2]

[1] Federal University of Technology, Minna, Nigeria
{Vnadama,ibrahim.shehu,solo.adepoju}@futminna.edu.ng
[2] University of Ilorin, Ilorin, Nigeria
jimoh_rasheed@unilorin.edu.ng

Abstract. A lot has gone into research aimed at establishing design guidelines to guide developers in developing mobile applications usable by low literate and novice users due to their technological inclination. However, despite quite a number of valuable usability constraints unveiled, corresponding recommendations made and a list of synthesized design guidelines established across various research works, those guidelines are still incomplete and not standardized. In a similar context, the World Wide Web Consortium (W3C), an international standards organization for the World Wide Web, has addressed a similar problem for web based applications. They developed a set of standard guidelines called Web Content Accessibility Guidelines (WCAG 2.0) that specifies how web content can be made more accessible to all types of user on the World Wide Web. The existence of such standard for mobile phones application would greatly impact mobile application development for such users. However none of such standards as WCAG exists for mobile applications development. It has been established that more effort is needed towards uncovering more low literate and novice user centered usability constrains with corresponding recommendations. Thus there exists the need in this research area towards achieving a set of standard guidelines for the development of mobile applications. This study aim to achieve four (4) objectives: i. to explore for low literate or novice user centered usability constraints in mobile applications and their associated design recommendations from existing literatures. ii. to build a mobile banking prototype based on design recommendations from existing literatures. iii. to perform empirical test on some selected banking applications against the developed prototype. iv. to evaluate (comparative analysis) of objective (iii.) aimed at exposing more novice user centered usability constraints using System Usability Scale (SUS) tool. Levels of significance were tested via a two sampled t-test for mean.

Keywords: Usability · Design recommendations · Mobile banking applications · Novice users · Low literate users

1 Introduction

The global mobile phone customer base has continued to grow with annual increment in the number of subscribers across both developed and developing countries [1, 2]. In

© Springer International Publishing AG 2017
A. Marcus and W. Wang (Eds.): DUXU 2017, Part II, LNCS 10289, pp. 181–197, 2017.
DOI: 10.1007/978-3-319-58637-3_14

the past three decades, three products had the most impact on the world: the internet, personal computers and mobile phones all in the Information and Communication Technology (ICT) sector [3]. Amongst these, the mobile phone has the highest penetration especially in developing and underdeveloped countries. To further explain on the penetration of mobile phones, an estimated figure of 487 million was sold across the world between July- September in 2011 [4, 5]. That was higher than the figures of personal computers (PCs) sold around the same time frame [4]. Recent statistics by the International Telecommunication Union (ITU) has shown a much higher penetration of mobile phones usage in the world, with an estimated worldwide subscription of over 7 billion in 2015 [6].

It is because of this robust mobile subscriber base that the attentions of many entities with global development focus have been gained over time. Such entities have seen the vast availability of mobile phones as an avenue to serve as a platform for delivering developmental services [7]. One of such entities is the banking sector amongst many others. Bank services are now widely available on mobile phones as a means to afford customers the opportunity to carry out transactions at their convenience, anywhere, anytime.

However, across developing and underdeveloped nations, there exist various categories of mobile phone users. Each category is determined by factors such as literacy level, and exposure level to the mobile phone technology. The tendency that such users are carried along in such developmental growth evidently tends to be low because of the low adoption levels [2]. Also, one of the difficulties to delivering such services in such parts of the world is that most of the population is non literate [8], and even majority of the literate are typically novice users of such technologies. Africa, being a continent of developing and underdeveloped countries that suffer such dilemma has the second largest mobile market in the world after Asia according to African Mobile Observatory 2011.

1.1 The World Wide Web Consortium (W3C)

The World Wide Web Consortium (W3C) is an international standards organization for the World Wide Web. It was founded by Tim Berners-Lee in 1994 with the main purpose of developing a set of standards guidelines that specifies how web content can be made more accessible to all types of user on the World Wide Web. This was to bridge a similar gap as to low literacy and technological inclination of users. The current version, WCAG 2.0, was published in December 2008 and became an ISO standard, ISO/IEC 40500:2012 in October 2012. Because of the benefits derivable from the use of such a guideline the Canadian Federal Government, the Australian Government and the Israeli Ministry of Justice, have over time mandated that all online web contents meet the accessibility requirements of WCAG 2.0.

There are a lot of ongoing research aimed at establishing design guidelines to guide developers in developing mobile applications usable by low literate and novice users. However, despite quite a number of valuable usability constrains unveiled and corresponding design recommendations made from various research work, those guidelines are still incomplete and not standardized [9–13]. Also, there is no standard for mobile phone applications development as WCAG 2.0 exists for web content development. It has been established that more effort is needed towards uncovering more low literate and novice user centered constrain with corresponding recommendations, in anticipation to gather sufficient data to help establish a standard such as WCAG 2.0 with respect to mobile phone application interfaces for all types of user.

1.2 Usability

There are various definitions of usability in the Human-computer Interaction community. There also exist frameworks for its specification and measurement. A few opinion from various standards are:

The IS0 9241-11 standard defines usability as: "The extent to which, a product can be used by specified users to achieve specified goals with effectiveness, efficiency and satisfaction in a specified context of use". ISO/IEC 9126-1, on the other hand defines usability as 'the capability of the software products to be understood, learned, used and be attractive to the user, when used under specified conditions'.

Usability is an important quality attribute of any given product be it a mobile phone or mobile application. This then implies that usability evaluation is highly necessary to ensure usable mobile phones and mobile applications. Over time quite a number of usability evaluation methods have been developed. Such usability evaluations can basically be classified into three categories: usability testing, usability inquiry, and usability inspection [14]. Usability testing entails engaging representative users in carrying out typical tasks through interactions with a system or a prototype. Common methods include co-discovery learning, question-asking protocol and shadowing method. In Usability inquiry, an interaction with users takes place as they interact with the system in real world settings. Users are asked questions in order to help understand their feelings about the system and their information needs. On the other hand, field observation, concentrates on focus groups, while questionnaire surveys are used to gather data on usability. Another method, usability inspection, employs the use of usability experts to analyze the usability-related aspects analytically. Common available techniques are cognitive walkthrough and heuristic evaluation. Research of [15] is of the opinion that there exist two more techniques, analytical modeling and simulation. The two aim at predicting usability by using user models and interface models.

2   Research Recommendations Established Thus Far for Designing Usable UI's for Low Literate and Novice Users

A research [16] more or less covers a lot of ground with regards to design recommendations for low literate and novice users thus far. Their research findings and recommendations not only confirm the vast majority of previous works, but expose more issues. However usability still remains a major hurdle to be crossed [12, 13].

The research [16] took two steps in evaluating how best to improve the usability of mobile interfaces for low literate and novice users. Firstly, the researchers undertook an ethnographic study with the aim to identify usability barriers face by the target audience.

Ninety (90) low-literacy subjects across India, Kenya, the Philippines, and South Africa were selected. Also, via another study by the same group involving seventy (70) subjects in India, they quantitatively compared the usability of different points in the mobile design space. They considered three text-free interfaces: spoken dialog system, graphical interface and live operator. Also, text interfaces such as Short Message Service (SMS), electronic forms and Unstructured Supplementary Service Data (USSD).

Results from the studies confirmed that textual based interfaces were found to be unusable by first-time and low-literate users. It was also established that they were more error prone for novice users [16]. In the healthcare domain, result showed that a live operator is as much as ten times more accurate and effective than text-based interface, and also proved to be more cost effective in countries such as India. The researchers established a higher task completion rate in the context of mobile banking via a graphical interface. However, subjects who understood the spoken dialog system could use it more quickly due to their comfort and familiarity with speech. Similarly, the results presented in [16] were also in research works by [17–21].

2.1 Challenges Encountered by Novice Users in the Ethnographic Study

There were a number of challenges encountered by subjects in interacting with the mobile banking services and navigating through mobile phones in general. The challenges encountered by the subjects are summarized in the study [16] and similar to other research [17–21] are as follows:

Scroll Bars. Vertical scrollbars were not at first understood by quite a number of subjects. They did not understand that there were functions underneath what was shown on the screen. The researchers had to explain in detailed demonstrations what scrollbars were and how to utilize them.

Nonnumeric Inputs. Most subjects utilized their phones for making and accepting voice calls only. This category was also high when studies were carried out in India, Kenya, and South Africa. Some were unable to type words on their phones, talk less of composing an SMS message. Performing a USSD operation involving digits and symbols ("*" and "#"), subjects could type digits but couldn't find the symbols.

Language Difficulties. All the mobile banking services under the study generated and issued SMS receipts on successful completion of transactions. The text messages were completely in English, except for one of the services provider (M-PESA) which also offered in Kiswahili. Most subjects were not fluent in English and consequently found it difficult to read and understand the receipts sent via text message. Even those who could read and understand English found it difficult understanding specialized/technical terms and receipts containing multiple transaction summaries.

Discoverability. It was confirmed also that functions hidden deep in any hierarchical structures were less discoverable by subjects. A similar constraint emerged from poor interaction design, for instances such as when functions were classified under apparently unrelated functions

Hierarchical Navigation. Most subjects at first were unable to comprehend and navigate hierarchical menus. This posed a problem even for basic tasks such as calling back a phone number from which a missed call was earlier received. As for non-users of mobile phones, none were able to navigate the menus, instead of simply using the call logs or address book which would have been much easier and effective, most of them dialled the numbers from scratch each time they needed to make calls. These were confirmation of some earlier research works on challenges of representing tree structures among literate but novice user [22].

Soft-key Function Mapping. Irrespective of those who owned mobile phones or not, the majority of subjects were able to effectively use "hard keys" (example of such are direct number entry and send/end keys). However, some subjects found it difficult to use soft keys mostly found beneath the screen to performed different function in different contexts. Subjects who needed to navigate through different layers of the user interface (UI) to send text message got lost and had no clue to which soft key to use in navigating.

2.2 Synthesized Design Recommendations

The six (6) challenges encountered by the novice user in the ethnographic study of [16] and related studies of [17–21] yielded corresponding design recommendations as follows:

- Provide graphical clues
- Provide voice annotation support where ever possible
- Provide local language support, both in text and audio
- Minimize hierarchical structures
- Avoid requiring nonnumeric text input
- Avoid menus that require scrolling
- Minimize soft-key mappings
- Integrate human mediators into the overall system, to familiarize potential users with scenarios and UIs

The items listed above therefore echo design recommendations from [16–21]. Thus an interesting research agenda is presented aimed to improve the usability of the items listed to make them more accessible for all type of users.

3   Research Method

This research conducted three (3) comparative studies. Each of these studies involved the comparison of two (2) simulated user interfaces. In each study the first UI was the simulation of an existing mobile banking application, tested against another simulated application developed base on the selected design recommendation discussed from past research targeted towards low literate and novice users. The design recommendations were selected based on applicability to the mobile banking context. However the scope of the research was limited to working with novice users only. Each comparative study was in two phases. The first phase of the comparative study was an exploration for possible usability constraints novice could encounter on navigating through the UI of the existing application while performing some predefined tasks. This is done to examine mockups also known as fidelity prototypes for design flaws and usability constraints. It is a standard evaluation procedure carried out on predesigned mockups by developers to check usability barriers. It helps save cost and time as it is carried out early in the development cycle before engaging programmers.

The second phase was the testing of simulated mobile banking applications against the prototype. Both simulations were carried out on novice users. The interaction with both applications was first aimed to establish the significance of the impact of design recommendations implemented. Secondly, it was aimed to afford the researchers the opportunity to explore for more novice user centered constraints as novice user interacted with both user interfaces. The same was carried out against the prototype in two more comparative studies in the same manner. Thus in each of the three studies, each groups tested the developed prototype (developed based on the selected recommendations) against an existing mobile banking application. To achieve the project aim and objectives, the research frame work in Fig. 1 was adopted.

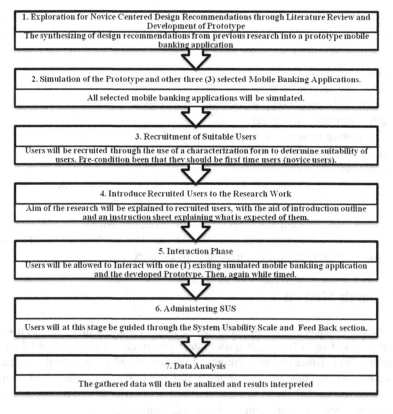

Fig. 1. Research Frame Work

3.1 Exploration for Novice Centered Design Recommendations and Development of Prototype

Analyzed through literature review, the prototype mobile banking application was developed based on five (5) out of eight (8) design recommendations related to the mobile banking application context were selected. The selected design recommendations were based on how they fit into the mobile banking context outlined below. Others were more applicable in the health domain and other contexts. Thus the implemented design recommendations are as follows:

- Provide graphical clues
- Provide voice annotation support wherever possible
- Minimize hierarchical structures
- Avoid requiring nonnumeric text input
- Avoid menus that require scrolling

3.2 Simulated Functionalities

In the interaction phase, the research work focused on predefined tasks (transaction tasks) on which users were tested. Selected were transactions that seemed to be the widest spread and carried out by users over the counter and through ATMs machines. They are as follows:

- Balance Inquiry
- Airtime recharge
- Intra bank transfer
- Interbank transfer
- Transaction History

3.3 Recruiting Suitable Users

The population of interest for this study was non mobile banking users also known as novice users or first time users. A total of 20 participants were randomly selected and recruited for each of the three (3) comparative studies. The groups consisted of individuals within and around Niger State, Nigeria. Suitable users were recruited through the use of a characterization forms. These were pre-test questionnaire, meant to ascertain most importantly that they were first time users. Also, demographic details and other information on their internet and banking experience were gathered.

3.4 Introducing Users to the Research Work

The recruited users on qualification were introduced to the overall aim and objective of the study via a guide line document. As any pre-meditated associations with respect to brand loyalty and experience would affect the research result, fictional banking names were given to the four simulated banking applications as shown in Table 1.

Table 1. List of existing Banks simulated and tested

Bank name	Details
BBank	Simulation prototype based on design recommendation gathered from previous research tested against other Banks in each comparative study
ABank	Simulation of an existing mobile banking application tested against BBank in the first comparative study
CBank	Simulation of an existing mobile banking application tested against BBank in the second comparative study
DBank	Simulation of an existing mobile banking application tested against BBank in the third comparative study

3.5   Interaction Phase

In order to further engage recruited users, an outlined scenario of a recently established bank was painted to the recruited users. The scenario explained that the bank wanted to select from two prototypes a mobile banking application for their customers. The bank hope to obtain user perception concerning the user interfaces designs. Recruited users were asked to assume recently enrolling with the bank. For the purpose of the evaluation, they were told they owned one (1) savings account and were already subscribed to the mobile banking option. A set of tasks on Table 2 expected of them to perform was outlined in an instruction sheet given and explained to them.

Table 2. List of tasks to be performed by users

Task	Task type	Task details
Task 1	Balance inquiry	Users were expected to check their account balance
Task 2	Airtime recharge	Users were expected to purchase airtime via the application
Task 3	Intra-bank transfer	Users were expected to transfer funds from their account to another person's within the same bank
Task 4	Inter-bank transfer	Users were expected to transfer funds from their account to another person's banking with another bank
Task 5	Transaction history	Users were expected to trace a past transaction from there transaction history log

3.6   Data Analysis and Method

On successfully completing the tasks, the System Usability Scale (SUS) tool questionnaire developed by Brooke in 1986 [23] was administered. The term "system" was replaced with "mobile application". The SUS tool is a 10-item questionnaire that reveals usability in terms of three (3) parameters; efficiency, effectiveness and satisfaction. Table 3 defines and gives the meaning of each parameter.

Table 3. Definition of SUS parameters

S/No	Parameters	Definition and Meaning
1	Effectiveness	The ability of users to complete tasks using the system, and the quality of the output of those tasks
2	Efficiency	The level of resource consumed in performing tasks
3	Satisfaction	Users' subjective reactions to using the system)

The SUS tool is deemed as highly robust, low cost, and versatile [24]. It has been tried and tested for almost 30 years and has proven dependable for evaluating the usability of systems compared to industry standards [24]. It gives a global view of subjective assessments of usability. It has been used in over 200 studies for usability evaluation. According to a research by Tullis and Stetson, SUS performs best across sample sizes of at least 12–14 participants [25]. Also according to [26] a sample size of 20 per group across the 3 groups is sufficient to run the needed quantitative analysis.

The data analysis for each comparative study were performed in four steps which are:

- SUS Scores Computation.
- Paired T-Test analysis on the SUS Scores.
- Average Task Completion Time Computation.
- Paired T-Test analysis on the Average Task Completion Time Computation.

3.7 Paired T-Test

On obtaining both SUS scores for both applications, the SUS scores were then subjected to a Paired T-Test to test for any statistical significant difference. The paired T-Test analysis assumed an alpha (α also known as Level of Significance or Level of Certainty) value of 0.05 (CI: 95%), and the results interpreted. The t-tests were conducted based on two hypotheses.

Firstly, the Null hypotheses, that there exists no statistical significant difference between the mean SUS scores of both banks tested ($H_o: \mu_1 - \mu_2 = 0$).

Secondly, the alternative hypotheses, that there exists a statistical significant difference between the mean SUS scores of both banks tested ($H_o: \mu_1 - \mu_2 \neq 0$).

3.8 Exploring for User Constraints Before the Comparative Study

The available Usability Inspection Methods (UIMs) are the Cognitive Walkthrough (CW) and Heuristic Evaluation (HE). The HEs are used by inspectors to examine Graphical User Interfaces (GUIs) seeking for possible usability constrains. When any usability constrains is found, it is reported in association to its corresponding violated heuristics. The CW on the other hand, are used by inspectors to analyze if a user can make sense of interaction steps and flow as they proceed in a pre-defined task.

The combination of HE and CW was employed to explore for more novice centered usability constraints before engaging recruited users. It involved the evaluation of screen shot (screen grabs), from specific task perspectives (as listed in Table 2 earlier) of the existing mobile banking applications transaction flow. They were arranged sequentially following the transaction flow sequence of each task and examined for possible usability constraints.

Secondly, to expose more novices centered usability constraints, additional feedback were gathered in a debriefing session. The debriefing session took the form of a semi structured interview, verbally interacting with users on successfully interacting with the simulated applications. This helped users convey their perception of both interfaces.

4   Result

Recruited users for all three (3) groups of the comparative study were novice. That is, first time user of the mobile banking application. Table 4 is a summary of their demographic details.

Table 4. Summary of the three groups demographic details and SUS Scores.

		Group 1		Group 2		Group 3	
Sex	M	8		10		9	
	F	12		10		11	
Age group	18–25	8		7		11	
	26–33	9		8		5	
	34–41	3		5		3	
	42 and Above	0		0		1	
SUS	SUS Scores	ABank	37.25	CBank	47.00	DBank	43.13
		BBank	85.25	BBank	85.25	BBank	83.88
		Diff	*48.00*	*Diff*	*38.25*	*Diff*	*40.75*

A total of 20 novice users were randomly recruited for each of the comparative study groups. According to the data gathered from the administered pre-test questionnaire, all participants had at least one active bank account at the time of participation with no mobile banking application experience. Participants had similar levels of experience in internet usage. Participation was entirely voluntary and each individual consented to participate in the study.

4.1   Group 1 (ABank Against BBank)

Figure 2 shows the mean SUS scores for the ABank and BBank interface. The score range is 0–100.

Figure 2 indicates an improved overall score and rating for the BBank (simulation of prototype mobile banking application base on design recommendations gathered from previous researches) interface compared to ABank (simulation of an existing mobile banking application). The mean SUS score for the BBank was 85.25 and that of ABank 37.25 with a difference of 48.00 observed between both the interfaces. To test the significance of the result, we conducted a paired t-test analysis with an alpha value of

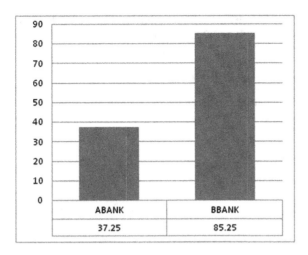

Fig. 2. ABank against BBank.

0.05 (CI: 95%). There was a significant difference in the scores for ABank (M = 37.25, SD = 22.37) and BBank (M = 85.25, SD = 11.64) interfaces; t(19) = −7.91, p <=0.001. The t-test analysis also showed a high degree of variance (ABank = 500.51, BBank = 135.46).

All participants managed to complete their given tasks in both interfaces. Figure 3 shows the average time spent in seconds for each task across participants.

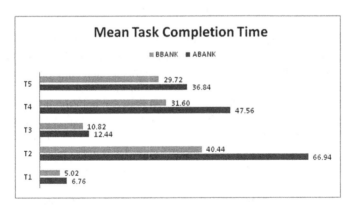

Fig. 3. ABank against BBank.

Figure 3 show's that participants in general completed the set tasks within a shorter period of time via the BBank interface. The mean completion time for ABank interface was 34.11 s and 23.52 s for the BBank interface. However a paired t-test analysis with an alpha value of 0.05 (CI: 95%) showed there was no significant difference between the mean task completion times for ABank (M = 34.11,

SD = 24.92) and the mean task completion times for BBank (M = 23.52, SD = 14.95) interfaces; t(5) = 2.22, p = 0.09.

4.2   Group 2 (CBank Againt BBank)

Figure 4 shows the mean SUS scores for the CBank and BBank interface. The score range is 0–100.

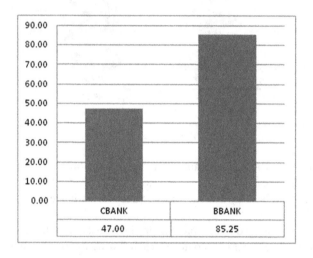

Fig. 4. CBank against BBank.

Figure 4 indicates an improved overall score and rating for the BBank (simulation of prototype mobile banking application base on design recommendations gathered from previous researches) interface compared to CBank (simulation of another existing mobile banking application). The mean SUS score for the BBank was 85.25 and that of CBank 47.00 with a difference of 38.25 observed between both the interfaces. To test the significance of the result, we conducted a paired t-test analysis with an alpha value of 0.05 (CI: 95%). There was a significant difference in the scores for CBank (M = 47.00, SD = 23.79) and BBank (M = 85.25, SD = 9.13) interfaces; t(19) = −7.66, p <=0.001. The t-test analysis also showed a high degree of variance (CBank = 536.55, BBank = 83.48).

All participants managed to complete their given tasks in both interfaces. Figure 5 shows the average time spent in seconds for each task across participants.

Figure 5 show's that participants in general completed the set tasks within a shorter period of time via the BBank interface. The mean completion time for CBank interface was 31.59 s and 22.40 s for the BBank interface. A paired t-test analysis with an alpha value of 0.05 (CI: 95%) showed there was a significant difference between the mean task completion times for CBank (M = 31.59, SD = 19.81) and the mean task completion times for BBank (M = 22.40, SD = 14.75) interfaces; t(5) = 3.97, p = 0.017.

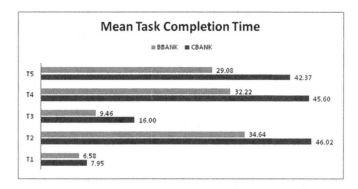

Fig. 5. CBank against BBank.

4.3 Group 3 (DBank Againt BBank)

Figure 6 shows the mean SUS scores for the DBank and BBank interface. The score range is 0–100.

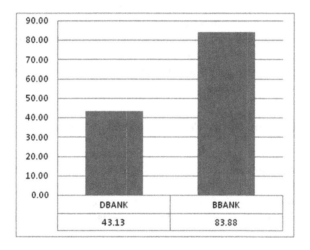

Fig. 6. DBank against BBank.

Figure 6 indicates an improved overall score and rating for the BBank (simulation of prototype mobile banking application base on design recommendations gathered from previous researches) interface compared to DBank (simulation of an existing mobile banking application). The mean SUS score for the BBank was 83.88 and that of DBank 43.13 with a difference of 40.75 observed between both the interfaces. To test the significance of the result, we conducted a paired t-test analysis with an alpha value of 0.05 (CI: 95%). There was a significant difference in the scores for DBank (M = 83.88, SD = 22.62) and BBank (M = 83.88, SD = 10.08) interfaces; $t(19) = -6.06$, $p <= 0.001$. The t-test analysis also showed a high degree of variance (DBank = 511.75, BBank = 101.62).

All participants managed to complete their given tasks in both interfaces. Figure 7 shows the average time spent in seconds for each task across participants.

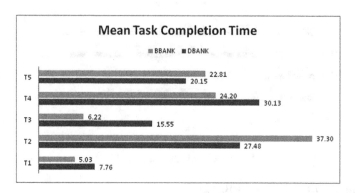

Fig. 7. DBank against BBank.

Figure 7 show's that participants in general completed tasks 1, tasks 2, tasks 4, within a shorter period of time via the BBank interface. However, it took longer time on task 2 and task 5. The mean completion time for DBank interface was 20.21 s and 29.22 s for the BBank interface. A paired t-test analysis with an alpha value of 0.05 (CI: 95%) showed there was no significant difference between the mean task completion times for CBank (M = 31.59, SD = 10.46) and the mean task completion times for BBank (M = 22.40, SD = 15.47) interfaces; t(5) = 3.97, p = 0.017.

4.4   Exploring for More Novice Centered Usability Constraints

Novice centered usability constraints were sought using various techniques before, during and after the comparative studies involving the recruited users. A combination of Cognitive Walkthrough (CW) and Heuristic Evaluation were employed to explore for usability constraints early before the prototypes were developed.

First noticed was the transaction flow length especially that of ABank. The transaction flow seems lengthy and was assumed to require quite an amount of patience and cognitive load most especially by novice users. Thus to remedy this, the research recommends for such target audience, transaction flow should be brief and short as adopted in the simulation of the design recommendation based prototype.

Secondly, inconsistency in keyboard input format of touch screen phones from ABank and DBank was observed. Input field such as account number and phone number simply requires a numeric keyboard format to pop up. However it was observed that in some transactions, such input field came up with an alphabetic keyboard format. This implies that users would need to be knowledgeable enough to re-format the on screen keyboard to a numeric keyboard format by toggling through. This clearly would require more time and patience by novice users to perform those transactions there by taking much more transaction time than necessary. This could also pose an inconvenience to a user who cannot toggle through the various available keyboard formats, frustrate those who can as they would need to input alphabets before realizing the need to reformate the keyboard and restart the entry all over again. As a remedy, it is recommended that there should be consistency in linking each input field to the most appropriate input keyboard format.

A number of other constraints observed were consistent with constraints already established from previous researches. Such were discoverability of functionalities, scroll bars, the use of graphical clues and audio annotation. Amongst all, the most prominent observed from the use of the prototype was the incorporations of graphical clues and audio annotations. They were clearly observed to have positively impacted the ease of use from the recruited users point of view. When asked for strengths of the prototype, majority of users mentioned the presence of these features and confirmed they made use of the prototype much easier to interact with. These were also observed to be responsible for the reason majority strongly responded positively to the SUS question number 1 (I think that I would like to use this application frequently).

Lastly, it was observed from the debriefing session that users would prefer a striped down version of mobile banking applications just as the prototype was based on. That is, a version void of functionalities they would rarely need. They admitted they would find such easer to interact with rather than surfing through deep hierarchical structures each time they needed to perform important functions, constantly distracted by functions they would rarely need.

5 Discussion

Results from data analysis proved the researcher's initial hypothesis to be true. The initial hypothesis that existing Nigerian mobile banking applications could be improved upon. This was based on the fact that there exist a wide gap between research based design recommendations prototype (BBank) and design prototypes of existing Nigerian mobile banking applications (ABank, CBank and DBank). Results show an improved usability especially in user satisfaction of BBank and this may consequently have a positive impact on the adoption and acceptance of mobile banking, particularly from a usability perspective. Participants spent less time in performing transactions on the BBank in groups 1 and 2. However, there was a statistical significant difference in mean task completion time of BBank only in group 2.

Results show they were a bit slower on task 2 and 5 in group 3, however still appeared to be more satisfied using the BBank interface. In addition to the previously established research based design recommendations, this research suggests the following design recommendation for mobile banking application development:

- That transaction length be kept as short as possible
- Input regions be properly and consistently formatted to corresponding appropriate keyboard formats especially for touch screen phones
- Functionality striped down versions of such applications is made available for such users (novice users) to reduce the complexity in their favor.

6 Conclusion

The prototype developed based on research (previously established) design recommendations performed well and better than the existing banking application prototypes across the three (3) comparative studies. Recruited users exhibited higher levels of satisfaction with the design recommendation based prototype than the existing applications. The researchers hope the results presented will draw the attention of mobile banking application developers and Managers of banks to the fact that there is a need to take seriously the peculiar needs of their customer base which includes all kinds of user. Majority are novice users and would only get the best out of mobile banking applications if the applications are developed based on established design recommendations from research. This will boost the adoption level and help achieve a deeper penetration of developmental services much needed across developing and underdeveloped nations.

References

1. UNCTAD: Science and Technology for Development: A New Paradigm for ICT. Information Economy Report, New York (2007). http://unctad.org/en/docs/sdteecb20071_en.pdf
2. Poushter, J., Oates, R.: Cell phones in Africa: Communication Lifeline. Pew Research Centre, Washington DC (2015). http://www.pewglobal.org/2015/04/15/cell-phones-in-africa-communication-lifeline/
3. Thulani, D., Tofara, C., Langton, R.: Adoption and use of internet banking in Zimbabwe: an exploratory study. J. Internet Bank. Commer. 14(1) (2009). http://www.icommercecentral.com/open-access/adoption-and-use-of-internet-banking-in-zimbabwe-an-exploratory-study.pdf
4. Bertolucci, J.: Smartphone Sales Boom - Who Needs A Laptop? (2012). http://www.pcworld.com/article/249313/smartphone_sales_boom_who_needs_a_laptop_.html
5. BBC: Global smartphone sales are up by nearly 50% (2012). http://www.bbc.co.uk/newsround/20330429
6. ITU: ICT Statistics newslog - m-banking (2015). http://www.itu.int/ITU-D/ict/newslog/CategoryView,category,m-banking.aspx
7. Donner, J.: Research approaches to mobile use in the developing world: a review of the literature. Inf. Soc. 24, 140–159 (2008). doi:10.1080/01972240802019970
8. UNESCO: UNESCO Institute of Statistics: Literacy data (2011). http://www.uis.unesco.org/FactSheets/Documents/FS16-2011-Literacy-EN.pdf
9. Boyera, S.: Mobile Web for Social Development Roadmap (2009). http://www.w3.org/TR/2009/NOTE-mw4d-roadmap-20091117/
10. Chittaro, L.: Designing visual interfaces for mobile applications. In: 3rd ACM SIGCHI Symposium on Engineering Interactive Computing System, pp. 331–332. ACM, New York (2011). doi:10.1145/1996461.1996550
11. Chaudry, B.M., Siek, K.A., Welch, J.L., Connelly, K.H.: Mobile interface design for low-literacy populations. In: 2nd ACM SIGHIT International Health Informatics Symposium, pp. 91–100. ACM, New York (2012). doi:10.1145/2110363.2110377
12. Matyila, P.M.L., Albert, R., Botha, A., Sibiya, G.: The design of accessible and usable mobile services for low literate users. In: International Conference on Adaptive Science and Technology (ICAST), pp. 1–6 (2013). doi:10.1109/ICASTech.2013.6707504

13. Biljon, J.V., Renuad, K.: Validating mobile phone design guidelines: focusing on the elderly in a developing country. In: Annual Conference of the South African Institute of Computer Scientists and Information Technologists, No. 44 (2016). doi:10.1145/2987491.2987492

14. Jeongyun, H., Ham, D.H., Park, S., Song, C., Yoon, W.C.: A framework for evaluating the usability of mobile phones based on multi-level, hierarchical model of usability factors. In: Interaction with Computer. ScienceDirect, pp. 263–275 (2009). http://dx.doi.org/10.1016/j.intcom.2009.05.006

15. Ivory, M.Y., Hearst, M.A.: The state of the art in automating usability evaluation of user interfaces. ACM Comput. Surv. **33**(4), 470–516 (2001). doi:10.1145/503112.503114

16. Medhi, I., Patnaik, S., Brunskill, E., Gautama, S.N.N., Thies, W., Toyama, K.: Designing mobile interfaces for novice and low-literacy users. ACM Trans. Comput. Hum. Interact. (TOCHI), Article No. 2 (2011). doi:10.1145/1959022.1959024

17. Grisedale, S., Graves, M., Grünsteidl, A.: Designing a graphical user interface for healthcare workers in rural India. In: ACM SIGCHI Conference on Human Factors in Computing Systems, Atlanta, USA, pp. 471–478 (1997). doi:10.1145/258549.258869

18. Warschauer, M.: Demystifying the digital divide. In: Scientific American, pp. 42–48 (2003). http://edf.stanford.edu/sites/default/files/Warschauer_2003_scientificamerican0803-42.pdf

19. Chipchase, J.: Understanding non-literacy as a barrier to mobile phone communication (2005). http://research.nokia.com/bluesky/non-literacy-001-2005/index.html

20. Thatcher, A., Mahlangu, S., Zimmerman, C.: Accessibility of ATMs for the functionally illiterate through icon-based interfaces. In: Behaviour and Information Technology, pp. 65–81 (2006). doi:10.1080/01449290500102128

21. Findlater, L., Balakrishnan, R., Toyama, K.: Comparing semiliterate and illiterate users' ability to transition from audio + text to text-only interaction. In: SIGCHI Conference on Human Factors in Computing Systems, pp. 1751–1760 (2009). doi:10.1145/1518701.1518971

22. Walton, M., Vukovic', V., Marsden, G.: Visual literacy as challenge to the internationalisation of interfaces: a study of South African student web users. In: CHI 2002 Development Consortium, Minneapolis, USA, pp 530–531 (2002). doi:10.1145/506443.506465

23. Qi, X.M., Uddin, M.N., Geun-Sik, J.: The wordNet based semantic relationship between tags in folksonomies. In: 2nd International Conference on Computer and Automation Engineering (ICCAE), Singapore (2010). doi:10.1109/ICCAE.2010.5451821

24. Fung, T.K.F.: Banking with a personalized touch: Examining the impact of website customization on commitment. In: Electronic Commerce Research, pp. 296–390 (2008)

25. Wessels, L., Drennan, J.: An investigation of consumer acceptance of M-banking. Int. J. Bank Mark. 547–568 (2010). http://dx.doi.org/10.1108/02652321011085194

26. Universal Access in Human-Computer Interaction: Universal Access to Information and Knowledge. 8th International Conference, Heraklion, Crete, Greece (2014). ISBN: 978-3-319-07440-5

Feasibility of Utilizing E-Mental Health with Mobile APP Interface for Social Support Enhencement: A Conceptional Solution for Postpartum Depression in Taiwan

Wen-Ko Chiou[1(✉)], Chun-Ying Kao[1], Liang-Ming Lo[2], Ding-Hau Huang[3], Ming-Hsu Wang[4], and Bi-Hui Chen[5]

[1] Department of Industrial Design, Chang Gung University, Tao-Yuan, Taiwan
wkchiu@mail.cgu.edu.tw
[2] Department of Obstetrics and Gynecology, Chang Gung Memorial Hospital, Taipei, Taiwan
[3] College of Management and Design, Ming Chi University of Technology, New Taipei, Taiwan
[4] Graduate School of Management, Chang Gung University, Tao-Yuan, Taiwan
[5] Department of Business Administration, Chihlee University of Technology, New Taipei, Taiwan

Abstract. Postpartum depression (PPD) is a common issue in global scale. Social support enhancement were proved to be effective for reducing PPD. Currently, there are few researches in Taiwan concerning the subject which were mentioned above. In the other hand, applying E-mental health (EMH) services for social support enhancement has become a trend in modern society. However, few EMH services were designed to target PPD audiences. This research aims to investigate the condition of PPD and social support in Taiwan, in addition, the research also took a look into local reception of EMH services. Questionnaire had been applied to 224 postpartum women through clinical field and forums on the Internet. The result indicates that 27.7% of participant shows potential high risk for PPD, the rate of potential high risk is higher than global average. Negative Correlation between PPD and social support were confirmed. Participants receive more informal social support compares to formal social support. Approximately 90% of the participants were user of EMH services (Social media, Chatroom, Internet forum/Bulletin Board System). About 30% of the participant utilize smartphone APP for EMH services, 25% the participant were unaware of the existence of smartphone APP for EMH services. According to the result, smartphone APP for EMH services were proposed to be a suitable solution for PPD in Taiwan.

Keywords: Mobile application interface · Postpartum depression · Social support · E-Mental health · Edinburgh postnatal depression scale

1 Introduction

1.1 Postpartum Depression

Postpartum depression (PPD) are categorized as one of the non-psychotic major depression, the global prevalence rate of PPD are approximately 10 ~ 15% [1–3]. The major

A. Marcus and W. Wang (Eds.): DUXU 2017, Part II, LNCS 10289, pp. 198–207, 2017.
DOI: 10.1007/978-3-319-58637-3_15

cause of PPD is believed to be rapid fluctuation of hormone in postpartum condition, other risk factors include a personal or family history of depression (prenatal depression included), low social support, impactful event during pregnancy, life pressure, and gestational diabetes mellitus [4, 5].

PPD often occurs in the postpartum period between 2–4 weeks to 1 year. The major symptoms of PPD include depressed mood, sadness, irritability, weeping, sleep and eating disturbances, feelings of worthlessness/excessive/inappropriate guilt, decreased concentration/ability to make decisions, feeling inadequate in taking care of the baby. The symptoms can persist for 2 weeks to months. For severe cases, the PPD patient has considered a plan to act on suicidal thoughts or has thoughts about harming her infant, thus, intervention such as medical assistant and care should be carried out.

The Edinburgh Postnatal Depression Scale (EPDS) [6] is a popular tool, which serves as a quick assessment for mental condition. The ideal screening time falls in the range between 2 weeks and 6 months after childbirth [7]. The woman who has been assessed with a positive result will be further evaluated by doctors, according to the Diagnostic and Statistical Manual of Mental Disorders, five edition (DSM-V).

Current treatment for PPD includes medicinal treatment and non-medicinal treatment. Although medicinal treatment is relative effective, the side effect of the medicine may raise the concern of breast-feeding mothers [8]. Non-medicinal treatment, in the other hand, is considered to be side effect free. Common non-medicinal treatment includes psychotherapy, supportive group, acupuncture, and yoga. Medical personnel often encourage postpartum to do activities, which concerns exercises, bask in the sun, and expand the comfort zone [9].

1.2 Social Support

Social support is believed to be one of a major factor that influences and indicates PPD condition [5, 10, 11]. Social support is generalized defined as material, cognition and emotional support provided by social network member or professionals [12, 13]. Social support can be divided into formal support and informal support, according to the source provider of support [14].

Formal support is provided by professionals (for example, medical personnel and social human service workers). Postpartum women often learn knowledge and skills from nurse or midwife, and being helped in the process transforming from women to a mother [15, 16]. Postpartum disease supportive group lead by professionals were effective in experiential support and reducing the sense of isolation for postpartum psychosis patient [17].

Informal support is provided by social network members (for example, family, friends, coworkers, supervisors, peers), and serves as the major source of support for postpartum women [18]. Influential of family members are believed to be the greatest [19], and practical support gained from partners and mother are considered very important [20]. In addition, peers provide emotional, information and evaluation support through experience sharing, and the degree of satisfaction are positive correlated with the among of time of the support [21].

1.3   E-Mental Health

E-Mental Health (EMH) system is a modern solution for psychological issues. The key functions of EMH system include information provision [22], assist of assessment, condition monitoring [23], intervention [24], and social support enhancement [25]. The tools and media such as Internet forum, chatroom, blog, and social media are often involved. Advantage of online community includes convenience, anonymous, interaction without opinion.

Social interaction for postpartum women is often reduced, for they tend to stay home for baby caring and physical recovery. By utilizing Internet, postpartum women can reach out to the world and establish connection with people, thus, sense of loneliness and depression can be reduced, as the result of social support and self-esteem enhancement [26]. For example, private group in Facebook are often used as a forum, user tend to exchange their opinion, and provide social support to each other [27, 28].

EMH services are flourishing in recent years, due to the widespread of smart phones and mobile applications (APP). Cost for development are comparatively low for APP compares to traditional mental health services. APP are not limited by location and time, thus it can be more reachable to the user. According to WHO, the key word "depression" hold the 2nd place for search popularity of mobile health APP, second only to "diabetes" [29]. Pregnant women tend to use smartphones for Internet browsing, and utilize APP for information gathering. However, for APP concerning depression, there are about only 23% percent of the app provides suitable functions and contents, and there are few supportive mobile health APP to be found [30].

1.4   Purpose of Research

There are few researches in Taiwan concerning PPD and social support currently, and there are little to none researches concerning suitability for utilizing EMH as a solution for PPD. The aims of this research are: (1) To investigate the condition of PPD in Taiwan, and try to comprehend the scope of the demand, (2) Inspect the condition of social support for postpartum women in Taiwan, and analyze the correlation between social support and PPD. (3) To investigate the utilization rate and circumstances of use for EMH in Taiwan, and consider whether it is suitable or not to utilizing EMH as a solution for PPD in Taiwan, and propose a fitting direction for EMH design.

2   Methods

2.1   Design

The course of survey started from October 2016 and finished in January 2017. Participants were asked to fill out an online questionnaire established with Google Forms.

2.2 Participants

Postpartum women were recruited in clinical field of Taipei Chang Gung Memorial Hospital and PTT Bulletin Board System (BBS). The criterions of eligibility for participant were: (1) Taiwanese only, due to the language barrier of foreigner. (2) Fluent with Chinese mandarin. (3) Age from 20 to 40 approximately. (4) Less than 1 year from date of childbirth. (5) Singleton baby only. (6) First-time mother and mother with multiple children were included.

2.3 Assessments

The questionnaire consist of 4 parts, which are: (1) Demographical data (age, education, occupation, number of children, age of infant, numbers of dates stayed in hospital after childbirth), (2) Multidimensional Scale of Perceived Social Support (MSPSS), (3) Taiwanese version of the Edinburgh Postnatal Depression Scale (EPDS-T), (4) the questionnaire of utilization rate and circumstances of use for EMH (social media, chatroom, forum/BBS) and related APP.

The Multidimensional Scale of Perceived Social Support (MSPSS) [31] is a 12-item research tool designed to measure perceptions social support. The subscales are categorized by 3 source provider of social support, which are: (1) medical personnel subscale (item 1, 2, 5, 10), (2) family subscale (item 3, 4, 8, 11), (3) friend subscale (item 6, 7, 9, 12). Score ranged from 1 to 7 were measured, and mean score were presented as result of MSPSS. Cronbach's α coefficient for the whole scale, medical personnel subscale, family subscale, and friend subscale were 0.88, 0.88, 0.89, 0.86 respectively.

The EPDS is a 10-item self-report instrument designed as a screening questionnaire to detect postnatal depression. In this study, we use Taiwan version of EPDS (EPDS-T) [32]. For each item, a positive score ranged from 0 to 3 were measured. Maximum score is 30, with a cut-off of 12/13. Participant with a score >12 are identified as mentally suffering, and should be aided by clinical intervention. In addition, a specific item in EPDS-T indicates suicidal tendency of the participant. Cronbach's α coefficient for EPDS-T is 0.89.

2.4 Data Analysis

The data collected were analyzed by SPSS 20.0.0 statistic software. Descriptive statistic were applied for basic data analyze, T-test was applied to analyze relationship between social support and PPD. Chi-square was applied to analyze detailed relationship between subscale of social support and PPD.

3 Results and Discussion

3.1 Demographic Characteristics

In this study, 224 postpartum women were recruited. The basic demographic characteristics of participant are listed below, please refer to Table 1 for additional information:

(1) Average age: 32.11 (SD 3.5), (2) numbers of dates stayed in hospital after childbirth: 4.09 (SD 1.4), (3) first-time mother: 74.6%.

Table 1. Demographic characteristic of the participants (n = 224)

Characteristic	Total		High risk group		Non-high risk group		χ^2	P
	n	%	n	%	n	%		
Number of participants	224	100.0	62	27.7	162	72.3		
Previous depression							7.120	.008
Diagnosed	9	4.0	6	9.7	3	1.9		
Non-diagnosed	215	96.0	56	90.3	159	98.1		
Age of maternal (in years)								NS
20–25	7	3.1						
26–30	65	29.0						
31–35	111	49.6						
36–40	41	18.3						
Age of infant (in months)								NS
0–3	125	55.8						
4–6	54	24.1						
7–9	25	11.2						
10–12	20	8.9						
Education								NS
High school	7	3.1						
Junior college	14	6.3						
College or university	129	57.6						
Graduate school	74	33.0						
Occupation								NS
Full-time	139	62.1						
Homemaker	85	37.9						

NS indicates not significant.

3.2 Prevalence of PPD

According to the point of cut off (12/13) of EPDS-T, participant with a score exceeding 12 are identified as high risk group for PPD. The result shows 27.7% of the participants were identified as high risk group for PDD. According to Table 2, the score for the participant ranged from 0 to 25.

Generally, previous studies indicate the rate for high risk group are ranged between 5.5–16.6%. A study concerning influence of postnatal depression on obstetric and perinatal outcomes, which involves 23220 participants, shows 10.4% rate of the participant scoring ≥12 [33]. A study involved 528 prenatal participant shows 5.5% for rate of high risk group [34]. 16.6% high risk rate were identified for a research concerning ethnic

Table 2. Percentage of EPDS score

Scores of EPDS	n	%
0–5	44	19.6
6–10	92	41.1
11–15	54	24.1
16–20	27	12.1
21–25	7	3.1

minorities in London [35]. According to Table 3, locally, result from previous studies in Taiwan indicated a range of 19.0–21.0% for PDD high risk rate.

Table 3. Prevalence of high risk of PPD in Taiwan

Author	Sample size	EPDS Cut-off	Time frame (days after childbirth)	High risk of PPD (%)
Huang and Mathers (2001)	100	12/13	0–3 months	19.0
Our study	224	12/13	0–3 months	14.7
Heh et al. (2004)	186	9/10	1–4 weeks	21.0
Our study	224	9/10	1–4 weeks	6.2

By comparing the result of this research and previous studies under the condition of equal cut-off point and timing, we found out that the local high risk rate has declined, but the high risk rate in Taiwan is comparative high than general high risk rate globally. The scope and severity of local PPD problem were demonstrated, a solution for the problem would be valuable.

The severity of depression is positively correlated with history of depression. The results of this study are consistent with previous study [4, 5]. According to Table 1, 4% of the participants were diagnosed with depression. The relative risk of participant with history of depression were 2.6 times higher than participant without history of depression.

Postpartum women stayed in hospital for only a short period (4.09 days in average), EPDS assessment are seldom applied widely in the period [38]. For the WHO suggestion, best screening opportunity are believed to be the return visit to the obstetrics in 4–6 week after childbirth, and the visit to pediatrics in 2 month after childbirth. Return visit to the obstetrics are often neglected or overlooked. As for the visit to pediatrics, attentions are paid mostly to the infant. Thus, mental state mother are not heeded [39]. According to the research result, smartphone APP is extensively accepted in Taiwan, suitability for applying EMH with APP interface as a convenient EDPS assessment interface were verified.

3.3 Social Support and PPD

According to Table 4, score of EPDS-T are negatively correlated with score of social support and its subscale (medical personnel subscale, family subscale, and friends subscale). The result indicates that enhancing social support is a suitable counter-measure for local PPD problem.

Table 4. Correlations between social support and PPD (n = 224)

Social support	High risk group (n = 62)		Non-high risk group (n = 162)		T test		Total		Correlation coefficient, r
	Mean	SD	Mean	SD	t	p	Mean	SD	
Total social support	4.65	0.89	5.11	0.80	−3.779	.000	4.98	0.85	−.320**
Formal support	3.80	1.30	4.33	1.19	−2.904	.004	4.18	1.24	−.184**
Informal support	5.08	1.00	5.52	0.84	−3.307	.001	5.40	0.90	−.323**
Family support	5.02	1.17	5.59	0.98	−3.743	.000	5.43	1.06	−.371**
Friend support	5.18	1.14	5.46	0.90	−1.949	NS	5.38	0.98	−.185**

** P < .01, NS indicates not significant.

Previous study shows informal support and PPD are significant correlated, on the other hand, correlation between informal support and PPD are insignificant [19]. In this research, social support of non-high risk groups significantly higher than high risk group. Postpartum women receive informal support (mean = 5.40, SD 0.90) more than formal support (mean = 4.18, SD 1.24). Reinforcement for formal support may be helpful for countering PPD problem.

For informal support, participant received more support from family than friends. Family and friends are proved to be major source of support for postpartum women [18]. Both family support and friends support are negatively correlated with PPD in this research, implying the feasibility of developing related EMH features for these targeted audiences.

3.4   Reception for EMH and Smartphone APP as EMH Interface

88.4% of the participants were identified as EMH services user (current user or former user). 71.4% were identified with experience of joining social media groups; 49.1% were identified with experience using chatroom; 74.6% were identified with experience using forum/BBS. the high reception of EMH indicates the proposal for EMH as PPD countermeasure can be perceived positively.

All of participants show the habit of using smarts phones. There is 66.5% being identified for using related app. Although the reception are positive, the content of EMH with APP interface were not perceive as trustworthy enough, only 35% of the APP were recognized for including information that is reliable or intact [40]. The 28.6% of participants are unaware of the existence of EMH APP. In addition, most of the participant are identified as member of online supportive group, such supportive group includes mother group, mother chatroom, APP for postpartum community, and forum/BBS. The reception of APP as EMH interface shows there are space for improvement, especially in information quality and availability for EMH with APP interface.

3.5 Limitations

The limitations of this research includes survey environment, category of EMH, and data analysis. (1) For survey environment, conditions were not equivalent between clinical environment and web survey. The researcher interprets meaning of question for participant in clinical environment, but not on the web survey. (2) The content of EMH have been slightly modified. There a no distinctive difference for contextual meaning between the word "Internet forum" and "BBS" in Taiwan in general, so the researcher made modification and combined the two word into a single one, which is "Internet forum/BBS". Blog is personal, and considered to be non-mainstream social media. In Taiwan, few people follow and subscribe bloggers proactively, so the item concerning blog in EMH was removed. For the reason mentioned above, the reliability and validity for questionnaires applied in this research should be verified in the future. (3) For data analysis, this research applied only correlation analyze between social support and PPD. Previous studies generally examine the relationship further by utilizing path analysis. Thus, path analysis should be carry in the future to inspect condition of influence between the two factors.

4   Conclusion

This research aims to investigate the condition of PPD and social support in Tai-wan. In addition, the research also took a look into local reception of EMH services. Based on the result, conclusions are made and listed as below:

1. The rate of PPD high risk group (Scoring >12 in EPDS-T) is comparatively high in Taiwan, and room for improvement exist for EPDS assessment. Indicating a serious problem concerns a large proportion of local population.
2. Social support is verified as a negative correlated factor for PPD, thus, it may be suitable to be manipulated as PPD countermeasure. Participants receive higher informal social support than formal social support. For informal support, participant received more support from family than friends.
3. A positively perceived opportunity gap exists in developing EMH for PDD, EMH with APP interface is suitable. For local participant, 88.4% were EMH user, 66.5% were user of EMH with APP interface, and 28.6% of the user are unaware of the existence of EMH with APP interface.

Acknowledgments. We have an appreciation for Drs. Zimet, Teng, and Shen, whom provide the permission of using the assessments. On the other hand, many thanks for Dr. Lo provide participants in the clinic to implement the experimental programs.

References

1. Wisner, K.L., Parry, B.L., Piontek, C.M.: Postpartum depression. N. Engl. J. Med. **347**(3), 194–199 (2002)

2. Gavin, N.I., et al.: Perinatal depression: a systematic review of prevalence and incidence. Obstet. Gynecol. **106**(5, Part 1), 1071–1083 (2005)
3. Vesga-López, O., et al.: Psychiatric disorders in pregnant and postpartum women in the United States. Arch. Gen. Psychiatry **65**(7), 805–815 (2008)
4. Milgrom, J., et al.: Antenatal risk factors for postnatal depression: a large prospective study. J. Affect. Disord. **108**(1), 147–157 (2008)
5. Robertson, E., et al.: Antenatal risk factors for postpartum depression: a synthesis of recent literature. Gen. Hosp. Psychiatry **26**(4), 289–295 (2004)
6. Cox, J.L., Holden, J.M., Sagovsky, R.: Detection of postnatal depression: development of the 10-item Edinburgh postnatal depression scale. Br. J. Psychiatry **150**(6), 782–786 (1987)
7. Boyd, R.C., Le, H., Somberg, R.: Review of screening instruments for postpartum depression. Arch. Women's Mental Health **8**(3), 141–153 (2005)
8. Hirst, K.P., Moutier, C.Y.: Postpartum major depression. Women **100**, 17–19 (2010)
9. Field, T., et al.: Yoga and social support reduce prenatal depression, anxiety and cortisol. J. Bodywork Mov. Ther. **17**(4), 397–403 (2013)
10. Beck, C.T.: Predictors of postpartum depression: an update. Nurs. Res. **50**(5), 275–285 (2001)
11. Robertson, E., Celasun, N., Stewart, D.: Risk Factors for Postpartum Depression (2003)
12. Gottlieb, B.H., Bergen, A.E.: Social support concepts and measures. J. Psychosom. Res. **69**(5), 511–520 (2010)
13. Thoits, P.A.: Mechanisms linking social ties and support to physical and mental health. J. Health Soc. Behav. **52**(2), 145–161 (2011)
14. Hogan, B.E., Linden, W., Najarian, B.: Social support interventions: do they work? Clin. Psychol. Rev. **22**(3), 381–440 (2002)
15. Logsdon, M.C., Davis, D.W.: Social and professional support for pregnant and parenting women. MCN Am. J. Matern. Child Nurs. **28**(6), 371–376 (2003)
16. Wilkins, C.: A qualitative study exploring the support needs of first-time mothers on their journey towards intuitive parenting. Midwifery **22**(2), 169–180 (2006)
17. Doucet, S., Letourneau, N., Blackmore, E.R.: Support needs of mothers who experience postpartum psychosis and their partners. J. Obstet. Gynecol. Neonatal. Nurs. **41**(2), 236–245 (2012)
18. Leahy Warren, P.: First-time mothers: social support and confidence in infant care. J. Adv. Nurs. **50**(5), 479–488 (2005)
19. Leahy-Warren, P., McCarthy, G., Corcoran, P.: First-time mothers: social support, maternal parental self-efficacy and postnatal depression. J. Clin. Nurs. **21**(3–4), 388–397 (2012)
20. Häggman-Laitila, A.: Early support needs of Finnish families with small children. J. Adv. Nurs. **41**(6), 595–606 (2003)
21. Dennis, C.-L.: Postpartum depression peer support: maternal perceptions from a randomized controlled trial. Int. J. Nurs. Stud. **47**(5), 560–568 (2010)
22. Santor, D.A., et al.: Online health promotion, early identification of difficulties, and help seeking in young people. J. Am. Acad. Child Adolesc. Psychiatry **46**(1), 50–59 (2007)
23. Heron, K.E., Smyth, J.M.: Ecological momentary interventions: incorporating mobile technology into psychosocial and health behaviour treatments. Br. J. Health. Psychol. **15**(1), 1–39 (2010)
24. Khanna, M.S., Kendall, P.C.: Computer-assisted cognitive behavioral therapy for child anxiety: results of a randomized clinical trial. J. Consult. Clin. Psychol. **78**(5), 737 (2010)
25. Scharer, K.: An internet discussion board for parents of mentally ill young children. J. Child Adolesc. Psychiatr. Nurs. **18**(1), 17–25 (2005)

26. Shaw, L.H., Gant, L.M.: In defense of the Internet: The relationship between Internet communication and depression, loneliness, self-esteem, and perceived social support. Cyberpsychol. Behav. **5**(2), 157–171 (2002)

27. Cavallo, D.N., et al.: A social media–based physical activity intervention: a randomized controlled trial. Am. J. Prev. Med. **43**(5), 527–532 (2012)

28. Herring, S.J., et al.: Using technology to promote postpartum weight loss in urban, low-income mothers: a pilot randomized controlled trial. J. Nutr. Educ. Behav. **46**(6), 610–615 (2014)

29. Martínez-Pérez, B., De La Torre-Díez, I., López-Coronado, M.: Mobile health applications for the most prevalent conditions by the World Health Organization: review and analysis. J. Med. Internet Res. **15**(6), e120 (2013)

30. Shen, N., et al.: Finding a depression app: a review and content analysis of the depression app marketplace. JMIR mHealth uHealth **3**(1), e16 (2015)

31. Zimet, G.D., et al.: The multidimensional scale of perceived social support. J. Pers. Assess. **52**(1), 30–41 (1988)

32. Teng, H.-W., et al.: Screening postpartum depression with the Taiwanese version of the Edinburgh Postnatal Depression Scale. Compr. Psychiatry **46**(4), 261–265 (2005)

33. Navaratne, P., Foo, X.Y., Kumar, S.: Impact of a high Edinburgh Postnatal Depression Scale score on obstetric and perinatal outcomes. Sci. Rep. **6** (2016)

34. Nielsen, D., et al.: Postpartum depression: identification of women at risk. BJOG Int. J. Obstet. Gynaecol. **107**(10), 1210–1217 (2000)

35. Onozawa, K., et al.: High EPDS scores in women from ethnic minorities living in London. Arch. Women's Ment. Health **6**, s51–s55 (2003)

36. Huang, Y.C., Mathers, N.: Postnatal depression–biological or cultural? A comparative study of postnatal women in the UK and Taiwan. J. Adv. Nurs. **33**(3), 279–287 (2001)

37. Heh, S.-S., Coombes, L., Bartlett, H.: The association between depressive symptoms and social support in Taiwanese women during the month. Int. J. Nurs. Stud. **41**(5), 573–579 (2004)

38. Horowitz, J.A., et al.: A community-based screening initiative to identify mothers at risk for postpartum depression. J. Obstet. Gynecol. Neonatal. Nurs. **40**(1), 52–61 (2011)

39. Nicole, L., et al.: Canadian mothers' perceived support needs during postpartum depression. J. Obstet. Gynecol. Neonatal. Nurs. **36**(5), 441–449 (2007)

40. Declercq, E.R., et al.: Listening to Mothers III: Pregnancy and Birth, p. 53. Childbirth Connection, New York (2013)

Exploring the Interaction Between
Visual Flux and Users on Mobile Devices

Shih-Wen Hsiao and Yi-Cheng Tsao[✉]

Department of Industrial Design, National Cheng Kung University, Tainan, Taiwan
swhsiao@mail.ncku.edu.tw, nyct.tw@gmail.com

Abstract. This research introduces the concept of visual flux to depict the process of the physical interaction between users and mobile devices in the scenario of controlled visual stimulation over various screen dimensions. Position sensors of mobile devices and motion sensors are applied in this research to incorporate the effects of corresponding distance and orientation between devices and users. A reconstruction system is established to provide a pragmatic approach to the process of user activities. The experimental results indicate that the participant performance under the condition of the same number and even size of stimulation decreases with increasing device dimensions, and the correlation between the angle of view and participant performance is revealed. Future research based on this concept could be conducted to extend the screen dimensions and thereby discover the entire spectrum of the informative glasses.

Keywords: User experience · Mobile touch device · Motion sensor

1 Introduction

The increasing demand for mobile computing has led to the presence of numerous handheld devices of different screen dimensions, from 4-in phones to 12.9-in tablets [1]. The diverse sizes of devices offer various options for customers according to individual preferences. However, the physical limitations of different dimensions constrain the display area and cause an inconsistent user experience across screens. The previous study indicated that larger displays offer a preferable user experience and a higher sense of immersion [2], yet the mobility of larger devices often fails in the tasks of daily portable usage. It is also a challenge for most mobile applications to offer a consistent user experience across devices under the fragmented conditions of screen sizes. Although it is possible and effortless to directly scale and resize the contents to fit different panels, a proper solution is to optimize the user experience across different displays [3]. Therefore, the approach to evaluating user feedback to the stimulations from various screen dimensions has become an important issue [4]. In addition to resizing the contents with a fixed ratio between targets and panels, the content adjustment between screens could utilize a fixed target size that reveals more content with increasing dimensions of different devices or even completely redesign the interface for the diverse panel sizes. In the situation of identical target sizes, the concept of flux could be adopted to explore the interaction between users and various sizes of displays.

© Springer International Publishing AG 2017
A. Marcus and W. Wang (Eds.): DUXU 2017, Part II, LNCS 10289, pp. 208–220, 2017.
DOI: 10.1007/978-3-319-58637-3_16

This research introduces the concept of visual flux to describe the process from controlled visual stimulation of mobile devices to brain recognition of information and explores the interaction between users and different screen sizes of portable devices. The communication of the information stream utilizes the device display to create visual stimulations on the retinas of the user's eyes, and the flow from different screen sizes and by various device orientations leads to the representation of this approach in the form of visual flux. User feedback is then provided to the devices after the information of visual flux undergoes the perception process of the human brain. This research analyzes the data of user feedback and visual flux and explores the user interaction between receiving and conveying information across different sizes of portable devices. On mobile devices, visual flux (J_v) could be defined as the amount (n) of effective information (q) passing through the area of the user's field of view (A) (Eq. 1):

$$J_v = n\frac{q}{A} \tag{1}$$

In this case, q represents the source of visual stimulations, or targets. This research utilizes the controlled dimension of visual stimulation (q) and discusses the user behavior with different numbers (n) of stimulations on different screen sizes (A) under the condition of respective unit visual flux (q/A). From the device aspect, A could be defined as the effective zone of the display area, not including the title bar or the control bar. From the user's perspective, considering the individual behavior with different postures for various sizes of portable devices, the definition of A could be represented as the angle of view of distinctive devices to the user. To consider the effects of the relation between the devices and the users, such as the corresponding distance and orientation between devices and users, the dimensions of different screen sizes, and the information stimulation from each device, this research incorporates the Kinect v2 motion sensor released by Microsoft Corporation and the orientation data from the position sensors of mobile devices and constructs a system for reconstructing the user's interactive behavior to explore the physical user activities with multiple dimensions of mobile devices; the study intends to investigate the process between the images generated by the devices and the information perceived by the human brain with the controlled stimulation over multiple sizes of mobile devices via the concept of visual flux.

2 Related Work

In the field of studying the interaction between portable devices and physical user behavior, the research focuses on discovering the viewing distance between handheld electronic devices and different groups of users to provide comprehensive findings [5], in addition to the relation between font size and viewing distance, a detailed study [6] offers the relation between one type of content and the viewing distance of a smart phone. However, the effect of cross-dimensional comparison with multiple sizes could offer a more exhaustive understanding of fragmented screen conditions. Research on the effect of different desktop screen sizes on human posture revealed that users tend to position larger displays at a greater distance [7], and it is valuable to extend this analysis to the field of mobile devices. Research on the minimum target size of mobile devices [8] offers a complete discussion on the effect of target size with one-thumb usage along with a wide range of applications. On the other hand, studies on human postures with mobile devices including head restriction while using a cell phone [9], muscle activity related to user posture [10], and the effect of typing related to upper body posture [11] are also exhaustive, and researches that attempt to utilize user skeleton data [12, 13] are also applicable not only in the discipline of human–computer interaction but in a wide range of applications. Regarding evaluation of user performance, Fitts' Law [14] indicates that the mean time (MT) of user reaction is a linear function of the index of difficulty (ID) and could be expressed in the form of $MT = a + b \cdot ID$ (a and b are experimental coefficients). The index of difficulty, ID, is the bit form of the ratio between target length and moving path, $ID = \log_2(1 + D/W)$, where D is the length of the moving path, and W is the target width. Hick's Law, with a similar form of prediction for user performance [15], focuses more on the condition of multiple choices. Both predictions are widely applicable to the domain of user performance. The computational model proposed in the research [4] attempts to establish a model of user experience on mobile devices and breaks down the user experience into usability, affect, and user value, which requires authentic quantitative inputs. Studies of user experience on touch devices are also fruitful; e.g., research that focuses on the gesture between touch [16] and slide provides a comprehensive study, and researches on virtual keyboards [17, 18] and different types of input methods [19] are also exhaustive. A valuable cross-platform comparison is conducted on three different mobile operating systems [20]—iOS, Android, and Windows—which compares the differences in virtual keyboards. In an era of fragmented devices, there is an urgent need for a user experience and performance comparison among multiple screen sizes.

3   Method

To achieve the purpose of capturing user posture and gathering the orientation of mobile devices, this research applies a Kinect v2 motion sensor in sync with the orientation data recorded by the position sensor of the mobile devices and establishes an integration

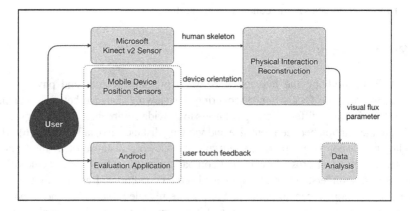

Fig. 1. Architecture of the approach used in this research

system to combine these two types of data and attempts to reconstruct the entire physical process of interaction between the users and the mobile devices. An evaluation application based on Android is programmed to control the output stimulation of the mobile devices and records the user feedback under the specific visual stimulation. Various dimensions of devices are selected as the equipment for this research to facilitate the understanding of the user interaction and performance under different screens. Figure 1 illustrates the architecture of the approach of this research.

3.1 User Posture Capture

Microsoft Kinect v2 sensors are applied in this research to extract the user skeleton information during the interaction process. As shown in Fig. 2, Kinect v2 sensors are capable of capturing 2D RGB color images and 3D depth information and extracting the position coordinates of the 25 spatial joints of the individual user, including the head, neck, pelvis, shoulder, elbow, and palm. This research focuses on the interaction between mobile devices and the user's upper body posture and extracts 17 upper body joint data to calculate the parameters of different user postures for different screens. The Kinect v2 sensor is positioned directly in front of the user at a proper distance that could capture the whole user body image and complies with the design specification of Microsoft Cooperation. The recorded 17 spatial joint data and relative time stamps are later converged in the integration system to reconstruct the user's activity.

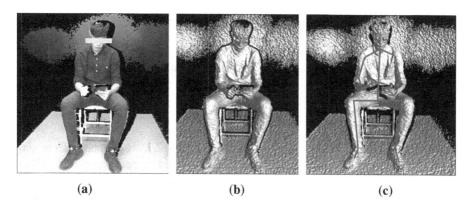

(a)   **(b)**   **(c)**

Fig. 2. Samples of the captured images from Kinect v2: (a) 2D RGB image, (b) 3D depth image, and (c) user skeleton joint data (Color figure online)

3.2 Mobile Application

Two functions of the mobile application are required for this research: (1) deriving and recording the orientation of the mobile devices and (2) providing controlled visual stimulation and recording the user feedback. The Android system is capable of calculating the relative angles between the device coordinates and earth—azimuth, pitch, and roll—via the position sensors, such as the geomagnetic field sensor and accelerometer (Fig. 3(a)). The recorded orientation data and relative time stamps are later merged with user skeleton data to reconstruct the user activity during the interaction process. For controlled visual stimulation, the tasks are designed as a single touch tap on numbered circular targets on a white background (Fig. 3(b)). Each target has the diameter of exactly 1 cm, representing the unit visual flux (unit J_v) corresponding to each device. Serial and distinctive numbers are rendered within each target as users are asked to touch each target to complete the task. When the largest (and last) target in the stage is finished, the next new stage with refreshed locations and colors of targets is immediately regenerated (Fig. 3(c)). Note that the number of targets is equal to the stage number: namely, the first stage contains one target, the fifth stage contains five targets, and the last stage, the twentieth stage, contains twenty targets. The locations of the targets are separately distributed over the screens and are randomly located to avoid the learning effect caused by repeated target locations. The colors of the targets are also randomly generated as red, blue, and green to simulate the daily usage of applications. User feedback, such as time, touch locations, successful targets and errors, is recorded during the process for later analysis.

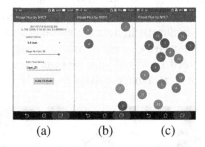

(a)   (b)   (c)

Fig. 3. Snapshots of the Android application: (a) orientation data and basic options, (b) stage 5 of the evaluation screen, and (c) stage 15 of the evaluation screen (Color figure online)

3.3 Physical Interaction Reconstruction System

After the data acquisition of the user's skeleton and the device's orientation, a reconstruction of the user's physical interaction behavior could be performed, and further related information could also be calculated. This research introduces the physical interaction reconstruction system, which integrates skeleton and orientation data and derive corresponding information, such as *angle of view* and *angle of skew*. The user's horizontal angle of view to the devices is represented as the angle of view (α), and the angle difference between the user's fixation at the center of the device and the normal direction of the device screens is represented as the angle of skew (θ). The angle of view, α, is defined as Eq. 2, where x is the width of the device screen, and l is the distance between the user's eyes and the device, or the viewing distance:

$$\alpha = 2\tan^{-1}\frac{x}{2l} \qquad (2)$$

The other parameter is the angle of skew, θ, which is defined as the angle difference between the normal direction of the device screen and the user's line of sight, as Eq. 3.

Vector $\vec{e}$ is defined as the vector pointing from the center of the device to the reference point of the user's eyes, and vector $\vec{d}$ is defined as the normal vector of the device screen. Due to the constraint of the experimental sensors, this research assumes that the reference point of the user's eyes is the geometric center of the user's head, which is captured by the Kinect v2 sensor as the coordinates of the head joint.

$$\theta = \cos^{-1} \frac{\vec{e} \cdot \vec{d}}{|\vec{e}||\vec{d}|} \tag{3}$$

The physical interaction reconstruction system of this research integrates the skeletal data and device orientation data and could clearly reconstruct the moments of physical interaction between the users and the devices. In-time parameters, such as angle of view and angle of skew per frame, are calculated immediately to assist a better understanding of user behavior. It is also able to freely rotate and observe the relation between user posture and device orientation from multiple directions (Fig. 4). Primary functions such as play at normal speed, fast forward, or jump to a specific frame are also useful for observers to gain a more detailed understanding of the physical interaction process.

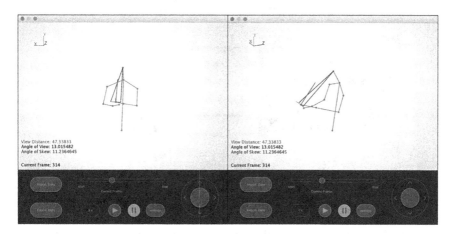

Fig. 4. Screenshots of the physical interaction reconstruction system

3.4 Experimental Procedure

This research focuses on the user's performance across multiple dimensions of mobile devices, and the experiments are conducted on 4 devices of different sizes: ASUS ZenFone GO (4.5-in), ASUS ZenFone 3 Max (5.2-in), ASUS ZenPad (8-in), and ASUS ZenPad (10-in). The effective display area for each device is 46.2, 59.8, 159.84, and 260.55 cm^2, respectively, and the average effective display ratio is 1.4375 with the standard deviation of 0.067 (all measurements of the effective display area exclude the title bar and the control bar). Fourteen subjects between 22 and 35 years of age (average age 26 years, standard deviation 2.75 years) participated in this experiment, 8 males and

6 females. One participant was left-hand dominant, while the other participants were right-hand dominant, and all participants exceeded 8 years of experience with touch-sensitive mobile devices. A 7-in non-experimental device was offered to participants for a free trial and to familiarize themselves with the operating process of the application. Participants were asked to finish tasks, touching the evaluating application targets throughout all stages in a natural gesture while the Kinect v2 sensor captured their image without any physical contact. An adequate rest between each task was given to eliminate visual fatigue and any carry-over effect, and two tasks were performed for each device dimension to minimize the situation of drift coordinates of skeleton joints by the Kinect v2 sensor. Participants were informed that they would be rewarded after the experiment to increase their willingness to participate. During the process, participants were asked to complete the tasks with the device in portrait orientation and use the dominant index finger to touch and the other hand to hold the device. The experiments were performed in a specially designed compartment with a unified lighting source, with three walls and the ceiling painted black to reduce the interference of additional light reflections. Adequate space was ensured so that no participant would feel stressed. Figure 5(a) shows the experimental setup and the controlled environment of this research; Fig. 5(b) shows the equipment used in this research, including four experimental devices and one non-experimental device for familiarizing users with the application.

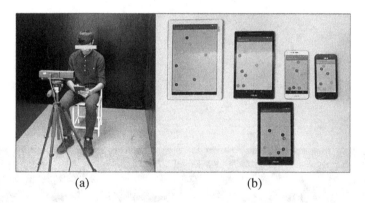

(a)   (b)

Fig. 5. (a) The experimental setup and (b) the experimental equipment used in this research

4   Result

The participant performance against different dimensions of mobile devices under controlled stimulation is analyzed in this research, and the results show that during the experimental time span (less than 5 min), participant performance—i.e., the average number of finished targets per second (TPS)—decreases with increasing size of the device display (Fig. 6). For the 4.5-in device, the average TPS of participants is 1.622 with a standard deviation of 0.189; for the 5.2-in device, the average TPS of participants is 1.484 with a standard deviation of 0.205; for the 8-in device, the average TPS drops to 1.209 with a standard deviation of 0.125; and for the 10-in device, the average TPS is 1.063 with a standard deviation of 0.096. Statistical analysis using repeated measures analysis of variance (rmANOVA) indicates that the average TPS differences between the four screens are statistically significant ($F_{(3,39)} = 135.84$, $p < .001$). Post-hoc comparison by Bonferroni corrections reveals that all average TPS differences among the four screens are statistically significant (4.5-in/5.2-in $p < .001$, 5.2-in/8-in $p < .001$, 8-in/10-in $p = .001$). Thus, it could be inferred that user performance drops with increasing effective display area under the condition of fixed target size in the mid-short term operating scenario.

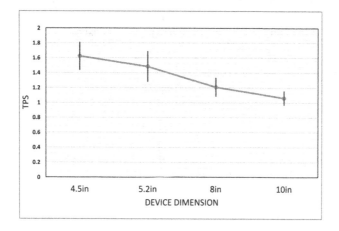

Fig. 6. The averaged TPS among four experimental devices

Regarding the number of touch screen errors recorded across different screen sizes of experimental devices, shown in Fig. 7, for individual participants, the majority of the participants tended to commit more errors with increasing device display. Furthermore, the average number of errors is also positively correlated to the dimensions of the

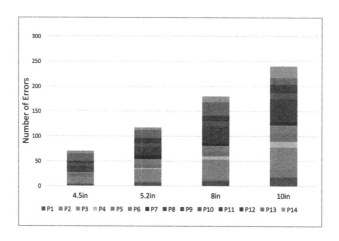

Fig. 7. The error counts among four experimental devices

devices. The statistical analysis using rmANOVA shows that the differences in the average number of errors across the four screens are statistically significant ($p < .001$).

Taking a closer look at the task process, the experiment reveals that participant performance declines on larger screens at each stage of the tasks. Figure 8(a) shows the completion time for each stage on the four different screens and reveals a negative correlation between participant performance and screen dimensions, which indicates that J_v could describe user performance under the same number (n) of controlled stimulations (q) over different screens (A). Linear correlations between the number of targets and completion time of the targets are shown in Fig. 8(b) and indicate good compliance with both Fitts' Law and Hick's Law of this experiment design.

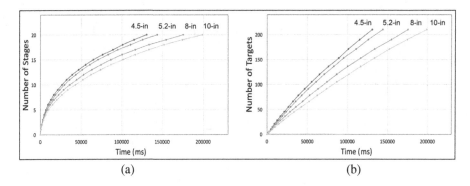

(a)   (b)

Fig. 8. User performance on four experimental devices: (a) number of stages as a function of time (ms) and (b) number of targets as a function of time (ms)

The relation between the averaged time of milliseconds per target (MPT) and the number of completed targets is shown in Fig. 9. This reveals that the average MPT increases with increasing number of visual stimulations across the four screens, and the differences among the devices become recognizable after approximately 5 stages (15

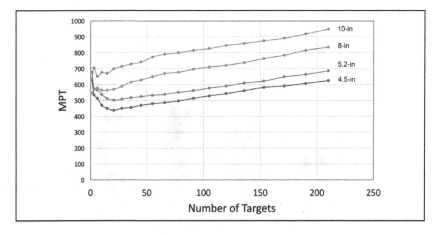

Fig. 9. The averaged MPT on four experimental devices as a function of the number of targets

target touches). The conjecture is that the unstable status before stage 5 is caused by the uneven distribution of visual stimulations.

Figure 10 shows the accumulated targets for one of the task processes at stage 5 and stage 10 of a certain participant (Fig. 10(a) and (b) respectively). It is evident that the number of targets before stage 5 is insufficient to cover the entire screen, and this is speculated as the main cause of the fluctuation of averaged MPT before stage 5 in Fig. 9.

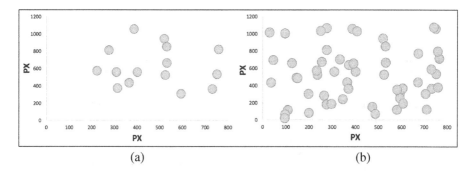

(a)   (b)

Fig. 10. Target distribution example of: (a) 0 to 5 stages and (b) 0 to 10 stages

The previous results indicate that participant performance under the condition of equal stimulation, same number and even size of stimulation, decreases with increasing device dimensions. This research further explored the effect of user posture with the detailed information of *angle of view* and *angle of skew*, both derived using the physical interaction reconstruction system. Although the pilot experiments show that increased angle of skew leads to decreased participant performance, the main experiment reveals that the average differences of angle of skew among the four devices are not statistically significant (the average is $14.01°$ with $0.74°$ standard deviation across four screens, $p = .516$ with rmANOVA). It may be practical for this research to neglect the effect of the angle of skew, but from the user-centered experience perspective, sudden and violent changes in angle of skew could offer precious information regarding the fluctuation in user experience since the dramatic change in angle of skew seriously affects the angle of view. In addition, the continuous quantitative data of angle of skew during the interaction process may be valuable for qualitative research of user behavior.

From the user's perspective, J_v could be further represented as the number of stimulations in the user's angle of view. The experimental results show that the average angle of view is $9.43°$ with a standard deviation of $1.85°$ for the 4.5-in device, $10.94°$ with a standard deviation of $2.14°$ for the 5.2-in device, $16.67°$ with a standard deviation of $3.38°$ for the 8-in device, and $19.54°$ with a standard deviation of $3.13°$ for the 10-in device. The performed rmANOVA indicates that the differences in angle of view among the four devices are statistically significant ($p < .001$). The MPT for èach participant as a function of angle of view is shown in Fig. 11(a), which reveals a positive correlation between angle of view and MPT. The normalized data show a clear correlation between MPT and angle of view as the ratio corresponding to the average value of individual participant; see Fig. 11(b).

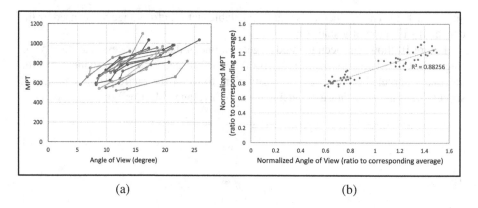

(a)   (b)

Fig. 11. The relation of (a) MPT as a function of angle of view and (b) normalized MPT as a function of normalized angle of view

In addition, the experiment reveals that participants tend to position different dimensions of mobile devices within a range of more similar angles of view, but not similar enough to obtain the exact same angle of view for different screens. Namely, for larger screens at further distances and vice versa, the tendency is consistent with the results of previous research on fixed displays [7]. A reference angle of view of the four devices, which is derived from the average viewing distance of each user, is depicted in Fig. 12 to contrast with the actual angle of view. Compared to the reference angle of view, which assumes that the devices are positioned at the same distance, this reveals that the actual angle of view covers a narrower range of angles and is more reflective of the certain conditions for the interactive process. The supposition is that users are familiar with particular viewing distances and have the tendency to position devices in the respective useful field of view (uFOV), and the reduced distance of eye movement facilitates user performance.

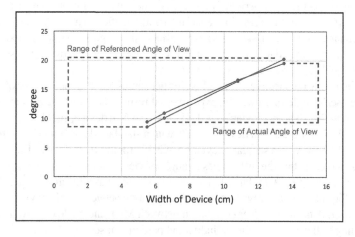

Fig. 12. Difference between range of actual angle of view and range of referenced angle of view

5   Discussion

This research introduces the concept of visual flux to describe the process of physical interaction between users and mobile devices and utilizes the unit visual flux as a datum to compare the user performance under different screen dimensions. This approach could depict the condition of receiving information under the mid-short time span (<300 s). Based on the data of device dimensions and relative user posture, this research proposes an alternative perspective for portraying users' physical interaction process with mobile devices. Under the specifically controlled stimulation, the proposed concept could offer a quantitative index for design across platforms in fields where the consistent user experience across different screen sizes is crucial, such as mobile gaming, in both hardware manufacturing and application development. Furthermore, the physical interaction reconstruction system of this research offers a more intuitive and detailed point of study for understanding the physical process of human–computer interaction. Future research based on this concept could be conducted to extend the screen dimensions to laptops, desktops, or even projectors or scale the sizes down to wearable devices and head-mounted devices to explore a deeper understanding between visual stimulation and user feedback across the entire spectrum of informative glasses.

Acknowledgements.   The authors would like to thank the Ministry of Science and Technology of Taiwan for supporting this research under project No. 105-2221-E-006-115-MY2.

References

1. Apple Inc. (2017). http://apple.com
2. Hou, J., Nam, Y., Peng, W., Lee, K.M.: Effects of screen size, viewing angle, and players' immersion tendencies on game experience. Comput. Hum. Behav. **28**(2), 617–623 (2012)
3. Supporting Multiple Screens, Android Developers (2017). https://developer.android.com/guide/practices/screens_support.html
4. Park, J., Han, S.H., Kim, H.K., Oh, S., Moon, H.: Modeling user experience: a case study on a mobile device. Int. J. Ind. Ergon. **43**(2), 187–196 (2013)
5. Wu, H.-C.: Electronic paper display preferred viewing distance and character size for different age groups. Ergonomics **54**(9), 806–814 (2011)
6. Bababekova, Y., Rosenfield, M., Hue, J.E., Huang, R.R.: Font size and viewing distance of handheld smart phones. Optom. Vis. Sci. **88**(7), 795–797 (2011)
7. Shin, G., Hegde, S.: User-preferred position of computer displays: effects of display size. Hum. Factors **52**(5), 574–585 (2010)
8. Parhi, P., Karlson, A.K., Bederson, B.B.: Target size study for one-handed thumb use on small touchscreen devices. In: Proceedings of the Mobile HCI 2006, pp. 203–210. ACM Press (2006)
9. Thumser, Z.C., Stahl, J.S.: Handheld cellular phones restrict head movements and range of visual regard. Hum. Mov. Sci. **32**(1), 1–8 (2013)
10. Werth, A., Babski-Reeves, K.: Effects of portable computing devices on posture, muscle activation levels and efficiency. Appl. Ergonomics **45**(6), 1603–1609 (2014)

11. Kietrys, D.M., Gerg, M.J., Dropkin, J., Gold, J.E.: Mobile input device type, texting style and screen size influence upper extremity and trapezius muscle activity, and cervical posture while texting. Appl. Ergonomics **50**, 98–104 (2015)
12. Barmpoutis, A.: Tensor body: real-time reconstruction of the human body and avatar synthesis from RGB-D. IEEE Trans. Cybern. Spec. Issue Comput. Vis. RGB-D Sens. Kinect Appl. **43**(5), 1347–1356 (2013)
13. Hsiao, S.-W., Chen, R.-Q., Leng, W.-L.: Applying riding-posture optimization on bicycle frame design. Appl. Ergonomics **51**, 69–79 (2015)
14. Fitts, P.M.: The information capacity of the human motor system in controlling amplitude of movement. J. Exp. Psychol. **47**, 381–391 (1954)
15. Seow, S.C.: Information theoretic models of HCI: a comparison of the Hick-Hyman Law and Fitts' Law. Hum. Comput. Interact. **20**, 315–352 (2005)
16. Tang, T.Y., He, M.Y., Cao, V.L.: "One doesn't fit all": a comparative study of various finger gesture interaction methods. In: Marcus, A. (ed.) DUXU 2016, Part III. LNCS, vol. 9748, pp. 88–97. Springer, Cham (2016). doi:10.1007/978-3-319-40406-6_9
17. Hakoda, H., Shizuki, B., Tanaka, J.: QAZ keyboard: QWERTY based portrait soft keyboard. In: Marcus, A. (ed.) DUXU 2016, Part III. LNCS, vol. 9748, pp. 24–35. Springer, Cham (2016). doi:10.1007/978-3-319-40406-6_3
18. Azenkot, S., Zhai, S.: Touch behavior with different postures on soft smartphone keyboards. In: Proceedings of the MobileHCI 2012, pp. 251–260. ACM, New York (2012)
19. Deniz, G., Onay Durdu, P.: Comparison of mobile input methods. In: Marcus, A. (ed.) DUXU 2016, Part III. LNCS, vol. 9748, pp. 3–13. Springer, Cham (2016). doi: 10.1007/978-3-319-40406-6_1
20. Korkmaz, Y., Onay Durdu, P.: Comparison of user performance and satisfaction of tablet virtual keyboards in three different OS environment. In: 2015 9th International Conference on AICT, pp. 269–273. IEEE (2015)

New Mobile Service Development Process

Hans-Peter Hutter[✉] and Andreas Ahlenstorf

School of Engineering, Institute of Applied Information Techology (InIT),
Zurich University of Applied Sciences (ZHAW),
Technikumstr. 9, Winterthur, Switzerland
{hans-peter.hutter,andreas.ahlenstorf}@zhaw.ch

Abstract. Mobile applications play an ever growing role in everybody's life around our globe and the leading app stores currently offer more than 2 million different apps each for their users. It is well accepted that the usage context is much more important in the UI and UX design of these apps than when designing desktop applications. It is important to realize that a lot of these apps are part of a mobile service that defines their usage context and the UX of the mobile app is not only determined by the interaction with it but by the value creation of the whole service. We therefore propose in this paper a joint service and app design process that not only optimizes the user interaction with the mobile app but also the UX of the whole service in order to provide an optimal value proposition to the service customer of the mobile service.

Keywords: Mobile service · Mobile app · Service design process

1 Introduction

Various user-centered design processes for applications and mobile apps have been proposed in the literature, e.g., [2,3]. These point out the importance of understanding the user and his needs as well as the usage context. These processes neglect, however, that mobile apps often are part of a mobile service and the usage context and user needs derive from the service needs. On the other hand, different service design processes have been described, e.g., in [1,5,6]. However, none of these processes describe how to derive the UI design requirements for the mobile app from the designed service concept so that the value proposition of the service concept is really achieved.

In this paper a new joint design process is described for mobile apps together with the services they support in order to provide optimal user experience and value proposition to the service customer and app user. First, the basic idea of the new service design process, in the following called InIT Service Design Process (ISDP), is explained.

The second part exemplifies how the ISDP can successfully be applied in a real project in the design of a service for the Swiss fair trade company gebana. The goal of this project was to develop an Access-To-Market (A2M) service for small holder organic farmers in developing countries in order to give them access to a fair trade market in Europe [4]. This service supports producers of

© Springer International Publishing AG 2017
A. Marcus and W. Wang (Eds.): DUXU 2017, Part II, LNCS 10289, pp. 221–232, 2017.
DOI: 10.1007/978-3-319-58637-3_17

organically farmed products to enable them to get access and relationship to a consumer market in the developed countries. It leads them trough the whole process of product tests, organic certification, and setup of the supply chain until a long-term producer-consumer relationship is established. This A2M service is based on a communication service named MOSAFA. For this service a mobile app had to be developed, that supports the farmers in developing countries to communicate and exchange information with gebana during the whole process.

2   Basic Idea

The basic idea of the ISDP is depicted in Fig. 1. In a first step the jobs of the targeted customers are identified. Jobs in this context mean e.g. something the customer wants to have done or a feeling he wants to have or to avoid, or an experience he wants to make. Related to these jobs the customers have specific pains and expect specific gains that should be addressed by a service.

For the jobs, gains, and pains that are important to the customer one or more service concepts are designed that have a clear value proposition regarding the jobs of the customer and his pains and gains. These service concepts are iteratively prototyped and evaluated with the customers until promising service concepts are found. A service concept normally addresses only a few jobs, pains or gains of the customer but does this in a convincing manner.

From these service concepts requirements are derived for the mobile app and the other IT systems needed. The mobile app can well support more than one service. The service concepts thereby exactly specify the usage context for the different interaction scenarios of the mobile app.

During the development of the mobile and other systems these are regularly tested in the context of the developed service concepts in order to optimize the user interactions with the app and other IT systems as well as the service concepts themselves.

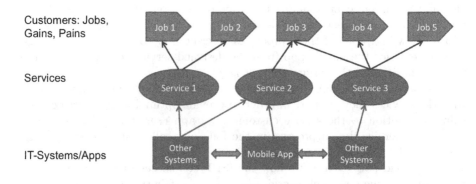

Fig. 1. Basic idea of the ISDP service design process

3   Overview on the InIT Service Design Process (ISDP)

The ISDP is customer centered from the very beginning and iterative by nature (Fig. 2):

In the Customer & Context Analysis phase the service customers and stakeholders are identified and their needs, skills, goals and contexts are investigated, e.g. with contextual interviews, customer journey and other user research methods (see e.g. [5]). The goal of this phase is to get a clear picture of the service customers and the usage context. The insights of this phase are summarized in service design personas for the different customer groups.

In the second phase, Service Innovation, the first step is to analyze the whole service system with the relevant service customers. Then, the jobs and outcomes of the different service customers are scrutinized in order to identify opportunities for value-creation for each partner in the service system. This can be done with one of the Universal Job Maps described in [3] depending on the innovation focus.

In the Service Design and Prototyping phase the new service concepts for the relevant service customers are iteratively designed addressing their high-opportunity jobs, gains, and pains. This is done in close collaboration with the targeted service customers in order to optimally support their jobs and to produce the expected outcomes so that the intended values are really created for each service partner. The service concepts are prototyped with value proposition canvases [4] and storyboards in early stages, later on with low-fidelity and high-fidelity prototypes and service blueprints.

In the evaluation phase, the different service prototypes are evaluated in usability tests and in field tests with real service customers in the real context. The phases Service Design & Prototyping and Service Evaluation are iterated until the service concept meets the customers' and stakeholders' expectations. If the Service Evaluation phase reveals that additional customer segments have to be addressed for the whole service system the overall service design process is iterated (see Fig. 2).

In the Service Implementation phase contextual stories for the personas developed in the Customer & Context Analysis phase and a domain model are derived from the service blueprints and other user research artifacts. The contextual stories describe the different service provider steps from the customer point of view whereas the domain model describes the universal domain language and, to some extent, the customer's mental model. Together with the service prototype they are part of the requirements for the design of the mobile app and the other IT-systems needed to optimally support the designed services. Finally, the mobile app is developed in an iterative user-centered manner like, e.g., described in [1,2]. The wireframes and mockups of the mobile app are regularly tested with service customers in the actual service context.

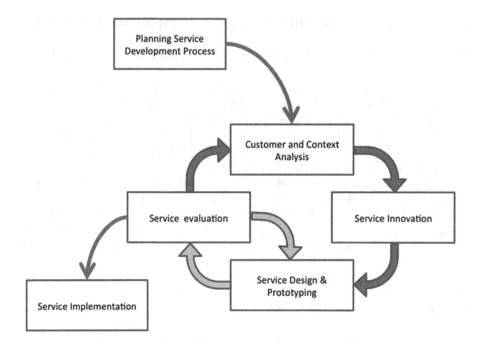

Fig. 2. ISDP overview

4 Application of the InIT Service Design Process to the MOSAFA Service

In the following it is shown how the different steps of the ISDP looked like in the sample service MOSAFA. The MOSAFA service should allow farmers in developing countries to exchange information with gebana employees in the context of the A2M service described in Sect. 1.

4.1 Customer & Context Analysis

In the Customer & Context Analysis phase different contextual inquiries were conducted with farmers in developing countries and the consumers in the developed countries but also with gebana employees in the developing countries and in Switzerland in order to

- Identify the different user groups and other stakeholders important for the MOSAFA service
- Understand the sociocultural and technical context of the users of the MOSAFA service
- Identify the jobs and outcomes (gains and pains) of the different service customers and stakeholders
- Elicitate other requirements for the MOSAFA service and app

The stakeholder map in Fig. 3 shows the various stakeholders identified during the contextual inquiries. These inquiries revealed that the most important customers of the MOSAFA service are the farmers in developing countries and the gebana management employees in Switzerland and in the developing countries. However, the inquiries also revealed significant barriers for the farmers in the developing countries to participate in the MOSAFA service:

- Language barriers: the farmers in developing countries often only speak their native language (e.g. Djoula in Burkina Faso) and hardly any major language like English or French. This problem may be alleviated in the future, as the kids of the farmers normally learn some English or French at school.
- Technical barriers: although most of the farmers have or at least have access to a mobile phone, they normally only use it for phone calls. Several of the interviewed farmers have neither experience with the internet nor with mobile apps.

Therefore, another customer group was introduced for the MOSAFA service: the agents. Whereas the gebana employees interact directly with the MOSAFA

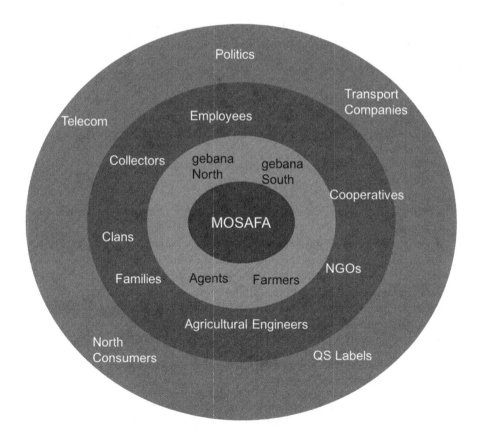

Fig. 3. Stakeholder map for the MOSAFA service

service, the farmers in the south normally do not directly interact with the MOSAFA app but through an intermediate, the so-called agent. An agent is responsible for a group of farmers that he regularly contacts and communicates with. The role of an agent may be taken over by a representative of the farmer cooperatives, a Collecteur (see below) or someone else who has good contacts to the farmers and is knowledgable in English or French and has some basic IT skills.

Other stakeholders of the MOSAFA and the A2M service worth mentioning here are:

– Collecteurs: these are persons that collect the harvested goods from the farmers and transport them to a processing station, e.g., a drying station, or a storehouse.
– Agricultural Engineers: these are persons paid by gebana in order to advise the farmers on organic farming.
– NGOs: they also have direct interest in the A2M service in two ways: On the one side they are looking for market access for their farmer groups in the developing countries, on the other side they are looking for fair trade projects in developing countries they could support.

During the Customer & Context Analysis phase also the technical context for a communication service like MOSAFA was analyzed. The major insights and conclusions of this analysis were:

– Messaging Services
  • The Data connection was normally stable enough to transmit messages. However, none of the Messaging Services tested (SMS, Pushy, Google Cloud Messaging) was reliable enough to transmit information without any losses.
  • There were very long delays (up to several days) in the data transmission and no guarantee for any upper limit.
– Data Connection
  • The quality of the data connections was quite variable even for the same connection.
  • Often there was no data connection at all for longer periods of time (days)
  • Outside gebana offices there was no WiFi connection available.
  • Breakdown rate during data transfers was high. Only 20% of the data transmissions (10 MB) were completed.
  • On average only 0.5 MB data could be transferred in one transmission.
  • Downstream: 10–100 MB per day could be transmitted.
  • Upstream: only up to 5 MB per week could be transmitted.

These insights lead to the following conclusion regarding the MOSAFA service and the corresponding mobile app:

– It is generally possible to exchange information digitally.
– Reliable exchange of digital information with partners in developing countries is a challenge.

- Information exchange with partners in developing countries via SMS or push notifications is not reliable enough.
- The best solution therefore seemed to be the following:
  - The applications involved in the data exchange must be resilient to frequent connection losses and should support partial data transmissions without the need for retransmissions.
  - Information exchange is therefore best done via a generic form app to be developed for smartphones. With this app partners in developing countries can collect the data directly on the mobile device on site. The data is first stored on the mobile device. As soon as an internet connection is available the data is automatically transferred to a server at gebana.
  - A web server at gebana offers a web service that can be called from the mobile app in the global south as many times as needed (pull service).
  - With this concept it should be possible to reliably collect data via a form app in reasonable time. However, there is no guarantee that time-critical information can be transmitted in time.
  - Large contents such as pictures or videos should only be transferred when a reliable WiFi connection is available, e.g., at the gebana offices.
  - All data transfers should be done automatically in the background (e.g., via the SyncAdapter in Android) in order to save battery on the mobile and to automatically transfer data as soon as a network connection is available.

Based on the results of the contextual inquiries the following three most important service customer groups of the MOSAFA service were identified: farmers, agents, and gebana employees. For each of these service customer groups a service design persona was developed.

4.2   Service Innovation

In this phase the jobs, gains, and pains of the three personas developed in the last phase were scrutinized. It is important to realize that the MOSAFA service system relies on three service customers, as depicted in Fig. 4. For each of this service customers an attractive value proposition had to be offered by the service so that these customers really participate in the service on a long-term basis.

The farmer provides information to the MOSAFA service needed by the gebana employee. The value he expects from the MOSAFA service is contacts to other farmers, agents, and gebana employees, information regarding organic farming and advice. The motivation of an agent to participate is – apart from money, contacts to farmers, and information – that he gets a smartphone and an influential role among the farmers. The gebana employee provides tasks for the agents and information to the MOSAFA service. The value he gets out of it is an easy way to run data collection campaigns and collect data from farmers and agents.

For each of these three service customers the different jobs they want to have done were identified together with the gains and pains related to these jobs.

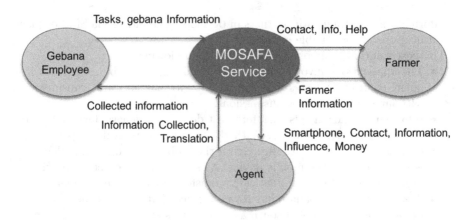

Fig. 4. Service system of MOSAFA

The prioritization of the gathered list of jobs and outcomes revealed the following jobs, gains, and pains that should primarily be addressed by the MOSAFA service:

- Gebana employee
  - Jobs
    - Run a data collection campaign
    - Collect farmer profiles
    - Collect agent profiles
    - Collect farmers' stock status
    - Collect photos/videos from farmers
    - Distribute information to farmers
    - Assign tasks to farmers
    - Assign tasks to agents
    - Remind agents
  - Pains
    - Effort to collect information
    - Time to collect information
    - Wrong information
    - Missing information
  - Gains
    - Easy verification of collection status
    - Flexible aggregation of the data
    - Easy visualization of the data
- Agent
  - Jobs
    - Collect farmers' contact info
    - Collect farmers profiles
    - Collect farmers' stock status
    - Distribute information to farmers

  * Collect other information from farmers (organic certification)
  * Verify/Update information on site
- Pains
  * Effort to collect information
  * Time to collect information
  * Information gets lost
  * Forget something to do
- Gains
  * Easy overview on open/closed tasks
  * Be perceived as reliable
  * Be perceived as trustful
  * Be influential
- Farmer
  - Jobs
    * Provide information to gebana
    * Receive instructions
    * Do organic farming
    * Sell products
  - Pains
    * Farming problems
    * Organic certification fails
    * No contact to agent
    * Low harvest
    * Low income
    * No market for product
    * Cannot sell whole stock
  - Gains
    * Get help with organic certification
    * Good price for products
    * Get help with organic farming
    * Exchange with other farmers
    * Regular contact to agent
    * Contact to gebana
    * Access to market in developed countries

In the following the job analysis focused on the core job of the gebana employee *Run a data collection campaign* together with the related jobs of the agents, and farmers. For this we analyzed the job steps of the gebana employee, the agent, and the farmer involved in this core job using the Universal Job Map proposed by Bettencourt [1]. For each of these jobs steps identified we again looked for the major pains and gains of the personas related to each job step.

From this job map of the core job *Run a data collection campaign* we also derived a service blueprint showing the most important steps of each of the service partners as well as the interactions between the personas and the MOSAFA app and MOSAFA server, resp. (see Fig. 5).

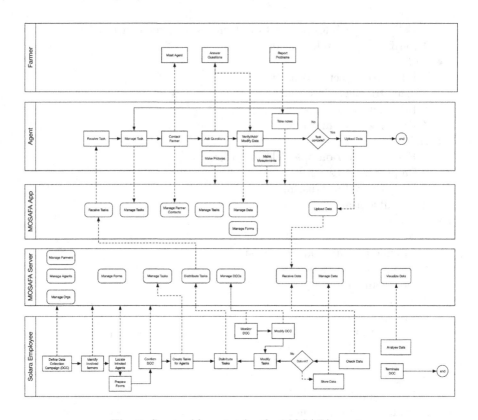

Fig. 5. Service blueprint for the MOSAFA service

4.3   Service Design & Prototyping and Service Evaluation

From the service blueprint in Fig. 5 contextual scenarios were developed for each interaction with the MOSAFA app and the MOSAFA server in the blueprint. In addition, a domain model was developed that shows all important concepts and their relations of the MOSAFA service form the user point of view (see Fig. 6). Based on these contextual scenarios and the domain model different mockups of the MOSAFA App and MOSAFA Server were iteratively developed. The mockups were evaluated in usability tests with real service customers in the context of the MOSAFA service.

4.4   Service Implementation

The service implementation of the MOSAFA service mainly comprised the development of the MOSAFA app and the MOSAFA server. The requirements for the app were derived from the contextual scenarios and the domain model of the service design phase. The contextual scenarios thereby describe the interaction dynamics where the domain model shows the static view of the problem domain.

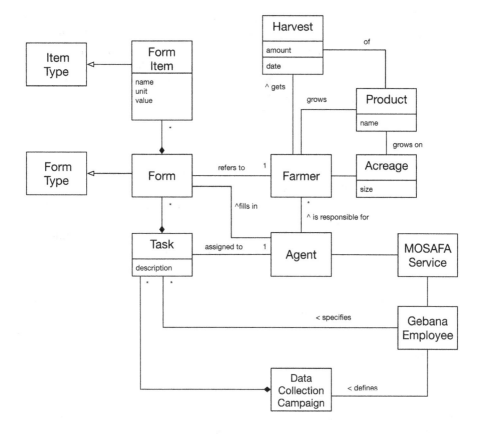

Fig. 6. Domain model for the MOSAFA service

Both are valuable inputs for the software development of the MOSAFA app and server in addition to the UI-mockups developed in the service design phase.

The resulting MOSAFA app is a generic form app for the agents that connects to the MOSAFA server as soon as an internet connection is available and automatically downloads the tasks for the agent. A task comprises the task's description and a form for each farmer the agent is responsible for and who is part of the data collection campaign. The agent can easily enter the data into the form while talking to the farmer. He can also take additional notes and pictures right in the form. The data entered is stored locally on the mobile device. As soon as the mobile device has internet connectivity the filled in forms are uploaded to the MOSAFA server. Pictures are only uploaded if there is a broadband connection to the MOSAFA server. Such a task can also be used to distribute information to the farmers or agents. The MOSAFA app gives the agent an easy overview of all his tasks and their status.

On the MOSAFA server the gebana employee can easily set up a data collection campaign selecting the corresponding farmers and agents. He then defines the task for the agents and selects or creates the corresponding form type. Based on this information the MOSAFA server automatically generates all individual tasks and forms for the different agents. Once the data collection campaign has started, the gebana employee has an easy overview on the status of the data collection campaign, i.e., which tasks are pending, which are completed, which forms have been returned, and so on.

5 Conclusion

This paper proposes the first time an overall design process model for a mobile app as a part of a mobile service which covers the whole process from the analysis of the service customers, their context, jobs, gains and pains, through the service design down to the interaction design and the development of the corresponding mobile app and other IT systems. This allows that the UX of the mobile app and the value proposition of the corresponding service are optimized in a joint effort.

Acknowledgement. This work was supported by the Consortium for Technology and Innovation CTI of Switzerland in the project CTI 16331.1 PFES-ES.

References

1. Bettencourt, L.A.: Service Innovation. How to Go from Customer Needs to Break-through Services. Mc Graw Hill, New York (2010)
2. DIN/EN/ISO: International Standard DIN EN ISO 2941–210:2010. Ergonomics of human-system interaction – Part 210: Human-centred design for interactive systems. International Organization for Standardization, International Electrotechnical Commission, Geneva (2010)
3. Direkova, N.: Design sprint methods (2016). https://developers.google.com/design-sprint/downloads/DesignSprintMethods.pdf
4. Hutter, H.P., Klammer, J., den Anker, F.V., Wiedmer, A.: Service platform for the exchance of services with developing countries. In: Tech4Dev 2016, UNESCO Chair in Technologies for Development International Conference, Lausanne. p. 127 (2016)
5. Osterwalder, A., Pigneur, Y., et al.: Value Proposition Design: How to Create Products and Services Customers Want. Strategyzer Series. Wiley, New Jersey (2014)
6. Stickdorn, M., Schneider, J.: This Is Service Design Thinking. Basics - Tools - Cases. BIS Publishers, Amsterdam (2011)

Designing User Experiences of Novel Technologies

Masayuki Ihara[✉], Takayuki Adachi, and Hiroshi Watanabe

NTT Service Evolution Laboratories, NTT Corporation, Yokosuka, Japan
{ihara.masayuki,adachi.takayuki,watanabe.hi}@lab.ntt.co.jp

Abstract. User experience is critical for the success of new services based on novel technologies. This paper analyzes user experience design for new services with the use case of behavior observation of smartphone-signage collaboration in public spaces. We employ the AIDA model with its four steps of attention, interest, desire, and action, to analyze the observation results of user behaviors in a public exhibition space.

Keywords: User experience · AIDA model · Smartphone-signage collaboration · Behavior observation

1 Introduction

In order to successfully launch a new service based on a novel technology, it is important that the issue of user experience be fully understood. If a similar service exists in the market and users have developed a mental model of its usage, it is easy for them to understand and thus accept the new service. However, a completely new service based on a novel technology makes service acceptance problematic, and in the worst case the service will not be recognized.

This paper analyzes how to design the user experience for a new service. It introduces the use case (includes behavior observation) of a smartphone-signage collaboration service for public spaces.

2 Background

There are two basic research and development strands; improvement and innovation. The former aims at improving the performance of an existing idea or technology so we can assume that users are familiar with the idea or technology. The latter targets novel concepts that are unknown to users and so the take-up rate can be an issue. Thus it is important to design not only the technology itself but also the user experience with consideration of user attributes and the expected use environment. For example, in the case of a new signage service for public spaces, there are many issues to be considered; age and gender of target users, context in which the signage will be encountered, and ambient factors such as other advertisement displays [1, 2].

© Springer International Publishing AG 2017
A. Marcus and W. Wang (Eds.): DUXU 2017, Part II, LNCS 10289, pp. 233–240, 2017.
DOI: 10.1007/978-3-319-58637-3_18

3   Smartphone-Signage Collaboration Technology

While some works on smartphone-signage collaboration are known [3, 5], we developed our own Wi-Fi based smartphone-signage collaboration technology, MPIS (Multi-Player Interactive Signage); it allows multiple users to interact with the system simultaneously [4].

A screenshot is shown in Fig. 1. Users can operate their own pointer on the signage display by finger flicks on their smartphone after connecting the smartphone to the signage Wi-Fi. This is a novel interactive operation method that allows users to overview a categorized menu on the signage and view detailed information of each category on their own smartphone. However, users don't know that they need to connect their smartphone to the signage nor that they can obtain detailed information from the signage because these functions are novel.

Fig. 1. A screenshot of developed technology, MPIS.

4   User Behavior Model

In order to analyze user behaviors when using MPIS, we employed the AIDA model as it is popular in a marketing filed for analyzing user behaviors as regards purchases. We thought that this model could be employed to our signage use case in public spaces in terms of the similarity of user focus on a single target among many contending stimuli. The AIDA model consists of the following four steps: Attention, Interest, Desire, and Action. Figure 2 shows the initial problems with MPIS as identified by the AIDA analysis.

In Fig. 2, Problem #1 in the Attention step is that a user does not pay attention to MPIS. This is a problem of general signage since he/she does not recognize the existence of MPIS service. That is, this problem does not depend on his/her evaluation for MPIS.

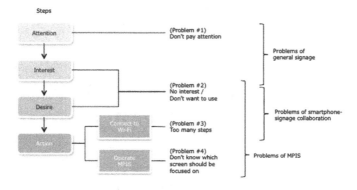

Fig. 2. MPIS problems identified.

Problem #2 in the Interest/Desire steps is that a user does not want to use MPIS due to lack of interest. This could be a problem with general signage, smartphone-signage collaboration or MPIS. This problem depends on why the user is not interested.

Problem #3 in the Action step is that the user gives up attempting to make the Wi-Fi connection due to too many operation steps for registration. This could be a problem with Wi-Fi use in smartphone-signage collaboration or MPIS.

Problem #4 in the Action step is that the user cannot correctly operate the smartphone because he/she does not know which screen should be focused on. This is a problem with the user interface design of MPIS.

5   Experiments: Behavior Observation

We conducted experiments in a public exhibition space of a museum. The aim of the experiments was to extract problems in the user experience design of MPIS not from subjects prepared for the experiments but from regular visitors to the exhibition space. These experiments were conducted on Jan. 11th 2015. We did not select nor control subjects in advance so their age and gender were not confirmed. A demonstration booth was set as one exhibit in a free special exhibition event of a professional sport team. Thus, most subjects seemed to be fans in their 20's to 40's from our observation.

All the exhibits presented items about the sport team. The content on MPIS included player profiles, play results, etc. The exhibit was in an open space where everyone can freely enter and exit so we could not accurately measure the number of visitors. From the Wi-Fi connection logs it seems that there were about 200 visitors experienced MPIS.

Figures 3 and 4 show a floor map and the booth of our exhibit, respectively. As shown in Fig. 3, this exhibit area has two entrances and was surrounded by walls, in front of which many types of exhibit were demonstrated such as picture panels, a display to play movies, an attraction based on face recognition technology, etc. An experimenter had a seat in the center of the area and observed user behaviors. An instruction to use MPIS was presented on a sheet of the stand beside a signage display (See Fig. 4) and was also presented as a slideshow in one of the cells on signage screen (hidden in Fig. 4).

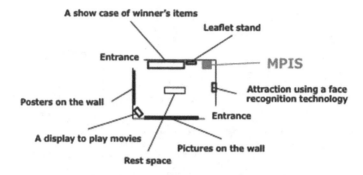

Fig. 3. Floor map of the MPIS exhibit area.

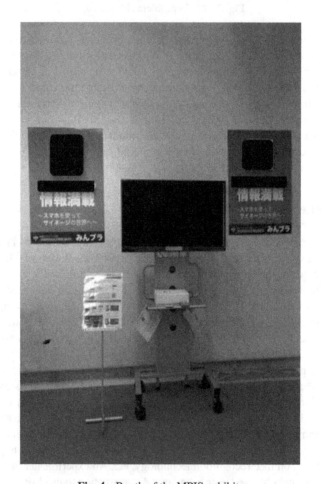

Fig. 4. Booth of the MPIS exhibit.

6 Analyses

In this section, we use the AIDA model to analyze the observed user behaviors. Table 1 summarizes the solutions for problems identified by the AIDA analysis.

Table 1. Solutions for problems identified by the AIDA analysis.

Step	Solution
Attention	Make a visually attractive guide near/on the signage display
Interest	Emphasize user benefits and attractive contents
Desire	Emphasize easy operation
Action	Ensure that the series of operations guides the user focus

6.1 Attention

We observed whether visitors stopped in front of the MPIS booth or not and found that 57 of 353 people (16%) stopped. This low ratio is because MPIS had a strong competitor; its neighbor was an exhibit that captured the visitor's face and displayed the famous sport player that most closely resembled the visitor. This result shows the importance of making a visually attractive guide near/on the signage display. This problem of "contending stimuli in the environment" would be more significant in the case of signage in a town, at a train station, etc. because many other visual/auditory advertisements occupy the same public space.

6.2 Interest and Desire

We observed how many people tried to use MPIS. 21 of the 57 people (37%) who stopped in front of MPIS tried to operate it. Most people did not recognize what services or contents MPIS would provide for them. Moreover, they seemed to have the impression that the signage would be difficult to use somehow. In order to attract more people, it is important to emphasize user benefits, attractive contents, and easy operation.

6.3 Action

To access MPIS service, the user had to perform two steps; connect to the MPIS Wi-Fi and then control the screen. In the exhibition, a free Wi-Fi service was provided and all exhibits needed Wi-Fi were based on the free Wi-Fi. When a visitor wanted to use the free Wi-Fi for the first time, registration was necessary. After finishing the registration, a portal page was shown on the smartphone. As shown in Fig. 5, forcing the user to navigate a long page sequence to start MPIS use is a significant problem. A system log showed that only 726 of 1691 (43%) attempts to connect to the MPIS Wi-Fi succeeded in reaching the portal page of MPIS.

Fig. 5. Long page sequence to start to use MPIS.

Next, we analyze the ease of operating MPIS. As mentioned in above, users needed to operate their own pointer on the signage display by finger flicks on their smartphone. This allowed users to overview a categorized menu on the signage and view detailed information of each category on their own smartphone. We assumed that users could operate the pointer without looking at their smartphone like a game controller. However, most users viewed the smartphone when entering finger flicks. Then, they were not able to see their own pointer move on the signage screen in response to their flick operation. Figure 6 shows a problem with the user's focus control in operating MPIS. The user could not understand when their focus should change.

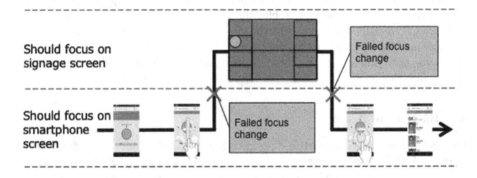

Fig. 6. User focus change in operating the MPIS

7 Discussion

It is expected that the MPIS service could be improved by applying solutions shown in Table 1 for each step of the AIDA model. In this section, we discuss one improvement. In the experiment, we found that most people noticed the existence of the signage display but did not pay attention to the instruction sheet on the stand beside the display. People glanced at the signage display, felt it was difficult to use, and gave up before checking the instruction sheet. Most people did not notice the existence of the instruction sheet as they were paying attention to the signage display. To solve this problem, one possible solution is to position the instruction sheet stand directly in front of and below the display, see Fig. 7. This is because it is not easy for humans to notice other object, printed material when concentrating on a display.

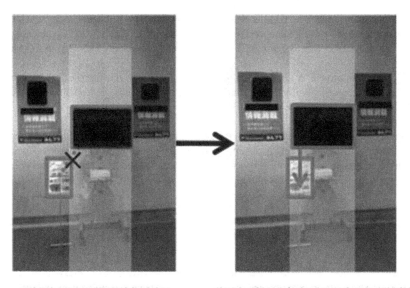

Place a stand beside a display   **Place a stand between a user and a display**

Fig. 7. Position change of instruction sheet stand.

8   Conclusion

This paper analyzed user experience design for new services with a use case of behavior observation of smartphone-signage collaboration for use in public spaces. We employed the AIDA model to analyze the observation results of user behaviors in a public exhibition space.

Future work includes improving the proposed smartphone-signage technology, MPIS, by applying the results of the AIDA analyses.

Acknowledgements.   This research is supported by the Ministry of Internal Affairs and Communications, Japan.

References

1. Alt, F., Schneegass, S., Girgis, M., Schmidt, A.: Cognitive effects of interactive public display applications. In: The 2nd ACM International Symposium on Pervasive Displays (PerDis 2013), Mountain View, CA, pp. 13–18, April 2013
2. Alt, F., Schneegaß, S., Schmidt, A., Müller, J., Memarovic, N.: How to evaluate public displays. In: the ACM International Symposium on Pervasive Displays (PerDis 2012), Porto, Portugal, Article 17, 6 p., June 2012

3. Davies, N., Langheinrich, M., Clinch, S., Elhart, I., Friday, A., Kubitza, T., Surajbali B.: Personalisation and privacy in future pervasive display networks. In: The SIGCHI Conference on Human Factors in Computing Systems (CHI 2014), Toronto, Canada, pp. 2357–2366, April–May 2014
4. Ihara, M., Seko, S., Miyata, A., Aoki, R., Ishida, T., Watanabe, M., Hashimoto, R., Watanabe, H.: Towards more practical information sharing in disaster situations. In: Yamamoto, S. (ed.) HIMI 2016, Part II. LNCS, vol. 9735, pp. 32–39. Springer, Cham (2016). doi: 10.1007/978-3-319-40397-7_4
5. Schwartz, L., Vagner, A., Kubicki, S., Altenburger, T.: Feedback on the definition and design of innovative mobile services. In: Proceedings of the 13th International Conference on Human Computer Interaction with Mobile Devices and Services (MobileHCI 2011), Stockholm, Sweden, pp. 525–528, August–September 2011

Do Car Drivers Really Need Mobile Parking Payment?

A Critical Evaluation of the Smart Service *apparkB* in Barcelona

Aylin Ilhan[✉], Kaja J. Fietkiewicz, and Wolfgang G. Stock

Department of Information Science, Heinrich Heine University Düsseldorf,
Düsseldorf, Germany
{Aylin.Ilhan,Kaja.Fietkiewicz}@hhu.de, stock@phil.hhu.de

Abstract. *apparkB* is a mobile parking payment application, which has been developed and implemented in the city of Barcelona, Spain. We empirically analyzed the awareness of Barcelona's citizens of this service, the users' satisfaction with it and their need to use it. Mobile applications are important services in smart cities, as they support citizens' daily tasks. To critically evaluate *apparkB* we deployed the information service evaluation (ISE) model. In order to get data on *apparkB* we applied an online survey, conducted interviews with Barcelona's smart city authorities, and performed rapid ethnographical field research in April 2016. Only a minority of Barcelona's citizens use this service, as they do not know it or do not use a car in the city. However, those who really use it articulate a need and are satisfied with *apparkB*.

Keywords: Smart service · ApparkB · Smart city · Mobile parking payment · Parking · Mobile service · Persuasive technology · Barcelona

1 Introduction

Why do we need more sustainable and commendable infrastructures in today's everyday life? One possible answer is that "population growth and increased urbanization raise a variety of technical, social, economic and organizational problems that tend to jeopardize the economic and environmental sustainability of cities" [1]. Who matches up to these challenges? For many researchers and practitioners, smart city developers do. They step up to the plate and do not only "monitor, understand, analyze and plan the city", but also create an infrastructure that "improve[s] the efficiency, equity and quality of life" for the people [2]. This article is a case study of the city of Barcelona, which is the 2nd largest city in Spain and is assumed to be one of the smartest cities in Europe [3]. As one of the smart services, Barcelona's citizens have the possibility to use a mobile application called apparkB to pay online for their parking ticket. Annoying situations like running back to the parking automat to prolong the ticket or the searching for the parking automat belong to the past. Which advantages has apparkB? Processes like paying, locating the parked car and prolonging the parking ticket are possible with only one mobile application, every time and everywhere. The basic idea of the smart application is easy to understand; however, do the citizens really use it? Our research is

© Springer International Publishing AG 2017
A. Marcus and W. Wang (Eds.): DUXU 2017, Part II, LNCS 10289, pp. 241–254, 2017.
DOI: 10.1007/978-3-319-58637-3_19

motivated by two questions. Do car drivers really need mobile parking payment? And, are the car drivers satisfied with this smart service?

1.1 Smart City and Smart Services

Up to date there is no clear definition of the term "smart city" and the concept is often characterized as fuzzy. According to Chourabi et al. [4], "the concept is used all over the world with different nomenclatures, context, and meanings." The improvement of the efficiency, sustainability and quality of life are aims of the smart city development projects. Fietkiewicz and Stock [5] summarized the existing definitions and introduced a comprehensive definition of "smart city." There are two sub-concepts – the broad and the narrow one. The latter concentrates on the green sustainable development of a city. Natural resources and energy, transport and mobility, and living conditions are in the main focus [1]. "[S]mart economy, smart people, smart governance, smart mobility, smart environment and smart living" are for Giffinger and Gudrun [6] essential and necessary components of a broader view on a smart city. Additionally, "education, healthcare, public safety" should also be recognized as essential infrastructure components [7]. The smart city in a broader sense is also labeled "Informational City," according to Castell's prototypical city of the network society [8]. Castell's theory defines two kinds of spaces: space of flows (flow of information, capital and power) and space of places (physical entities). Smart city research arrived at a new scientific discipline, namely "informational urbanism" [9].

The "smartness" of a city is defined by cognitive and the digital infrastructures [5]. For this case study, digital infrastructure (the information and communication (ICT) infrastructure) is the determining one. However, the best smart city concept or implementation of ICT is pointless if the citizens as well as the companies are not aware of the transformation of "their" city into a smart city. As Neirotti et al. [1] point out, "cities that are more equipped with ICT systems are not necessarily better cities." Developers require the right and needed ICT systems and smart services that are not isolated from each other and adapted to the needs of a specific target group. "A smarter city should be viewed as an organic whole – as a network, as a linked system" [10]. Cities that are equipped with ICT have three attributes: they are instrumented, interconnected and intelligent [11]. It is important to give the citizens the chance to "participate in the governance and management of the city" [4]. ICT is one – indeed important – aspect, but the use of ICT is another [12].

Mobile payment (m-payment) is a service which can be applied in smart cities [21–23]. M-payment organizes the interconnection between users' "credit or debit cards, phone bills, or prepaid deposits" and the mobile device [24]. It offers a convenient paying method from wireless devices related to different kinds of purchases. The Near Field Communication (NFC) supports m-payment. NFC "mobile payment has been emerging as a noticeable phenomenon that can enable consumers to turn their smartphone into digital wallets" [13]. But not only NFC enables mobile payment, other short-range wireless technologies such as Bluetooth, Infrared Data Association (IrDA) and Radio-Frequency Identification (RFID) enable mobile payment, too [14]. Hu, Li and Hu [15] confirm that users from all over the world appreciate mobile services such as mobile banking and m-payment. PaybyPhone enables to pay a ticket by mobile phone and makes the traditional parking meter obsolete. Mainetti et al. [16] stressed out that with the upcoming of smart cities intelligent parking systems boast necessity. "Drivers can spend a significant amount of time searching for available spots" [17] while producing and disseminating real-time information to drivers [17]. Related to parking meters, "over the years, the number of parking-system-related technologies has increased" [18]. Fraifer and Fernström [18] introduce different options of smart parking systems, such as Global Positioning Systems (GPS), RFID and other wireless sensor network-based services. With the use of such systems, the user is able to be informed about location and availability of parking spaces [18]. ApparkB is an application of mobile payment used to pay for parking in Barcelona.

1.2   Barcelona

Barcelona has a long history and an infrastructure that developed since centuries. Due to its geographical location, it became the main port, a popular touristic place and one of the leading industrial clusters of Spain. "Barcelona is considered as a success story in urban development across Europe" [3]. The city does not only get attention due to its transformation into a smart city. "The popularity of Barcelona noticeably increased, and it became attractive not only for tourism but also for talented people and business" [32]. Barcelona's path to a smart city is also supported by the fact that the Smart City Expo and World Congress took place for the first time in Barcelona in 2011 [19]. Barcelona's transformation into a smart city is characterized by "having a simple and effective, closer to citizens, connected, ubiquitous, and innovative public (local) administration" [20]. Smart Services in Barcelona represents a broad spectrum, e.g. Barcelona WiFi, Open Government (Open Data), Sharing Bicing Service and intelligent parking services. Some of the smart city programs of Barcelona and the including projects did not only improve the quality of life and the economic growth but also created 1,870 new jobs there [19]. Barcelona transformed its old and obsolete industrial zone "Poblenou" into a digital district, called 22@district [21]. To be equitable towards today's challenges, the 22@ district represent a "new model [of] knowledge urban space that encourages collaboration and synergies between universities, government and companies with the aim of developing innovation and entrepreneurship together with the creation of a good quality of life for its citizens" [21]. Considering the fact of the fast-growing developing progress and implementation of services, the 22@ district creates an "urban laboratory for testing future infrastructure and services" [21], called 22@ Urban Lab. Here, companies get the chance to develop new products and to conduct tests with pilot projects. The focus of these pilots is set on "the environment, energy, mobility, urban development and telecommunication" [22]. Strength of the 22@district, besides promotion of talents, is the enablement of clusters. According to Etzkowitz and Piqué [23], it is important to connect different facilities (like universities, institutions and companies) within one cluster. This way, the collaboration and the flow of knowledge between them is established and supported. Besides technical progress, it is also important to promote the ICT skills. According to Fontova [24], the Media-TIC in the 22@district is characterized as the main central point of the ICT community. Looking at the city's internet presence, it seems that the local government sees the necessity to keep up with other cities and advanced trends, as it presented a *Digital City Plan* from 2017–2020 with the aim "to drive technological sovereignty for citizens."

1.3 apparkB

The mobile application apparkB enables citizens of Barcelona to pay for their parking time via smartphone. It is freely available both for Android and for iOS users. To use the application to the fullest a registration is necessary. The registration process demands information such as name, personal identification number and approval number of the vehicle. In a next step, one has to enter the bank or credit card information. For the use of apparkB, it is necessary to be connected to the internet. ApparkB users profit from the possibility to prolong the parking time with their smartphone and not at the parking meter on the street. Comfortable paying is also guaranteed. ApparkB's users can prolong the digital parking ticket from everywhere and every time, depending on the parking time conditions. Furthermore, as the application works with GPS, it can help the user to find the parked car. Additionally, the application operates as an alerting service. The user can set the time when he wants to be remained of the remaining parking time. The traffic control checks whether the parked car has a digital parking ticket also with a mobile device [25].

To start the parking time, the user has to open the application, choose the parking zone as well as the vehicle and push the button to start the parking counter. Figure 1 (left) shows that the user has a parking duration of 42 min. To complete the payment and stop the parking the user must click on the blue button. The picture on the right of Fig. 1 shows the location map around the parking lot.

Fig. 1. Surface of apparkB – payment process (left); location map (right). Source: http://apps4bcn.cat/esp/app/apparkb-1/373/ (Color figure online)

2 Methods

The offer of smart services as apparkB in Barcelona does not necessarily have to be successful considering the needs and satisfaction of citizens in smart cities. ApparkB represents a mobile application that supports the mobile payment and mobile prolonging of parking tickets and the locating of the parked car. Our theoretical model framework enabled us to evaluate users' experience with this application.

2.1 Theoretical Model Framework

We have chosen the Information Service Evaluation (ISE) model [12] (Fig. 2) as our evaluation framework. The dimension 1 (D1) of the ISE model concentrates on information services in general. According to Venkatesh and Davis [26], the success, the adoption and the use of information technology is dependent on two important factors: perceived usefulness and perceived ease of use. Perceived ease of use describes whether a service operates efficiently or not [26]. Referred to the e-commerce, Gefen, Karahanna, and Straub [27] point out that the factor trust is important as well. D1 measures the perceived smart service quality and includes the aspects ease of use, usefulness and trust.

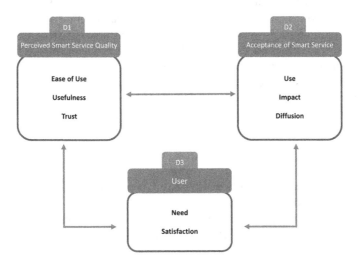

Fig. 2. Our research model

ISE's dimension 2 (D2) represents the acceptance of a smart service. According to Schumann and Stock [12], the dimension of acceptance includes the aspects of adoption, usage, impact and diffusion. It is important to distinguish between adoption and usage. Schumann and Stock [12] describe it concisely: "One can adopt a service and stop to use it. And one can adopt it and use it permanently." Within their evaluation framework, the regular usage in everyday life usually results in behavior changes of some kind. This phenomenon is called impact. If someone accepts a service, uses it and is satisfied with it, then it is likely that he or she will recommend it to friends or family (the so-called 'diffusion'). Every service needs a recommendation, as Venkatesh and Davis [26] explained, that "a superior or co-worker suggests that a particular system might be useful, a person may come to believe that it actually is useful, and in turn, form an intention to use it." D2 measures the acceptance of a smart service and includes the aspects use, impact and diffusion.

ISE's dimension 3 (D3) represents the residents of a smart city. For our investigation, it is important to find out if there is a correlation between perceived smart service quality and the user's need and satisfaction. The original dimension 'information user' by Schumann and Stock [12] was adapted for this purpose. This case study concentrates on the satisfaction of the users with the service, as it is an important indicator for the product's success. "To avoid wasting resources in this way it is useful to survey the user satisfaction and to use the findings to inform the planning of product development" [28]. Satisfaction includes an element of need, because "if the system does not provide the needed information, the user will become dissatisfied and look elsewhere" [29]. According to Lee and Pow [30], the satisfaction referred to a system is related "to the ease of accessing, learning and using the system, user control, flexibility, robustness, and so on." Therefore, it is necessary to evaluate the satisfaction of users and to analyze the aspects, which deteriorate or improve the satisfaction of a user. Furthermore, Doll and Torkzadeh [31] point out that the analysis of the satisfaction of a user could be compared with different aspects as "content, format, accuracy, ease of use, or timeliness." In this way, the third dimension (D3) in this framework model inquires the subjective satisfaction of the user and his or her needs.

The following research questions (RQs) are either general questions on Barcelona as a smart city and on apparkB's usage (RQ1 and 2) or aspects regarding the interrelationships between the dimensions of the ISE model (Fig. 2); they are the foundation of this investigation.

- RQ1: Background information: How many people in Barcelona realize that they are living in a smart city?
- RQ2: D2/Acceptance of apparkB: How many people use apparkB? How often do they use it? Why do some people refuse to use it?
- RQ3: Are there correlations between the perceived smart service quality of apparkB (D1), the acceptance of this smart service (D2) and the user characteristics in terms of needs and satisfaction (D3)?

2.2 Practical Framework

In order to answer the three research questions an online survey was developed and distributed in Barcelona using social media and e-mail contacts. The online survey was based on a seven-point Likert scale (1 – "Strongly disagree" up to 7 – "Strongly agree").

Furthermore, to understand the progress and concept of Barcelona's smart city it was essential to conduct a case study combined with a rapid ethnographical field research before the survey was developed. Case studies are used to develop a theory based on the executed case study. The data collected in a recently executed case studies leads to a theory based on "novelty, testability, and empirical validity, which arise[s] from the intimate linkage with empirical evidence" [32]. A case study is a good way to gather information on unexplored or marginally explored research fields and develop a theory based on the gathered data. Furthermore, the case study "is useful in early stages of

research on a topic or when a fresh perspective is needed, while the latter is useful in later stages of knowledge" [32]. The aim of this case study is to find out if the residents of Barcelona use some of the smart services, if so, how often do they use them and why, or what are the reasons for not using the services. The results of the research are of importance for either improving or implementing smart city services in other cities or countries, especially pertaining to their advantages or disadvantages. The case study and the ethnographical field research, which is "a style of research that lays down the procedural rules for how to study people in naturally occurring setting or 'fields' by means that capture their social meaning and ordinary activities" [33] enables a real impression about the city, citizens and services by being on location. We conducted a "rapid" ethnography. Baines and Cunningham [34] describe the rapid ethnographical research as "a form of multi-method ethnography involving data collection from numerous sources over a relatively short period including interviews, participant observations, document review and sometimes surveys and focus groups." According to Millen [35], the rapid ethnographical field research has the potential "to provide a richer field experience for a smaller amount of time in the field."

Both strategies, the case study as well as the ethnographical field research, employ interviews as a research method. Qu and Dumay [36] point out that this kind of method is one of the strongest ones to collect qualitative data. The interviews with authorities responsible for the Barcelona smart city strategy and services enable a good understanding of the goals and vision of the project. The semi-structured interview method includes prepared questions, which are "guided by identified themes in a consistent and systematic manner interposed with proves designed to elicit more elaborate responses" [36].

Barcelona was visited in April 2016 for eight days, and nine authorities of Barcelona's smart city services were interviewed on-site. Additionally, 131 participants from Barcelona completed the questionnaire.

3 Results

3.1 Perceived Smartness of Barcelona (RQ1)

It is interesting to analyze if residents living in Barcelona also know that their city is labeled as a smart city and what a smart city is exactly. Figure 3 shows that 57% of 131 participants know that Barcelona is labeled as smart city and 49% have basic knowledge on the definition of a smart city. Since even researchers are not in agreement about smart city's definition, this is a surprising result.

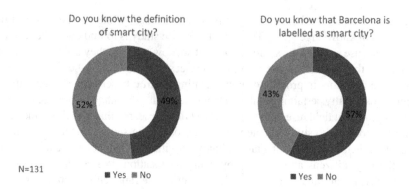

Fig. 3. Awareness of smart city definition and Barcelona being a smart city

3.2 Usage of apparkB (RQ2)

Related to apparkB, Fig. 4 shows that only 8% do actually use the application for paying their parking ticket or to locate their parked car. 27% do know the application, but do not use it. Why most respondents do not use apparkB? Many participants (62%) do not know the app. Other participants stated that they do not need the app, as they do not drive into the city or only use free parking places (Fig. 5). Other occasionally mentioned reasons are that the participants are not satisfied with the application as it does not work properly or that the application requires too much personal information.

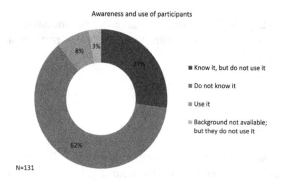

Fig. 4. Using distribution related to apparkB

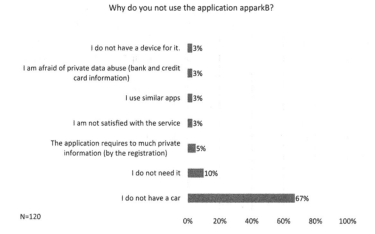

Fig. 5. Reasons for rejecting the apparkB; multiple answers were possible (non-users only)

Figure 6 shows that two out of eleven active apparkB customers use the application several times a day (18%). The second most used time interval is several times a week. 18% of the customers use the app once a week. However, the majority of participants use apparkB less than once a week (36%).

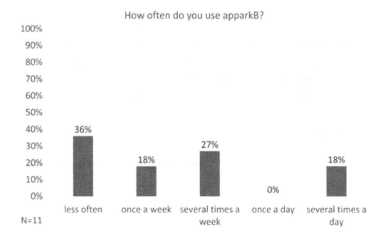

Fig. 6. Use distribution related to apparkB (users only)

Now we arrive at users' assessment of the apparkB project. For the analysis of each statement listed in Fig. 7, the median values were computed. The statements about apparkB generate an impression how the participants perceived the service's impact and functions. Participants confirm the usability of the application as they agree that it is easy to use (median: 6). Also, the service of locating the parked car is very well received (6). The customers nearly always confirm that the payment via the application does work without technical problems (6). However, apparkB does not offer the feature of finding a free parking space (3), and users would welcome such a service. One of the project's main impacts is the replacement of the manual parking meter (7). The function to prolong a ticket does not fully convince the residents, when looking at the median value (4.5). However, participants emphasize the usability of the app, since prolonging the parking ticket with the application is easier than with the manual parking meter (6). It is easy to register as a user (6). Furthermore, the users have no trust problems to transmit the credit card and bank information (6). The participants confirm that the application satisfied their demands (6). They would recommend the service to friends or family members that do not know it (6). In the end, the participants totally agreed that they would recommend apparkB for other cities, too (7).

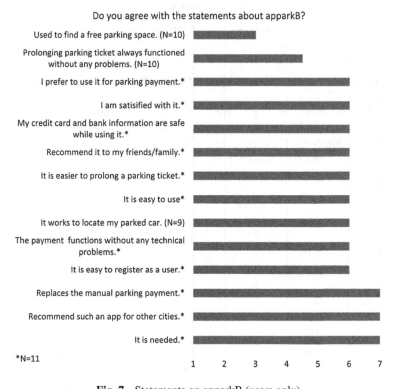

Fig. 7. Statements on apparkB (users only)

3.3 Correlations Between apparkB's Perceived Quality, Acceptance and Users' Characteristics (RQ3)

The survey included several different questions about the apparkB. The internal consistency of the dimensions was tested with Cronbach's α. A positive correlation has to be interpreted bidirectional as the variance is not calculated by deeper analysis. As our data are on an ordinal scale, we calculated a rank correlation applying Spearman's rho.

Is there a rank correlation between the perceived smart service quality (D1) and the acceptance of smart service (D2)? The only indicator from D1 that significantly

correlates with indicators of D2 is *Usefulness* (+.654* with *Impact*, +.730* with *Diffusion* and even +.762** with *Use*) (Table 1). The more apparkB is perceived as useful, the more it is used, has more impact and tends to diffuse into society, generally, the more it is accepted. Perceived ease of use only plays a minor role when it comes to acceptance of this smart service. Considering the correlations between D1 and D3 (user), again *Usefulness* is essential. It correlates significantly with both, *Satisfaction* (+.614*) as well as *Need* (+.759**). The more apparkB is perceived useful the more it is satisfying and meets the users' needs.

Table 1. Bivariate rank correlation (Spearman's rho) between perceived smart service quality (D1), smart service acceptance (D2) and user (D3)

	Dimension 1			Dimension 2			Dimension 3	
N = 11	Ease of use	Usefulness	Trust	Use	Impact	Diffusion	Need	Satisfaction
Ease of use	1	.544	.206	.130	.481	.332	.337	.564
Usefulness	.544	1	.244	**.762****	**.654**	**.730***	**.759****	**.614***
Trust	.206	.244	1	−.010	.257	.333	.306	.366
Use	.130	**.762****	−.010	1	.298	**.785****	**.845****	.276
Impact	.481	**.654***	.257	.298	1	.234	.394	**.629***
Diffusion	.332	**.730***	.333	**.785****	.234	1	**.824****	.579
Need	.337	**.759****	.306	**.845****	.394	**.824****	1	.393
Satisfaction	.564	**.614***	.366	.276	**.629**	.579	.393	1

* $p < .05$, ** $p < .01$, *** $p < .001$

For indicators of D2 and D3, there is a strong correlation between *Need* and *Use* (+.845**), *Need* and *Diffusion* (+.824**) as well as between *Satisfaction* and *Impact* (+.629*). The more apparkB is needed by the users the more the customers will use it and it will diffuse to new users. The more users are satisfied the more impact apparkB has on them. Additionally, there is an important significant correlation between two indicators within dimension 2. *Diffusion* highly correlates with *Use* (+.785**), meaning the more apparkB is used the more it will diffuse into society. If a smart service as apparkB satisfies the users' needs, it is perceived as useful. Usefulness in turn has strong relations to use, impact and diffusion. Ease of use and trust only exhibit weak relations to acceptance.

4   Discussion

Rapid ethnographical field research and semi-structured interviews showed that Barcelona is not overloaded with high number of ICT services. ICT related services are merely implemented in areas where the residents really need them. One interviewee defined this idea as "the development and implementation of a symmetrical infrastructure." Being able to decide, if services need to be implemented in specific areas is important to avoid unnecessary costs and to ensure the maximum benefit for the citizens.

The critical evaluation of the service apparkB in Barcelona shows that only a minority of the participants use this application, because the majority simply has no car in the city (it is not fun to drive in Barcelona). Nevertheless, 8% of all our participants are satisfied with the smart city service and do need it. Obviously, apparkB satisfies those users' needs and leads to its use. Based on the outcomes of the survey, it is not the missing satisfaction, the trust or the ease of use why people avoid the application. The pivotal question is, "is there a need to drive and to park in the city?" Citizens in metropolises often use public transport possibilities and leave the car at home. Traffic jam, no parking places or too expensive parking spaces are typical motives to not use a car. During the rapid ethnographical field research, we observed a lot of citizens using a bicycle or public transport possibilities. They obviously do not need apparkB. It also raises the question, whether smart city projects should encourage car holders to drive into the city, by offering such applications. Smart city idea is also linked to a sustainable development and green city infrastructure. Therefore, it is more advisable to allocate the resources and ICT technology to developing a more efficient public transport, supporting car-sharing, or use of alternatives to the own car. Making the usage of cars in the city center easier with help of parking applications contradicts this idea. Divorced from the smart city context, it is indeed a good and convenient alternative to manual parking meters.

Nevertheless, by using and implementing ICT (like the introduced mobile applications) manual procedures like parking meters become obsolete. As today the most people have a mobile phone, developers use this possibility to improve the life quality by simplifying the daily tasks. In the current state of technology, a mobile phone is not only a device for communication it also could be used as a digital wallet, since payment for parking time is possible. Additionally, the results show that parking applications do not only offer a comfortable payment, but also prolonging of the parking time and ticket.

This research makes clear that the critical evaluation of services in smart cities is not only a "nice" option but rather a necessity. With the use of evaluation models, developers and researchers get a feedback, if the citizens really need such services. Furthermore, our research shows that the success of a service depends on different indicators, including the users' needs, the service's perceived usefulness, its impact on users' behavior, and the extend of use.

References

1. Neirotti, P., De, M.A., Cagliano, A.C., Mangano, G., Scorrano, F.: Current trends in smart city initiatives: some stylised facts. Cities **38**, 25–36 (2014). doi:10.1016/j.cities.2013.12.010
2. Batty, M., Axhausen, K.W., Giannotti, F., Pozdnoukhov, A., Bazzani, A., Wachowicz, M., Ouzounis, G., Portugali, Y.: Smart cities of the future. Eur. Phys. J. Spec. Top. **214**, 481–518 (2012). doi:10.1140/epjst/e2012-01703-3
3. Bakici, T., Almirall, E., Wareham, J.: A smart city initiative: the case of Barcelona. J. Knowl. Econ. **4**, 135–148 (2013). doi:10.1007/s13132-012-0084-9
4. Chourabi, H., Nam, T., Walker, S., Gil-Garcia, J.R., Mellouli, S., Nahon, K., Pardo, T.A., Scholl, H.J.: Understanding smart cities: an integrative framework. In: Proceedings of the Hawaii International Conference on System Sciences, pp. 2289–2297. IEEE Computer Society (2011)
5. Fietkiewicz, K.J., Stock, W.G.: How "smart" are Japanese cities? An empirical investigation of infrastructures and governmental programs in Tokyo, Yokohama, Osaka, and Kyoto. In: Proceedings of the Hawaii International Conference on System Sciences, pp. 2345–2354. IEEE Computer Society (2015). doi:10.1109/HICSS.2015.282

6. Giffinger, R., Haindlmaer, G.: Smart cities ranking: an effective instrument for the positioning of cities? Archit. City Environ. **4**, 7–25 (2010)
7. Washburn, D., Sindhu, U.: Helping CIOs understand "smart city" initiatives. Forrester Research (2009)
8. Castells, M.: The Informational City: Information Technology, Economic Restructuring and the Urban-Regional Process. Blackwell, Oxford (1989). doi:10.2307/2073712
9. Stock, W.G.: Informational Urbanism. Syst. Cybern. Inf. **13**, 62–69 (2015)
10. Kanter, R.M., Litow, S.S.: Informed and interconnected: a manifesto for smarter cities. Harvard Business School Working Paper, No. 09-141 (2009)
11. Harrison, C., Eckman, B., Hamilton, R., Hartswick, P., Kalagnanam, J., Paraszczak, J., Williams, P.: Foundations for smarter cities. IBM J. Res. Dev. **54**, 1–16 (2010). doi:10.1147/JRD.2010.2048257
12. Schumann, L., Stock, W.G.: The information service evaluation (ISE) model. Webology **11**, 1–20 (2014). doi:10.3233/ISU-140759
13. Pham, T.T.T., Ho, J.C.: The effects of product-related, personal-related factors and attractiveness of alternatives on consumer adoption of NFC-based mobile payments. Technol. Soc. **43**, 159–172 (2015). doi:10.1016/j.techsoc.2015.05.004
14. Leong, L.Y., Hew, T.S., Tan, G.W.H., Ooi, K.B.: Predicting the determinants of the NFC-enabled mobile credit card acceptance: a neural networks approach. Expert Syst. Appl. **40**, 5604–5620 (2013). http://dx.doi.org/10.1016/j.eswa.2013.04.018
15. Hu, X., Li, W., Hu, Q.: Are mobile payment and banking the killer apps for mobile commerce? In: 41st Hawaii International Conference on System Sciences, pp. 84–94. IEEE Computer Society (2008)
16. Mainetti, L., Marasovic, I., Patrono, L., Solic, P., Stefanizzi, M.L., Vergallo, R.: A novel IoT-aware smart parking system based on the integration of RFID and WSN technologies. Int. J. RF Technol. **7**, 175–199 (2016). doi:10.3233/RFT-161523
17. Nawaz, S., Efstratiou, C., Mascolo, C.: Smart sensing systems. Pervasive Comput. **15**, 39–43 (2016). doi:10.1109/MPRV.2016.22
18. Fraifer, M., Fernström, M.: Investigation of smart parking systems and their technologies. In: Thirty Seventh International Conference on Information Systems. IoT Smart City Challenges Applications (ISCA 2016), Dublin, Ireland, pp. 1–14 (2016)
19. Gascó, M.: What makes a city smart? Lessons from Barcelona. In: HICSS 2016 Proceedings of the 2016 49th Hawaii International Conference on System Sciences, pp. 2983–2989. IEEE Computer Society (2016)
20. Gascó, M., Trivellato, B., Cavenago, D.: How do southern European cities foster innovation? Lessons from the experience of the smart city approaches of Barcelona and Milan. In: Gil-Garcia, J.R., Pardo, T.A., Nam, T. (eds.) Smarter as the New Urban Agenda. PAIT, vol. 11, pp. 191–206. Springer, Cham (2016). doi:10.1007/978-3-319-17620-8_10
21. Piqué, J.M., Pareja-Eastaway, M.: Knowledge cities on smart cities: transferring the 22 @ Barcelona model. In: 30th IASP World Conference on Science and Technology Parks - Work. 2 new role STPs Driv. city Chang. Recife, Brazil, pp. 1–14 (2013)
22. Majó, A.: 22@Urban Lab, the example of Barcelona. In: Col·legi d'Economistes de Catalunya (ed.) Knowl. Econ. Territ., 64th edn. Revista Econòmica de Catalunya, pp. 101–105 (2014)
23. Etzkowitz, H., Piqué, J.M.: 22@ Barcelona: a knowledge city beyond science parks. In: Catalunya C d'Economistes de (ed.) Knowl. Econ. Territ., 64th edn. Revista Econòmica de Catalunya, pp. 171–182 (2014)
24. Fontova, R.: The Media-Tic building, a "medusa" in 22@ (2009). http://lameva.barcelona.cat/bcnmetropolis/arxiu/en/page43d3.html?id=22&ui=304&prevNode=33&tagId=23

25. Ajuntament de BarcelonalBarcelona de Serveis Municipals SA ApparkB. https://www.areaverda.cat/en/operation-with-mobile-phone/apparkb/
26. Venkatesh, V., Davis, F.D.: A theoretical extension of the technology acceptance model: four longitudinal field studies. Manage. Sci. **46**, 186–204 (2000). doi:10.1287/mnsc.46.2.186.11926
27. Gefen, D., Karahanna, E., Straub, D.W.: Trust and TAM in online shopping: an integrated model. MIS Q. **25**, 51–90 (2003)
28. Bramwell, B.: User satisfaction and product development in urban tourism. Tour. Manage. **19**, 35–47 (1998). doi:10.1016/S0261-5177(97)00091-5
29. Ives, B., Olson, M., Baroudi, J.: The measurement of user information satisfaction. Commun. ACM **26**, 785–793 (1983). doi:10.1145/358413.358430
30. Lee, M.K.O., Pow, J.: Information access behaviour and expectation of quality: two factors affecting the satisfaction of users of clinical hospital information systems. J. Inf. Sci. **22**, 171–179 (1996). doi:10.1177/016555159602200303
31. Doll, W.J., Torkzadeh, G.: The measurement of end-user computing. Manage. Inf. Syst. Q. **12**, 259–274 (1988). doi:10.2307/248851
32. Eisenhardt, K.M.: Building theories from case study research. Acad. Manage. Rev. **14**, 532–550 (1989). doi:10.5465/AMR.1989.4308385
33. Brewer, J.: Ethnography. Open University Press, Buckingham (2000)
34. Baines, D., Cunningham, I.: Using comparative perspective rapid ethnography in international case studies: strengths and challenges. Qual. Soc. Work. **12**, 73–88 (2013). doi:10.1177/1473325011419053
35. Millen, D.R.: Rapid ethnography: time deepening strategies for HCI field research. In: Proceedings of the Conference on Designing Interactive Systems: Processes, Practices, and Methods Techniques, pp. 280–288. ACM New York (2000). doi:10.1145/347642.347763
36. Qu, S.Q., Dumay, J.: The qualitative research interview. Qual. Res. Acc. Manage. **8**, 238–264 (2004). http://dx.doi.org/10.1108/11766091111162070

The Study of Factors Affecting Minimum Center Distance of Mobile Touch Screen

Hong Ji[✉], Jingqin He[✉], Hong Sun[✉], and Jie Yin[✉]

Shanghai Research Institute of China Telecom Corporation Limited, Shanghai, China
jihong@sttri.com.cn, wanztzd13@163.com,
{sunhong,yinjie}@chinatelecom.cn

Abstract. The research takes the key center distance as the object and having a dynamic regulation through operation of performance result and get minimum center distance. Furthermore, the influence factors of the minimum center distance are explored based on the combination of the key speed and the subjective score. The results showed that: (1) the four assignments, discrete thumb, the thumb series, discrete index thumb and index series, have the minimum center distance that severally are: 4.17 mm, 6.30 mm, 3.38 mm and 5.40 mm. (2) The two factors of task type and operation finger have influence on minimum center distance. The results of this experiment can provide a scientific basis for the small key in touch screen and standardized design of the layout.

Keywords: Touch screen · Center distance

1 Introduction

With the development and popularization of smart phone more and more application transferred into mobile phone from computer in the field of social networking, such as shopping and so on. However, compared with the traditional computer screen, touch screen of mobile phone intelligent interactive space is much smaller. It's inevitable to rise new problem in operation between the rich content and the limited space, such as malfunction, low incoming efficiency (Wang Haiyan 2012). To this end, researchers have done a lot of research on the touch screen interaction problems, such as the influence factors of touch screen performance.

Related research has mainly focused on the impact of the size of key and the key spacing on the performance of the operation. For example, Parhi et al. (2006) used single click on the target (discrete) and serial click on the target (continuous), these two tasks were had a systematic research on the best mobile handheld touch key target size equipment under the single hand thumb operation. The result shows that subjects of the task completion time will reduce with the increase of the size of the object.

When the target is higher than a certain size (the size of discrete click operation button is 9.6 mm, the size of continuous click operation is 7.7 mm), it has no significant difference between various size level of click operation error. Key spacing refers to the distance between the two button edge that is another important design parameter frequently combined in size of the key. Zhang Wenlin (2011) recorded touch point offset,

© Springer International Publishing AG 2017
A. Marcus and W. Wang (Eds.): DUXU 2017, Part II, LNCS 10289, pp. 255–261, 2017.
DOI: 10.1007/978-3-319-58637-3_20

error rate and subjective assessment of the tested finger under the condition of in 3 key dimensions (4, 6 and 8 mm) and 3 kinds of spacing (0, 1 and 2 mm) using the thumb click task operation. The result shows that the size of the button has a significant impact on click operation drop point offset of click operation and error rate.

When the target size is larger, the placement of the offset and the error rate is lower. Besides, the effect of key space on performance is affected by the size of the button, when the key size is less than 6 mm, it should reduce the key space as much as possible to improve the operation correctness. Otherwise, the key space should be relaxed as much as possible.

Previous studies have verified that the size of key and the key space have a significant impact on the clicking operating performance of the touch screen. The larger the size of the target or the key space, the better the performance of the operation and the satisfaction of the subjective experience. However, further analysis shows that the existing studies have the following deficiencies. First of all, the key size and key space are independent research objects but they have reciprocal effect on both the spatial design and task performance in past study. Secondly, the best key is explored mainly through the control of fixed key size (key space level) and size he present study mainly through the control of a plurality of/key space level and click on the performance results of comprehensive comparison in each level. But these results can be different due to the different size of the variation level which leads to the instability results. Finally, the thumb was mostly used at click task operation in past research (Zhang Wenlin 2011; Park and Han 2010). The index finger is also used in the operation of finger except thumb in actual operation. In addition, although the clicking operation is the most basic operation mode and the actual operation is more complex, such as continuous digital input, text input, etc.

2   Experiment

2.1   Objective

This study will use the key center distance in touch screen as the research object through the operation of performance results to dynamically adjust the level of the center distance. Accomplish the operation of performance and subjective assessment results according to the thumb discrete, index finger discrete, thumb series and index series these four typical scenes.

2.2   Research Method

Subject. It have 31 internal students in the experiment (male: 16, female: 15) and they are all handedness who are at the age between 19–29 with normal vision and are able to use the mobile phone for the key operation. 14 of them had the experience of touch screen operation.

Experimental Equipment and Procedures. The experiment has four mobile phone running prototype test program, four mobile phone screen that have capacitive touch screen. The size of the screen is the representative in current market (mainly represents the prophase research on Hangzhou mobile phone stores based on specific parameters). Details are in Table 1.

Table 1. Phone parameters

Model	Size (inch)	Resolution (pix)	Length width (mm)
SE LT18i	4.2	480 * 854	93 * 52
SE X10i	4	480 * 854	89 * 50
HTC G13	3.7	480 * 800	82 * 49
SamsungI9000	4	480 * 800	87 * 52

In this study, the prototype program is composited by the C# language button test program which can be run under the Android system. The program interface mainly includes task prompt area and key operation area and shows in the Table 1.

The contents of the task prompt area will present the corresponding operation based on different types of tasks.

The length and width of keys in the operating area are equal. The distance between keys is 0 pixels. Every key center distance adjustment is according to the results of task completion rate after accomplished key task as the red line represents the distance between the two key centers that shown in Fig. 1. The initial parameters involved are converted to the corresponding pixel values, in order to maintain consistency between the various mobile phones.

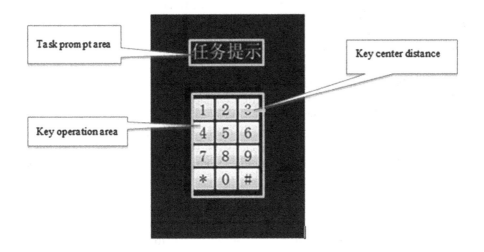

Fig. 1. Key test program of schematic diagram.

Experimental Variable and Design. The independent variables are operating finger and task type. Operating finger includes thumb and index finger of tested handedness. Task types include discrete tasks and a series of tasks. Four kinds of typical tasks are composed by two variables, which is the thumb discrete, thumb series, index discrete and index series. The subjects are designed in the experiment. It means all the subjects are required to through task operation under these four scenarios.

The dependent variable includes task completion rate in different center distance and the current subjective evaluation scores, it recorded automatically by the prototype program. The task completion rate refers to the percentage of correct responses to the 20 key tasks in each center distance. Subjective evaluation score refers to the key comfortable score to each center distance (Grade 5 score, 1 point means not satisfied, 5 points means very satisfied). Previous studies have found that the best key size is about 10 mm (Parhi et al. 2006). So the initial center distance of this study is set to 10 mm. The experimental implementation is adjusted by binary method according to every 20 task performance results in the center distance. The specific methods are as follows.

Take the current center for 10 mm at the first task operation, when task correct rate >=90% after the 20 consecutive tasks operation, the next operation of the center distance adjust to the center point of 5 mm 0 and 10 mm, otherwise, it should adjust to 12.5 mm which is the center point 10 mm and 15 mm. Repeated cycle test until the correct rate of <90% when passing a center distance and stop the task when two consecutive central distance of the correct rate of operation is >=90%. Finally, the linear interpolation method is used to find the center distance of the 90% corresponding.

Experimental Task. Under the condition of the designated center distance, the subjects touched by thumb and index finger for 20 times in consecutive. This operation includes discrete tasks and series of tasks of the two tasks.

The discrete task requires subjects to continuously press the corresponding key quickly and accurately with using the pulp of thumb and index finger according to the procedures task were presented randomly in the mission area (for example: "1" content of the task is single digits or symbols).

Series tasks requires subjects to successively press the corresponding key quickly and accurately with using the pulp of thumb and index finger according to the procedures task were presented in the mission area t (for example: "246#" means the content of the task is 4 digit or character combination).

The maximum reminded duration time for discrete tasks is 3 s and 12 s respectively. The interval time of these two tasks are fixed for 2 s. The task failed when the task failed to complete the corresponding key operation according to the task instructions in the task display time.

Experimental Procedure. Before the experiment, the subjects signed the Agreement and the Statement and the User Background Questionnaire. The experimenter read the experimental guide language to the subjects and open test program with clicking "practice experience" after the subjects understood the instructions. The subjects did two tasks of the practice for 3 times respectively. In the formal experiment, the experimenter fills the experimental parameters. The subjects continuous operate for 20 times in the specified key center distance. The subjects give a comfort evaluation about the key, after the completion of the operation and adjust the center distance according to the correct result rate of the operation. Repeat until the completion of all tasks. After the completion of all tasks, the subjects signed the registration form then receive remuneration.

In the progress of the experiment, the subjects used their handedness to hold the mobile phone and keep doing single hand operation. In order to balance the influence of each level, the task type and the operation order of the fingers are using ABBA balance technique.

The experimental results were processed by the SPSS17.0 software package. The three data, outside of standard deviations (about 3.2%), were respectively disposal which used in the thumb and index finger discrete tasks. The data, a series of center distance, the corresponding task completion rate, and the subjective evaluation score, is obtained after each test in the experiment. We use linear interpolation method to convert the data into the corresponding subjective evaluation score the minimum effective center distance. The main methods are as follows.

First of all, make the center distance as the abscissa, the 20 task to operate the correct rate as the ordinate, draw a broken line. As it shows in Table 2, to determine a point which correct rate is less than 90% and is the minimum distance of center after passing the first turning point, solid circles such as the (42,80%) and (43100%) in the dotted circle. The 90% corresponding of maximum center distance is acquired according to linear interpolation method: the formula $(y - y0)/(x - x0) = (y1 - y0)/(x1 - x0)$.

Table 2. Results of mean value, standard deviation of the minimum center distance (M+SD) and other targets under the condition of four tasks

	Thumb		Index finger	
	Discrete	Series	Discrete	Series
Minimum center distance (mm)	4.17 (1.25)	6.30 (1.29)	3.38 (0.59)	5.40 (1.32)
Operating evaluation score (1–5)	2.7 (0.87)	3.4 (0.75)	2.4 (0.95)	3.2 (0.79)

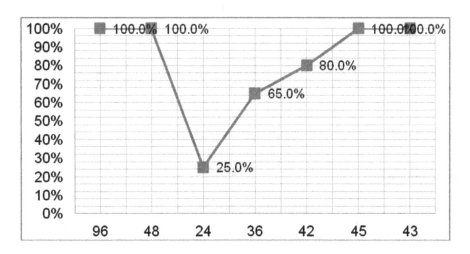

Fig. 2. Schematic diagram of minimum effective center distance

42.5 pixels of minimum center distance is based on the method above, and the mean value of the center corresponding to 42 and the 43 pixels is the current minimum center distance score (Fig. 2).

After the analysis above, we got minimum of center distance of four task scenarios (thumb discrete, index finger discrete, thumb series and the Index finger Series) according to the conversion rate of mobile phone pixel by pixel unit will center distance into mm. We got score data of the operation experience the mean and standard deviation of the results that are shown in Table 2.

3 Result

3.1 Minimum Center Distance

As it shown in Table 2, the results of the meaning value minimum center distance in 90% task completion rate is the index finger discrete (3.38 mm), thumb discrete (4.17 mm), index series (5.40 mm), and thumb series (6.30 mm). The analysis to the repeating method of minimum center distance of 2 (operation finger) *2 (task type) shows the nearly remarkable result: $F (1.30) = 17.58$, $p < .01$, $\eta2 = 0.37$. The result shows that the minimum center distance required by thumb operation is significantly larger than the center distance required by the index finger operation. The main effect of type is significant: $F (1.30) = 206.92$, $p < .01$, $\eta2 = 0.873$. It shows that the minimum center distance required by series of mission operations was significantly greater than that discrete tasks required from center distance. There was no significant interaction between finger and task type ($p > .05$).

3.2 Subjective Evaluation Score

It can be seen from Table 2 that the mean scores subjective feeling of the minimum key center under four kinds of task scenarios from high to low can be arranged as the thumb series (3.4), index finger series (3.2), thumb discrete (2.7) and index finger discrete (2.4).

The analysis of variance of repeated measurement on the subjective score were 2 (operation finger) *2 (task type), the main effect of finger operation is nearly significant, $F (1.30) = 3.97$, $p = 0.056$, $\eta2 = 0.117$. It shows that the subjective feelings task operation with thumb of the subjects is better than the subjective feelings in the discrete task. The main effect of the task type is significant, $F (1.30) = 31.84$, $p < .01$, $\eta2 = 0.515$. It shows that the subjective feeling of subjects in a series of task operation is better than it in the discrete tasks. There was no significant interaction between finger and task type ($p > .05$).

4 Conclusion

From the results above we can draw these conclusions:

The minimum of the key center distance results under the four task scenes, index finger discrete (3.38 mm), thumb discrete (4.17 mm), index series (5.40 mm) and the index finger series (6.30 mm) can be used as design basis when doing the design of operation key which use the small capacitive touch screen as the representing. But the specific design should be based on these parameters. Should enlarge the distance between the center of the button as much as possible, to ensure that the user's higher subjective experience.

References

Wang, H.Y.: Interaction design research of touch-screen mobile phone in mobile environment. Master's Thesis. Beijing University of Posts and Telecommunications (2012)

Zhang, W.L.: Effects of button and gap sizes on task accuracy for keyboard of touch sensitive mobile phone. Master's Thesis. Taiwan University of Science and Technology (2011)

Parhi, P., Karlson, A.K., Bederson, B.B.: Target size study for one-handed thumb use on small touchscreen devices. Paper Presented at the Proceedings of the 8th Conference on Human-computer Interaction with Mobile Devices and Services, Espoo, Finland, September 2006

Park, Y.S., Han, S.H.: Touch key design for one-handed thumb interaction with a mobile phone: effects of touch key size and touch key location. Int. J. Ind. Ergon. **40**(1), 68–76 (2010)

Mobile Phone – Offers Exchanged as Cultural Practice

Arminda Guerra Lopes[✉]

Madeira Interactive Technologies Institute, Madeira, Portugal
aguerralopes@gmail.com

Abstract. Mobile technologies are already modifying well-established communication patterns, amplifying and substituting them. Participating in the mobile information society is not only a matter of getting a phone call or a phone, but how it is used in everyday life. The use of mobile phone is a question of culture since they allow new habits, postures, communication, and behaviors that contribute to society transformation. The paper focuses on a study about mobile phones' use among young people. Particularly, we were interested in the text messages, treated as offers, sent by mobile phones. The paper concludes by presenting the design of an engagement conceptual framework, which can be a reflection point to consider within the design process of future interfaces. Conversely, this framework can also be a learning tool either for understanding the usability principles of an interactive interface or as an instrument to teach and motivate students in a knowledge exchange situation of collaborative work.

Keywords: Mobile technologies · Gift giving · Offering · Engagement conceptual framework · Cultural practices · Learning tool

1 Introduction

In the new vision of computation technology there is a force that shapes our individual and social lives. We are facing a corporative context where the mobile technologies modify the established standards of communication, increasing and substituting them. We never imagine the things that technology allows us to do. The social dynamics resulting from the use of some communication tools created a changing paradigm in people relationships. Conversely, culture, constructed by human beings in interaction between each other, became significant for interface design, as well as, for the given interpretations of cultural practices of groups when they use a product or service. In recent years, human computer interaction (HCI) and related fields, for example computer supported collaborative work, interaction design, and participatory design have produced an increasing interest focusing on efficiency, functionality and usability, towards an increasing preoccupation in the aspects related to the users' experience of technology and digital artifacts [1]. A social obsession of being in contact with others is imperative. It is this interconnectivity that defines culture today. The fundamental issues of technology media development have extended from traditional usability problems to wider social aspects of interpersonal contact, information sharing, participation and culturally inherent needs [2–5]. Cultural preferences have become one of the most

© Springer International Publishing AG 2017
A. Marcus and W. Wang (Eds.): DUXU 2017, Part II, LNCS 10289, pp. 262–274, 2017.
DOI: 10.1007/978-3-319-58637-3_21

significant subjects and focuses of technology development, as it slowly turns away from issues of usability to issues of fulfilling users' cultural and social needs [6, 7].

This paper focus on the technology that changed people lives in terms of communication and interaction – the mobile phone. We describe a study about mobile phones' use among young people (artifacts that contributed to frame culture). The activities mediated by telephone are an example of life routine, organization and structure around the mobile phone. In particular, in engagement practices, telephones as well as, some text messages sent by mobile phones are treated as offerings. Some aspects are seen, in more detail; such as, the meaning of these practices, the voluntary exchange, the acceptance/rejection, the pact and relationship that is established, the status and competition that is assumed, the pretending figure that can be implicit and the value of the exchanges.

2   Background and Related Work

Teenagers have provided a rich source of data about social practices in everyday life carried out through mobile technologies. Comparing with other nation, the number of mobile phone per head of population in Finland was the highest in the world [8]. Young people are considered to be a significant factor in the mobile phone business, because they have quickly learned how to operate them to an extreme. The popularity of mobile phones, in Korea, was most evident among young people and males [9].

A review of research literature related to gift–giving is widely accepted and documented. Of the little research on the design of gifting technologies that exists, among the most relevant is the work of Taylor and his colleagues [10–12] in which they concentrate on a model of gifting giving that emphasizes exchange and reciprocity in the context of teenagers "messaging" each other on their mobile phones. Through the data, they suggested that teenagers use their phones to participate in social practices that closely resemble forms of ritualized gift giving. Such practices shape the way teenagers understand and use their phones. They considered that this insight into everyday, phone-mediated activities has practical implications for mobile phone design. Using an example, they described how teenagers' gift giving practices could inform design, providing an initial means to conceptualize future emerging technologies. Traditional gifting is based on direct reciprocity within close-knit and relatively small "circles", while online gifting has the potential of bonding unfamiliar people together on a much larger scale [13]. They considered the use of gift giving, as a theoretical and conceptual framework, for analyzing social behavior in online networks and communities. Chakrabarty and Berthon also presented the notion of gift giving by showing that much of the gifts exchanged in social media are driven by social emotions [14]. Other studies on this subject presented the Finish cultural discourses about mobile phone communications with a detailed presentation regarding the use of mobile phone in different countries and the symbolism of its use [15]. English children's use of mobile phones in managing and maintaining friendships and relationships in their everyday lives is also available [16]. Two-thirds of the teen texters said they were more likely to use their cell phones to text their friends than talk to them by cell phone [17]. Nearly one in four teenagers are almost constantly online as their lives are swallowed up every move by their mobile phone [18]. More deeply related to our study, we highlight Sun who described the success of text messages compared with the usability weakness of mobile phones such as the small display, poor input methods, moving environments, and noisy surroundings [19]. In his opinion, the explanation is in socio-cultural contexts of use. All human activities are embedded in socio-cultural contexts, which are not only created by local cultural and historical practices, but also co-created by each participant's history and life experiences in the use of a technology.

3   Mobile Technologies – Cultural Approach

The innovative technology, mobile communications play a role in most people's daily lives, being applied in diverse directions. As a result, social activities and cultural values have been manifestly influenced. The mobile mobility is more a cultural than a techno-logical question. Mobile phone migrated from its initial function of a communication device and became a symbol of style and taste of the user. However, there are some nuances in its use, for example: there are people that use it more than a personal computer to send emails: there are countries where it can only be used in specific locations. It has become an icon or symbol of status. It does not represent only communication but also a question of social acceptance and popularity. There are those who create affection towards it and do not seek anything else, those who identify themselves in a personal way, and there in increasing of intimacy with the others created through the use of this piece of technology. The mobile phone became the cultural icon of the digital generation.

The goals of designing interactive product are concerned primarily with user's expe-rience, which means creating systems that are: satisfying, enjoyable, helpful, motivating, emotionally fulfilling and fun. This involves understanding the nature of the user's experience as well as the user or people 's expectations facing a product; in which means, after, during and before the 'spectacle'. However, understanding a user's actions is very difficult for the reasons of people being of different sexes, genders, sexual orientations, ethnicities, nationalities, religions, social classes and educational, technical, occupa-tional and experiential backgrounds and have or not have disabilities. Meaning that, there is a diversity of cultural levels that must be considered within interaction design in which it is not easy due to culture also being dynamic. Conversely, the cultural component of designing user interfaces is very important as well as user's physical capabilities and cognitive functions, but also, the cultural background and social situa-tion of the user at the time of using the product or service. Cultural preferences have become one of the most significant subjects and focuses of technology development. As it slowly turns away from issues of usability to issues of fulfilling users' cultural and social needs [20–22].

Applications of mobile technologies serve groups of people in shared activities, in particular geographically dispersed groups who are collaborating on some task in a shared context [23]. An important characteristic of those social applications is the continuous interaction between people and technology to achieve a common purpose. Interaction is a general model of socio-cultural phenomena. It needs the signification and meaning interchanged that occurs in a space dimension of norms, values, and meaning. New technologies are offering enormous opportunities for supporting people in their everyday lives; in which has brought a wider set of concerns and focuses on improving efficiency and productivity at work.

In this paper we follow Jenkins et al. cultural approach: participatory culture. Participatory culture viewpoints suggest a culture in which artistic expression and civic engagement are valued; private individuals do not act as consumers only, but also as contributors or producers, that enables people to work collaboratively; spaces or processes give people the means to take part and contribute; the challenger is on the consumer culture, wherein individuals do not act merely consumer but also participate in cultural commodities as contributors [24]. For Jenkins participatory culture has the following characteristics: low barriers for engagement, strong social connections among members, a belief in collective effort, and informal mentoring among members [25].

The approach was born to focus on culture and social media, however we are more concerned with participatory culture and technology. Technology enables different forms of communication and collaboration and it also allows a user centered design perspective on designing new products or services. With this study we wanted to understand how teenagers, using a mobile phone specially during text messaging, could contribute with their cultural expressions to the design of new technologies.

There are several definitions of culture. In general, we are talking about behaviors found in groups of people, the artifacts use in which cultural achievements are embodied. The culture texts, values the way that every act they due affects culture cultural roles (active or passive users).

3.1 Gift-Giving/Offers

People are accustomed to think in terms of what they can benefit from a given situation. Within gift giving paradigm, the gift permits to approach each person with another attitude, "What can I create? What can I give?" making part of the gift environment. Gift giving literature presents several models of gift explanation [26–29].

Gift giving, traditionally, refers to an object given from one person to another; with regards to increasing the amount of happiness in their life, or just decreasing the amount of sadness. This includes special days and occasions, and when somebody might need a lift. Gift giving is one of the symbolic forms of exchange between groups either physically distributed or approached. These practices have roots in old practices where they were executed ceremoniously, to establish alliances and rivalries. The giving is among other purposes, confined to help, council, share, or anything else that provides value to the recipient. The gifts are exchanged as a social practice show, and teenagers in activities mediated by telephone keep a kind of ritual of `gift-giving', and their participation in these activities has a significant impact in the form they see and understand the use of mobile phones. The gift exchange has nothing to do with goods exchange, but with mutual recognition. In the mindset of gift-giving, first, there are the thoughts and feelings of the gift giver and then there are the thoughts and feelings of the gift receiver, and then what the giver thinks the receiver is thinking, and then when the receiver opens the gift, it's what that person thinks the giver what thinking…it's all very complicated.

We prefer to consider, instead of gift, offer. Offer is voluntary but conditional submitted by someone to another for acceptance, and which becomes rightfully imposed if accepted by the offeree. An offer is a clear indication of the offeror's motivation to enter into an agreement under specified terms, and is made in a manner that a reasonable person would understand its acceptance.

Offers normally include a departing date, and they are an act of devotion or loyalty. They can have several interpretations like: presented for acceptance or rejection; to put forward for consideration; propose; presented in order to meet a need or satisfy a requirement as an act of respect. If we consider, superficially, one of the differences between gift and offer, one can say that if we put something in someone's hand expecting them to take it, and they do take it, we don't say that an offer was made to them. We say that someone gave it to them.

Another reason for the use of offer is based on the context we are studying, which is 'technology offer' in this domain, clients, customers, users, business, are strategies considered. Customers engage, choose and stay loyal to something as a service.

4   The Study, Methods and Methodology

The aim of this research was to understand how teenagers behaved using mobile phones during messages exchange. The study included 24 people with ages from 13 to 17 years old. The simple random sampling technique was used to select the teenagers. We observed them during the act of sending and receiving messages over a period of two months when they were at public places. The research methods were a combination of observations, questionnaires and interviews. Interviews were conducted face to face and by email. The interview questions were about strategies and corresponding features they used when sending and receiving a message.

Questions were for example, about teenagers awareness about text messaging; The frequency of sending and receiving; What did they think about text messages and the way it affects people relationships; What kind of habits and behaviors teen experienced; How often did they communicate with friends; Does it affects over the language spelling; Were they addicted to their mobiles; and finally, we posed questions concerning mobile usability (Mobile phones have different features. Can you use your phone easily?).

The data gathered and analysis was made using Grounded Theory Methodology. Grounded Theory Methodology (GTM) is a general method to use on any kind or combination of data, and it is particularly useful with qualitative data [30]. GTM is only one of several different qualitative research methods available to those conducting exploratory research [31]. It offers a comprehensive and systematic framework for inductively building theory. In order to generate GTM, the researcher engaged in a rigorous and iterative process of data collection and constant comparative analysis. Essentially, each line, sentence, paragraph etc. was read in search of the answer to the repeated question "What is this about? What is being referenced here?" GTM specify analytic strategies [32].

The responses, discussions, and archive materials were coded and analyzed with respect to gifting motivations, features, and usage.

5   Discussion and Results

The activities mediated by telephone are an example of life routine, organization and structure around the mobile phone. In particular, in engagement practices, telephones as well as, some text messages sent by mobile phones are treated as offerings. This section presents the main results we got from the data analysis on the study. The responses given by teenagers are considered the correct way to perceive, feel, think and act and these are passed on the whole partners. Culture determines what is acceptable or unacceptable, important or unimportant, right or wrong.

60% of the interviewed teenagers think that they are not 'cool' if they don't have the latest technology in mobile phones. Keeping up with the latest technology has become a very important status symbol to many teenagers. It makes part of the emancipation process. They keep all the savings to purchase the new mobile version, since it is fashionable (the old phone will be used by other family members, younger or older), this group of teenagers said that is was important to impress others, reason why they enjoyed showing their mobiles off (it made them feel important and trendy) when walking, in a bus station, leaving it on the table when they eat, etc. They were used to use accessories as an attempt to personalize their devices and be different.

We did not explore the content of text messages, but ways text message habits have changed over the last decade as it has become more popular. Finally, we offer design suggestions for future mobile communication tools.

Our results suggest that students communicate with a large number of contacts for extended periods of time, they engage in simultaneous conversations, and often use text messaging as a method to switch between a variety of communication mediums.

According our study, texting is the most common use of the mobile phone among teenagers (91%). The main reason to text is social reason: they talk with friends, and they talk about anything: sentiments, school, family.

The data show that 85% teenagers who text, are texting with their friends more than twice a day. Those who have a boyfriend or girlfriend send or receive texts everyday, several times a day. 48% of teenagers text with their parents at least once a day. The data did not helped to understand the frequency with which teens text. Girls are more likely than boys to use both text messaging and voice calling and they do it more frequently. We noticed that teens attaint the limits of text messaging plans.

Although voice interaction provides them with access to friends and parents, they prefer, however, texting since they feel that they have more freedom, they can pretend easily, and they do not have to show their mood (girls are prone to use emotions in their message). For teenagers, mobile phone gives them a new degree of freedom. More freedom because they can stay in touch with parents no matter where they are. They feel also safer because they can always use the mobile phone to get help.

Text is used in situations when it is discourteous or prohibited, to talk on the mobile phone, when teens are at the movies, school and when they do not want to show the surroundings.

Messages are to exchange information. Short messages are to report where they are, to check in on where someone else is. Long messages are exchanged to discuss important personal matters. Videos and pictures are exchanged less often due to technological limitations. Texting is also a method for managing schoolwork and to make appointments. Although forbidden, 15% of teenagers reported that they use mobile phone at school and they text in class without being caught (under desktops, inside bags, behind stacks of books).

The mobile phone and the act of sending messages have positive aspects in teenagers' opinion: make easier to change plans quickly; helps them to entertain themselves when they are bored; is important to exchange and to comment a joke; keep them busy, which is sometimes nice when for example, mom ask for help on cleaning situations.

Conversely, mobile phones and the constant connectivity bring some conflicting situations and emotions. For example, teenagers are convinced of: a text message interrupts what they are doing; Sometimes it is difficult to establish shared meaning through texting, especially with the tone of a message, i.e., some arguments create types of misunderstanding emerging from single punctuation use or the lack of it. Sending a text to the wrong person is a common problem that can lead to regret. This can happen as a result of confusion from trying to maintain multiple threads of text based conversation with multiple partners at once. Teenagers reported regret over text messages they have sent.

Concerning Language usage: for quick messaging short word, misspellings are used. There is the fear that this "new language" may replace standard language and young people will become unable to use language properly. According 12% of the interviewees, texting makes teen lazy because it does not force them to use proper grammar and spellings. Sometimes, teenagers write the way they text as it becomes permanently stored in their brain.

We have found that there are, actually, positive effects of texting for teens, from improved language skills to emotional relief, and even added benefits for the especially introverted teen. They can interact with others and understand their views and their knowledge. Conversely, the use of abbreviations in the professional writing the individuals may be the creative, and texting and 'textisms' may actually serve as a way to increase reading skills, literacy, and spelling fluency. Textese is an abbreviated vocabulary that includes letter/number, contractions or shortenings of words, emoticons (symbols for representing emotions such as ⊗ for sad), and vowels, punctuation, and capitalization.

Table 1 summarizes the main results we obtain from data analysis.

Data gathered and analysis permitted to build several categories, within GTM, which contributed to the design of the framework presented in Fig. 1 whose content is adapted from Taylor [11]. Some aspects are seen, in more detail; such as, the meaning of these practices, the acceptance/rejection, the voluntary exchange, the pact and relationships that is established, the status and competition that is assumed, the pretending figure that can be expected and the value of the exchanges.

Table 1. Cultural practices

Frequency of text messages	Limits of text messaging plans
What about text messages	More freedom Safe When it is discourteous or forbidden
Behaviors & Relationships	Pretending Hide mood Emotions exchange Entertainment Jokes exchange Keep busy
How often they communicate	More than twice a day – friends Extended periods – boyfriends/girlfriends Once a day - parents
Language spelling	Short word Misspelling Abbreviation
Addition to mobiles	Be cool Emancipation Fashion Personalization Social reason
Mobile usability	Easy to use Experience Need more 'intelligence'

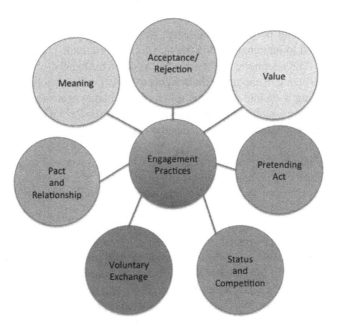

Fig. 1. Engagement practices

Offering sustains meaning – The act of offering converts something within people and with their relationships with who receives the offer. The offer helps to organize people's memories into things that can be reached and kept. Offering allows something to continue available for a period of time. It is through the offer that the offer acquires its meaning. The meaning is expressed not only in the offer but also through its giver and receiver, and in the occasional ceremony in which the exchange took place.

Acceptance/Rejection – in reply to offer, the receiver is obliged to accept it, i.e. to answer. The reception of the offer demands the acknowledgment and the participation of the giver in the occasion. However, when an offer (message) is made, the receiver can choose to accept or reject it. The acceptance of the offer is necessary to start the relationship. The acceptance is communicated through an answer (another offer). The receiver can terminate an offer on the grounds of rejection if he does not accept the offer, i.e. if he/she does not answer the message in a short period of time. The social expectations that are created by constant connectivity are evident: teens narrated about friends and acquaintances that get insulted, angry or upset if a text message is not responded. That is why they fell obliged to return texts. We are facing an act of devotion and loyalty.

Voluntary exchange – voluntary but conditional for acceptance. It will be enforceable if accepted by the offeree (sender). Voluntary exchange contrasts with an exchange that is mandated, for example, a parent message. Voluntary exchanges are the basis of a free communication.

Pact and relationship – this mechanism allows sharing emotional experiences and interchanging objects with personal meaning. The telephones can circulate and be changed without argument or negotiation (to see, to copy files, to change numbers…). The exchange implicitly demonstrates the privacy between one and the others.

Status and competition – the offer is exchanged through the reciprocity principle, in which the link among people is established through an apparent contradiction. The receiver is obliged to interchange the offer as a form of gratitude placing itself in inferiority position. The telephone and its content as other exchanged objects are mechanisms through which one can make these fights of power and competition. The proper situation of having a mobile phone, as a belonging, makes teenagers feel older and independent. Having a mobile phone means had no excuses for not telling teenagers 's parents where they are and that it provides their parents easy way to monitor on their teens.

Pretending act – during messages exchanges, both the giver and receiver can have diverse roles: they can pretend or act as different actors. The scenario may never be identified. In this situation a fallacy world will be created propitiating several pretending stories.

Value – the offer exchange objects by telephone confer value. The text messages, for example, can be seen as greater or lesser value if they are written in some way (capital letters, without punctuation…). For the offers as the text messages, the value is associated with who gave the offer and with the context in which it was sent and received. These considerations were only based on examples of text messages shown by teenagers within their mobile phones. We could also verify what happens in relation to other object exchanges such as: touches, images, music, videos, etc., but it was out of the scope of this study.

Teenagers consider the mobile phone as an adequate tool to share information. The usability aspects are not important. The focus is on the service. They considered that experience is the main point to get used and friendly with the mobile phone. Questions such as small display, poor input methods, moving environments and noisy surroundings do not interfere when using a mobile phone.

The results can take us to design a learning tool to use within the community of students and teachers to engage them within collaboration

From our perspective a framework does several things. The main one is to provide a set of activities to analyse information definitions for the information required in the design process phases. A list of framework requirements followed by a set of specific classifications that define the framework;

- It ties together the components of the offering technologies into learning components, making both processes more useful.
- It forces a design team to consider the presented categories in a way that promotes learning and more understandable interfaces.
- It may contribute to improve design practices taking into consideration that people will value design outputs.

The proposed framework (Fig. 2) consists of several inter-related strands, which can be synthesized, in – communication, collaboration, creativity and culture (Four Cs) [33]. Each strand is seen of equal importance and is composed by actions and/or situations to provide guidance for a design process interface.

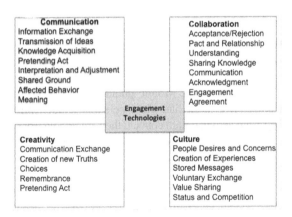

Fig. 2. Engagement conceptual framework for learning

Communication and Culture – communication is used to give and exchange information. The practice of communication is akin to engagement technologies as well, to learning in the way that both are skills or abilities, which are acquired and developed. Information is exchanged between individuals through a common system of symbols, signs, opinions or behaviors. From the transmission of messages, one person affects behavior to another. Communication is a cultural practice. Culture and cultural values play influential roles in almost all aspects of human life and technologies are not exempt from these cultural effects. People own cultural values, concerns and preferences influence interface design qualities and approaches. People create culture, as they create experiences and meaning for themselves and others.

Collaboration gives us a better understanding of how people work, use technologies, share knowledge, and communicate. The level of engagement denotes the alliance and obligation to react to communication. Cooperation can be associated with the cooperative principle, which regulates the exchange of information between individuals involved in interaction [6].

Creativity was used as a process with one of its ingredient - communication. Each idea was visible, communicable and understandable. Each feature which surround the engagement technologies' action and their circumstances give meaning to the learning event. It contains the main objectives of mobile offer technology, which are the same of an intended learning platform. For the interface technology design, situations like (within communication) degrees of privacy, flexibility and security, and a more functional environment for collaborative learning should be considered.

Each feature surrounding the offering action and their circumstances give meaning to the learning event. Each feature contains the main objectives of mobile offering technology and is the same of an intended learning platform. For the interface technology design, situations like considering (within communication) degrees of privacy, flexibility and security, and a more functional environment for collaborative learning should be considered.

The framework provides a comprehensive approach to consider in the design of new socio interfaces for learning.

6   Conclusion

The engagement practices are longstanding, however, they still frame the way people use technology in social interaction. Mobile phones have been appropriated for use within intimate relationships, to mediate close personal relationships, for family and friends separated by distance to maintain contact, they are popular for online dating, and for friend's finder, among other purposes. Offers either visual or text message are linked to objects related with the individual or group life galleries, with remembrances albums, with packages of experiences, and with unintended culture sharing.

The presented study shows how teenagers behave using their mobile phone when sending text messages. Teenagers share (offer) information with meaning and accept or reject the offers they receive. The offer is voluntary but conditional for acceptance. The established pact dictates the future of the relationship. They feel free and safe when they own the offer technology. Their emotions are shared and exchanged and better, they can pretend and have different roles and positions. Partners, friends and family have the position in their lives that they attribute them, according time schedules imposed. Experiences are exchanged. Teenagers learn what they want as they want with others from different communities and cultures, and they converse by being or pretending to be someone else. A series of exchanged situations can occur whether they are speaking of an engagement through offers, remembrances, and generate obligations.

Usability questions are never thought: since they start using the mobile phone is just a question of time to be a user expert. The concern is with Internet, limits of text messaging plans and speed.

The analyzed data permitted us to think about a learning tool either to adapt for teaching classes or to take into account when designing new technologies.

After all this paper does not contribute to new knowledge in the domain of interactive design. However it stressed important cultural information and social issues in the world of engagement technologies according our case study.

Acknowledgements. We thank all the volunteers who participated in this study.

References

1. McCarthy, J., Wright, P.: Technology as Experience. MIT Press, Cambridge (2004)
2. Herman, L.: Towards effective usability evaluation in Asia: Cross-cultural differences. In: Proceedings of the 6th Australian Conference on Computer-Human Interaction, pp. 135–136. IEEE Computer Society, Washington, DC (1996)
3. Yeo, A.: Cultural effects in usability assessment. In: CHI 98 Conference Summary on Human Factors in Computing Systems, pp. 74–75. ACM, New York (1998)
4. Barber, W., Badre, A.: Culturability: The merging of culture and usability. In: Proceedings of the 4th Conference on Human Factors and the Web (1998). http://zing.ncsl.nist.gov/hfweb/att4/proceedings/barber/. Accessed 20 Dec 2016
5. Clemmensen, T., Shi, Q., Kumar, J., Li, H., Sun, X., Yammiyavar, P.: Cultural usability tests – how usability tests are not the same all over the world. In: Aykin, N. (ed.) UI-HCII 2007. LNCS, vol. 4559, pp. 281–290. Springer, Heidelberg (2007). doi:10.1007/978-3-540-73287-7_35
6. Bourges-Waldegg, P., Scrivener, S.A.R.: Meaning, the central issue in cross-cultural HCI design. Interact. Comput. **9**(3), 287–309 (1998)
7. Strøm, G.: Interaction design for countries with a traditional culture: A comparative study of income levels and cultural values. In: McEwan, T., Gulliksen, J., Benyon, D. (eds.) People and Computers XIX - The Bigger Picture, pp. 301–316. Springer, London (2006)
8. Puro, J.P.: Finland: A mobile culture. In: Katz, J.E., Aakhus, M. (eds.) Perpetual Contact: Mobile Communication, Private Talk, Public Performance, pp. 19–30. Cambridge University Press, Cambridge (2002)
9. Kim, S.D.: Korea: Personal meaning. In: Katz, J.E., Aakhus, M. (eds.) Perpetual Contact: Mobile Communication, Private Talk, Public Performance, pp. 63–80. Cambridge University Press, Cambridge (2002)
10. Berg, S., Taylor, A., Harper, R.: Mobile phones for the next generation: Device designs for teenagers. In: Proceedings of the ACM Conference on Human Factors in Computing (CHI), Ft. Lauderdale, 5–10 April 2003, pp. 433–440 (2003)
11. Taylor, A., Harper, R.: Age-Old practices in the "new world:" A study of gift-giving between teenage mobile phone users. In: Proceedings of the ACM Conference on Human Factors in Computing Systems (CHI), Minneapolis, 20–25 April 2002, pp. 439–446 (2002)
12. Taylor, A.S., Harper, R.: The gift of the gab?: A design-oriented sociology of young people's use of mobiles. Comput. Support. Coop. Work Int. J. **12**(4), 267–296 (2003)
13. Skågeby, J.: Gift-giving as a conceptual framework: Framing social behaviour in online networks. J. Inf. Technol. **25**(2), 170–177 (2010)

14. Chakrabarti, R., Berthon, P.: Gift giving and social emotions: Experience as content. J. Public Aff. **12**(2), 154–161 (2012)
15. Poutiainen, S.: Finnish cultural discourses about the mobile phone communication. Doctoral Dissertations Available from Request. AAI3289237 (2007). http://scholarworks.umass.edu/dissertations/AAI3289237
16. Bond, E.: Managing mobile relationships: Children's perceptions of the impact of the mobile phone on relationships in their everyday lives. Child. Glob. J. Child Res. **17**(4), 514–529 (2010)
17. Lehnard, A., Ling, R., Campbell, S., Purcell, K.: Teens and Mobile Phones: Text Messaging Explodes as Teens Enhance it as the Centerpiece of their communication Strategies with friends. New Research Center & American Life Project, USA (2010). http://pewinternet.org/Reports/2010/Teensand-Mobile-Phones.aspx. Accessed Nov 2016
18. Bates, D.: Is your Teenager Addicted to their Mobile? (2015). Dailymail.com
19. Sun, H.: Bring socio-cultural contexts into activities – A localization study of mobile text messaging use. ACM SIGCAPH Newslett. **75**, 19–20 (2004)
20. Bourges-Waldegg, P., Scrivener, S.A.R.: Meaning, the central issue in cross-cultural HCI design. Interact. Comput. **9**(3), 287–309 (1998)
21. Strøm, G.: Interaction design for countries with a traditional culture: A comparative study of income levels and cultural values. In: McEwan, T., Gulliksen, J., Benyon, D. (eds.) People and Computers XIX - The Bigger Picture, pp. 301–316. Springer, London (2006)
22. Sawyer, S.: Design observations regarding public safety networks. In: Proceedings of the 12th Annual Digital Government Research Conference: Digital Government Innovation in Challenging Times. ACM (2011)
23. Rheingold, H.: Smart Mobs: The Next Social Revolution. Perseus Publishing, Cambridge (2003)
24. Jenkins, H., Purushotma, R., Weigel, M., Clinton, K., Robinson, A.J.: Confronting the Challenges of Participatory Culture: Media Education for the 21st Century. MIT Press, Cambridge (2009)
25. Jenkins, H.: Fans, Bloggers, and Gamers: Exploring Participatory Culture. New York University Press, New York (2006)
26. Berking, H.: Sociology of Giving. Sage, London (1999)
27. Godbout, J., Caillé, A.: The World of the Gift. McGill-Queen's University Press, Quebéc (1992)
28. Kolm, S.-C.: Introduction: The economics of reciprocity, giving and altruism. In: Gérard-Varet, L.-A., Kolm, S.-C., Mercier-Ythier, J. (eds.) The Economics of Reciprocity, Giving and Altruism, pp. 1–44. MacMillan Press Ltd., London (2000)
29. Klamer, A.: Gift economy. In: Towse, R. (eds.) A Handbook of Cultural Economics, pp. 241–247. Edward Elgar Publishing, Cheltenham (2003)
30. Glaser, B.: Doing Grounded Theory: Issues and Discussions. Sociology Press, Mill Valley (1998)
31. Denzin, N.K., Lincoln, Y.S.: Introduction: Entering the field of qualitative research. In: Denzin, N.K., Lincoln, Y.S. (eds.) Handbook of Qualitative Research. Sage, Thousand Oaks (1994)
32. Charmaz, K.: Constructing Grounded Theory: A Practical Guide Through Qualitative Analysis. Sage, London (2006)
33. Lopes, A.: Design as Dialogue: Encouraging and Facilitating Interdisciplinary Collaboration: VDM Verlag Dr. Muller, USA, UK, p. 336 (2009)

The Smartwatch in Multi-device Interaction

Donald McMillan[✉]

Mobile Life Centre, Stockholm University, Stockholm, Sweden
donald.mcmillan@dsv.su.se

Abstract. Wearable devices are typically not used on their own. Indeed, many are sold specifically as companion devices to mobile phones. Here, we take a close look at smartwatch use in its natural multi-device context, building on a corpus of 1009 in vivo smartwatch use incidents recorded with twelve participants over 168 h. We examine closely four exemplar clips, exploring glances for information during other tasks, maintenance tasks that allow the allocation of spare attention, the smartwatch in conversation around media consumption, and the physical constraints of its embodied use on the wrist alongside other devices. Our study sheds light on current smartwatch use practices alongside devices with more established use scenarios, and on how the smartwatch changes and disrupts those practices.

Keywords: Smartwatch · Video analysis · Multi-device interaction

1   Introduction

The adoption of smartwatches is increasing quickly, with the estimated 18 million units in 2015 [48] up from 6.8 million in 2014 [49] and moving towards Gartner's estimate of 50 million in 2016 [47]. This rapid adoption presents some interesting user research questions. For example, what does a wrist worn technology add to current practices of technology use? How does a smartwatch change the social interaction we have learned to build around other form factors such as the smartphone, tablet, personal computer, or connected television?

We provided 12 participants with a smartwatch for one month, with the final three days of use recorded with pairs of wearable cameras. These recordings were combined with interviews with each participant. This data gives us a uniquely detailed view on how smart watches are used, what for and in what context. From 34 days of recording we have over 168 h of recording, including 1009 incidents of watch use – or around 6 uses per hour, with each use being on average 6.7 s long.

In previous work we have used this corpus to examine how the smartwatch fitted into, and changed, our participants daily routines [38], and how the social context and wearer activity influences how the watch is used [30]. Here we take a closer look at how the watch is used in conjunction with, and alongside other technology.

© Springer International Publishing AG 2017
A. Marcus and W. Wang (Eds.): DUXU 2017, Part II, LNCS 10289, pp. 275–287, 2017.
DOI: 10.1007/978-3-319-58637-3_22

2 Background

The current generation of smartwatches from Pebble, Apple, and the variety of manufacturers building on Google's Android Wear platform has been increasing in popularity [39]. Running in parallel, there has been an increase in the amount of wrist worn non-watch wearables – primarily aimed at health, fitness, and the quantification of personal action [43]. This form factor has seen a lot of research in the HCI community. The mechanics of touch on small devices have been examined in detail [5, 19, 20] as has text entry for small devices [9, 12, 21, 25, 35] as well as other input modalities such as tilting and twisting the screen [46], tracing letters on other surfaces with your finger [34], interacting around the device [26, 36], interacting with just gaze and attention [1], and even blowing on the watch [10]. Given the amount of work done on input and output from smartwatches, there has not been a great deal on the use of the smartwatch. Lyons [27] looked at traditional watch wearers' practices in order to learn lessons that could be applied to the smartwatch. Giang et al. compared the amount of distraction notification's caused from smartwatches and smartphones [13], Cecchinato et al. [8] and Schirra and Bentley [42] interviewed smartwatch wearers to better understand how and why they used the device. Schirra and Bentley emphasised the importance of notifications as a watch function, as well as the importance of appearance in choosing a watch device. The smartwatch finds itself in an already busy technological space, where users necessarily have a smartphone to provide connectivity to the watch. Different constellations of devices in concurrent use have been explored [22], as well as the reasons and motivations for such use [11, 37], such as the suitability of the device to the task or environment. Tasks are divided between devices, with each one having its own role in the pattern of use [11, 14, 40]. Such patterns can be sequential [24], however parallel patterns have been shown to be more common with modern devices [32, 40]. Although these practices have been shown to be different between individuals and professional groups [11, 24, 40]. A common task, and difficulty, has been managing content across devices [11, 32, 37, 40], including the synchronization of meta-data such as interaction history [11, 23, 37].

The configuration of the set of devices changes with person and location. On the go this set of devices has been referred to as a Mobile Kit [28], however managing all the different device configurations can require significant effort and planning [37].

In HCI there have been a variety of systems, interfaces, and interaction methods proposed to support computing with multiple devices, and while these are generally not directly supported currently on the watch platform they provide an interesting lens through which to see multi-device use. One avenue explored was that of binding devices together, ranging from scanning for available proximate devices to connect wirelessly to physical methods, such as synchronous touching of a button or alignment [45]. Transferring content between screens as a result of direct user action [33], and migratory interfaces [2] exemplify techniques for moving between devices. Managing and switching tasks in multi-device computing environments has also been explored [3]. Collaborative systems with multiple devices and multiple users have also been developed [44].

3 Methods

To understand smartwatches in vivo, we wanted to record how the watches were used, what they were used for, and the wider context they were used in. Tracking of mobile devices, using logs and other means, has grown in popularity as devices have become important parts of almost all aspects of life [6–8, 18, 29]. Our use of naturalistic video recording of mobile device use has advantages in that it affords the opportunity to capture and analyse the moment-by-moment details of how the environment, the people, and device are connected to the use [4]. For this study, we had participants wear multiple portable wearable cameras that recorded their actions relatively unobtrusively, while allowing us to see and understand smartwatch use "in vivo" [29]. We made a small 'sensor bag' which contained two police issue cameras with long-life batteries that allowed them to record for eight hours each. One of the cameras was directed to record the scene around the participant (pointing forward). The second camera was connected to a small 'stalk' camera that was mounted at the shoulder of the participant (looking downwards), so as to capture the participant's body and wrist where the watch was attached.

Full details of the data collection and analysis can be found in [30, 38], in summary we recruited twelve participants with a median age of 30, with five out of the twelve participants being students. Seven of the twelve participants were female. All participants regularly used an iPhone, and had not previously owned a smartwatch. Three of them regularly wore wristwatches. Participants were given an Apple Watch, with a choice of small (38 mm) or large (42 mm), and were asked to use it for a month. The last three days of use were recorded using our camera setup. On the third day, the cameras and the smartwatch were collected by a researcher and, for most participants, an interview was carried out there and then.

Our analysis started by watching the video and extracting clips for each interaction with the watch. Each clip was logged with details including who was present, the type of watch interaction, other devices being used, and the length of interaction. For our analysis sessions, all authors collectively watched all 'watch use event' clips, around 8 h of video in total.

For this paper three clips have been selected for closer analysis clips, these were deemed to be particularly insightful of the nature of watch use alongside the participants' use of other devices. We drew on interactional analysis and the broader body of work in HCI that looks closely at the moment-by-moment interaction with technology [7, 13, 15–17]. Each extract is thus looked at as an individual, unique incident of use – but also inspected for exemplifying patterns that we can extrapolate to be present in other situations.

4 Results

We focus on three detailed analysis of examples of use. The first is the glancing interaction, where the watch is looked at as a timepiece or to quickly sate the users curiosity over the topic or origin of an incoming notification. These interactions are generally short (under 3 s) and do not involve interaction with the watch. The second is a watch initiated short interaction, mostly resulting from incoming notifications, that involves interaction with that message or clearing the message drawer. The third type of interaction we look at here is where the watch is an instigator of further social interaction.

4.1 Glancing

Figure 1 shows an example of the shortest of the watch-initiated types of use, the notification glance. By looking at the detailed timings of this interaction we can start to unpack this interaction and how it fits into the on-going task of working with the laptop. For the sake of space and readability, in this paper we have removed the second camera view which, in this case, showed part of the laptop screen and a train carriage. One point to notice is that this interaction, from the moment that the wrist starts to move until the participant has resumed working on the laptop, takes 3.34 s. The time that the user takes to decide that the message is of lower priority than the task currently at hand is somewhat less than 1.45 s – the time between the animation displaying the message beginning and the participant starting to dismiss the notification, and the watch, by moving their hand back to the keyboard. The notification on the Apple watch comes in three stages; the first stage is the indication that a notification is incoming (given with haptic feedback on the wrist, an audio alert, or both). The second stage is the first part of the animation where the message source is displayed with the icon of the application triggering the notification. In the third stage the notification digest scrolls onto the watchface, showing the sender (if applicable) of the message and a message digest consisting of the first 100 characters if text or a thumbnail for image data. In our corpus 19% of incidents of use (178 clips) are of glancing at an incoming notification, with a median length of 6.69 s.

Fig. 1. 7.29 s into the clip, wrist starts to move. Gesture complete at 7.86. Message animation complete at 9.26, gesture to move back begins at 9.31. Typing resumes at 10.63

In the example shown in Fig. 1 the participant responds to the first stage by bringing their watch up, waits through the second stage (not dismissing the notification based solely on its source), and only after the message digest is displayed dismisses the message. Given the timing of the user action and an estimated reading speed of around 3 words per second [41] with small text on mobile devices we can be reasonably sure that this message was dismissed on the recognition of less than 3 words, suggesting that the title or the sender were enough for the participant to, in this case, decide that the message didn't need immediate action on her part.

4.2 Maintenance

For our second example, shown in Fig. 2, we are also examining the use of the smart-watch alongside the users laptop computer. However in this case the use is on the couch at home and the participant is simultaneously watching television. This is a much longer interaction, taking 26.24 s in total.

Fig. 2. Watch lights up unexpectedly due to user movement at 1.53, User tilts hand at 3.56 and noticing 'red dot' raises wrist to interact, swiping to reveal notification at 4.9. The message digest is tapped to show the full message at 9.6, with the crown used from 10.8 to 22.8 to scroll and read the message. At 23.59 the user taps to dismiss, then at 24.9 uses the physical buttons to (inadvertently) take a screenshot in an attempt to return the watch to sleep. The previous activity is resumed at 29.8.

Here the user is engaged in maintenance work with the watch, specifically the noti-fications tray which holds notifications until they are dismissed (read and unread). As the user types the motion of their hand triggers the watch, possibly tricking the accel-erometer based algorithm tuned to detect the action of raising and twisting the wrist to see the time as one would with a traditional watch when the watchface was out of the line of sight. Part of the watch interface is the 'red dot' which appears top and centre of the watch face to indicate that the notification tray has an unread notification in it – which happens when a notification is pushed to the watch and the user does not activate the watch screen within 20 s to trigger the notification animation as shown in the previous example.

The activation of the screen caught the attention of the user, and as they glance at the screen the Red Dot is visible. This triggers the reorientation to the watch and prep-aration to interact – positioning both hands in such a way that the watch screen is avail-able for touch interaction.

Swiping down on the watch face brings up the notification drawer, and further swiping allows the participant to scroll through the notifications stored there. This 4.4 s activity is aided by the interface, in this screen the read notifications are shown with slightly muted colours to distinguish them from unread messages. Upon finding the brighter unread message the user taps it and is then able to scroll through the text of the message using the rotating bezel on the side of the watch, an activity which takes a full 12 s. This is a short message, yet despite this the participant scrolls up and down twice as if she has lost her place while reading the message. From this we can extrapolate that the television in the background is competing for her attention. Since this whole sequence of maintenance was not triggered by an incoming message this lack of urgency gives it a lower priority than the similar interaction we will see in the next example.

This is an example of a common maintenance task that we see with the Apple watch – clearing the red dot. Given that one of the most compelling reasons for owning a smartwatch is the notification system allowing for ease of triage, the managing of missed notifications was a surprisingly common activity comprising of 9% (88 instances) of smartwatch use recorded in our corpus, with a median length of 16.57 s.

The end of this sequence highlights a common problem that almost all of our participants encountered – confusion around turning the watch 'off.' That the default state for the watch involves the screen being off means that this is the state our participants wanted the watch to be in when they ended their interaction with it. In much the same way as they would press the lock button on their mobile phone to turn off the screen a number of attempts to do the same with the smart watch was observed. The methods to turn off the screen of the watch are to turn your wrist away from your body (in which case it is not turned off while still visible to the user) or to cover the watchface with the palm of the opposing hand. The watch, however, has two seldom used physical buttons. In the operating system version current at the time of data collection the rotating crown could be pressed to bring up the application launcher screen, and the button on the opposing side of the watchface could be pressed to bring up a quick-menu for contacting friends (much like a speed-dial). Upon pressing both buttons simultaneously a screenshot of the watchface is taken and transferred to the paired smartphone's photo application. In our data all three of the actions bound to the physical buttons were activated more in attempts to turn off the screen of the watch than in on purpose. This shows that, as well as the physical buttons not being bound to the most useful actions, patterns of use and interactional expectations are transferred from current touch-screen (specifically smartphone) practice to this new device. The envisaged use of the watch does not include the 'turn off' action at the end of an interactional episode, instead this would be inferred by the position of the hand or the device being covered by clothing. This mismatch of designer expectations and user training may be expected to be 'solved' by retraining of the user of the new device however this was not seen even after a month of constant use of the smartwatch. One reason for this could be that the 'wrong' pattern of use was continuously reinforced by the participants daily use of their other devices – mainly smartphones and tablets – where this was, in fact, the 'correct' pattern of use.

4.3   In Conversation

In our third example, shown in Fig. 3, we see one of our participants on the couch with her partner with a blanket over them watching television in the evening. The blanket, as it happens, covered the second camera leaving us with one angle of this interaction.

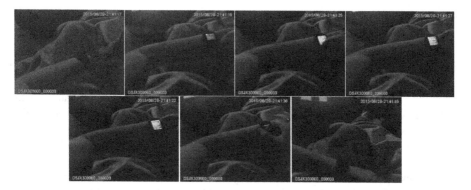

Fig. 3. Watch raised at 1.6, notification tray swiped down at 3.2. Notification tapped at 4.0 and scrolled down until 8.3. The user then scrolls back to the top of the notification (9.53) and proceeds to read the message to her partner until 18.2, gesturing to the message with the hovering finger. 20.2 she taps dismiss, 20.9 presses the buttons to return the watch to its rest state.

While the television program is playing the wearer receives a notification on the watch of an incoming text message. This is ignored until the currently absorbing scene on the television is over, and attention can be turned to the watch. By then the period in which the watch would automatically open the incoming message on activation was over, so our participant opened the notification drawer and immediately tapped the new message to open it. After silently reading through the message once, which takes just over 4 s, she proceeds to scroll back to the top of the message and read it out to her partner. The message, from her mother, talks of another live television program on at that time showing scenes of her hometown. This sparks a short conversation with her partner on the topic of this television program during which she taps the message to dismiss it and (as in the previous example) attempts to turn off the watch screen. The short conversation concludes when the sound level of the television program they are watching together rises in the background causing both to return their attention to the program. 28% (272 clips) of watch use in our corpus was in the presence of others, with 15% happening while the wearer was in conversation with a co-present other.

This example shows two interesting things about the smartwatches place in the constellation of devices used during second screening. The first is that the incoming notifications are not always immediately attended to, even through they are more personal (by being on your body) than those arriving to a mobile phone. The participant is able to fit the reading and managing of incoming notifications around the rhythm and flow of the program. The second is that, as has been noted previously [7], mobile devices have a privileged place in conversation, providing topics as well as tickets to talk about those topics. The couple here are able to manage their conversation and use of technology around what is happening on screen, as opposed to simply being distracted from the on-going show.

5 Discussion

The short glances, of which clip one above is an example, when including the 50% user initiated glances to check the time or to check for notifications, make up 72% of all instances of watch use we recorded. The very short interactional glances in response to incoming notifications are one of the most interesting uses of the smartwatch. Even though these uses do not involve any interaction with the watch or the incoming notification. This gives users the ability to quickly sate the curiosity caused by a notification on the mobile phone, potentially reducing the overall distraction from the incoming message as this can be done in around 3s.

This also gives the user the opportunity to effectively triage incoming messages, even when waiting for an important message which may have caused them to turn to their mobile phone with every audio or vibration alert they can continue the task at hand with very minimal interruptions until the channel or sender matches what they are waiting for. This could help with the types of on-going task where the distraction of mobile phone notifications was longer and more disruptive [31] when the user had to disengage with the primary task for a system generated or impersonal message, while allowing them to attend to the messages from family and friends that were not felt to be as disruptive during the task.

While there is some differentiation between the haptic alerts from, for example, a news application and an incoming text message this could be taken further to allow users to effectively pre-triage notifications on the wrist without interrupting the task at all. At the moment any notification that is ignored or postponed in this manner is put, unread, into the notifications drawer – necessitating carrying out the maintenance. By allowing users to dismiss notifications unseen, depending only on the haptic alert, through a gesture or a touch pattern the number of glances that need to be attended to and the number of maintenance tasks that need to be done by the user could be reduced significantly.

5.1 Maintenance

However, looking at Metrotra et al.'s finding that the distraction was felt to be greater depending on the timing within the on-going task [31], the inbuilt insistence that comes with the notification method with the Apple watch may make it more disruptive than it would appear at first glance. When a notification is new then glancing at it triggers an animation, and the direct access to the notification without the need for direct manipulation of the watch face. This also results in the watch marking that notification as read. If this is put off in order to focus on the task at hand then the notification is placed in the notification drawer unread – causing the 'red dot' to appear front and centre on the watch face.

This red dot is the trigger for many of the maintenance interactions, and from the interviews was seen to be something that was conflated with negative ideas of having 'missed something' or 'being behind.' Therefor, the question poses itself as to if users' actions to avoid the red dot includes performing glances at times when, if they were responding to notifications on the mobile phone they would not.

The reasons for starting a maintenance task vary. One reported motivation was simply to 'get rid of' the red dot given that its appearance means that one or more unread messages exist it must be cleared to serve its purpose as an indicator of unread messages. This means that it can happen, as in clip two, when the user notices that notifications are waiting, or it can be initiated to pass the time when the user was not otherwise engaged. We have seen this sort of down-time interaction with the notification drawer in queues in shops, waiting for public transport, and waiting between tasks in the kitchen.

Another motivation for this maintenance, beyond being able to use the red dot as an indicator of a new missed notification, was to make the use of the notification drawer itself easier. Given the small size of the screen on the Apple watch only one notification is fully visible at a time in this view. This means that if the notifications in the drawer are allowed to build up the user may be forced to scroll passed a lot of messages to find the unread one. While it is possible to 'force touch' – or press hard on the screen – to dismiss all the messages in the notification tray, if a user wants to find the unread notification (as ones that are seen with a glance still make their way to the drawer, they are simply marked as read and don't result in the display of the red dot) they must manually find it first.

At the moment there is a lack of third part apps running on the watch, but interaction in this space is one where the user has time and attention to spare. This would be a good candidate for interaction with an experience sampling application to elicit further information from participants.

5.2 The Watch in Conversation

The watch has a different place in conversation and co-located interaction than the smartphone. This is in part due to physicality of the watch. The device is designed to be orientated to a single user wearing it on their wrist, so turning one's wrist to allow another party to see the screen causes the watch to detect that it is no longer the focus of attention of its wearer – and this causes the operating system to turn off the screen. As we have seen [7] the smartphone, and the information on screen, often orientated around in conversation however this is not readily available when using the smartwatch. As seen in the clip in Fig. 3 this doesn't have to hinder conversational gambits which use the incoming messages by transforming them to reported speech, or as a topical resources. However, improving the gesture recognizer on the smartwatch to detect such an action, or providing a more direct method (such as holding a physical button or temporarily locking the screen on in much the same way as one would lock the rotation on a smartphone) would make the watch fit better with current practice.

Conversely the location of the smartwatch on the wrist, in the same location and mimicking the style and function of a traditional wristwatch, means that it comes with the baggage of long standing social conventions in speech and interaction which can be disrupted by the additional functions that technology has added. Where the mobile phone opened a new space in bodily interaction in social situations, the smart watch must contend with the meanings people would read into the same bodily interactions conducted with a traditional wristwatch.

When the smartwatch is set to provide only haptic feedback, inaudible to others, then the action of glancing to check an incoming notification can be read as the action of glancing to check the time – indicating impatience, boredom, or the intention to begin a closing sequence in the conversation. All but one of our participants reported turning off the audio alerts of incoming notifications in this way.

Connecting the new affordances of the smartwatch with the practices of the wrist-watch is somewhat more difficult. The social signals of performing a time-check are still available, however most other interactions with the watch overlap this signal. One possibility suggested by a participant during their post trial interview would be to add a second screen on the inside of the wrist allowing interactions with the smart functions of the watch to be obviously different.

6   Conclusion

In this paper we have gained a greater understanding of where the smartwatch sits in the technological landscapes in which users interact with them. By focusing on glancing and maintenance behaviours, accounting for the majority of use, we are able to compare the use of the smartwatch to that of other readily available devices in the home and on the body.

By looking at the physicality of the smartwatch, and its place not only on the body but in social expectations, norms, and constraints we can see that when designing an augmented, or smart, version of something already woven into our lives the current practices must not only be understood, but taken into account. Simply labelling change as 'disruption' is not enough. In the case of the smartwatch, users and those that they interact with must learn and adapt to their new affordances and build social practice and norms around them. One barrier to adoption often overlooked is the cost early adopters pay in continually breaking social practice until such norms come into being. By carefully designing for this transition process, taking into account that which is being disrupted as well as where and for whom, a major barrier for adoption of new technology could be significantly lowered.

References

1. Akkil, D., et al.: Glance awareness and gaze interaction in smartwatches. In: Presented at the Proceedings of the 33rd Annual ACM Conference Extended Abstracts on Human Factors in Computing Systems (2015)
2. Bandelloni, R., Paternò, F.: Migratory user interfaces able to adapt to various interaction platforms. Int. J. Hum Comput Stud. 60(5–6), 621–639 (2004)
3. Bardram, J.E.: Activity-based computing for medical work in hospitals. ACM Trans. Comput. Hum. Interact. 16(2), 10:1–10:36 (2009)
4. Brown, B., et al.: iPhone in vivo: Video analysis of mobile device use. In: Proceedings of CHI 2013, Paris, France. ACM Press, New York (2013)
5. Baudisch, P., Chu, G.: Back-of-device interaction allows creating very small touch devices. In: Presented at the Proceedings of the SIGCHI Conference on Human Factors in Computing Systems (2009)

6. Brown, B., et al.: 100 days of iPhone use: Understanding the details of mobile device use. In: Presented at the Proceedings of the 16th international conference on Human-computer interaction with mobile devices & services (2014). doi:10.1145/2628363.2628377

7. Brown, B., et al.: Searchable objects: Search in everyday conversation. In: Presented at the Proceedings of the 18th ACM Conference on Computer Supported Cooperative Work & Social Computing (2015)

8. Cecchinato, M.E., et al.: Smartwatches: The good, the bad and the ugly? In: Presented at the Proceedings of the 33rd Annual ACM Conference Extended Abstracts on Human Factors in Computing Systems (2015)

9. Cha, J.-M., et al.: Virtual sliding QWERTY: A new text entry method for smartwatches using Tap-N-Drag. Appl. Ergon. **51**, 263–272 (2015)

10. Chen, W.-H.: Blowatch: Blowable and hands-free interaction for smartwatches. In: Presented at the Proceedings of the 33rd Annual ACM Conference Extended Abstracts on Human Factors in Computing Systems (2015)

11. Dearman, D., Pierce, J.S.: It's on my other computer!: Computing with multiple devices. In: Proceedings of the SIGCHI Conference on Human Factors in Computing Systems, pp. 767–776 ACM, New York (2008)

12. Dunlop, M.D., et al.: Towards high quality text entry on smartwatches. In: Presented at the CHI 2014 Extended Abstracts on Human Factors in Computing Systems (2014)

13. Giang, W.C.W., et al.: Smartwatches vs. smartphones: A preliminary report of driver behavior and perceived risk while responding to notifications. In: Presented at the Proceedings of the 7th International Conference on Automotive User Interfaces and Interactive Vehicular Applications (2015). doi:10.1145/2799250.2799282

14. Grudin, J.: Partitioning digital worlds: Focal and peripheral awareness in multiple monitor use. In: Proceedings of the SIGCHI Conference on Human Factors in Computing Systems, pp. 458–465. ACM, New York (2001)

15. Heath, C., et al.: Configuring awareness. Comput. Support. Coop. Work (CSCW) **11**(3), 317–347 (2002)

16. Heath, C., Luff, P.: Technology in Action. Cambridge University Press, Cambridge (2000)

17. Hennfng, R.A., et al.: Microbreak length, performance, and stress in a data entry task. Ergonomics **32**(7), 855–864 (1989)

18. Hey, T., Trefethen, A.: The data deluge: An e-Science perspective. In: Grid Computing: Making the Global Infrastructure a Reality, pp. 809–824. Wiley (2003)

19. Holz, C., Baudisch, P.: The generalized perceived input point model and how to double touch accuracy by extracting fingerprints. In: Presented at the Proceedings of the SIGCHI Conference on Human Factors in Computing Systems (2010)

20. Holz, C., Baudisch, P.: Understanding touch. In: Presented at the Proceedings of the SIGCHI Conference on Human Factors in Computing Systems (2011)

21. Hong, J., et al.: SplitBoard: A simple split soft keyboard for wristwatch-sized touch screens. In: Presented at the Proceedings of the 33rd Annual ACM Conference on Human Factors in Computing Systems (2015)

22. Jokela, T., et al.: A diary study on combining multiple information devices in everyday activities and tasks. In: Presented at the Proceedings of the 33rd Annual ACM Conference on Human Factors in Computing Systems (2015)

23. Kane, S.K., Karlson, A.K., Meyers, B.R., Johns, P., Jacobs, A., Smith, G.: Exploring cross-device web use on PCs and mobile devices. In: Gross, T., Gulliksen, J., Kotzé, P., Oestreicher, L., Palanque, P., Prates, R.O., Winckler, M. (eds.) INTERACT 2009. LNCS, vol. 5726, pp. 722–735. Springer, Heidelberg (2009). doi:10.1007/978-3-642-03655-2_79

24. Karlson, A.K., et al.: Mobile taskflow in context: A screenshot study of smartphone usage. In: Proceedings of the SIGCHI Conference on Human Factors in Computing Systems, pp. 2009–2018. ACM, New York (2010)

25. Komninos, A., Dunlop, M.: Text input on a smart watch. IEEE Pervasive Comput. **13**(4), 50–58 (2014)

26. Kratz, S., Rohs, M.: HoverFlow: Expanding the design space of around-device interaction. In: Presented at the Proceedings of the 11th International Conference on Human-Computer Interaction with Mobile Devices and Services (2009)

27. Lyons, K.: What can a dumb watch teach a smartwatch? Informing the design of smartwatches. In: Presented at the Proceedings of the 2015 ACM International Symposium on Wearable Computers (2015)

28. Mainwaring, S.D., Anderson, K., Chang, M.F.: Living for the global city: Mobile kits, urban interfaces, and ubicomp. In: Beigl, M., Intille, S., Rekimoto, J., Tokuda, H. (eds.) UbiComp 2005. LNCS, vol. 3660, pp. 269–286. Springer, Heidelberg (2005). doi:10.1007/11551201_16

29. McMillan, D., et al.: From in the wild to in vivo: Video analysis of mobile device use. In: Presented at the Proceedings of the 17th International Conference on Human-Computer Interaction with Mobile Devices and Services (2015)

30. McMillan, D., et al.: Situating wearables: Smartwatch use in context. In: Proceedings of the 2017 CHI Conference on Human Factors in Computing Systems. ACM (2017)

31. Mehrotra, A., et al.: My phone and me: Understanding people's receptivity to mobile notifications. In: Presented at the CHI 2016 CHI Conference on Human Factors in Computing Systems (2016)

32. Müller, H., et al.: Understanding tablet use: A multi-method exploration. In: Proceedings of the 14th International Conference on Human-computer Interaction with Mobile Devices and Services, pp. 1–10. ACM, New York (2012)

33. Nacenta, M.: Cross-display object movement in multi-display environments. Ph.D. thesis, University of Saskatchewan (2009). http://library2.usask.ca/theses/available/etd-01062010123426

34. Marmasse, N., Schmandt, C., Spectre, D.: WatchMe: Communication and awareness between members of a closely-knit group. In: Davies, N., Mynatt, Elizabeth D., Siio, I. (eds.) UbiComp 2004. LNCS, vol. 3205, pp. 214–231. Springer, Heidelberg (2004). doi: 10.1007/978-3-540-30119-6_13

35. Nebeling, M., et al.: WearWrite: Orchestrating the crowd to complete complex tasks from wearables. In: Presented at the UIST 2015 Adjunct Proceedings of the 28th Annual ACM Symposium on User Interface Software & Technology (2015)

36. Oakley, I., Lee, D.: Interaction on the edge: offset sensing for small devices. In: Presented at the Proceedings of the SIGCHI Conference on Human Factors in Computing Systems (2014)

37. Oulasvirta, A., Sumari, L.: Mobile kits and laptop trays: Managing multiple devices in mobile information work. In: Proceedings of the SIGCHI Conference on Human Factors in Computing Systems, pp. 1127–1136 ACM, New York (2007)

38. Pizza, S., et al.: Smartwatch in vivo. In: Proceedings of the 2016 CHI Conference on Human Factors in Computing Systems, pp. 5456–5469. ACM, New York (2016)

39. Rawassizadeh, R., et al.: Wearables: Has the age of smartwatches finally arrived? Commun. ACM **58**(1), 45–47 (2014)

40. Santosa, S., Wigdor, D.: A field study of multi-device workflows in distributed workspaces. In: Proceedings of the 2013 ACM International Joint Conference on Pervasive and Ubiquitous Computing, pp. 63–72. ACM, New York (2013)

41. Schildbach, B., Rukzio, E.: Investigating selection and reading performance on a mobile phone while walking. In: Proceedings of the 12th International Conference on Human Computer Interaction with Mobile Devices and Services, pp. 93–102. ACM (2010)

42. Schirra, S., Bentley, F.R.: It's kind of like an extra screen for my phone: Understanding everyday uses of consumer smart watches. In: Presented at the Proceedings of the 33rd Annual ACM Conference Extended Abstracts on Human Factors in Computing Systems (2015)
43. Swan, M.: Sensor mania! The internet of things, wearable computing, objective metrics, and the quantified self 2.0. J. Sensor Actuator Netw. 1(3), 217–253 (2012)
44. Terrenghi, L., et al.: A taxonomy for and analysis of multi-person-display ecosystems. Pers. Ubiquit. Comput. 13(8), 583–598 (2009)
45. Uzun, E., et al.: Pairing devices for social interactions: A comparative usability evaluation. In: Proceedings of the SIGCHI Conference on Human Factors in Computing Systems, pp. 2315–2324. ACM, New York (2011)
46. Xiao, R., et al.: Expanding the input expressivity of smartwatches with mechanical pan, twist, tilt and click. In: Presented at the Proceedings of the SIGCHI Conference on Human Factors in Computing Systems (2014)
47. Gartner Says Worldwide Wearable Devices Sales to Grow 18.4 Percent in 2016. Gartner (2016)
48. Media alert: Apple shipped two-thirds of all smart watches in 2015. Canalys (2016)
49. Top 10 Smartwatch Companies 2014 (Sales). Smartwatch Group

The Interaction Design of Mobile Apps for Chinese Early Education

Qiong Peng[1,2(✉)]

[1] Chengdu University of Information Technology, Chengdu, China
q.peng@tue.nl
[2] Eindhoven University of Technology, Eindhoven, Netherlands

Abstract. Based on the current status of children's abundant exposure to mobile devices and the massive using apps as early education method in our daily life, this research explores the relationship between preschool children's cognitive characteristics and styles and interaction design of early education applications, with different qualitative research methods, to evaluate the interaction design for some representative apps. And then guidelines for the interaction design of mobile apps for early Chinese education is proposed and evaluated. This research aims to supply a reference for interaction design for early education apps, hoping that better and appropriate early education apps for children will be provided in the future.

Keywords: Interaction design · Cognitive style · Early education · Mobile apps

1 Introduction

As the fast development of science technology and the improvement of Chinese people's daily life, preschool children nowadays have more opportunities to using some of the modern mobile devices and the apps as well. According to the data of 2015, there were more than billion preschool children in China. With the traditional value that don't let children lose at the starting point, parents always put hopes on their children. So they pay more attention to education, especially the early education for preschool children. Parents not only spend much money on children's learning and training at school or from other agencies, but also prefer buying devices or tools to help children to learn. People believe that good preschool education will promote children's development and get better learning in the future. It's not strange that the preschool children can use smart phones or ipad very well. They can play games and get learning with many different apps.

Human beings get the fundamental learning through the intuitive cognition process which combines the external and internal information got by individual sensors. Children, especially the preschool children develop their abilities of independent and abstractive thinking after they have perceptions. Thus, they can learn through interacting with the interactive devices such as smart phone and iPad. These digital and interactive education products should meet the needs of natural learning, comfortable using and satisfaction. Early education products for preschool children usually combine the

© Springer International Publishing AG 2017
A. Marcus and W. Wang (Eds.): DUXU 2017, Part II, LNCS 10289, pp. 288–299, 2017.
DOI: 10.1007/978-3-319-58637-3_23

advantages of modern digital technology, with the benefits of promoting intelligence, enlightenment, and teaching. There is huge needs and potential in the early education product market. However, compared with other digital products, early education products for preschool children are mostly CDs which should be played with a computer and a screen. The problems such as lacking proper development, less and bad interaction design, limitation in time and place, lacking good guideline for product design, have existed for a long time. Apps not only own the advantages of mobile devices which are light and easy to take with, but also are flexible to be used at any time and any place. So it is necessary and important to develop more useful apps for early education to attract children's attention and improve learning effects.

Until the end of 2016, there have been 1.08 billion children in China, and more than 10,000 mobile apps both on Android and iOS platforms for preschool children's early education. It is estimated that more than 70% of these apps are designed by foreign companies mostly in North America and Europe. The ones developed by Chinese companies occupied small percentage in the market even through the app industry develops well in recent several years. This gives rise to a problem that not all the apps are suitable for preschool children in China. Since there are not only the language differences, but also some other problems such as different cultures, values, different living environment, various education types both at school and home, and behavior models, which may have influence in preschool children's cognitive development and the effect of early education. Thus, it should be taken into account that the general characteristics of cognitive development and the difference between Chinese children and children in western countries when making the interaction design for Chinese preschool children' early education.

In this paper, it aims to make research for interaction design of mobile apps for early education for Chinese children based on the cognitive development and Chinese preschool children's particular characteristics, through multiple research methods including both qualitative and quantitative research methods. The guidelines for interaction design of early education apps are proposed and tested with the hope to provide a reference for app interaction design, so that the preschool children in China can enjoy happy use and good learning by using these apps.

2   Related Literature Research

2.1   Cognitive Process and Cognitive Style Models

Children usually can be classified into five different groups: infant group (from 1 to 1 year old), baby group (from 1 year to 3 years old), children (from 4 years old to 6 years old), pupil (from 7 years old to 12 years old), and middle school children (from 13 years old to 18 years old). Preschool children usually include children from 5 to 6 years old.

In Psychology, cognition is the process of information acquisition and processing, organization, and application [1]. American cognitive psychology scholars believe that it is the information processing psychology and can be analog by a computer as the process of information input, code, processing, save and output. Jean Piaget holds the opinion that the cognitive process is the one during which human beings' adaptation of needs, so it is necessary to pay importance to psychological factors such as intelligence and thinking [1]. In cognition process, there are three phrases: feeling—perception–classification, feeling means human being get contact with the information in the environment through the sensory system. Feeling is the real impression from external stimulates. Perception is awareness activities which mean information obtaination and application. For children, the process of absorbing meaningful information is perception, and it is influenced by attention and previous experience. The accuracy of perception improves as children grow up. Attention as one of the critical checkpoints in information process is divided into three different types including selective attention, distributive attention, and sustained attention. The selective attention means filtering information, and then memory can save subjective experience. Wicken (1992) propose the information processing model means cognition is a complicated process [1].

Cognitive psychologists stress active learning process, and the cognitive styles influenced by individual character, motivation, emotion and cognitive ability which have a high impact on information process. Cognitive style is generalization methods in cognition and individual stable psychological inclination [1]. Allport proposed that cognitive style is the model of personal solving problems, thinking, perception and memory. We present the cognitive style model as Fig. 1 shows.

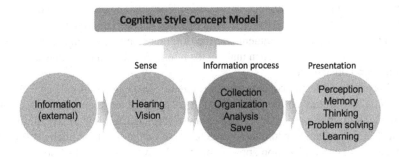

Fig. 1. Cognitive style concept model

There are different classifications of cognitive styles such as field independent-dependent type,

Analysis—non-analysis type, text-image type. Ridding and Cheema (1991)proposed two-dimensional cognitive style mode: [Whole-Analysis]-[Text-Image] [2], as Fig. 2 shows. In [Whole-Analysis] dimension, Whole means viewing information as whole; Analysis means dividing information into different groups and people usually only pay attention to one or two groups once. In [Text-Image] dimension, Text means people incline thinking about what they see, read and hear in a text, however, image means people prefer images to understand what they get from the external environment. Ridding also came up with CSA tool to analyze cognitive styles.

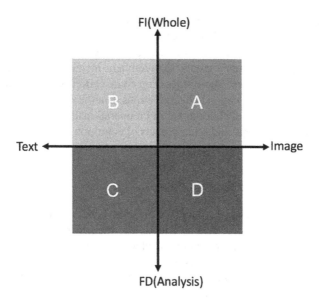

Fig. 2. FI-FD and text-image two dimensional model

2.2 The Cognitive Development of Preschool Children

In Piaget cognitive development theory, there are four stages in children's cognitive development process: Sensorimotor stage (from birth to 2 years old), Preoperational

Characteristics of Preschool children in Preoperational Stage
1. Focus on one characteristics of an object
2. One-way thinking, lacking reversibility
3. The sign system starts to form
4. Can choose middle size objects out of different ones with various sizes
5. Own memory for one to two years
6. Can distinguish red, yellow, blue and green colors
7. Can describe the lacking part in one picture
8. Can make supplement of the lacking parts in a human figure
9. Can distinguish right and left, sunny day and cloudy day

Fig. 3. Characteristics of preschool children in preoperational stage

stage (from 2 to 7 years old), Concrete operational stage (from 7 to 12 years old), and Formal operational stage (from 12 to 15 years old) [3]. Piaget believes that psychological development is a successive internal organizing or reorganizing process. Through it is a continuous process, children's mental development includes four stages due to the interaction of different factors. These stages can come earlier or later because of difference in the environment, education and motivations. But the sequence of the four stages cannot be changed. Preschool children are in Preoperational stage, and they have their characteristics in color, shape and other aspects of cognition, which has been summarized in Fig. 3 shows.

2.3   Early Education for Preschool Children

Learning is an abstract thinking activity. For preschool children, their abstract thinking ability is limited. So it calls for special attention to their learning methods. There are three popular education theories for children, which explore education for children from different perspectives. The first one is Theory of multiple intelligences (MI or MQ) proposed by Howard Earl Gardener (1993). In his book Frames of Mind, an intelligence is the ability with which people can solve problems or create useful products under a value criteria in a distinctive social and cultural environment. The eight abilities to meet the criteria include verbal-linguistic, musical-rhythmic, logical-mathematical, visual-spatial, bodily-kinesthetic, interpersonal, intrapersonal, and naturalistic [4]. MI theory, been viewed as the guideline of education innovation in many western countries, emphasize that the period from birth to 7 years old is the crucial time for children's development, thus it is very vital for children's future life.

The second one is Maria Montessori's education theory, which has two core principles: children engage in psychological self-construction through interaction with their environments, and children, especially under six years old, have an innate path of mental development [5]. This theory advocates that children's driving behavior in sensitive periods are significant and education for children should respond to and facilitate their expression. The third one is Fredrich Forbel's education theory, which laid the foundation for modern education [6]. He created the first kindergarten and developed learning toys known as Froebel Gifts [6]. In his theory, children have unique needs and capabilities [6], and the education should make use of games to guide children's activities, development and social involvement. All of the education theories lay emphasis on the role of games for education. As researchers' expression of games as happy and exciting activities which can be adaptive with children's cognition development, games are the most important method for children's socialization and cognition development. Games are the primary method for the children's education.

The literature review gives us inspiration for the interaction design of educational apps. It can be explained in two aspects: one aspect is that it should focus on children's cognition development and different cognitive styles. Preschool children are in such a special stage that they have intense curiosity in everything. Games can meet their interest and help their cognition development through personal involvement in games. Another aspect is that children's education should be designed as edutainment [7] which is the combination of entertainment and teaching. Games with multiple forms are the tool of children's development and a good style of edutainment. In a word, the interaction design of early education apps should be based children's cognition characteristics and make full use of games to attract children's interest to help children easily and happily to learn through edutainment.

3 Research Method and Process

In this research, there are several steps including existing products investigation, expert evaluation, interview, questionnaire and children's cognitive style test. Both qualitative and quantitative research methods such as observation, interview, questionnaire have been used. It is designed like this aiming to explore the relationship between preschool children's cognitive style and interaction design of early education apps, so that the guideline for interaction design can be proposed and demonstrated.

3.1 Existing Apps Investigation

There are five kinds of early education apps: apps for mathematics, apps for language learning, apps for identification and memory, apps for logic training and apps of integrated functionalities. These apps are designed both on iOS iPhone, iPad and Android devices. In recent many years, as mobile devices are available for everyone, apps have become the best way for children's early education. According to the results of some online survey, children in the major cities in China get more contact with early education apps compared with the ones in other small and rural areas. The apps for early education parents choose for their children mostly focus on storytelling, literacy, arithmetic, and music. Data also shows that until the end of 2015, children use these apps twice a day on average and 12 min every time.

However, even though early education apps on mobile devices have been very popular, good and bad ones mix. The low threshold of app development results in products' homogeneity. Parents show their concerns that which app should be chosen for children. Parents, who can decide whether to use apps and which one should be used for children, prefer the education apps with excellent functionalities and more user-friendly interfaces.

Results from an online survey and a questionnaire, 15 apps for early education have been recommended as the best choice for Chinese children and parents: (1) BabyBus (the best recommended app in App store in China, which using sound, text and images to develop children's multiple cognition development); (2) PlayKids (prevalent in more than 26 countries, with good stories and games); (3) Magikid (an app developed by Chinese company, stressing color, shape, number and logic development); (4) Montessori Crosswords (a proper application of Montessori education theory to help children to read, spell and pronunciation; (5) Elmo Loves 123 s(a good application of edutainment through games, cartoons and free creation); (6) Agnitus Kids Learning Program (a comprehensive application of English enlightenment); (7) Moose Math (an app to help train children's interest in math with games); (8) Donut's ABC(especially for children's English learning); (9) Music 4 Kids (an app for developing children's music learning);

(10) Scribble My Story(an app to help children create their own stories); (11) Distant Suns Lite (an app to help children to get to know Astronomy and the nature); (12) Smartots App(Smartots is the biggest mobile education platform for children. There are a series of useful apps); (13) Hay Day(an app analog management through games); (14) Wisdom Apps(one of the best popular early education apps in Apple store in China); (15) The Robot Factory(an app for 6 years old children to make their own robots).

3.2 Interview with Preschool Teachers and Parents

An interview aiming at getting more details of preschool children's cognition characteristics and opinions on existing early education apps was made in the same kindergarten. Five teachers with two years' working experience on average participated in the interview. 30 parents took part in the questionnaire research. The results show that there are some unique cognitive characteristics for preschool children, for example, preschool children can focus on stimulus for a long time, they have already known how to sequence, how to make classification, they can name colors, they have interest in words and graphs, and they can distinguish reality and imagination. According to Piaget's theory, preschool children's cognitive styles have been developed enough to own their individual characteristics. It gives us support to make research of the relationship between children cognitive style and early education apps interaction design.

3.3 Expert Evaluation

The 15 apps have been chosen out as recommended best early education apps. Giving the age and unique cognitive characteristics of preschool children, not all of them are suitable for preschool children. Then five apps (as Fig. 4 shows, BabyBus, Smartots app, Playkids, Magikid, and Montessori Crosswords) were chosen out for an expert evaluation. Five experts with three years' interaction design experience on average were invited for evaluation. The evaluation is designed to a 5-point scale adapted from

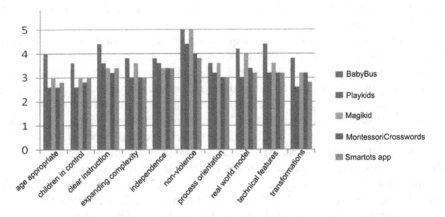

Fig. 4. Experts' evaluation result

Haugland/Shade's criterion for children's education software/applications [8]. The scale covers ten main aspects for children's interaction with software and applications, including age appropriate, children in control, explicit instruction, expanding complexity, independence, non-violence, process orientation, real world model, technical features and transformations. Combined with the results of think aloud during the evaluation and the means of the five apps, three apps (BabyBus, PlayKids, and Magikid) were chosen out as the samples for test, as Fig. 4 shows.

3.4   Children's Cognitive Style Test

Thirty preschool children (fifteen boys and fifteen girls) took part in this test. All of them are five to six years old with normal intelligence and vision, from the same kindergarten in one of the big cities in China. The cognitive style analysis tool (CSA), which has been viewed as one of the best tools with good reliability and validity, was adapted with a combination of the two dimensions of [Whole-Analysis] and [Text-Image]. In [Text-Image] test, different units of images, pictures, texts, and numbers were presented to these thirty preschool children and asked them to find out the right ones. The time was recorded for comparison as Fig. 5 shows.

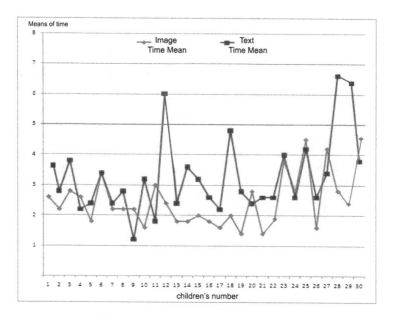

Fig. 5. Time means of [Text-Image] test

In [Whole-Analysis] test, field independence and field dependence are the two dimensions. Embedded Figure Test was used to ask the children to find out the embedded simple graphs. The one using less time to find out the right graphs gets higher points. More than 80% accuracy is viewed as field independent style.

After these two tests, the results and distribution in four quadrants of these 30 children's cognitive styles are presented in Fig. 6. In FI and FD dimension, there·is no superior for one to the other one. It only shows individual cognition style. Preschool children have already experienced development in cognition and acclimated experience from daily life. With some other factors such as personal character, living environment together, there are a different distribution in FI and FD dimension. For the children with FI style, they prefer independent activities, while FD style children need external help and guide which means more interaction with the external environment. For interaction design of early education apps, it is necessary to pay attention to this difference as

well as the external cultural influence, since there are differences in the behavior and interaction with external environment for Chinese children and children in western countries. Generally speaking, Chinese children mostly follow the rules, thus, more outer tips or remind can encourage their interaction. It means in the apps' interaction design, interactive feedback and effective feedback should be attached attention. In [Text-Image] dimension, more children are image style. Preschool children, even though, most of them can read text and characters, they prefer the concrete images which are easy to understand.

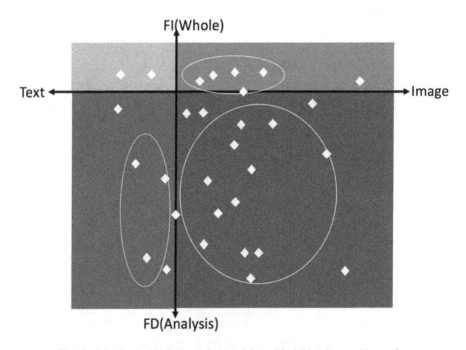

Fig. 6. Distribution in four quadrants of these 30 children's cognitive styles

It told us that when making interaction design for preschool children, images should be given priority to, supplemented with simple text or sound help. Concrete images have similarity with their real life, which can help children to imagine and learn. The interface should be designed with vibrant colors, which can attract children's attention easily because children are sensitive to warm and bright colors.

3.5 Guidelines for Interaction Design of Early Education Apps

We came up with guidelines for interaction design of early education apps based on children's cognitive style test and the typical characteristics of cognition development in three aspects with a more detailed explanation as Fig. 7 shows.

Aspects	Guidelines	Explanation
1. **Information** **Architecture**	1.1 Clear navigation	1.11 Easy to get in and out, easy to be back
		1.12 Navigation is clear and easy to understand
	1.2 Simple hierarchy	Appropriate number of hierarchy (2 to 3 is enough)
	1.3 Classify information	Appropriate classification of information based on reality
	1.4 Trackable	To let children to know current status
2. **Information** **presentation**	2.1 Information Visualization	2.11 Present information in real and concrete images
		2.12 Present selections in graphical style
		2.13 Vivid animations, good interaction
		2.14 Rich colors(using brighter colors, high purity colors)
		2.15 Delicate design for graphs
		2.16 Icons and symbols should designed easy to understand
	2.2 Operation Instruction	2.21 Give hints or help in simple and clear graphs or icons
		2.22 Icons are big enough to recognize
		2.23 Voice help
		2.24 Avoid using menu list
3. **Efficiency of** **interaction**	3.1 Effective Feedback	3.11 Every operation is visible
		3.12 Objects moving and change in size, color and shapes is visible
		3.13 Rapid and clear feedbacks
		3.14 Feedback should be designed in graphs or images, less text
		3.15 Voice feedback
		3.16 Give feedback in an encouragement style.
		3.17 Learning gradually step by step, from easy to difficult.
	3.2 Feel of control	3.21 Children can using independently.
		3.22 Customization of difficulty levels, numbers and languages
	3.3 Happy experience in interaction	3.31 Attractive, support constant use
		3.32 Pleasure in using
		3.33 Teaching useful concepts and values

Fig. 7. Guidelines of interaction design for early education apps

3.6 Evaluation for the Guidelines

To evaluate the feasibility and validity of the guidelines, the same 30 children took part in the test by using the three apps selected by expert evaluation. Researchers asked the children with different cognitive styles to using apps and recorded the whole process with video. Considering the children are too young to finish a five-point scale, researchers gave the points according to the observation of the process and interview as a supplement. Then the guidelines were evaluated by descriptive statistic analysis and ANOVA analysis in SPSS. The results show that all the P numbers are bigger than 0.05 and there is no significant difference. It means all the 27 guidelines are suitable for preschool children with different cognitive styles.

4   Conclusion

Interaction design of early education apps not only influences children's using experience but also is viewed as a weighting factor for the success of app design. The conclusions of this research are drawn as follows:

Firstly, there is a significant influence of cognition development and cognitive style to early education apps' interaction design. To some extent, the development of these apps can meet the cognitive requirements based on different cognitive styles. Even though there are limited children for the test, the results of cognitive styles are enough and representative. No matter what kind style a preschool child will have, there is a limitation in their ability of cognition and understanding for most preschool children, so their cognitive styles tend to be image and field-dependent. Thus, interaction design of early education apps should be guaranteed to be suitable for most of the cognitive styles. It is valuable to propose the interaction design guidelines which can support reference for design practice.

Secondly, due to the immaturity and instability of children's cognition, they have a higher dependence on concrete images and graphs. The presentation of pictures, icons, charts and so on should be taken seriously in interaction design, which means these visual symbols for feedback and operation should be designed in a concrete and straightforward style to reduce children's cognitive burden.

Thirdly, rapid and efficient feedback and interaction are necessary and important. Not only images, sound, and voice should also be advised to use. The feedback in an encouragement style can trigger children's more interaction with the apps.

Lastly, the significance of interaction is to bring happiness, attraction and flow to users, which can influence users' decision of using again or not and control whether and how much they can get. Compared with adults, preschool children with limited patients, are curious with new, concrete and interactive things, so attractiveness should be taken into account in interaction design. As the development of mobile technology, more productive interactions can be considered to use to meet the needs of attractiveness.

5   Discussion and Limitation

In this research, existing early education apps are investigated, guidelines for interaction design are proposed and evaluated. Due to the limited time, the available number of children and some other factors, there is still limitations in three aspects:

Limitation 1. Cognition is part of psychological research, which is a concept with personal influence. Classification of individual cognitive style can be decided only by statistical data. Cognitive style has uncertainty because of individual difference. The results in subjectivity in research purpose and can only be solved by using the accepted cognitive style testing method.

Limitation 2. The reason for choosing preschool children as the research target lies in the importance of cognition development in preschool period and lacking related research achievements. Researchers hope to fill the gaps in this field. However, preschool children are too young to express themselves clearly and accurately, which resulted in the difficulty in the evaluation. The researcher can only give the assessment based on the observation of children's facial expression and their behaviors. It may influence the rigor of the research to some extent.

Limitation 3. Strictly speaking, the better result usually needs a large number of samples to support. However, we can only get thirty children for the test due to various reasons. We only focus on Chinese children because we believe there are some differences in early education and children's cognition in China and western countries because of a different cultural environment. However, there is not enough deep research in this aspect to be used as strong support.

This research focuses on visual aspects of interaction design. There is still space for research of interaction design based on other sensory organs such as acoustics and touch, or multiple combinations. The proposed guidelines can be used as reference or support when making interaction design not only for preschool children but also for all the children in Preoperational stage since there is much similarity in children's cognition in this stage. Researchers have already made plans for the next step. The application of the proposed guidelines did not be applied in researchers' interaction design projects due to limited time. It will be implemented and improved in the next research plan.

Acknowledgement. The research reported in this paper was supported by the 2016 project (16ZB0217) of Sichuan Province Department of Education and 2014 project (GY-14YB-13) of Industrial Design Research Center of Sichuan Province Department of Education. Thanks to all who were involved in this research.

References

1. Peng, D., Zhang, B.: Cognitive Psychology, Zhejiang Education Express (2004)
2. Rayner, S., Riding, R.: Towards a categorization of cognitive styles and learning styles. J. Educ. Psychol. **17**(1–2), 5–27 (1997)
3. https://en.wikipedia.org/wiki/Piaget%27s_theory_of_cognitive_development
4. https://en.wikipedia.org/wiki/Theory_of_multiple_intelligences
5. https://en.wikipedia.org/wiki/Montessori_education
6. https://en.wikipedia.org/wiki/Friedrich_Fr%C3%B6bel
7. https://en.wikipedia.org/wiki/Educational_entertainment
8. Haugland, S.: The best developmental software for young children. Early Childhood Educ. J. **25**(4), 247–254 (1998)

Breaking Through the Traditional Form of News Communication—User Experience Design of Live Broadcast

Xueting Xie[✉]

Design Department, Netease Media Technology (Beijing) Co., Ltd., Beijing, China
448106070@qq.com

Abstract. With the development of science and technology, the integration of traditional media and digital media, as well as the diversification of the way users read, many mobile news platform including NetEase News begin to try new ways of content transmission. Live broadcast is one of them. As we know, the core elements of news are timeliness, authenticity and accuracy, which have been made to a great extent by live broadcast. This article will use real cases including the trial of two directions from the PGC and UGC to share the user experience design methods in news live broadcast.

Keywords: Live broadcast · User experience · Design · News · UI design

1 Background

1.1 Advantages of Internet News Live Broadcast

In terms of television news, news live broadcast has been a very common program. Its effect and influence is more than revealing the result of event but leading the viewers and audience to experience the event at the scene. Meanwhile, the broadcast would be unpredictable, fresh and full of suspense, which would be quite attractive for the viewers. News live broadcast not only satisfies audience's curiosity and meet their demands on interactions but cater for their fast and comprehensive access to information. So to say the live broadcast is a very attractive and catching approach for news presentation.

In China, the television news live broadcast mainly covers two types; one is ritual television news live broadcast and the other is event television news live broadcast. Although television news live broadcast is tending to be normalization, ritual news live broadcast is more common while the event news live broadcast is rare. A majority of television news broadcast has become pre-edited "live show". Since timeliness is the eternal pursuit of news production, when a hot topic is approaching, people want to obtain first-hand news and information, however, such "live show" is second-hand materials after edition plus extra verification and correction and its single perspective, this kind of news lose its effects of timeliness, which cannot meet viewers' expectation.

Speaking of timeliness, the Internet has a natural advantage. Every day there are countless messages spread on the Internet, but the valuable news is usually not the first

A. Marcus and W. Wang (Eds.): DUXU 2017, Part II, LNCS 10289, pp. 300–309, 2017.
DOI: 10.1007/978-3-319-58637-3_24

time to be on the TV screen; break news even more so. In this regard, the Internet is always faster than the traditional TV media step, because it has a massive UGC (User Generated Content) as a strong content support. With the reduction of equipment costs, recording live as everyone can pick up the phone can easily complete the matter.

1.2 Conception of NetEase News Live Broadcast

NetEase News is professional news & information platform with professional edit teams and many We Media as well as large quantity of users. Based on natural advantages, we parallel PGC and UGC to create a news live broadcast ecology providing good experience. Live broadcast is no more the privilege of television and anybody or group can be a starter of news live broadcast. And perhaps in the future, there will be a large army of new live broadcast consisting of media group, content teams, media professionals, ordinary PGC, UGC, college students and others. The whole society of people would do news live broadcast.

2 Definition of Product Modality

2.1 Users Demand Generation

As mentioned above, the facts through ages have proved that live broadcast would enable users to feel reality of the news, to know and experience the living stories. Does that mean everything succeeds as we transport the live broadcast model of TV or PC age to mobile terminal? Of course not, it is irresponsible for the users. Now, let's reconstruct live broadcast.

The traditional live broadcast is that the anchor showed the video and audio of occurrent events to the viewers, in which process the anchor would explain and remark on the event. The viewers, as acceptors, can only watch what was going on in the video. Through out observation, we found that if more viewers watched same news together, they would communicate, comment, cheer or stamp one's feet… on the events and sometimes they would share other relevant information from other channels; thus it would be more lively. For example, here is a familiar scene, when you are watching sports game in a bar or your house with a couple of friends, you always comment the players performance with people around you during the game. And all these interactions and behaviors will enrich the live broadcast content invisibly and also allow the receiver or acceptor to become the participant of live broadcast, which would improve viewers' experience and satisfaction.

Therefore, when watching live broadcast, it's very important for viewers to start and participate in the interactions more than just watching and receiving information. So I wondered it would be a great idea if I transfer this behavior during our daily life to the online platform.

2.2   Interactive Model of NetEase News Live Broadcast Products

News live broadcast is always a presentation way in NetEase news, but the old and single state of "play on platform and audience watching" cannot perform the potential of live broadcast. The former modal issues are mainly as follows: anchor and viewers can only release content within limited styles and it is hard for users to generate contents; the interactions between anchors and users are quite rare, which not only constrain the production of more news but bad for stimulating user's passion; thus various possibilities of transforming to live broadcast cannot be realized. Hence, in the revision, we have made great attempts regarding these two matters:

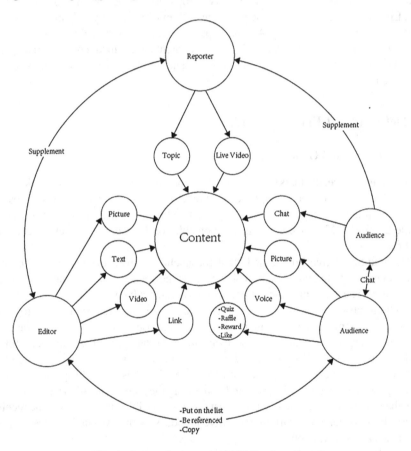

Fig. 1.   Interactive status of PGC live broadcast

We produce and generate content via three channels of reporter's live video broadcast, anchor's releasing content and audience's assist in posting content. Thus it would create a strong interactive broadcast circle of multiple channels with on-going communication between anchor and viewers and between viewers and viewers (See Fig. 1). Reporters explore live broadcast topic and collect live video resources at the spot;

editors, as the anchors, tells content of live broadcast with supplementary materials, like graphs, texts, videos and links; Through this production circle of broadcast content, there are more valuable content can be generated by reporters and editors.

There are multiple kinds of interactivities between viewers and anchors, like guessing, lucky draw, data competition; and the viewers can also add like or credit for anchor; viewers can have interactive communications, upload pictures or videos; viewers and anchors can have timely interactions in which they can quote each other's words and those excellent lectures can be stick.

To ensure the excellent content can be viewed by more users, and what's more, in order to make the content abundant, we allow and encourage the We media who can create the channel of new live broadcast. At the meantime, those channels can be subscribed to satisfy the user individuals favor (See Fig. 2).

Fig. 2. The We media

Except PGC, we also bring in UGC resources. We develop another application called Radish which provide the users a tool and a platform to transcribe and upload videos. This application is connected with Netease News application, the best videos are chosen to recommended on Netease News application so other users can watch them. The broadcasting room for UGC resources is more interactive and entertaining for users.

2.3 Function Design

According to the analysis of interactive model in the last chapter, users' behaviors mainly include the following five types: viewing, browsing, inputting, uploading and interaction. Based on these five principal behaviors, we deduced five major functions of the product and they are video playing, information flow display, inputting text, uploading graphs, texts and voice and configurable plug-ins.

Layout Design. As we mentioned in the abstract, the three core elements of news are timeliness, authenticity and accuracy, which are also our design goal. Before we start to design, we should think how to reflect and balance the three elements in experience design.

For timeliness, each broadcasting room has a report who is always online releasing the latest news. In our layout, we design the report's modules to information flow pattern to make sure users are able to catch up the latest information.

For authenticity, we design a video playing module is each broadcasting room. When the events take place in different places, we even provide a multi-channel video switch function for people to get information.

For accuracy, we bring in UGC resources that make it possible for users to release the information they achieve directly, and the reporter can quote the information.

Among all behaviors of users during watching live broadcast, watching the video is the most persistent behavior. Therefore, the video playing module is at the top stability zone. During the live broadcast, anchor would explain for the video and upload pictures, videos and even links to supplement information. Thus, the anchor studio is just below the video module so that the information from the anchor can be presented in the way of information flow.

At the same time, audience can look through anchor's information out of their own needs. In the last chapter, I mentioned about users' interaction demands while watching live broadcast, yet this behavior is intermittent. So there is no need to put this function module at the most direct position. We set the chat room as the second option underneath the video module. Users can look through the chat information of the audience with manual switch to the "chat room".

However, inputting and uploading can happen any time no matter it is during watching video, browsing or chatting. So the input box and upload entrance are fixed at the bottom of the screen and they wouldn't hide themselves because of tab switch. As for guessing, lucky draw, reward and other interactions, they would vary with the content of live broadcast. Thus these functions are designed in some floating icon, which is quite flexible and feasible and some of them are designed as top news or plug-in (Fig. 3).

As we mentioned, we provide another type of content production called UGC. This type of broadcast is different from PGC, so does design. According to the user's behavior, it will make it more real for people to communicate face to face. So we design a fullscreen video playing layout which is quite different from the PGC broadcasting room. And the chat flow and the interactive button such as thumbing up, sending flowers is floating on the screen which the users can chat and interact with the host (See Fig. 4).

Fig. 3. Layout design

Fig. 4. Pic.2 layout design

Details Design. The live broadcast of NetEase News covers news events, entertainment stars, sports event, press conference, variety activities and others. As different types of live broadcast have different demands, we need a layout design to meet all various demands. For event news, there are multiple live broadcast sources at most times. For example, the American presidential election, users would switch to check every state election status and reporters at different states would release different videos. Under such circumstance, we need to provide multi-channel video switch function (see Fig. 5). While for sports event live broadcast, especially for player killing or competition, users would like to know the scores timely; and we shall provide scores showing plug-in for this kind of live broadcast.

Fig. 5. Multi-channel video switch function

Additionally, live broadcast can be divided into notice, on air and review on the basis of live broadcast status. In each phase, there are different content. For the notice phase, the precedent information for users are the start time for live broadcast and it is necessary to provide remind function and make brief introduction for the live broadcast content. At this phase, there is not source for video resource and the video display module is replaced with some banner displaying live broadcast content. When it is on air, as mentioned above, there are five function modules on the screen. During the review, users focus more on watching and reading important information. Therefore, we provide key points focus viewing function (see Fig. 6).

The third detail of design I want to mention here is minimize the playing video area. We balance the layout of video and information feeds flow for the most users. In the otherwise, we provide another option for the user who want to focus on the feeds flow (see Fig. 7).

Fig. 6. Key points focus viewing function

Fig. 7. Minimize the playing video area function

Fig. 8. UI design

UI Design. The UI design of news live broadcast also follows the three core elements of news which are timeliness, authenticity and accuracy. We simplify the most design elements to make the information more obvious. The unified controls of button and icon reduce the cost of users cognition and development both. And we create a label of live to let user recognize the news type and status in the broadcasting list. And the animation effect make the user experience more smooth (see Fig. 8).

In the page of broadcast live, we design the timeline of each single information to show the timeliness of news. And every single information show as a card which is more easier to read (see Fig. 9).

Fig. 9. Timeline design

3   Conclusion

News live broadcast is a way of news presentation rather than a special type of news. The paper is just tentative exploration for news live broadcast experience design at mobile terminals, we will continue to develop better interactive model based on practical data and real use condition of all users.

With the development of science and technology and changes of media, there will be more diverse types of live broadcast. I believe the new AR and VR technology would bring new change in news live broadcast and we will advance with the times to create better live broadcast experience.

Innovation Design in Personal Center Interface of Mobile Application

Xin Xin[✉], Wei Zhou, Mengfan Li, Haozhi Wang, Han Xu,
Yuwei Fan, Weizheng Ma, and Di Zhu

Beijing Normal University, Beijing, China
xin.xin@bnu.edu.cn

Abstract. Nowadays, Mobile Internet has changed the Chinese shop mostly. The appearance of e-commerce mobile applications greatly overthrows the consumption structures and patterns in Chinese society. Merchandises consumers could only buy at malls before; they can now get them by simply touching the screen, and then receive at next day. Shopping efficiency has been enhanced significantly. Personal Center page, where viewing and tracking orders, payment and other acts needed to be done, plays a key role in mobile applications of e-commerce. So far, however, far too little attention has been paid to Personal Center pages. They are complex, short of ideas, and have too many levels with unfriendly interface. It is hard to give users good experience. Based on the Personal Center of the Pinzhi 365 mobile application, this innovation design, by the analysis of similar competing products, enhanced their accessibility, efficiency, memorability and friendliness, which create a model of innovation design in Personal Center interface.

Keywords: Interface design · Mobile application · Personal center

1 Background

Pinzhi 365 Mall has 12 main categories included home appliances, phones and digital, body care and makeup, costumes and lingerie, shoes and bags, food and drinks, home daily, home textiles, outdoor sports, accessories and watches, infant toys, nutrition and health care [8, 23], has amounted to more than 50,000 items and more than 500 companies sign up merchants.

When we were doing revision design, we found that the Personal Center interface of Pinzhi 365 is simple but characteristic, although it is not good enough on visual effects and interaction [5].

Excellent apps of e-commerce can be found everywhere these days. A considerable amount of optimization has been done in core processes of purchase but few focuses on Personal Center.

Our desk research indicated that Personal Center page composed by orders, tools, personal information and other features, is the most frequently accessed page in addition to purchase page [16].

In this revision design, in order to make Pinzhi 365 mobile app into users' life, not only the process of purchase has been optimized but also the Personal Center interface.

© Springer International Publishing AG 2017
A. Marcus and W. Wang (Eds.): DUXU 2017, Part II, LNCS 10289, pp. 310–323, 2017.
DOI: 10.1007/978-3-319-58637-3_25

2   Design Features in Personal Center Interface of E-Commerce Mobile App

In the first place, a few Personal Center interfaces of e-commerce apps both in China and around the world were analyzed. The result shows that the frequency of interactions is extremely high [1, 9], such as when viewing shopping car, orders, collection clip, history commodity and address management; purchase, logistic view are also high frequency behaviors; for personal information edit, for contacting customer service, for recharging and setting, they are all common features when users are online shopping.

It will lead the convenience of shopping and user experience to a higher level [22] if we make innovation design and optimize the features of Personal Center interface so that it can meet users' needs better at any time and a wealth of user traffic, then profits will follow at last.

We did desk research between two dimensions: features and interface design, in which interface design is divided into three small dimensions: page layout, color and icon. Then we compared and analyzed seven commonly used apps in China and around the world as cases.

2.1   Analysis of Personal Center Interfaces of Mainstream Mobile Apps in China

Taobao (Fig. 1). Taobao is one of the largest E-commerce shopping platform, which emerged from an amount of E-commerce platform by excellent price and rich categories.

In the aspect of features, the Personal Center interface of Taobao include core features (e.g. order view) and extended features (e.g. collections). However, there are so many extended features that they make it inconvenient for users and lower availability factor [2]. The key problem with this interface is that the meaning of extended feature icons is not clear and users cannot know the feature of this module by simply reading the words under the icon [13].

In the aspect of layout, nine patch is used in Taobao's Personal Center, which is clear but lack of innovation. There is now rules in the arrangement of extended features though they divided features by using different colors. Another problem in this design is redundant contents, resulting in more

Fig. 1.

typesetting items, which is adverse to enhance the users' experience.

As for colors, the user center follows Taobao's business marked orange, which can help consumers to feel closer and increase their shopping desire.

In icon design, silhouette-type icons are simple and with strong moral but lack of new ideas.

Pinduoduo (Fig. 2). Pinduoduo is a shopping e-commerce mobile app in China with a feature of group purchase online.

In aspect of features, its Personal Center has basic features and special features based on its business (e.g. my group purchase). It is simple and easy to use with no odd extended features, which occupy less cognitive resource and enhance user experience [19].

In the aspect of layout, Pinduoduo list every feature one by one, which is clear and makes it convenient for users to use.

The Personal Center interface of Pinduoduo use red as the main color. Red is a traditional color in China, which represent joy and abundance. Red can make user feel pleased and comfortable and easily promote consumption [28].

Silhouette-type icons are used here, which are simple with strong moral.

Dangdang   (Fig. 3). Dangdang   is   an e-commerce shopping platform in China, mainly selling books, audio & video products.

Dangdang's Personal Center interface provide a wide range of basic features but less extended features. It satisfied users' basic needs with lower cognitive resource.

As for the layout, nine patch and ranked list mode are used. It is clear and user-friendly to search features [14].

Red is used as the main color, which makes user feel pleased and can promote consumption [27].

Silhouette-type icons are used here, which are simple with strong moral and easier for users to identify and search [2].

Fig. 2.

Fig. 3.

JD.com (Fig. 4). JD.com is an e-commerce shopping platform, mainly selling electronic products.

In the aspect of features, similar to Dangdang, Personal Center interface of JD.com has core features (e.g. order information and asset information) and few basic extended features, which will reduce users' cognitive burden, compared to Dangdang.

Personal Center of JD.com used ranked list layout mode. There is some information next to the personal pictures.

Orange red is used as the main color of its interface. Some geometry elements are used in personal information column, which highlight the science and technology feeling, fitting the basic orientation of JD.com's main goods [9].

Silhouette-type icons are used here, which are simple with strong moral.

Summary. Overall, there are some characteristics of e-commerce mainstream mobile apps we can conclude:

Fig. 4.

In the aspect of features, basic features of e-commerce app in China include order information, collection, and property information. They are the core features in Personal Center, which users use frequently.

Those extended features that e-commerce apps love to add but users rarely use and even do not know how to use, complicate the whole interface and increase users' cognitive burden.

Through the interface design, nine patch and ranked list are usually used in this type of apps. Too many extended features, lack of order, unclear classification require more cognitive resource.

Warm colors, like orange and red, fit appreciation of the beauty of Chinese, are beneficial to earn users' identity, increase shopping passion then promote consumption.

As for icons, most of them used silhouette-type icons and various apps basically approaches unity on icon design (especially on the icon design of basic features). This not only enhances the coordination of the system and the reality, gives the icon a clear meaning, standardized design, but also allows users to use the interface information obtained to clarify its understanding, identification and search.

2.2 Analysis of Personal Center Interface of Mainstream Mobile Application in Foreign Market

Amazon (Fig. 5). Amazon is an international e-commerce platform. There are many differences between domestic e-commerce apps. First, from the features, its Personal

Center interface does not have many redundant feature icons, but only contains individual related content, which made it seem concise. Putting 'Contact Us' in a more obvious position indicates the attention Amazon's paid to users.

In the aspect of layout, by using the list, the unique feature of Amazon's Personal Center interface is there is the interval between the items, which provides consumers with greater fault tolerance [17], so that it wouldn't be easy to make mistakes when users click on a feature.

In the aspect of color, intending to stimulate shopping appetency of users by the effect of visual sense, red and orange, as based hue, are used in most Chinese e-commerce apps. Nevertheless, the Personal Center interface of Amazon obeys the minimal style with black and gray hue which made the interface refreshing, and provided consumers a rational consumption pattern [8, 9].

For icon design, Amazon Personal Center interface maintains a high degree of consistency. With concise and intelligible icon, the significance of its graphics and symbols is conducive to visual search of consumer [5].

eBay (Fig. 6). Same as Amazon, eBay is a mainstream international e-commerce application. Its composing type of Personal Center adopts a list shape containing six major features, like Watching and Purchases, which basically are able to meet all the needs of users. Same as Amazon, eBay also attaches great importance to user feedbacks and needs, and that is the reason it puts Help & Contact on obvious location. The trait of eBay is abandoning the icon design in Personal Center interface. In addition to settings and messages, other content only use text cues. With simple operations, it will not produce unnecessary cognitive burden. The separation distance between projects is also relatively large which

Fig. 5.

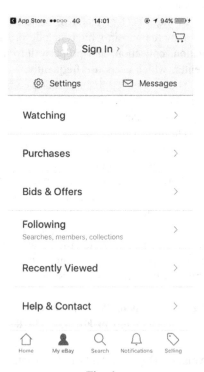

Fig. 6.

help consumers feel freer to use within the limited mobile phone screen. Such a simple interface can improve the user's search efficiency [5].

Regards color, eBay's Personal Center interface uses simplex color aiming at providing a way that user can find the needs of the feature clearly with ease, not prone to error. But to some extent, the simplex tone would affect the aesthetic level of the interface and lead to the difficulty about attracting the attention of users [21].

Wish (Fig. 7). The features of the Wish are the same as the two applications above. The interface is very simple, clear-oriented as well. The difference is that it has one more social features named Invite Friends in a bid to enhance the socialization of the software.

In the layout, Wish's Personal Center interface used same list shape with other apps, but the difference is the interaction gesture of the menu, which account for about two-thirds of the left side of the screen part, is sliding to right. When we are reading, the general reading habits are from left to right, which makes users always pay their attention on the left side rather than right when they are looking at an interface [8]. The interface design like Wish could sharpen users' focus to content.

The layout styles of icons are simple as well, and at the same time, enhanced the aesthetic level of the interface.

Blue and white are the main color of Wish's interface. Light-colored background contributes to improve user's search efficiency [23], but also more in line with Western aesthetic.

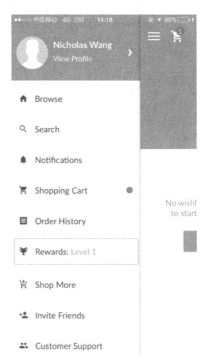

Fig. 7.

Summary. In summary, in the international market, the Personal Center interface of mainstream e-commerce mobile applications has the following characteristics:

First, the content of such apps' Personal Center interface features are concise and use list type for typesetting mostly. On the contrary, Chinese e-commerce applications have many redundant features, which hinder users operating, and reduce the search efficiency as if a user wants to use a feature, the extra feature will interfere with the individual's search behavior. Therefore, such a simple interface can improve user's search efficiency.

Secondly, e-commerce applications' interface color need to put more emphasis based on users' preference and culture characteristics in the color of international e-commerce applications' interface, compared to Chinese, are more inclined to the concise style and cool colors [17].

Furthermore, at the bottom of several applications' Personal Center interface listed above, there is a clear feature linking between customer service and get user feedback. Therefore, if users encounter any problems or have any suggestions, they could find feedback channels directly to improve the user experience of the application.

2.3   The Summary Analysis of International and Chinese Mainstream E-commerce Mobile Applications' Personal Center Interface

See Table 1.

Table 1.

	Evaluative Dimension	Layout			Feature			
APP		Composing	Color	Icon Design	Order Inquiry	Favorite	Asset	Extended Features
National	Taobao	Nine Patch Mode; Redundancy of Overall Content; Irregular Layout	Main Color: Orange	Silhouette-type	√	√	√	Redundant; Low Efficiency
	Pinduoduo	List Mode; Clear;	Main Color: Red	Silhouette-type	√	√	√	Less
	JD.com	List Mode;	Main Color: Jacinth Add Geometric Elements;	Silhouette-type	√	√	√	Less
	Dangdang	Nine Patch & List Mode Overall layout is clear;	Main Color: Red	Silhouette-type	√	√	√	Less
International	Amazon	List Mode; Large Icon Interval, High Fault Tolerance;	Main Color: Black & Gray Concise Interface Contribute to Rational Consumption	Graphic Symbols, Strong Implications;	√	√	√	Less
	eBay	List Mode;	Main Color: White Single color, User-friendly Query Information, Lack of Beauty;	No Icon Design, Only Text Clues;	√	√	√	X
	Wish	List Mode; Occupy Left Side of Screen Two-thirds Area	Main Color: Blue & White	Concise, Unified Style;	√	√	√	X

3   Pinzhi 365 Current Personal Center Interface Analysis

The Personal Center page of Pinzhi 365 (Fig. 8) include conventional features of general e-commerce applications, such as settings, orders, coupons, attention and so on. However, the arrangement of the list hides most of the detail features, resulting in a problem that there is a number of sub-logic level in Personal Center, which runs counter to the flat trend design [19]. It is an unfavorable factor in presenting features.

In the aspect of icon, morphological features are not clear enough and lack of consistency. Using four different background colors affected the silhouette-type icon recognition [11].

For the color, the overall tone of the interface is dim with old-fashioned color. Icon background color is not uniform and no rules can be found, which will reduce user's visual search efficiency.

Compared with all the Personal Center interfaces mentioned above, Pinzhi 365 Personal Center interface is extremely functionalized but lack of details.

Fig. 8.

4   Innovative Design in Personal Center Interface

4.1   Feature Design

In the innovation design in Personal Center interface of Pinzhi 365, we consider satisfying user's feature requirements. What feature design needs to consider is to meet user's needs as far as possible and to avoid redundant levels, so that users can quickly find the features they need. In the design process, we used affinity diagram to define goals, then we listed all the elementary feature points and did Priority Ranking based on frequency of use in order to combine features that user rarely use. It could not only make the interface simple and clear with practicability, but also solve the problem of wasting too many cognitive resources.

4.2   Layout Design

As shown in Fig. 9, circular divergent overturned traditional multiple listing page. The center of the circle is located at about eight-fifths of the layout, which is the visual

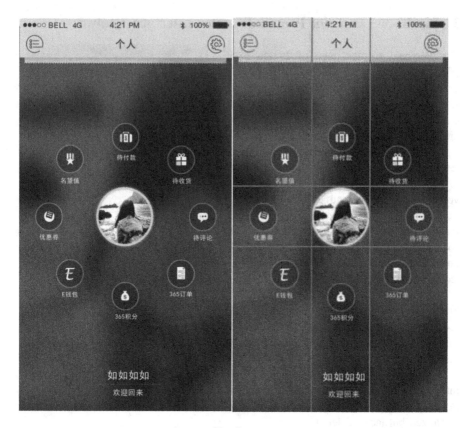

Fig. 9.

center of the page (the viewpoint). Putting personal image in this position highlights the theme 'Personal Center', which express the concept of user center. Besides, the lively bounce motion effect shown when you open this page enhances the sense of interaction, which will give users a new experience the first time the use [24].

4.3   Icon Design

Usually, icons users can be recognize intuitively by users better than text. Thus, concision, usability and efficiency are the features should be pursued by designers, rather than a complex artistic one [22]. There are several principles considered in designing Pinzhi 365 Personal Center page (Fig. 10):

Identifiable. First of all, rather than pursuing the special effects which would attend to trifles and neglect the essentials, we focus on the substantial features. The feature of 365 score in this interface for example. Users would be clear the concept that points worth money at the first glance.

Fig. 10.

Differences. In a series icon, each icon should be significantly different with each other, so that users can recognize the represent meaning quickly and accurately. Pinzhi 365 Personal Center has consistent style formed by the same color and size of the ring. However, each icon has its own graphics with corresponding meaning, which is easy to compare the differences between the various.

Uniform Style. While accomplishing the principle of differences, icon also need to maintain the overall uniform style by common elements, like graphics and colors. Such design of each icon used white and yellow surrounded by same size and thickness of yellow circle [21].

Environmental Coordination. According to Tolman's cognitive theory, also known as the field theory, each icon does not exist alone, since the environment easily affects people's cognition. So icons and the environment should be related. For example, color studies have shown that yellow is recognized easily in most distinctive in the black background, especially in the interface with gray, yellow and white (text color). So each icon is corresponding to three colors in harmony with the environment [6, 9].

Moderately Complex. Icons, after meeting the basic principles of aesthetic, would increase the degree of complexity. However, complexity and recognition are considered as a normal distribution, as shown in Fig. 11. So increasing the recognition degree of moderate complexity will increase interest and attract users.

4.4   Color and Image Design

Using a personal picture in Gaussian blur effect as background would in accordance with avatars, which would, made them more prominent.

Brightness play a key role in attracting attention of consumers (Fig. 12), thus yellow as the symbol of the sun, which express hope and optimism, and inspire creativity and energy, used as the main interface color of Pinzhi 365. Combining black and white with part of the red as embellishment create a positive, warm and dynamic keynote of Pinzhi 365 [24].

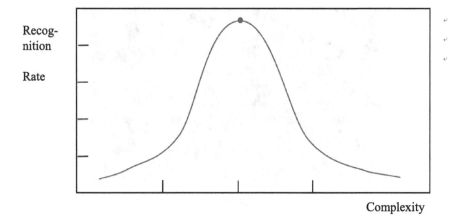

Recog-
nition

Rate

Complexity

Fig. 11.

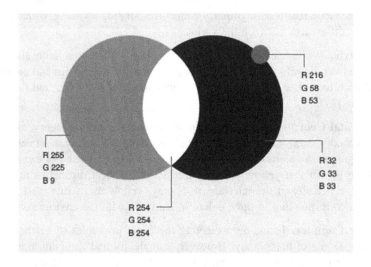

Fig. 12.

4.5 Other Design Details

The curtain effect on the top of the page let title bar and the bottom interface have a sense of convergence and gives users a sense of kinship.

Edge of the avatar glowing design highlights the user center philosophy and the surrounding feature is listed starting from the user, the user name on the bottom with "welcome back" banner that interface will not have problem of top-heavy, and add users to the human intimacy. User name and slogan between the boundaries so that the whole interface does not seem too scattered and have a sense of the rules, the other is not a simple line of the boundary blunt interface will be cut, but the use of the center, the gradual disappearance of both ends of the effect. To ensure the integrity of the entire interface.

5   Design Evaluation

5.1   Evaluation

Usability and Accessibility. The visual elements in Pinzhi 365 mobile app Personal Center are oriented, resulting in lower learning cost. Icon style is uniform and easy to remember with high recognition and strong usability. Meanwhile, the interface has great visual cues, whose graphical symbols have implications with moderate complexity, which connect to the real world. Yellow, black and white are used. Using similar color in similar feature makes the interface easy to use [8, 17].

Efficiency. The round divergent arrangement provides users necessary and frequently used quick entrance, which greatly raises using efficiency, so that users do not have to find a required feature level by level. Meanwhile, the entire interface has a strong consistency: same color represents the same graphics the same feature, same operation used in the same task, which greatly raises using efficiency.

Memorability. A recognizable visual language is used in the interface, which is easy to recognize and interesting. For example, the icon of 'receiving' is a small present symbol. It contributes to users' memory but there is no need for them to memorize it. The position of quick entrance would never change so that users can easily find them at any time [17].

Friendliness and Satisfaction. Users are the center of the Personal Center page. Frequently used entrances are put in the most sensible position. Icons are designed with moderate complexity. They are clear and easy to recognize with sharp colors, which makes the interface user-friendly. Using Gaussian blurred avatar as background, highlight the theme and has a great characteristic. The bounce effect shown when user open the page, let users feel lively and modern.

5.2   Summary

Overall, the innovation design in Personal Center interface of Pinzhi 365 Mobile APP is with great beauty and metaphor, whose visual elements has a certain continuity. The operation is simple and directly, with good feedback. Users would feel as if they have fully control.

6 Prospect

The innovative design of Pinzhi 365's Personal Center has broken the traditional rules of Personal Center interface design. By using innovation design in layout and micro-interactive animation, the page was designed smooth, natural and correspond with users' characteristic behavior. Expect for the product page, users click Personal Center page the most. Design in Personal Center will affect the user experience in mobile app directly. In the future, we expect more innovation design in Personal Center interfaces of mobile app to start from layout and interaction.

Acknowledgement. The publication of this research project was supported by the Fundamental Research Funds for the Central Universities.

References

1. Aprile, W., van der Helm, A.: Interactive technology design at the Delft University of Technology - a course about how to design interactive products. In: Proceedings of the E&PDE 2011, London (2011)
2. Arvola, M.: Interaction design qualities: theory and practice. In: Proceedings of the NordiCHI 2010, pp. 595–598. ACM Press (2010)
3. Liu, D., Cheng, X.: The mobile phone interface icon visual design analysis. Jiangnan University School of Design (2012)
4. Liu, D.: 3G mobile phone user interface design methods and design process. Hunan University (2007)
5. Wen, F., Xu, Y.: Application of personality traits in human-computer interface interaction. Chin. J. Psychol. (02), 398–400 (2006)
6. Yang, F.: Research on APP layout design based on user interactive experience. Art Technol. **29**(9) (2016)
7. Goldman, S.L., Nagel, R.N., Preiss, K.: Agile competitors and virtual organizations: strategies for enriching the customer. Van Nostrand Reinhold (1995)
8. Ma, H.: Less is more - on the flat interface design style advantages. Mod. Decoration (Theory) (12), 87–88 (2013)
9. Pang, J.: 3G mobile e-commerce platform user interface design. Jiangnan University (2010)
10. Li, J.: The application of color in UI design. Henan Polytechnic University (2016)
11. Johannsen, G.: Knowledge-based design of human-machine interfaces. Control Eng. Pract. **3**(2), 267–273 (1995)
12. Kamba, T., Elson, S.A., Harpold, T., et al.: Using small screen space more efficiently. In: Conference on Human Factors in Computing Systems: Common Ground, CHI 1996, Proceedings, Vancouver, BC, Canada, 13–18 April 1996, pp. 383–390 (1996)
13. Tan, K., Hong, Z., Li, Y.: Research on the APP interface design under the context of "inheritance and innovation". Packing Eng. (08), 60–63 + 115 (2015)
14. Hao, K.: Micro-Bo APP interface optimization design. Kunming University of Science and Technology (2015)
15. Zhang, L.: Phone software interface design method based Intelligent System Exploration. Packaging Eng. (24), 58–61 (2010)
16. Liu, L.: Based on the brand recognition mobile phone APP interface visual design study. East China University of Science and Technology (2015)

17. He, L.: Web-based design of visual information to convey the effectiveness of. Zhejiang University (2006)
18. Li, N.: Mobile e-commerce terminal interface design. Shanghai Jiao Tong University (2014)
19. Norman, D.A.: Emotional design: why we love (or hate) everyday things (2004)
20. Gao, P., Yang, Z.: On flatness and quasi-materialization in UI design. Art Educ. Res. (10), 60 (2014)
21. Saffer, D.: Designing for Interaction: Creating Smart Applications and Clever Devices. Peachpit Press, Berkeley (2006)
22. Tian, S.: Analysis of the role of color psychology in network marketing. Northeastern University Qinhuangdao School of Economics and Trade (2013)
23. The icon design principles. http://www.uimaker.com/uimakerhtml/uistudy/2010/0506/3433. html, Zhan Ku
24. Li, T.: Based on the user experience of smart phone APP interface design. Taiyuan University of Technology (2015)
25. Visual composition. http://www.chinaz.com/design/2015/0922/449483_2.shtml, 25 school
26. Webster, J., Trevino, L.K., Ryan, L.: The dimensionality and correlates of flow in human-computer interactions. Comput. Hum. Behav. 9(4), 411–426 (1993)
27. Xiong, X.: The user interface in the mobile phone icon design rescue. Jiaxing College of Design (2016)
28. Xu, Y.: Study on the relationship between color app and user experience in mobile terminal health class. Art Technol. 29(1), 113 (2016)
29. Wang, Y.: Analysis and research on the visual art elements of app interface based on Andrews platform. Wuhan University of Technology (2013)
30. Wei, Y.: 3G smart phone interface visual design. East China University of Technology (2012)
31. Lee, Y.E., Benbasat, I.: A framework for the study of customer interface design for mobile commerce. Int. J. Electron. Commer. 46(3), 79–102 (2003)

Applying Working Memory Theory to Redesign a Mobile Application User Interface: Take a Handicraft Self-learning Page as an Example

Jun Xu[1(✉)], Sicong Liu[1], and Xiaozhen Fu[2]

[1] Nanjing College of Information Technology, Nanjing, People's Republic of China
xujun@njcit.cn
[2] Independent Researcher, Hangzhou, People's Republic of China

Abstract. This paper studies the issue of applying working memory theory to redesign a mobile application information construction to improve the information delivery for the novices who have less design literature. The aim is to gain a graphic and words information design method and rules for handicraft self-learning page on mobile context.

With the rapid development of China's creative industry and motivation of a series of policies, a mass of novices rush into creative products design fields. They participate in competitions and exhibitions, but most of them lack basic knowledge and skills. Mobile application is considered a useful tool to help them begin. This research takes a handicraft self-learning page of a mobile application prototype as an example, which is included two kinds of visual information: graphics and words. By explicating the relationship between working memory theory and user interface information design, stating the importance of using this theory, this research indicates that using working memory theory in user interface design has been aware of an everyday tool which designers can motivate the information delivery effectively and increase work performance.

By using two main characters of working memory, limited capacity and volatile in mobile context, the research summarize principles for reconstruct the page wireframe and typography, redesign fronts, color and graphics. In the examination stage, researchers propose a hypothesis, comparing with the original page, participants' handicraft process recognition and learning transfer had improved, time-costing of remembering the full page had reduced.

A behavior experiment is used to verify the theory which raised in this research. 49 college students take part in this study as volunteers. Their ages vary from 18 to 23 with a mean age of $20.1 + 1.5$ years. All of them have no experiences in doing handicraft. At the beginning of the experiment, a page of the mobile application is displayed to the volunteers who are required to remember the main processing steps of the handicraft which listed on the page. After a brevity rest, a redesigned page is shown to the volunteers which the same demands are required. Two factorials are measured in this experiment: (1) times of fully remembered processing steps which instructed on the application page;(2) how many steps could be recalled by volunteers after the fixed time. Those two factorials would be measured twice: one is after the original page displayed another one is after the redesigned page showed. These factorials could reveal that the effects of information delivering with one page of the mobile application, how

© Springer International Publishing AG 2017
A. Marcus and W. Wang (Eds.): DUXU 2017, Part II, LNCS 10289, pp. 324–332, 2017.
DOI: 10.1007/978-3-319-58637-3_26

much information could be delivered by a single page of the mobile application. The differences between the two measures would suggest that the effects of information transferring whether be improved after the page redesigning by using working memory theory.

The results of this research suggest that both the total time of fully remembered steps and the steps could recall by volunteers after a fixed time have significant improvement after the redesigning.

According to these results, we draw the conclusion that the mobile application page redesigning with the help of working memory theory could improve the recall of handicraft process obviously.

Keywords: Working memory · User interface · Handicraft learning

1   Introduction

Working memory, as a part of cognitive psychology plays a positive role in user interface design when using it in a correct way. It supports and augments human memory rather than burdening or confusing it. Working memory is the part of activated in the sensor and long-term memory which users are conscious of in a short term (Johnson 2010). It combines attention which we are aware of at given moment. Working memory has close relationship with many advanced cognitive abilities, such as inference, problem-solving and learning. As a consequence, it has become the core of human cognitive activities (Zhao and Zhou 2010; Cai and Su 2008; Li, et al. 2014). Working memory has two characteristics, limited capacity and volatility, it implicates user interfaces which should help users remember essential information from one moment to the next, not to remember system status or what they have done (Johnson 2010).

Limited capacity of working memory determines how much information the users can remembered. Miller (1955) proposed that the average of humans' short-term memory capacity was around 7 ± 2 chunking, Cowan (2011) transformed the short-memory span into 4 ± 2 chunking according to quantities of experiments. Volatile character of working memory influences the users' attention. Focusing on new information turns it away from some of what it was focusing on (Johnson 2010). In the research of working memory contents, users tend to remember the regular graphics, its regular feature does not influent the spatial working memory. (Wenchun and Yueliang 2013)

In recent years, China's culture and creative industry has stepped into a rapid development stage. The government has actively promoted policies, such as the famous police, "mass entrepreneurship and innovation" on cultural and creative industry, which created new opportunities for the public. Students, from primary school students to college students are encouraged to participate into these creative activities. However it is hard for these novel designers who lack basic design knowledge, skills capabilities to do such a professional activities.

In today's mobile internet era, people are in habit of getting information from their mobile devices ubiquitously and fragmentarily. Learning activities has changed as well. In our previous work, we proposed an interactive diagram for Chinese craft self-learning by the mobile application. By analysis learning outcome datum, we found image-text information is easy to remember and recognize, but it is very hard to gain well-developed skills only by using this App (Xu 2016). Consequently, we developed a mobile phone application (App) prototype to help novices to gain design knowledge and skills and participate into creative product design. By the case research, the image-text information remembers and reorganization design methods and rules for handicraft self-learning page on mobile context can be presented.

As mentioned before, working memory has closed relationship with user interface, especially for learning software. On the mobile device, physical context, social context, contextual context and time context have been changed. Smaller screen size influences the numbers of chunking which users can catch. Users' reading behaviors have also changed, they can read while walking, traveling, using their finger to zoom in and zoom out or flip over the page. However, few researches apply working memory theory in user interface of the mobile handicraft learning application. These studies will focus on applying working memory theory to redesign a handicraft learning page, then to exam the hypothesis, which is the time users took in remembering and recall the process by using the new page designed will be less than the original page.

The entire research has 4 parts. Section 1 reconstructs the page layout in mobile context to help users remember the steps of handicraft easier. Section 2 presents the experiment, which include participants and experiment paradigm. In Sect. 3 the result had been analyzed. In Sect. 4, it discusses the result from working memory theory, and do summarizers.

2 User Interface Redesign for Mobile Phone

2.1 Grid View for Handicraft Process

According to working memory theory, users have limited memory capacity to remember what they see in a moment. The capacity is approximate 6 chunking. In the handicraft process learning task by using mobile phone application, an objective cause to the novices who are hard to remember the process is that the handicraft process is complex.

Additionally, the mobile phone screen space is limited, therefore users can only view a small of content at a time. List view displays the process in a single list. Generally, designers use texts and small icons. Compared with list view, grid view displays more efficient layout for browsing the whole content in reasonable pages. In addition, grid view has priority at images because handicraft process presented in images is more accessible than icons or texts.

In the respect of mobile context for handicraft process learning, most users do not have plenty of time when they are on a mobile application. Grid view can provide fast scan and choose when users are walking or on transport. Aside from aspect above, grid view works best for examining specifics in this single content-handicraft process. When users scan the page, less relevant images have been filter out.

Figure 1 is the layout of original page, it arranges the image-text contents in the handicraft process order. Users have to scroll a lot to see all images, because of the limited screen space. This kind of layout increases the cognitive load, users need to remember images which they saw before scrolling. Famous user interface principles, recognition rather recall and help users recognize, diagnose and recover from errors (Nielsen 1995) are all based on working memory theory. Good user interface can help users remember what they have done before.

Fig. 1. The layout of the original Page

In the redesign layout (Fig. 2), the process images and the explanatory texts are combined into one chunking. The images are zoomed in, and the texts underlie the

Fig. 2. The layout of redesign page

images. In this handicraft case, it has 6 steps. When we redesign the layout, all of the steps can be in one page.

2.2 Emphasize the Essential Information

As mention before, working memory has the other characteristic, volatility. That is to say, when users focus on new information, the old one will be forgotten. In the case, the original user interface has few mistakes to barrier memory. Firstly, in step figures, some irrelevant information in the images distracts users' attention on the main information. For example, in the first step figure, an animal model appeals to users' attention by its size and figure. It barriers the main information——the shape of the clay (Fig. 3). Secondly, when we consider the reading-pattern aspect, people tend to follow an F-shape pattern when they looking at different pages (Nielsen 2006). The beginning of each line on the left is noticed more. Using this F-Shape pattern in the case, our version will be attracted by three red circles with the same size. However, the red circle and the red circle with ordinal number index different information. Its same size and the same position disrupt users' vision.

Fig. 3. The original page

Based on the issues on the user interface above, the page has been redesigned, and shows the final version below (Fig. 4). In order to help users pay more attention to the main information of each step figure, the irrelevant parts of each step figure have been cut. It provides the information non-disruptively to increase users' memory.

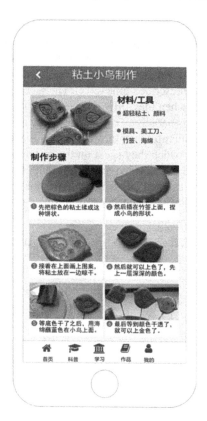

Fig. 4. The redesign page

According to the F-shape pattern, the size and position of the red circle had been reformed. The two red circles on the top are smaller than the one with numbers. The reasons have two, one is processes of the handicraft are more important than items of materials and tools. The other reason is a number with circle need bigger size.

3 Experiment Design

3.1 Participants

49 volunteers took part in the experiment, (mean age 20.1 + 1.5 years) which includes 22 females. All of them had no formal learning experiences in any handicraft. They were required to follow the instruction of the mobile applications which include the original

UI design and the redesigned one and answer some questions at the end of the experiment. All participants had no history of neurological or psychiatric illness. Informed consent was obtained before participation.

3.2 Experiment Paradigm

In this study, there are two different types of paradigm would be used. The first paradigm was designed to explore the difference of the accurate rate between the original UI design and the redesigned one when subjects were required to remember the more steps as possible as they could at the prescribed time (20 s). The second one is to test the amount time of the volunteers used when they fully received the information which sent from the mobile application. In this paradigm, participants were asked to recall the orders of the making steps of the handicraft when they confirmed that they had fully remember the entire process. The time which they spent on the remembering would be recorded and the same process would be executed again, but the UI of the mobile application would be changed to the redesigned one which follows the instruction of the working memory theory. The process of the experiment was shown in Fig. 5

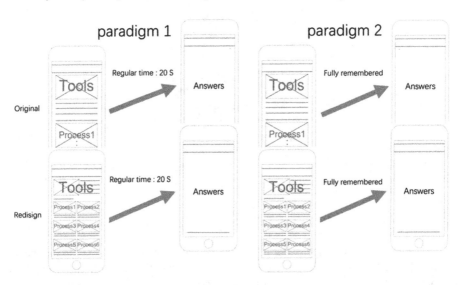

Fig. 5. Theprocess of two paradigms

4   Result Analysis

The average of correction rate of the original is 29% and the average of the redesigned is 74% in the paradigm 1, but according to the result of the independent t test analysis, the difference between two types was not significant ($p < 0.133$). The mean value of the time which is used on the redesigned is 7.91 s while the average of the original is 11.98 s. An independent t test analysis was utilized to explore the difference between two kinds of design type. The result suggested that there was a significant difference between two sorts of designs (p < 0.001). The average of the two paradigms is showed in the Fig. 6.

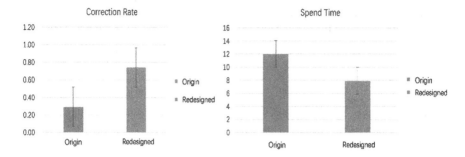

Fig. 6. For the paradigm 1 which displayed in the left, the correction rate was explored which the average of the original design was 29% ± 3% and the result of the redesigned was 74% ± 9%, but the difference between them was not significant (p < 0.133). For the paradigm 2 which showed in the right, the mean time which the volunteers spent to remember the steps of artware was recorded. The average time of the original is 11.96 ± 53.6 s and the result of the redesigned one is 7.91 ± 15.18 s. An independent t test was also used to explore the difference between two design types which the result suggested that two design sorts had the significant difference (p < 0.001). The error bar represent the STE.

5   Discusses and Summarize

One of the purposes of the user interface design is to communicate the information to the users more quickly and economically. In this study, we found that the effects of the information communication was affected by the structure of pages which the consumed time spent by subjects was significant difference. However the traditional web user interfaces was not suited for the modern mobile application context. Comparing with using web page to remember a handicraft process, it has many differences when users use mobile application. The case we are discussing in the paper is a small part of Chinese traditional handicrafts, and it is simple. Many other handicrafts have long and complex processes. It's impossible to organize a complex handicraft process into one page. These types of handicrafts have not been involved in the experiment above, and whether the new structure of the page can improve complex information communication does not be confirmed. In the design practice, UI designers have applied some useful ways, such as the step thumbnail to help users remember the long and complex information.

According to the working memory theory, the memory capacity at the short-term time (<20 s) could maintain 4~6 items. The traditional design usually adapted the flow-layout in the mobile application design which in some complex situation might lead to the page too long and such long page was causing users spent too much time to read. Such design was not considering the memory limitation of the human brain. To overcome the disadvantages, the design paradigm needs to change.

In order to help novices obtain the efficient information when they use mobile application to learning a handicraft, this study uses working memory to redesign a page.

Two ways were used, the gird view replaced the list view; emphasized the essential information to improve users memories. In experience period, it chose participants, set two paradigms. By analyze the correction rate and the time which testees fully remember the entire process, the conclusion was draw, the mobile application page redesigning with the help of working memory theory could improve the recall of handicraft process obviously.

References

Nielsen, J.: F-Shaped Pattern For Reading Web Content, vol. 4 (2006). https://www.nngroup.com/articles/f-shaped-pattern-reading-web-content/

Johnson, J.: Designing with the Mind in Mind, pp. 79–84. Elsevier, Amsterdam (2010)

Wenchun, W., Yueliang, S.: The influence of graph's regulation character on storage of object and spatial working memory. Stud. Psychol. Behav. **11**, 205–210 (2013)

Zhao, X., Zhou, R.L.: Working memory: Critical role in human cognition. J. Beijing Normal Univ. (Soc. Sci.) **5**, 38–44 (2010)

Xu, J.: The prototype building for Chinese traditional craft interactive diagram and the effect study. Beauty Times **6**, 97–99 (2016)

Xu, H., Chunyan, G.: Capacity and resource allocation of visual working memory. In: Advances in Psychological Science, vol. 21, pp. 74–81 (2013)

Bettini, C., Brdiczka, O., Henricksen, K., Indulska, J., Nicklas, D., Ranganathan, A., Riboni, D.: A survey of context modelling and reasoning techniques. Pervasive Mobile Comput. **6**(2), 161–180 (2009)

Designing the Playing Experience

A Systematic Review of Geolocated Pervasive Games: A Perspective from Game Development Methodologies, Software Metrics and Linked Open Data

Jeferson Arango-López[1,3](✉), Cesar A. Collazos[1], Francisco Luis Gutiérrez Vela[2], and Luis F. Castillo[3]

[1] Departamento de Sistemas, Facultad de Ingeniería Electrónica y Telecomunicaciones – FIET, Universidad del Cauca, Cl. 5 #4-70, Popayán, Cauca, Colombia
{jal,ccollazo}@unicauca.edu.co

[2] Departamento de Lenguajes y Sistemas Informáticos, ETSI Informática, Universidad de Granada, c/Periodista Daniel Saucedo Aranda, s/n, 18071 Granada, Spain
fgutierr@ugr.es

[3] Departamento de Sistemas Informáticos, Facultad de Ingeniería, Universidad de Caldas, Calle 65 # 26-10, Edificio del Parque, Manizales, Caldas, Colombia
{jeferson.arango,luis.castillo}@ucaldas.edu.co

Abstract. Pervasive games are a new way of social interaction through new technologies such as sensors, software applications and network communication that can be found in mobile devices. Those games allow us to do daily activities in a natural way and arise as a new option of entertainment. For that reason, we decided to do a systematic literature review to identify the methods and metrics used in the development of pervasive games and how they relate to Linked Open Data (LOD). This review presents findings to confirm the need of methodologies to develop applications related to games and entertainment of pervasive nature, and incorporate all its characteristics, which make them different from traditional software.

Keywords: Pervasive games · Game development · Semantic web · Game metrics · Systematic review

1 Introduction

The majority of mobile devices nowadays harness location and orientation-sensing capabilities [1, 2] such as GPS (Global Positioning System), compass and accelerometer to provide information about the current context of players and deliver a gaming experience [3]. This is how mobile devices have become in fundamental part of our lives, allowing that much of the activities we carry out every day are sensible to the context where we do them. Due to the wide availability of personal communication devices, there is an increase in the demand for mobile services based on location [4]. We use mobile devices to work, communicate with family and friends and even for entertainment through games. It allows that each context takes advantage of communication networks. Focused in entertainment, it is feasible to think of applications that contain

© Springer International Publishing AG 2017
A. Marcus and W. Wang (Eds.): DUXU 2017, Part II, LNCS 10289, pp. 335–346, 2017.
DOI: 10.1007/978-3-319-58637-3_27

virtual worlds inviting users to be part of them. That is how people make an absolute immersion, and when that happens there is a disconnection of the real world. That is why computer games and related technologies are being used in research of applications with different aims, like teaching, health and tourism, and not totally centered on entertainment [5].

This document considers a pervasive digital game as a game in which the player's experience is extended to the real world. That is possible through the use of device's sensors [6]. These games are a recent form of entertainment that brings the game experience out of the device and into the physical world, integrating both virtual and physical realms [7]. In addition, it introduces a new game experience that is possible to play wherever and whenever the user wants, this combines virtual and real objects, places and people, and even the gaming time with real events. Pervasive games break the boundaries of the circle that is around classic games [8].

In the following section, we present a contextualization of research topics. Section 3 describes the planning of the systematic literature review. In Sect. 4 are shown the data extraction activities from relevant papers that were found in Sect. 3. In Sect. 5 we present the analysis of search execution and their outcomes, relations and figures. Finally, in the Sect. 6 we discuss about conclusions and future work.

2 Background

2.1 Pervasive Games

Pervasive games represent a radically new game form that transfers gaming experiences out into the physical world, weaving ICTs into the fabric of players' real environments [9]. Many different forms of gaming have been grouped under the concept, including the massively collaborative troubleshooting games (The A.I. Game), the location-based mobile games (Botfighters), the games augmenting the reality with ludic content (Visby Under) and the games staged with a combination of virtual and physical elements [8]. Currently mobile devices are the main elements to achieve pervasive games objectives, because these are linked directly and naturally. Mobile devices are currently the main driver to fulfil the promises of pervasive game playing because they are naturally networked, full of sensors, widespread, and easily accessible [7]. Due to the necessity for a corresponding infrastructure, short-range proximity sensors are not ideal for implementing pervasive games; thus GPS and Wi-Fi form the basis of most recent location-aware games [10]. Emerging pervasive games use sensors, graphics and networking technologies to provide immersive game experiences integrated with the real world [11].

These games may involve one or more players who may be distributed or co-located, and where game play can take place in the broad variety of locations and contexts where one might expect such mobile devices to be used [12]. Games have not received the full attention of the requirements engineering community. This scenario is becoming more critical as we move towards newer forms of games, such as pervasive games [7].

2.2   Software and Game Development Methodologies

Especially, in recent years, the use of mobile applications has increased dramatically along with the concept of 'smart' phone [13], these applications allow the continuous communication and information exchange between mobile devices through wireless technologies, that interaction can be detailed on Fig. 1.

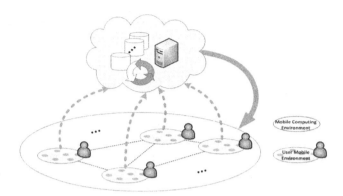

Fig. 1. Movement on mobile computing environment [13]. Figure shows the interaction between users and devices through internet connection.

Most software development organizations make use of a standard set of practices when developing software [14]. Although, Software developers rarely adopt systems and software development methods outright, but rather filter and combine elements from these methods to fit their needs [15]. For pervasive games based on location it is not different, they are implemented using traditional methodologies of software development. In addition, developers do not consider the HCI (Human-Computer Interaction) concepts, which neither are contemplated by those methodologies. Is important to take them into account because the user's requirements and their needs must be explored to improve them applying HCI techniques [16].

2.3   Game Metrics

Game metrics are interpretable measures of something related to games. More specifically, they are quantitative measures of attributes of objects. A common source of game metrics is telemetry data of player behavior [17]. There are three types of metrics used by Game User Researchers: User Metrics (metrics related to people playing the game), Performance Metrics (metrics related to the performance of software or hardware of the game) and Process Metrics (metrics related to the process of developing the game) [18]. When the game is measured, aspects of the game itself must be included, but there is something that is more important: the player experience. For this topic, metrics known as "playability metrics" appear [19] that allow to measure the fun created by a game in a player.

2.4   Linked Open Data

Model Driven Software Development (MDSD) & Domain Specific Modeling (DSM) are means to overcome software development challenges [20]. Semantic web allows knowledge representation through elements and conceptual relationships (modeling).

Knowledge generated recently is available in Linked Open Data (LOD) standards which allow to have free access to such knowledge. In addition, LOD connects local information with other data sources through key terms. The main reason why semantic web and web 3.0 are important to improve human performance is known as cognitive overload [21].

3   Systematic Review

A systematic literature review is a method to analyze, evaluate and interpret all relevant studies to a particular research question, or specific area, or phenomenon of interest [22]. This type of process had their origin in medicine, due to continuous advance of such area, it is necessary to address a research towards a not researched specific topic. There are some proposals to apply these protocols in software engineering. Kitchenham and Charters [23] propose a set of phases to do it. In this document is used those phases, the process is shown next.

3.1   Literature Review Need

A consequence of the current wide adoption of mobile computing is the emergence of mobile and pervasive gaming [12]. It is necessary to get information about pervasive game, software development methodologies – The emergence of pervasive technologies has led to an increased interest in both the design and the development of pervasive games [24] –, game metrics – qualitative and quantitative metrics [18] –, and location techniques through mobile devices.

3.2   Research Questions

The main objective of this systematic literature review was to get most important scientist data to identify current status of pervasive game development. In consequence, it was necessary to research about methodologies to develop that kind of games. In addition, we searched frequently used metrics to evaluate performance, usability, process resources, etc. Finally, we found semantic web applications that produce a better design and implementation of pervasive games.

- **RQ1:** ¿Are there specific methodologies to develop pervasive games based on location?
- **RQ2:** ¿Which metrics are most used to evaluate a software development methodology and their products?
- **RQ3:** ¿Are there ontologies to store data produced by pervasive games based on location?

Continuing with the methodology phases given by [23] and conduct this review, we considered to apply PICOC [24] to define main concepts. Table 1 shows these concepts.

Table 1. Definition of concepts using PICOC.

Criterion	Description
Population	Researchers, students and game developers.
Intervention	Game development methodologies supported by linked open data and their metrics.
Comparison	Other methodologies used to develop games.
Outcome	List of methodologies, metrics and semantic resources to game implementation.
Context	Academic level, research level and industrial level.

3.3 Search Terms

With PICOC analysis, arise a set of general concepts. These concepts are defined as related terms between them. Next list shows terms:

– Pervasive games
– Geolocation games
– Ontology pervasive games
– Pervasive games methodology
– Software methodology metrics
– Software development
– Software design

3.4 Search Process

Based on search terms and their synonymous, the complete query string was generated, which was complemented with logic operators. We considered published papers, whose publication date was since 2012. This string was executed, and only 3 papers were obtained. For that reason, we decided to split the first query string in three main topics (Pervasive games based on location, software development methodologies and software metrics, and Linked Open Data in games). When we did that on 25th August, 2016, we got the following results:

– **Pervasive games based on location**

   (((geolocation) **OR** pervasive) **AND** gam*)

– **Software and games development methodologies and software metrics**

   (((((game) **OR** software) **AND** methodology) **AND** metrics) **AND** (((software) **OR** game) **AND** ((((((development) **OR** implementation) **OR** construction) **OR** design) **OR** planning) **OR** methodology)))

– **Linked open data in games**

((((((("semantic web") **OR** ontology) **OR** "semantic repository") **OR** "linked open data") **AND** game*))

In addition, for best results, we applied filters. Those filters were defined as inclusion criteria and exclusion criteria. The next sections show a list of each criterion type.

3.5 Inclusion Criteria

1. Paper published between 2012 and current date.
2. Paper published as result of conferences, congress or journals.
3. Paper written in English.
4. Paper included into databases shown on Table 2.
5. Paper associated with these topics: HCI, Computer, Informatics Engineering and related.

Table 2. Used databases. Specific data of each database where were executed the query strings.

Name	URL	Acronym
Springer link	http://www.springer.com/	Springer
Scopus	https://www.scopus.com/	Scopus
IEEE xplore digital library	http://ieeexplore.ieee.org/	IEEE Xplore
ACM digital library	http://dl.acm.org/	ACM
Web of science	https://webofknowledge.com/	Web of Science

3.6 Exclusion Criteria

1. Paper only with content table or resume.
2. Paper not related to a research.
3. Paper not related to software or game development, LOD or software metrics.
4. Paper which does not fulfill at least one of inclusion criterions.

3.7 Extracting Information

Process of systematic literature review used different databases, some free access and other private access. Table 2 shows each database information.

Table 3. Results of queries. Matrix of results for each databases and query strings.

String database	Pervasive games	Methodologies and metrics	Linked open data	Total
IEEE xplore	90	30	50	170
ACM	126	47	19	192
Springer	170	383	120	673
Scopus	65	68	45	178
Web of science	41	68	16	125
Total				1338

Through the search executed for each database on Table 2, the results shown on Table 3 were obtained. Graphic representation is on Fig. 2. To reduce the number of results, the inclusion and exclusion criteria were applied.

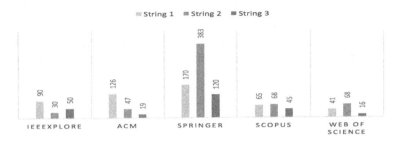

Fig. 2. Database results by string query. For each database three query strings were executed, which showed related papers. String 1: pervasive games based on location, String 2: game/ software development methodologies and game/software metrics, String 3: LOD related to games.

4 Data Analysis and Results

4.1 Additional Filters

According to Table 3, where total results are presented, we analyzed each paper evaluating its title and abstract. We read all titles, checking that each one had relation with the topic research. All results are presented in Table 4.

Table 4. Title and abstract analysis results. This table shows accepted and rejected papers, in addition are presented duplicated papers.

Databases	Total	D[a]	%D	A[b]	%A	R[c]	%R
IEEE xplore	170	16	9.4	39	22.9	131	77.1
ACM	192	0	0	19	9.9	173	90.1
Springer	673	12	1.8	15	2.2	663	97.8
Scopus	178	30	16.8	26	14.6	152	85.4
Web of science	125	14	11.2	11	8.8	114	91.2
Total	1.338	72	5.4	110	7,8	1228	92.2

[a]Duplicated: When a paper was included in result list more than once.

[b]Accepted: a paper that meets the requirements given by exclusion/inclusion criterions

[c]Rejected: a paper that does not meets the requirements given by exclusion/ inclusion criterions.

In Table 4, we present percentages related with analysis results based on total papers for each database, and categorized by type (Accepted, Rejected, Duplicated). However, some papers were rejected (R) and found in different databases (D). For that reason, there is a difference between the total number of paper shown in Table 4 and total papers in Table 3.

4.2   Process Description

After applying first extra exclusion criterion (based on title), the number was reduced from 1338 to 557 papers. With second extra exclusion criterion (based on abstract), the number of papers was reduced to 115. Next, these 115 papers were read to achieve the third extra exclusion criterion (based on full text). Finally, 110 papers were selected to answer the research questions. In this phase, we were sure of relevance that each paper had with research topics. In Fig. 3 a resume of complete process on systematic literature review is shown.

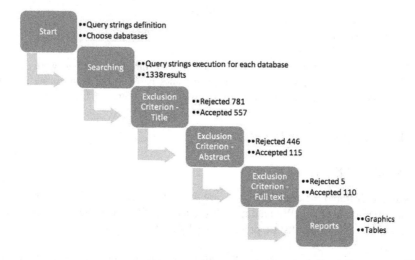

Fig. 3.   Search process description and application of exclusion criterion.

With that process, we can define that numbers with most relevance are associated with accepting percentage, 7.8% is a good result, corresponding to 110 papers. Classification made subsequently is represented in Table 5. To know the complete list of paper and codes is necessary to see appendix A.

Table 5.   A portion of categories of topics and papers.

Category	Subcategory	#	Studies (View appendix A)
Pervasive games	PG Meaning	37	0001, 0004, 0010, 0023, 0027, 0032, 0037, 0039, 0040, 0056, 0068, 0071, 0073, 0078, 0083, 0171, 0174, 0175, 0185, 0202, 0367, 0368, 0369, 0376, 0398, 0399, 0489, 0514, 0523, 0528, 0530, 0532, 0535, 0539, 0541, 0542, 0551
	Augmented Reality	6	0056, 0175, 0276, 0368, 0376, 0864
	PG Design	20	0001, 0004, 0010, 0027, 0071, 0078, 0180, 0185, 0226, 0276, 0368, 0369, 0489, 0514, 0523, 0528, 0530, 0535, 0842, 0861
	PG in Health	5	0004, 0027, 0190, 0402, 0839
	PG in Education	13	0073, 0127, 0147, 0188, 0348, 0530, 0532, 0535, 0539, 0633, 0641, 0868, 0893

In order to explain better the results in Fig. 4, a general description of found categories is presented. There is evidence of a little bit of work that has been done to achieve an implementation of a methodology related to pervasive games, however, there is also an important number of prototypes in that area.

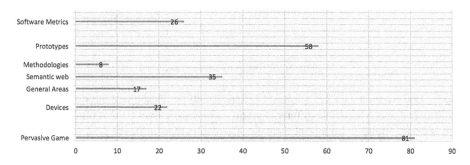

Fig. 4. Results by research topic. The 110 papers are presented grouped by category.

4.3 Results

Based on the systematic literature review and its results, the research questions are answered below.

RQ1: We found that software development methodologies used in pervasive games implementation are the same used by the development of desktop applications, information systems on web environment, among others. That is, there was not referenced a methodology or software process that considered pervasive games development. However, agile software processes adapted to game development were found, although those software processes do not contemplate features and special elements games have. In addition, we found prototypes without following a methodology, in consequence of that, these prototypes have quality troubles. Most studies using methodologies for prototype development use Scrum and Waterfall.

RQ2: Due to there are no software development methodologies focused on this kind of games, consequently, metrics used to measure functioning are the same used to measure quality, performance and resources. Design and implementation for especial features are not considered, even less, features of devices where games are executed. There are a lot of software metrics, which have been adapted according to the needs of projects. Most used metrics on games development are quality metrics as shown in Fig. 5. Based on that figure, we can conclude that there are little studies about user experience metrics. Similarly, performance metrics are not given enough importance, although, these metrics are fundamental in pervasive computing environments due to limited hardware resources on mobile devices.

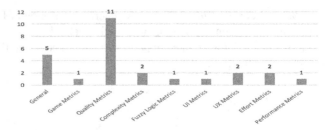

Fig. 5. Software metrics results.

RQ3: Linked open data has allowed to share results to researchers through standards fulfillment that can associate different systems. The videogames field, it is not an exception, we have found an important increase of semantic repositories in games, even more in pervasive games. This systematic literature review presents a direct relationship between these knowledge areas, having greater impact in health and education fields. In Fig. 6 we can see that 19% of game prototypes are associated with LOD.

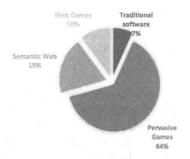

Fig. 6. Found prototypes percentages.

5   Conclusions and Future Work

The main objective of this research was to identify a specific software development methodology to create pervasive games based on location. Also, to find metrics to apply in a methodology and their products. Due to the absence of this methodology, we support the hypothesis presented in [6], where researchers mention the need to have a methodology that take into account all variables and features of pervasive games.

It is important to consider new technologies to use them as a whole, and thus, to support activities of our life such as learning, health and tourism. To achieve that, we think that using Linked Open Data standards is possible to improve those processes, due to their capabilities of semantic and cognitive power.

Mobile devices give more options to social interaction, but, in the same way they allow a total immersion in virtual worlds. According to needs of current society, where is necessary that people interact with others and mobile devices and pervasive games can help to achieve this objective through the integration of virtual and real elements.

As future work, we think that new software processes and software development methodologies that allow to consider different variables and elements own of pervasive games are necessary, specifically games based on location, using mobile devices, GPS sensor and beacons.

Also, it is necessary to define metrics to adapt them to especial needs given by games and their technological challenges. On the other hand, in order to help to give a solution in an identified problem by the systematic literature review (the meaning of pervasive games), we believe that is necessary to give a meaning to pervasive games depending of specific features, not only for each field of knowledge.

Appendix A

This information is available in: http://tinyurl.com/PG-paper-hci2017-appendix-A

References

1. Lochrie, M., Pucihar, K.C., Gradinar, A., Coulton, P.: Designing seamless mobile augmented reality location based game interfaces. In: International Conference on Advances in Mobile Computing & Multimedia, pp. 412–415 (2013)
2. Corral, L., Sillitti, A., Succi, G.: Software assurance practices for mobile applications a survey of the state of the art. Computing **97**, 1001–1022 (2014). Springer
3. Sekhavat, Y.A.: KioskAR: an augmented reality game as a new business model to present artworks. Int. J. Comput. Games Technol. **2016**, 12 (2016)
4. Ahmadi, H., Tootaghaj, S.Z., Hashemi, M.R., Shirmohammadi, S.: A game attention model for efficient bit rate allocation in cloud gaming. Multimed. Syst. **20**, 485–501 (2014)
5. Davies, M., Callaghan, V., Shen, L.: Modelling pervasive environments using bespoke and commercial game-based simulators. In: Li, K., Li, X., Irwin, G.W., He, G. (eds.) LSMS 2007. LNCS, vol. 4689, pp. 67–77. Springer, Heidelberg (2007). doi:10.1007/978-3-540-74771-0_8
6. Viana, R., Ponte, N., Trinta, F., Viana, W.: A systematic review on software engineering in pervasive games development. In: Brazilian Symposium on Computer Games and Digital Entertainment, pp. 51–60 (2014)
7. Valente, L., Feijó, B., do Prado Leite, J.C.S.: Mapping quality requirements for pervasive mobile games. Requir. Eng. **22**, 137–165 (2015)
8. Montola, M.: Exploring the edge of the magic circle: defining pervasive games. In: Proceedings of DAC, vol. 1966, pp. 16–19 (2005)
9. Kasapakis, V., Gavalas, D.: Pervasive gaming: status, trends and design principles. J. Netw. Comput. Appl. **55**, 213–236 (2015)
10. Magerkurth, C., Cheok, A.D., Mandryk, R.L., Nilsen, T.: Pervasive games: bringing computer entertainment back to the real world. Comput. Entertain. **3**, 1–19 (2005)
11. Sra, M., Schmandt, C.: Expanding social mobile games beyond the device screen. Pers. Ubiquit. Comput. **19**, 495–508 (2015)
12. Soute, I., Bakker, S., Magielse, R., Markopoulos, P.: Evaluating player experience for children's outdoor pervasive games. Entertain. Comput. **4**, 25–38 (2013)
13. Eom, H.-E., Lee, S.-W.: Human-centered software development methodology in mobile computing environment: agent-supported agile approach. EURASIP J. Wirel. Commun. Netw. **2013**, 1–16 (2013)

14. Crookshanks, E.: Development methodologies and SDLC. In: Crookshanks, E. (ed.) Practical Enterprise Software Development Techniques, pp. 37–59. Apress, Berkeley, CA (2015). doi: 10.1007/978-1-4842-0620-1_4
15. Babb, J.S., Hoda, R., Nørbjerg, J.: XP in a small software development business: adapting to local constraints. In: Commisso, T.H., Nørbjerg, J., Pries-Heje, J. (eds.) SCIS 2014. LNBIP, vol. 186, pp. 14–29. Springer, Cham (2014). doi:10.1007/978-3-319-09546-2_2
16. Zaina, L.A.M., Álvaro, A.: A design methodology for user-centered innovation in the software development area. J. Syst. Softw. 110, 155–177 (2015)
17. El-nasr, M.S., Drachen, A., Canossa, A.: Game Analytics. Sprint, New York (2013)
18. El-nasr, M.S., Durga, S., Shiyko, M., Sceppa, C.: Data-driven retrospective interviewing (DDRI): a proposed methodology for formative evaluation of pervasive games. Entertain. Comput. 11, 1–19 (2015)
19. González Sánchez, J.L., Gutiérrez Vela, F.L., Montero Simarro, F., Padilla-Zea, N.: Playability: analysing user experience in video games. Behav. Inf. Technol. 31, 1033–1054 (2012)
20. Guo, H., Trætteberg, H., Wang, A.I., Gao, S.: PerGO: An Ontology towards Model Driven Pervasive Game Development, pp. 651–654. Springer, Heidelberg (2014)
21. Kay, R.: Semantic Web. Computerworld. 32 (2006)
22. Paz, F., Pow-sang, J.A., Universidad, P.: A systematic mapping review of usability evaluation methods for software development process. J. Softw. Eng. Appl. 10, 165–178 (2016)
23. Kitchenham, B., Charters, S.: Guidelines for performing systematic literature reviews in software engineering. Engineering 2, 1051 (2007)
24. Chamberlain, A., Martínez-reyes, F., Jacobs, R., Watkins, M., Shackford, R.: Them and us: an indoor pervasive gaming experience. Entertain. Comput. 4, 1–9 (2013)

A Conceptual Model for Educational Game Authoring: A Showcase in Math Games

Johan Baldeón[1,2(✉)], Anna Puig[2], Inmaculada Rodríguez[2],
Cristian Muriel[2], and Leandro Zardain[2]

[1] Avatar Group, Informatic Section, Engineering Department,
Pontificia Universidad Católica del Perú,
Av. Universitaria 1801, Lima, Peru
johan.baldeon@pucp.edu.pe
[2] WAI Research Group, Department of Mathematics and Computer Science,
IMUB and UBICS Research Institutes, University of Barcelona,
Gran Via, 585, 08007 Barcelona, Spain

Abstract. The educational game development is a multidisciplinary software engineering process, where participate instructional and game designers, artists and programmers. Nevertheless, educators, who have an important role in the process, have limitations in authoring games at any moment to adapt them according to key educational aspects such as intended learning outcomes and their metrics, students' learning styles, teaching and learning activities and embedded assessment. We propose a conceptual domain model that supports the development process of educational game authoring tools taking into account both educational and game domains. We consider authoring in two domains. In the educational domain, teachers configure/modify either generic activities with any curricular content, or specific learning activities with a concrete one. In the game domain teachers configure/modify game elements and challenges. Finally, we present two educational game authoring tools in the domain of maths supported by the proposed conceptual model.

Keywords: Serious game · Game-based learning · Educational game authoring

1 Introduction

The use of educational games for learning, known as Digital Game-Based Learning (DGBL), has increased over the last few years [27]. Some of the reasons are that educational games not only serve to entertain but also contribute to facilitate interactivity during learning, overcome the lack of commitment on the part of students, provide opportunities to think and reflect deeply and perform a positive change in behaviour [15].

Educational games development process follows the classical game development process [5,25]. In pre-production phase, the game is designed according

© Springer International Publishing AG 2017
A. Marcus and W. Wang (Eds.): DUXU 2017, Part II, LNCS 10289, pp. 347–361, 2017.
DOI: 10.1007/978-3-319-58637-3_28

to educators' requirements, which define learning outcomes, interactive learning activities, and their evaluation metrics. In the production phase, the game is constructed by game developers, and validated by teachers through an iterative and incremental process. Finally, in the distribution phase, support and training are carried out accompanied by instructional designers. Nevertheless, teachers are usually dependent on developers to update or modify the game to better fit learners and learning outcomes of each session or academic unity. As a consequence, educational games may have short-life usage in the classroom. To overcome this limitation, several educational games platforms offer authoring tools by mean of scripting, visual editors and mods components, with the drawback of being intended for users with technical, artistic or programming skills.

Authoring tools have been successfully proposed to assist the development of a game in different ways, either from scratch or by means of editing already generated content and game mechanics, abstracting the technical aspects of game development for non-programmer users.

There are different approximations to educational game authoring. First, successful commercial games, such as *Minecraft: Education Edition*[1] and *SimCityEdu*[2], allow teachers create new scenarios or customise pre-existing configuration levels to learners using embedded educational mods.

Second, other tools let the edition of the concrete game features on pre-built games such as scenarios, characters, and dialogues. *SeGAE* is a serious game authoring environment that offers instructors the options to modify the game design by defining rules and game objects such as characters, objectives, victory conditions and authorised actions even after the development stage [28]. *SHAI Scenario Editor* allows instructors design educational scenarios from high-level logic diagrams to low-level logic structures [26]. *e-Adventure* is an educational game authoring tool that adds the possibility of exporting the game to an LMS (Learning Management System) [24].

Finally, there are approaches that propose tools for building games from scratch, incorporating both learning and gaming aspects from early stages in the development process. Roungas and Dalpiaz [19] developed a web-based environment that assists game designers in the creation of a game design document based on a conceptual model for educational games. Kirkley et al. [16] propose a wizard tool that allows both instructional designers and game designers to link instructional design elements and game events. Tang et al. [23] developed a model-driven serious game development platform supported by a game content model [22] in the design specification. *StoryTec* uses a visual programming approach to allow teachers without programming skills to specify generic games activities (e.g. puzzle, quizzes) applicable to any discipline. Then, teachers have to define concrete instructional content for those activities, according to the Intended Learning Outcomes (ILOs) [17]. As this process of defining instructional content for the game can be arduous and time-consuming, an alternative authoring approach can be based on embedded specific curricular activities. By embedded specific curricular activities, we mean digital teaching and learning

---

[1] https://education.minecraft.net/.

[2] https://www.glasslabgames.org/games/SC.

activities (TLAs) integrated into the game and directly related to a concrete content of a discipline, such as fractions in maths, human muscles in natural sciences, etc. Therefore, the authoring tool allows teachers configure some properties of the TLAs. For example, in a fractions game, the teacher can specify the values of denominators that he wants students to practice in the game challenges.

In this work, we propose a conceptual model that integrates both game and educational concepts with the purpose of guiding the development of an educational authoring tool. The model is defined to cover two different authoring domains (educational and game domains). In the *educational domain*, the authoring consists in create/edit either generic activities of any discipline (i.e. puzzle mechanics to be applied to reach different ILOs) or embedded specific curricular activities (already designed activities, integrated into the game, to achieve concrete ILOs). In the *game domain*, the authoring focuses on create/edit game elements and activities, e.g. challenges, characters, levels, etc. Additionally, and as a proof of concept, we show two authoring applications of this conceptual model in the domain of maths.

This paper is structured as follows. Section 2 presents a proposal of the educational game authoring process. Section 3 presents our conceptual domain model that supports instructional designers in game authoring taking into account the Outcome-Based Education (OBE) approach. Section 4 illustrates the applicability of our proposal through a serious game authoring platform about mathematics concepts. Finally, Sect. 5 gives conclusions and future work.

2 Educational Game Authoring Development Process

In the process of educational game authoring development, we should consider both the educational and the game domains to identify the elements of each domain susceptible of being authored. To identify these elements, we pass through the classical development process of a digital educational serious game, which has got three phases: pre-production or planning phase, production or construction phase, and distribution or delivery phase [5,15].

In the pre-production phase, the game concept is developed. In this phase, from the point of view of the educational domain, instructional designers define elements such as Intended Learning Outcomes (ILOs), their metrics, Learning Styles (LS), Teaching and Learning Activities (TLAs) to be considered and how to assess the learning [14]. From the game domain viewpoint, designers define elements including the concept, flow, game objectives related to learning outcomes, and players information such us: age, gender, preferences and player types. In this phase, game design starts defining the genre, goals, some aesthetics, mechanics, dynamics, number of players, the input device, feedback elements and description about the game impact. At this stage, it should be defined the domains of authoring (educational and/or game domains), and the elements of these domains to be authored.

In the production phase, the design, programming, art and quality assurance of the digital serious game is carried out taking into account the authoring domains defined in the previous stage. Additionally, and in parallel, the authoring tool is designed and developed in the specified authoring domain.

Finally, in the distribution phase, diffusion management, support and training are performed accompanied with instructional designers. At that phase, the validation of the proposed learning assessment is a key factor to get an early feedback to adapt either the gameplay or the learning activities included in subsequent iterations of the development. In this phase, we propose that, once the game is finished and the authoring tool is deployed, the instructor uses it to tune some game parameters (i.e. in a game about geometry topics, the teacher can configure the inclusion of embedded learning competences in the game challenges such as identification of 2D shapes and their properties, and he can specify the proportion of activities for each ILO). Additionally, it is possible to include either personalised activities for each student or activities of specific ILOs for the entire class, to suit teacher's own pace.

Phases in the afore-described process should follow principles of User Centered Design (UCD), with a strong focus on users during all the steps of the development, and with the aim of evaluating as early as possible prototypes to get fast and valuable feedback from users.

As the target group of an educational authoring tool are teachers, usability criteria such as easy to learn, error prone, efficacy and efficiency are critical to design a product that fits their needs and values.

The design of the educational game, with a target group of students aiming at both learning and especially having fun, takes a broader perspective. It also focuses on usability criteria but takes into account hedonic factors closely related to the experience of the user (UX) in the game, such as game play as well as immersion, and emotions. In the literature, the research on these (and other) factors provides heuristics to assist game design development [9].

3   A Conceptual Model for Educational Game Authoring

Our proposal is a conceptual domain model for educational game authoring based on the Outcome-Based Education (OBE) approach, which supports educators in the elaboration of digital instructional design [20].

Our conceptual domain model for educational game authoring presents three main components. Figure 1 depicts a simplified version of the model that will be further detailed in the following subsections: The OBE Educational Model (OEM), that considers the instructional design; the Game Design Model (GDM), that addresses the digital game-based design; and the Digital Game-Based Learning Model (DGBLM), that defines the Digital Game-Based Learning (DGBL) approach supported by both OEM and GDM.

3.1   OBE Educational Model (OEM)

The Outcome-Based Education (OBE) is an educational approach that focuses on the process of learning followed by each student. OBE proposes three guided stages that identify the key elements of the deployment of the educational curriculum: the Intended Learning Outcomes (ILOs), the Teaching and Learning Activities (TLAs) to lead to the ILOs, and how the students are assessed [6].

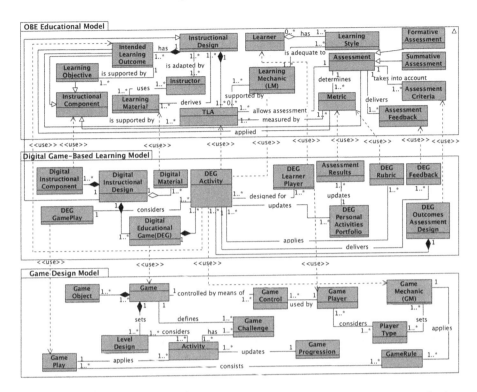

Fig. 1. Main conceptual model components for supporting educational game authoring.

In the first stage, the educator designs the syllabus and classes of an outcomes-based curriculum regarding the learner's accomplishment [3,21]. Therefore, ILOs describe the competencies that students must achieve as well as teachers must be able to measure students' learning achievement. Then, at this stage, instructional designers ought to define metrics to monitor student learning during the ongoing process (*formative assessment*), and also to evaluate student learning at the end of the process (*summative assessment*) [13].

In the second stage, the educator defines Teaching and Learning Activities (TLAs) to achieve the ILOs taking into account the learning styles (LS) of students. In the cognitive domain, TLAs can be deployed using different categories of the revised Bloom's taxonomy [1]. Each category involves the use of its own specific Learning Mechanics (LMs) [2,4].

Finally, the third stage focuses on the deployment of the TLAs and the learning assessment which implies collecting, analysing, interpreting and using information to improve students' learning ongoing process [11].

Model in Fig. 2 depicts entities that support the instructional design process in the OBE educational approach, and takes into account well-known methodologies used in teaching: ADDIE Model [18], the Dick and Carey Systems Approach Model [10], the Gagné's 9 Events of Instruction [12] and Bloom's Taxonomy [7].

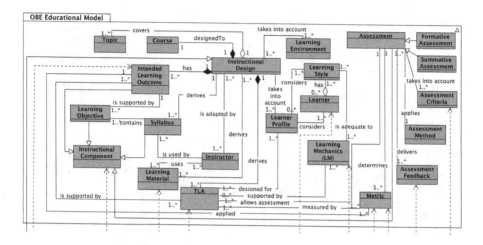

Fig. 2. OBE Educational Model (OEM).

The instructional designer starts the process of elaborating the *Instructional Design* for a *Course* considering *Topics*, *Intended Learning Outcomes* in knowledge, skills and attitudes that learners have to achieve, *Learning Objectives*, analysis of *Learners* regarding *Learning Styles* and *Learner Profile*, *Learning Environment*, designing *Formative* and *Summative Assessment* with *Criteria*, *Method* and *Feedback*, and designing Teaching and Learning Activities (*TLAs*) with their *Learning Mechanics (LM)*, *Metrics*. The *Instructional Design* is adapted by the *Instructor* to derives a *Syllabus* and uses *Learning Materials*.

Some of the just mentioned concepts are candidates to be configured by teachers and so be incorporated in an authoring tool. For example, *TLAs* are closely linked to *game challenges* and *game mechanics* in the game domain, and can be as generic such as *puzzles* or *quizzes*, or domain-specific (i.e. dependent on the learning subject) such as construct a 3D building using basic shapes.

3.2 Game Design Model (GDM)

This model contains entities that define main components in the game design process, such as the *Game*, analysis of *Game Requirements*, *Game Players*, their *Player Types* and *Game Controls*, outline the *Game Challenges*, makes a *Game Narrative* and *Game Presentation*, define the *Artistic Style*, *Characters* and *Game Objects*, design the *User Interface*, *Environment*, *Levels* with *Music*, *Maps*, *Activities* with *GamePlay*, *GameRules*, *Game Mechanics* and *Progression* (See Fig. 3).

Some of these game entities are susceptible of being configured by the teacher and then can be incorporated in the authoring tool. For example, a teacher can configure the time to finish a *Game Challenge*.

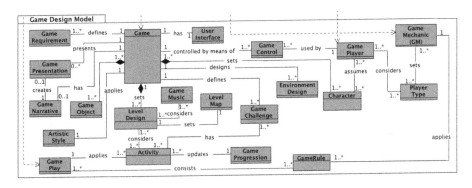

Fig. 3. Game Design Model (GDM).

3.3 Digital Game-Based Learning Model (DGBLM)

This model contains entities that integrate elements of the OBE Educational Model (OEM) and Game Design Model (GDM). It focuses on relevant components which can be considered by authoring tools.

When instructional designers or instructors assume the role of game author, they take into account *Digital Instructional Components*, *Digital Guidances*, *Digital Materials* and *Technology*, as well as *Context Requirements* to define the *Digital Instructional Design*, which relies on *Digital Educational Games (DEG)* including *DEG Activities* according to teaching and learning activities (*TLAs*), *Learning Mechanics (LM)* and *Game Mechanics (GM)*.

The learners are also players (*DEG Learner Player*) and they have a *DEG Personal Activity Portfolio* about performance in academic and game progression, the *DEG Learners/Players* can be grouped according to their characteristics (*DEG Learner Player Group*). The *DEG Outcomes Assessment Design* generates a *DEG Assessment* supported by results of *DEG activities* following a *DEG Rubric* giving *DEG Feedback* both in the game and academic progression. The *Digital Educational Games (DEG)* included in the *Digital Instructional Design* can have different *DEG Activities* with *DEG Activity Types* based on learning styles and player types, hence, different *DEG GamePlay*. According to Kapp [15], the types of game activities for learning games are *Building*, *Role-Playing*, *Exploring*, *Strategising*, *Puzzle*, *Allocating*, *Collecting* and *Matching* games (See Fig. 4).

4 Authoring Tools in Practice

In this section, we show how the conceptual authoring model just presented materialises in two math games and their corresponding authoring tools. Both authoring proposals support the edition of specific curricular activities in the educational domain. In the first game, named Fracsland, we put the focus on fractions concept and present the learner an adventure in an island with fractions

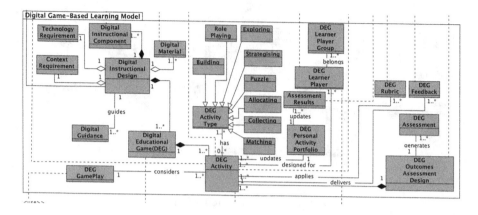

Fig. 4. Digital Game-Based Learning Model (DGBLM).

related challenges. The second game, called GeoPieces, is related to geometry learning both in 2D and 3D. Both games are addressed to 10–12 aged children.

In the following, we refer in italics those concepts of the domain model proposed in the previous section (see Fig. 1) that have been used in Fracsland and GeoPieces authoring tools.

4.1 Fracsland

This game is an adventure serious game where the players assume the role of a shipwreck survivor with the goal of escaping from an island. They collect pieces of a boat engine by interacting with game characters and solving fraction quests.

In this game, the *Intended Learning Outcome (ILO)* is to be able to understand and apply the fraction concept in practice. To cover this ILO, teachers usually define a *TLA (Teaching and Learning Activity)* as a puzzle based on the manipulation of materials (e.g. wooden sticks, pies) and also use the blackboard [8].

This puzzle is mapped in the educational game as a challenge the player has to complete interacting with "fractionable interactive objects" (e.g. bridge) using an inventory of tools shown in the HUD (See Fig. 5).

The HUD includes resources collected during the game (such as rope, wood, knife) and fractions tools (2/9, 6/9, ...). These tools can be used to select those parts of the resources that are needed to solve challenges (e.g. use a part of the wood to complete a bridge in construction).

The parameter of the challenge that will be configurable by the teacher is the denominator of the fraction that the educator wants their pupils to work with. Eventually, the teacher can define the solution of the quest (i.e. both numerator and denominator). Another parameter that the teacher can define is how to represent the fractions in the game (pie or bars).

Fig. 5. Screenshots of fractions' challenges in Fracsland: an adventure serious game in maths.

As shown in Fig. 6, Fracsland authoring platform allows configuring the *DEG Learner/Player Group*. In this case, the teacher can upload either an excel file with all the class or add each student manually.

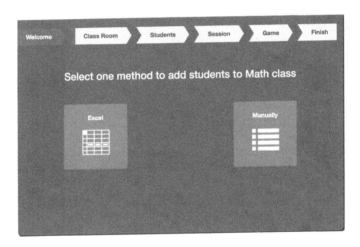

Fig. 6. Fracsland authoring tool: DEG learner/player group.

Figure 7 shows three *DEG Activities* corresponding to three game challenges configured by the teacher. The first *DEG Activity* shows that the teacher wants their students work with $x/2$ fractions where x representing any possible numerator in the game challenges. The same for the rest of the challenges, $x/5$ and $x/7$. These activities will be included in the game that the teacher can automatically generate for the entire classroom. Additionally, the teacher can personalise quests individually. Figure 8 depicts *DEG Personal Activities Portfolio* that contains the set of challenges the teacher assigns to one of the students (i.e. named Iker). Figure 9 depicts in green dotted lines, those entities of the proposed conceptual model developed in Fracsland.

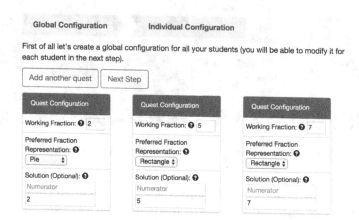

Fig. 7. Fracsland authoring tool: DEG activities.

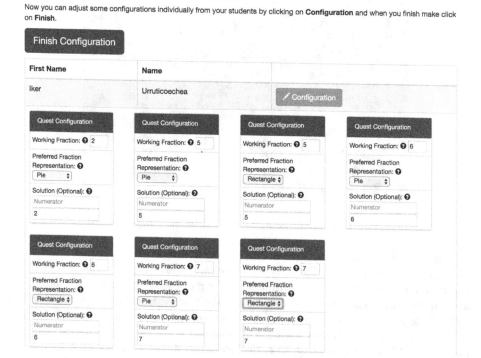

Fig. 8. Fracsland portfolio.

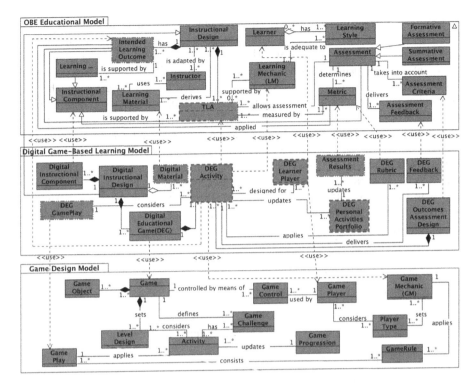

Fig. 9. Main conceptual model for supporting educational game authoring. The entities in green and red dotted lines were developed in Fracsland and GeoPieces respectively. (Color figure online)

4.2 GeoPieces

The game consists of a series of campaigns that the students will have to finish in order to obtain complex 3D objects from simpler three-dimensional shapes. To gain them, it will be necessary to get first some 2D shapes and then build basic 3D objects through unfolding (See Fig. 10). Each campaign covers a set of ILOs (Intended Learning Outcomes).

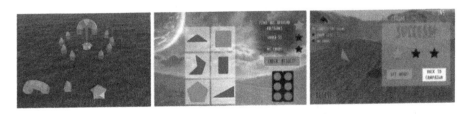

Fig. 10. Screenshots of GeoPieces game.

This game is designed to support the following *ILOs*: identification of 2D shapes and their properties, such as symmetries, angles, perimeters and areas, the identification of 3D objects and their relationship to 2D and 3D shapes. In this game, the authoring tool allows teachers to define the ILOs that are deployed in form of game activities (campaigns) and let assess learner progression, that is, the teacher can say "let my students play only with challenges related to certain learning competences, such as identification of 2D shapes and their properties". Then after some days, when new knowledge is acquired by the children, the teacher can enable the following learning competences related to 2D and 3D shapes. Alike Fracsland where the teacher configures TLA's parameters that map directly to game components (i.e. modifying working fractions in the game with new values), GeoPieces authoring hides the details of the game activities from the teacher. Additionally, as a campaign focuses on a set of ILOs, teachers can weight ILOs to be deployed in the game. For example, in a 2D geometry learning session, if the ILOs named "Classification, Angles and Parallelism" were weighted by 40% and "Symmetry, Rotation, and Proportions" ILO by 60%, and the rest of ILOs by 0%, the number of game activities included in the campaign would be proportional to these weights.

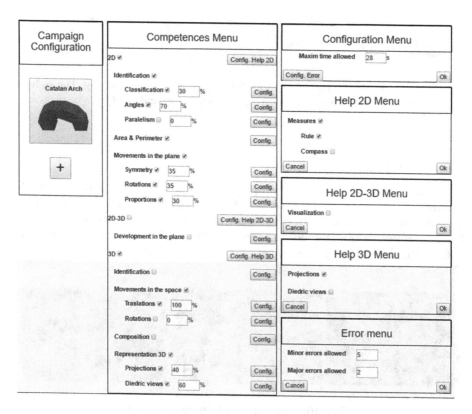

Fig. 11. GeoPieces authoring tool.

As can be seen in the left part of Fig. 11 the teacher can select the campaign (i.e. the 3D object to be constructed) between a set of predefined campaigns, or can select to create a new one using the button "+". The middle part shows the percentage of each ILO that will be used to generate game activities (i.e. *DEG-Activity*) for the selected campaign. In the right part of the Figure, teachers can configure some properties of the activity, such as time constraint (*DEG-GamePlay*), and interactive helpers (e.g. rule, compass), represented as *Digital Material*. In the bottom right part, the error menu specifies the number of minor and major errors that will trigger a reporting alarm to the teacher (*Assessment Results*). Figure 9 depicts in red dotted lines, those entities of the proposed conceptual model developed in GeoPieces.

The play list in Youtube "*A Conceptual Model for Educational Game Authoring: a Showcase in Math Games*"[3] shows videos about the games Fracsland and GeoPieces.

5   Conclusions and Future Work

In this paper, we propose a conceptual model that supports the development of educational game authoring tools to allow educators customise game activities according to their intended learning outcomes. Although state of the art approaches consider educational aspects, these leave aside key elements about the educational approach such as intended learning outcomes and its metrics, learning styles, teaching and learning activities mapped into the game, game mechanics matched with learning mechanics according to Bloom's taxonomy in the learning domain, player types, and embedded assessment in digital learning activities. Furthermore, the proposed model is designed to support different domains of authoring: educational (generic and specific curricular learning activities) and game (scenarios, characters, challenges, etc.) domains.

Finally, as a proof of concept of the authoring tool in the educational domain, we present two examples of maths games that can be configured by teachers, either editing game activities' parameters related to the Teaching Learning Activities (TLAs), or defining the percentage of Intended Learning Outcomes (ILOs) that will guide the generation of number and type of game challenges. Moreover, this generation can be personalised according to students' profile.

As on-going work, we are further developing the educational game authoring platform based on the proposed conceptual model, and plan to deploy and validate it with teachers in classrooms.

Acknowledgments. We thank projects TIN2012–38876–C02–02, 2014SGR623, TIN2015–66863–C2–1–R (MINECO/FEDER), Carolina Foundation, Sergi Cebrian, David Rausell and the contribution of Avatar Group members for supporting the development of this research.

---

[3] https://goo.gl/0UXYlU.

References

1. Anderson, L.W., Krathwohl, D.R., Airasian, P.W., Cruikshank, K.A., Mayer, R.E., Pintrich, P.R., Raths, J., Wittrock, M.C.: A Taxonomy for Learning, Teaching, and Assessing: A Revision of Bloom's Taxonomy of Educational Objectives. Longman, New York (2001)
2. Arnab, S., Lim, T., Carvalho, M.B., Bellotti, F., Freitas, S., Louchart, S., Suttie, N., Berta, R., De Gloria, A.: Mapping learning and game mechanics for serious games analysis. Br. J. Educ. Technol. **46**(2), 391–411 (2015)
3. Baldeón, J., Rodríguez, I., Puig, A.: LEGA: A LEarner-centered GAmification design framework. In: Proceedings of 17th International Conference on HCI. ACM (2016)
4. Baldeón, J., Rodríguez, I., Puig, A., Gómez, D., Grau, S.: From learning to game mechanics: the design and the analysis of a serious game for computer literacy. In: 11th Iberian Conference on Information Systems and Technologies (CISTI), pp. 1–6 (2016)
5. Bethke, E.: Game Development and Production. Wordware Publishing Inc., Plano (2003)
6. Biggs, J.: Aligning Teaching for Constructing Learning, pp. 1–4. The Higher Education Academy, Heslingtonpp (2003)
7. Bloom, B.S., Engelhart, M.D., Furst, E.J., Hill, W.H., Krathwohl, D.R.: Taxonomy of Educational Objectives: The Classification of Educational Goals, Handbook 1: Cognitive Domain. Longmans, Green and Co., London (1956)
8. Canals, M.: Fracciones. Los dossiers de Maria Antonia Canals (2009)
9. Desurvire, H., Wiberg, C.: Game usability heuristics (PLAY) for Evaluating and designing better games: the next iteration. In: Ozok, A.A., Zaphiris, P. (eds.) OCSC 2009. LNCS, vol. 5621, pp. 557–566. Springer, Heidelberg (2009). doi:10.1007/978-3-642-02774-1_60
10. Dick, W., Carey, L., Carey, J.O., et al.: The Systematic Design of Instruction, vol. 5. Longman, New York (2001)
11. Erwin, T.D.: Assessing student learning and development: a guide to the principles, goals, and methods of determining college outcomes (1991)
12. Gagne, R.M., Briggs, L.J.: Principles of Instructional Design. Rinehart & Winston, Holt (1974)
13. Harlen, W., James, M.: Assessment and learning: differences and relationships between formative and summative assessment. Asses. Educ. Princ. Policy Pract. **4**(3), 365–379 (1997)
14. Hays, R.T.: The effectiveness of instructional games: a literature review and discussion. Technical report, DTIC Document (2005)
15. Kapp, K.M.: The Gamification of Learning and Instruction Fieldbook: Ideas into Practice. Wiley, New York (2013)
16. Kirkley, S.E., Tomblin, S., Kirkley, J.: Instructional design authoring support for the development of serious games and mixed reality training. In: Interservice/Industry Training, Simulation and Education Conference (I/ITSEC). Citeseer (2005)
17. Mehm, F., Konert, J., Göbel, S., Steinmetz, R.: An authoring tool for adaptive digital educational games. In: Ravenscroft, A., Lindstaedt, S., Kloos, C.D., Hernández-Leo, D. (eds.) EC-TEL 2012. LNCS, vol. 7563, pp. 236–249. Springer, Heidelberg (2012). doi:10.1007/978-3-642-33263-0_19

18. Morrison, G.R., Ross, S.M., Kemp, J.E., Kalman, H.: Designing Effective Instruction. Wiley, New York (2010)
19. Roungas, B., Dalpiaz, F.: A model-driven framework for educational game design. In: De Gloria, A., Veltkamp, R. (eds.) GALA 2015. LNCS, vol. 9599, pp. 1–11. Springer, Cham (2016). doi:10.1007/978-3-319-40216-1_1
20. Spady, W.G.: Outcome-Based Education: Critical Issues and Answers. ERIC, Arlington (1994)
21. Surgenor, P.: Teaching Toolkit, Planning a Teaching Session, 1st edn. UCD Teaching and Learning, Dublin (2010). http://www.ucd.ie/t4cms/UCDTLT0022.pdf
22. Tang, S., Hanneghan, M.: Game content model: an ontology for documenting serious game design. In: Developments in E-systems Engineering (DeSE 2011), pp. 431–436. IEEE (2011)
23. Tang, S., Hanneghan, M., Carter, C.: A platform independent game technology model for model driven serious games development. Electron. J. e-Learn. **11**(1), 61–79 (2013)
24. Torrente, J., Del Blanco, Á., Marchiori, E.J., Moreno-Ger, P., Fernández-Manjón, B.: <e-adventure>: introducing educational games in the learning process. In: IEEE EDUCON 2010 Conference, pp. 1121–1126. IEEE, April 2010
25. Van Eck, R.: Digital game-based learning: it's not just the digital natives who are restless. EDUCAUSE Rev. **41**(2), 16 (2006)
26. Van Est, C., Poelman, R., Bidarra, R.: High-level scenario editing for serious games. In: GRApp, pp. 339–346 (2011)
27. Wiggins, B.E.: An overview and study on the use of games, simulations, and gamification in higher education. Int. J. Game-Based Learn. (IJGBL) **6**(1), 18–29 (2016)
28. Yessad, A., Labat, J.M., Kermorvant, F.: Segae: a serious game authoring environment. In: 2010 10th IEEE International Conference on Advanced Learning Technologies, pp. 538–540. IEEE (2010)

The Shape of Challenge

Using Affordance Design to Create Challenge Within Games

Michael Brandse[(✉)]

Digital Hollywood University, Ochanomizu Sola City Academia 3F, 4-6 Kandasurugadai,
Chiyoda-ku, Tokyo 101-0062, Japan
michaelbrandse@dhw.co.jp

Abstract. Challenge design is in many ways unique to design in that it is created to throw obstacles in the way of the player rather than focus on an experience that tries to eliminate them. Challenge is a necessity to games, since many players of games derive the majority of the entertainment from the challenges they find in a game. Due to its nature, challenge has largely been misunderstood, both by researchers and game designers alike. It is often assumed that usability is a non-issue for games due to the presence of challenge, which is a false assumption. Furthermore, oftentimes challenge is erroneously defined through its difficulty. To battle these misconceptions, we have devised a model that explores the shape of challenge, concentrating on how it is designed. With this model, we attempt to dispel the idea that usability is a non-issue and identify that difficulty is just a single element of challenge. Using our model, we will enable a deeper understanding of game design as well as open up future venues of challenge design research.

Keywords: Patterns of DUXU practice and solutions · Game design · Challenge design

1 Introduction

Since the earliest games like the famous Pong from the 1970's, games have developed into a huge industry that is now catering to millions of people. Within this timeframe, the industry has gone through many transformations and innovations. Not just in the sense of scope, but also in how games are being designed. One element that has not changed is how challenge remains a core component to the majority of games. However, while the need for challenge has not diminished with the majority of modern games still containing competitive elements, the ways challenges are designed has. Back in the earliest renditions of games, game design knowledge was sparse. The result was a large variety of games that were too difficult to play, impossible even. Since many of those extremely difficult games were development for the Nintendo Entertainment System, these kind of difficult games became well known as "Nintendo Hard" games [1] in popular culture. Furthermore, during those days, games were often played in game arcades. Since games in arcades cost money to operate, designers would often make extremely difficult games to increase profit, since the more difficult a game was, the

© Springer International Publishing AG 2017
A. Marcus and W. Wang (Eds.): DUXU 2017, Part II, LNCS 10289, pp. 362–376, 2017.
DOI: 10.1007/978-3-319-58637-3_29

easier it was for the player to fail and have to retry. As the industry started to move away from game arcades and game designers gained more experience and more resources to work with, the difficulty issue largely remedied itself. This gave designers a large variety of ways to incorporate challenge into their games. However, despite the advances in game design, a formal definition of challenge was never established.

The primary focus of challenge is to supply obstacles that the players need to exert effort in order to overcome it. Players of games generally do not find this a hassle, and instead, consider this an important source of enjoyment. Suits B. referred to this as the lusory attitude [2]. The importance of challenge is further confirmed by Cox, who argues that the Theory of Flow is important to the immersion of gamers, which includes challenge as one of its components [3] as well as Juul, J., who included player effort in his own definition of games.

> *"Player effort is another way of stating that games are challenging, or that games contain a conflict, or that games are "interactive". It is a part of the rules of most games (except games of pure chance) that the players' actions can influence the game state and game outcome. The investment of player effort tends to lead to an attachment of the player to the outcome since the investment of energy into the game makes the player (partly) responsible for the outcome"* [4].

In this paper, we aim to model challenge after established affordance models for games. We will be looking at how challenge is designed as an encounter, both in how challenges connect to one another as well as the elements present within a challenge. Using this, we will be able to create a challenge framework that will be essential in creating effective challenges that will be enjoyable to players of games. We will be building on our preliminary findings, where established a basic model for challenges in games [5]. We intend to further explore the elements within the model, and update the model where necessary.

2   The Locked Door and the Puzzle

2.1   Challenge as Affordance

In our preliminary study, we explored challenge as a collection of affordances within games. For this, we relied on the cognitivist theory of affordances for games [6]. Cardona-Rivera identified three core concepts:

- Real affordances are what is actually possible in an interactive virtual environment.
- Perceived affordances are what players perceive to be possible.
- Feedback is the perceptual information used in the game to advertise the real affordances.

Furthermore, we also drew from the work of Pinchbeck [7], who established a taxonomy of game objects in regards to affordances in games. We concluded that in order to form a challenge, two elements were required. The first element is an obstruction, something that will stop the player from being able to progress. The second is the process to finding a means to dissolve the obstruction. While one could argue that the means is what is important, we argue that once the player finds the means, the player has already received everything that is required to dissolve the obstruction. In other words, the means is the proof that the player can continue. Since the process in getting the proof to continue is often where the game requires the player to perform tasks in order to process and therefore makes up the majority of the gameplay within a game, we argue rather that the means, the process of getting that means is more important to the shape of the challenge. We named these two required elements the locked door and the puzzle (see Fig. 1), named after a very basic challenge often found in games; a locked door. When the player encounters a locked door in a game, the player cannot continue until the player has the means to open this door; a key-like object. In order to progress, the player then has to search for the key-like object and once the player successfully completes his search, the player is rewarded with the key to open the locked door.

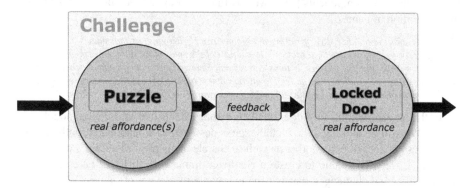

Fig. 1. The locked door and the puzzle.

2.2 The Locked Door

The locked door is a real affordance that denies the player the ability to progress until the associated puzzle has been successfully cleared. Each challenge only has a single locked door.

2.3 The Puzzle

The puzzle is a task or a set of tasks that have to be fulfilled successfully in order to dissolve the locked door. The affordances present within puzzles are real affordances. Tasks don't necessarily have to be fulfilled in sequence or even in the same space (some tasks can persist throughout the entire game). Puzzles largely define the form of the challenge the player needs to complete and is where the game employs the core gameplay to its fullest. Through the tasks required to complete a challenge, one can determine what kind of challenge categories the game employs. Tasks require interaction with real affordances to be completed. In each puzzle, at least one affordance needs to be present for it to be a puzzle. Generally, when a puzzle has been successfully completed, feedback is given to the player to alert them of this. Oftentimes, feedback is also given during the puzzle in the case the puzzle contains multiple affordances.

It should also be noted that even though we named the basic form of challenge the locked door and the puzzle, this serves as a metaphor. It doesn't necessarily have to be in that literal shape. While we were successful in our initial research to establish a basic shape for challenge, it was beyond the scope of that research to define challenge in-depth. For that reason, we did not thoroughly research the puzzle and the elements that make up a puzzle. Since the puzzle is integral to challenge, this research focuses on examining and defining the various elements present within the puzzle, so we can make a complete definition of challenge.

3   Method

For our research, we have conducted a thorough analysis of a large list of game software in order to establish major design trends regarding challenge design elements, which we will use to construct our framework with. To add further credence to our findings, we will present a game scenario that we will analyze through the proposed framework.

3.1   Data Analysis

For our initial study, a number of games were analyzed based on the main means of interaction made available to the player for a particular game, also known as the core gameplay. Gameplay present outside of the core gameplay, such as mini-games, were not included in the analysis. Games across a variety of genres was analyzed, in order to ensure the creation of a framework that can be used for any type of game. We focused on single player games only.

3.2   Equipment

For the games that were analyzed, we used the hardware on which the games were released. For the games for which we could not acquire hardware or the games for which we lacked the required aptitude, we used internet resources. Common resources we used was video footage in the form of "let's plays," which are videos of players playing through the game, often commenting on their progress while playing.

3.3   Protocol Design

For the initial research, we have attempted to analyze an as broad a selection of games as possible, across various genres, in order to get an as complete an understanding as possible about challenge design trends within games. See Table 1 for a selection of the games that were surveyed.

Table 1. Sample of surveyed games

Hardware	Survey type	Game surveyed
Super nintendo entertainment system	Hardware	Crono Trigger, Smash TV, Zombies ate my neighbors, Lost Vikings, Super Mario World, Super Mario Kart, Terranigma, Mega Man X
Nintendo DS	Hardware	Magnet Loop, Contra 4, Phoenix Wright Ace Attorney, Castlevania Dawn of Sorrow, Elite Beat Agents, Advance Wars Dual Strike, Big Bang Mini, Space Invaders Extreme
Nintendo 3DS	Hardware	Bravely Default, Luigi's Mansion Dark Moon, Super Mario 3D Land, Yo-kai Watch, Mario vs. Donkey Kong: March of the Minis
Nintendo Wii	Hardware	Disaster Day of Crisis, Metroid Prime 3 Corruption, Muramasa the Demon Blade, Little King's Story, Super Monkey Ball Banana Blitz, Rayman Raving Rabbids, Wii Sports, Zack and Wiki Quest for Barbaros Treasure, Super Mario Galaxy
Sony PlayStation	Hardware and video	Tekken 3, Resident Evil, Silent Hill, Metal Gear Solid, Wild Arms, Alundra, Legend of Mana, Vagrant Story, Suikoden II
Sony PlayStation 2	Hardware and video	Okami, Viewtiful Joe, Prince of Persia The Sands of Time, God of War, Devil May Cry, Dark Cloud 2, Breath of Fire Dragon Quarter, Radiata Stories
Sony PlayStation 3	Hardware and video	Puppeteer, Folklore, Ni no Kuni Wrath of the White Witch, Little Big Planet, Uncharted Drake's Fortune, Valkyria Chronicles, Batman Arkham Asylum, Demon's Souls
Personal computer	Hardware and video	Mark of the Ninja, Dishonored, Plants versus Zombies, Super Meat Boy, Braid, Left 4 Dead, The Binding of Isaac, Mini Ninjas, Overlord, The Secret of Monkey Island Special Edition, Cave Story, La Mulana

4   Case Analysis: The Legend of Zelda: Ocarina of Time

Within the puzzles of challenges, we have identified five major elements that make up a puzzle and have used those to reconstruct our locked door and puzzle model (see Fig. 2). We found that in order for a puzzle to be effective, each puzzle needs at least one of every element.

- **Challenge Objects** are the elements with which the player can interact.
- **Flow Control** is used to bind the challenge objects together.
- **Boundaries** are used to host all the challenge objects and connections.
- **Difficulty** is used to make game objects and the connections harder to overcome
- **Rewards** are used to provide the player with incentives to clear the challenge.

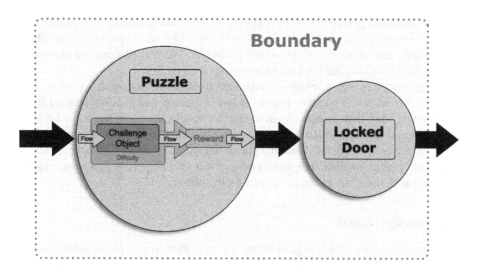

Fig. 2. Reconstruction locked door and puzzle model.

In the coming chapters, we will further elaborate on the various elements, using an obstacle found within The Legend of Zelda: Ocarina of Time [8] to illustrate the elements with examples. In The Legend of Zelda: Ocarina of Time, players are tasked with finding artifacts in environments the game refers to as temples. In order to traverse all these temples and get their hands on the artifacts however, players have to overcome the obstacles within them. At the end of each temple, the player will encounter a giant monster. This monster serves as the final and most important obstacle within the temple.

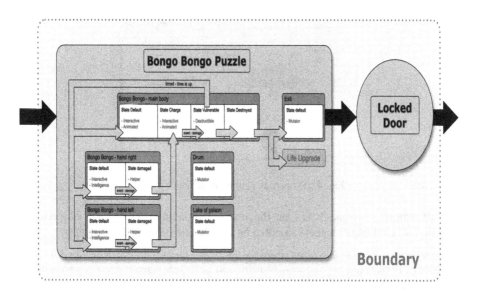

Fig. 3. Bongo Bongo puzzle breakdown.

One of the temples players will visit is known as the Shadow Temple and, as its name implies, its theme has to do with darkness and invisibility. At the end of this temple, a giant monster called Bongo Bongo awaits the player. We will be using the encounter with the monster to explain the various elements (see Fig. 3).

Bongo Bongo is a giant creature suspended from the ceiling, with a gigantic eye instead of a head. It has no arms. Instead, it has two hands that are disconnected from the main body and float around. Apart from the creature, the room has a giant bongo placed in the middle of it, which serves as the main battlefield for the player. Surrounding the bongo is a pool of poison. Once the player has entered the room with the creature, escape becomes impossible. The locked door of this challenge is Bongo Bongo itself; if it is defeated, the game generates an exit for the player.

4.1 Challenge Objects

Challenge objects are all the objects within a puzzle that the player can interact with. They form the majority of the puzzle and allow the player the show mastery of the skills required for the game. For this reason, challenge objects can be considered to be the most important component in a puzzle. Over the years, a large variety of game objects have been created to challenge the player. Due to this, challenge objects can have a variety of properties (see Fig. 4).

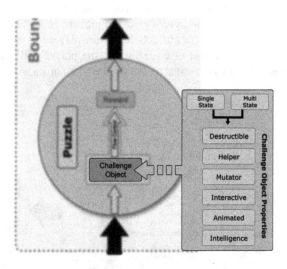

Fig. 4. Properties within challenge objects.

Furthermore, drawing from Dan Pinchbecks taxonomy of gameplay objects, we argue that all challenge objects can either be single state or multi-state objects.

"To begin with, all ludic objects can be divided into those with one state and those with at least two states. A state is defined as a set of properties that defines the object and its relationship to its context. Objects with only one internal state are those whose affordances only take one form

and cannot be altered by gameplay. Multiple state objects, in contrast, are those in which the affordances can be altered, the simplest form of which is being removed from the world" [7].

In the coming chapters, we will further elaborate on the possible properties we observed within challenge objects present within games.

Destructible. Destructible is a property assigned to challenge objects that have an arbitrary number assigned to them. This number, when reaching zero, results in a "destroyed" state. The destroyed state generally causes the object to generate an event outside of the player's control. In the most common application, the number is reduced through gameplay by causing the object "damage." This damage can be influenced through arbitrary properties the game can assign as weaknesses or strong points.

In the Bongo Bongo fight, while observing the main body of the creature, we found that the body had four states. One of those states had a destructible property. The main goal of the battle was to get Bongo Bongo's main body into the state with that property, so the player could finally damage the main body. Once the body has switched to its "destroyed" state, this obstacle is considered cleared and the player can progress further into the game.

Helper. Helper is a property assigned to challenge objects that allows those objects to support the player. The effect of helpers is instantaneous and limited to once per activation. Helpers can come in many form. Common applications include providing the player with ammunition for a tool with finite uses, if the tool is necessary for solving the puzzle. This is done to prevent the player from getting stuck in a certain segment of the puzzle, rendering the puzzle insolvable until the player procures new ammunition. Other common applications include providing the player with hints or removing challenge objects from the puzzle if this means the puzzle becomes easier.

During the fight with Bongo Bongo, if the player wishes to damage Bongo Bongo's flying hands, the player needs to use a long range weapon. In The Legend of Zelda: Ocarina of Time the player has a number of long range weapons, but many of them have as limitation that they can only be used when the player has sufficient ammunition for them. To prevent the challenge from becoming impossible to solve, when the player damages one of Bongo Bongo's hands, the hand has a chance of giving new ammunition to the player. In this case, Bongo Bongo's hands also serve as helpers.

Mutator. Mutators influence the player is various ways without the player having any influence over it. The change is always gradual and while it can affect the player's means of interaction with the game world, it can never outright change it. A common example is a floor of ice, often found in platforming games like Super Mario Brothers. On a floor of ice, the player character's acceleration and braking speed is generally greatly affected making it hard to navigate ice covered floors. It does, however, not change the way the player is controlled.

The lake of poison present within the boundary in which the player finds Bongo Bongo is considered to be a mutator. While the lake has no influence whatsoever over the player's movement, the lake will instead deal damage in constant intervals as long as the player is touching the lake of poison.

Interactive. The interactive property means that the player can interact with it, if the player chooses to do so. Having the choice of interaction is key to this property. With this we mean that the player has to perform a specific action in order to start interaction, such as pressing a button or clicking something within the game world. While the interactive property has some parallels with the mutator property, the major difference is that the mutator property only affects the player to a certain degree, but has no power to completely change the form of interaction, like the interactive property does.

The main body of the Bongo Bongo monster is an interactive challenge object. If the player uses a special item, the player can turn the visibility of the main body on and off. By default, the main body of Bongo Bongo is invisible, though upon entering the room the player is made aware that the main body exists and merely became invisible (hinting to the interactive property of the body). Furthermore, the hands of Bongo Bongo can be considered interactive as well. While the hands normally attempt to attack the player, when damaged, the hands stop doing so. Lastly, when Bongo Bongo's main body is trying to charge the player, the player can damage a weak point on the main body. If the player successfully manages to do so, the main body's state will switch to vulnerable.

Animated. The animated property gives the challenge object the ability to alter its own position, rotation, scale or combination of those over time. Animated objects can either contain a looping animation, in which case these objects generally don't have a complex pattern and stay to a fixed path, or a non-looping animation.

The main body of Bongo Bongo can be considered to have an animated property as well. While Bongo Bongo's main body is in the default state, it is constantly moving out of reach of the player, while being confined to the contours of the drum, in order to make sure that the main body cannot be damaged. Furthermore, once both hands of Bongo Bongo have been damaged, Bongo Bongo will charge the player. This charge is a simple animation of Bongo Bongo moving in a straight line towards the player. Since this is the only animated behavior the main body exhibits, we considered it the main body to have an animated property rather than an intelligence property (which we will further discuss in the next chapter).

Intelligence. A special property has been reserved for intelligence, be it either through populating the challenge object with another human player or through artificial intelligence. In the case of a human opponent, the challenge object that is chosen often resembles that of the player, affording the other human opponents the same kind of gameplay possibilities as that of the player. In this sense, the player can also be considered a challenge object. In the case of artificial intelligence, this concerns an object that can move by itself and has at least got a basic ability to make decisions. The main difference between an object with artificial intelligence and animated objects is that objects with artificial intelligence are designed to either directly oppose or help the player.

The hands of Bongo Bongo have the ability to make basic decisions. The two hands of Bongo Bongo change their actions based on how many hands left undamaged. If both hands are undamaged, the hands will alternate between attacking the player and drumming the drum. If one hand is damaged, the hand will attack and then pause, after which it repeats the process. Furthermore, the type of attacks also change. When both hands are undamaged, the hands tend to attack together.

4.2 Flow Control

Flow control is responsible for binding all the elements within a puzzle together, while also determining how the linked objects relate to one another. There are various ways to do this, and we have identified the following to have been employed by games previously (see Fig. 5).

- **Timed** is a connection that has a time limit associated to it. When the time limit has passed, it either calls a state on the attached challenge object responsible for resetting the object, punishes the player, or both.
- **Fixed order** is a connection that requires the player to operate challenge objects in a specific order. If the order is not done correctly, a reset state will be called for the connected objects and the player will have to restart the puzzle. In certain cases, punishment of the player can be associated with this connection as well.
- **Event** is a connection that is called when the challenge object's state has changed.
- **None** is a connection that is always active, regardless of the player's actions.

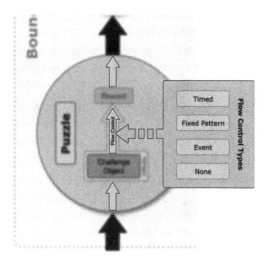

Fig. 5. Types of flow control.

When the player has managed to shoot the main body's weak point when the creature charges the player, Bongo Bongo's main body will fall to the ground and an invisible timer will start. During this time, the player can deal damage to Bongo Bongo. If the player deals enough damage to defeat it, the player clears the obstacle however, if the timer runs out before the player is able to damage Bongo Bongo sufficiently, Bongo Bongo's main body and the hands will be reset (with the exception of Bongo Bongo's incurred damage) and the player will have to start over the process of making Bongo Bongo vulnerable.

4.3   Boundaries

A boundary is the area in which the challenge and the puzzle is contained (see Fig. 6). This means that the boundary is not just limited to challenge objects, but also contains the obstruction (the locked door) of the challenge. Boundaries can either be open or closed. When a boundary is closed, it contains an obstruction to impede the progress of the player (i.e. the locked door). All challenges required to complete a game are challenges with closed boundaries, though it doesn't mean that all challenges with closed boundaries are required to clear a game. Open boundaries don't contain a clear obstruction and are generally introduced as optional elements within the game; a player is not required to clear challenges with an open boundary.

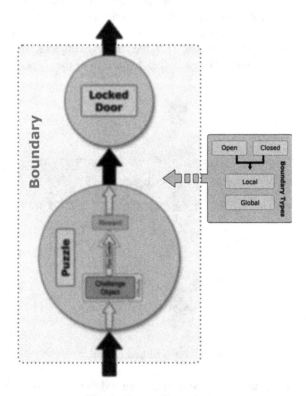

Fig. 6. Types of boundaries.

There are two types of boundaries; a local and a global boundary. A local boundary is a boundary in which the challenge is contained within an area clearly visible to the player. Within a local boundary, not more than one challenge with one outcome can be present. Within a global boundary on the other hand, the boundary is not immediately obvious to the player. A global boundary can contain multiple challenges with multiple obstructions and oftentimes, solving every single one of these separate challenges are required to get the means to solve the global boundary challenge. A challenge with a global boundary should at least contain one challenge with a local boundary; otherwise it should be considered a challenge with a local boundary.

In the fight with Bongo Bongo, players find themselves in a local boundary. Upon entering the room with the creature, players will be able to see everything there is to see in the room; both the elements critical to clearing the obstacles as well as the elements that are not.

4.4 Difficulty

Something that has been difficult to define up until now has been difficulty in games. Now that we have defined the various elements within puzzles, we can look at difficulty and how it is born. After our analysis, we found that difficulty is present within challenge objects and flow control. Furthermore, difficulty is caused by two means (see Fig. 7). The first means is the room for error that the player is allowed; the room for error can affect both challenge objects and flow control. The second is the punishment that the player incurs when the player is unable to finish a task successfully, which is primarily activated within flow control. By increasing or decreasing the room of error and altering the severity of the punishment, the difficulty in games can be increased or decreased.

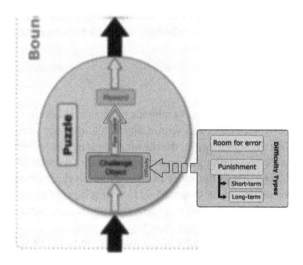

Fig. 7. Types of difficulty.

A good example of this is the game Dark Souls, a game series whose primary selling point is its difficulty. What can be observed in this game is that while the game does not offer any unique game mechanics as compared to other games in the same genre, the one way in which it differs is the high amount of punishment the player incurs when the player does something wrong as compared to other games. Furthermore, Dark Souls also offers a very low room for error, with challenge objects only giving very small windows of opportunity in which the player is able to successfully clear a challenge object. In analyzing difficulty, we found that there are two ways in which a game designer can administer punishment to a player.

- **Short-term punishment** punishes a player by providing the player character with negative effects, making the player redo the challenge in its entirety or certain parts of it. Short-term punishment is instantaneous; the player will be able to continue the game after the punishment has been incurred. This type of punishment is limited to the scope of the challenge.
- **Long-term punishment** generally forces the player to restart the game from the last part where the player saved his or her game data. The effects of long-term punishments can be diminished by introducing check points, which are points in the game where the game automatically saves the player's data so the player can restart at this point upon incurring a global punishment. Long-term punishment can also be applied after the game or a segment of the game has been completed. This is often done through ranking the player's results and penalizing the final result.

The Bongo Bongo fight relies on timing to create difficulty. In order to deal damage to the hands as well as make the main body of Bongo Bongo vulnerable, the players are only given a small window of opportunity in which they have to aim their weapon at the monster and fire it. Punishment to the player is given in the form of damage to the player's life. If the player's life reaches zero before Bongo Bongo is defeated, the player will be moved back to the entrance of the Shadow Temple and the player will have to navigate back to the room with Bongo Bongo, who will be fully recovered by the time the player enters again.

4.5 Motivator

A motivator serves as the motivation for why the player should overcome the challenge. While multiple motivators can exist within any challenge, one motivator should be responsible for either giving the player the means of clearing the locked door associated with the challenge, or presenting player with appropriate feedback in the locked door being cleared. We have based the types of motivators on the emergent, retained and revised reward type taxonomy as proposed by Cody Phillips [9] (see Fig. 8).

In The Legend of Zelda: Ocarina of Time, rewards are very common with varying levels of desirability. One reward that is especially sought after is an upgrade to the player's life points, which can dramatically impact the ability of the player to compete with the obstacles within the game world. The Legend of Zelda: Ocarina of Time refers to these upgrades as "Heart Containers." Once the player defeats Bongo Bongo, the player is rewarded one of these heart containers.

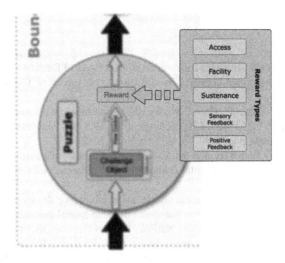

Fig. 8. Reward types

5 Conclusion

Challenge, even to this day, serves as a very important yet vastly misunderstood design element in games. By defining challenge as something that can be designed, we will be able to see that challenge is not something that is present within the entire game, but something that is contained on its own. This will certainly clear away the misunderstandings that have until now plagued challenge, and will open up new venues such as more focused usability research for games or affordance research for games. Furthermore, we believe that challenge is one of the most important components in game design and is what sets games apart from other interactive products or other entertainment media. Understanding what challenge is will play an essential role in creating more effective game content. While this will be of use to anyone involved with game design, this will be especially beneficial to fields that require more concrete evidence of effectivity, such as serious games. We hope that future work will be able to further validate and develop this model, as well as serve as a basis for challenge design research.

6 Limitations

We believe that the elements we defined for puzzles within challenges are exhaustive. However, since this study relies on analysis of games already produced, we cannot say the same for the properties we defined within the various elements. Since new game types are still being created to this day, there's a chance that new properties for the defined elements may be created. While minor, we do believe that this constitutes as a limitation to our current study.

References

1. Enger, M.: What is "Nintendo hard"? (2012). http://www.giantbomb.com/profile/michaelenger/blog/what-is-nintendo-hard/98057/. Accessed 15 Dec 2015
2. Suits, B.: The Grasshopper: Games, Life and Utopia. University of Toronto Press, Toronto (1978)
3. Cox, A., Cairns, P., Shah, P., Carrol, M.: Not doing but thinking: the role of challenge in the gaming experience. In: CHI 2012 Proceedings of the SIGCHI Confèrence of Human Factors in Computing Systems, pp. 79–88. ACM, New York (2012)
4. Juul, J.: The game, the player, the world: looking for a heart of gameness. In: Copier, M., Raessens, J. (eds.) Level Up: Digital Games Research Conference Proceedings, pp. 30–45. Utrecht University (2003)
5. Brandse, M.: The locked door and the puzzle: using affordance design to create compelling game design. In: ADADA 2015 Proceedings of the 13th annual conference of Asian Digital Art and Design Association, Chonnam National University, ADADA, pp. 256–261 (2015)
6. Cardona-Rivera, R., Young, R.: A cognitivist theory of affordances for games. In: Proceedings of the 2013 DiGRA International Conference: DeFragging Game Studies (2014)
7. Pinchbeck, D.: An affordance based model for gameplay. In: Proceedings of the 2009 DiGRA International Conference: Breaking New Ground: Innovation in Games, Play, Practice and Theory. Brunel University (2009)
8. Nintendo, E.A.D.: The Legend of Zelda: Ocarina of Time (Software). Nintendo, Japan (1998)
9. Phillips, C., Johnson, D., Wyeth, P.: Videogame reward types. In: Proceedings of the First International Conference on Gameful Design, Research, and Applications, Gamification 2013, pp. 103–106. ACM, New York (2013)

Co-designing a Civic Educational Online Game with Children

Ana Claudia da Costa[1(✉)], Francisco Rebelo[2,3], and António Rodrigues[4]

[1] Câmara dos Deputados, Brasília, Brazil
analustosa12@gmail.com
[2] Faculdade de Motricidade Humana, Universidade de Lisboa, Estrada Da Costa, 1499-002
Cruz Quebrada - Dafundo, Portugal
frebelo@fmh.ulisboa.pt
[3] Centro de Investigação em Arquitectura, Urbanismo e Design, Universidade de Lisboa, Rua Sá
Nogueira, Alto da Ajuda, 1349-063 Lisboa, Portugal
[4] Laboratório de Pedagogia, Faculdade de Motricidade Humana e UIDEF, Instituto de Educação,
Universidade de Lisboa, Cruz Quebrada, Portugal
arodrigues@fmh.ulisboa.pt

Abstract. This study presents the co-design process of an educational game for citizenship, involving children aged 10–14 years old. The game project was born in the context of "Plenarinho", a portal of the Chamber of Deputies of Brazil. Several authors have shown that using digital games has great teaching potential, as they have important principles of different learning theories. However, the creation of an educational game is a complex process that must focus itself on the educational goals of the demanding organization and on final users' interests. Notwithstanding, in educational game design, target groups rarely contribute since the beginning of design phases. Facing this, we decided to explore the co-design methodology as a way to find answers to the following question: What type of contributions can a creation process involving children bring along to the design of an educational game? Our study was constituted by two stages. The first stage was made up of meetings with the organization's team and it was dedicated to the definition of the game requirements. The second stage was the one of co-design with children and was dedicated to collective creativity throughout the design process. It was constituted by six meetings. Results suggest that co-designing with younger users is a promise to successfully conciliate learning into fun and engaging games. Users, despite their age, can provide us information about various game mechanics characteristics, visual and narrative characteristics, helping us to design solutions, which considered both pedagogical and playful sides.

Keywords: User centered design · Co-design · Child users · Educational games · Citizenship education

© Springer International Publishing AG 2017
A. Marcus and W. Wang (Eds.): DUXU 2017, Part II, LNCS 10289, pp. 377–386, 2017.
DOI: 10.1007/978-3-319-58637-3_30

1   Introduction

Several authors have shown that digital games have great teaching potential, as they have in themselves important principles of different learning theories [10, 11, 16, 19, 23]. This can explain the growing interest in serious games or gamification of educational contents. In the case of civic content, it's not different. Previous studies have shown that digital games can incorporate learning methods that have been found to be effective in research on civic education in the classroom [3, 21, 24]. Among them, we can point out fostering youths' competences to discuss and express their opinions about current events, practice civic problem-solving and decision-making, and simulations of real-world civic events [2, 15, 17].

However, the creation of an educational digital game is a complex process that, beyond its multidisciplinary character, must focus itself on the curriculum educational goals and, at the same time, on the expectations and interests of the users [7]. This article describes on the co-design process in which concepts for a civic educational game were defined based on user-centered approach.

We focused on civic learning because of its importance in democratic societies [12, 15]. The lack of interest in politics concerning Brazilian students may be partly due to the difficulties school had to deal with during the formation of active citizen [18]. The game to be developed is a demand of Plenarinho - www.plenarinho.leg.br, the children's political website of the House of Representatives in Brazil. The website was launched in 2004, and it is a commitment made by this Institution to create mechanisms to promote political education and active citizenship.

The decision to design a digital game was supported by recent studies [3] showing that decreasing interest of young students in political issues can be fought with educational games. On one hand, "Compared with more traditional media formats these games draw attention, enhance engagement in their topic and induce a positive attitude toward learning and behavioral changes [4]."

On the other hand, it has been recognized that putting together learning and fun is quite a challenge [14]. Many educational games are criticized for failing in achieving their entertaining goals [25]. In order to create a compelling game experience by designing an effective educational tool - ensuring knowledge acquisition and improved attitudes, we decided d to rely on an user-centered design approach, bringing users and the demanding institution into the design process, since its initially phases [9, 22].

User centered design methods emphasize the importance of investing time and energy in understanding users and in bringing them into the design process [1, 8, 9, 13, 22]. Nonetheless, in educational game design, children and other stakeholders rarely contribute since the early design phases [25]. As a result, many technological innovations, designed with educational purposes, are carried out without taking students' needs and abilities into consideration.

Excluding users from the early concept and design phases, often leads to game designer's self-referential definitions [1]. Misconstructions about (child) user can contribute to make the game fail in its educational goals, especially because the intrinsic difficulties in conciliating fun and learning.

The question of how to bring and involve children users in the development process of an educational game arises. To address this question, we decided to use a co-design method as a framework to involve child users and stakeholders in a manner that maximizes the value of their contributions and the use of collective creativity shape the game. [13, 25]

Both, users and stakeholders, took part as informants. "Informant design" approach is, according to Scaife [22], the best method "for the design of interactive software for non-typical users or those who cannot be equal partners (e.g., children)". As an informant, they can have a bigger impact on the direction of the development of the game.

In this article we describe the third phase of a larger study dedicated to the design of a civic educational game aiming students aged 12 to 14 years. The other two phases are described in previous articles [5, 6], and are dedicated to the creation of three children-persona, which supported some final decisions concerning game design.

Thus the aim of this study is twofold: it describes a case study that used a methodological co-design framework for educational game, involving child users, and the concept of a citizenship educational game generated during its implementation.

2 Methodology

The third phase, presented here, was organized in two stages. The first stage was made up of two meetings with the organization team and it was dedicated to the definition of the educational game's requirements. The second stage was the one of co-designing with children and was dedicated to collective creation throughout the design process. It was constituted by six meetings, which involved organization's team, including game designer/developer and children.

The first stage focused on defining organization's learning goals and its connection with Brazilian curriculum. Two members of Plenarinho's team participated in two different sessions. In total, each session lasted approximately two hours.

At the first session, the three children-persona resulted from the previous phases were presented as an input to the discussion, in order to enable a better understanding of the target users. Personas, as fictive characters based on factual information (archetypal user), help the team to deep understand end-users and their likes, dislikes and capabilities [1, 8, 20]. The advantage of discussing learning goals with inputs provided by personas is that they bring into discussion relevant characteristics that can lead the team to reconsider and redefine some of these goals [1].

During the second stage (co-creation with child-users), we ran five focus groups sessions with students, and three game developers/designers of Plenarinho's team; we conducted one interview with one student, and four meetings with Plenarinho's game designers, pedagogue and director.

A total of 17 students participated in the co-creation session. All participants were middle school students and were between 10 to 14 years of age. Six participants were girls. To recruit them, we sent an email to all the House of Representatives' functionaries, inviting them to bring their child to participate in a game design process. The emails were selected on a first-come, first-served basis. Five focus groups took place at the House of Representatives, and one interview was conducted at the students' house. The brainstorming sessions were recorded, coded and analyzed by the researchers.

The first focus group lasted for three hours, with a 30 min lunch break. The 12 participants were 10 boys and 2 girls of age 10 to 13. The procedure was: (1) *Warming and Introductory Round.* First we presented the reasons why we invited them to participate and our educational goals. After, as an icebreaker, we played a game that helped participants to know each other and better engage in the following activities. Next, we started a conversation about their civic knowledge. To facilitate it, we asked them three questions: (i) What comes to mind when you listen to the word politics? (ii) What games can teach? (iii) Can a game teach politics or civic behavior? They were not obliged to answer and they could bring a different subject as well. The warming and introductory round took around 35 min, including the chat. (2) *Big Circle.* It was how we called the beginning of each focus group. It was the moment when we would talk about the last meeting and prepare the actual one. On the first day, because we were mainly interested in helping them to reflect about civic subjects in order to broaden the space of possibilities to the game, we proposed a finish me story activity. We gave them the beginning of a story, which has a civic context, and they have to finish it. *Big Circle* lasted around 45 min. (3) *Thinking and Designing the Game.* The student group was divided into two subgroups and each group was invited to brainstorming about a game to teach civic behavior and knowledge. They received paper and black pencil and were invited to prototype the ideas that we have shared during the previous moments, mixing it with their game preferences. This round lasted around one hour.

The second focus group took place one week later with ten students, nine boys and one girl of age 10 to 13 years. The procedure was: (1) *Big circle.* We discussed the previous session, its outputs, and we presented some mockups designed by Plenarinho's team, based on students' prototypes and suggestions. Because we had two different prototypes, one for each subgroup, they voted for the best solutions. We alternated phases of diverging (creating choices) and converging (making choices) [8]. *Big circle* lasted around one hour. (2) *Thinking and Designing the Game.* We split them in three sub-groups. They were given paper and black pencil. Based on their decisions concerning the results of our previous meeting, they were oriented to come up with game concepts, each prototyping their own ideas about civic problems, creating narratives, solutions, difficulty levels, game mechanics, etc. They were not constrained in the creation and conceptualization of those prototypes. This phase lasted around one hour and a half.

The third focus group happened with a smaller number of students, three boys and one girl of 10 to 13 years. The procedure was the same of the second meeting, but we didn't need to split the group. (1) *Big Circle.* We discussed the results of previous session, making choices about the solutions they have presented. (2) *Thinking and Designing the Game.* They were encouraged to think of the further steps of the game concept. Each session lasted around one hour.

After those three focus groups, the results were analyzed and presented to the members of Plenarinho's team during two different meetings. In both, they were asked to review the learning goals with regard to the solutions proposed by the students. New storyboards were created in order to articulate content and game mechanics.

The fourth focus group took place one month after the third one. A total of four students, three boys and one girl, between ages of 10 to 13, participated in this session. Procedures were the same from previous sessions. (1) *Big Circle*, we presented some Plenarinho's comics and discussed with the students their use as reference to the game narrative and characters. They all agreed. Big Circle lasted around one hour. (2) *Thinking and designing the game*, when they were told to discuss and refine game mechanics and narrative. Plenarinho's game developers took part in this sessions, redesigned the previous storyboards in order to register new solutions. This session lasted around one hour and a half.

Fifth meeting was an interview with a 10 years old girl. She couldn't participate in the last focus group, but would like to contribute with us. We went to her house, presented her the last storyboards and asked her to evaluate. We analyzed together the storytelling, game missions, rules, tutorials, buttons and navigation. This meeting lasted around two hours.

Sixth and last focus group was carried out with four girls, aged 10 to 14 years. The procedures were the same from previous sessions (*Big Circle* and *Thinking and Designing the Game*) and we carried on refining the game. This meeting lasted around 2 h and half.

After concluding the focus group phase and analyzing all the data we gathered, we organized two more meetings with only Plenarinho's team. We discussed all the solutions (game characteristics) presented by the students and its integration with the original learning goals.

3   Results

Sessions with Plenarinho's team were crucial to determine game's learning goals: (1) Game should function as motivational tool to arise interest and engagement in citizenship behaviors; (2) Should help players make connections between individual actions and larger social consequences; (3) Should induce think reflection about civic behavior and how it can be practiced in children context; (4) Should better understand concepts as democracy, authoritarianism, politics, citizenship; (5) Power and life in the game should explore citizenship behaviors (cooperation, persuasion, negotiation, mobilization, conflict solutions, etc.).

Based on these goals, game requirements that should be used during the co-design phase were defined: (1) Game missions should provide students with citizenship challenges that are connected to real world events; (2) Game should be located within a fantasy world, using Plenarinho's characters and narratives as reference to the game design; (3) Could be played outside formal school context. Even though we recognize that teachers and peers are very important to make meaning of the game experience, the organization didn't want to depend on teachers' adherence to the game to achieve its educational goals.

The co-design focus groups with students and Plenarinho's team resulted in an adventure game concept that was composed by five different phases, corresponding to five different levels of growing difficulties. The game was conceived to be played on tablet or mobile.

Users decided that game scenario would be an archipelago (Fig. 1) in where each island were facing a social different problem. When the game begins, players would informed about a problem they have to solve (main mission). As they play the game, many challenges would come their way, and apart from having to find out the origin of the main social problem, they must help to fulfill some basic needs of citizens in the island, such as needs for food, water, and housing. Players could choose when to accomplish these smaller missions, but if they take longer, problems would go grow bigger, and they will need much more (citizenship) energy to solve them. Such events include epidemics, invasion by a neighboring island, environmental accidents, etc. Feedbacks should be provided by alerts, short animations that would pop up on the screen and also by changing scores in the resource bar (Fig. 2). Checking points were suggested in order to avoid restarting from the beginning levels. Rewards should be useful within the game context and missions, but they also advocated in favor of easter eggs or free mode moments.

Fig. 1. Story board created by children. Focus group 2

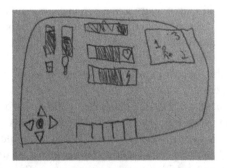

Fig. 2. Ressource bar designed by children (focus group 2)

4   Discussion

Overall, the results revealed a variety of ideas that could put together fun and learning, showing considerable promise on this kind of cooperative methodology to design educational games. *"We are making a game that people will play for real"* (boy, 10 years old, focus group 1); *"I like this game because it will be a bit of adventure and strategy"* (boy, 10 years old, focus group 2); *"When playing, if you do not help people, the game does not tell you that you have done the wrong thing. But, if you keep not doing it, after a while, you receive alerts that warn you if you have done the right thing or the wrong thing* (Girl, 10 years old, focus group 4).

The first two focus groups with more than 10 students was less effective and has brought us some difficulties in controlling the activities. Students were easily distracted, making us spend a lot of time to reorganize them. Our experience with 5 or 4 children were much more productive.

During the meetings, in what concerns students civic knowledge, we were surprised by their awareness about national social political issues, even though their speech showed a tendency to reproduce what is contained in the media (or parents) discourse. *"Politics is a total mess"* (boy, 10 years old, focus group 1); *"... It is an attempt to organize a big country like ours"* (boy, 12 years old, focus group 1), *"I think of deputies"*, *"I think of elections... is to choose a representative for yourself"* (boy, 10 years old, focus group 1), *"Politics is an opportunity that can or can't be used"* (boy, 11 years old, focus group 1), *"It is a country choosing someone to govern it... It depends on whether you are choosing right or wrong..."* (girl, 10 years old, focus group 1). Those results reinforce our understanding that it is important to contribute with educational technologies that can help them to think critically about this subject.

Results also indicated that co-design sessions with children have the potential to determine game elements that can answer user's needs and preferences, and, at the same time, provide the leaning goals aimed by the organization. The variety of ideas generated during the co-design with end-users and stakeholders, in this study represented by Plenarinho's team, showed considerable promise to successfully conciliate learning into fun and engaging games. Some comments made by students during our meetings can highlight this perception: *"Oh, I can't wait it to be finished, I want to play it as soon as possible, please!"* (Girl, 10 years old, focus group 5); *"I told my friend what we are doing here and everyday he asks me when he can play this game ..."* (boy, 10 years old, focus group 5).

However it is important to remark that many game concepts that younger participants suggested resembled their best preferred games. So this was also a topic discussed with them and again, they surprised us with their knowledge when talking about copyright. *"Yes, we must be very careful to avoid problems with copyrights!"* (boy, 13 years old, focus group 2). We stressed that we could be inspired by those games, but that we couldn't make a version of them.

Users, as they listen to stakeholders, they can better understand the learning goals of the game, and thus better integrating them with their game preferences: *"Oh, I see... It's like in the game that I prefer to play. You are the son of a resistance movement member and you have to kill the dictator. But here our game is not going to be a killing or murder one, thinks has to be done in another way, right?"* (Boy, 13 years old, focus group 1). On the other hand, when stakeholders and the design team can listen to and discuss solutions with users, they can put their own expertise in developing products that will appeal to the target audience.

5   Conclusion and Future Work

This article reported upon a co-design methodology for a civic educational game, in which children and the game demanding institution were involved since its initial phases.

Firstly, two meetings with Plenarinho's team were held in order to define game requirements and clear learning goals. Results of these meetings were used in all co-design phases enabling children to clearly understand the civic goal of this educational game. This is especially important when different stakeholders have different interests or the content has a broader concept. Plenarinho's team was focused on the game content, didactic and practical requirements, while children were interested in having fun.

Secondly, the focus groups sessions and interview with children provided us with game mechanics that meet previous established pedagogical goals and requirements. Results revealed that children tend to use their previous gaming experiences and preferences to choose game mechanics. Some game concepts were completely detached from the learning goals and we had to discuss it with them in order to make more appropriate decisions and choices. Possibly more input can be gather using game design techniques adapted to younger users.

The challenge of putting fun in an educational game remains. However, this was an innovative experience if we consider the participation of children on the design of educational games. This was a choice made based on the idea that only users can provide us with information about their preferences. Kids don't play for learning, they play for fun. If we do not bring them into the design process, who would inform us about what motivate them to play? On the other hand, educational content cannot be abandoned at the expense of fun aspect. Different stakeholders can help us finding that balance, since each one can contribute with their knowledge on the topic.

To conclude, results of the co-design methodology allowed us to infer that this can be a way to deal with the apparent contradiction in designing educational and fun games. Although this study focused on the co-design of civic educational game, we believe that this framework can be used for any educational game project. As highlighted by human centered design approach, for an effective technology, end users must take part during design processes Nevertheless, more experiences like this as well as empirical evaluations are needed in order to build basis for a more consistent co-design methodology for educational games.

Consequently, future work should focus on evaluating game prototype and discussing it with educators. We know their value in helping students to make meaning of their game experience, encouraging them to think over the game subject, and make connections with real world issues. They should take part in any educational game design process.

References

1. Antle, A.N.: Child-personas: fact or fiction? In: Proceedings of Designing Interactive Systems, Penn State, pp. 22–30 (2006)
2. Bash, E.: Flow and cooperative learning in civic game play. Ph.D. Proposal, 1, pp. 1321–1338 (2015). http://doi.org/10.1017/CBO9781107415324.004
3. Blevins, B., LeCompte, K., Wells, S.: Citizenship education goes digital. J. Soc. Stud. Res. **38**(1), 33–44 (2014). http://doi.org/10.1016/j.jssr.2013.12.003
4. Bourgonjon, J., Valcke, M., Soetaert, R., Schellens, T.: Students' perceptions about the use of video games in the classroom. Comput. Educ. **54**, 1145–1156 (2010)
5. da Costa, A.C., Rebelo, F., Teles, J.: Child-persona: what I think to what they are. In: Rebelo, F., Soares, M. (eds.) Advances in Ergonomics in Design. AISC, vol. 485, pp. 43–51. Springer, Cham (2016). doi:10.1007/978-3-319-41983-1_5
6. da Costa, A.C., Rebelo, F., Teles, J., Noriega, P.: Child-persona: how to bring them to reality? Procedia Manuf. **3**, 6520–6527 (2015). http://doi.org/10.1016/j.promfg.2015.07.943
7. Chee, Y.S., Mehrotra, S., Liu, Q.: Effective game based citizenship education in the age of new media. Electron. J. e-Learn. **11**(1), 16–28 (2013)
8. Cooper, A., Reimann, R.: About Face 2.0: The Essentials of Interaction Design. Wiley, San Francisco (2003)
9. Druin, A.: The role of children in the design of new technology. Behav. Inf. Technol. **21**(1), 1–25 (2002). http://doi.org/10.1080/01449290110108659
10. Gee, J.P.: Bons Videojogos e boa aprendizagem. Edições pedago, Portugal (2010)
11. Gee, J.P.: Lo que nos enseñan los videojuegos sobre el aprendizaje y el alfabetismo. Granada, Espanha: Colección aulae (2004)
12. Gibson, C., Levine, P.: The civic mission of schools. New York, Washington DC: The Carnegie Corporation of New York; the Center for Information (2003)
13. Geit, K. Van, Cauberghe, V., Hudders, L., Veirman, M. De.: Using games to raise awareness. how to co-design serious mini, 532–540 (2012)
14. Lavigne, M.: Jeu, éducation et numérique - Approche critique des propositions logicielles pour l'éducation, du ludo-éducatif aux serious games. Les enjeux de l'information et de la communication, 49–71 (2013)
15. Lenhart, A., Kahne, J., Middaugh, E., Rankin Macgill, A., Evans, C., Vitak, J.: Teens, video games, and civics: teens' gaming experiences are diverse and include significant social interaction and civic engagement. Pew Internet Am. Life Proj., 1–64 (2008). http://doi.org/10.1016/j.chembiol.2006.01.005
16. Malone, T.W.: What makes things fun to learn? Heuristics for designing instructional computer games. In: Proceedings of the 3rd ACM SIGSMALL Symposium and the First SIGPC Symposium on Small System, pp. 162–169. ACM Press, New York, (1980)
17. Niemi, R.G., Junn, J.: Civic Education: What Makes Students Learn. Yale University Press, New Haven (1998)
18. Pacheco, J.: A educação para a cidadania: o espaço curricularmente adiado. Teias, Rio de Janeiro, Ano **1**(2), 99–133 (2000)
19. Prensky, M.: Digital Game-Based Learning. McGraw-Hill, New York (2001)
20. Pruitt, J., Grudin, J.: Personas: practice and theory. In: Proceedings of DUX 2003: Designing for User Experience Conference (2003)
21. Raphael, C., Bachen, C., Lynn, K.-M., Mckee, K., Baldwin-Philippi, J.: Games for civic learning: a conceptual framework and agenda for research and design. Game Cult. **5**, 199–235 (2010)

22. Scaife, M., Rogers, Y.: Kids as informants: telling us what we didn't know or confirming what we knew already? pp. 1–26 (1998). http://discovery.ucl.ac.uk/1324103/
23. Squire, K.: From content to context: Videogames as designed experience. Educ. Researcher **35**(8), 19–29 (2006)
24. Westheimer, J., Kahne, J.: What kind of citizen? the politics of educating for democracy. Am. Educ. Res. J. **41**, 237–269 (2004)
25. Zaman, B., Poels, Y., Sulmon, N., Annema, H., Verstraete, M., Grooff, D.D., Desmet, P.: Concepts and mechanics for educational mini-games: a human-centered conceptual design approach involving adolescent learners and domain experts. Int. J. Adv. Intell. Syst. **5**(3), 567–576 (2012)

Improving the Usability in a Video Game Through Continuous Usability Evaluations

Corrado Daly, Claudia Zapata[✉], and Freddy Paz

Engineering Department, Pontificia Universidad Católica del Perú,
Av. Universitaria 1801, Lima, Peru
{cdaly,zapata.cmp}@pucp.edu.pe, fpaz@pucp.pe

Abstract. User experience in a software product - like a videogame - has a great impact on the success and acceptation of it. Players feel better when they can learn and understand easily the game's goals and how to reach them. The purpose of this study is to show evidence that continuous user experience tests combined with software improvements can make that acceptation reached in a smarter way. These tasks are accomplished integrating usability techniques and Agile Methodology.

Keywords: Videogames · Usability evaluation · User experience (UX) · Agile methodologies · Scrum

1 Introduction

The development of video games usually includes the following major activities: game design, development, testing and deployment. The development phase involves creating the necessary graphics and sounds as well as building the software that implements the video game [8]. Like any software, a video game must be created applying a development methodology but as a highly interactive element, such methodology should be a flexible process that allows usability activities to be introduced.

According [2], a videogame is an interactive software conceived "to make the player feel good when playing it", unlike other interactive software that are made for accomplishing tasks in a specific context.

Usability is a software-product quality measure system, used to ensure that users reach objectives in an efficient, effectively and satisfactory way in a specific context [3]. This means that a videogame quality cannot be ensured using usability, it needs a broader concept like user experience.

This paper describes the experience of making a high-level acceptation videogame, combining a software methodology with continuous user experience test iterations. In further sections development methodology and testing instruments will be described, and finally results will be discussed.

© Springer International Publishing AG 2017
A. Marcus and W. Wang (Eds.): DUXU 2017, Part II, LNCS 10289, pp. 387–397, 2017.
DOI: 10.1007/978-3-319-58637-3_31

2   Methodology

In this section we will describe Usability and the Agile Methodologies, as well as the integration of both techniques for the development of the tool that is part of the present study.

2.1   Usability

According to [3], the definition of usability is: the effectiveness, efficiency and satisfaction with which certain users reach the specified goals in particular environments.

In [4], Nielsen indicates that usability engineering is not a single activity that takes place before the launch of the product, on the other hand is a set of activities that take place throughout the product life-cycle management.

Nielsen presents the following steps as part of the life cycle model of usability engineering:

1. Know the user.
2. Competitive analysis.
3. Set usability goals.
4. Parallel design: Develop multiple versions of a parallel interface, compare the results and take the best aspects of each.
5. Participatory design: Involve the user as part of development and allows developers to have a group of users available to make queries.
6. Coordinated design of the entire user interface: Coordinate and centralize aspects of the interface to maintain consistency throughout the application.
7. Apply guides and perform heuristic analysis.
8. Prototyping.
9. Empirical evidence.
10. Iterative design: The application must be developed in test and correction cycles based on the results of the empirical tests.
11. Collect feedback from field use.

Rubin and Chisnell [5] defines user-centered design as techniques, processes, methods and procedures for designing usable products and systems as well as the philosophy that places the user at the center of this design process.

The proposed lifecycle by [9] as the user-centered development lifecycle is shown in the Fig. 1.

Both documents [4, 9] propose common tasks such as:

– Knowledge of the user, necessary when defining requirements of any type of tool.
– Usability testing.
– Prototyping.
– Heuristic evaluation.
– Iterative design.

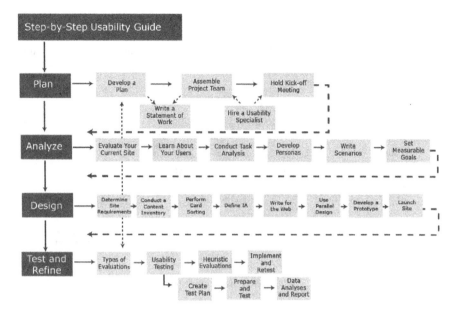

Fig. 1. User-Centered Design Process Map [9]

2.2   Agile Methodology

Agile methodologies are a group of software development methods that emphasize [2]:

- The collaboration between the programming team and the business experts.
- Communication face to face.
- Rapid delivery of value for the business.
- Self-organized teams.
- The quick response to change.

The most used agile methodologies are XP and Scrum [7]. The latter allows organizing medium teams so it was a matter of our interest.

Scrum [6] is an agile approach for product and service development. The work is done in sprints that are fixed periods of time of between 1 to 4 weeks during which a multidisciplinary team does all the work. At the end of each period the team must have built a potentially deliverable product.

In Scrum [6], user stories that an application must deploy are placed in a product backlog consisting of a prioritized list of features. The activities that are carried out in Scrum and that allow to advance the product backlog are:

- Product backlog grooming: new functionality of the product backlog is added or removed.
- Sprint planning: planning phase prior to each iteration.
- Sprint: an iteration during which the product is built.
- Daily scrum: 15-minute daily meeting of the team, during which the best way to move towards the solution is reviewed.

- Sprint execution: construction activity of the development team.
- Sprint review: inspects and adapts the product at the end of each iteration.
- Sprint retrospective: the construction process is reviewed and adapted at the end of each iteration (Fig. 2).

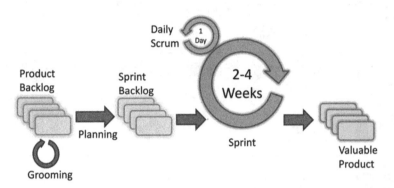

Fig. 2. Scrum life cycle [6]

The roles in this methodology [6] allow to properly coordinate the team and are the following:

- Product Owner: The person responsible for product leadership and define what features should be built, in what order to build and prioritize.
- Scrum Master: A person who provides leadership to the team, acts as coach of the principles of Scrum, it helps solve blockers and the team achieve its best performance.
- Development Team: The self-organized team who is responsible for designing, building and testing the desired product.

2.3   Integrating Usability and an Agile Methodology

The proposed integration is based on a case study by Aguilar and Zapata [1], in which the XP design process is improved through the use of UCD tools. The difference for the present work is that when developing a video game, we are facing a more extensive application in development time and work equipment, so it was decided to use Scrum instead of XP as shown in Fig. 1. In this sense, "Interviews" will not be used because the requirements were obtained from the game design but "Personas" and "Scenarios" were used because they helped to represent different groups of users and their needs. This allowed bettering defining the game mechanics as the forms of interaction and the design of the interface.

"User Evaluations" will go hand in hand with development iterations and participants will be required to evaluate the degree to which the product meets predefined usability criteria (Fig. 3).

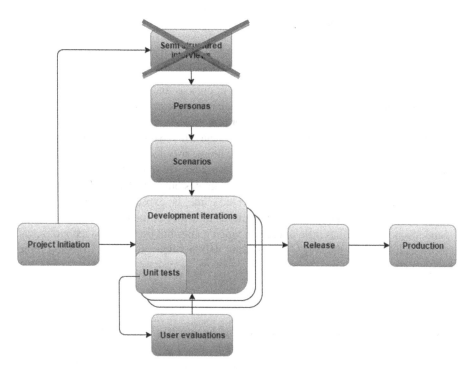

Fig. 3. Adaptation of integration proposed [1]

3 Development Process

The objective of the project was to develop a videogame that motivates high school students to learn more about Mariano Melgar, who was an important poet during the Independence of Peru. The platform game is placed in a dream of the character and through the levels moves from Mariano Melgar's love conflicts to his surrender for the freedom of his country. The Fig. 4 shows some stages of the game.

Fig. 4. First level of the videogame

3.1 Personas and Scenarios

The group of high school students who are wanted to reach are adolescents between 13 and 16 years and designed the following possible profiles:

– Students with good performance: organized, curious and with great motivation for reading. When faced with a video game you are interested in deepening its content (story, characters and possible related stories).
– Students disinterested: unmotivated and dedicated to leisure activities, whose objective is only to approve the courses but not necessarily to learn. When faced with a video game he wants to be entertained and does not see it as a learning tool.
– Students gamer: has a great interest in video games but has a hard time seeing them as a learning tool. When faced with a video game, he expects to have high quality graphics and music and that the mechanics and history of the game are fun.
– Students not gamer: has little interest in video games but uses various technological tools such as social networks. When faced with a video game, it is expected to be easy to play.

3.2 Iterations

The video game has two levels: the first shows the user how to use the commands and meet the objectives; on the other hand the second level gives more information about the character and his role in the Independence of Peru. These levels were developed in four iterations where, after each one, user evaluations were performed.

3.3 Continuous Evaluations

The objective of the evaluations done was to obtain information about the user experience in the game. This experience includes the understanding of the main goal of the game, and learning the actions/movements made by the character.

People for the first three iterations were chosen randomly, only with the requirement that they can operate a computer, so their experience in previous games can be similar or different. It was expected that they learn themselves to discover how to achieve the main goal and the tasks need for that. Except for a unique user case, users chosen for one test didn't participate in other tests. For the fourth iteration, it was proposed an age and gender balanced group high school students, as well as possible.

The tests consisted in a time-taken playing session, with a limit of 30 min in a test scenario. It is expected that the player accomplish the main goal, but it's considered other possibilities, like the player needs a "little help" or the user leaves the game cause frustration. It's important to remark that all the sessions were filmed so they can be reviewed after. Users were located in an isolated room, in a computer with the game installed and running. The only other people allowed to be there were the observers as shown in Fig. 4.

The first iteration was made in a black-backed scenario in one single space that can be scrolled horizontally; it was only for testing commands and movements. Further versions included full graphical scenario with doors, elevators, high and low points, objects to be collected and a statue for path indications. Latest version also includes initial and final video sequences and a floating book for command help. All movements are not allowed at the start of game, they are gradually enabled and explained by the help system, so, for example, character can't move objects before it's allowed, even if there are objects that can be moved.

Before each test, users were informed about the most important facts of the test: they will play a game, they must self-learn how to move, how to take objects, how to jump and how to reach the goal-point. Also, they were provided with a pre-test questionnaire requesting information about:

- Gender
- Age
- Formal studies
- Game playing experience, including weekly playing time, and some types of games previously played.

During the test the information collected was reported by observers, and includes how the user completed the tasks, and how easily was for him/her. The tasks include some actions like:

- Move (left/right)
- Jump
- Hang up
- Pull
- Push
- Go up
- Other general aspects of the game

After each test, user was prompted for a post-test questionnaire, which requests information about his/her experience playing the game, this includes the facts of:

- How useful was the help and if it was in the appropriate moment
- How appropriate was the command-key layout
- How the character movement was perceived
- How the character reacted to commands
- How easily the tasks (move, jump, hang up, pull, push and others) were made
- Best and worst facts perceived by the user about the character control
- What is the main goal of the game
- What is the user perception about the main character

The first iteration provided useful information about the commands for realize the actions and how quick or easily the user learned about it. This iteration was applied to two young-mid age users.

Second and third iterations used full graphical interface (Fig. 5), and considered one scenario with many rooms, connected by doors. In each room there are objects to be collected, dangerous places, help for commands, moving objects (acting as elevators), and decorative objects. In this scenario, user must distinguish what is useful and what is not, and find the way through the rooms. These two iterations provided very useful information about difficulties previously not seen, and also help and navigation issues. The second iteration was applied to three mid-age users and the third one was applied to a teenager (Fig. 6).

Fig. 5. First iteration: user test

Fig. 6. Second and third iterations: user test

The last iteration was made to a group of 24 teenagers. As before tests, this was conducted in computer laboratories with the testing version of the game previously installed. Time was extended to 40 min. Only users and observers were allowed to stay in. The profile of the tested users is showed in the Table 1.

Table 1. Last-iteration user profile by gender, age and declared playing time

Gender	Male	Female	Total	
	11	13	24	
Age	13	14	15	Total
	4	17	3	24
Average gaming time in hours (declared)	0-2	3-5	5-8	Total
	17	4	3	24

4   User Evaluations Results

Each iteration exposed some issues and difficulties found playing the game. There was a place for comments that brought feedback for improvements in the game, and those improvements made changes in later test questions, so improvements in user experience features can be tested.

The first iteration showed confusion about movements. Because they were applied to previously-experienced gamers, the layout was not as they expected. Also, users noticed that the movements are not felt natural, dangers are difficult to see, and also it was difficult to difference between movement and actions like push or pull.

In the second iteration (full scenario and graphical interface), the users also perceived not natural movements but with less intensity than the first iteration. Improvements noticed include more natural hang up and a better help. One user left the game, and the other two ended with a bit of help. In this case, other issues were discovered, most important were:

- Help, even improved, was not easily understood.
- Directions for path are not clear, "help" points to the final destination but not to the nearby path.
- Users don't know what the objects in the inventory are and how they get there.
- Users have unlimited lives, it was perceived boring for one of them.
- There are checkpoints in some places, but they are not adequately placed.
- It's very difficult to guess some actions: how to pull a box that is over another one?
- It's not clear if a long jump requires previous running for taking "impulse".
- The user wants to make the character run, but it only walks.
- Time for final stage was too short, and don't left time for the user to think or plan a strategy.

In the third iteration, applied to a teenager, most of the issues were corrected, but the game was not finished successfully, the main reasons include help was still difficult to understand.

The fourth and last iteration was made to a group of teenagers, with all the observations and issues fixed and/or improved. Almost all the issues were fixed, but the "running" feature wasn't added, instead, there's a "slow move" and a normal faster move. In this case, they were mostly experienced players (see Table 2). In this iteration users noticed:

- Help was very clear for half of the users, and clear for the rest. No one noticed some issue.
- Path indications were mostly clear.
- Movement commands were easily learned and done, even if they are not equal to other games played before by the users.
- There's still a perception that the character's reaction was not natural as it's expected.
- 11 players ended the game successfully before the expected time limit (30 min).
- Three users understood easily all the facts of the game and finished quickly without external help. Others accomplished tasks in more time.
- Eight users required external help but accomplished the tasks.
- Two users tried to do movements that are not allowed at that time.
- The video sequences helped to understand the story around the main character.
- One player abandoned the game at 26 min.
- Players who completed the game showed an average time of 33,8 min.
- Nobody noticed the need of run.

Table 2. User perception of the game in the last iteration. In a scale of numbers, 1 means "most difficult" or "never", 5 means "most easy" or "always".

		1	2	3	4	5	Total
1.	Movement indications are clear			4	8	12	24
2.	Path indications are clear	1	2	2	11	8	24
3.	Command layout is adequate		2	6	11	5	24
4.	Character can be moved in different ways	3	1	3	10	7	24
5.	Objects can be pushed by the character		2	4	11	7	24
6.	Objects can be pulled by the character		1	7	8	8	24
7.	Character movements are natural		1	11	6	6	24
8.	Character can jump to the platforms		1	5	11	7	24
9.	Character can hang up to the platforms		1	4	13	6	24

5   Conclusions

Use of user experience (UX) integrated with software development stages was useful since it provided quick information regarding user experience issues and make the development process fix those issues while improving new features.

Earlier test iterations showed important improvements in user experience, so these features were available quickly in another testing iteration. Because they were applied to previously-experienced gamers, the command layout was not as they expected. Also, users noticed that the movements are not felt natural, dangers are difficult to see, and also it was difficult to difference between movement and actions like push or pull.

In the last version, almost all the issues were fixed. Help and path indications were almost clear all users for the rest, movement commands were easily learned and done, even if they are not equal to other games played before by the users, even if there's still a perception that the character's reaction was not natural as it's expected.

Final iteration provided broader results in target users, and all of them never played the videogame, so their feedback provided very useful information about user experience features and improvements, and also gave the research team a path to add new features.

Video games are not unrelated to the techniques of agile software development and usability techniques on the contrary the application in its development cycle is very beneficial to obtain a better quality of product without neglecting the other aspects of this type of software.

References

1. Aguilar, M., Zapata, C.: Integrating UCD and an agile methodology in the development of a mobile catalog of plants. In: Soares, M., et al. (eds.) Advances in Ergonomics Modeling, Usability & Special Populations. AISC, vol. 486, pp. 75–87. Springer, Cham (2017)
2. Alliance, A.: The Agile Alliance. http://www.agilealliance.org
3. ISO: 9241–11. Ergonomic requirements for office work with visual display terminals (VDT's), Berlin, Germany (1998)
4. Nielsen, J.: Usability Engineering. Morgan Kaufmann, Burlington (1993)
5. Rubin, J., Chisnell, D.: Handbook of Usability Testing: Howto Plan, Design, and Conduct Effective Tests. Wiley, Hoboken (2008)
6. Rubin, K.S.: Essential Scrum: A Practical Guide to the Most Popular Agile Process. Addison-Wesley, Boston (2012)
7. Salvador, C., et al.: A systematic review of usability techniques in agile methodologies. In: Proceedings of the 7th Euro American Conference on Telematics and Information Systems. pp. 17:1–17:6. ACM, New York (2014)
8. Tschang, F.T.: Videogames as interactive experiential products and their manner of development. Int. J. Innov. Manag. **09**(01), 103–131 (2005)
9. U.S. Department of Health & Human Services: User-Centered Design Process Map (2014). https://www.usability.gov/how-to-and-tools/resources/ucd-map.html

Connecting Through Kinect: Designing and Evaluating a Collaborative Game with and for Autistic Individuals

Kristen Gillespie[1(✉)], Gabriel Goldstein[2], David Shane Smith[1], Ariana Riccio[1],
Michael Kholodovsky[2], Cali Merendino[2], Stanislav Leskov[2], Rayan Arab[1],
Hassan Elsherbini[2], Pavel Asanov[1,2], and Deborah Sturm[2]

[1] Department of Psychology, CSI/CUNY, New York, NY, USA
Kristen.Gillespie@csi.cuny.edu
[2] Department of Computer Science, CSI/CUNY, Staten Island, NY, USA
Deborah.Sturm@csi.cuny.edu

Abstract. We are developing a game to help autistic people collaborate with their siblings and peers while improving their social-communicative skills. Autistic college students have been involved in game design and evaluation since the project's inception. They have provided invaluable feedback that we are incorporating with their help. By involving autistic students in game design and evaluation, we are helping them develop employment-readiness skills while ensuring that the game is well designed to teach autistic people.

Keywords: Autism · Participatory research · Game design · Collaboration · Emotion recognition · Autistic college students

1 Introduction

Autism Spectrum Disorder (ASD) is defined by reduced social-communication skills and restricted and repetitive patterns of behavior and/or focused interests [1]. ASD is also associated with a number of strengths, including attention to detail, honesty, and enhanced ability to recognize and create patterns [2–4]. Autistic people often (but not always) express their focused interests through a systematic approach to learning and a strong affinity for computers [5]. Computer-based information is organized according to predictable rules that may be well matched to the systematic processing styles of many autistic people [6]. Heightened affinity for computers may make many autistic people well suited to careers in STEM (science, technology, engineering and math) fields. Indeed, while autistic people are *less* likely to enroll in college overall than non-autistic people, they are *more* likely to enroll in STEM majors than students with other disabilities *and* students without disabilities [7]. Although a growing number of autistic college students are graduating from college with marketable STEM skills, young people with ASD remain chronically underemployed as they face pronounced struggles developing the interpersonal skills needed to obtain and maintain competitive employment [8–10]. We are developing a video game to help autistic youth improve their social understanding and collaboration skills. By involving autistic college students in the design and evaluation of this game, we hope to help the students who are involved in the project

© Springer International Publishing AG 2017
A. Marcus and W. Wang (Eds.): DUXU 2017, Part II, LNCS 10289, pp. 398–413, 2017.
DOI: 10.1007/978-3-319-58637-3_32

develop employment-readiness skills while using their feedback to ensure that the game is well designed to teach autistic people.

Challenges collaborating with others and difficulties communicating in ways that are well matched to social contexts are core aspects of the diagnostic criteria for ASD [1]. Autistic people often become depressed because they wish to make friends but have difficulty recognizing the subtle social cues one must interpret in order to forge close relationships [11]. In contrast to the difficulties autistic people experience adapting to offline social contexts, many autistic people report that they can communicate effectively through computer-mediated communication [5]. Not only do computers provide new social horizons for autistic people, interventions delivered via computers can be more motivating for autistic people than interventions delivered in-person [12]. Consequently, families have been quick to adopt computer-mediated supports for autistic people and research evaluating computer-mediated interventions for autism is burgeoning [13].

Despite great excitement about computer-mediated interventions for autism, evidence that computer-mediated interventions are effective in helping autistic people develop *generalizable* social-communicative skills that are apparent outside of the computer-mediated contexts in which they are trained remains very limited [14]. Troublingly, given that generalization has long been recognized as a limitation of many in-person interventions for autistic individuals (e.g., [15]), few assessments of computer-mediated interventions for autistic people include evaluations of whether increased social-communicative skills when engaging with computers generalize to in-person social interactions [16]. In the relatively few studies that do assess generalization, benefits of computer-mediated interventions for autistic people are often apparent when participants are tested with the stimuli they viewed during the intervention but gains are often no longer apparent when participants are asked to generalize trained skills to new stimuli [17]. Nevertheless, a computer-based face processing training program, *FaceSay*^{TM}, has consistently been associated with improvements in the real-world social skills of autistic children [e.g., 18]. Whyte and colleagues speculated that the paucity of studies demonstrating that autistic people generalize skills from computer-mediated to face-to-face situations may be attributable to flaws in game design [14]. Key elements known to be important motivational aspects of computer games more generally, such as opportunities to play the game with peers, clear and consistent rewards, a storyline, and customizability, are often lacking in games designed by researchers for autistic people.

1.1 Why Is Participatory Research for and with Autistic People Needed?

Interdisciplinary participatory research wherein autistic people are involved as active collaborators in game design and evaluation may be needed to address the disconnect between the apparent potential of computers to help autistic people and the limited benefits of computer game-based interventions for autistic people documented thus far [e.g., 19]. Indeed, Parsons and Cobb [20, p. 427] proposed a "triple-decker sandwich" wherein effective technologies to support autistic people are developed by aligning three principles: (1) Theory (i.e. top-down insights derived from research), (2) Technologies (i.e. the affordances of technologies), and (3) Thoughts (i.e. the situated perspectives of members of the autism community).

Opportunities for autistic people to be meaningfully involved in all aspects of technology design and evaluation can greatly improve the alignment between technologies and the needs and perspectives of autistic people. Involvement of autistic people in game design is also likely to be empowering; prior work with autistic children has revealed that active participation in the process of game design improves collaboration skills and confidence [e.g., 19]. Nevertheless, a recent literature review of participatory research involving adults with autism revealed extraordinarily few empirical studies utilizing a participatory approach [21]. The authors of the review emphasized the importance of involving autistic people as true partners in autism research (e.g., in the development of research questions and analytic strategies) rather than only involving them in lower level aspects of the project (e.g., data coding). The paucity of participatory autism research may arise because opportunities to help design and conduct research are not always structured to include direct benefits for the autistic people who are considering involvement. A key point from an article describing a uniquely effective research collaboration between autistic and non-autistic people, AASPIRE, was that clearly defined and mutually respectful roles are needed in order to support effective collaborations between autistic and non-autistic researchers [22].

Interdisciplinary collaborations may be particularly important for helping autistic people to be meaningfully involved in the design and evaluation of technologies to support them as interdisciplinary collaborations allow insights about how to successfully involve autistic people, and the benefits of such involvement, to be communicated across disciplines [23]. In a recent paper describing an interdisciplinary seminar series[1] examining technological innovations to support autistic people, the authors emphasized both potential benefits (e.g., empowerment, social inclusion, and socially valid technologies) and potential challenges (e.g., variation in the skills of different autistic people and potential disagreements between different groups of stakeholders and/or the researchers) of involving autistic people in the design of technologies to support them. For example, autistic youth and researchers may disagree about what they would like the game to teach people [e.g., 20]. These differences in opinion can elucidate ways in which a proposed technology may lack social validity in the community it is designed for (e.g., an intention to use technology to normalize autistic people may conflict with the desire of some autistic people not to be normalized).

In addition to potential difficulties integrating diverse perspectives, process oriented and outcome oriented assessments do not always align. For example, autistic people may learn collaborative skills and gain self-confidence through the process of helping to design new technologies but the end product may not always have the impact on other autistic people that the researchers were seeking [e.g., 19]. Given potential disjunctions between processes and outcomes, the authors emphasized the importance of carefully documenting the contributions of each member of the team in order to be able to track ideas from the process of development to the final product.

Despite the relative lack of data-driven participatory research with autistic adults [21], a small but growing number of feasibility/usability studies document the process of involving autistic children and adolescents in the design of technologies for autistic

---

[1] www.digitalbubbles.org.uk.

people [19, 20, 24–32]. Benton and colleagues [19, 24, 25] noted that participatory design can help researchers design technologies to reach the very diverse types of people who share an autism diagnosis. They speculated that participatory design remains infrequently used with autistic people because the social-communicative challenges and rigidity that define autism can make it difficult to involve autistic people in design. They developed a successful approach, Interface Design Experience for the Autistic Spectrum (IDEAS), to include autistic children in the participatory design of a math game. IDEAS merged participatory design strategies developed with non-autistic youth with principles of a widely-used intervention for autism, TEACCH [33]. The IDEAS method involves four steps: (1) introducing each design session with a visual timeline (with tasks to tick off) and a recap of prior meetings, (2) demonstrating/discussing software relevant to the focus of the session, (3) generating design ideas (with examples of technologies that are and are not effective and idea generation templates as needed) and (4) drawing out the idea agreed upon. Although the process was effective in involving autistic children in game design both individually and in groups, the end game was more appealing to the autistic students who had been involved in designing it than it was to other autistic children. Given that autistic people are often attached to their own idiosyncratic preferences, opportunities for customization are likely to be essential when designing games for autistic people [28].

Truly participatory research reframes the traditional power dynamic of "technology user" and "technology creator/expert" by empowering "users" to co-discover the potential of technologies while collaboratively deciding how to transform them [20]. Although most of the research documenting participatory research with autistic youth has focused on usability/feasibility studies, Parsons and Cobb recently wrote a paper documenting insights derived from a highly systematic and data-driven example of participatory technology development and evaluation with autistic youth, COSPATIAL (*Communication and Social Participation: Collaborative Technologies for Interaction and Learning*) [20]. Their project provides an excellent example of the aforementioned "triple-decker sandwich" wherein effective technologies are developed by aligning theories, the affordances of technologies, and the thoughts of users. The theoretical framework driving their project was constructivist; they viewed learners as actively constructing their own skills through interactions with others. To match this theoretical perspective, they selected technological platforms that promoted collaborative interaction (e.g., collaborative virtual environments). They captured the perspectives of community members by involving them in design and usability testing. In the first year of the project, they conducted observations of autistic children and needs assessments with teachers to identify key learning goals (i.e. collaboration and social conversation). They also obtained feedback on game design from teachers, 5 autistic and 6 non-autistic students. In the second year of the project, they obtained usability data from 6 autistic and 8 non-autistic students. In the third year of the project, they conducted an educational evaluation of the impact of the technology on 22 autistic students. After observing conflicts between the ways teachers wished to develop the technology (i.e. a desire for controlled activities to guide the learners toward specific learning objectives) and the students' preferences (i.e. a desire to make the game as flexible as possible to allow exploration), the core design team (which included 5 teachers) decided to prioritize the goals of teachers. The researchers highlighted the complications inherent in trying to develop technology in response to conflicting stakeholder perspectives and emphasized the importance of transparency when communicating the aims of a participatory research project, the perspectives of the researchers, and the reasons certain recommendations are and are not taken. When discussing tensions between process oriented and product oriented research, they indicated that careful documentation of both the process of technology development and the impacts of the technology on outcomes may help to alleviate these tensions.

1.2 Research Aims

Our research is both process and product oriented. The aims of our research are: (1) to document the process of including autistic youth in the design of a game to help autistic people understand complex emotions and collaborate and (2) to determine if an emotion matching game that autistic individuals can play with peers and siblings is effective at scaffolding collaboration and recognition of complex facial and bodily emotions. Over the past year and a half, the principal investigators (an autism researcher/psychologist and a professor of computer science) have been developing this game in collaboration with Pavel Asanov, a technology innovator. Autistic college students in Dr. Gillespie-Lynch's mentorship program, Building Bridges Project REACH, have been providing feedback on the design and evaluation of the game. Meaningful inclusion of autistic students in game design and evaluation allows them to gain valuable employment skills and also ensures that the game is well-matched to the interests of the individuals it is designed to support.

2 Game Design

The game is designed to support the development of generalizable social-communicative skills in two ways: (1) by providing participants with an immersive intervention wherein they can simultaneously engage with a peer or sibling digitally and in-person and (2) by teaching participants how to interpret complex emotions using varied cues (facial cues, bodily cues, and context cues). Evidence suggests that immersive computer-mediated interventions, such as virtual reality interventions, are more effective at promoting generalization among autistic individuals than less dynamic computer-based interventions [16]. Whyte and colleagues recommended that computer-mediated games to help autistic people transfer skills to the real world include multiple players (as most games for autistic people focus on individual instruction) and blended computer and in-person interactions [14]. Our collaborative game is immersive and dynamic. Standing near one another, participants complete collaborative emotion matching puzzles by moving images on a screen using Kinect technology. Because participants are acting together upon a digital world while standing next to one another in the "real world", they have many opportunities to engage with one another in-person while receiving digital scaffolding to help them solve increasingly complex collaborative emotion matching tasks. Not only is the opportunity to simultaneously engage in-person and online likely to promote generalization of social-communicative skills, our game is designed to address inter-related core challenges associated with ASD. While autistic people often do not struggle with interpreting simple emotions, such as happiness or sorrow, they do struggle with interpreting complex emotions, such as shame or surprise, which provide important but subtle clues about how to adapt to social contexts [34].

Our game is being developed by an interdisciplinary team using the Unity engine with scripts written in C#. The platform is a Windows PC with the Kinect gesture-based user control system. This hands-free control has two major advantages over mouse/ keyboard/controller for autistic individuals: (1) it eliminates an additional device that players often have difficulty manipulating and (2) it incorporates exercise into game-play, which is thought to be helpful for autistic players [35].

An introductory visually guided tutorial lets players acclimate to the Kinect environment by using animations to show the player how to move and place game objects. In the core game, two players stand side by side using hand gestures to move the pieces of a puzzle. Each puzzle depicts the outline of a figure in an emotionally valenced context (e.g., a bear in the background to depict fear). After players construct the body of the figure, they must agree on the correct emotion for the face of the figure by selecting from three displayed emotions. When players master a skill, an audio-visual film clip or mini-game appears as a reward. These emotions become increasingly complex over the course of the game. In addition, the depiction of the emotions shifts from cartoons to photo-realistic displays in order to build from a widely documented interest in cartoons among autistic people [36] toward photorealistic emotions they will encounter in everyday life. Similarly, puzzles early in the game include overlapping cues to the appropriate emotion to agree upon (e.g., a background image of a group of peers excluding the main character and a body cue of sadness) while later levels contain only one cue (e.g., just the body cue of sadness) to encourage recognition of complex bodily and facial emotions based on limited cues. In order to motivate all players to persist and learn, our approach to game design follows well-regarded principles outlined by Gee [37] such as coding for "Empowered Learners" with levels that are pleasantly frustrating while incorporating 'just in time' instruction. Our game design is guided by the principles of Serious Games that Whyte suggested may be particularly useful for autistic players [14] such as including scenarios to elicit emotion recognition and building games with two players playing cooperatively.

The collaborative component of our game was adapted from a less immersive collaborative picture-matching task that was effective at promoting collaboration among minimally verbal young children with autism. Holt and Yuill [38] noted that many of the "collaborative games" developed to help autistic individuals engage with one another do not actually require any collaboration as one participant can dominate the game without any feedback from the other player. To address this, they developed a truly collaborative picture-sorting task that required children to collaborate by indicating agreement at key points. Four minimally verbal autistic preschoolers showed more engagement with and awareness of one another when playing the game that was truly collaborative than when playing a so called "collaborative game" that did not actually require the children to indicate agreement.

Holt and Yuill's innovative game supported collaboration among children who do not typically collaborate with one another [38]. However, it was delivered to children seated next to one another in front of laptops who had to manipulate a mouse to operate the game. Participants in our game are standing and must use large hand movements to manipulate pieces rather than clicks of the mouse. It is important to encourage autistic individuals to move physically and to provide activities that they can access with a range of motor skills as sedentary behaviors and motor difficulties are common in autism [39, 40]. Indeed, one of the four autistic children in Holt and Yuill's original study struggled with using the mouse; in a subsequent study, which replicated the original benefits of their collaborative technology, Holt and Yuill evaluated a touch-screen collaborative interface [41]. Our game, which is entirely nonverbal with audio-visual scaffolding and feedback, addresses a core difficulty in autism with successively more difficult emotion matching tasks. Therefore, it has the potential to be useful for autistic people at many different stages in development and across cultures.

2.1   Participatory Feedback from Autistic College Students

We invite autistic college students enrolled in the Project REACH mentorship program to provide feedback on our game at key junctures in game design, compensate them (with gift cards) for their time, and invite them to become more deeply involved in game design or research depending on their level of interest. Two autistic college students and their mentors provided feedback on very early stages of the game last spring. One of the autistic students provided extensive feedback which included: (1) Making the sound effects louder and the images bigger, (2) Providing demonstrations of how to pick up objects, (3) Making clearer whose hand operates each hand on the screen, (4) Motivating players with virtual rewards, and (5) Selecting backgrounds that match the desired emotion. For example, images of fall and sunsets conjured up happiness for him. He could not commit to greater involvement in the project in the spring. However, he returned this fall to provide more feedback and indicated that he is now very interested in becoming more involved in game design.

This fall, five autistic students and two of their mentors were videotaped while playing the game (to allow us to code interactions) and participated in structured interviews about the game. Their overall response to the game was positive. Four of the students mentioned the collaborative aspect of the game. One commented, "Most games where there are two players... make you feel frustrated about the other player playing with you. You rage at missed opportunities and have a scapegoat to blame when you lose. (This game) teaches you to really work together." Students provided detailed suggestions about how to improve the look, feel and content of the game which included: (1) Providing demos about each level of the game, (2) Reducing the lag between player movements and the Kinect response, (3) Making the faces bigger, (4) Allowing players to customize the characters, (5) Making coins meaningful by pairing them with prizes, (6) Designing images for the background rather than "google images" and improving the quality of images (to "make it seem like it's 2016 these days and I'm not playing like a 1990's game"), (7) Making the game more difficult using a timer, more puzzle pieces or by asking participants to recognize blended emotions, (8) Providing opportunities to select expressions that do not match the context and/or each other ("a lot of people get some sort of kick out of seeing situations and people in them with expressions that don't really match"), (9) Providing situations that young people commonly experience (e.g., getting caught cheating on a test), (10) Allowing players to express negative emotions that they can't explore in day-to-day life ("like Grand Theft Auto"), and perhaps most importantly, (11) Giving the game a storyline showing how the characters progress.

Two of the authors of this report qualitatively coded the videos of the autistic and non-autistic college students playing the game. They obtained reliability on seven coding categories for the behaviors of the autistic students: (1) looking at the screen, (2) looking at their partner, (3) showing positive emotion, (4) expressing frustration, (5) asking for help, (6) turn taking behavior, and (7) conversation/commenting. All of the autistic students were highly visually engaged with the screen; they typically attended to the screen for the entire duration of each observation period. Although they rarely looked at their partners during game play, three of the five autistic students looked at their partner at least once. Most of the autistic students frequently communicated verbally during game play. However, they had been prompted to comment on their ongoing perceptions of the game. Although the students did not express frustration during game play, they remained fairly taciturn overall while playing. However, all five of the students expressed positive emotion at least once when playing. Only three autistic students exhibited explicit turn taking behaviors. However, we had prompted the non-autistic player to let the autistic player make each move first which may have diminished turn taking.

The ease with which researchers attained reliability on the coding scheme suggests that it is a promising foundation for larger scale assessments. Our difficulties interpreting some of the results of the coding due to prompts we had given the players to interact in specific ways taught us that we should initially allow players to play the game without any verbal directions in the future. Although the fact that the players displayed some positive and no negative emotions is promising, we hope that positive emotions will occur more frequently as we make the game more engaging by incorporating students' recommendations. Although it is promising that the autistic players were highly engaged with the screen when playing the game, we may wish to embed prompts for players to look at one another in future iterations of the game in order to maximize benefits of interacting via the screen and in-person simultaneously.

Many of the autistic students gave valuable feedback regarding the look and feel and content of the game. They liked the Kinect interface and enjoyed controlling items with their hand. The tutorials helped them understand how to select and release objects. They suggested improving the tutorial by animating the object to grab (instead of only the hand moving). Students suggested scenarios that might be more relevant for other autistic youth (e.g., interactions at school) than the scenarios we had initially developed (e.g., a person in the woods with a bear).

When asked the purpose of the game, autistic students typically realized that emotions were involved. However, two autistic students thought the game was designed to promote motor coordination and one student reported motor difficulties playing it. Autistic students also noted distracting details more frequently than non-autistic students (e.g., coding text that was accidentally visible at the bottom of the screen). Although the autistic students all said that the emotions depicted by the puzzle characters were clear, a few autistic students (but not mentors) misidentified the valence of emotions (e.g., happy instead of ashamed), thus supporting the need for this type of game. All of the autistic students approved of the purpose of the game. Two students suggested that we also use the game to teach literacy and creativity.

Three autistic students indicated that they were interested in becoming involved in game design or research. These students have been invited to attend our first planning meeting of the spring term where they will receive training in the roles they wish to take on. Pronounced variation in the abilities of these students may create challenges when initially developing their roles but will help us develop the game towards the diversity of the spectrum. We will use the IDEAS model to create opportunities for autistic college students with diverse skills sets to help with game design by (1) introducing each session with a visual timeline (with tasks to tick off) and a recap of prior meetings, (2) demonstrating/discussing relevant software, (3) providing examples/idea generation templates to support students in generating and evaluating ideas and (4) exploring ideas we agree upon through multiple modalities (e.g., drawing, speaking, writing and/or demonstrating).

2.2 Changes Based on Feedback

While observing novice players testing our game, we realized that we needed a more extensive tutorial level to introduce them to the Kinect interface. In general, players were not familiar with how to grab, move and release objects. We created three tutorials with animated demonstrations for the user to copy. In the most basic level we show an animation of a hand moving; a second level shows the animated hand opening and closing to demonstrate grabbing; a third level teaches the player to place an emotional face in the puzzle. These tutorials were modified in response to user feedback and from watching the players interact with the game and one another. For example, originally we used an animated hand to show how to move an object. However, some players did not understand that they needed to grab the piece and place it. Figure 1 shows a snapshot of an updated animation that demonstrates the placement of a face puzzle piece. We used a faded (somewhat transparent) puzzle piece to show the desired move/interaction.

Fig. 1. Tutorial to demonstrate placement of faces

The most essential change in game design initiated by student feedback was to develop a storyline for the game with a consistent main character whose gender and race will be customizable. In early iterations of the game, each level of the game portrayed a different character in a different situation. The autistic students noted that they would prefer to choose among different main characters who varied in race and gender. They also indicated that the game would be more relevant to players if it more closely mirrored the lived experiences of urban youth yet had a fantastical element. Therefore, we created a story focused on a single customizable protagonist facing a challenge that many autistic youth face, exclusion and bullying, and how friendship (with a friendly purple dragon) can help one overcome bullying (See Fig. 2).

Fig. 2. Two scenes (fear and shame) from the first version of the game are on the left. Two scenes (sadness and anger) from the revised game with a storyline are on the right.

Players recommended increasing the sizes of the emotional faces so they could be read more easily and improving the overall quality of the images. Therefore, we increased the head size of the main character and began to use Illustrator rather than Photoshop as the primary illustration tool (as it is more flexible). We are also planning to change the shape of the puzzle pieces of emotional faces so that they are all half circles which are larger than the face itself (aren't closely cut out) so that the shape of the face doesn't influence which face is correct (and the player can focus instead on the emotion).

Our original design had a numeric point system with a running score. Students recommended using pictorial feedback instead so we changed the point system to coins that float up when the correct puzzle piece is placed. Players then reported that it was unclear *why* the coins appeared or what *function* they served. Students recommended collecting the coins at the top of the screen and allowing players to use them to purchase tools that can be used in the game (e.g., a shield). We are planning to implement these suggestions.

Players were sometime confused about which hand on the screen they were controlling so we placed color-coded hands on each side of the screen so that each player knows which hand is theirs. We subsequently moved these hands to the top of the screen after realizing that the players didn't notice them when they were at the bottom of the screen.

One very significant change we made was based on watching the way novice Kinect players positioned their hand during play. We noticed that when their hand was not completely closed, Kinect was interpreting any motion as a grabbing motion. This sometimes led to puzzle pieces moving when the player did not intend to move them. We changed the code to recognize only 2 hand position modes - grab and release; anything in between (lasso) is now interpreted as release.

Although not a design issue per se, we are also working intensively on a coding issue that multiple autistic students highlighted as a key "glitch" to address. This coding issue sporadically introduces a lag between players' movements and the resultant Kinect-mediated motion of puzzle pieces. A number of students indicated that they were distracted by this "glitch" so we have been working intensively on improving it.

3   Planned Game Evaluation

In order to systematically evaluate both the process of game design and the learning outcomes associated with playing our game, we adapted the evaluation strategy developed by Parsons and Cobb [20]. After we have documented the process of developed a polished version of the game guided by our autistic collaborators, we will evaluate the usability of the game in order to refine it further (e.g., planned usability study) and then conduct an assessment of its efficacy (e.g., planned efficacy study). In order to develop meaningful roles for autistic college students who are interested in helping to evaluate the game, we will adapt strategies from participatory action research. For example, we will provide autistic researchers with "potentially wrong" versions of outcome goals and assessments (i.e. stated learning objectives and standardized measures that they may feel are not ideal) and will ask them to edit the outcomes and assessments to make them more effective [42].

3.1   Planned Usability Assessment

In our usability study, we will determine if our Kinect-based game is more engaging than identical in-person emotion-matching tasks while obtaining feedback on game design from a large number of individuals with and without ASD. Dyads, comprised of 60 autistic college and high school students and 60 neurotypical peers, will participate in a single session consisting of a pre-test, computer-based and in-person emotion matching tasks, and a post-test. Students will be paired with a peer of approximately the same age. Modality of collaboration will be a within-subjects variable; dyads will be randomly assigned to complete either an in-person or a Kinect-based series of emotion-matching tasks first followed by the other modality of tasks. The specific emotion matching activities they encounter in the computer-based and in-person versions of the game will be counterbalanced. Type of dyad will be a between-subjects variable:

(1) Twenty autistic students paired with twenty autistic peers, (2) twenty autistic students paired with twenty non-autistic peers and (3) twenty non-autistic students paired with twenty non-autistic peers. By comparing engagement across computer-mediated and in-person versions of the game for different dyad types, we can determine if the intervention is uniquely beneficial for autistic people.

All participants will be video-taped and audio-recorded during a 5 min free play activity prior to the pre-test, during the emotion matching tasks, and during a 5 min free play activity after the post-test. Research assistants who attain research reliability on the following codes will qualitatively code the videotapes: (1) fidelity of administration of tasks, (2) looking at the screen, (3) looking at their partner, (4) showing positive emotion, (5) expressing frustration, (6) asking for help, (7) turn taking behavior/collaboration, (8) conversation/commenting, and (9) joint engagement with positive affect. The number and type of tasks that participants successfully complete together will also be assessed. All participants will be asked what they liked and did not like about the game and how to improve it.

We expect that increased collaboration, engagement during and completion of complex emotion recognition tasks will be apparent in the Kinect-based version of the tasks relative to the in-person version. We expect that benefits of the Kinect-based game will be most apparent for dyads containing one autistic and one neurotypical peer. Few prior studies have examined communication between two autistic individuals although it is a topic of high interest given that autistic people often, but not always, report feeling more comfortable engaging with other autistic people [43].

3.2   Planned Assessment of Efficacy

After incorporating feedback from participants in the usability study, we will conduct a more focused and intensive study to examine benefits of repeated engagement with the program for minimally verbal younger autistic individuals and their siblings. Participants will include 40 minimally verbal autistic children (4–12 years of age) who have a sibling and their 40 siblings. Dyads will be randomly assigned to either receive the Kinect-based intervention immediately (playing the game for 5 h a week for 6 weeks) or to a wait list control group. Pre-test and post-test measures will consist of assessments of Theory of Mind, recognition of simple and complex facial and bodily emotions, a parent-report of autism symptoms and the gold standard behavioral measure of autism symptoms (the Autism Diagnostic Observation Schedule). The qualitative behavioral measures described in the usability study will be obtained during pre-test and post-test free play sessions and during game play. Parent and sibling reports of the frequency with which siblings play with their autistic sibling will also be obtained.

We expect that participation in the Kinect-based training will be associated with improvements in complex facial and bodily emotion recognition, Theory of Mind, collaboration and sibling engagement. Although we expect improvements to be more pronounced for autistic siblings, we also expect improvements among non-autistic siblings given that challenges with Theory of Mind are an aspect of the Broader Autism Phenotype [43].

4   Conclusions

Our participatory research project is designed to document both the process of involving autistic college students in the design and evaluation of a game to help other autistic people develop social-communicative skills and the degree to which the game is effective in actually helping other autistic people develop collaboration and emotion recognition skills. So far, our autistic college student collaborators have provided very useful suggestions that have led to extensive improvements in game design. Their suggestions have often (but not always) been compatible with the suggestions of other autistic students and our aims as researchers. In fact, the autistic students reminded us to include key design principles (e.g., a storyline and an interpretable reward system) in our game that are believed to promote generalization of skills but are often lacking in games designed for autistic people [14] and were initially lacking in earlier versions of our game as well. Therefore, the autistic students effectively guided us to make our work more consistent with theoretical principles of learning.

The autistic students also provided some recommendations that we may not be able to incorporate into the storyline we developed without introducing confusion (e.g., providing opportunities to select emotions that don't match the context). We will need to discuss the process of evaluating recommendations to decide which to use during our game design meetings with our autistic collaborators. Importantly, all of the autistic students agreed that the learning goals of the game would be helpful for other autistic people.

We are attempting to navigate the tension that Parsons and Cobb described between process oriented and outcome oriented research [20] by documenting the empowering process oriented aspects of participatory research with a small group of autistic college students, evaluating if the game is engaging for a broader population of autistic students, revising the game accordingly, and then evaluating if it is effective in promoting social development among autistic people who struggle to express themselves. Unlike other participatory research studies which have involved autistic *children and adolescents* in game design, we hope to use the insights that accomplished autistic *adults* have derived from their life experiences to develop a game that is engaging and effective for autistic youth who are not able to express themselves through spoken speech. Autistic people report that they gain understanding of themselves and others with development [e.g., 45]. Therefore, autistic adults may be uniquely capable of melding insights derived from the lived experience of being autistic with a gradually developed understanding that other autistic people may have different perspectives than their own in order to help us adapt the game to the needs of autistic people who can't express their own preferences easily. Our project is designed to investigate the possibility that autistic adults can provide unique insights into the top level of Parsons and Cobb's "triple-decker sandwich" of effective technology design by helping us gain greater understanding of the learning processes of minimally verbal autistic people in order to design our game to better serve their needs.

Acknowledgements. This project has been supported by a CUNY Interdisciplinary Research Grant (#2316) awarded to Kristen Gillespie-Lynch and Deborah Sturm, a PSC-CUNY Award (RF-CUNY award # 67108-00 45), jointly funded by the Professional Staff Congress and the City

University of New York, awarded to Deborah Sturm and a grant awarded by the FAR Fund to Kristen Gillespie-Lynch to support Project REACH, the mentorship program we are recruiting autistic collaborators from. We would like to thank Patricia J. Brooks, Bertram Ploog, Christina Shane-Simpson, Rita Obeid, Danielle DeNigris, Jonathan Pickens, and mentors and mentees from Building Bridges Project REACH for initial feedback on study design.

References

1. American Psychiatric Association APA: Diagnostic and statistical manual of mental disorders, 5 (2013)
2. Mottron, L., Dawson, M., Soulieres, I., Hubert, B., Burack, J.: Enhanced perceptual functioning in autism: an update, and eight principles of autistic perception. J. Autism Dev. Disord. 36(1), 27–43 (2006)
3. Sodian, B., Frith, U.: Deception and sabotage in autistic, retarded and normal children. J. Child Psychol. Psychiatry 33(3), 591–605 (1992)
4. Baron-Cohen, S., Ashwin, E., Tavassoli, T., Chakrabarti, B.: Talent in autism: hyper-systemizing, hyper-attention to detail and sensory hypersensitivity. Philos. Trans. R. Soc. London B Biol. Sci. 364(1522), 1377–1383 (2009)
5. Gillespie-Lynch, K., Kapp, S.K., Shane-Simpson, C., Smith, D.S., Hutman, T.: Intersections between the autism spectrum and the internet: perceived benefits and preferred functions of computer-mediated communication. Intell. Dev. Disabil. 52(6), 456–469 (2014)
6. Murray, D., Lesser, M.: Autism and computing. In: Autism 99 Online Conference Organised by the NAS with the Shirley Foundation (1999)
7. Wei, X., Jennifer, W.Y., Shattuck, P., McCracken, M., Blackorby, J.: Science, technology, engineering, and mathematics (STEM) participation among college students with an autism spectrum disorder. J. Autism Dev. Disord. 43(7), 1539–1546 (2013)
8. Burgess, S., Cimera, R.E.: Employment outcomes of transition-aged adults with autism spectrum disorders: a state of the states report. Am. J. Intell. Dev. Disabil. 119(1), 64–83 (2014)
9. Baldwin, S., Costley, D., Warren, A.: Employment activities and experiences of adults with high-functioning autism and Asperger's disorder. J. Autism Dev. Disord. 44(10), 2440–2449 (2014)
10. Bublitz, D., Fitzgerald, K., Alarcon, M., D'Onofrio, J., Gillespie-Lynch, K.: Verbal behaviors during employment interviews of college students with and without ASD. J. Vocat. Rehabil. (In press)
11. Müller, E., Schuler, A., Yates, G.B.: Social challenges and supports from the perspective of individuals with Asperger syndrome and other autism spectrum disabilities. Autism 12(2), 173–190 (2008)
12. Moore, M., Calvert, S.: Brief report: vocabulary acquisition for children with autism: teacher or computer instruction. J. Autism Dev. Disord. 30(4), 359–362 (2000)
13. Fletcher-Watson, S.: A targeted review of computer-assisted learning for people with autism spectrum disorder: towards a consistent methodology. Rev. J. Autism Dev. Disord. 1(2), 87–100 (2014)
14. Whyte, E.M., Smyth, J.M., Scherf, K.S.: Designing serious game interventions for individuals with Autism. J. Autism Dev. Disord. 45(12), 3820–3831 (2015)
15. Harris, S.L.: Teaching language to nonverbal children-with emphasis on problems of generalization. Psychol. Bull. 82(4), 565 (1975)

16. Gillespie-Lynch, K., Brooks, P., Shane-Simpson, C., Gaggi, N.L., Sturm, D., Ploog, B.O.: Selecting computer-mediated interventions to support the social and emotional development of individuals with autism spectrum disorder. In: Silton, N. (ed.) Recent Advances in Assistive Technologies to Support Children with Developmental Disorders (2016)

17. Golan, O., Baron-Cohen, S.: Systemizing empathy: teaching adults with Asperger syndrome or high-functioning autism to recognize complex emotions using interactive multimedia. Dev. Psychopathol. **18**(02), 591–617 (2006)

18. Hopkins, I.M., Gower, M.W., Perez, T.A., Smith, D.S., Amthor, F.R., Wimsatt, F.C., Biasini, F.J.: Avatar assistant: improving social skills in students with an ASD through a computer-based intervention. J. Autism Dev. Disord. **41**(11), 1543–1555 (2011)

19. Benton, L., Johnson, H., Ashwin, E., Brosnan, M., Grawemeyer, B.: Developing IDEAS: supporting children with autism within a participatory design team. In: Proceedings of the SIGCHI Conference on Human Factors in Computing Systems, pp. 2599–2608. ACM, May 2012

20. Parsons, S., Cobb, S.: Reflections on the role of the 'users': challenges in a multi-disciplinary context of learner-centred design for children on the autism spectrum. Int. J. Res. Method Educ. **37**(4), 421–441 (2014)

21. Jivraj, J., Sacrey, L.A., Newton, A., Nicholas, D., Zwaigenbaum, L.: Assessing the influence of researcher–partner involvement on the process and outcomes of participatory research in autism spectrum disorder and neurodevelopmental disorders: a scoping review. Autism **18**(7), 782–793 (2014)

22. Nicolaidis, C., Raymaker, D., McDonald, K., Dern, S., Ashkenazy, E., Boisclair, C., Baggs, A.: Collaboration strategies in nontraditional community-based participatory research partnerships: lessons from an academic–community partnership with autistic self-advocates. Prog. Community Health Partnerships **5**(2), 143 (2011)

23. Brosnan, M., Parsons, S., Good, J., Yuill, N.: How can participatory design inform the design and development of innovative technologies for autistic communities? J. Assistive Technol. **10**(2), 115–120 (2016)

24. Benton, L., Johnson, H., Brosnan, M., Ashwin, E., Grawemeyer, B.: IDEAS: an interface design experience for the autistic spectrum. In: Extended Abstracts CHI 2011. ACM (2011)

25. Benton, L., Vasalou, A., Khaled, R., Johnson, H., Gooch, D.: Diversity for design: a framework for involving neurodiverse children in the technology design process. In: Proceedings of the 32nd Annual ACM Conference on Human Factors in Computing Systems, pp. 3747–3756. ACM, April 2014

26. Bossavit, B., Parsons, S.: Designing an educational game for and with teenagers with high functioning autism. In: Proceedings of the 14th Participatory Design Conference: Full papers - Volume 1 (PDC 2016), vol. 1. ACM, New York, NY, USA, pp. 11–20 (2016). doi:http://dx.doi.org/10.1145/2940299.2940313

27. Cobb, S., Beardon, L., Eastgate, R., Glover, T., Kerr, S., Neale, H., Reynard, G.: Applied virtual environments to support learning of social interaction skills in users with Asperger's Syndrome. Digital Creativity **13**(1), 11–22 (2002)

28. Frauenberger, C., Good, J., Alcorn, A., Pain, H.: Conversing through and about technologies: Design critique as an opportunity to engage children with autism and broaden research (er) perspectives. Int. J. Child-Comput. Interact. **1**(2), 38–49 (2013)

29. Keay-Bright, W.: The reactive colours project: demonstrating participatory and collaborative design methods for the creation of software for autistic children (2007)

30. Millen, L., Cobb, S., Patel, H.: A method for involving children with autism in design. In: Proceedings of the 10th International Conference on Interaction Design and Children, pp. 185–188. ACM, June 2011

31. Neale, H.: Using virtual reality to teach social skills to people with Asperger's syndrome: explaining virtual reality and user-centred methodology. In: Proceedings of the 12th Annual Durham International Conference on Autism, April 2001
32. Piper, A.M., O'Brien, E., Morris, M.R., Winograd, T.: SIDES: a cooperative tabletop computer game for social skills development. In: Proceedings of the 2006 20th Anniversary Conference on Computer Supported Cooperative Work, pp. 1–10. ACM, November 2006
33. Mesibov, G.B., Shea, V.: The TEACCH program in the era of evidence-based practice. J. Autism Dev. Disord. **40**(5), 570–579 (2010)
34. Capps, L., Yirmiya, N., Sigman, M.: Understanding of simple and complex emotions in non-retarded children with Autism. J. Child Psychol. Psychiatry **33**(7), 1169–1182 (1992)
35. Levinson, L.J., Reid, G.: The effects of exercise intensity on the stereotypic behaviours of individuals with autism. McGill University (1992)
36. Grelotti, D.J., Klin, A.J., Gauthier, I., Skudlarski, P., Cohen, D.J., Gore, J.C., Schultz, R.T.: fMRI activation of the fusiform gyrus and amygdala to cartoon characters but not to faces in a boy with autism. Neuropsychologia **43**(3), 373–385 (2005)
37. Gee, J.P.: Learning by design: games as learning machines. Interact. Educ. Multimedia **8**, 15–23 (2010)
38. Holt, S., Yuill, N.: Facilitating other-awareness in low-functioning children with autism and typically-developing preschoolers using dual-control technology. J. Autism Dev. Disord. **44**(1), 236–248 (2014)
39. Jasmin, E., Couture, M., McKinley, P., Reid, G., Fombonne, E., Gisel, E.: Sensori-motor and daily living skills of preschool children with autism spectrum disorders. J. Autism Dev. Disord. **39**(2), 231–241 (2009)
40. Must, A., Phillips, S.M., Curtin, C., Anderson, S.E., Maslin, M., Lividini, K., Bandini, L.G.: Comparison of sedentary behaviors between children with autism spectrum disorders and typically developing children. Autism **18**(4), 376–384 (2013). doi:10.1177/1362361313479039
41. Holt, S., Yuill, N.: Tablets for two: how dual tablets can facilitate other-awareness and communication in learning disabled children with autism. Int. J. Child-Comput. Interact. (2016)
42. Fine, M., Torre, M.E., Burns, A., Payne, Y.A.: Youth research/participatory methods for reform. In: Thiessen, D., Cook-Sather, A. (eds.) International Handbook of Student Experience in Elementary and Secondary School, pp. 805–828. Springer, Dordrecht (2007)
43. Schilbach, L., Timmermans, B., Reddy, V., Costall, A., Bente, G., Schlicht, T., Vogeley, K.: Toward a second-person neuroscience. Behav. Brain Sci. **36**(04), 393–414 (2013)
44. Tsang, T., Gillespie-Lynch, K., Hutman, T.: Theory of mind indexes the broader autism phenotype in siblings of children with autism at school age. Autism Res. Treat. (2016)
45. Jones, R.S., Huws, J.C., Beck, G.: 'I'm not the only person out there': insider and outsider understandings of autism. Int. J. Dev. Disabil. **59**(2), 134–144 (2013)

Engagement in a Virtual Reality Game with Gesture Hand Interface. An Empirical Evaluation of User Engagement Scale (UES)

Irma C. Landa-Avila[✉] and Maria-Luisa Cruz[✉]

Facultad de Ingeniería, Universidad Panamericana campus Guadalajara,
Prolongación Calzada Circunvalación Poniente 49,
45010 Zapopan, Jalisco, Mexico
{ilanda,mlcruz}@up.edu.mx

Abstract. The combination of virtual environments and gesture control inter-face has increased in the past years. It is believed that these technologies could increase user engagement and the user experience. However, there is still no standard scale to measure user engagement in those systems. The User Engagement Scale UES, proposed by O'Brien is a multidimensional scale for engagement measurement. It had been tested in different conditions and systems, such as web pages and social networks, keeping consistency in its result. We apply the UES to a virtual reality game with gesture hand control, to evaluate its viability in this kind of system. A sample of 164 individuals, who attended a huge technology trend and information event, completed a questionnaire after playing the game. The game includes puzzle solving using hand gesture inter-face. The questionnaire was adapted from the original proposed by O'Brien, to fit the videogame application. The UES scale is composed of six aspects or subscales: Perceived Usability (PU), Aesthetics (AE), Novelty (NO), Felt Involvement (FI), Focused Attention (FA), and Endurability (EN). The analysis results indicated that the scale had good reliability for all the aspects or sub-scales included. As a result of applying the principal component analysis, we found that the FA and AE components retained all its items. Meanwhile, the PU sub-scale is divided into three different components, and the NO, FI and EN subscales are combined in a new component. We establish a discussion of the characteristics and usability of virtual reality systems and gesture hand control that could cause these variations in the UES components. Also, we discuss the context as a potential key factor to influence engagement and user experience.

Keywords: User engagement · User Engagement Scale · Virtual Reality · User Experience

1 Introduction

Human Computer Interaction (HCI) is evolving continuously. Nowadays the "third wave" of HCI studies is dominated by user experience (UX), virtual environments and brain-machine or gesture-control interaction [4] UX is concerned with how people interact with technologies and how these interactions are shaped by human values, contextual constraints, and society.

© Springer International Publishing AG 2017
A. Marcus and W. Wang (Eds.): DUXU 2017, Part II, LNCS 10289, pp. 414–427, 2017.
DOI: 10.1007/978-3-319-58637-3_33

New technologies and interactions are demanding new methods to be really understood and holistically evaluated. Authors like Sweetser and Wyeth [21] claimed that understanding game usability had priority over understanding game enjoyment, but nowadays the study of just the usability dimension it would leave out of the analysis important factors. A discipline like UX field has offered a series of methods and tools; there are still some other aspects of the interaction that need to be explored. Among these is user engagement, which is focusing on offering a more robust measure of experience [14]. According to Lalmas, O'Brien and Yom-Tov [10] user engagement is the emotional, cognitive, and behavioural experience of a user with a technological resource that exists, at any point in time and over time and makes "the user wants to be there" (Jones n.d.).

User engagement cannot replace user experience or vice versa; thus there is no direct correlation between them, the aim of the interface design is to generate engaging experiences, although there is not a clear path to guide the design process. User engagement has been recognized as key factor to understand the user behaviour and overall efficacy in video games [6]; a positive video game experience provides an engaging and enjoyable time [5] that cannot be understood only in terms of usability analysis. There is a demand for deep understanding of its behaviour and of what makes a game enjoyable to the users [23], though users are demanding not only functional but also engaging applications.

Among the interfaces that are calling to generate a more engaging game experience are Virtual Reality (VR) and Head-Mounted Displays (HMD's) to generate a full immersion of the user [3, 23]; however, it is also important to consider the way that a user interacts with the VR game. One of the possibilities is through a Leap Motion Controller (LMC) that is designed to track hand movement inside a small workspace and is capable of fine movement tracking. It is showing a great performance in small virtual environments, compared to Kinect, which only provides the means to detect body gestures [7].

As result, virtual game designers are seeking to generate engaging experiences, but they lack precise knowledge about how to generate and evaluate it. Even if most of the options that are available at the moment are questionnaires, there are few of them that are focused on video games. One example is the Flow State Scale (FSS) that was originally developed for physical activities but is now being used in video games. This leaves the need to further explored auto report methods to have and clear and agile instrument that can be used in the context of a video game.

O'Brien and Toms [15] have been developing the user engagement scale (UES), an interesting tool to report user engagement. Their approach explains engagement as a combination of six factors: Focused Attention (FA), Perceived Usability (PU), Aesthetics (AE), Endurability (EN), Novelty (NO) and Felt Involvement (FI) [16]. Their scale consists of a 31 item self-reported questionnaire that offers an overall evaluation of the experience, but also of user perceptions of each attribute. Even though the scale has been validated, mostly in shopping, social networking and news websites [2, 13, 14, 16] there are few studies that validated it as a helpful instrument for video game development [23].

The aim of this study is to contribute to the current knowledge of user engagement in games in the context of virtual reality environment with and HMD-LMC interface, by focusing on validating the UES for this kind of system.

2 Methodology

2.1 Participants

The simple consisted of 164 participants who attended the event "Jalisco Campus Party 2016", an international event of high technology celebrated in Guadalajara, Mexico from June 29 to July 3, that brought together young talent of the technological and entrepreneurial community. The survey was applied to some attendants to the Universidad Panamericana stand who chose to play the game. The age range of the participants was between 16 to 35 years old (Median of 21.7 years old, Standard Deviation of 4.9). The sample was composed of 36 women and 124 men.

None of the participants had played the game before; also, it is important to mention that, as the video game is controlled by hand gesture interface (LMC), which is still little used in the Mexican technological community, most of the participants in this study did not have a previous experience with this controller.

2.2 Stimuli: Virtual Reality Game

The participants played a logic/ability virtual reality game named Fixer [19].

Fig. 1. Screen shot of Fixer game, developed by UP Media Lab.

The game included a virtual reality environment with a hand controlled interface. The goal of the game is to assemble two different puzzles into one (Fig. 1). Each puzzle was composed of small cubes arranged to form the half of a bigger cube. Only four hand movements are recognized, vertical and horizontal cube rotations and push and pull actions over the cubes. The rotation of the cube is achieved moving both hands in the opposite direction while a pinching gesture, with the thumb and index finger, is done. The pull and push moves are accomplished making a natural movement of pushing and pulling the cube with the extended hand. The gamers had one minute to play the game, with an unlimited number of attempts. If the two puzzle halves were not correctly aligned, the assembly failed and the user needed to separate the pieces and start again; after the pieces were correctly joined, a new and more complex level appeared automatically. They were 16 different levels in the first version of the game.

2.3 Hardware

The virtual reality environment consisted of an Head-Mounted Display, of the brand Oculus Rift 2. The hand controller interface was implemented with a Leap Motion Controller. This device employs two infrared cameras and three infrared emitters; according to the manufacturer, it has a 100o of field of view and a refresh rate of 75 Hz [20]. Both devices were connected through USB ports into a desktop computer. The gamer takes a seat in front of the computer; the depth distance from camera to the user was calibrated as a new gamer took place in front of the computer.

2.4 User Engagement Scale

The User Engagement Scale was measured by a 7-point Likert scale. The scale was based on the Wiebe, Lamb, Hardy and Sharek adaptation [22] that was modified to fit the video game context. From that base, the scale was translated into Spanish and presented on paper.

Table 1 shows the original scale, its adaptation to game experience and the Spanish version used in this study. Also, the engagement factors that are related to each item are included. Each item was named with the corresponding letter to the subscale and a consecutive number. Some of the items were originally formulated in negative mode, but they were inverted before the analysis; these cases are marked with a z in the name.

2.5 Test Procedure

Participants were invited to play the game. Before the HMD was placed, a small introduction about the game was given verbally. At the beginning of the game, a screen with instructions was presented for a couple of seconds, during the game, no help was provided, but in the game screen, a timer and the level indicator were displayed above the puzzle cube.

According to flow studies [10], it is suggested to administer the questionnaire at the end of the game. Otherwise, it could result in negative ratings for user engagement due to the interruption rather than the actual experience. So, when the game was over, the participants left the seat and answered orally some demographic queries. As people tend to give more positive answers if the questionnaire is completed through an electronic device [9], the use of a paper-based instrument for this study was selected. The participants were required to respond each of the UES items marking the number on the scale; there were not time limit, and they could ask anything related to the scale, but no description of the item was given.

Table 1. User Engagement Scale adaptation.

Items		Factor
1	I lost myself in this shopping experience I lost myself in this game experience Me perdí a mi mismo en esta experiencia del juego	FA1
2	I was so involved in my shopping task that I lost track of time I was so involved in the activity of the game that I lost consciousness of time Estaba tan involucrado en la actividad del juego que perdí la conciencia del tiempo	FA2
3	I blocked out things around me when I was shopping on this website I blocked things around me when I was playing the game in the exhibition stand Bloqueé las cosas alrededor de mi cuando estaba jugando el juego en el stand	FA3
4	When I was shopping, I lost track of the world around me When I was playing, I lost track of the world around me Cuando estaba jugando, perdí sentido del mundo alrededor de mí	FA4
5	The time I spent shopping just slipped away The time I spent playing the game just slipped away El tiempo que pase jugando el juego pasó volando	FA5
6	I was absorbed in my shopping task I was absorbed in the activity of the game Estaba absorto en la actividad del juego	FA6
7	During this shopping experience I let myself go During this gaming experience I let myself go Durante esta experiencia de juego simplemente me deje llevar	FA7
8	I felt frustrated while visiting this shopping website I felt frustrated while I was playing this game Me sentí frustrado mientras estaba jugando este juego	PU1z
9	I found this shopping website confusing to use I found the game confusing to use Encontré el juego confuso de usar	PU2z
10	I felt annoyed while visiting this shopping website I felt annoyed while I was playing Me sentí desorientado mientras estaba jugando	PU3z
11	I felt discouraged while shopping on this website I felt discouraged while I was playing Me sentí desanimado mientras estaba jugando	PU4z
12	Using this shopping website was mentally taxing Using the game is mentally taxing Usar el juego es mentalmente agotador	PU5z
13	This shopping experience was demanding The game experience was demanding La experiencia del juego fue demandante	PU6z
14	I felt in control of my shopping experience I felt in control of the experience Me sentí en control de la experiencia	PU7

(continued)

Table 1. (*continued*)

Items		Factor
15	I could not do some of the things I needed to do on this shopping website I could not do some of the things that need to be done in the game No pude hacer algunas de las cosas que se necesitan hacer en el juego	PU8z
16	Shopping on this website was worthwhile Playing this game at the Campus Party was worth it Jugar este juego en el campus party valió la pena	EN1
17	I consider my shopping experience a success I consider my experience a success Considero mi experiencia un éxito	EN2
18	This shopping experience did not work out the way I had planned This experience did not work out the way I had thought Esta experiencia no funcionó de la forma en que pensaba	EN3z
19	My shopping experience was rewarding My experience of the game was rewarding Mi experiencia del juego fue gratificante	EN4
20	I would recommend shopping on this website to my friends and family I could recommend playing this game to my friends and family Podría recomendar jugar este juego a mis amigos y familiares	EN5
21	I continued to shop on this website out of curiosity I could continue to play this game out of curiosity Podría seguir jugando este juego por curiosidad	NO1
22	The content of the shopping website incited my curiosity The content of the game incited my curiosity El contenido del juego incito mi curiosidad	NO2
23	I felt interested in my shopping task I felt interested in the gaming experience Me sentí interesado en la experiencia del juego	NO3
24	I was really drawn into my shopping task It was really drawn is the experience of the game Estaba realmente sumergido es la experiencia del juego	FI1
25	I felt involved in this shopping task I felt involved in this activity Me sentí involucrado en esta actividad	FI2
26	This shopping experience was fun The experience of the game was fun La experiencia del juego fue divertida	FI3
27	This shopping website is attractive The game was attractive El juego fue atractivo	AE1
28	This shopping website was aesthetically appealing The game was aesthetically stimulating El juego fue estéticamente estimulante	AE2
29	I liked the graphics and images used on this shopping website I liked the graphics and images used in the game	AE3

(*continued*)

Table 1. (*continued*)

Items		Factor
	Me gustaron las gráficas e imágenes usadas en el juego	
30	This shopping website appealed to my visual senses	AE4
	The game appealed to my visual senses	
	El juego estímulo mi sentido visual	
31	The screen layout of this shopping website was visually pleasing	AE5
	The design of the game screen was visually pleasing	
	El diseño de la pantalla del juego fue placentera visualmente	

At the end of the event, the surveys were captured in a database, and the results were analyzed through the SPSS software.

2.6   Data Analysis

The data were analyzed to determine if the UES could be used to measure engagement in a virtual reality video game with an LMC interface. The reliability analysis was done following the steps proposed by [16], which include the examination of the reliability of the subscales, using the guidelines of DeVellis [8] and the application of the factor analysis of the data.

3   Results

3.1   Reliability Analysis

Table 2 presents the descriptive statistics and correlations between the subscales, as they were defined in O'Brien and Toms [16]. The reliability was analyzed using Cronbach's alpha coefficient and it is included in Table 2. According to DeVellis guidelines [8] a Cronbach's alpha coefficient between 0.7 and 0.8 is respectable and between 0.8 and 0.9 is very good.

Table 2. General statistics of the sample

	N	M	SD	α	NO	FA	AE	FI	EN	PU
Novelty (NO)	164	6,01	1,24	0,807	–					
Focused Attention (FA)	164	5,31	1,33	0,855	0,471	–				
Aesthetic Appeal (AE)	164	5,39	1,36	0,865	0,667	0,485	–			
Felt Involvement (FI)	164	5,8	1,19	0,700	0,695	0,610	0,598	–		
Endurability (EN)	164	5,61	1,12	0,742	0,716	0,446	0,558	0,718	–	
Perceived Usability (PU)	164	4,69	1,23	0,787	0,271	0,098	0,219	0,344	0,528	–

Table 2 also shows the correlation between the subscales. The EN, NO and FI subscales presented the higher values of correlations over 0.7, so it is suspected that there is some overlapping among these subscales in the factor analysis. Another six moderate correlations were detected with a range of values between 0.4 and 0.6. The PU subscale was the one that exhibited the lowest correlations with the others subscales.

3.2   Factor Analysis

As aforementioned, the UES originally is divided into six subscales, Novelty, Focus Attention, Aesthetics, Felt Involvement, Endurability, and Perceived Usability.

As the objective of this study was to validate the UES to be applied in video games with an HMD-LMC interface, a factor analysis was applied to determine if the subscales are still differentiable. Oblique rotation with a Direct Oblimin was selected in SPSS [18], thus in these studies of generalizability, oblique rotations are preferred. In the oblique rotations, the factors were not considered orthogonals, so the scales were not completely independent between them. All the subscales were oriented to measure the engagement variable, so they must present some correlation between them.

The resulting component matrix of the factor analysis is presented in Table 3. The analysis converged after 25 iterations, and six factors were detected. The items of the subscales NO and FI were distributed in different factors.

In the case of NO, two items (NO1 and NO3) were loaded in factor 1 together with the EN and FI items. While the last item (NO2) was loaded on factor 5 with the AE items. The items FI2 and FI3 were loaded on factor 1 with EN and FI items, while FI1 was loaded on factor 3 with FA items. Meanwhile, the items of the subscale PU were loaded in factors 2, 4 and 6. The distribution of the PU subscale items will be analyzed with more detail in the discussion section.

O'Brien and Toms [18] presented a comparative table between different studies. In which, the subscales of AE, FA and PUs presented a stable behaviour across five studies. Meanwhile, in just three studies the FI, EN, and NO subscales were loaded in the same factor; in addition, in the others studies, these subscales kept their structure and their items were loaded on different factors. The merge of three subscale items was also present in this study. Table 4 shows the distributions of the original items, proposed by O'Brien and Toms [16], the rearrangement by other three different studies and the result in this study. All these studies included the merging of EN, FI and NO items in one factor.

Five principal factor groups were detected in this study. Also, the NO2 item was loaded with the AE subscale but in the others, it was associated with the factor that merged FI, EN and NO. However, this item also presented a good value to associate it to the merged factor (Table 3). Three studies eliminated three items from the total scale, reducing the number items from 31 to 28. Some of the eliminated items were

Table 3. Factor analysis of the data

Variable	1	2	3	4	5	6
EN1	**0,570**	0,125	0,071	−0,261	0,289	0,050
EN2	**0,653**	−0,059	0,055	0,437	−0,088	0,108
EN4	**0,772**	0,035	0,056	0,100	0,096	0,003
EN5	**0,433**	0,074	−0,044	−0,088	0,493	0,044
FI2	**0,642**	0,065	0,083	−0,029	0,209	0,018
FI3	**0,833**	0,019	−0,010	0,087	0,033	−0,090
NO1	**0,426**	0,318	0,020	−0,229	0,326	−0,035
NO3	**0,741**	−0,023	0,088	−0,097	0,177	0,026
EN3z	−0,006	**0,514**	0,017	0,427	0,034	−0,041
PU1z	0,086	**0,687**	−0,069	0,223	0,089	0,067
PU3z	0,046	**0,866**	−0,004	−0,083	−0,055	−0,066
PU4z	0,141	**0,674**	0,028	−0,034	−0,102	−0,141
PU5z	−0,205	**0,819**	−0,036	0,123	0,109	0,081
FA1	0,015	−0,061	**0,841**	0,108	−0,030	0,015
FA2	0,161	0,096	**0,744**	−0,133	−0,024	0,170
FA3	0,126	−0,115	**0,650**	0,076	0,141	−0,346
FA4	−0,233	−0,124	**0,759**	0,167	0,117	−0,237
FA5	0,114	0,309	**0,420**	−0,297	0,192	0,063
FA6	−0,004	−0,014	**0,735**	−0,056	0,034	0,121
FA7	0,360	0,171	**0,621**	−0,195	−0,129	0,174
FI1	0,109	0,218	**0,486**	−0,040	0,102	0,417
PU2z	0,082	0,339	−0,099	**0,628**	0,131	0,068
PU8z	0,050	0,138	0,101	**0,692**	−0,013	0,058
AE1	0,152	0,050	0,134	−0,059	**0,676**	0,086
AE2	−0,063	0,154	0,054	0,062	**0,797**	0,142
AE3	0,026	0,042	−0,097	−0,131	**0,666**	−0,137
AE4	0,126	−0,150	0,061	0,118	**0,750**	−0,036
AE5	0,035	−0,103	0,211	0,258	**0,768**	0,066
NO2	0,395	−0,038	−0,002	−0,147	**0,440**	0,225
PU6z	0,185	0,293	−0,027	0,400	−0,133	**−0,531**
PU7	0,085	−0,073	−0,026	0,355	0,005	**0,720**

loaded in the merged factor in our analysis. In the four studies, the item EN3z is load in the same factor that the PU subscale. In all studies, except the one of the Wiki-Search, the FI1 item is loaded with the FA subscale.

Table 5 shows the groups generated according through the factor analysis. The GF6 was an alternative proposal that was obtained after different trials.

Table 4. Across studies comparison

Items	Video Games HMD-LMC	Video Games [22]	WikiSearch [13]	Shopping [12]
EN1	GF1	GF1	GF1	GF1
EN2	GF1	—	GF1	GF1
EN4	GF1	GF1	GF1	GF1
EN5	GF1	GF1	GF1	GF1
FI2	GF1	—	GF1	GF1
FI3	GF1	GF1	GF1	GF1
NO1	GF1	GF1	—	—
NO3	GF1	GF1	GF1	GF1
EN3z	GF2	GF2	GF2	GF2
PU1z	GF2	GF2	GF2	—
PU3z	GF2	GF2	GF2	GF2
PU4z	GF2	GF2	GF2	GF2
PU5z	GF2	GF2	GF2	GF2
FA1	GF3	GF3	GF3	—
FA2	GF3	GF3	GF3	GF3
FA3	GF3	GF3	GF3	—
FA4	GF3	GF3	—	GF3
FA5	GF3	GF3	GF3	GF3
FA6	GF3	GF3	GF3	GF3
FA7	GF3	GF3	—	GF3
FI1	GF3	GF3	GF1	GF3
AE1	GF4	GF4	GF4	GF4
AE2	GF4	GF4	GF4	GF4
AE3	GF4	GF4	GF4	GF4
AE4	GF4	GF4	GF4	GF4
AE5	GF4	GF4	GF4	GF4
NO2	GF4	GF1	GF1	—
PU2z	GF5	GF2	GF2	GF2
PU8z	GF5	GF2	GF2	GF2
PU6z	GF5	GF2	GF2	GF2
PU7	GF5	—	GF2	GF1
	31	**28**	**28**	**28**

Table 5. Factors detected by FA

New factors	O'Brien subscales [18]	Media	SD	α
Factor analysis results				
GF1	EN(1,2,4,5), NO(1,3), FI(2,3)	5,9	0,500	0,915
GF3	FA(1,2,3,4,5,6,7), FI1	5,3	0,480	0,870
GF4	AE(1,2,3,4,5), NO2	5,4	0,288	0,875
GF2	PU (1z,3z,4z,5z), EN3z	5,1	0,493	0,818
GF5	PU (2z,6z,7,8z)	4,1	0,381	0,544
Alternative proposal				
GF6	PU(1z,2z,3z,4z,5z,6z,7,8z),EN3z	4,6	0,650	0,808

4 Discussion

4.1 General UES Performance

During the recollection of the data of this study, the UES had an overall acceptance of the people who answered the questionnaire. However, there were some complaints about the length of the test, and a couple of items were misunderstood. The last point should be seriously taken into consideration, insomuch as the communication and consistency in defining constructs affect measurement [9]. Other studies that have discussed the duration of the test [2, 17, 18] have determined that it could be reduced to 19 items for the case of information searching [17] or even to 10 items, as it was used for Levesque et al. [11] when a haptic interface was tested. The high correlation between the items of FA and AE suggest that it is possible to reduce the items in these factors without affecting the final measurement.

4.2 Reliability Analysis

The reliability of the scale was examined using Cronbach's alpha coefficient, which measures internal consistency for each subscale. The overall reliability of the scale was 0.860. All the factors presented an acceptable grade of reliability with Cronbach's Alpha coefficient over 0.7. These values suggest that the results of the UES could be used in an initial test of engagement in video games with HMD and LMC with good confidence.

4.3 Factor Analysis

The factor analysis generates a different construct scale, which is an important issue to discuss. The factor analysis generated six factors that were different from the original scale [16] A high similitude in the scale construction was observed with the Wiebe study [22], while was divided into three factors in this study according to the factor analysis. The principal difference between both studies was the interfaces used, while the video-game Block Walk used a keyboard controller, Fixer used LMC. In general, there is a high consistence on the EN, FI and NO items that were loaded in the same factor across all the studies. These items were pick up from EN (1,2,4,5), NO (1,3) and FI (2,3). The result present in the factor analysis agrees with [13]. They present other two cases of studies where the merge of EN, NO and FI subscales are present, and they suggest to redefine the UE Scale as a four-factor experimental scale with FA, AE, PUs, and EN/FI/NO subscales.

Another difference is related to the behavior of Perceived Usability. All the studied consulted grouped together all the PU items, but in this case, the result was divided into three groups. In the first one, were PU1, PU3, PU4 and PU5 (coefficient of 0.818), in the second one were PU2 and PU8 and finally, PU6 and PU7 were together. After other re accommodations trials, two possibilities were found, the first one was to keep the first group and join the last two groups into one with a coefficient Alfa of 0.544. The second option was to put together all the PU factors as other previous studies have done, but the coefficient was reduced to 0.808 (Table 5). The first option was considered the best as long as the coefficient was higher that in the first option.

The four items that were put together in this new group were related with confusing to use (PU2), demanding (PU6), felt in control (PU7) and could not do things (PU8). These items could be related to a particular aspect of the usability. The general definition (ISO/IEC 9126) points that the usability is the capacity of an interfaced to be understood, learned, used and generated attraction. According to this, this group seems to be related with the understood and used of the game. On the contrary, the remaining group has items related to felt frustration (PU1), felt annoyed (PU3), felt discourage (PU4) and mentally taxing (PU5) that seems to have relation with the satisfaction/attraction dimension of the usability.

This difference was not previously showed in any other study. Thus there must be a particular factor causing this. There are two main possibilities, the first one is the HMD-LMC interface [1], and the other one is the duration of the stimuli. No other study has proved the UES in virtual reality environments, which can be a significative difference among the other studies. Even if the instrument had demonstrated to be reliable for this context, further research must be developed to identify which factors of the scale are more related to the virtual reality stimuli. Also, the time of this test was significantly shorter than in other studies, and normally this affects the efficiency dimension of the usability, so is also suggest making future research with different time of the experience.

5   Conclusion

The reliability analysis showed a respectable and very good alpha coefficient for all the subscales; this value shows that the scale could be applied in this way to video games with virtual reality environment and hand controlled interfaces.

After the factor analysis, the items were rearranged in five factors, Table 5. The reliability analysis for each new factor was calculated and the Cronbach's alpha coefficient increased for the first four factors to values over 0.8 and lowering the acceptable value of 0.6 for the five factors. The factor that merges the EN/NO/FI subscales increased from an average of 0,747 to a value of 0.915, the second factor related to PUs went from 0,787 to 0.818, the third factor related to FA items went from

0.855 to 0,870, and the four factor related to AE went from 0,865 to 0.875. The items related to the five factor are also related with the PUs subscale as the factor two, but its behavior is different.

The factor arrangement calculated in the factor analysis is consistent with the scale structure present by Wiebe [22] when the UE scale was also applied in a video-game context. This similitude in the structure reinforces the scale validity in the video-game context.

The results suggest that the HMD-LMC and the time of the stimuli could be the cause for the arrangement of the factors (Perceived Usability), but there is needed further analysis to identify the particular elements that are causing that phenomenon.

Finally, the results for the perceived usability factor suggest that could be divided into two sub dimensions, one related to the direct use of the game, while the other will be associated with emotional or satisfaction aspects. Also, this last one group (PU1z, PU3z, PU4z, and PU5z,) seem to present a redundancy between the items, so it could be probable removed one of them to reduce the overall number questions.

This study found that the UES could generate confident results in general about the engagement in video games with an HMD-LMC interface. However, it is desirable to modify some items of the UES to include new elements present in this kind of systems. Also, it is necessary to carry out more studies about how new technologies such as HMD and LMC could influence in the engagement of video games and general software.

Acknowledgements. The authors want to thank the developers of the Fixer virtual reality game, Arturo Jafet Rodríguez M.Sc., and Enrique Alberto Rosales M.Sc., from UP-Medialab, for providing access to the game. Also, we thank Allen Galaviz Gerardo for the help of database capturing.

References

1. Bachmann, D., Weichert, F., Rinkenauer, G.: Evaluation of the leap motion controller as a new contact-free pointing device. Sensors (Basel, Switzerland) **15**(1), 214–233 (2015). doi:10.3390/s150100214
2. Banhawi, F., Ali, N.M.: Measuring user engagement attributes in a social networking application. In: 2011 International Conference on Semantic Technology and Information Retrieval, STAIR 2011, pp. 297–301 (2011). doi:10.1109/STAIR.2011.5995805
3. Beattie, N., Horan, B., McKenzie, S.: Taking the LEAP with the Oculus HMD and CAD - plucking at thin air? Procedia Technol. **20**(1), 149–154 (2015)
4. Bodker, S.: Second wave hci meets third wave challenges. In: NordCHI 2006 Extended Abstracts on Human Factors in Computing Systems, NrodiCHI 2006, pp. 1– 8. ACM (2006). doi:10.1145/1182475.1182476.1
5. Boyle, E.A., Connolly, T.M., Hainey, T., Boyle, J.M.: Engagement in digital entertainment games: a systematic review. Comput. Hum. Behav. **28**(1), 771–780 (2012)
6. Boyle, E., Connolly, T.M., Hainey, T.: The role of psychology in understanding the impact of computer games. Entertain. Comput. **2**(2), 69–74 (2011). doi:10.1016/j.entcom.2010.12.002

7. Ebert, L.C., Flach, P.M., Thali, M.J., Ross, S.: Out of touch – a plugin for controlling OsiriX with gestures using the leap controller. J. Forensic Radiol. Imaging **2**, 126–128 (2014)
8. DeVellis, R.: Scale Development, Theory and Applications, p. 121. Sage Publications, Chapel Hill (1991)
9. Kelly, D., Harper, D.J., Landau, B.: Questionnaire mode effects in interactive information retrieval experiments. Inf. Process. Manage. **44**(1), 122–141 (2008)
10. Lalmas, M., O'Brien, H., Yom-Tov, E.: Measuring User Engagement. Morgan & Claypool Publishers, San Rafael (2015)
11. Levesque, V., Oram, L., MacLean, K., Cockburn, A., Marchuk, D.J., Colgate, J.E., Peshkin, M.: Frictional widgets: Enhancing touch interfaces with programmable friction. In: Proceedings of the SIGCHI Conference on Human Factors in Computing, pp. 1153–1158 (2011)
12. O'Brien, H.L.: The influence of hedonic and utilitarian motivations on user engagement: the case of online shopping experiences. Interact. Comput. **22**(1), 344–352 (2010)
13. O'Brien, H.L., Cairns, P.: An empirical evaluation of the User Engagement Scale (UES) in online news environments. Inf. Process. Manage. **51**(1), 413–427 (2015)
14. O'Brien, H.L., Lebow, M.: Mixed-methods approach to measuring user experience in online news interactions. J. Am. Soc. Inform. Sci. Technol. **64**(8), 1543–1556 (2013). doi:10.1002/asi.22871.20,84
15. O'Brien, H.L., Toms, E.G.: What is user engagement? A conceptual framework for defining user engagement with techonology. J. Am. Soc. Inform. Sci. Technol. **59**(6), 938–955 (2008)
16. O'Brien, H.L., Toms, E.G.: The development and evaluation of a survey to measure user engagement. J. Am. Soc. Inform. Sci. Technol. **61**(1), 50–69 (2010)
17. O'Brien, H.L., Toms, E.G.: Measuring interactive information retrieval: the case of user engagement scale. In: Proceedings of the 2010 Conference of Information Interaction in Context, pp. 335–340 (2010b)
18. O'Brien, H.L., Toms, E.G.: Examining the generalizability of the User Engagement Scale (UES) in exploratory search. Inf. Process. Manage. **49**(1), 1092–1107 (2013)
19. UP-Media Lab: FIXER (Version 1.0), Zapopan, Jalisco, Mexico (2016)
20. Riftinfo: Oculus Rift Specs DK1 vs DK2 comparison (2016). http://riftinfo.com/oculus-rift-specs-dk1-vs-dk2-comparison. Accessed 8 Feb 2017
21. Sweetser, P., Wyeth, P.: GameFlow: a model for evaluationg player enjoyment games. Comput. Entertain. **3**(3), 1–24 (2005)
22. Wiebe, E.N., Lamb, A., Hardy, M., Sharek, D.: Measuring engagement in video game-based environments: investigation of the user engagement scale. Comput. Hum. Behav. **32**(1), 123–132 (2015)
23. Yannakis, G.N., Hallam, J.: Towards optimizing entertainment in computer games. Appl. Artif. Intell. **21**, 933–971 (2007)

Effect of Playing Factors and Playing History on Game Flow and Companionship Levels for Online Pets

Elena Carolina Li[1(✉)] and Ding-Bang Luh[2]

[1] Department of Information Communication, Yuan Ze University, No. 135, Yuandong Rd.,
Zhongli Dist., Taoyuan 320, Taiwan (R.O.C.)
helena1799@gmail.com
[2] Department of Creative Product Design, Asia University, Taichung, Taiwan (R.O.C.)

Abstract. Electronic robots and virtual pets are used for enjoyment and even companionship. Studies have demonstrated that flow experience and companionship can affect whether players continue interacting with their robots and virtual pets. One study also revealed a positive relationship between flow and companionship regarding online pet games. However, the playing factors and elements of playing history (for example game types, playing time, flow factors, or companionship factors) that significantly increase players' flow and companionship levels are unclear. This study used a questionnaire survey to identify playing factors that may affect players' flow and companionship levels. This study utilized two scales (flow and companionship) to evaluate the flow and companionship states of online pet game players. A total of 204 valid questionnaires were collected. The results revealed that (1) time distortion and concentration were the crucial factors for increasing flow experience; (2) attractiveness was the crucial factor for increasing players' sense of companionship with their online pet; (3) spending more playing time with their online pets every day significantly increases players' levels of flow and companionship; and finally, (4) players who thought themselves to have high flow and companionship levels did actually have higher flow and companionship levels, which indicated that self-reporting of flow and companionship levels was a reliable method. These results can serve as a reference for online pet game designers and in relevant research fields.

Keywords: Companionship · Flow · Online game · Virtual pet

1 Introduction

Companion robots can play a crucial role in therapy and care, and one of their key characteristics is to give users a positive interaction experience (Larriba et al. 2016; Lorenz et al. 2016). Bernabei et al. (2013) reported that animal-assisted intervention has a positive effect on people with dementia and improves the quality of their social interactions. This applies to virtual pets as well as to physical companions and pet robots. Tsai and Kaufman (2014) demonstrated that taking care of a virtual pet can increase children's empathy and humane attitude scores. Children bond emotionally with their virtual pets and believe that virtual pets have their own particular personalities (Tsai and Kaufman 2014). Byrne et al. (2010) revealed that a mobile phone game can

© Springer International Publishing AG 2017
A. Marcus and W. Wang (Eds.): DUXU 2017, Part II, LNCS 10289, pp. 428–442, 2017.
DOI: 10.1007/978-3-319-58637-3_34

encourage children to practice healthy eating habits through allowing them to care for a virtual pet.

Whether concerning a companion robot or a virtual pet, the aforementioned studies all demonstrated that nonliving pets can have a positive effect on their owners. Crucial to these nonliving pets achieving their design purposes—such as providing therapy, care, health, education, company, or social interaction—is the establishment of a relationship between user and pet and the motivation of the user to continue using the product, software, or game.

Compared with embodied companion robots or electronic pets, virtual pets are cheaper and easier to purchase and thus have more users (Li and Luh 2011). Smart phone development has led to the release of various mobile phone games, of which virtual pet games such as My Boo, Bubbu Cat, and My Virtual Pet Shop are examples (App Store 2016).

Relevant studies have demonstrated that flow experience and companionship are crucial factors that encourage players to continue interacting with their virtual pets (Lawson and Chesney 2007a; Luh and Li 2015; Luh et al. in press). Most online pet games provide a virtual game environment or allow players to freely design their own game scenes. The environment settings in an online role-playing game can affect players' self-presentation, which in turn can enhance players' trust regarding the game content and game community (Park and Chung 2011). Therefore, players may use virtual pet games for self-presentation, and this may affect players' levels of motivation to continue playing the game.

Interaction frequency, game activity diversity, and relationship with game avatars are all factors that can affect the levels of intimacy between players and their game roles (Zhao et al. 2010). Thus, interaction frequency and the relationship with a virtual pet can both affect the intimacy between a player and that player's virtual pet. These discussions demonstrate that various factors affect the relationship between users and their virtual pets. However, what kind of playing experience enhances virtual pet players' flow and companionship levels has not been deeply studied.

We have previously conducted studies evaluating players' flow experiences with online pet games and their feelings of companionship with their online pets. Luh et al. (in press) confirmed that players experienced true flow while playing online pet games. Li and Luh (2015) also revealed that a high flow state enhances a player's feeling of companionship with the online pet, whereas a low flow state results in low level of companionship. Strong feelings of companionship cause a high flow experience, whereas weak feelings of companionship result in a low flow experience (Li and Luh 2015). Furthermore, Li and Luh (in press) determined that players had different flow and companionship levels depending on their motivations for playing the game.

All these previous studies revealed that players experience flow and companionship with their online pets, and that a positive relationship exists between flow and companionship levels. However, it is unknown what types of flow and companionship factors significantly enhance players' gaming experiences and whether game model, playing years, and playing time affect players' flow and companionship levels. If a factor is discovered to affect players' flow and companionship levels, it can be used to enhance game experience through appropriate game design.

We previously used flow and companionship scales to evaluate players' flow and companionship levels (Li and Luh 2015); however, there is no standard scale for such an evaluation for players' flow and companionship levels. Therefore, we asked players to evaluate their own flow and companionship levels (as high or low). Whether this classification method is a useful standard is further discussed. The players who considered themselves to experience a high level of flow and a strong feeling of companionship had significantly higher levels in all flow and companionship factors than those who classified themselves as in the low flow and companionship group. This classification method can thus be used to distinguish players' flow and companionship levels in relevant research fields.

This study explored these issues; the purposes were to determine (for online pet games) (1) whether game model affects players' flow and companionship levels; (2) whether playing history (for example, playing years and playing time) affects players' flow and companionship levels; (3) what kinds of flow and companionship factors affects players' flow and companionship levels; and (4) whether players who considered themselves to have high flow and companionship levels did in fact have a significantly higher level of flow experience and companionship. The results are expected to aid in the development of more types of robots, products, and applications that can improve people's quality of life: for example, a robot or application to help manage the health of patients or the elderly by interacting with companion objects; a learning tool or application for students and children through which they interact with virtual pets; or an artificial reality (AR) or virtual reality (VR) product that can help those in the medical field to understand or experience the therapeutic effect of virtual pets.

2   Literature Review

2.1   Online Pet

The National Taiwan University Hospital Yun-Lin Branch cooperated with a Taiwanese university to design an app called Pet Running (Li 2016). With this app, users can raise virtual pets through their own physical exercise: when a user engages in a physical activity, the virtual pet grows. This app demonstrates that virtual pets can not only serve as companions, but can also improve user health. Numerous studies have also revealed that interacting with a virtual pet can benefit users, having health, educational, or psychological effects (Lawson and Chesney 2007a, b; Luh et al. 2015).

This study classified online pet games into four types according to their game models. In some games — for example, in the games Pet Society and Meromero — players can own only one online pet at a time, whereas players can own more than one online pet in other games such as My Fishbowl. Similarly, some games (e.g., My Fishbowl) include only one species of pet, whereas players can raise numerous species and can own pets of more than one species in games such as Neopet and FarmVille. Table 1 summarizes the four types of online pet games and lists examples of each type. In this study, all four types of online pet games were used as samples.

Table 1. Types and examples of online pet games

Types of pet species	Number of pets that a player can raise in a game	
	One	More than one
One	• Dog Sweetie	• My fishbowl • Neko Atsume: Kitty Collector
More than one	• Pet Society • Meromero • Neopet	• FarmVille

2.2 Flow

Bressler and Bodzin (2013) reported that mobile AR science games can increase students' interest in science and help them acquire collaboration skills if the students achieve flow while playing the game. Su et al. (2016) discovered that human–computer interaction, social interactions, skills, and challenges positively affected flow experience and in addition were found to positively affect a player's loyalty to a mobile game. Chang (2013) reported that flow experiences increased users' intentions to continue playing social network games. These studies indicated that flow experiences can have positive effects for users and encourage them to continue using a system or game.

Flow is the state wherein a person is fully immersed in an activity and has an energized focus (Csikszentmihalyi 1975). Flow was previously described to involve three phases (Chen 2000): flow antecedents, flow experience, and flow consequences. In this flow model, the flow antecedents lead to a flow experience, and flow experience then causes various flow consequences.

Different activities require various flow antecedents and can produce different flow consequences (Chen 2000; Choi and Kim 2004; Csikszentmihalyi 1990; Finneran and Zhang 2005; Ghani 1995; Hoffman and Novak 1996; Novak et al. 2000; Skadberg and Kimmel 2004; Sweester and Wyeth 2005). Therefore, flow antecedents and consequences alone cannot be used to confirm whether players experience flow. Compared with its antecedents and consequences, the flow experience is a superior indicator of a player flow state.

In our previous studies (Li and Luh 2015, in press), we identified four main factors in the flow experience of online pet games: concentration, time distortion, loss of self-consciousness, and telepresence. In this study, these four factors were used to evaluate players' flow states.

2.3 Companionship

Real pets such as cats provide companionship that enriches the lives of their owners (Dabritz and Conrad 2010; Wood et al. 2015). Aguiar and Taylor (2015) reported that a virtual pet provides entertainment and companionship to preschool children. Companionship is a crucial relationship based on shared experience and is found in relationships with partners, family, friends, lovers, pets, or others. Companionship can take three relationship forms: one-to-one, one-to-many, and group relationships (Li 1999). In this study, we focused on the companionship game players felt from their online pets, which reflected a one-to-one or one-to-many (one owner to many online pets) relationship.

Zasloff (1996) developed the Comfort from Companion Animals Scale (CCAS) to measure the companionship between real pets and their owners. Libin and Libin (2003) developed the person–robot complex interactive scale (PRCIS) to assess the interaction between users and newly developed robots and to evaluate the advantages and disadvantages of robots. PRCIS can be used to determine the feasibility of robotic psychology and robotherapy. According to the CCAS, PRCIS, and relevant companionship theory, we developed the companionship scale for artificial pets (CSAP; Luh et al. 2015). This previous study proposed that users establish a companionship with electronic and virtual pets. The CSAP comprises 34 items and includes the three factors of enjoyment, satisfaction, and responsibility, which positively affect the development of companionship. In developing and applying the CSAP, our study demonstrated that some players do feel companionship with their online pets (Luh et al. 2015; Li and Luh 2015).

2.4 Previous Studies

In our previous study (Li and Luh 2015), scales were designed and used to identify the relationship between flow experience and companionship. One scale was used to evaluate participants' flow experiences, and the other was used to evaluate participants' feelings of companionship with their online pet(s).

The previous study used the narrative (survey) method, asking participants to recall their overall flow experiences for an online pet game. The flow experience scale included four factors: concentration, loss of self-consciousness, time distortion, and telepresence. There were 22 items in the flow experience scale, and these 22 flow items were again used to evaluate players' flow states in this study. To evaluate players' flow experience levels, we asked the players to classify their flow levels as high or low. The question asked was: "When I play this online pet game, [option 1] I feel that I am in flow with the game; [option 2] I feel that maintaining a flow in this game is hard (Li and Luh 2015)." We used these two questions again in the present study to determine players' flow levels and divide players into two groups (high and low flow level).

To evaluate companionship, the previous studies used the CSAP, which had 34 items for the evaluation of players' feeling of companionship with their virtual pet(s) (Luh et al. 2015; Li and Luh 2015). The questionnaire also asked the players to evaluate their companionship levels. The question asked was: "What is my attitude toward my pet? [Option 1] It does not matter to me whether I often interact with my pet. [Option 2] My pet is interesting and I often interact with it." In the present study, the CSAP was again used to evaluate players' states of companionship with their online pet(s). The questions were used to distinguish players' companionship levels and divide players into two groups (high and low level of companionship).

3   Data Analysis Method

This study performed statistical analysis on the data collected in our previous study (Li and Luh 2015). The flow and CSAP scales were used to determine whether relevant playing factors and playing history affect players' flow and companionship levels. The analysis items in the flow (22 items) and companionship (34 items) scales were the same as were used in our previous study (Li and Luh 2015). A 7-point Likert scale was used to measure the agreement of the participants, with a high score indicating a high level of agreement.

The present study also analyzed information about the participants, including gender, age, favorite online pet game, playing years (number of years they have played such games), and daily playing time. Furthermore, the items listed in Sect. 2.4 were used to assign players to high and low flow and companionship level groups. The present study aimed to identify what factors and playing history increased players' levels of flow and companionship, and some hypotheses were proposed.

The first hypothesis was based on the four game models defined in Sect. 2.1; it stated that two game models would result in significantly higher levels of flow and companionship: (1) players raise only one pet at one time and there are many pet species in the game and (2) players can raise many pets at one time but there is only one pet species in the game.

The second hypothesis stated that players with more playing years and playing time would have significantly higher levels of flow and companionship. The third hypothesis stated that the four flow factors (concentration, time distortion, loss of self-consciousness, and telepresence) and three companionship factors (enjoyment, satisfaction, and responsibility) would significantly increase players' levels of flow and companionship. Our final hypothesis stated that players who considered themselves to have a high flow (companionship) level would exhibit significantly higher levels of all flow (companionship) factors than the low flow (companionship) group.

Two items from the CSAP scale were used to test the validity of the questionnaires. If the item responses conflicted (subtracting the two scores ≥ 3), then the completed questionnaire was considered invalid. The completed questionnaires were also considered invalid if the responses to all questions were the same.

The participants in the study were required to be online pet game players. Statistical Package for the Social Sciences (SPSS) 22.0 was used for the statistical analysis. Descriptive statistical analysis was performed on information about the participants: gender, age, game types, playing years, and daily playing time. This study asked participants to complete the questionnaire while considering their favorite online pet games, each of which was classified as one of four game types (Table 1).

Cronbach's α was employed to evaluate the reliability of the flow and companionship scales, and a Cronbach's α of more than 0.7 indicated that a scale had a high coefficient of internal consistency (Chiou 2006). Exploratory factor analysis was conducted to test the validity of the flow and CSAP scales. A principal component method was employed. According to the statistical standard, the factor loading of each item in the three scales had to exceed 0.32 (Chiou 2006) to indicate that it sufficiently contributed to the scale validity. Moreover, the Cronbach's α of each factor in the three scales had to be higher than 0.7, and the cumulative variance had to be higher than 50%, which indicated that a scale was valid for testing a single concept (Chiou 2006). After factor analysis was performed, the items with the highest factor loadings were selected as the basis for identifying and interpreting factors in this study.

After the factor analysis, we used within-subject analysis of variance (ANOVA) to determine which flow and companionship factors were crucial for increasing players' flow and companionship levels; the significance level α was set at .05, and the Bonferroni method was employed for post hoc tests. Additionally, we used the T-test to identify whether game types, playing years and playing time had any significant positive effects on flow and companionship levels, wherein the significance level α was also set at .05. We also used a T-test to discover whether the high flow and companionship level groups had higher levels of flow and companionship regarding each flow and companionship factor.

4   Results and Discussions

4.1   Results

After invalid questionnaires were removed, there were 204 valid questionnaires for use in the statistical analysis. Of the valid participants, 64.2% were female (n = 131) and 35.8% (n = 73) were male. Regarding age, 56.3% (n = 116) of the participants were young adults (16–24 years old), and 43.7% (n = 88) were adults (25–45 years old). The other playing experience data are presented in Table 2. Fewer than ten participants played games of two of the four types; therefore their data was omitted because further statistical analysis could not be performed. The two game types that were thus disregarded were "players raise only one pet and there is only one pet species in the game" (n = 8) and "players can raise many pets and there are many pet species in the game" (n = 5).

Table 2. Participants' playing history

Variables	Groups	Numbers of participants	Percentages of participants
Game types	Players raise only one pet and there are many pet species in the game (GT1).	94	46.1
	Players can raise many pets at one time but there is only one pet species in the game (GT2).	110	53.9
Playing years	<1 year (PY1)	116	56.9
	≥1 year (PY2)	88	43.1
Playing time	<1 h /day (PT1)	103	50.5
	≥1 h /day (PT2)	101	49.5
Flow level	High (FH)	116	56.9
	Low (FL)	88	43.1
Companionship level	High (CH)	135	66.2
	Low (CL)	69	33.8

The Cronbach's α values of the flow and CSAP scales were 0.906 and 0.961, respectively, indicating that the two scales had high reliability. Factor analysis revealed factor loadings for all items of 0.44–0.87. The total variance of each scale was higher than 61%, further confirming the validity of the two scales. The results of the factor analysis are presented in Table 3. The flow experience scale comprised 22 items, and the first factor analysis revealed that two items ("It was no effort to keep my mind on what was happening" and "I was worried about what others may have been thinking of me") of the flow experience scale were classified as one factor. However, one factor must have at least three items (Chiou 2006); therefore, the two items were deleted, leaving 20 items in the flow experience scale (Table 3). The original CSAP included three factors; however, there were four factors in this study after factor analysis. The companionship factors in this study were based on the factor loadings of each item and its content.

Table 3. The results of factor analysis

Scales	Factors	Items	% of Variance	Cumulative %	Cronbach's α
Flow	Telepresence/loss of self-consciousness	12	27.943	27.943	.913
	Concentration	4	18.176	46.119	.863
	Time distortion	4	15.582	61.701	.816
CSAP	Attachment	16	26.888	26.888	.953
	Attractiveness	6	17.248	44.135	.844
	Uniqueness	6	10.146	54.281	.829
	Reality	5	10.049	64.331	.854

Within-subject ANOVA and the post hoc Bonferroni test were performed to determine which flow factors elicited a flow experience and which companionship factors enhanced participants' feelings of companionship with their online pet(s). Tables 4 and 5 present the within-subject ANOVA results based on the methods for testing other factors.

Table 4. Within-subject ANOVA summary of flow factors

Source	SS	df	MS	F	Post hoc test: Bonferroni
Between (A)	147.823	2	73.912	147.044***	Time distortion
Within-Subjects					$(M = 4.63, Sd = 0.08)$,
Between-Subjects (S)	590.864	203	2.911		concentration
Error (A*S)	204.075	406	.503		$(M = 4.53,$
Total	942.762	710			$Sd = 0.08)$ > telepresence / loss of self-consciousness
					$(M = 3.54, Sd = 0.08)$

*** $p < .001$

Regarding the flow experience factors ($p = .000 < .001$, F = 147.044; Table 4), the players experienced significantly higher levels of time distortion ($M = 4.63$, $Sd = 0.08$) and concentration ($M = 4.53$, $Sd = 0.08$) than a sense of telepresence and loss of self-consciousness ($M = 3.54$, $Sd = 0.08$). Regarding the companionship factors ($p = .000 < .001$, F = 133.660; Table 5), players rated attractiveness as having a much more significantly positive effect on their feelings of companionship ($M = 4.91$, $Sd = 0.07$) than the other factors; thus, attractiveness is a crucial factor in the building of companionship between players and their online pets. A sense of attachment ($M = 3.45$, $Sd = 0.09$) was the factor discovered to have the weakest effect for players.

Table 5. Within-subject ANOVA summary of companionship factors

Source	SS	df	MS	F	Post hoc test: Bonferroni
Between (A)	203.051	2.809	72.278	133.660***	Atractiveness ($M = 4.91$,
Within-Subjects					$Sd = 0.07$) > Reality
Between-Subjects (S)	760.866	203	3.748		($M = 4.47$, $Sd = 0.09$),
Error (A*S)	308.389	570.289	.541		Uniqueness
Total	1272.306	776.098			($M = 4.44$, $Sd = 0.08$) > Attachm ent ($M = 3.45$, $Sd = 0.09$)

*** $p < .001$

The T-test results revealed that playing time had significant effects on flow and companionship levels, but game type and playing years did not (Table 6). Players who spent longer playing with their online pet(s) every day had higher flow and companionship levels. Regarding gender and age, the T-test did not achieve significance (defined as $p < .05$), indicating that neither gender nor age affected the participants' flow and companionship levels.

Table 6. T-test results regarding participants' playing history

Aspects	Factors	Groups	n	M	Sd	T values
Flow	Game types	GT1	94	4.03	0.89	0.624
		GT2	110	3.95	0.84	
	Playing years	PY1	116	3.98	0.85	−0.078
		PY2	88	3.99	0.89	
	Playing time	PT1	103	3.85	0.80	−2.236*
		PT2	101	4.12	0.91	
Companionship	Game types	GT1	94	4.14	1.03	0.724
		GT2	110	4.03	1.10	
	Playing years	PY1	116	4.00	1.08	−1.157
		PY2	88	4.18	1.04	
	Playing time	PT1	103	3.93	1.04	−1.985*
		PT2	101	4.23	1.07	

* $p < .05$

The T-test also revealed that players who spent longer interacting with their online pets had significantly higher concentration levels, experienced more time distortion and attachment, found their pets more attractive, and felt that their online pet was more unique (Table 7). Therefore, if players can be encouraged to spend more time each day interacting with their pets, their flow experience and feeling of companionship will be enhanced.

Table 7. T-test results regarding playing time

Aspects	Factors	Groups	n	M	Sd	T values
Flow	Telepresence/loss of self-consciousness	PT1	103	3.46	1.01	−1.022
		PT2	101	3.62	1.18	
	Concentration	PT1	103	4.31	1.04	−2.788**
		PT2	101	4.75	1.18	
	Time distortion	PT1	103	4.37	1.07	−3.150**
		PT2	101	4.89	1.27	
Companionship	Attachment	PT1	103	3.36	1.17	−2.102*
		PT2	101	3.72	1.24	
	Attractiveness	PT1	103	4.68	1.02	−3.407***
		PT2	101	5.14	0.91	
	Uniqueness	PT1	103	4.25	1.17	−2.392*
		PT2	101	4.63	1.11	
	Reality	PT1	103	4.37	1.09	−1.251
		PT2	101	4.58	1.33	

$* p < .05; ** p < .01; *** p < .001$

The T-test results confirmed that the players who believed they had high levels of flow or companionship did actually have significantly higher levels of flow or companionship. Furthermore, the levels of the three flow and four companionship factors were higher for the players in the high flow/companionship groups than for those in the low flow/companionship groups (Tables 8 and 9).

Table 8. Factors affecting flow level

Aspects	Factors	Groups	n	M	Sd	T values
Flow		FH	116	4.39	0.74	9.167***
		FL	88	3.45	0.72	
Flow factors	Telepresence /loss of self-consciousness	FH	116	4.00	0.99	7.879***
		FL	88	2.93	0.92	
	Concentration	FH	116	5.02	0.95	8.105***
		FL	88	3.89	1.03	
	Time distortion	FH	116	5.09	1.05	7.059***
		FL	88	4.02	1.11	

$*** p < .001$

Table 9. Factors affecting companionship level

Aspects	Factors	Groups	n	M	Sd	T values
Companionship		CH	135	4.48	0.88	9.440***
		CL	69	3.22	0.91	
Companionship factors	Attachment	CH	135	3.95	1.09	8.263***
		CL	69	2.65	0.97	
	Attractiveness	CH	135	5.24	0.83	7.896***
		CL	69	4.21	0.95	
	Uniqueness	CH	135	4.77	1.04	6.663***
		CL	69	3.73	1.06	
	Reality	CH	135	4.82	1.10	6.654***
		CL	69	3.72	1.13	

*** $p < .001$

Enhancing the effect of flow and companionship factors on a player encourages the player to continue playing a game because the player experiences flow and companionship with the online pet. Furthermore, the T-test results indicated players' self-ratings of flow and companionship levels were reliable and can be used to classify players' levels of flow and companionship.

4.2 Discussions

Regarding the flow factors, concentration ($M = 4.53 > 4.00$, $Sd = 0.08$) and time distortion ($M = 4.63 > 4.00$, $Sd = 0.08$) were discovered to be crucial for increasing players' flow experiences. The results thus indicated that interacting with online pets may help a player to concentrate on the game and distort that player's sense of time (Luh et al. in press).

The telepresence/loss of self-consciousness factor ($M = 3.54 < 4.00$, $Sd = 0.08$), which included 12 items in the flow scale, was not identified as a crucial factor for increasing players' flow experience. According to the content of various online pet games, we concluded that game scenery and online pet appearance are both critical for players' sense of telepresence (Luh et al. in press). However, the appearance factor was not crucial for increasing players' flow experience. Thus, game scenery design and online pet appearance does not help players gain a high level of telepresence or experience a large loss of self-consciousness, so game scenery design and online pet appearance must be further investigated.

Among the four companionship factors, game or pet attractiveness ($M = 4.91$, $Sd = 0.07$) was crucial if players were to feel companionship for their online pet. Therefore, continuing to increase attractiveness for players will help them feel companionship with their online pet.

Compared to pet's attractiveness, reality, and uniqueness factors, sense of attachment ($M = 3.45 < 4.00$, $Sd = 0.09$), which included 16 items in the CSAP scale, was not discovered to be crucial for companionship. We inferred two possible reasons for this: (1) players expect to feel attached to their online pet, but the studied online pet games cannot fulfill this expectation effectively; or (2) players did not originally expect to feel attached to their online pets and did not subsequently gain any such attachment.

Only 13 participants played the games wherein (1) players could raise only one pet and only one species was available or (2) players could raise many pets and numerous pet species were available. This may indicate that these two types of games find it difficult to attract players. The other two game types, GT1 and GT2, had a total of 204 players (Table 2), indicating that these game types attracted more players. No significant differences were found in the flow and companionship levels of players of game types GT1 and GT2 (Table 6). Therefore, both types of game enabled players to achieve flow and feel companionship with their online pets.

T-test results revealed that how many years the participants had been playing online pet games did not affect players' flow and companionship levels, the reason for which should be discussed in the future. The T-test also demonstrated, however, that when players spend longer interacting with their online pet each day, they experience more flow and companionship. This was especially true regarding the following factors: concentration, time distortion, sense of attachment, pet's attractiveness, and pet's uniqueness.

Game designers wanting to increase players' flow and companionship levels should focus on encouraging players to spend more time interacting with their online pets daily, but game designers may need not emphasize involving players in online pet games over long periods (such as one or two years). The players' levels of flow and companionship did not differ considerably between the genders, with results similar to those of Lawson and Chesney (2007b), which focused on the effect of gender on sense of companionship with Nintendogs.

According to the T-test (Tables 8 and 9), players who believed they had high flow and companionship levels were confirmed to actually have high flow and companionship levels. Thus, the players' feelings are a reliable indicator. Nonetheless, we suggest that scales should include additional two or three items to identify players' flow and companionship levels; for example, "Compared with other players, I believe I have high levels of flow/companionship when playing the game." Using multiple items to determine whether a player belongs to high or low flow/companionship groups is more objective than relying on self-reporting.

This study used data collected in our previous study (Li and Luh 2015), and most of the games played by the participants were PC games. Currently, there are more than one hundred mobile games, and whether the results of this study are applicable for mobile pet games requires further investigation and discussion. Furthermore, the playing history factors discussed in this study only included gender, age, game type, playing years, and daily playing time. Other relevant factors, such as individual online pet games, playing days per week, and lifestyle can also be studied in the future.

5 Conclusions

This study evaluated what types of playing factors and playing history factors affect players' flow and companionship levels. The results revealed that concentration and time distortion were crucial for increasing players' feelings of flow. Pet attractiveness, reality, and uniqueness were discovered to be the crucial factors for building players' sense of companionship with their online pets. Furthermore, more time spent playing with online pets each day resulted in significantly higher flow and companionship levels. Finally, players who self-rated themselves as having high flow and companionship levels were confirmed to actually have higher flow and companionship levels than those who self-rated their levels as low.

The results of our previous studies (Li and Luh 2015, in press; Luh et al. 2015, in press) and this study collectively demonstrated that players truly achieve flow while interacting with their online pets and that some players feel companionship with their online pets. In addition, flow and companionship were revealed to have a positive relationship when considering online pet games. Different game motivations were discovered to result in different flow and companionship levels in players. Finally, game designers can enhance players' flow and companionship levels by strengthening some crucial playing factors and playing history factors.

The results of these studies can serve as a developmental reference for designers of games in which players own a virtual pet, such as online, VR, and AR games. Moreover, these results will also be useful in the development of companion robots, robot pets, and virtual pets for company functions, health management, and e-learning. Product, system, and game designers can utilize the relevant flow and companionship factors to enhance users' motivation and help them build more intimate relationships with their companion products or virtual pets.

References

Aguiar, N.R., Taylor, M.: Children's concepts of the social affordances of a virtual dog and a stuffed dog. Cogn. Dev. **34**, 16–27 (2015)

App Store: App Store iTunes (2016). https://itunes.apple.com/tw/genre/ios/id36?l=zh&mt=8. Accessed 20 Dec 2016

Bernabei, V., De Ronchi, D., La Ferla, T., Moretti, F., Tonelli, L., Ferrari, B., Forlani, M., Atti, A.R.: Animal-assisted interventions for elderly patients affected by dementia or psychiatric disorders: a review. J. Psychiatr. Res. **47**(6), 762–773 (2013)

Bressler, D.M., Bodzin, A.M.: A mixed methods assessment of students' flow experiences during a mobile augmented reality science game. J. Comput. Assist. Learn. **29**(6), 505–517 (2013)

Byrne, S., Wagner, E., Gay, G., Humphreys, L., Retelny, D., Pollak, J.: It's time to eat: Using mobile games to promote healthy eating. IEEE Pervasive Comput. **9**(3), 21–27 (2010)

Chang, C.-C.: Examining users' intention to continue using social network games: a flow experience perspective. Telematics Inform. **30**(4), 311–321 (2013)

Chen, H.: Exploring web users' on-line optimal flow experiences. Unpublished Ph.D. Dissertation, School of Information Studies, Syracuse University, Syracuse, NY (2000)

Chiou, H.: Quantitative Research and Statistical Analysis in Social & Behavioral Sciences. Wunan Publishing, Taipei (2006)

Choi, D., Kim, J.: Why people continue to play online games: In search of critical design factors to increase customer loyalty to online contents. Cyberpsychol. Behav. **7**(1), 11–24 (2004). doi: 10.1089/109493104322820066

Csikszentmihalyi, M.: Beyond Boredom and Anxiety. Jossey-Bass Publishers, San Francisco (1975)

Csikszentmihalyi, M.: Flow: The Psychology of Optimal Experience. Harpers Perennial, New York (1990)

Dabritz, H.A., Conrad, P.A.: Cats and toxoplasma: implications for public health. Zoonoses Public Health **57**(1), 34–52 (2010)

Finneran, C.M., Zhang, P.: Flow in computer-mediated environments: promises and challenge. Commun. Assoc. Inf. Syst. **15**, 82–101 (2005)

Ghani, J.A.: Flow in human computer interactions: test of a model. In: Carey, J. (ed.) Human Factors in Information Systems: Emerging Theoretical Bases, pp. 291–311. Ablex Publishing Corporation, New Jersey (1995)

Hoffman, D.L., Novak, T.P.: Marketing in hypermedia computer-mediated environments: conceptual foundations. J. Mark. **60**(3), 50–68 (1996)

Larriba, F., Raya, C., Angulo, C., Albo-Canals, J., Díaz, M., Boldú, R.: Externalising moods and psychological states in a cloud based system to enhance a pet-robot and child's interaction. BioMed. Eng. OnLine **15**(1), 72 (2016). doi:10.1186/s12938-016-0180-3

Lawson, S., Chesney, T.: The impact of owner age on companionship with virtual pets. In: Proceedings of the 15th Europe Conference Information Systems (ECIS 2007), St. Galen, Switzerland, pp. 1922–1928 (2007a)

Lawson, S., Chesney, T.: Virtual pets: great for the games industry but what's really in it for the owners? In: Proceedings of the 19th Women in Games 2007, Newport, Wales (2007b)

Li, E.C., Luh, D.-B.: From real to virtual pets- the evolution of artificial companions as pet. In: Proceedings of IASDR2011 the 4th World Conference on Design Research, pp. 1–12 (CD format) (2011)

Li, E.C., Luh, D.-B.: The relationship of flow level and companionship level for online pet games. In: 2015 The International Conference on Applied System and Innovation, Japan (2015)

Li, E.C., Luh, D.-B.: Effect of game motivation on flow experience and companionship: the online pet games as the example. Interaction Studies (In press)

Li, J.-S.: Exercise is no longer alone, virtual pets with you! (2016). http://udn.com/news/story/7266/1535044-運動不再孤單-虛擬寵物陪你!. Accessed 10 Jan 2017

Li, P.-Y.: Interpersonal theory. Test. Couns. **152**, 3152–3156 (1999)

Libin, E., Libin, A.: New diagnostic tool for robotic psychology and robotherapy studies. Cyberpsychol. Behav. **6**, 369–374 (2003)

Lorenz, T., Weiss, A., Hirche, S.: Synchrony and reciprocity: key mechanisms for social companion robots in therapy and care. Int. J. Soc. Robot. **8**(1), 125–143 (2016). doi:10.1007/s12369-015-0325-8

Luh, D.-B., Li, E.C., Dai, C.-C.: Game factors influencing players to continue playing online pets. IEEE Transactions on Computational Intelligence and AI in Games (In press)

Luh, D.-B., Li, E.C., Kao, Y.-J.: The development of a companionship scale for artificial pets. Interact. Comput. **27**(2), 189–201 (2015)

Novak, T.P., Hoffman, D.L., Yung, Y.-F.: Measuring the customer experience in online environments: a structural modeling approach. Mark. Sci. **19**(1), 22–42 (2000)

Park, S., Chung, N.: Mediating roles of self-presentation desire in online game community commitment and trust behavior of Massive Multiplayer Online Role-Playing Games. Comput. Hum. Behav. **27**(6), 2372–2379 (2011)

Skadberg, Y.X., Kimmel, J.R.: Visitors' flow experience while browsing a web site: its measurement, contributing factors and consequences. Comput. Hum. Behav. **20**(3), 403–422 (2004)

Su, Y.-S., Chiang, W.-L., Lee, C.-T., Chang, H.-C.: The effect of flow experience on player loyalty in mobile game application. Comput. Hum. Behav. **63**, 240–248 (2016)

Sweester, P., Wyeth, P.: Game Flow: A model for evaluating player enjoyment in games. ACM Comput. Entertain. **3**(3), Article 3A (2005)

Tsai, Y.-F., Kaufman, D.: Interacting with a computer-simulated pet: factors influencing children's humane attitudes and empathy. J. Educ. Comput. Res. **51**(2), 145–161 (2014)

Wood, L., Martin, K., Christian, H., Nathan, A., Lauritsen, C., Houghton, S., et al.: The pet factor - companion animals as a conduit for getting to know people, friendship formation and social support. PLoS ONE **10**(4), e0122085 (2015). doi:10.1371/journal.pone.0122085

Zasloff, R.L.: Measuring attachment to companion animals: a dog is not a cat is not a bird. Appl. Anim. Behav. Sci. **47**(1), 43–48 (1996)

Zhao, Y., Wang, W., Zhu, Y.: Antecedents of the closeness of human-avatar relationships in a virtual world. J. Database Manage. **21**(2), 41–68 (2010)

Game Worlds and Creativity: The Challenges of Procedural Content Generation

Rafael Pereira de Araujo[(✉)] and Virginia Tiradentes Souto

Institute of Arts, University of Brasilia, Brasília, Brazil
rafael.pereira.87@hotmail.com, v.tiradentes@gmail.com

Abstract. Videogames have evolved considerably over the last few years in terms of content creation and the possibilities provided by the evolution of hardware and software capabilities. As independent studios rise in popularity and distribution becomes available for the general audience (De Jong 2013), developers large and small focus on creating enduring game experiences with perceivable value for customers. One of the most commonly used methods of generating additional content for a game is procedural generation, which consists of using algorithms and modular game assets to create seemingly endless game areas, characters or challenges (Shaker et al. 2016). While this allows developers to increase game content, the use of procedural content generation also creates some challenges in terms of game balance, narrative quality and several other aspects intrinsic to game design. This paper analyses previous studies in procedural content generation. In addition, it discusses the impact of procedural generation in the creative process of game-making, proposing a "less-is-more" approach to increase value by investing in content quality over content quantity.

Keywords: Videogames · Interface · Information design · Creative process

1 Introduction

Over the last 30 years, videogames have evolved from toys aimed at children and young adults to complex entertainment platforms that impact the lives of millions of people from different backgrounds throughout the world; they are responsible for major financial results, runner-up only to the military and automotive industries (Santaella and Feitoza 2009). The ascension of videogames as a relevant medium has brought more than just many new players and products: the increase in competition, studio budgets and marketing stunts has turned the market into an intense, performance-driven race to win consumers' attention among a long list of options that are chosen and consumed fiercely. Making a good game is not only a matter of good game design, but also a demonstration of whether the said game's quality stands up to its competitors.

While this is true of many entertainment products and media such as movies and music, videogames rely heavily on technological advances to be able to provide new experiences once thought unimaginable. High-quality virtual reality (VR) experiences, for example, are only now becoming more popular thanks to large investments by relevant players in the market. Even more, internet and connectivity options have blurred

© Springer International Publishing AG 2017
A. Marcus and W. Wang (Eds.): DUXU 2017, Part II, LNCS 10289, pp. 443–455, 2017.
DOI: 10.1007/978-3-319-58637-3_35

the line between multiplayer gaming and social media, creating new challenges for experienced game makers.

Among the challenges presented to game developers, one in particular deserves attention as it impacts not only the way games are developed, but also what is at their core: game length and content. As game studios became larger, games became more complex and long, with single-player gameplay times going from a few minutes (as seen in games such as "Pitfall") to hundreds of hours (such as "The Witcher 3: Wild Hunt" and "The Elder Scrolls V: Skyrim"). This increase in game time is a reflex of increased content generation. In a role-playing game such as those mentioned above, developers have to create a large, believable fictional world with characters, interactive assets and stories, and that is highly demanding in resources and development times. Unsurprisingly, game development teams have grown from small teams of up to five people to a staff of hundreds of developers; Ubisoft Montreal, the studio behind recent games such as "Watch Dogs 2", has a workforce of more than 2,500 people.

In this race for increased content quantity, a particular technique is used and has been enhanced over the years: "procedural-content generation" (PCG). PCG consists of algorithms used by a software, in conjunction with several pre-made assets, to generate game content without direct intervention from a developer (Hendrickx et al. 2011). By using PCG, developers can program pre-made behaviours and assets for a game (such as different character traits and landscape features like forests and caves), and the algorithms will generate combinations of these assets to create infinite, endless maps or characters to interact with. In game development lingo, one can refer to content created by PCG as "procedural content".

Procedural content can be seen at different levels in many games throughout the years. In "Grand Theft Auto: San Andreas"[1], for example, the game map is predefined and modelled by developers, but the inhabitants of the fictional city in which the game takes place are procedurally generated – save for those more closely connected to the game story. Other games, such as "The Elder Scrolls V: Skyrim"[2], use algorithms to generate "quests" - adventures in which the player fights against foes and explores caves and mysterious places. By this means, there are literally an infinite number of adventures the player can enjoy while playing the game, each time in a different place and with different foes.

While this may seem like an attractive option for developers for saving time and budget in development, there are risks in the use of PCG, most notably the quality of the content and the replayability[3] of the game relying on its game mechanics within a procedural world.

---

[1] 2004 videogame developed by Rockstar Games. In "GTA", the player takes the role of a character involved in criminal activity. The game takes place in a large, realistic city, and offers the player a wide range of missions and different objectives.

[2] 2011 videogame developed by Bethesda Game Studios. Skyrim is a "role-playing game" in which the player creates a character, within a limited set of features, to explore a fantasy world with several adventurous quests.

[3] Word commonly used to describe the game's quality of being played more than once after being finished for the first time. A game that the player can enjoy more than once is considered a "replayable" game (or a game with "high replay value").

In this paper, some of these challenges will be addressed, with the goal of helping developers in adopting PCG according to their real needs, avoiding the risks of bad use of this technique. To do so, a case study with the recent game "No Man's Sky"[4] is presented, highlighting the use of PCG and the positive and negative aspects of its use. Furthermore, a study in state-of-the-art procedural generation is presented, in order to help developers have a better understanding of its use and possibilities.

2 Uses of PCG in Games

Procedural content general can be implemented in several different ways, according to the nature of the project and the hardware and software capabilities available. Some of the possible combinations of PCG in games include (but are not limited to):

- Map and level designs
- 'Quests' or challenges
- Character traits, appearance or names

Each of these categories contains several challenges and possibilities that can be highlighted, notably for their relevance in the game as a whole. Adopting each of these tools gives developers the possibility of extending plots, maps or world assets in a way that the core mechanics can be enjoyed over a long span of time by gamers.

2.1 Procedurally-Generated Map and Level Designs

The use of procedural map designs gives developers two main possibilities to work with: extending replayability value within a closed game, or allowing players to enjoy an "endless" game. To better illustrate both cases, known games are presented next.

"Diablo"[5] is a classic game known for the use of procedurally-generated maps. While the game offers a closed plot and gameplay length (divided into several acts with a unique foe to be defeated at the end of each act), the challenges and adventures lived through in each act happen in maps formed by combinations of map tiles that are randomized during each gameplay.

These random maps always offer similar experiences, such as special rooms with rewards for players, areas with stronger enemies and a way in and out of each "dungeon". However, since their layout is procedural, players have to discover their way out of the mazes and caves every time they play, thus reducing some common practices in meta-games that change the way experienced players enjoy the game. Figure 1 shows a scene from "Diablo 2".

---

[4] 2016 videogame developed by Hello Games. The game offers a seemingly infinite space for the player to explore, with literally billions of different planets with different flora and fauna created by PCG algorithms.

[5] 1996 videogame developed by Blizzard Entertainment. "Diablo" is a game set in a fantasy world, in which the player controls an adventurer who fights demons and other creatures in dungeons, catacombs and caves while upgrading the character's equipment and powers to face stronger foes.

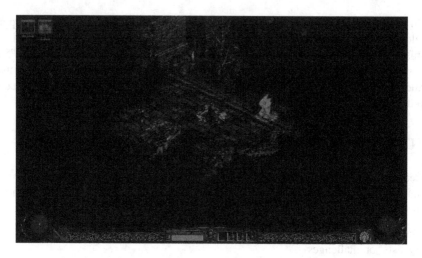

Fig. 1. "Diablo 2" (Source: Destructoid)

The use of randomly generated maps in "Diablo" comes with two notable characteristics. First of all, the increase in replayability is noticeable as it adds more variety during each playthrough. Seasoned players, familiar with the items and enemies in the game, will still have to face new challenges and discoveries even after several experiences with the game.

On the other hand, since the map works with predefined assets and structures, there is a lack of landmark spots or points of interest. Because of that, "Diablo" relies on preset special areas (such as boss stages or other fixed structures to support the plot) that do not follow the algorithms used to generate the maps. This is an interesting design decision, since it allows developers to work on a complex plot with characters that interact with pieces of the scenery without compromising the PCG and the story presented to the player.

The second game example refers to the use of PCG to create a seemingly endless game that can be explored and enjoyed infinitely. "Minecraft"[6] (Fig. 2) - a game that focuses on gathering resources and surviving in a lush green world - uses one of these algorithms to create a world so large it is, in fact, endless (save for occasional glitches and software limitations on console ports). Players can enjoy the game and its adventures – including one of the possible endings – just by staying in a relatively small area. Other players can explore, build and travel as far as their time and dedication allows, increasing the replayability of the game.

Again, there are considerations to be made on this game design decision. "Minecraft" is a game in which players are not given a strict goal; there is no complex plot or deeply-engineered characters to interact with. Because of that, the idea of an endlessly large

---

[6] 2011 videogame developed by Mojang. In "Minecraft", players explore a procedurally-generated world and build structures while surviving through several days, battling monsters and gathering resources.

Fig. 2. Minecraft (Source: Digital Foundry)

world with mineral resources, animals and plants fits in to the game's enjoyment without harsh consequences.

The same formula could not be applied in other games where core mechanics rely on more complex interactions, or more diversity in terms of scenery and landscapes. In that case, the PCG used in "Diablo" might be a more appropriate choice, giving developers more flexibility when needed.

2.2   Quests' and Challenges

Several games within many of the more popular genres (such as action and RPG games) have their core gameplay rely on a "quest" system. That is, while the player has the freedom to play the game, develop a character and visit different parts of a game world, it is only by partaking in given challenges or 'quests' that he can be rewarded for his efforts. In other words, 'quests' are the missions given to the player within a game world.

A recent example of procedural 'quests' or missions within a complex world is presented in "The Elder Scrolls V: Skyrim". In "Skyrim", the player enters a fictional world of adventures where a main storyline is supported by the possibility of having the player also enjoy "sidequests" or additional missions that will allow them to explore the world of Skyrim further.

Bethesda developed an algorithm called "Radiant Quest System" (Maciak 2011) to generate endless adventures in the world of Skyrim (Fig. 3). By combining several of the game assets – including a large number of voice acting lines – the characters are able to give the player entirely new missions that extend the gameplay time for as long as desired. As an example, a character that becomes a 'Dark Brotherhood' member (a guild that takes on assassination contracts in different parts of the fictional world) may talk to his contractors to receive missions such as "eliminate character X in part of the world Y".

Fig. 3. The Elder Scrolls V: Skyrim (Source: Game Pressure)

In "Skyrim", this quest system is used in complement to the main game plot – in which characters have unique names and interactions – allowing players to become stronger, collect more items and explore the large world of Skyrim.

On the other hand, a quest system that provides an endless number of quests also falls short in giving them a deeper significance. Players know how far these quests go, to the point of knowing that they will not affect the status quo of the world significantly – in a similar fashion to what happens in Massively Multiplayer RPG games (in which the "persistent" game world must not change much in order to give new player a similar first-time experience).

2.3   Character Traits, Appearance or Names

Developing characters for a new game is often a complex part of game development, requiring a large effort by the writing and design team. Complex characters feel life-like, and players can relate to them on an emotional level and thus obtain good enjoyment from the game (Brown and Cairns 2004).

By using PCG, developers can combine several different personality traits in order to create an infinite number of game characters, be it to provide a large world that feels lively or to work within a limited world, increasing the replayability factor by generating random scenarios in which the player will have different interactions and challenges each time they play the game.

The most notable example for this use of PCG is the strategy game "Crusader Kings". In this game, the player assumes the role of a ruler in medieval Europe and must develop their own nation, interact with other rulers and, if necessary, wage war with them. These interactions with other rulers (Fig. 4) is complex and takes into account several character traits – such as age, behavior, health, family lineage and even private life (to the point of including love interests as part of character descriptions), which the player can use to their advantage when necessary.

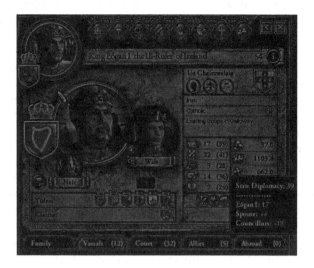

Fig. 4. Character description in "Crusader Kings" (Source: Game Pressure)

In "Crusader Kings", these interactions with other characters, despite their complexity, do not get to the point of direct interaction (such as voiced dialogue or real-time combat). Because of that, characters are described by players as lively and believable, since they stray from typical formulae of character creation by mixing different characteristics that result in "human" characters with flaws and peculiarities. Other players point out that the algorithm used in the game allows for so much randomness in character generation that uncanny scenes and stories may take place within the game. There are forums on the internet dedicated to describing some of the tales of the game characters.

By analysing the games presented and the different uses of PCG, it may be clear that the use of this technique allows for an increase in game content quantity, and if correctly applied it can support a well-written plot and game world. Relying on it, though, might prove to be a disadvantage if it is used as main storytelling tool, as seen in the next topic.

3   Challenges of PCG and the "No Man's Sky" Case

Procedural content generation is a powerful tool to enhance the game time and the possibilities provided by a solid game world. By using algorithms, developers can extend the life cycle of a game, allowing players to enjoy a well-developed game mechanic infinitely, without relying on expansion packs or online-dependent content (which may run offline sometime in the future or when a new game comes out).

On the other hand, relying on said content as a main feature might also prove to be a disadvantage in two specific situations: flawed implementation and lack of quality in the core mechanics. To better illustrate these flaws, here we present a recent game that was taken for a "promising" new title, but which received harsh critiques from the media and gamers, including a notable amount of refund requests throughout the world, pointing out that the game was not "up to the promises" it made during development stages.

"No Man's Sky" is a game developed by Hello Games and released in 2016 for the PC and the Playstation 4. In this game, the player controls a space explorer that must repair his ship and visit many different worlds in search of unique new specimens, as well as logging the many different planets they land on. There is an optional plot that players can take part in, travelling ever further towards the centre of the galaxy to uncover a mystery.

The main selling point in "No Man's Sky", though, is the creation of procedurally generated planets. By using an algorithm to generate planets, the game offers the notable figure of 18,446,744,073,709,551,616 planets to be explored (Murray 2014). Naturally, these planets were not crafted individually by the developers, but rather generated by the computer. The catch behind this particular use of PCG is that all the players in the world play the game with the same PCG "seed" (a number that triggers the different combinations generated by the algorithm). Also, each player starts a new game in a different part of the virtual galaxy, in a unique, unclaimed planet.

Because of that, and in addition to the game's internet connectivity features, "No Man's Sky" allows players to name each planet they land on and explore, sharing the data obtained with the game server. In other words, the game community can help in "charting" the unique and huge universe created.

The downside of the system created as the core mechanic of the game, though, received a backlash from the media and gamers for being overly simple and not allowing for much variety – as one would expect from a game based on space exploration (Kollar 2016). The planets created by the game vary in their weathers (some colder, some hotter), their unique creatures and landscapes, but they do not have enough diversity to truly represent the plethora of possibilities gamers expected from a giant uncharted universe (Fig. 5).

According to game reviewer Kollar (2016), all planets look and feel similar, with just different colour schemes and weather figures as the only differences between them. There is no mention of extreme landscapes, more complex life forms, or even planets with more unexpected compositions or characters with different behaviours.

Despite the commercial result of the game and the fact that the development team was small, this case indicates that the reliance on PCG as a core mechanic must necessarily be combined with gameplay mechanics that are complex enough to support the relatively bland set of combinations that come with the procedurally generated universe of "No Man's Sky".

In order to help developers in evaluating their reliance on PCG for their games, Table 1 provides recommendations and points out important aspects of implementation of PCG within games. It is divided into three PCG usages (basic, intense, core) and it shows the desired effects. The table is based on the analysis of the games previously mentioned and on the description of uses of PCG by Karonen (2013) and Hendrickx (2011), and takes into account a similar size of development team, budget and time.

Fig. 5. A planet in No Man's Sky (Source: Playstation Lifestyle)

Table 1. Reliance on PCG and basic effects

PCG usage	Desired effect
Basic	Shorter game, focus on predefined writing and game mechanics
Intense	PCG as support element for a separated plot or game architecture
Core	Strong game mechanics relying on long game times for optimal enjoyment

These three PCG usages are explained below.

Base usage of PCG

When using little or no PCG in creating game elements, most game assets, stories, characters and maps must be crafted individually, generating unique pieces. By doing so, developers can fine-tune combinations, relationships and game balance. While this option seems optional in terms of quality, it must be noted that "handcrafted" assets demand more production time and budget (Hendrickx 2011). For a smaller studio, this may mean that a game with little or no reliance on PCG should be shorter and more focused on the positive aspects of the game core design – be it an interesting plot or game mechanics that thrive with fine adjustments for a nearly-perfect experience within the limits of the game. Larger studios with heftier budgets may be able to handcraft content to create games large enough to be considered long, expansive experiences by players and media. One notable example from 2015 is "The Witcher 3: Wild Hunt", by Projekt CD Red, which offers completely unique content – including voice acting and animations – clocking over 200 h of game time (Tach 2015). As a suggestion for smaller developers, this option is the most recommended one if the studio aims to deliver unique, enthralling experiences.

Another reasonable base usage of PCG is in generating content during development stage. Instead of using predetermined "seeds" to generate content on-the-go according to players' actions, PCG can be used to create a large game area or non-playable characters. By doing so, developers can work with a predetermined template and build up on it, instead of creating every asset from scratch. That is an adequate solution in many cases, for it reduces time spent during initial stages of design.

Intense use of PCG

Just as seen in "Skyrim" and its "Radiant Quest System", PCG can be a powerful asset to extend game time and enjoyment beyond the base experience. Also, just as seen on "Diablo", an intense use of PCG is desirable when it does not detract from the possibilities provided by the game. Keeping core points from plot and game universe separate can help in obtaining the best of both worlds, giving room to writers working on a plot or a more complex game element, while still allowing players to have an "endless" area or experience in which they can hone their skills or just enjoy the gameplay further when not focusing on the main plot – be it for greater enjoyment or for "late-game" performance.

Core use of PCG

When procedurally generated content is at the core of a game, it is essential that the core gameplay mechanics must be strong enough to support worlds and assets that are clearly detracted from a dedicated writing. This level of reliance on PCG requires a larger amount of fine-tuning and game balance to keep the player's interest in the game stable over the expected course of gameplay. Csikszentmihalyi's (1990) description of the state of Flow points out that, to achieve such a state of immersion and engagement, the user must be faced with a balanced level of difficulty and stimuli, so their mind is always on a comfortable "edge". Using PCG as a core element requires, above all, solid gameplay that can overcome the test of time and be enjoyable over long game times, not only a game which "feels good for a few hours".

It should be noted that the recommendations provided are not the only aspects that must be taken into account when making design choices during the development of a game.

Each game is unique in its own design, and therefore aspects that range from budget to marketing plan must be taken into account, so players will be familiar with what to expect from the game, avoiding unpleasant experiences like the public backlash "No Man's Sky" suffered. The game, designed with several design choices in mind, was marketed under the banner of a large company, raising expectations far beyond the capabilities of a smaller studio (Kollar 2016). In the end, "No Man's Sky" was perceived by the general public to be a game with little content and gameplay possibilities, but it was extended immensely thanks to procedurally-generated worlds that allow gamers to play it infinitely without ever experimenting all that the game has to offer.

This leads to a relevant discussion of the role of procedurally generated assets in a game, and how they affect not only how it is played but also the very essence of some particular experiences.

4   Discussion

When working with procedurally generated content for a game, one of the most relevant concerns is the impact of the use of algorithms and predefined assets in the creative process of a game.

First and foremost, it must be taken into account that using these assets could ultimately mean a more repetitive – and less creative – approach to the establishment of fictional worlds. Since games have become longer and more complex over the years, there is an increased need to explore game mechanics, plots and game worlds.

As happens in literature, music and other media, game content should not be measured by sheer quantity, but rather evaluated for the quality and content of a given piece. By using procedurally-generated assets, there is an intrinsic risk of creating uninteresting and unoriginal content. While this may seem obvious when discussing the creation of core assets (like the main characters in a story-driven game), it is not as obvious when dealing with second-class assets such as the population of a fictional world.

"The Elder Scrolls V: Skyrim", while using PCG to create missions and adventures, does not use procedural generation for most of the world content. Each city has lively inhabitants with names and personalities. Gamers throughout the world discuss stories involving these characters, and they are distinct from one another during gameplay (despite the use of PCG for some traveller characters that appear in a few places). This allows for a deeper interaction with the world, a world in which every piece of knowledge adds to the narrative.

PCG can be positively used for an improved experience in several other ways. The previously mentioned examples of games like "Minecraft" and "Diablo 2" show that games with a heavy focus on gameplay or on building a narrative out of the player experience can benefit from the endless possibilities of a world created from scratch every time.

Thus, it can be pointed out that the biggest hurdle in creating an interesting world when using PCG is the balance between the need for a long game experience and the idea of creative, authorial writing to fill in the game world with interesting stories and elements.

With the ascension of independent game studios, which benefit from the increase in digital distribution options and social media to reach out to more gamers, it is important for small and new developers to find a position in the market where they can actively engage with their games by providing pleasant, memorable experiences. This paper intends to point out that procedural generation, while alluring for developers because it may create seemingly endless content, might make it impossible for them to work on authorial content or finely crafted experiences.

Several recent independent games have received critical acclaim and player fidelity for delivering short, yet meaningful, experiences to gamers. One of the reasons that "indie" games have reached this status relates to the lack of corporate demands that generally affect large "triple-A" titles. With a reduced need to appeal to corporate goals and more creative freedom, developers can focus on core aspects of gameplay, experiment with unique game mechanics and focus on writing and world-creating in shorter experiences.

It is notable that games that rely heavily on procedural generation might fall into the trap of creating a huge amount of content that may eventually not be backed by compelling gameplay or an audiovisual experience that provides the player with enough enjoyment to keep playing. The previously mentioned case of "No Man's Sky" fits in that example, with the additional fact that the developers of the game were backed by a larger studio, which helped boost the game's publicity prior to its release by announcing features and possibilities that would not be available in the final game.

The discussion also occupies a different level when it comes to the debate on how authorial and unique a videogame should be. As a powerful medium, it allows content creators to think of many different ways of presenting content to players, but it could be argued that any automatic or artificial content would lack the artistic value of an original creation.

Videogames have evolved from experiences created solely by programmers to multidisciplinary pieces that can provide gamers with joyful moments, convey emotions and even spark debates on heated topics. Focusing on these experiences and emotions allows developers to make much more meaningful games – and that has been proved a positive outcome of development effort in many recent independent games.

5   Final Remarks

This paper has as its main goal the discussion of the effect of procedural generation in creating original content for games. While this may seem relatively trivial, it is important to spark the discussion on the nature of content created by developers – especially the ones in the independent games scene – who come from different backgrounds and whose work reflects on the very essence of games.

By taking into account the table presented and the case studies of recent games, this paper provides developers with insight into the effects of PCG and offers recommendations based on what developers want for their games. PCG can affect the general perception of the world by gamers, who will explore and be inspired by the content created and aimed at them. More importantly, it is vital to take into account that games offer developers a huge array of possibilities, experiences to be created and shared with the world, and that unique, creative content has proved to be a desirable feature of modern games, despite some recent cases of games considered unoriginal and uninspired.

Future work based on this paper can be developed, given time and resources, especially in analysing the direct effect of PCG in numbers, evaluating the increase in development time and using player reception metrics to evaluate their enjoyment throughout gameplay. Another relevant topic for further discussion is the market effect of game length – or whether long games fare better in sales compared to regular-sized or short games, naturally within similar core mechanics or themes.

References

Brown, E., Cairns, P.: A grounded investigation of game immersion. In: CHI 2004, Vienna. ACM Press (2004)

Csikszentmihalyi, M.: Flow: The Psychology of Optimal Experience. Harper and Row, New York (1990)

De Yong, J.: Indie issues: the meaning of 'indie' games, and their incorporation into the 'mainstream' media. Master Thesis, Faculty of Humanities, Universiteit van Amsterdam (2013)

Hendrickx, M., et al.: Procedural content generation for games: a survey. ACM Trans. Multimedia Comput. Commun. Appl. (2011). ACM

Karonen, I.: Random/procedural vs previously made level generation (2013). Gamedev StackExchange http://gamedev.stackexchange.com/questions/58306/random-procedural-vs-previously-made-level-generation

Maciak, L.: Skyrim: radiant quest system (2011). Terminally Incoherent http://www.terminally-incoherent.com/blog/2011/12/16/skyrim-radiant-quest-system/

Murray, S.: Exploring the 18,446,744,073,709,551,616 planets of No Man's Sky (2014). Playstation blog https://blog.eu.playstation.com/2014/08/26/exploring-18446744073709551616-planets-mans-sky/

Santaella, L., Feitoza, M.: Mapa do jogo: a diversidade cultural dos games. Cengage Learning, São Paulo (2009)

Shaker, N., et al.: Procedural Content Generation in Games. Springer, Cham (2016)

Tach, D.: Why the Witcher 3 is 25 or 200 hours long (2015). Polygon http://www.polygon.com/2015/4/14/8406525/witcher-3-length-how-long-wild-hunt

Yannakakis, G., Togelius, J.: Experience-driven procedural content generation (extended abstract). In: Proceedings of the Sixth International Conference on Affective Computing and Intelligent Interaction (ACII) (2015)

Designing Game Controllers in a Mobile Device

Leonardo Torok, Mateus Pelegrino$^{(\boxtimes)}$, Daniela Trevisan,
Anselmo Montenegro, and Esteban Clua

Computing Institute, Federal Fluminense University,
Av. Gal. Milton Tavares de Souza, s/n°, São Domingos, Niterói,
RJ 24210-346, Brazil
{ltorok,daniela,anselmo,esteban}@ic.uff.br, mateuspelegrino@gmail.com
http://www.ic.uff.br

Abstract. The creative process behind new videogames always encouraged the development of innovative gameplay mechanics. However, the gamepad used to play is frequently overlooked, used only as a simple input device. This work proposes an improvement to an adaptive interface [12], using a smartphone as gamepad, with machine learning algorithms employed in real-time to tune the interface to the ergonomic needs of the current user. Now it includes an API that allows the game to change the interface elements anytime, creating a new gaming experience. Several statistics about the interaction with this interface were logged during test sections with 20 volunteers, with different levels of gaming experience. With these data, we seek to determine how to tune the interface in order to improve the experience, resulting in an iterative approach to controller design.

Keywords: Adaptive interface · Gamepad · Virtual gamepad · Touchscreen

1 Introduction

Innovation is at the heart of game development. Since the early days, where characters were represented by a few pixels, until the era of 4K gaming, more and more titles arrive in the market with groundbreaking innovations regarding level, character and sound design, gameplay mechanics and even introducing completely new game genres. However, even when a new game is revolutionary, the input device used to play it hardly is. Mouses and keyboards remained basically the same on the last few decades, only adding extra keys for shortcuts to allow quicker actions. The joystick, the most iconic interface used by consoles or PCs, also did not change that much. If one compares an original DualShock controller, launched in 1997 for the first PlayStation console, and a modern DualShock 4 [6], introduced in 2013 for the PlayStation 4, it is easy to see that they are strikingly similar. If we go as far as 1983 with the Nintendo Entertainment System, we can see that modern controllers only improved ergonomics and added more buttons [7].

© Springer International Publishing AG 2017
A. Marcus and W. Wang (Eds.): DUXU 2017, Part II, LNCS 10289, pp. 456–468, 2017.
DOI: 10.1007/978-3-319-58637-3_36

Of course, it would not be accurate to claim that nobody tried to disrupt the joystick paradigm in the last decades. In 2006, Nintendo launched the Wii, a console that included a revolutionary controller: the Wiimote. Using accelerometers and infrared sensors to detect motion, the Wii allowed gamers to interact using gestures that were more intuitive and natural than simply pressing a button. The console became a resounding success, selling more than 100 million units [3]. As this trend was quickly replicated by its competitors, a new gaming audience appeared: casual gamers [3]. This market segment wanted simplified experiences, avoiding the complexities of regular games and gamepads that demanded quite a bit of dexterity from players to interact with multiple buttons simultaneously [5]. This trend continued with the rise of smartphones, making gaming more accessible than ever before.

In our previous work [12], we introduced a new type of gamepad. This new game controller is a mobile app running on a smartphone or tablet, displaying a virtual gamepad on its screen. This app communicates with a game running on a PC using sockets over a local Wi-fi network, sending all button presses to the computer. The traditional gamepad is replaced by a smartphone, while the game on the PC only has to implement a simple API to communicate with the new controller. This new gamepad is context-sensitive, showing only the buttons that the game needs in a simplified and more casual-friendly interface. It can also show GUI elements such as switches and dials, not possible on regular controllers, creating a completely new experience. This controller also includes several machine learning routines to correct and adjust its interface to the interaction patterns of a user, in real-time, avoiding interaction errors that occur on touch based interfaces. These corrections have the potential to significantly improve the experience [12], but they take some time to reach a better interface. The user has to, at least momentarily, deal with a sub-optimal UI design.

As we are dealing with a full touch interface, several data about the interaction between gamer and gamepad can be collected. While this was used before to fine tune the interface [13], this data will now be used to propose new designs for the adaptive game controller, using testing sections to determine troublesome UI decisions that will be fixed in a next version, proposing an iterative approach to controller design. These new and optimized layouts will then become the new default, potentially decreasing the time that the interface needs to adapt to a new user and solving the initial issue of playing with a sub-optimal UI. This process can then be repeated, until reaching the best layout for the gamepad.

This work will start discussing the related literature regarding touch interfaces and video game controllers. In the next section, the adaptive interface will be presented in details, showing how it can change the way we play videogames. We will then show the methodology used for our tests and the results of our testing sections, with the new proposed designs and the reasoning behind each changes.

2   Related Work

There are several works that try to address the impact that the lack of haptic feedback has on touchscreen interfaces, that normally results in more user mistakes. In this work, it will be measured as the success rate, the percentage of touches that correctly performed an action (in our case, the ones that hit any button instead of an empty screen area).

Rogers et al. [10] proposed models that treat touch input during the handover of control between user and system, trying to correct inputs when interacting with a map mobile application. Weir et al. [14] used machine learning to treat specific models of touch input, remapping incorrect touches to a different location on the screen, based on historical input data. A different approach was presented on Bi et al. [2], that improved touch accuracy using a Bayesian target selection criterion to treat input. Virtual keyboards are another important real-world application that has to deal with incorrect inputs. Solutions like key-target resizing [1] have been applied to increase the accuracy.

The approach on this work is the same used on Torok et al. [12], proposing machine learning routines to redesign the interface of a virtual gamepad in real-time, increasing the success rate. This solution will be described with more details in Sect. 3.2. When comparing this interface to a traditional gamepad, the first notable thing that it lacks is the haptic feedback that a physical button provides. Zaman and Mackenzie [15] compared a virtual gamepad with different physical controllers, showing that using a touchscreen for gaming decreases the in-game performance of users. While this application is different, since the game runs on a PC screen (avoiding the problem caused by the fingers concealing part of the screen), the lack of haptic feedback still is an issue. However, the tests performed in the previous work showed that the success rate of a simple virtual gamepad can be substantially improved using an adaptive interface with machine learning routines to improve the performance of a user.

While the lack of haptic feedback is clearly a disadvantage, this controller has a significant improvement when compared with the previous version. Now the game can configure the controller layout anytime, allowing the controller to display a simplified and casual-friendly interface that contains only the buttons that are necessary at the moment. A regular gamepad has to provide a large set of buttons since it is a generic interface used by a plethora of games, having to work with the simplest platforming game and with the most complex strategy game. When we reduce the amount of options displayed on the screen, a virtual interface on a mobile device can outperform a traditional controller due to demanding less mental effort [8]. We will discuss this aspect in Sect. 3.1

3   Adaptive Controller and Game

3.1   Game Context Adaptation

The adaptive controller, based on a full-touch interface on a mobile device, creates several new possibilities [9]. The first one is that it can display only the buttons that are necessary in the current section of the game, while a traditional gamepad has dozens of buttons regardless of how many the current game actually needs, being more intimidating to novice players. The second improvement is the possibility to display GUI elements on the screen that are not possible on traditional controllers, like switches, dials and gesture areas. With these new elements, we can map in-game actions to a more natural interface, an approach similar to the one introduced by motion controls. With a simplified interface and less buttons, we will try to bring the simplicity of mobile gaming to PC and console games, creating a more attractive experience to a new generation of casual gamers.

As the game itself can determine every element of the controller layout, being able to radically change it anytime, this new gamepad is adapted to the game context. This means that the controller becomes part of the gameplay and of the game challenges. With this interface, the game designer now can develop the game and the controller used to play it at the same time, creating an entirely new experience. Figure 1 shows a gamer using the controller to play our game, illustrating how radically the interface can change during the game.

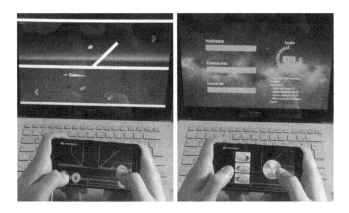

Fig. 1. A player using the adaptive controller to play our prototype game in two different moments.

3.2   User Behavior Adaptation

According to Langley [4], an adaptive interface is an interactive software system that aims to improve its interaction with a user based on a partial experience. In our case, we will use the input data of the current interaction to perform adjustments to the controller layout. This fine tunning happens constantly, always using the latest data to improve the interface. The proposed controller is fully virtual and touch based, lacking any kind of haptic feedback (except for vibrating when a button is pressed). So, unlike what happens on a traditional gamepad, the user can miss buttons when trying to interact.

The adaptive controller employs several tactics to improve the interface. The first one is touch approximation: when the user misses a button, the touch is associated to the closest button. This guarantees that mistakes will be corrected. The second tactic is preventive instead of corrective [13], analyzing the user behavior to determine how to improve the interface. All touches are used as input for a K-means clusterization [11], where K is the amount of buttons on the screen that were used at least once. This results in K clusters, each one with a centroid. As the touches are normally located close to (or inside) a button, the clusters also end up close to their boundaries. The centroids will then be associated to the closest button, and the app will start moving the buttons towards its associated centroids. The size of each button is also changed: the 1/3 most used buttons will receive a slight size boost, becoming 50% bigger. This tactics are the same employed in [12].

3.3   Prototype Game

For the testing sections, a prototype game was developed for the adaptive controller, called Guardians of Eternity. The objective is to escape the planet with the main character. It's a simple game, with two stages. The player just has to reach the far right of the stage to finish it, avoiding getting hit by enemies or colliding with obstacles. Each hit decreases its health bar (or kills it instantly on level 2). If the player dies, he will return from the last checkpoint. In level 1, the player controls a robot and has to perform simple platforming tasks to defeat enemies and avoid hazards. The controller uses a simple layout with two directional arrows and a jump button, plus a transform button. Pressing the latter changes the character to the spaceship form. Now the gameplay is a classic dual-stick shooter and the controller layout changes to two analog sticks (left one to move the ship and right one to shoot at any direction). Figure 2 shows the game screens for this stage while Fig. 3 shows the respective controller layouts used to play.

After completing the level, the main character is too damaged to keep going and it is necessary to disable several of its weapons and powers. In Fig. 2 we can see the minigame screen, where the player has to turn off the switches on the controller and turn down the power using the dial. This is an example of the kind of direct and natural interaction that this controller provides (as shown on Fig. 3), mapping a real-world action to an interface that is way more similar to real devices than mere buttons on a gamepad. The player, now stuck in the spaceship form, proceeds to enter a maze, where he has to avoid colliding with walls or asteroids. The weakened guardian has troubles to fight the effects of gravity. The player must constantly press "up" to avoid falling to the ground. The controller (as seen in Fig. 3) has buttons to control the vertical and horizontal movements, separated in the opposing sides of the interface in an attempt to provide a more ergonomic alternative to a regular d-pad.

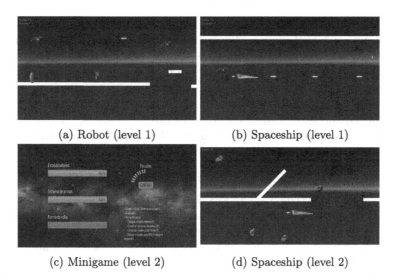

(a) Robot (level 1)   (b) Spaceship (level 1)

(c) Minigame (level 2)   (d) Spaceship (level 2)

Fig. 2. Game screens for both levels. Level 1 has two gameplay modes: platforming as robot (a) and dual-stick shooter with the spaceship (b). After finishing this stage, the player enters a minigame (c) that precedes the second level (d).

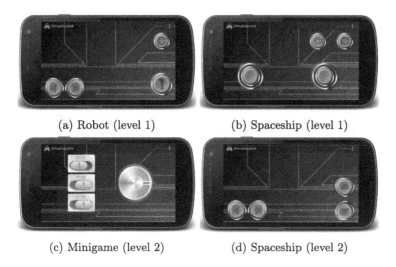

(a) Robot (level 1)   (b) Spaceship (level 1)

(c) Minigame (level 2)   (d) Spaceship (level 2)

Fig. 3. The layout displayed by the adaptive controller during the different stages of the game.

4   Experiment

The tests were performed with 2 groups of 10 users each. The first one represented the advanced players: people that play videogames as a hobby, several hours per week, and usually expend a fair amount of money in gaming hardware (consoles or GPUs for PCs) and games. The second group was the less experienced users, or casual players. These volunteers rarely play games and never expend any cash on gaming hardware, usually playing only in their smartphones.

All users had a single task: to finish the Guardians of Eternity game using the adaptive controller. Each level was preceded by screens explaining the plot of the game and teaching how to control the characters. In addition, as soon as a level started, we explained briefly the objective and gameplay mechanics to the users. A 20 min hard time limit was also defined in case any user failed to complete the game. However, as it was pretty short, no user failed to complete the task.

The mobile app collected a large variety of logs about the interaction, like the number of touches on the screen and its coordinates, the current active controller layout and several in-game events, like deaths and checkpoints. These data will be used for the evaluations in the next section.

The smartphone used as gamepad was a Motorola Moto X Play, running Android 6.0.1. It has a multitouch 5.5′ full HD display. The game was running on a laptop with a Core i7 3537U CPU, 6 GB of RAM and a Nvidia GeForce GT735M GPU. The operating system was Ubuntu 16.04.

5   Results

With all testing sections performed, all the log files were gathered and we started evaluating which kind of improvements to the interface could be made. This analysis started by grouping the touches for all users of each group, creating a heatmap that showed which points of the screen were being touched more frequently. In the same heatmaps, the positions that the buttons reached during their real-time optimization were also mapped. These two information combined will be used to improve the layout of the controller. Heatmaps were created for all layouts, except the ones used on menus or in the minigame, since these screens only demanded a few touches in the screen. The second part of our analysis will be a detailed evaluation of the data in the log files, verifying how the changes in the controller interfered with the success rate (that is the percentage of touches that correctly hit any button and performed an in-game action).

5.1   Heatmaps

Figure 4 shows the heatmaps for the layout used to play as the robot on level 1. The scale goes from blue (lower concentration of touches) to red (higher concentration of touches), with a yellow cloud showing the positions occupied by the center of the buttons when trying to adapt to the interaction patterns. In this case, we can see that the more experienced users had a more consistent pattern of touches, focused on a smaller area, indicating that they are generally more precise when hitting the screen. In both groups, we saw a tendency to approximate the right-side buttons, allowing the player to reach both buttons with less effort and more agility. This is a case where the original interface was not very

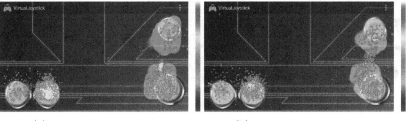

(a) Less experienced users   (b) More experienced users

Fig. 4. Heatmaps for the layout used to play as robot, for both groups. The yellow clouds show the areas that the button occupied when adapting its position, while the colored regions show the heatmaps for the touches of the users. (Color figure online)

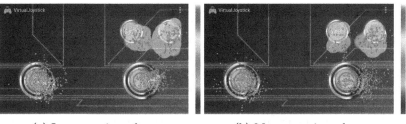

(a) Less experienced users   (b) More experienced users

Fig. 5. Heatmaps for the layout used to play as the level 1 spaceship, for both groups. The yellow clouds show the areas that the button occupied when adapting its position, while the colored regions show the heatmaps for the touches of the users. (Color figure online)

well designed and the controller automatically fixed this mistake and reached a more ergonomic position. Also, as all tests where performed with a 5.5′ phone, we could theorize that on a smaller device this effect would not be so aggressive since the buttons would not be so far apart. Anyway, it shows that this adaptation can also be useful when dealing with devices with different screen sizes.

The layout for the level 1 spaceship resulted in the heatmaps displayed on Fig. 5. Both groups showed again a tendency to bring the upper side buttons closer to the right analog stick, decreasing once more the effort to reach multiple buttons. The more experienced users, however, maintained the distance between the transform and super buttons, while the less experienced group tried to get them closer. A stark contrast is on the right analog stick, with the less experienced users showing way more touches. This was caused by a big difficulty in understanding how to play a dual stick shooter among the less experienced users. While the expert players already knew how to play such type of game and simply pointed the right analog stick towards the enemies, the less experience players tried to press the right stick as if it was a button each time they intended

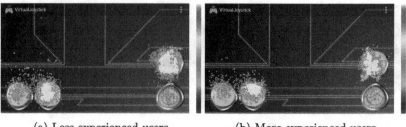

(a) Less experienced users   (b) More experienced users

Fig. 6. Heatmaps for the layout used to play as the level 2 spaceship, for both groups. The yellow clouds show the areas that the button occupied when adapting its position, while the colored regions show the heatmaps for the touches of the users. (Color figure online)

to fire the main weapon, even after being informed about the correct way to play several times. Their lack of gaming skill and experience made this kind of control too complex. This showed that maybe the less experienced players should receive a different layout, simplified, with a normal button to simply fire forward instead of the more advanced gameplay mechanics of dual stick games. Providing different interfaces for more casual or more experienced gamers is one of the possibilities that the adaptive controller brings to gaming.

The level 2 ship controller resulted on the pattern indicated by Fig. 6. As the buttons are already close to each other, we did not have a lot of variation in the positions. The more experienced players rarely used the down button, while the less experienced players relied on it more constantly. Indeed, it is not mandatory to use this button, since the stage already has a gravity effect so the ship is always gently going down. The experienced players usually only moved up moderately and calculated their movements so most of the times they had to lower the position of the ship, it could be done with the natural force of gravity (showing superior skills). The less experienced players usually lacked this kind of control and had to compensate constantly their less gracious movements to avoid colliding to the walls.

5.2 Detailed Log Analysis

We also investigated if changes in the controller layout are influencing the game performance. One user from each group was selected. The more experienced user chosen for this analysis (Fig. 7a) had the lowest success rate between his group and the third lowest overall, being a special case. The initial black area is the time on menus, where the user was experimenting with the interface and missed some keys. As soon as he starts playing, the success rate constantly increases until he changes the interaction form (from robot to spaceship). From this moment on he starts missing buttons until the interfaces adapts to his behavior and improves his performance, a tendency that remains mainly stable until the next level. However, he misses a button when playing as robot almost at the same time

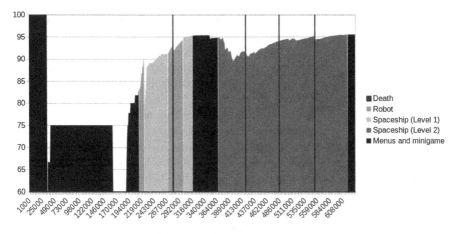

(a) More experienced user

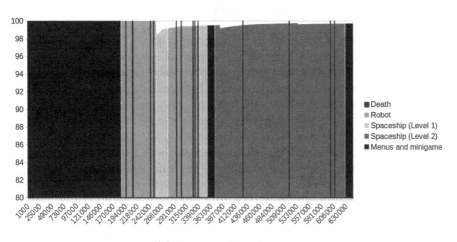

(b) Less experienced user

Fig. 7. Complete history for the test session of one of the more experienced users (a) and one of the less experienced users (b). The X-axis is the time, in milliseconds, while the Y-axis is the success rate at that time. The color of the plot area shows which layout was active, while the dark blue horizontal lines mark each time the user died in the game. (Color figure online)

that he dies, indicating that these events may be correlated. On stage 2, the controller keeps improving its success rate, but this time we have 2 deaths close to moments where he missed buttons. This shows that, for some users, it still is necessary to adjust the layouts to reach a more optimal performance and the results of the heatmaps can be a first step to improve these layouts.

On the other hand, the less experienced user shown on Fig. 7b keeps its success rate at 100% until changing form to the spaceship. As the layout changed, he gets momentarily lost. As he adapted to the interface and the controller adapted itself to his behavior, he regained his full success rate. The only other radical decrease is on the beginning of level 2, showing a consistent pattern. He missed buttons when the interface changed, but his performance quickly improved due to his own learning of a new interface and the controller adaptations. Also, we did not have any situation where he missed buttons and died shortly afterwards, indicating that the interface was not an issue for this user.

In both cases, we can notice that the success rate tends to fall when a new interface is introduced. After the machine learning algorithms fixed the layout, the success rate starts to improve until stabilizing at a high value. This provides an interesting motivation to create a new and fine-tuned initial layout for the adaptive controller, decreasing the initial frustration with a new interface by providing a semi-optimized version as default, that is the exact concept of this work and the objective of the final section.

6   Conclusion and Future Work

Using the touch pattern displayed by the heatmaps (Sect. 5.1), improved versions of our controller layouts were created. The layout used to play in the second stage will remain unchanged, since the proximity of its buttons already resulted in a heatmap without any significant patterns to indicate potential improvements.

When playing as the robot in level 1, the players showed a tendency to bring both action buttons together, allowing faster access to both buttons. Figure 8 shows the result of the first correction proposed in this new iterative process. The tendency of decreasing the distance between buttons is also apparent for the spaceship layout, but the clear difficulty in using a second analog stick to shoot for the less experienced users made us create two separate layouts, one for each group, as seen on Fig. 9.

In both cases, we approximated all action buttons following the pattern displayed on the heatmap. As the groups positioned the action buttons similarly, we decided to use the same position for both cases, keeping the two layouts as similar as possible. While the more experienced group will keep the dual stick mechanics, we decided to replace the second stick with a single "Fire" button that shoots straight forwards for casual players. Of course, this layout removes

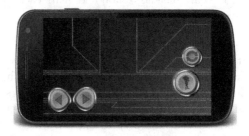

Fig. 8. New controller layout for the robot on the first level.

(a) Less experienced users   (b) More experienced users

Fig. 9. New controller layouts for the spaceship on the first level.

some extra shooting features, but simplifies the task of hitting enemies by letting the less experienced players focus only on moving the ship instead of dealing with complex mechanics.

The game can show a screen before level 1 allowing the player to chose how he wants to play or simply relate these layouts to its difficulty settings. Per instance, when a user plays on "Easy", the game could use the simplified layout, assuming that a casual user will play. Selecting "Normal" or "Hard" would also select the dual stick layout, assuming that we now have a more skilled player. The latter approach will be used in the next version of the testing game.

This new iterative approach to controller design intends to improve an interface using data obtained directly from usability testings. By using all input patterns of these gameplay sessions, new interfaces that match more accurately the real behavior of the players can be designed. These results will become the new default layouts for the controller. While the machine learning routines will still optimize it for each user, the starting point will be much closer to an optimum value, shortening the time it takes to become optimized to a user and avoiding the initial decrease in the success rate when interacting with a new layout (Sect. 5.2). This process can be repeated after applying the changes, until the controller reaches the best default layout for a comfortable gaming experience.

Future developments of this research includes the application of this approach in different types and genres of games, evaluating how it can impact the development of controller interfaces. Another interesting research is to apply the concept of having different controller layouts for specific user profiles, such as simplified interfaces for casual users, evaluating how it impacts their performance and enjoyment of different games.

Acknowledgments. We would like to thank our volunteers for their participation in our testing sessions. We are also grateful to CAPES, CNPQ and FAPERJ for their financial support.

References

1. Baldwin, T., Chai, J.: Towards online adaptation and personalization of key-target resizing for mobile devices. In: Proceedings of the 2012 ACM International Conference on Intelligent User Interfaces, pp. 11–20. ACM (2012)
2. Bi, X., Zhai, S.: Bayesian touch: a statistical criterion of target selection with finger touch. In: Proceedings of the 26th Annual ACM Symposium on User Interface Software and Technology, pp. 51–60. ACM (2013)
3. Hollensen, S.: The blue ocean that disappeared-the case of nintendo wii. J. Bus. Strategy **34**(5), 25–35 (2013)
4. Langley, P.: Machine learning for adaptive user interfaces. In: Brewka, G., Habel, C., Nebel, B. (eds.) KI 1997. LNCS, vol. 1303, pp. 53–62. Springer, Heidelberg (1997). doi:10.1007/3540634932_3
5. Marshall, D., Ward, T., McLoone, S.: From chasing dots to reading minds: the past, present, and future of video game interaction. Crossroads **13**(2), 10 (2006)
6. Merdenyan, B., Petrie, H.: User reviews of gamepad controllers: a source of user requirements and user experience. In: Proceedings of the 2015 Annual Symposium on Computer-Human Interaction in Play, pp. 643–648. ACM (2015)
7. Mott, T.: 1001 Video Games You Must Play Before You Die: You Must Play Before You Die. Hachette, UK (2011)
8. Oshita, M., Ishikawa, H.: Gamepad vs. touchscreen: a comparison of action selection interfaces in computer games. In: Proceedings of the Workshop at SIGGRAPH Asia, pp. 27–31. ACM (2012)
9. Pelegrino, M., Torok, L., Trevisan, D., Clua, E.: Creating and designing customized and dynamic game interfaces using smartphones and touchscreen. In: 2014 Brazilian Symposium on Computer Games and Digital Entertainment, pp. 133–139, November 2014
10. Rogers, S., Williamson, J., Stewart, C., Murray-Smith, R.: Fingercloud: uncertainty and autonomy handover incapacitive sensing. In: Proceedings of the SIGCHI Conference on Human Factors in Computing Systems, pp. 577–580. ACM (2010)
11. Smola, A., Vishwanathan, S.V.N.: Introduction to machine learning, vol. 32, p. 34. Cambridge University, UK (2008)
12. Torok, L., Pelegrino, M., Lessa, J., Trevisan, D.G., Vasconcelos, C.N., Clua, E., Montenegro, A.: Evaluating and customizing user interaction in an adaptive game controller. In: Marcus, A. (ed.) DUXU 2015. LNCS, vol. 9188, pp. 315–326. Springer, Cham (2015). doi:10.1007/978-3-319-20889-3_30
13. Torok, L., Pelegrino, M., Trevisan, D.G., Clua, E., Montenegro, A.: A mobile game controller adapted to the gameplay and user's behavior using machine learning. In: Chorianopoulos, K., Divitini, M., Hauge, J.B., Jaccheri, L., Malaka, R. (eds.) ICEC 2015. LNCS, vol. 9353, pp. 3–16. Springer, Cham (2015). doi:10.1007/978-3-319-24589-8_1
14. Weir, D., Rogers, S., Murray-Smith, R., Löchtefeld, M.: A user-specific machine learning approach for improving touch accuracy on mobile devices. In: Proceedings of the 25th Annual ACM Symposium on User Interface Software and Technology, pp. 465–476. ACM (2012)
15. Zaman, L., MacKenzie, I.S.: Evaluation of nano-stick, foam buttons, and other input methods for gameplay on touchscreen phones. In: International Conference on Multimedia and Human-Computer Interaction-MHCI 2013, p. 69-1 (2013)

Designing the Virtual, Augmented and Tangible Experience

The Importance of Specific Usability Guidelines for Robot User Interfaces

Julia Ramos Campana[1,2(✉)] and Manuela Quaresma[1]

[1] LEUI—Laboratory of Ergodesign and Usability Interfaces,
PUC-Rio University, Rio de Janeiro, RJ, Brazil
mquaresma@puc-rio.br
[2] 13 Robotics Robótica Ltda., Rio de Janeiro, RJ, Brazil
juliarcampana@gmail.com

Abstract. In the field of robotics, user interfaces have the important role of aiding humans in better interactions with robots. Hence, until full autonomy becomes a reality, user interfaces are an essential way to communicate necessary information to interact with robotic systems. This article examines which principles of design have been used in Human-Robot Interaction (HRI) to understand further how can usability guidelines can improve the development of user interfaces built to integrate solutions considered as "complex systems"; simultaneous compositions of software behaviors, present in a great deal of industrial solutions and HRI research.

Industrial robots have been used in a variety of situations, ranging from *in Situ* maintenance, to space exploration and the central role of humans in the interaction with automated systems is to undertake what is called supervisory control through monitoring and supervision of operational tasks. Research in interface design can contribute significantly to increase system performance and collaboration between man and robots. As robotic systems evolve the goal for human-in-the-loop activities should not be to eliminate the human, but rather to create human-system collaboration with greater capabilities than the individual components. Therefore, the investigation of guidelines for the elaboration of the more efficient interface in the interaction with robots can greatly contribute with usability principles.

Keywords: Robots · AI agents · DUXU · Robot user interface · Design guidelines · Usability principles

1 Introduction

One of the purposes of this study is present a literature review that examines the principles of design that have been used in Human-Robots Interaction (HRI) guidelines for the development user interfaces for the interaction with robots. Within the interface design theme, the study of the visual conception of robotic systems happens in a similar way to many other human-computer interaction (HCI) systems such as the web and applications for mobile phones or tablets. What changes is how interactions between humans and robots occur compared to interactions between man and computer. For Scholtz [1], HRI

© Springer International Publishing AG 2017
A. Marcus and W. Wang (Eds.): DUXU 2017, Part II, LNCS 10289, pp. 471–483, 2017.
DOI: 10.1007/978-3-319-58637-3_37

differs from HCI because "it concerns complex systems, which have dynamic control systems, present autonomy, and can operate in changing real-world environments". These differences can be seen through different spectrums of the interaction and its agent roles, along with physical nature of robots, number of systems a user may be asked to interact with, and the environment of interaction.

Robotic systems are a combination of different sensors; electronics and mechanical parts, and most of time the innovation is constituted through the way its components are being grouped for a specific purpose. This work is concerned with the design of software interfaces that is embodied in industrial robots as part of greater solutions. In other words, the interface of systems, which interact with other physical and virtual components and require their functionalities to be grouped into one place. The goal of the article is to examine ergonomic aspects of interfaces designed to let users control robots either manually or autonomously. It also concerns the simplest case of HRI [2], which occurs when one human works with one robot, which in this case, is a manipulator robot. Robot manipulators are widely used in research and development (R&D) and suited for a variety of tasks and commonly adapted as part of a greater solution in robotics.

If at first robots were created in the industry to release humans from risk and dangerous tasks, they are now getting closer of tasks related to all kinds of human needs [3]. On the other hand, even though intelligent systems become more and more reality, completely autonomous systems are far from being the norm. In actual fact, we need to have humans who monitor the systems, intervening when necessary [1] as well as design systems, that can be used by domain experts but not robotics experts. It is important to establish a partnership between humans and robots with greater capabilities than the individual components.

The challenges presented in the development of these interfaces range from the aspects of interaction to the composition of teams; certain software's may require training and learning from human operator, as well as the adaptation or creation of design guidelines aligned with the needs of a given project. Also, robotic user interfaces have a rarer character in terms of design output, a niche market more specific and with team compositions often structured in software engineering and mechatronics, but lacking designers to deal with usability and aesthetics aspects in such projects [4]. Thus, many times these interfaces are designed and developed by the same individuals who developed and built the robot.

2   Ergonomics and HRI

Human-robot interaction (HRI) can be defined as "the study of the humans, robots, and the ways they influence each other" [6]. As a discipline, it regards the analysis, design, modeling, implementation, and evaluation of robots for the use of humans. The field is strongly related to human-computer interaction (HCI) and human-machine interaction (HMI). Nonetheless, it is distinct in some aspects of its interactions; robots may present dynamic systems with varied levels of autonomy that operate in real-world world environments. Another characteristic that distinguishes models are the differences that occur in the types of interactions and its roles respectively, the physical nature of robots, the quantity of systems the user may have to interact with at the same time, and the environment that these interactions may occur [6].

Human-computer interaction is the term most commonly used to indicate a computer application and files associated with the objects manipulated, not a physical system controlled by a computer [2]. The concept of human-robot interaction only became possible in the last decade as advances were accomplished in field robotics such as reasoning, perception, and programing that made semi-autonomous systems feasible [6]. At first, HRI was solely associated with teleoperation of factory robotic platforms but sooner, as the interest in robotics and its possible applications grown, the importance of research in usability and interface design become a crucial contributor to effectiveness in the performance of complex systems.

To examine guidelines that are important for the development of solutions composed of other parts, by a robot manipulator, it is necessary to define the context of interaction and interaction roles playing apart in the operation. The interest of this study is in collaboration between humans and manipulator robots to accomplish remote tasks where the operator cannot be present, conceding a set of autonomous behaviors to be executed by the robot. This could vary from a robot responding to precise commands from a human about some the position of a controlled arm to a more complex robot system planning and executing trajectory [6].

2.1 Interaction with Manipulator Robots

With the evolution of robotics research, the later incorporation of industrial robots into other types of production processes created new requirements that called for more flexibility and intelligence in industrial robots. These new trends in robotics Research have been denominated service robotics because of their general goal of getting robots closer to human social needs [3]. In a world where robots maximize capabilities and can

Fig. 1. Man and a robot manipulator collaborating in a task. (Source:Gizmodo)

perform more tasks in an autonomous manner, it is important to think about interactions between humans and robots that are aligned with the software architecture and interface design that may accommodate the human-in-the-loop [6].

More complex tasks can be solved if humans and industrial robots combine their individual skills and merge workspaces (Fig. 1) [5]. This is primarily because the weaknesses of one partner can be complemented by the strengths of the other. For instance, from an ergonomic perspective, humans are not suited for heavy and repetitive handling tasks whereas robots do not tire because of repetitive material handling [6]. To ensure that the efficiency of overall systems is as high as possible, it is necessary that the human operator feels comfortable when interacting with the robot.

In the beginning, robot tasks we taught using a teaching pendant. Driving individual joints and bringing the tool centering point to the desired location moved the robot accordingly. Once the location was correct, the robot joint were values stored in a file [7]. Thus, a typical robot program would inhere of a list of move instructions. Within the growing demand for robot applications, programming languages were created to facilitate complex task descriptions. Nonetheless, as industries looked to robotics to improve their revenue and release humans from risk, the disadvantages of online teaching emerged; programming online represented downtime for the robot once the costly equipment would be used for the preparation of and development instead of production [7]. In addition, program quality was not consistent and heavily relied on programmer and feedback was poor. Offline programming was then a solution for these issues, and different robot programs were created enabling different applications from textual programming interfaces to the simulation of environments in 3D graphical systems. As robotics research evolved so did the devices and graphical representation of 3D spacing computer-aided production engineering (CAPE), making interface design a topic of great importance for robot controlling and interaction.

From the perspective of an efficient interaction, ideally, the presence of a robot is transparent to the human, which interacts directly with the world. The human explores the world through some elements of control and gathers information about it through some element of information presentation. A remote human cannot interact directly with the world but instead, interacts with the world through the robot as an intermediary. In such a situation, the control commands are passed from human to robot, modulated by the autonomy of the robot and then executed in the world. In the other spectrum of interaction, information returns directly to the human but is obtained through robot sensors where they are interpreted and perhaps used to identify a robot's behavior. In this context, there are two circuits of interaction: the human interacts with the robot through the interface, and the robot interacts with the world through the autonomous mode. The robot has limitations in relation to what it can do autonomously, how it can act and where it can function autonomously. In the same way, the interface is also inclined to limitations.

2.2 Supervisory Control

The central role of humans in systems that have automation is to assume so-called supervisory control [8]. This control establishes a new relationship between humans and machines as their interaction differs from the traditional human-machine-task model where the human performs a task from a computer or system with lower capabilities. In the supervisory control paradigm, the human or operator becomes a strategist, interacting at the beginning and at the end of the operation, delegating to the machines all the operational steps.

Per Parasuraman [8], the human supervisory control paradigm is characterized by the concept of automation, where the human stop being the main actor of the task, becoming the strategist. At this point, the human plans, monitors, and controls the necessary actions, delegating the operational part to the robot. Supervisory control interfaces are designed for high-level command generation. To effect supervisory control, the operator divides a problem into a sequence of sub-tasks, which the robot then executes on its own. Thus, it requires that the robot can achieve goals (even limited ones) while keeping it safe.

To develop more useful and acceptable robotic user interfaces that will allow the better interactions with industrial robots is necessary to consider the complex systems, in which these robots are integrated, as a simultaneous composition of software behaviors, that must be understood in the context and dimension of the interaction model of HRI. "This changes the user's role from being in control to monitoring and intervening when necessary. This introduces the concept of 'being-out-of-the-loop' and raises the issue of how to alert the user to an exception and how to bring the user up to speed to quickly and effectively intervene" [1].

2.3 Situational Awareness in HRI

This study is interested is the simplest case of HRI, which occurs when one human works with one robot. More precisely by calling out distinct needs of consciousness to the human and the robot, this "base case" makes clear the unequal consciousness relationship between both agents. Drury [2] points out that given one human and one robot collaborating in a task, HRI awareness is the understanding that the human has information about location, status, and surroundings of the robot; along with the knowledge that the robot received from the human the necessary commands to direct its activities and restraints in which it will operate.

Supervisory control interfaces are well-suited for applications that must operate remotely, and the awareness factor is extremely important to select guidelines and metrics that are in accordance with the level of robot's autonomy [8] and consequently how interface design elements must structured and to an efficient interaction. Situational Awareness (SA) [9] constitutes an important human factor in the interaction with supervisory control of remote applications. It represents a continuous diagnosis of the state of a dynamic world [7]; thus, is quite distinct from the choice or decision of what action to take because of the diagnosis. The accurate choice will then depend on good SA, but choice is not the same as SA. Therefore, HRI awareness focuses on the person who most directly controls the robot's activities, which is the operator. For this reason, awareness for HRI analysis can help determined the most of the critical incidents with robot manipulators in remote operations.

2.4   Robot User Interfaces (RUI's)

Robot user interface (RUI) specifies a user interface (UI) that supplements virtual access to human operators interacting with robots working in challenging environments such as *In situ* maintenance or rescue missions [10]. In other words, RUI's are developed and deployed to play an important role in controlling robots and ensuring security in complex environments. The advance in robotic applications naturally created the need to interface different parts of integrated solutions in virtual environments. With the advent of devices with physical and visual feedback to our lives, these interfaces are presented under different outputs such as computers, smartphones or tablets.

Currently, RUIs are often difficult to understand and grasp as they require some training and learning from human operators. These interfaces end up being designed and developed by the same people who built the robot [10], which usually results in un-intuitive and without standard interfaces and creates cognitive handling issues for the operators [5]. The goal of RUI's built to interface systems, which interact with other physical and virtual components and require their functionalities to be grouped into one place. RUI's are usually refined in applied research and development, which implies distinct character in terms of design production output (Fig. 2).

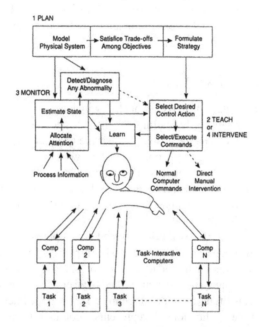

Fig. 2. Diagram of general functions of the supervisory control paradigm. (Source: Parasuraman, 2006.)

Nearly, RUI's are developed to play the crucial role of controlling or monitoring operations via remote interface. In his article about multi-robot interface design, Naveed [10] conducted a survey of HCI principles to improve an existing RUI's used to control a team o mobile exploratory robots. Considering an interaction with multiple robots the main issue he had was that the map-view, robot camera view and sensor data of the system would not appear on the same screen. Therefore, the constant need to switch between windows create a burden to the user. The RUI proposed as a solution (Fig. 3) provided all relevant information in the one single display, a recurrent and important principle when interacting with complex systems.

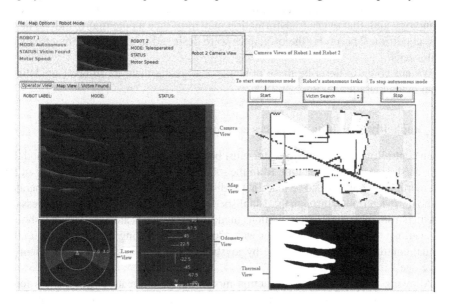

Fig. 3. The new design of RUI by providing all the relevant information on a single display [10].

3   Principles of Interaction for Efficient Interface Design

Guidelines are general rules, pieces of advice to enforce a certain principle with the intent to obey to a good foundation of work. This study aims to present a literature review that examines the principles of design that have been used in HRI guidelines for the development of RUI's. The goal is to illustrate how designers can apply this knowledge in practice when developing robotic interfaces.

Interface design research has different authors who proposed principles of usability to better interaction with products and systems. In this context, ideas and principles to facilitate the overall use and satisfaction of systems may encounter some repetition throughout literature. In other words these principles are similar in some ways but approached in different perspectives. HCI fields has produced most of the guidelines for interface design [14, 15], but authors like Norman [11, 12] defined more generic principles that can be related to the interactions with physical and computer systems, which perhaps allows a relationship with the HRI model once it approaches systems and elements in real time.

In the field of HRI, the importance of supporting human interaction with robots naturally evolved through the concept of better communication and use of systems, which is directly connected with the efficient user interfaces. Literature review in HRI shows that many authors proposed guidelines for more efficient interaction between humans, robots. Goodrich and Olsen [16] highlighted the importance of creating the metrics of neglect tolerance and efficient interfaces. They compiled their findings in a set of principles for efficient interactions in HRI. In this case, the principles are since human intent is transformed and restricted by the availability of technology and, that every transformation may introduce a potential workload or an error condition. Therefore, the principles were designed to act against the effects of bottlenecks.

We are going to describe these principles and relate them to different guidelines found in the literature review.

3.1 Implicitly Switching Interfaces and Autonomy Modes

When controlling a robot, the operator must be able to change forms of control and the ways he/she receives information from the robot. These changes are often imposed by the environment but can also be made at the discretion of the human being. The operator is who must determine, through the established operational context, when it is necessary to switch from manual to an autonomous mode. Mode changes are necessary but should not overload the operator, if the user wants to change operating mode, picking up the manual control (which can be done by joystick, for example) should be sufficient to prove one's intention.

Allowing an implicitly of interaction modes means to create efficient ways for a human controller to interact with robots or (semi) autonomous machines [6]. It also can be related to the decrease of cognitive load and provide detailed and complete control capability of what can be accomplished [15, 17, 18]. In terms of interface design, it should then acknowledge the changes made to avoid any confusion from the user's part. When it comes to cognitive processing, the user does not need a mental model that tells them the steps necessary to alternate modes of interaction, which evokes the idea of the lower cognitive load.

3.2 Use Natural Human Cues

Our natural interaction with people brings us vast experience in dealing with each other and a natural set of forms of expression. Nonetheless, natural language is an indescribable goal, and many other forms of natural expression are useful to as such visual feedback and gestures. With regard to the processing of cognitive information, naturalness means that one's mental model and the proposed system are aligned, making attention to sensory stimuli, and short-term memory uses a practice employed. Thus, naturalness is compatible with effective interaction because it invokes the generation of an intuitive response.

Many types of research describe forms of making interactions more natural and overall usability of systems friendlier. Fong, Thorpe and Baur [5], pointed that interfaces must be designed such that users can unambiguously impart intentions and receive feedback. Also, human-computer dialogue requires a vocabulary, which associates labels with concepts (e.g., command words) and sequences of actions (grammar) allowing a natural cognitive relationship to accomplish tasks with the system [8]. Interface designers who wish to use this principle should be aware of visual representations that are disseminated in our lives through visual languages and devices we use; maps are a good example of how visual repertoire and well-adjusted presentations can help in the ease of use of systems [6, 8, 18].

3.3   Directing Manipulating the World

The purpose of interacting with a remote robot is to accomplish some task in the world. Therefore, RUI's should be designed to allow tasks to be accomplished, rather than drawing attention to the robot or the interface per se. In terms of cognitive information processing, interacting with the robot-world requires a mental model while interacting with the robot requires another separate model. If the robot is transparent to the user, then only one model is necessary. This principle entails that working memory is less likely to be overloaded [15, 18] with extra data in short-term memory and extra mental models. Thus, transparency is a desired element during the interaction.

3.4   Manipulate the Robot-World Relationship

Support autonomy that directly supports the world manipulation is not an easy task. Under these circumstances, human attention may need to be drawn to the robot, and it is most helpful if this attention remains focused on pertinent elements of the world and the task. More precisely, information regarding the status of the robot in relation to a goal state or information that relates robots pose to world coordinates is useful. Thus, the user understands the world through the representation of the robot, and regarding cognitive information processing, the relationship between the robot and world must be known before the user can plan what the robot should do.

3.5   Information Is Meant to Be Manipulated

One primary purpose of RUI is to present information about the world to the user, as well as the relationship between the world and the robot, and solely about the robot. When information is displayed to a user the purpose is to support decision making by the user at perhaps the most fundamental level; this information is used to determine environment path and eventual obstacles that may be present. For example, if an obstacle is presented than the user may wish to guide the robot around it, thus its necessary spatial information about robot´s surroundings [17], so the user is aware [2] of how to guide the robot towards his goal. In terms of cognitive information and processing model, if information can be manipulated directly there is no need for a mental model that translates this information into an action that will occur in a different modality.

3.6 Externalize Memory

One of the difficulties with teleoperation a robot via a camera perspective is that the user cannot see where the robot's parts are [20]. A common occurrence in HRI is when the user projects himself into the machine so under his perception the machine becomes an extension of the user [21]. This greatly simplifies the task of keeping the correct mental model resident in working memory, but it is limited if the sense of priority and perception is missing. Without this sense, the user must either (a) maintain all relevant information in short-term memory [19] and then integrate this information into a mental representation [18], or (b) consult other sensors and integrate all sensors into a consistent whole [22]. This can make the task of guiding a robot all compassing. One form of simplifying cognitive loading associated with navigation is to externalize memory.

3.7 Support Attention Management

Attention seems to be a major bottleneck in cognitive information processing. As mentioned before situation awareness is a human factor of extreme importance when dealing with supervisory control [2, 8]. Even if sufficient information is presented to the user if there's no attention on the provided information than incorrect decisions can be made. In terms of interface design, it is important to manage a user's attention by providing status of the system functioning [6].

4   Evaluation

A comparative analysis (Table 1) was made to illustrate a relationship of different HRI guidelines presented in literature examine the reviewed articles. Based on supervisory control, recurrent aspects of interaction were selected and then group accordingly. Furthermore, it was evaluated what would represent a combination of

Table 1. Acomparative analysis of HRI guidelines table related to the supervisory control.

Principles for efficient HRI interfaces	[2]	[5]	[6]	[11]	[16]	[17]	[18]	[22]	[23]	[24]
Implicitly in switching modes	x	x			x					
Reduce cognitive load				x	x		x	x	x	x
Enhance awareness	x				x	x				
Visibility of system status	x		x		x					x
Availability of required information	x					x				x
Avoid multi-window approach	x				x	x				
Reduce interactive steps				x						x

these factors and what must be taken into consideration that may not be present on available guidelines. In this case, the base of reference is the interaction of one human working with one robot and related guidelines and principles around supervisory control interactions in remote operations.

When examining different guidelines around the same theme, it is possible to note certain recurrence and redundancy once the main objectives that permeate similar ideas. To enhance system performance is a principle mentioned by authors in both fields of HRI [2, 17] and HCI [11–15];it has a direct relationship with the design more efficient user interfaces and reducing the number of interactive steps [11, 24]. Considering supervisory, interfaces would include the availability of required information to make the right decision [2, 17], as well as access time to the interface for the needed actions and the amount of any distraction or attentional shift between the robot scene and the control interface [2, 5]. The presentation of information is then an important principle to remote operations [18, 23, 24]; visibility of system status [2, 6, 24] and implicitly of switching interfaces and autonomy mode [16] are essential to an efficient collaboration with robot manipulators in a remote work environment [5]. Furthermore, other guidelines on HRI can be related to this goal; to avoid any deadlock circumstances [2, 16]; providing all relevant information in one single display [18, 22, 23] allows the operator to have necessary means to plan, teach, monitor and intervene when necessary.

5   Conclusion

A literature review was conducted with articles regarding interface design for HRI to collect guidelines that could be useful for the development of RUI's in remote operations with robot manipulators. The objective of this analysis is to be able to comprise guidelines that support better HRI interfaces but also to identify aspects that are recurrence and therefore important for monitoring this kind of robots in remote operations. The table shows recurrence of guidelines that refer to awareness creating a relationship with the supervisory control and the function of monitoring a single robot operating in the remote environment the factors of awareness can provide a significant framework to evaluate the needs of the operator. It also shows a recurrence of guidelines that required all relevant information displayed to a user with intent to support decision-making, which reducing the workload of the operator and diminishes the number of interactive steps, consequently improving system performance.

Interface designers involved in the construction and development of RUI's under the mentioned circumstances should be then, able to provide all relevant information in one single display, organizing system information per its relevance steps that must be taken further for the effectiveness of the system. An interface designer should be able to represent robot world in a natural perspective; the perception of robot world does not require a different mental model, which brings a fluid interaction and avoid bottlenecks in the system. Therefore, directly present information about this relationship as such messages of notifications regarding actions and system status must be clear to the user.

Acknowledgment. 13 Robotics Robótica Ltda. is gratefully the financial support of Energia Sustentável do Brasil and the ANEEL R&D program (contract COPPETEC/UFRJ JIRAU 09/156631-0003/2015) project EMMA 02 – Protótipo para Revestimento Robótico de Turbinas In Situ.

References

1. Scholtz, J.: Evaluation methods for human-system performance of intelligent systems. In: Proceedings of the 2002 Performance Metrics for Intelligent Systems Workshop, Gaithersburg (2002)
2. Drury, J.L., Scholtz, J., Yanco, H.A.: Awareness in human-robot interactions. In: IEEE International Conference on Systems, Man and Cybernetics, vol. 1, pp. 912–918. IEEE, October 2003
3. Garcia, E., Jimenez, M.A., De Santos, P.G., Armada, M.: The evolution of robotics research. IEEE Robot. Autom. Mag. **14**(1), 90–103 (2007)
4. Murphy, R.R.: Rescue robotics for homeland security. Commun. ACM **47**(3), 66–68 (2004)
5. Fong, T., Thorpe, C., Baur, C.: Collaboration, dialogue, human-robot interaction. In: Jarvis, R.A., Zelinsky, A. (eds.) Robotics Research. STAR, vol. 6, pp. 255–266. Springer, Heidelberg (2003)
6. Scholtz, J.: Theory and evaluation of human robot interactions. In: Proceedings of the 36th Annual Hawaii International Conference on System Sciences, p. 10-pp. IEEE, January 2003
7. Regev, Y.: The evolution of offline programming. Ind. Robot **22**(3), 3 (1995)
8. Parasuraman, R.N., Sinderman: Human-Automation Interaction. Hfes, Santa Monica (2006)
9. Parasuraman, R., Sheridan, T.B., Wickens, C.D.: A model for types and levels of human interaction with automation. IEEE Trans. Syst. Man Cybern. Part A Syst. Hum. **30**(3), 286–297 (2000)
10. Naveed, S., Rao, N.I., Mertsching, B.: Multi robot user interface design based on HCI principles. Int. J. Hum. Comput. Interact. (IJHCI) **5**(5), 64 (2014)
11. Norman, D.A.: The psychopathology of everyday things. In: Levitin, D.J. (ed.) Foundations of Cognitive Psychology: Core Readings, pp. 417–443. MIT Press, Cambridge (2002)
12. Norman, D.A.: Design principles for human-computer interfaces. In: Proceedings of the SIGCHI Conference on Human Factors in Computing Systems. ACM (1983)
13. Jordan, P.W.: An Introduction to Usability. CRC Press, New York (1998)
14. Shneiderman, B.: Designing the User Interface: Strategies for Effective Human-Computer Interaction. Pearson Education India, New Delhi (2010)
15. Nielsen, J.: Usability inspection methods. In: Conference Companion on Human Factors in Computing Systems, pp. 413–414. ACM, April 1994
16. Goodrich, M.A., Olsen, D.R.: Seven principles of efficient human robot interaction. In: IEEE International Conference on Systems, Man and Cybernetics, vol. 4, pp. 3942–3948. IEEE, October 2003
17. Drury, J.L., Hestand, D., Yanco, H.A., Scholtz, J.: Design guidelines for improved human-robot interaction. In: CHI 2004 Extended Abstracts on Human Factors in Computing Systems, pp. 1540–1540. ACM, April 2004
18. Nam, C.S., Johnson, S., Li, Y., Seong, Y.: Evaluation of human–agent user interfaces in multi-agent systems. Int. J. Ind. Ergon. **39**(1), 192–201 (2009)
19. Keyes, B., Yanco, H.A., Drury, J.L., Micire, M.: Improving human-robot interaction through interface evolution. In: Chugo, D. (ed.) human-robot interaction, pp. 183–202. INTECH Open Access Publisher, Vienna (2010)

20. Yamanouchi, W., Yokokura, Y., Katsura, S., Ohishi, K.: Bilateral teleoperation with dimensional scaling for realization of mobile-hapto. In: 34th Annual Conference of IEEE on Industrial Electronics, IECON 2008, pp. 1590–1595. IEEE, November 2008
21. Salaberry, M.R.: The use of technology for second language learning and teaching: a retrospective. Modern Lang. J. **85**(1), 39–56 (2001)
22. Bahadur, S., Sagar, B.K., Kondreddy, M.K.: User interface design with visualization techniques. Int. J. Res. Eng. Appl. Sci. **2**(6), 53–55 (2012)
23. Clarkson, E., Arkin, R.C.: Applying heuristic evaluation to human-robot interaction systems. In: Flairs Conference, pp. 44–49 (2007)
24. Chen, J.Y., Haas, E.C., Barnes, M.J.: Human performance issues and user interface design for teleoperated robots. IEEE Trans. Syst. Man Cybern. Part C (Appl. Rev.) **37**(6), 1231–1245 (2007)

Discounted Prototyping of Virtual Reality Solutions for Science Education

Ghislain Maurice Norbert Isabwe[✉], Margrethe Synnøve Moxnes,
and Marie Ristesund

University of Agder, Grimstad, Norway
maurice.isabwe@uia.no, {msmoxn03,mriste03}@student.uia.no

Abstract. Science education requires experimental work for learners to achieve the intended learning outcomes, which sometimes involve abstract concepts by nature. Advances in digital technology can help learners to undertake experimental work, which would otherwise be costly, either due to the scarcity of laboratory equipment or safety requirements. However, one of the major concerns resides into how to design usable learning solutions from the users' perspective. That would require the involvement of users at all stages of design and development process, even if the technology itself could still be in its infancy. It can be very helpful to present the new design concepts to potential users at a very early stage, with rough models or low fidelity prototypes just to communicate the solution ideas. Such a prototype helps to better understand users' needs and requirements as well as to test and evaluate perceived usability as well the user experience at early stages of the human-centred design process. This work presents a cost-effective approach to low fidelity prototyping for virtual reality based solutions. Virtual reality is modelled through physical objects to allow sample users feel and experience the learning of chemistry concepts through active experimentation. The prototype is made out of everyday components to create an experience of virtual reality in a real physical world. That included paper, prints, boxes, bottles and a book to represent a chemical bonding experiment in an outdoor scenario. User testing proved this prototyping technique to be very practical as well as cost effective.

Keywords: Virtual Reality · Low fidelity prototype · Human-Centred Design

1 Introduction

Traditionally, teaching and learning science subjects has relied on physical laboratory settings to carry out experimental work. Chemistry is one of the subjects thought at junior high school level. Chemistry is quite abstract and consists of a vast amount of theoretical curriculum. However, students do only a few experiments related to chemical bonding and chemical reactions. This is due to the fact that some of the chemical substances are quite expensive and they can also be dangerous for students. The substances must be stored correctly and labelled according to the CLP (Classification, Labelling and Packaging of Substances and Mixtures) regulations [1, 2]. According to Kjemisk Institutt at the University of Oslo, the junior high-school

© Springer International Publishing AG 2017
A. Marcus and W. Wang (Eds.): DUXU 2017, Part II, LNCS 10289, pp. 484–498, 2017.
DOI: 10.1007/978-3-319-58637-3_38

students are not allowed to do experiments with substances that are corrosive, poisonous, explosive and allergenic [3]. One of the approaches to increase students' abilities to perform experiments is to use digital media supported learning solutions. For example, a virtual learning environment where students could perform required experiments. This kind of virtual environment should allow students to explore, combine substances, experience and reflect upon the chemical reactions. Furthermore, in a virtual environment the students should be able to do experiments with dangerous substances without the risk of getting hurt.

This work aims to explore how to effectively design a virtual reality based solution to support the learning of chemistry in junior high school. Virtual Reality (VR) is a technology where users can access a virtual environment and experience it as if they are physically there. VR can be used for both entertainment and education [4]. VR in education is mostly used as a simulation tool, for example to experience traveling to different countries or going back in time.

Several Virtual Reality devices were released in 2016 by renowned brands such as Sony, Oculus and HTC [5]. In 2016 several options for a Virtual Reality device became available for purchase: Google Cardboard [6]; Google Daydream [7]; Samsung Gear VR [8], powered by Oculus [9]; Playstation VR [10]; Oculus Rift [11]; HTC Vive [12]. The sales of VR equipment are rapidly increasing. Statista [13] found that the worldwide shipment of VR head-mounted displays was 140.000 in 2015; 1.43 million in 2016 and it is expected to be 6.31 million in 2017.

Many VR devices are still expensive, ranging from $5 to $799. In addition, when purchasing a VR device there is also a need to buy hardware that can run VR applications. This could be either a smartphone or a computer. On one hand, schools may not have enough funding for purchasing VR devices and other necessary equipment. On the other hand, schools may not be willing to invest into this kind of technology unless they are confident that VR-based solutions are likely to improve the teaching and learning. Even though some of the students may be familiar with latest digital technology solutions, teachers are not likely to conversant with the use of VR in education. Thus, it might be costly and time-consuming to use the system.

There have been considerable advances in development of Virtual Reality devices, however the technology for full immersive experience is still missing. In addition to hardware limitations, it is challenging to design VR based solutions with sufficient user involvement in order to achieve higher user satisfaction. Emerging technology solutions such as virtual reality sets, are not yet widely available to the research and design community. In virtual reality settings, users interact with objects within an environment beyond screen-based single user interfaces, but rather a combination of several interface types as well as interaction styles [14]. The methods for prototyping such contexts of use are still limited, and design teams can struggle to discuss and evaluate early design concepts with stakeholders. Designers should adopt a participatory design approach with special consideration to the target users: On one hand, to find out whether the users would have the same mental model as designers (to understand the design concept), but on the other hand to assess if the users are likely to accept and use the proposed technology based solution.

This paper presents a new approach to prototyping virtual reality based solutions using a use case from chemistry education. The emphasis is on the value of prototyping physically situated interactions beyond screen-based user interfaces. Gill [15] argued that "unfortunately, screen based prototypes are not very good at simulating user interactions because our physical interaction with a product has a pronounced effect on our cognition". He suggests that while screen based prototypes are good for stimulating products where the user has to point, press or manipulate a screen button, they are not good enough to simulate situations that involve grabbing with a hand. We argue that this line of thought can be extended to virtual reality, since this involves manipulation of physical objects such as joysticks to manipulate, move or explore virtual objects.

The main goal of this study is to provide an answer to the research question:

"How to create a low fidelity prototype for virtual reality solutions that support users' interactions within a three-dimensional multisensory space"?

The next section discusses the human-centred design process along with methods that were used in this work. Section 3 presents the low fidelity, discounted prototyping approach for virtual reality solution. In Sect. 4, the findings from user studies are discussed. Finally, Sect. 5 suggests conclusions and gives indications of future work.

2 Human-Centred Design of Virtual Reality Based Solutions

The design of any interactive system for human use should always thrive to create a solution that is usable and provide a high level of satisfaction for the intended users. Therefore, it is important to use a process which involves users at all stages of the design: the human-centred design process (HCD) as shown in Fig. 1.

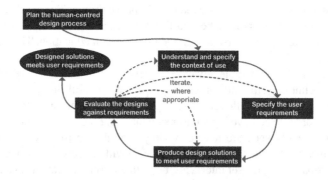

Fig. 1. Interdependence of the HCD activities. Adapted from [16]

2.1 From Needs to User Requirements

The HCD process has to be thoughtfully planned and managed during the whole process to be successful. The process ensures that the artifact is structured and designed in regards to the users and their needs [17]. Relevant data needs to be collected in order to understand and specify how the artifact should be used [14]. The data supports finding the target audience (population) and their goals for using the artifact. Furthermore, the data can be collected by conducting structured or semi- structured interviews, or by handing out questionnaires. The questions can be open and closed questions. Open questions allow the participants to elaborate on their answer, however the closed questions are either multiple choices or Likert scales. Likert scales should have at least five responses, either with numbers or indicate how much the participants agree or disagree, approve or disapprove. With Likert scales the participants can give a degree of opinion in their answers [18]. In structured interviews the interviewer usually asks closed questions, similar to questions from a questionnaire. With semi-structured interviews, the interviewer might ask both closed and open questions. For this research, a junior high-school teacher explained what the students learn in regards to chemistry and chemical bonding in 8th, 9th and 10th grade. The teacher explained that the school does not perform many experiments, instead the students use a molecule set to create and explore the molecules. Moreover, the students can explore molecules using applications (apps) on a tablet.

When designing an artifact that is meant to support the users, it is important to know who is the target audience and what type of support should be provided. This is the foundation for the requirements and to determine how to design and develop the product. The requirements are established through data gathering and analysis [14].

James and Suzanne [19] created the Volere requirements template, comprising of requirements shells like the one shown in Fig. 2.

Requirement #: 8   **Requirement Type**: 9   **Event / Use case**: 1

Description: Students should see the molecules and atoms for the chemicals.

Rationale: To be able to physically see how the molecules and atoms are built up.

Originator: UX Designer and Software Developer

Fit criterion: When the user interacts with objects in the system, the molecule or atoms for the substance will be visible and attached to the selected object. The user can pick up the object and have a closer look at the molecule or atom.

Customer Satisfaction: 5   **Customer Dissatisfaction**: 5

Priority: 5

Conflicts: -

Supporting materials:

History: November 15th, 2016

Fig. 2. Functional requirement shell

The Volere requirements support testing as soon as they have been established. A requirement is testable through its fit criterion. If the fit criterion cannot be met, it means that the requirement is either not concrete or too ambiguous. Software Requirement Specification (SRS) [20] is a software system description for a system that includes specific functions. The supplier and/or the customer can write the SRS. The SRS includes information regarding functionality, external interfaces, performance, attributes and design constraints. The Volere Requirements have been chosen for this research, since adding, editing and deleting requirements through the iterative HCD process are more efficient than they are with the SRS. Functional and non-functional requirements can be established efficiently with the use of the Volere Shell Template. The requirements are iterated further in regards to the results from the user tests.

2.2   Producing Design Solutions and User Testing

After the requirements are established, working on the design solution was started by creating scenarios, a storyboard, use cases and prototypes. Conceptual scenarios can be used for creating design ideas and establishing requirements [21]. Any person, regardless of computer skills, can try the VRBS (virtual reality based solution) with some input from the facilitators or teachers. The students can explore the scene, walk around and touch objects with the controller in order to receive information about substances and chemicals. Furthermore, they can select an object and place it with another object in order to experience and learn from the chemical reactions, when the objects are combined. In regards to Kolb's Experiential Learning Cycle [22] the students should be supported in creating a concrete experience when combining the objects. After the chemical reaction has occurred, the student will be asked by the professor why the reaction happened. Then, he/she has to respond out loud what he/she thinks could be the reason for the chemical reaction. This supports the students in reflecting upon their experience. Moreover, the activity allows students to reflect upon the experience in a way that matches the "Reflective Observation" phase from Kolb's Experiential Learning Cycle [22]. Concrete scenarios can be used in regards to prototyping, generating ideas and evaluation [21]. The concrete scenario for this research was created as follows:

"During chemistry class Peter has received a task from his teacher to explain what carbon monoxide can do to humans and how the molecule is built up. Peter wants to engage with the VRBS in order to do the task. He needs to experience the chemical substances in a virtual reality environment, to get a better image of how all the chemicals are connected in a real world. Peter puts on the VR gear and starts exploring the scene. A professor tells him to help him out of the tent since there is too much carbon monoxide inside. Peter drags the professor out of the tent. Suddenly a sound clip plays. The professor thanks Peter for rescuing him from CO poisoning and is grateful for giving him access to oxygen (O_2). In addition, information about oxygen and the O_2 molecule are visible. Peter touches a disposable grill, which is inside the tent, with the controllers and receives detailed information about CO (Carbon Monoxide) substance, molecule structure and that it is dangerous to have it inside the tent. Peter now has enough information about CO to do the task he received from his teacher. He removes the VR gear and starts working on the task that his teacher gave to him".

Based on the scenario, sample uses cases are defined in order to describe user and system tasks for the design solution. Table 1 presents an essential use case, from which a storyboard was created to visualize the design concepts.

Table 1. Essential use case for the VR system

User intention	System responsibility
Explore and find information about Carbon Monoxide	Display the scene and available objects
Help the professor out of the tent	Play audio clip with instructions
Touch the disposable grill with the controller	Display Carbon Monoxide information and molecule. Play audio clip about Carbon Monoxide
Read the experiments from the book	Display the book
Touch the gasoline can with the controller	Display text information about C_8H_{18}, and the molecule. Play audio clip with information about C_8H_{18}
Pick up the gasoline can	Display hint in the book if the user has not finished the experiment during the next 60 s
Throw the gasoline can on the campfire	Display an explosion and play explosion sound. Play "Why did this happen" audio clip
Answer the professor, and explain why the explosion happened	Future Work: Play sound to inform user if he/she is right or wrong

A storyboard is an efficient and effective technique to showcase the ideas and thoughts of the product [23]. For the VRBS, a storyboard consisting of drawings was created as shown in Fig. 3.

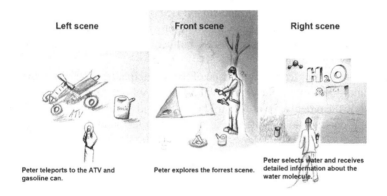

Fig. 3. The storyboard where the user is exploring the forest scene

The storyboard is a collage of sketches showcasing how a user is exploring the forest scene and performing tasks. The storyboard helped visualize the forest scene with all the necessary objects for task executions. As seen in Fig. 3, the middle sketch called Front scene, displays a VR user exploring the scene. The scene consists of a tent with a man and disposable grill inside, a campfire and trees behind the user showcasing that it is a forest scene. The scene to the right called Right scene displays a user selecting the water and receiving the water molecule symbol and text information. Next to the water is a bucket that the user can fill with water. The left sketch called Left scene, displays the user who has teleported to the All Terrain Vehicle (ATV) and gasoline can.

An important part of the design process is prototyping, which encourages designers to reflect upon the created product [24]. A prototype allows the stakeholders to interact with and explore the functionalities within the product. The product should be tested to identify potential usability problems early in the design process. With a prototype the users can interact with the system and test if it matches the requirements. The quickest and cheapest option is produce a Low-Fidelity prototype (for example paper prototypes) [25]. Many design flaws and issues can be addressed early in the design process, before the development process starts. A low-fidelity prototype does not necessarily resemble the final product. It can be made out of cardboard and paper instead of using a digital tool. The use of such a prototype is mainly for exploration, to try out new ideas and alternative designs in a cheap and effective manner. Examples of low-fidelity prototypes are storyboards and paper prototypes. A storyboard is a sequence of events that the user has to go through in order to achieve tasks. A paper prototype can be created to test the physical design for the product. It is made of sketches, prints and sticky notes illustrating the interface in different settings [14, 26] Further on, cheap and fast prototypes can be produced for special contexts of use, such as those requiring interactions in multisensory environments. Users in such environments expect to experience interactions through, for example, a combination of visual, tactile and auditory senses among others. Typically, users of a VR solution for science education would expect to be able to see different scenes, hear some sounds, touch physical objects and move in a physical space. Therefore, a low-fidelity prototype for the VR solution should provide for those user expectations including the mobility requirements. Based on a storyboard for user interactions in a virtual reality environment, a low fidelity prototype was created with pictures, paper figures, a cardboard box and empty soda bottles. Thereafter, user based testing and evaluation was carried out.

Participants to user testing comprised of five participants: two schoolboys aged 13–16 years, and three science teachers from 30–50 years old. One of the teachers was a woman, while the other two were men. The testing and evaluation was done by a mixed methods approach, including the use of observation techniques, interviews and questionnaires.

3   Cost Effective Prototype for Virtual Reality Based Solutions

Based on the ideas and user feedback on the storyboards, a low-fidelity prototype was created with prints, paper, boxes, empty soda bottles and a book as shown in Fig. 4.

This prototype should allow test users to perform chemical experiments involving mixing of different chemical substances and experiencing chemical reactions as proposed in the "essential use case". Obviously, some of the user interactions such as audio-based messages would be delivered by the research team during user testing. The components in this prototype were mainly selected based on the user requirements, the availability of the components and the familiarity of target users with regards to the concepts under study. For instance, the left part of Fig. 5 shows a single use disposable

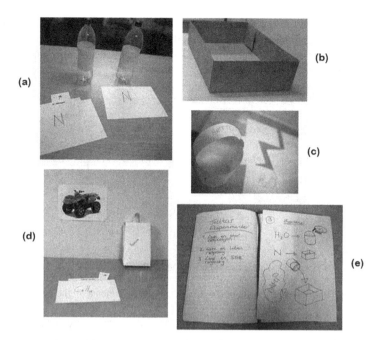

Fig. 4. (a) Nitrogen bottles and information about Nitrogen, (b) nitrogen container, (c) a bucket of water and papers indicating a lake, (d) print of an ATV, paper fuel can and information about octane and (e) a book with experiments and a hint.

grill ("engangsgrill") with the writing "CO" placed in a tent. This is to allow test users to easily recognize a familiar scene: the generation of carbon monoxide if a burning source is left in a place with low levels of oxygen (a tent in this case). Next to the tent, is the letter "N" which stands for the chemical element "Nitrogen" and an arrow showing the user where to get additional information about this element.

Fig. 5. To the left: The professor in the tent with a disposable grill and carbon monoxide. To the right: The chemical formula for Nitrogen. Underneath is a sheet of paper with more information and an arrow indicating more information can be found.

Figure 6 shows a professor's notebook from which a test user can get a list of tasks related to learning chemical reactions. The notebook also illustrates a hypothesis of what would happen if a test user mixed given chemical substances (water, nitrogen) at a certain temperature (100 °C).

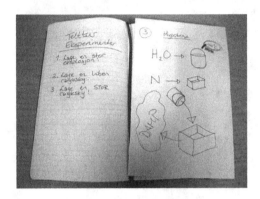

Fig. 6. The professor's notebook with the list of experiments on the left page.

Since the scenario of use involves fire, an inextinguishable torch was fabricated using a paper-stick and a printout. Then, the fire picture is mixed with more pieces of paper to illustrate a campfire in the vicinity of a tent as shown in Fig. 7. The main intention is to provide a mental image of an outdoor scenery, in which the test users could identify themselves with and inherently understand better possible chemical reactions that might occur.

Fig. 7. To the left, a paper tent with a stick figure and a paper disposable grill. To the right, a campfire and information about carbon monoxide. The inextinguishable paper torch

A virtual reality prototype should provide a feel of being in a virtual environment, and in this case the technology under investigation would include a head mounted device (HMD). Hence, the experimental setup for user testing involved the wearing of a slalom helmet with goggles, on which an action camera (GoPro) was mounted. This setting is very practical for both the test users and the researchers. The former would get a near real experience of wearing a HMD (the weight, the straps, limited field of view etc.), while the latter can collect rich experimental data as seen by the test users.

Once all the pieces and bits of a low fidelity virtual reality prototype are in place, it is important to create an environment that allows the user to perform physical manipulation of objects as well as support mobility in space. Figure 8 shows a test environment that affords test users to move around while performing user tasks as it would happen if an interactive system was provided.

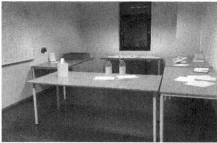

Fig. 8. To the left, a slalom helmet with goggles and the mounted action camera on top. To the right, the physical space to support user mobility

4 Experimental Setup and Findings

User testing was carried out in a controlled room environment, in which test users were introduced to the idea of using virtual reality in teaching and learning of chemistry. Following a set of user tasks, the design concept was introduced through the use of the low fidelity prototype. All user testings were video recorded using a fixed video camera and a moving camera mounted on a helmet worn by test participants as shown in Fig. 9.

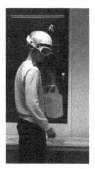

Fig. 9. User testing: user interactions with a virtual reality prototype

The younger participants from early junior-high school needed more help than the older students. To minimise users' discomfort, the facilitators were quick to give them guidance or hints in the book if they said that they did not know what to do, or if they stood still without trying to solve the tasks. Hence, all the users were able to perform the tasks. One of the users found it difficult to orientate in the room and to find objects when wearing the goggles. In order to make it less challenging for the participants, they could have been told that the helmet and goggles could be removed if necessary.

Before the tests, it was assumed that the users would put out the campfire by pouring a bucket of water over it. The campfire is necessary to perform task #1 and #3. Therefore, an inextinguishable torch was placed near the campfire, so the user could set fire to the campfire if they had extinguished the fire. During the first user test, the torch was confusing to the user who though it was to be used as a tool for every experiment. In addition, the participant never put out the campfire. Hence, the torch was removed to avoid any confusion during the next user tests.

All of the participants, except from one, walked back and forth between the professor's notebook and the objects. The other participant took the hint sheet from the book and walked around with it during the tasks. This resulted in a faster tasks completion if compared to others. For this reason, in the high-fidelity prototype the book with tasks and hints will always be available for the user on the left-hand controller. For future work, the user will be asked if they are left or right handed. The placement of the book will be determined by the input response from the user. All the participants could complete the first experiment (create a huge explosion) without any hints. Test users needed hints to resolve two experiments with nitrogen and water. The hints were illustrations of drawings showing the user how to perform the tasks. All participants managed to understand the illustrations, hence all of them successfully completed the given tasks.

For the second task, vapor cloud was written as the reaction between nitrogen and water, assuming this was the correct term after reading in the science textbook for teachers. One of the participants (a science teacher) informed that it should be called a smoke cloud instead. Therefore, the text was changed to smoke cloud. During the next user tests the participants thought that the smoke cloud would be created when they put out the campfire. Another participant was asked, also a science teacher, what the cloud should be called. The participant said that the word gas cloud would be a more accurate name for the reaction between nitrogen and water. In addition, the user informed that during science classes at school the students are well informed about the different characteristics of substances, like solid, liquid and gas. Thus, the name was changed from smoke cloud to gas cloud. In addition, the description was changed to: "Create a gas cloud by using N". Thereby, the users also got an indication of how to perform the experiment. Observing that many participants had trouble with the third experiment (Create a huge gas cloud by using N"), another experiment was created for the high-fidelity prototype. The new experiment was to boil water. Then the last task was to create a big gas cloud by using N and H_2O 100 °C (Fig. 10).

To be able to illustrate that the molecules would show up when the user pointed at objects in VR, one of the facilitators was standing next to the participants with sheets of paper with illustrations of molecules. When a participant looked at an object, the facilitator would show them the sheet of paper illustrating the corresponding molecule. One of the participants took the paper and wanted to bring it along. This was an unforeseen experience. The facilitator allowed the participant to take the papers, but took them back as soon as the participant started to move. Furthermore, in order to indicate liquid Nitrogen, empty 1,5 l soda bottles were used. The soda labels were removed and a taped note was added that said Liquid Nitrogen. Most users unscrewed the soda bottles cork in order to

Fig. 10. User testing: user experience within a physical prototype of virtual reality

pour an imaginative Nitrogen liquid. This was unforeseen since it was assumed that the participants would simulate poring nitrogen without unscrewing the corks.

The paper objects in the scene did not have a correct scaling to the real world, which seemed to confuse the participants. The tent and the professor had a very small size in regards to other objects and to the participants. In addition, many participants did not understand that there was CO inside the tent because of the disposable grill. Assuming that the size would not be a major issue, and to avoid using too much time creating the scene, some objects were smaller than the real world. Many participants had trouble finding the tent and the professor. Hence, the facilitators had to guide them for finding the objects. Therefore, a small note was attached to the disposable grill with the text: "CO" and taped to the grill. For future prototype testing, facilitators should consider creating more accurate scaling of objects. It might be easier for the test participants to find and use the paper objects correctly. To illustrate a man (professor), a paper stick figure was cut out. Several participants were unable to understand that this was a person. Therefore, a face was drawn on the paper figure including glasses and some hair. During the following user testings there were no problem for the users to understand that the paper figure was the professor.

Moreover, there were several sheets with information about different chemicals. These sheets were placed behind the corresponding sheet containing the chemical formula, for example H_2O for water. The sheets were made visible showing a headline and the first sentence. Although the first participant made a thorough orientation in the scene, he/she never viewed the sheets information. For that reason, arrows were placed on the sheets pointing upwards, indicating that the sheets could be moved in order to read additional information about the chemical. Which resulted in one of the participants pulling out the sheets to read about the chemicals. Hence, being able to complete the tasks.

A container was placed next to the water and a bucket next to the nitrogen bottles. The idea was that the users would fetch water with the bucket and pour nitrogen into the container. The placement of the items was confusing for the first participant during the user test. Therefore, the bucket was moved next to the water and the container next to the nitrogen. During the next user tests the participants interacted with the items that were placed next to the objects. Thus, supporting the participants to complete the tasks effectively.

It was important that the science teachers approved the tasks, since most of the tasks were created from the teacher's textbook. In addition, the teachers had to confirm that the molecules and text information about each substance was correct. The teachers also had to approve of the nitrogen atom's construction. All the participants understood and completed the tasks. Furthermore, they thought the tasks were useful and fun to perform. Also, the teachers approved the tasks. Hence, the development of the VRBS could continue.

5   Conclusion and Future Work

This work has investigated the design process of a virtual reality (VR) based solution for science education. Usually, designing a human-centred interactive system requires user involvement throughout the design process. However, VR presents a particular challenge given that it is still a relatively new, expensive technology, which requires interactions beyond the traditional two-dimensional user interfaces. Many designers may not have adequate tools for fast, and easy creation of cost-effective artifacts for involving users in designing usable solutions. This article proposes the use of everyday objects to create models of multisensory virtual reality environments. Using a case study of learning chemistry at junior high school level, this work developed a VR based solution concept that involves students performing chemical experiments in a virtual outdoor environment. This research paper shows a practical approach to develop a VR prototype at very low cost, which is also referred to as a "discounted prototype". User based testing of the prototype has provided invaluable feedback to revise the user requirements and refine the interaction design. This prototype helped in engaging key stakeholders to test the solution concept and find out usability problems very early in the design process. It was found that, most importantly, the users understood the solution concept and suggested necessary adjustments. In most of cases, users managed to complete the given user tasks and appeared to behave like they are immersed in a virtual reality environment. There are indications that any effective low fidelity VR prototype should support multisensory interactions such as the manipulation of objects, movements of test participants as well as auditory and visual interactions. This work can be extended by investigations into how to create reusable assets for low fidelity prototyping of VR in the same way as it is done with mockups and wireframing for screen based interactions. Research could establish an inventory of objects, which could be matched and mixed in the prototyping process. Such objects should be flexible enough to represent several application scenarios. One option for creating a low-fidelity prototype for virtual reality solutions can be adding easily accessible objects in a room. The user can interact with the objects in the room in order to complete the given tasks. In addition, when the users are wearing a helmet with a mounted action camera, facilitators can efficiently collect and analyse data from the usability test.

References

1. Universitetet i Oslo - Kjemisk Institutt. Oppbevaring og håndtering. http://www.mn.uio.no/kjemi/forskning/grupper/skole/ressurser/hms/kjemikalier-grunnskole/kjemikalier-ungdomstrinn/oppbevaring-og-handtering.pdf
2. Miljødirektoratet. Klassifisering og merking i CLP. http://www.miljodirektoratet.no/no/Publikasjoner/Publikasjoner/2011/Mars/Klassifisering_og_merking_i_CLP/
3. Universitetet i Oslo - Kjemisk Institutt. Regler og ansvar på naturfagrommet. http://www.mn.uio.no/kjemi/forskning/grupper/skole/ressurser/hms/kjemikalier-grunnskole/kjemikalier-ungdomstrinn/regler-og-ansvar.pdf
4. Aabakken, L.: virtuell virkelighet i medisin - Store Norske Leksikon, 09 April 2015. https://snl.no/virtual_reality. [Cited: 21 August 2016]
5. Swanson, J.: The Year of Virtual Reality – KnowledgeWorks, 11 May 2016. http://knowledgeworks.org/worldoflearning/2016/05/virtual-reality-2016/. [Cited: 12 September 2016]
6. Google. Google Cardboard. https://vr.google.com/cardboard/. [Cited: 21 August 2016]
7. Daydream - Headset (2016). https://vr.google.com/daydream/headset/
8. Samsung. Samsung Gear VR. http://www.samsung.com/global/galaxy/gear-vr/. [Cited: 21 August 2016]
9. Oculus Gear. Gear VR powered by Oculus. https://www3.oculus.com/en-us/gear-vr/. [Cited: 21 August 2016]
10. Sony. Playstation VR - Virtual Reality headset for PS4. https://www.playstation.com/en-us/explore/playstation-vr/. [Cited: 21 September 2016]
11. Oculus. Oculus Rift. https://www3.oculus.com/en-us/rift/. [Cited: 21 August 2016]
12. HTC Vive. Vive. https://www.htcvive.com/us/. [Cited: 21 August 2016]
13. Statista. Forecast unit shipments of virtual reality head-mounted displays worldwide from 2015 to 2017 (in million units). http://www.statista.com/statistics/509154/head-mounted-displays-worldwide-shipments/. [Cited: 21 August 2016]
14. Sharp, H., Rogers, Y., Preece, J.: Interaction Design - Beyond Human-Computer Interaction, 3rd edn. Wiley, West Sussex (2014)
15. Gill, S.: PAIPR prototyping: some thoughts on the role of the prototype in the 21st century. In: Valentine, L. (ed.) Prototype: Design and Craft in the 21st Century. Bloomsbury Academic (2013)
16. International Standard Organization. Ergonomics of human-system interaction - Part 210: Human-centred design for interactive systems (ISO 9241-210:2010), October 2010
17. Maguire, M.: Methods to support human-centred design. Int. J. Hum. Comput. Stud. **55**(4), 587–634 (2001)
18. Likert, R.: A technique for the measurement of attitudes. Arch. Psychol. **22**, 136–165 (1932)
19. Robertson, J., Robertson, S.: Volere Requirements Specification Template. [Template], 16th edn. Atlantic Systems Guild, London (2012)
20. IEEE Computer Society. Software Engineering Standards Committee & IEEE-SA Standards Board. IEEE Recommended Practice for Software Requirements Specifications. Institute of Electrical and Electronics Engineers (1998)
21. Benyon, D.: Designing Interactive Systems: A Comprehensive Guide to HCI, UX and Interaction Design, 3rd edn. Pearson Education Limited, Harlow (2014)
22. Kolb, D.A.: Experiential Learning, Experience as the Source of Learning and Development, pp. 26–33. Prentice Hall PTR, New Jersey (1984)
23. Barakat, R.A.: Storyboarding can help your proposal. IEEE Trans. Prof. Commun. **32**(1), 20–25 (1989)

24. Schön, D.: The Reflective Practitioner: How Professionals Think in Action. Basic Books, New York (1983)
25. Rettig, M.: Prototyping for tiny fingers. Commun. ACM **37**, 21–27 (1994)
26. Grady, H.M.: Web site design: a case study in usability testing using paper prototypes. In: Proceedings of IEEE Professional Communication Society International Communication Conference and Proceedings of the 18th Annual ACM International Conference on Computer Documentation: Technology & Teamwork, pp. 39–45. IEEE Educational Activities Department (2000)

A Natural Interaction VR Environment for Surgical Instrumentation Training

Adalberto Lopes[1(✉)], Antônio Harger[1], Felipe Breyer[2], and Judith Kelner[1]

[1] Universidade Federal de Pernambuco, Recife, Brazil
{apsl2,ahr,jk}@cin.ufpe.br
[2] Instituto Federal de Pernambuco, Recife, Brazil
fbb3@cin.ufpe.br

Abstract. This paper details the process of prototyping a Surgical Instrumenta-tion Simulator using Virtual Reality and a gesture-based natural interaction. Our prototype used a cost-efficient mobile headset along with a telephone screen for a stereoscopic display, thus creating a low-cost. We applied an iterative approach to our prototyping process, and user testing included both students and profes-sionals from the Health field. Results showed proposed interactions techniques as satisfactory according to users. In addition, the low-cost hardware choice proved sufficient in quality to support an immersive experience.

Keywords: Interaction design · HMD · Natural user interfaces

1 Introduction

Since their arrival in the early 2010s, Head Mounted Displays (HMDs) have gained relevance in the industries of video games, simulators, health, and education. They differentiate by allowing greater immersion to users in first-person experiences. Further-more, advances in interaction and visualization technology for HMDs allowed users to feel closer to a real environment. Specially in systems using body tracking devices that transfer user's hands or their entire body to the virtual world. Immersion was also improved by progress on graphical engines and HMD screen resolutions, promoting visual realism in such experiences.

Examples of interaction techniques for Virtual Reality (VR) exist in both academia and commercial applications. They use a variety of interaction technologies such as camera tracking, navigation systems, single-hand sensory controllers, and traditional game controllers. Each device supports different functionalities and degrees of immer-sion to the user [1].

In this article, we first document current use of HMDs for medical training. Medical applications using HMDs include endoscopy surgery [2], image examina-tion, tridimensional mapping in high-risk locations [3], and surgery simulators. Later, we later detail the construction and user testing of a surgical instrumentation simulator with health students and professionals. It is necessary for health students to train the recognition and organization of surgical instruments. Such instruments are expensive to purchase, and educational institutions, in some countries, do not

© Springer International Publishing AG 2017
A. Marcus and W. Wang (Eds.): DUXU 2017, Part II, LNCS 10289, pp. 499–509, 2017.
DOI: 10.1007/978-3-319-58637-3_39

provide students with necessary time to practice using them. Thereby, developing such a low-cost simulator would not only reduce costs in acquiring surgical materials but also allow students to learn from their homes.

2 Presence and Interaction

An interaction designer strives to build interactive products that are easy to learn, effective, and pleasant to use. The benefits of good interaction design to a VR system include greater immersion in the virtual environment, a better sense of presence, a smoother learning curve, and better general usability. According to Bowman [4], an interaction technique is a method that allows a user to carry out a task through a user interface. An interaction technique includes both hardware and software. It maps information from an input device to an action, then to the system output in a way that the output devices can interpret. Thus, interaction design seeks performance, usability, and utility [4].

Performance is how well a user and the system perform an action, and it reflects the efficiency and precision of the product. Usability indicates if an interactive product is pleasant, easy to use, and effective to users. Utility means that the developed interactions fully support, or complete, the user's goals.

The main goal of VR technology is to recreate the sense of presence for users. Hence, it immerses them in a virtual environment so that they suppose being in a "real" world [5]. VR is an advanced interaction technique that allows immersion, navigation, and interaction in a synthetic tridimensional computer-generated environment, using multi-sensorial channels [6]. Accordingly, users seek immersive experiences in VR.

Through technology such as body tracking and haptic feedback, interactive devices can aggregate senses to VR experiences when combined with an HMD. Such is the case with the Oculus Rift controller. VR applications can use input from its touch and movement sensors to render an accurate representation of the user's hands. If the user has a closed grip on the controller, the game shows their hands closed. The Leap motion is another example of a device that enables hand presence, although it does its tracking through infra-red cameras. It detects a multitude of gestures through high-precision hand and finger tracking, and it is a low-cost device for VR. When used with VR, the Leap motion is placed in the HMD providing a 150-degree range of detection.

3 Related Work

The paper "Virtual Training of Fire Wardens Through Immersive 3D Environments" [7] presents an immersive interface using Oculus Rift and a Leap Motion. They presented gesture-based interaction for choosing paths and actions in a fire escape simulation. In the simulation, users selected one out of two or three pre-defined paths through their choices. Similarly, our work also uses the Leap Motion as an input device, and gestures for actions such as moving to waypoints in the virtual space.

In their study, Dorabjee et al. [8] analyzed ten applications using Leap Motion and an HMD. They presented design suggestions and tendencies for creating natural interfaces. Following Wixon and Wigdor, they claimed that natural interfaces do not need to be natural, but rather need to make the users behave naturally while interacting with the product. Wixon and Wigdor also say that five basic characteristics are necessary for an interface to be considered natural. The first characteristic is "Evocative" since the interface evokes a natural behavior for the user to interact with the system. "Unmediated" is the second characteristic, meaning the users must interact with the system without a secondary system, using their hands or body instead. Next, there is "Fast and few", as the user should interact with the objects through fast interactions related to their natural properties instead of a set of commands. Contextual, the fourth characteristic, prescribes that the interface presents an ambient where the user naturally knows how to realize the actions. Lastly, the fifth characteristic is Intuition: the objects respond to the actions how the user would expect them to. In this paper we describe a prototype that employs a natural interface with Wixon and Wigdor's five characteristics.

Experiences with HMDs may cause undesirable physical symptoms to the user, which Davis et al. [9] names cybersickness. The symptoms include nausea, vomiting, and eyestrain, and they occur due to the disconnection between the virtual and real experiences. For instance, if a user is motionless in the real world, but moving in the virtual world, this confuses their brain and might cause cybersickness. Factors that affect chance of cybersickness include user age, playing stance, and hardware framerate and latency.

Settgast et al. [10] compared the level of immersion of two VR systems, DAVE and HMD, for scenarios of observation, emotion, and interaction. Users were also checked for cybersickness on after each session. Results showed that for all tasks users preferred the DAVE system because they perceived their actions and the visuals as "more realistic". They attributed this to the screens in the DAVE system, which rendered images in larger scale. Their tests showed, however, that users presented slightly higher levels of cybersickness after the DAVE session than with HMDs. During our tests, we inquired users about cybersickness symptoms after using the low-cost equipment prototype.

4   Objectives

In this paper, we present and evaluate a surgery instrumentation simulator prototype with educational purposes. The prototype aims to promote immersion and procedures close to the real experience while maintaining a low cost. Thus, we checked the participant for cybersickness symptoms after the tests.

5   Methodology

Our methodology had four stages: Technology Selection, Prototype Construction, User Tests, and Feedback and Data Analysis. We first observed existing interaction techniques from academia and the industry, identifying the hardware most suited to our project. Then we developed the prototype aided by interaction design and level design techniques. During the prototype's construction, we performed preliminary tests to iterate over the interaction techniques and level design. With the prototype completed, we started user tests to evaluate interactions and hardware components.

5.1   Technology Choice and Prototype Development

For the prototype's hardware, our team investigated market options regarding price and user evaluations. We chose a U$ 45.00 basic mobile HMD, of the Brazilian brand Beenoculus, alongside a U$ 150.00 LG Nexus 4 smartphone, and a U$ 79.99 Leap Motion. A computer was also necessary for rendering the video and streaming it to the smartphone using the Trinus VR app through a Wi-fi or USB connection.

We chose to develop the prototype using the Unity 5 Game Engine because it was a free platform with great support for VR and the Leap Motion. The engine's illumination features were also decisive, allowing for a good level of visual fidelity. Thus, the project setup is shown in Fig. 1. It uses the mobile HMD with a Leap Motion attached and using the Smartphone as a stereo screen.

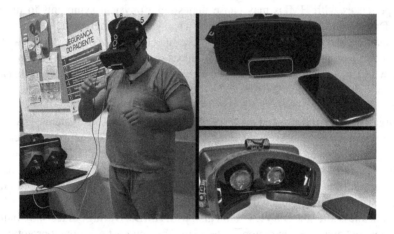

Fig. 1.   Prototype. (Source: author)

The prototype was developed through an iterative process. We generated test builds for small groups of users to evaluate the interaction techniques and complexity of the tasks. During these iterations, we adjusted, added and removed interactions and changed the task order. Sections 5.2 and 5.3 detail the changes made and their motivations.

5.2   Step Descriptions

The goal of the prototype was to simulate the organization of surgical instruments in a desk. Our first iterations of the prototype had the player taking objects from an unorganized desk, then placing them on another. However, the users expressed discomfort in moving between the tables frequently, so we split the process into two tasks: Categorization and organization. In the former, the user takes objects from the unorganized desk separating them in groups. Next, in the organization step, the user repositions the objects, sorting them accordingly.

The prototype initially had 41 objects which the user had to organize in sectors, one for each category of tools. However, due to users struggling to differentiate small instruments of similar size, 8 objects were removed, leaving 41-8 in the final iteration. Figure 2 shows the layout of the table.

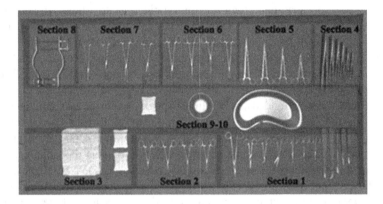

Fig. 2. Layout of the table (Source: Author)

In the Categorization phase, the user collects the objects belonging to each category and places them in a floating tray. Incorrectly categorized objects return to their initial position in the table, and the player receives a new, empty tray for each category. A text indicator for the current category shows the amount of remaining objects. Due to table size, the user must move through the virtual space during this test, which is done by pointing (Fig. 3).

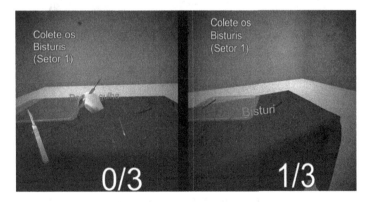

Fig. 3. Left: The floating tray. Right: A text indicator for the current category shows the amount of remaining objects (Source: Author)

In the organization phase, the user has a tray with objects to place on the table. The table has slots for the tools that change color to show whether the order the objects are in the correct order. When the user completes a section, they move automatically to the next one, until all are complete.

5.3   Interaction Techniques

We started the prototype development by implementing tool manipulation. The user could pinch objects carry them, then release the pinch to drop them. In addition, we prototyped a looking interaction to show object details when the user looked at them. Our initial tests showed that, although the pinch interaction was effective and intuitive, a fraction of the users naturally tried to grab objects by grasping them, so we added that grasp interaction. Furthermore, we noticed users had difficulty grabbing small objects when they were close to each other. To mitigate this problem, we added a highlight to the closest object. We also added that highlight to places where the tools could be placed.

Early in testing, it became clear that the natural reach of the user's hands was insufficient for manipulating distant objects. Making the user move around the virtual space would be undesirable, so we prototyped interactions for moving the table instead. We prototyped an interaction where the user would grab specific spots at the table to drag it. This, however, showed to be unintuitive and hard to convey visually, so it was discarded. Next, we tested an interaction to move the user instead: If they pointed at a destination for a while, they would move to it. Our tests showed that it was effective, so we kept it. The final interactions of highlight, movement, and object manipulation are shown in Fig. 4.

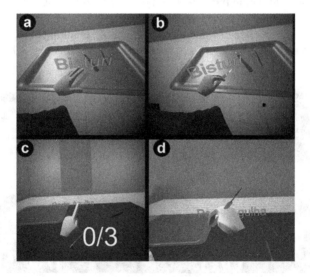

Fig. 4. A: Highlight, B: Pinch, C: Point, D: Grab (Source: Author)

5.4   Metrics

For the usability analysis of this prototype, we used Sauro and Lewis's PSSUQ (Post-study System Usability Questionnaire) [11]. The survey had 16 questions about usability on a 0 to 7 Likert scale, where 0 and 7 corresponded to "completely agree" and "completely disagree". Similarly to Davis et al. [9], our cybersickness evaluation was done by asking "Have you felt any discomfort using this prototype?" to which the user would answer a number from 0 to 10 where 0 meant "I had no discomfort" and 10 meant "I feel sick". We analyzed participant answers and complaints to identify problems in the prototype.

5.5 User Tests

The prototype's user sample comprised of 19 users (11 males), of which 8 were health students or professionals. Of the users within the care sector, 2 were heart surgeons, 1 was a resident doctor, 4 were medical students and one was a nursing student. The remaining participants were students of either computer science, law, or electronic engineering. Users were between 20 and 31 years old, with an average of 24 (SD = 3.9). We executed test sessions in a hospital room, in the GRVM research group and in the house of one of the developers, and Fig. 5 shows test sessions. After completing the tests, the users answered a survey about discomfort and prototype usability. We organized the data in table form, which the next session will detail.

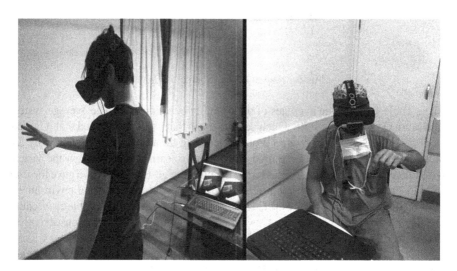

Fig. 5. User tests (Source: author)

6 Results

6.1 Data Analysis

The duration of the experiments occurred with time minimum of 16 min and maximum of 35 min. Users spent an average of 23 min (SD = 4.1) to complete the test. Looking at the Fig. 6, we noticed that 14 users had total comfort or the least discomfort when using the prototype. They scored the level of nausea at 1 or 2 on the scale where 1 means "no discomfort" and 10 means "I am nauseous (vomiting)". Only one participant (female) was unable to complete the test. She had symptoms of nausea and dizziness after 5 min of use and gave up the tasks. The participant did not respond to the PSSUQ questionnaire because she did not complete the test. Another participant, also female, presented dizziness problems soon after finishing the test and removed the HMD. She affirmed loss of spatial orientation after leaving the virtual environment and punctuated the discomfort with note 8.

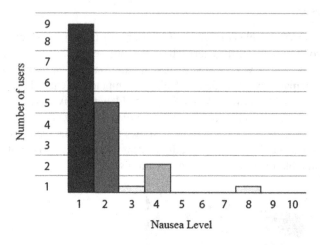

Fig. 6. Nausea Level. (Source: Author)

The Table 1 shows the averages of the usability questionnaire. The average system usage score (SysUse) was 1.79, which demonstrates that users have stated that it is easy to use the prototype. Users had no problem learning the interactions proposed by the simulator. The command that required more time to learn was to walk in the virtual environment. This interaction worked from the pointing gesture. When we gave the user the "walk" command, most of them felt they were present in the virtual environment and walked forward in the real world. The interaction also presented problems because some participants stretched the arm forward making it impossible for the sensor to visualize the user's hand.

While executing some gestures, the users reported the absence of error messages when software problems happened. The main problem in the prototype occurred in the Grab interaction. Participants had their hand mirrored by the Leap Motion when picking up instruments. This problem caused dropping of objects, and frustration in users. In addition, an error has occurred caused by the limitation of the Leap Motion range. Users moved their hands to a position out of bounds of the sensor and caused non-rendering of hands in the simulator. However, in developing the prototype tasks the system reported errors to users. For example, if the user placed some object in the wrong order the system would display the color red at the piece slot. Looking at item 7 of the table (), we can see that the users defined the error messages as bad. Scores for this item resulted in an average of 3.66. This happened because users who dealt with implementation errors or Leap Motion sensor problems gave high marks for error messages.

Overall, users have approved the system interface. Observing the data from the table, it can be stated that users gave good marks for Interface Quality (intQual), obtaining an average of 1.81. The users assimilated the highlight function, the positioning of the target

Table 1. PSSUQ (Means)

Item	Item text	Mean	SD
1	Overall, I am satisfied with how easy it is to use this system	2.11	1.50
2	It was simple to use this system	1.66	0.76
3	I was able to complete the tasks and scenarios quickly using this system	2.44	1.14
4	I felt comfortable using this system	1.61	1.14
5	It was easy to learn to use this system	1.33	0.48
6	I believe I could become productive quickly using this system	1.61	1.28
7	The system gave error messages that clearly told me how to fix problems	3.66	1.81
8	Whenever I made a mistake using the system, I could recover easily and quickly	2.44	1.50
9	The information (e.g., online help, on-screen messages, and other documentation) provided with this system was clear	1.81	1.33
10	It was easy to find the information I needed	1.72	1.12
11	The information was effective in helping me complete the tasks and scenarios	1.50	1.04
12	The organization of information on the system screens was clear	2.00	1.18
13	The interface of this system was pleasant	1.50	1.24
14	I liked using the interface of this system	1.55	1.24
15	This system has all the functions and capabilities I expect it to have	2.38	1.28
16	Overall, I am satisfied with this system	1.77	1.30
Scale	Scale scoring rule	Mean	SD
SysUse	Average Items 1–6	1.79	0.40
InfoQual	Average Items 7–12	2.19	0.78
IntQual	Average Items 13–15	1.81	0.49
Overall	Average Items 1–16	1.94	0.57

texts, and the help that existed through the colors. The Information Quality (InfoQual) score were also good with 2.19 average. To complete the tasks the users needed to know the name and type of the instruments they were manipulating. However, the team noted that some users were unable to see the names of the objects in the scenario. This was because some users did not regulate the convergence lens correctly.

The interface did not have a reticle in the center of the screen. The absence of this component in the interface generated an interactive problem. To know the name of a certain surgical instrument the users had to centralize the object on the HMD screen. However, some participants did not center the object by moving the head. They just moved their eyes inside the HMD and could not know the name of the object they were looking at. After completing all the tests, the development team realized the need to add a reticle in the interface. This component would make users know specifically where to look. Users identified a display issue on their smartphone screen because it was small at 720p resolution. This made some visualization tasks difficult. One participant commented, "The resolution was so low that sometimes I could not distinguish the difference between haemostat and surgical scissors".

7 Discussions

The team developed the project in about 5 months and evaluated interactions with 19 users who approved the interactive project. A small part of the sample (2 users) suffered problems of cybersickness. However, the vast majority of users felt that the hardware did not generate physical problems. Therefore, the low cost setup it is safely for use. Participants spent an average of 23 min to complete the test. Users spent more time doing the first task than in the second. This happened because the first task required users to become familiar with the movement, visualization, and interactions of the virtual environment.

Range, occlusions or leap motion sensor failures were the main usability problems. At times, users placed their hand out of range of the sensor, resulting in tracking failures. At other times, one hand could create occlusion over the other. This happened when the user placed one hand in front of the other causing the non-visualization of a hand in the virtual environment. The team was able to avoid the problem of accuracy of the leap motion after reducing the number of objects from 41 to 33. This helped to make the pinch interaction more accurate.

While developing the prototype, the team realized that users found the grab interaction more natural than the pinch interaction. The team added in the project the two gestural forms to perform the pick-up action. However, the grab technique generated leap motion failures because the sensor could not identify the thumb of the users. Sometimes, the leap motion mirrored users' hands and caused objects to drop on the table.

Not implementing a reticle on the simulator screen caused interface problems. Some users could not which object was in the center of the HMD screen. Users were able to memorize actions intuitively. However, the development team noticed problems in the interaction of pointing to walk. The users caused leap motion failures by stretching the arm and getting out of bounds.

Highlights marked components locations. Snaps and waypoints have helped users to complete tasks. At the first moment of the research, the team planned the level design with a single phase. The goal was to give full freedom for the user to make the decisions to choose by which task to begin. The team realized that users were feeling tired due to the large number of goals, and the need for constant movement. Therefore, the development team decided to split the level into two levels. Separating the complex task of organizing a surgical instrumentation table into several mini-tasks optimized the users' time.

8 Conclusions and Future Work

This research successfully built the intended prototype. The low-cost setup proved sufficient for an immersive experience. From analyzing the test results and feedback, we concluded that most users were satisfied by the system usability and found the interface pleasant. However, two of the 19 participants showed cybersickness symptoms, which might hinder such a product's accessibility.

As future works, we intend to solve issues found by our testers and run more tests using a larger sample of health care professionals. Our software should be refined to solve problems caused by jitter in the Leap Motion input and prevent errors that hinder the user experience. Regarding the prototype hardware, we would like to use a smartphone with a 1080p resolution screen to ease observation tasks. Finally, improvements to the interface would include a reticle for a more clear indication of the looking interaction and a range indicator for the maximum hand distance.

References

1. Anthes, C., Hernández, R., Weidemann, M., Kranzlmuller, D.: State of the art of virtual reality technology. In: 2016 IEEE Aerospace Conference, At Big Sky, MT, USA (2016)
2. Sony introduces a medical head mount display system for use in endoscopic surgery (2014). http://www.sony.co.uk/pro/press/pr-sony-head-mount. Sony
3. Google Cardboard saves baby's life (2016). http://edition.cnn.com/2016/01/07/health/google-cardboard-baby-saved/. CNN
4. Bowman, D.A., Kruijff, E., LaViola Jr., J.J., Poupyrev, I.: 3D User Interfaces: Theory and Practice. Addison-Wesley, Westford (2004)
5. Slater, M., Wilbur, S.: A, framework for immersive virtual environments: speculations on the role of presence in virtual environments. Presence Teleoperators Virtual Environ. **6**(6), 603–616 (1997)
6. Burdea, G., Coiffet, P.: Virtual Reality Technology. Wiley, New York (1994)
7. Diez, H., García, S., Mujika, A., Moreno, A., Oyarzun, D.: Virtual training of fire wardens through immersive 3D environments. In: Web3D 2016, Anaheiim, CA, USA, 22–24 July 2016
8. Dorabiee, R., Bown, O., Sarkar, S., Tomitsch, M.: Back to the future: identifying interface trends from the past, present and future in immersive applications. In: OzCHI 2015, Melbourne, VIC, Australia, 07–10 December 2015
9. Davis, S., Nesbitt, K., Nalivaiko, E.: A systematic review of cybersickness. In: IE 2014, Newcastle, NSW, Australia (2014)
10. Settgast, V., Pirker, J., Lontschar, S., Maggale, S., Gütl, C.: Evaluating experiences in different virtual reality setups. In: Wallner, G., Kriglstein, S., Hlavacs, H., Malaka, R., Lugmayr, A., Yang, H.-S. (eds.) ICEC 2016. LNCS, vol. 9926, pp. 115–125. Springer, Cham (2016). doi: 10.1007/978-3-319-46100-7_10
11. Sauro, J., Lewis, J.R.: Quantifying the User Experience: Practical Statistics for User. Elsevier, Waltham (2012)

Visual and Interactive Concerns for VR Applications: A Case Study

Francimar Maciel[✉], Alvaro Lourenço, Paulo Carvalho, and Paulo Melo

Samsung SIDIA, Manaus, Brazil
{francimar.m,alvaro.abl,p.carvalho,paulo.melo}@samsung.com

Abstract. Virtual Reality has enabled the evolution of distributed information architecture in the three-dimensional environment. It means that interface elements like buttons or menus are not restricted to 2D-dimensional environments: they can be now immersed in 3D space with arbitrary position and orientation. This scenario implies a need to think about different paradigms to be designed in regard to several aspects like location, field of view, selection, movement, attention etc. The present paper aims to present some aspects of information arrangement and content management in Virtual Environments, as well as provide advice for testing the effectiveness of those systems using the application RIO 360 for virtual reality as reference.

Keywords: Virtual Reality · Information architecture · Visual design · Virtual environments

1 Introduction

The word VR (Virtual Reality) has gained a lot of attention and excitement over the last years. The power of the technology to create impressive and unexpected digital experiences surely is one of the main reason for this scenario [1]. This technology's strength comes from a broad venue for creativity, freedom and multimedia capabilities that, however, happen under a heavy cost of learning curve, caveats and experimentation [2]. Although it presents a sort of opportunities for creating engagement and new experiences immersion, this event brings relevant questions like: what are the new paradigms for information arrangement in regard to the 3D space? What are the differences from interactions with 2D space? Based on a systematic literature review, this essay aims to share the discoveries of a design team when building VR Rio 360 [3], a tourism VR app focused on Rio de Janeiro and its famous attractions. Rio 360 was the first app built by a mobile solutions team in transition to create solutions for VR. The core findings were result of a multidisciplinary effort of concept design, software development, and user research studies.

© Springer International Publishing AG 2017
A. Marcus and W. Wang (Eds.): DUXU 2017, Part II, LNCS 10289, pp. 510–523, 2017.
DOI: 10.1007/978-3-319-58637-3_40

2   From 2D to 3D

Information spaces support intuitive computing interaction by mapping information to real world space, allowing us to look beyond the boundaries of the computing device and perceive information where it belongs – in the surrounding environment [8]. Several frameworks related to spatial and mixed reality interactions have previously been developed for immersive virtual environments [8]. Modern graphical user interfaces are object-oriented; the user first accesses the object of interest and then modifies it by operating upon it. After gathering the information, VR Rio 360 ideation process found its way by role-playing tasks like what users should do to reach, open, preview and explore each of the touristic features. These early exercises generated insights from visual and information designs to interaction and development approaches that were reproduced in 3D environments with rough boxes and planes and very little visual concern.

Traditional app development is usually defined by the co-work of designers and engineers in an established framework remarkably segregated by competency and tools. Deliverables are often communicated remotely with little sharing of perspectives and concerns over the complexities and limitations of each side's technology. VR, and most specifically the concept design of Rio 360, forced the whole team to break down this barrier, rethink its tools, and interact deeply on how to materialize which composition should come to life. This collaboration did not mean a complete blur of the distinct expertizes, but definitely challenged designers and engineers to exercise rationale and empathy over each other's concerns. This way, the project gained substantial improvements from a technical sense behind designers' decisions, and sharper instinct with refinements of developers' routines.

There are several reasons for going with an object-oriented interface approach for graphical user interfaces. Thus, icons are good at depicting objects but often poor at depicting actions, leading objects to dominate the visual interface. Software like Unit 3D played a central role in the team's experimented workflow, for the common interface they offer to distinct professionals like technical 3D artists, content strategists, interaction designers and front-end developers. In the task of composing a world for Rio de Janeiro, environment designers could place map elements like epic places and geographic references; they adjusted and balanced overall proportions in the same interface used by content strategists to position touristic pins and define overall place of findings across the map; yet the very same interface in which math developers exposed core variable adjustments to control movement speed and acceleration parameters that were then finely tuned by interaction designers concerned about other aspects such as motion sickness and discoverability.

3   Cognitive Aspects of Information in Virtual Environments

Research and experimental studies have clarified some cognitive aspects of information access on VE, some of them are listed below:

3.1 Perception

In virtual environments, the frequent problems with alignment and convergence, three-dimensional models and texture maps are topics that place substantive constraints on the role of bottom-up data processing in perception. Moreover, we also must considerer that we are living in a society of digital artifacts with a sort of representations and associations [9]; it means that we are able to interpret the meaning on television, smartphones, tablets, desktops but we also are learning how to interpret information and extend our actions into a virtual environment. Much of this can actually be inherited from mental models and affordances of the real world, but also can portray potential spots for confusion as the digital language ends up mixed with simulated realities, absent of anchors (corners and edges) that usually frame conventional squared interfaces.

In Rio 360 it became necessary to create a round stereotyped version of the map, emphasizing the city's most relevant places as main visual anchors/clues that would help users to situate themselves from practically everywhere. The stylized map also dealt with the distribution of information, ensured scattered experience spots were in similar distances from each other, hooked visual compositions from one spot to nearby ones in near, mid, and far FOVs and ultimately shaped an experience of a constant rhythm for content discovery.

Furthermore, map boundaries received a special behavior combining an invisible collider and an animated cursor to signalize navigation constraints and ensure that users would remain inside the content area. When selecting and interacting with these contents, a mixed approach of 'pin-over-map' icon was engineered to behave as an animated character capable of drawing attention when a user gets nearby, present the title for the experiences with additional feedback for gaze interactions. All this combined approach of map and icon in a free walking experience is essentially a translation of bidimensional map interface to a reality-inspired referenced and explorable place.

3.2 Attention

A VE system can give accessible clues about the focus of a user's attention that are not available in an ordinary desktop screen. Due to the field of view and resolution provided by those applications, users carry out navigation and orientation actions. These actions constitute an announcement, a sort of nonverbal protocol about what the user is currently attending. Some guidelines are suggested to optimize perception, attention and action [12]:

- Consider using primarily red colors and lighting for dark scenes to maintain dark adaptation while maintaining high visual acuity for foveal vision.
- Don't expect users to notice or remember events just because they are within their field of view. Use salience, e.g. colorful object or a spatialized sound to capture a person's attention.
- Consider getting a user's attention first through spatialized audio to prepare them in advance for an event.
- Attention can also be captured by objects that seem out of place and by putting objects where users expect them.
- Collect data to build attention maps to determine what actually attract users' attention.

3.3 Learning and Memory

Although a number of research projects have studied the VE, some issues remain unsolved. In regard to the Rio 360 app, one of the core issues was: how much fidelity is required to produce desired levels of satisfaction and learning? Which type of input offers special advantages for conveying the information available? The approach for this project assumed that experienced navigators – those familiarized with Rio touristic icons – would have an easier exploring curve to find desired locations while the less experienced ones would end up discovering things by serendipity. In both cases, visual clues for lead experiences like the Sugarloaf, Christ the Redeemer, and *Pedra da Gávea*, would end up serving as placed references for users to locate themselves, remember the experiences they visited, and locate the next available ones. By making use of repeated gaze interaction patterns, the application's concept model also made sure each new spot would be immediately familiar to the previous ones, in a seamless flow of exploration.

3.4 Knowledge

For each type of information that can be addressed to or learned by a user in a VE, there are potential issues to be addressed in a way to attend the cognitive processes properly. This can be viewed as a matrix of cognitive processing issues by types of information [9], some of these issues are listed below:

- Location knowledge: many VEs allow their participants to easily change their location and their orientation while observing objects in the environment. This model of interaction can offer the user the location of objects, as well as bring and access them.
- Part-whole knowledge: When less familiar complex objects are presented in an environment, it may be necessary to give the participant means for exploring part-whole relationships. One such means is to give the user the ability to move objects [9].
- Procedural knowledge: it is listed to provide action sequences in order to guide the user how to perform a desired task. It must be considered that some tasks/actions will be prioritized higher than others, in regard to time, effectiveness and context of application.

4 UX for VR

4.1 Vision of the Future

People are accustomed to 1st person narratives of cinema and video games, and although they may serve as a starter point to think about VR, they do not suffice to fully understand the sense of a virtual presence. 1st person is often about the fruition of a mixed 2D/3D interface with a simulated character whose vision is translated to a squared canvas.

Two of these concepts sets 1st person apart from VR experiences: visual language and field of view. On a square canvas, visual language often makes use of letterings and infographics that usually refer to margins and corners of the screen in a way to create referential spaces for certain types of information. Unaware of the conceptual models these layouts are able to create, and of the eye's instinctive capability to zap between and change from one scope to another, one can easily misevaluate what means to be presented. The truth is that most of nowadays' screens exceeds the eye's field of view (FOV), which is actually very small. So, when living the 1st person narrative, one is constrained to the eye's limitation, with no auxiliary Field of View (FOV) and extra information, while deprived from referential screen spaces like corners and sides. It is a world, and it changes everything from the very visualization, to the entire language, which performs messages, interfaces, and visual schemas.

VR presence means that elements otherwise hooked into screens corners will have to be spatially placed in order to create a quick and instinctive referral for users. Attaching interface elements onto user FOV is often distracting and confusing, as user's cognitive resources will be spent to constantly filter a cluttered vision and concentrate/ explore through the main spatial elements. This leads to the first brand new interaction task introduced by VR: the "gaze".

In severe contrast with the general sense of mobile app developments, users now are bound to look around, and to constantly explore away. This also means that the available information has to be well designed into VR space, not in concepts like screens or user vision; and in this matter, the development team ended up realizing nuances of this new composition paradigm. As placing things to explore all throughout the environment can sound as a good approach to VR information design, too many details or vastness of space can also alienate users, depriving them of quick recognition of current and next/ possible locations, which would ultimately affect core heuristics like the ability to return and to understand current system status.

In regard to a big city like Rio de Janeiro, the strategy was to limit the content for 12 touristic spots that would not work alone without a modification of the map to maintain a certain average of space between all available spots (Fig. 1). Design for the 1st person means to design a specific place, made to be digitally explored. This matter can possibly open research venues to correctly relate other environment and architecture disciplines.

Fig. 1. Rio 360 map with some of available spots, in red. (Color figure online)

4.2   It Feels like Reality

If good enough, a virtual interface will submerge users into a flow of signals, actions, and feedback that ultimately get them to skip their natural human perception of surroundings in favor of a distinct reality. And although this is indeed possible up to a variable extent, Rio 360 presented the team to a catchy underlining of this interaction: the balance of assumption control vs. wish fulfillment. If "real" enough, a virtual environment can potentially raise expectation towards affordances and possibilities that were not really implemented by software. And the peculiar freedom of VR presence often allows users to try those presumed tasks, which can lead to a sequence of failures and undesired frustration. So as the team gathered these early user insights, the idea of controlling user's assumptions with a consistent interaction pattern pointed out as the solution to lead users' attention and provoked them into features that are actually feasible. This approach performed a core function in Rio 360, as the pattern recursively endorsed itself along distinct places and objects in the environment, which fueled users into a flow of successful and enjoyable actions of controlled and fulfilled expectations.

In an attempt to smoothen the learning curve even further, the team opted to take additional advantage of gaze interaction - perhaps the most intuitive of VR tasks - to move users from one location to another. So in practical terms, users would just have to look to both move, open, enter, load, and exit from distinct content across the map. This means that users are constantly moving, as long as they are looking for something new, stopping by when the desired/selected spots fit inside their field of view. Although succeeding on taking first VR users to accomplish most of the proposed tasks, the movement paradigm faced adoption issues as gaze exploration is rarely matching users movement decisions. So even when successfully figuring out the gaze-movement approach, users complained about having controls to decide when to stop and start moving again.

5   Rio 360 Development

The goal of Rio 360 was to create an exploratory experience in first-person perspective to give the user an immersed view of some areas in Rio de Janeiro. Four types of media were used: photos, audio, video and 3D graphics. The main aspects of visual information were developed in such a way to achieve the appropriate quality for the app are listed below.

5.1   Information Arrangement

Concept design for Rio 360 offered users an opportunity to freely fly over an interactive map to discover more about the city. However, Rio de Janeiro has a remarkably narrow map, which was more suggestive to a linear and driven exploration. So, to ensure complete user freedom, the map was put into aspherical mold so as to preserve referential relationships amongst touristic icons across the city. The impact of this transformation was not sensitive to users as immersion loosens their perception of the map as a whole, but it guaranteed the rhythm and balance for information discovery in whichever direction users choose to navigate. In order to act quickly so as to verify the idea's validity, as well as possible failures, the team managed to translate the concepts of 2D wireframing and prototyping into functional VR environments made of rough blocks. Such approach sped up the conclusions about required interaction improvements and anticipated many of the caveats/blockages that VR concepts usually offer.

5.2 Immediate Distance

VR introduces an update to traditional foreground and background concepts of cinema and game scenes. The immediate plan is central for the feeling of presence, and elements in that range offer an increased sense of "coexistence" for users (i.e.: a plane at 35,000 ft impresses way less than another at a landing distance). Conversely, even detailed 3D elements tend to be flattened when put far from the camera, as interpupillary distance fails to generate distinct information for perspectives of each eye.

5.3 Level of Detail (LoD)

It was important to save precious computing resources by giving less polygons and details for elements that users will never get close to. Furthermore, it is important to attribute a fair amount of detailing for elements in the foreground, with really sensitive adjustments to LOD as eye capacity to capture them grows exponentially as they get closer to the user's vision. Textures also play an important role on this, as 2D volume faking techniques are still effective at enriching an element's reality. The use of VR early in the design process forced the detailed development of the interior space as much as the exterior. By having the opportunity to "go inside" the design and see it from within, the designer was forced to solve complex connections and details, which would not have been apparent with other media. The design was developed much more than those of other students not using VR as a design medium. With VR, the designer had to develop the entire three-dimensional model to a convincing level of detail, whereas other students concerned themselves with only specific views and details. Once the model was colored and detailed such that there were more than 10,000 polygons to be rendered, the simulation was slowed down to unacceptable frame rates (3–4 Hz).

In order to continue developing the design in greater detail, a separate model was generated representing a portion of the design. This second model was then developed to a high level of detail not easily accomplished by traditional architectural modeling methods. When this was simulated, we found that the Spaceball and monitor (non-immersive VR) aided in the perception of details and connections, but it was quite difficult to maneuver in tight spaces. It was necessary to view the model more intuitively so that the details and connections could be more easily studied. At this point, we attempted immersive simulation with a tracked HMD and wand. This was a whole new paradigm for evaluating spatial qualities of the design.

The frame rate was extremely low (1–2 Hz) and therefore quite disorienting, but we were able to inspect details and connections quite competently by having more intuitive control over the viewpoint. In both the immersive and non-immersive VR, flying through the design, as opposed to walking through it, had some advantages as well as some disadvantages. Flying provided a means of adopting viewpoints that could not be easily achieved in the real environment. This was useful for inspecting interior details, or for evaluating the exterior of the building from a number of viewpoints. However, there was a certain loss in the sense of scale due to the absence of any effort required to move to a location. This suggested a need for some type of treadmill to improve the navigational interface. However, once a critical threshold of detail was represented in VR, the designer was able to perceive spatial characteristics of the design that may not have been apparent with other design media. Before the complexity of the model reached a certain level, the use of VR as a design tool seemed to be a viable, but not unique, tool of representation.

The real-time simulations became more useful as a design tool as the level of detail of the model (color, transparency, and geometric complexity) increased. However, the level of detail needed to be kept in check to keep the frame rate at an acceptable level. The challenge presented by this conflict required both the generation of a second, more detailed model, and the skills of the designer to abstract the models. Although more powerful geometry engines are continually being developed, it is unlikely that we will ever be satisfied with the level of detail that can be simulated in real time. This may indicate a need for new ways to display complex geometry to the viewer, both in terms of rendering algorithms and in terms of the arrangement of the database [7].

5.4   Low Resolution

The need for details is handicapped by the amount of screen pixels that are actually able to fit in the Field of View (FOV), which opposes to the standard mobile and desktop mainstream paradigm, in which higher pixel densities are consistently reached year over year. The lack of pixels, along with immediate distance heuristics, creates a tricky approach to achieve pixel perfection levels and crisper details, taking long hours to be refined. Text readability is especially critical in that sense, as they are primarily composed by a sequence of narrow lines and gaps which can easily fail in blurred and poorly aliased situations.

5.5   Movement and Scale

Moving the user camera in Rio 360 generates an extra level of complexity to distance fine-tunings: defining dynamic scene shots. As users are able to reach a given content from any of its sides with varying distances, all composition would have to change in an indefinite number of situations. In order to work around this, Rio 360 makes use of distinct distance definitions, object scales and pixel densities for UI and landscape elements so that the composition among them will never hit, collide or overlap with each other.

A complex 3D-model is derived from a solid material by carving and sawing. This is promising for the design of highly detailed objects. Through the use of interpolated voxels and textures, Wang & Kaufman attempt to generate realistic looking results [5]. For our purposes we don't need such fine graduation in design. Our approach is from the opposite end - the coarse, simply 'bordered' model, the elementary form. The above approaches aim for 'near-as' photorealistic virtual images. This brings with it the resulting well- known problems associated with rendering time, resolution, texturing, etc. The second major criticism is the limited ace of the users action/movement. Most of today's VR applications are desktop-based, some allowing the user to interact on a one square-meter. We want to emphasize the space required for Doing. That means that we want to support a 1:1 experience for the user/actor [6].

5.6 Sound

Researches related to intersensory research concluded that certain perceptual qualities perceived by one sensory system can be influenced by the qualities of other sensory systems [9]. In terms of auditory-visual interaction, there are many similarities between visual and auditory perceptual groupings. Studies suggest that the auditory and visual modalities seem to interact in order to specify the nature of certain events within a perceiver's environment [10]. As a way to provide information, a combination of direct and indirect sound can be used; this model is largely used in VE for games. In regard to the context, some experts say that sound can be 50% of the VR experience, if a user hears a sound that doesn't match a typical human experience in a world that feels like a human experience, it tends to cause confusion and sounds unrealistic [11]. The authors also recommend to be careful to spatialize sound and align it to the directions the characters face, objects and content position.

5.7 Controlling Sickness

Camera movement, as one of the paradigms to explore virtual environments, offers a dramatically positive impact in user immersion. However, it also has possibly the highest of the development tradeoffs: motion sickness and control paradigms. By deploying a really granular control for modeling acceleration math, Rio 360 offered a great deal of experience in avoiding motion sickness. Everything is really eased and capped to avoid involuntary bumps, breaks, and sidewalk sensations, enabling difficult transportation tasks through the horizontal and vertical axes. As VR is quite new to most people, supporting users with distinct levels of sensitivity and familiarity to simulations is highly recommended. Several studies according to recommendations by Oculus [4] discuss how the camera movement is one of the major factors for the occurrence of motion sickness in virtual environments, stating that less movement will result in less discomfort.

6 UX Evaluation

For creating a measurement system on VE applications, two levels of measures should be considered. The primary level measures focus on outcome, indicating what the user accomplished in the VE system. The secondary measures help us interpret and elaborate on why performance was successful or not [9]. Aiming to identify points of improvement focusing on content comprehension, interaction flows, and overall usability, two processes of evaluation in different stages were conducted. Firstly, UX sessions were conducted with 9 internal employees, based on a qualitative task analysis when the final release was ready. The task analysis process was used to observe the participants while they performed the tasks required. Secondly, aiming to contribute for the first app update an expert review was applied.

6.1   UX Sessions

The study was conducted with 5 male, and 4 female individuals, ranging between 19 and 44 years old. Android was mentioned by most of them as their main operational system, while Samsung was the most used smartphone brand. Aiming to cover the aspects related to touristic interests in Rio de Janeiro, most of users had the habit of travelling. When asked about their planning process and if there was some kind of service that they would like to have, the most common request was for a service that would gather different types of information in only one place, e.g., city attractions and nearby restaurants. When asked about their experience with VR and devices related to it, there were 3 main answers: never used it (2 users), brief experience (4 users) and experienced (3 users). Users who were experienced had contact with contents from more than one device, e.g., Oculus rift, HTC VIVE and Gear VR. The study was split into three stages: initially, the participants were requested to explore the content freely for at least 1 min. Secondly, they were invited to talk about what they were figuring out into the new place and its surroundings and to perform a set of tasks:

- Move in different directions.
- Identify the Interface components. (e.g. landmarks, connection buttons).
- Access the videos.
- Identify the information available on videos.
- Access the postcards.
- Identify the information available on postcards.

At the end, a self-report per participant was applied aiming to obtain responses for points of improvements and additional information needs. The sessions lasted 1 h and 20 min (in average). Rio 360 is a VR application developed by SIDIA (Samsung R&D Center in Brazil) for Samsung Gear VR. Therefore, the participants tested the content through this device.

6.1.1   UX Sessions, Results

From the UX sessions it was possible to identify major points of improvements mainly related to navigation and speed, interaction with video, markers, and tutorial.

The issues were classified into three categories: major, minor and cosmetics.

- Major issues: mainly related to navigation and speed. Some users felt some level of motion sickness while on the application's initial screen, mostly because of the involuntary movement. They complained about the navigation speed. Defining it as inconsistent, most of them said that the speed made navigating uncomfortable - they were also unable to stop on particular spots; once inside the video, users had difficulty exiting it. They did not properly understand the video's exit display - some thought that it was signaling the tourist spot's actual location on the video and others thought that they would find more content through it; the display's color (green) an its icon was also mentioned by the users, according to them it did not seem like an exit method.

- Minor issues: mainly related to the comprehension of information available on the postcards' tips (Fig. 2). According to the users, the tips seemed to be links to more content elsewhere or even on the application itself. Most users spent some time looking for a way to close the card, instead of instantly looking away from it to close it. Two users did not find a way to return to the map. With a sort of possibilities to be presented, maps are a powerful way to provide information and familiarity to users. However, some principles must be considered when these tools are implemented on VE: spot on the map where you want to go, provide a sense of overall space - even if the user tries to explore a detail, they must know how to go back to the original position. Focus on primary content, watch out for redundant information [12]; they also mentioned that the options' colors were not clear and commented that it seemed like each function had its own color, or that the option in red was inactive/ had an error. In regard to the connection window's position (Wi-fi and 3G), users said that it was high enough so it would not get in the way of navigation. Some of them commented that they did not expect to find this type of settings' options there.

Fig. 2. Rio 360 postcards

- Cosmetic issues: mainly related to map markers. Users mentioned that some markers were placed in odd places. The major complaint about the markers was that some, even with their red color, seemed to be hidden. Users said that they could be placed higher on the map to make it easier to find them.

Additionally, the users were invited to suggest improvements after using the app. They highlighted the following topics:

- A tutorial could be created to explain how to navigate and interact with the items available on the application.
- An option could be added to choose the application's navigation speed as a whole, e.g. YouTube's video speed system.
- Some participants imagined that each option on the Connection Window (Wi-fi and 3G) could have individual switches.
- The application's options (regarding navigation and connection) could be bundled in only one menu.
- It would be interesting to have an area of the application with a list with all the tourist spots available, so it would become easier to find experiences. Users also mentioned that this list could have indicators of which experiences were already seen/visited, in order to keep track of how much of the application had already been explored.
- In order to avoid motion sickness, there could be an option to navigate by teleporting the user from one point to another.

6.2 Usability Inspection

After the first release, aiming to minimize the effects related to motion sickness while playing the videos, a cognitive walkthrough (CW) was applied. Usability specialists analyzed the 12 videos, focusing on: identifying system lag and latencies, verifying warning for videos with susceptibility to motion sickness, and overall visual problems. During this approach, the four CW questions [13] were also considered: 1. Will the users try to achieve the right effect? Does the user know what to do? Is it the correct action? 2. Will the user notice that the current action is available? Is the action visible? Will users recognize it? 3. Will the user associate the correct action with the effect to be achieved? If the action is visible, will the user understand it? 4. If the correct action is performed, will the user see that progress is being made toward the solution of the task? Is there system feedback to inform the user of their progress? Will they see it? Will they understand it?

6.2.1 Usability Inspection, Results

Most videos presented motion sickness issues in three or two moments, mainly due to rapid movements, low frame rate, and proximity with people on the scene recorded. Overall visual problems were related to transition between videos and contrast of colors - some footage seems to have washed out colors. It was observed that the footage quality, in regard to bright, luminance, shadow and others factor during the scene recording totally affect the quality of color in the VE videos.

7   Conclusions

VR Rio 360 became an opportunity to research, review and learn important aspects for developing a tourism application for a virtual environment. Initially, our main challenge was how to set the camera's movement to as natural as possible. We did not have a clear idea about which type of patterns users could have about VR usage. Would they know how to use a touchpad? Due to this, it was decided to focus the interaction of movements and control through the eye position, disregarding other models. After UX sessions, it was observed that other models could be explored. Our next steps will consider this.

Due to the lack of reference standards on VEs, some users initially mentioned they did not have previous ideas about the position of items like the tutorial or connection window button. From these results, it was possible to identify opportunities for future studies aiming to comprehend how core information could be presented/selected in regard the VEs. E.G. Where could a tutorial appear? Does it go away after selection or can it remain visible?

Due to the diversity of human factors that can influence the possibility of motion sickness occurrence (like gender, age, postural instability, high anxiety, exposure schedules, psychological characteristics such as fatigue, concentration, etc.), research which may indicate some level of susceptibility in regard to all of those factors can help all the VR community to increase the quality of interaction and information assessment into VEs.

In addition to that, we also observed how sound can decrease or increase discomfort while navigating. During the UX sessions, the background music seemed familiar and relaxing for some people, and perhaps it helped them while they explored the map. It could be an interesting topic for our next studies. Research can also be conducted to contribute on the development of a framework for evaluating virtual environments, especially one aiming to measure the level of effort required to comprehend and gain information regarding different types of stimuli and media.

Acknowledgement. The conception of this essay was the result of the combined efforts from SIDIA's Solutions Team and UX & Design team. It is also important to highlight the company's performance in supporting and promoting research and development for systems that are present in the domestic market's leading technology products. For all those people involved in this project, our sincere appreciation is made manifest here.

References

1. Chahal, M.: Why 2016 will be virtual reality's breakthrough year (2016). https://omobono.com/insights/blog/designing-vr-applying-usability-heuristics-virtual-reality. Accessed 2 Dec 2016
2. Chan, C.S.: Virtual reality in architectural design. In: Liu, Y.T., Wang, T.C.C., Hou, J.H. (eds.) CAADRIA 1997 Workshops, pp. 1–10. Hu's Publisher Inc., Taipei (1997)
3. Rio 360 VR App on Oculus Store. https://www.oculus.com/experiences/gear-vr/1105507662843899/. Accessed 2 Dec 2016
4. Oculus Best Practices Version 310-30000-02. https://static.oculus.com/documentation/pdfs/intro-vr/latest/bp.pdf. Accessed 2 Dec 2016
5. Wang, S.W., Kaufman, A.F.: Volume sculpting. In: Proceedings of the 1995 Symposium on Interactive 3D Graphics. ACM Press, Monterey (1995)
6. Donath, D., Regenbrecht, H.: VRAD (Virtual Reality Aided Design) in the Early Phases of the Architectural Design Process (1995). https://cumincad.architexturez.net/system/files/pdf/8955.content.pdf

7. Campbell, D., Wells, M.: A Critique of Virtual Reality in the Architectural Design Process (2003). http://papers.cumincad.org/data/works/att/0e58.content.pdf
8. Ens, B., Ramos, J.D.H., Irani, P.: Ethereal Planes: A Design Framework for 2D Information Spaces in 3D Mixed Reality Environments (2014). http://hci.cs.umanitoba.ca/assets/publication_files/EP-SUI-CR__website_version.pdf. Accessed 6 Feb 2017
9. Lampton, R.D., Bliss, J.P., Morris, C.S.: Human performance measurement in virtual environments. In: Handbook of Virtual Environments Design, Implementation, and Applications. Lawrence Erlbaum Associates, Inc. (2002)
10. Bregman, A.S.: Auditory Scene Analysis. MIT Press, Cambridge (1990)
11. Fictum, C.: VR UX: Learn VR UX, Storytelling & Design. CreaterSpace Independent Publishing Platform (2016)
12. Jerald, J.: The VR Book: Human-Centered Design for Virtual Reality. Association for Computing Machinery and Morgan & Claypool, New York (2015)
13. Lewis, C., Wharton, C.: Cognitive walkthroughs. In: Helander, M., Landauer, T.K., Prabhu, P. (eds.) Handbook of Human Computer Interaction, 2nd edn. Elsevier, New York (1997)

Algorithm Experimental Evaluation for an Occluded Liver with/without Shadow-Less Lamps and Invisible Light Filter in a Surgical Room

Hiroshi Noborio[1,2(✉)], Kaoru Watanabe[1,2], Masahiro Yagi[1,2],
Shunsuke Ohira[1,2], and Katsunori Tachibana[1,2]

[1] Department of Computer Science, Osaka Electro-Communication University,
Neyagawa, Japan
[2] Department of Biomedical Engineering, Osaka Electro-Communication University,
Neyagawa, Japan
{nobori,kaoru,tatibana}@oecu.jp

Abstract. In this paper, we investigate our proposed motion transcription algorithm that helps develop a virtual liver model from a real liver; the virtual liver is designed using the STL-polyhedron in an experimental surgical room. If we do not use any shadow-less lamps in the room, the algorithm correctly copies the translational/rotational motions from the real liver to the virtual liver. However, if we use one or two shadow-less lamps during the surgery, the copy quality decreases significantly, and consequently, our surgical navigation is sometime dammed. To overcome this problem, we attempted to overlap the shadow-less lamps with light-blocking filters. The purpose of using the light-blocking filter is to eliminate the unsuitable wavelength of shadow-less light for our camera system, the Microsoft Kinect v2. It is equipped with three types of cameras: an RGB camera, an infrared camera, and an infrared laser projector. The Microsoft Kinect v2 detects the infrared rays reflected from the object in front of it, estimates all the depth distances within all the pixels, and tracks 3D objects with several shapes. As a result, using one of the two light blocking filters, the camera Microsoft Kinect v2 captures all depths at all pixels stably on a 3D liver model, and consequently, our motion transcription algorithm plays an active role in the experimental procedure.

Keywords: Occluded liver experimentation · Shadow-less lamp · Invisible light filter

1 Introduction

In the past two or more decades, many fast and robust approaches have been developed for surface registration [1–7]. However, these approaches adopt three-dimensional (3D) point-point matching and irregular (x, y, z-axes) 3D matching. These approaches are quite time consuming, and consequently, they are not suitable for surgical navigation in real time. To overcome this drawback, we propose an approach where the movements of a real liver in an operating room are replicated by the

© Springer International Publishing AG 2017
A. Marcus and W. Wang (Eds.): DUXU 2017, Part II, LNCS 10289, pp. 524–539, 2017.
DOI: 10.1007/978-3-319-58637-3_41

movements of a virtual liver simulated on a PC. This motion transfer function is important for developing a surgical navigation system.

Our algorithm involves two types of parallel processing: depth difference calculation for all pixels by z-buffering with a graphics processing unit (GPU) and selecting the best neighbor from a large number of neighbors using the multicores on a GPU. In the former procedure, we use two-dimensional (2D) depth-depth matching between a real depth image in the real world and its virtual depth image, which is developed automatically by z-buffering in the virtual world. This type of matching comprises regularly arranged one-dimensional (z-axis = depth) matching. Therefore, all the matches for a vast number of pixels can be calculated in parallel by z-buffering on the GPU. In the latter procedure, we perform a rapid search for the best neighbor whose difference between real and virtual depth images is to be the minimum/medium/average/maximum. The real depth image is captured by the camera, and the virtual depth image is calculated by the z-buffering. The best neighbor is selected within a large number of neighbors based on six degrees of freedom (DOFs) that determine the translational/rotational movements in space in parallel using the multicores on the GPU. Thus, we successively find a position/posture that is most likely to exist based on various differences between the depth image captured by a Kinect v2 in the real world and the image captured by the GPU in the z-buffer in the virtual world. To eliminate the local minima, we use two types of randomization processes in the steepest descent method.

A practical system for surgical navigation requires several basic functions. Therefore, we are now developing several types of software, hardware, sensing equipment, and control schema. In this paper, firstly, we explain our navigation system with many software/hardware/sensing items in Sect. 2. Then, we test our algorithm for a liver occluded by a cover in a real surgical room both with and without the shadow-less lamps and/or two light blocking filters in Sect. 3. Thereafter, in Sect. 4, we conclude by presenting the types of experimental results obtained.

2   Our Motion Transcription Algorithm

From the past three years, we have been developing a surgical navigation system [8–10]. In this system, we pay attention to an automatic machine tracking a real organ by using its virtual organ model as shown in Fig. 1. For this purpose, we theoretically and practically investigated the two-dimensional (2D) depth-depth matching between a real depth image in a real environment, which is captured by a depth camera, such as Kinect v2, and its virtual depth image in the graphical environment, which is captured automatically by z-buffering of the GPU (Fig. 2).

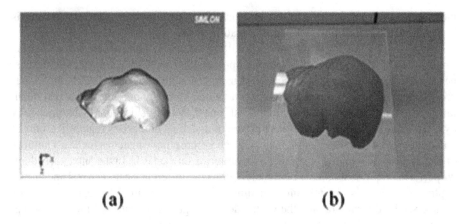

Fig. 1. (a) A polyhedral liver with STL format, and (b) its printed plastic liver.

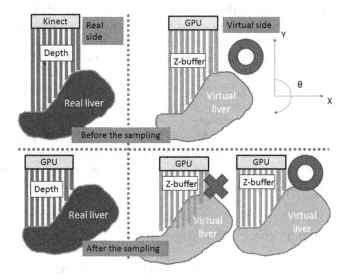

Fig. 2. By matching the real and virtual depth images, we can find a better position/orientation of virtual liver against that of the real liver.

Our algorithm performs a rapid search for the best neighbor, where the difference between the real and virtual depths is the minimum/medium/average/maximum compared with a large number of neighbors based on six degrees of freedom (DOFs) translation/rotation movements in space in parallel using the multicores on the GPU (Fig. 3). Thus, we successively find a position/posture that is most likely to exist based on various differences between the depth image captured by a Kinect v2 in the real world and the image captured by the GPU in the z-buffer in the virtual world. To eliminate the local minima, we use two types of randomization processes in the steepest descent method (Fig. 4).

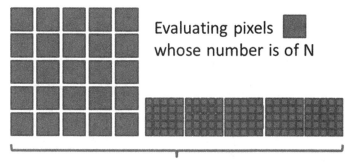

Evaluating images whose number is of M

Fig. 3. In our algorithm, we randomly select a set of pixels whose number is N in each image, and evaluate the minimum, median, or average of difference distribution between their master and slave depths. Furthermore, we select the minimum, median, or average of evaluation values in many images whose number is M. The kinds of randomizations escape from a local minimum among motion space in our 2D depth-depth matching algorithms.

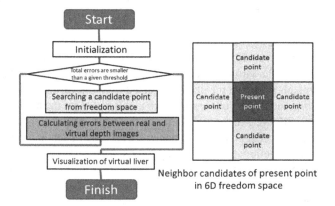

Fig. 4. (a) The flowchart of our depth-depth matching algorithm, (b) 24 neighbor candidates whose dimension is 6 represented by 3 translational degree-of-freedoms and 3 rotational ones.

Finally, in our navigation study, a 3D computer-generated (CG) virtual environment that is controlled by the OpenGL platform on the GPU is theoretically adjusted for a 3D real camera environment, which is controlled by the Kinect SDK and Kinect Studio API. Thus, the virtual 3D coordinate system is roughly consistent with the real 3D world. Furthermore, a user can make out the differences between the depth images of the real and virtual livers in the 3D real and virtual environments, according to various color types used in the Kinect v1 [10] (Fig. 5).

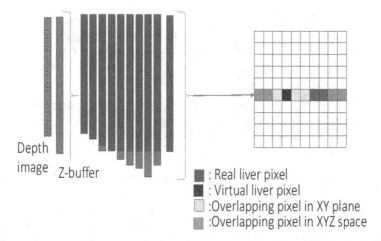

Depth
image   Z-buffer

■ : Real liver pixel
■ : Virtual liver pixel
□ :Overlapping pixel in XY plane
▨ :Overlapping pixel in XYZ space

Fig. 5. In our experiment, we evaluate our motion transcription algorithm by the calculation of overlapping ratio (the number of green pixels)/(the number of blue pixels) * 100. This refers to the extent to which a virtual 3D liver overlaps its corresponding real 3D liver during a surgical navigation (Color figure online).

While observing the colors, a user can select several parameters related to the 3D CG virtual environment according to the consistency between the real liver in the camera coordinate system and the virtual liver in the graphics coordinate system. In the image, the blue and red pixels represent the pixels projected from the virtual and real 3D livers, respectively. Furthermore, the yellow and green pixels represent the pixels overlapping the virtual and real 3D livers in the XY plane and the XYZ space, respectively. If depth differences between the real and virtual images are less than 1 cm at a pixel, the pixel color is changed from yellow to green. Many liver surgeons said that an error of 1 cm is acceptable during a liver surgery. In this image-based position/orientation adjustment system, the CG virtual world captured artificially by the z-buffer of the GPU should agree with the real world captured by a real depth camera [10].

Furthermore, by calculating (the number of green pixels)/(the number of blue pixels) * 100, we can evaluate the ratio of a 3D real liver that overlaps its corresponding 3D virtual liver (Fig. 5). In the following section, by using the overlapping ratio during an experimental operation in a surgical room, we can evaluate our motion transcription algorithm with no, one, two shadow-less lamps, as well as without them, and with invisible light filters. It is quite obvious that the evaluation area is defined as a circle in which we can see the 3D liver through an occluding object.

3   Our Experimental Results for an Occluded Liver with/Without Shadow-Less Lamps and Invisible Light Filter

In this section, many realistic experiments are conducted, not in the laboratory, but in the medical surgical operation room. The overall layout of the experimental equipment is shown in Fig. 6. In order to move the liver, an acrylic plate that is 25 cm in length,

25 cm in width, and 2 cm in thickness was placed on the operating table, and a real object liver model was placed on the top of the plate. Migration of the liver was carried out by moving the acrylic plate instead of moving the actual liver model itself. Moreover, for experiments involving occlusion, a cardboard sheet containing a hole of 10 cm in diameter was placed on the real liver model. The surface of this corrugated board was colored in light orange color using a coloring spray to make it look like human skin. Kinect, which was attached to a vertically movable robot, was able to change the distance from the real liver model according to the situation. Kinect was placed horizontally with respect to the operating table at a height of 84 cm from the bottom of the actual liver model. The camera system was fixed by attaching metal fittings to a metal rod. The metal rod-fixed Kinect was attached to the robot. The distance from the robot to Kinect was 32 cm.

Fig. 6. In our navigation study, we evaluate our motion transcription algorithm in a real surgical room with two shadow less lamps covered by two kinds of invisible light filters. In our navigation, a 3D liver is always obstructed by a cardboard box with a circle. Through the circle, the camera can capture a part of the 3D liver. In another experiment, we evaluate the motion transcription algorithm by changing the size of circle.

In the experimental procedure, first, the initial positions of the real liver model and the virtual liver model were matched. Then, the real liver model that was placed on an acrylic board was covered with corrugated cardboard and was subjected to translational and rotational movement within the corrugated cardboard box. Prior to the movement, the actual liver model was installed, so that it could be seen from the whole hole of the cardboard. It was done to ensure that the range visible from the hole of the cardboard did not become less than half after the movement of the model. The offset value was 10 mm for real and virtual depth images against the 3D real liver and its polyhedron with the STL format in our surgical navigator. The model was moved by 5 cm in the y-axis direction during the parallel movement, and it was rotated 45° around the z-axis center during the rotational movement. Each coordinate axis is shown in Fig. 6.

First, we explain the differences between this experiment and our previous experiments [8–10]. The main difference is the use of a real surgical room with one or two shadow-less lamps (Fig. 6). All the previous experimental results were obtained in our research room under daylight and/or fluorescent lamps for a 3D liver opened perfectly (which is not occluded by any other object).

In the following paragraphs, we successively discuss the following: observation without any lamp, observation with one lamp, observation with two lamps, observation with two lamps covered by an infrared shielding filter TS6080, which is manufactured by SyberLeps Co, and the observation with two lamps covered by an invisible light filter SL999 developed by Nexfil Co. for pairs of translational and rotational movements of the 3D liver (Fig. 7).

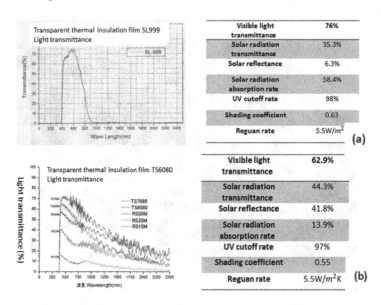

Fig. 7. (a) Light transmittance and several specs of SL999, (b) Light transmittance and several specs of TS6080.

3.1 Surgical Observation Without Any Lamp

The experiment was carried out in the surgical operation room without any shadow-less light.. The state of translating and rotating the 3D real liver model was captured with Kinect Studio and the experiments were performed using the data taken. Accuracy evaluation was performed using the overlapping ratio from the time of initial position adjustment to the time of parallel movement and after rotational movement (Fig. 8).

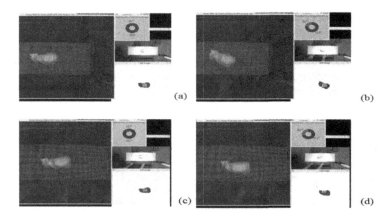

Fig. 8. A real red liver obstructed by a box with a circle window is followed by its virtual blue liver formed by STL polyhedron in a surgical operation room with one shadow-less lamp. (a), (b) The liver is rotationally moved before and after a surgical operation, respectively. (c), (d) The liver is translationally moved before and after a surgical operation, respectively.

The real liver model and the virtual liver model were interlocked, and it was confirmed that it moves in the same way while rotating and translating. Before moving (Fig. 8(a)), as shown in Fig. 10(a), the overlapping ratio was 99.5%, which is considerably high. When moved (Fig. 8(b)), the overlapping ratio was affected, and after movement it became 95.4%, as shown in Fig. 8(b). Figure 10(a) is a graph showing the transition of the overlapping ratio from the end of the initial alignment to the end of the movement. No significant change in the coincidence ratio was calculated from the end of the initial alignment until after the movement. In our steepest descent method, although the liver navigator also showed a decrease in the overlapping ratio during the translational movement, there was no drop in the overlapping ratio during the rotational movement.

It was confirmed that when the real liver model was moved, the virtual liver model moved in parallel in the same way. Before the movement, as shown in Fig. 8(c), the overlapping ratio was 98.6%, which was considerably high. When the model was moved, as shown in Fig. 8(d), the overlapping ratio decreased, and after the movement, it became 88.3%, as shown in Fig. 10(b). Although the decrease in the overlapping ratio is seen when compared with the same ratio before the movement, the result shows a high overlapping ratio that exceeds 80%. Figure 10(b) is a graph showing the transition of the overlapping ratio from the end of the initial alignment to the end of the movement. During the movement, the overlapping ratio dropped sharply by approximately two times. It was approximately 30% lower than the initial alignment, and a maximum reduction of approximately 60% was observed. However, the overlapping ratio stabilized and improved at each elapsed time interval, and after the movement, it showed a high value that approached the overlapping ratio after the completion of the initial position adjustment.

3.2 Surgical Observation with One Lamp

In this part, we use the operating room with one shadow-less lamp for conducting several experiments. As compared with the no lighting case, our algorithm's performance decreases, unfortunately, due to the influence of some unsuitable wavelengths emitted by the shadow-less lamp (Fig. 9).

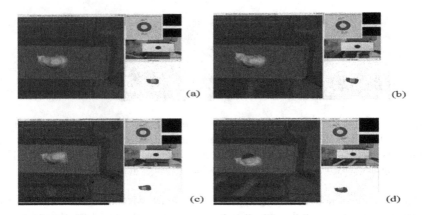

Fig. 9. A real red liver obstructed by a box with a circle window, is followed by its virtual blue liver formed by STL polyhedron in a surgical operation room without any shadow less lamp. (a), (b) The liver is rotated before and after a surgical operation, respectively. (c), (d) The liver is translationally moved before and after a surgical operation, respectively (Color figure online).

The real liver model and the virtual liver model were interlocked, and it was confirmed that it moves in the same way when rotating and translating. Prior to the movement, as illustrated in Fig. 9(a), a very high coincidence ratio of 98.2% was observed. During movement, the overlapping ratio fluctuated, and after movement, as shown in Fig. 9(b), it was reduced to 77.3%, as shown in Fig. 10(c). It is a graph showing the transition of the overlapping ratio from the end of the initial alignment to the end of the movement. A decrease in the overlapping ratio was observed every time it was moved, and it decreased to 50% at the maximum. However, as the movement ended, the overlapping ratio increased, showing an overlapping ratio exceeding 70%.

It was confirmed that when the real liver model was moved, the virtual liver model moved in parallel, in the same way (Fig. 9(c), (d)). Prior to the movement, as shown in Fig. 10(d), a very high coincidence ratio of 100% was observed. During movement, the coincidence ratio fluctuated, and after movement, it was reduced to 83.4%, as shown in Fig. 10(d). Although the decrease in the overlapping ratio is seen while comparing it with the same ratio before the movement, the result shows a high overlapping ratio exceeding 80%. Figure 10(d) is a graph showing the transition of the overlapping ratio from the end of the initial alignment to the end of the movement. Although there was no significant decrease in the overlapping ratio as there was in the case of no lighting, a decrease by approximately 15% in the overlapping ratio was observed. No increase was observed after the decrease in the overlapping ratio, and

0 lamp

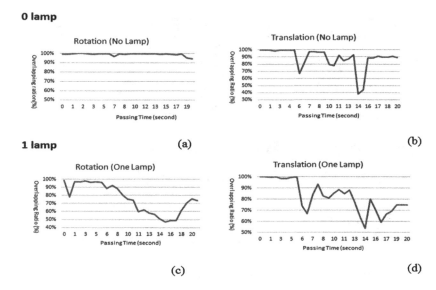

(a)   (b)

1 lamp

(c)   (d)

Fig. 10. (a), (b) The overlapping ratio is changed during a surgical operation if a human moves a 3D liver rotationally and translationally, respectively, in a surgical room without any shadow-less lamp. (c),(d) The overlapping ratio is changed during a surgical operation if a human moves a 3D liver rotationally and translationally, respectively, in a surgical room with one shadow-less lamp.

the overlapping ratio after the movement was 83.4%. The difference was not very significant when compared with the state when the shadow-less light was not used.

3.3 Surgical Observation with Two Lamps

A real liver model is moved rotationally, and then its virtual liver model follows the real liver following our motion transcription algorithm. Prior to the rotational movement, as shown in Fig. 11(a), the overlapping ratio is 95.9%, which is considerably high. When moved (Fig. 11(b)), a variation in the overlapping ratio is observed, and after the movement, it increases to 97.6%, as shown in Fig. 13(a). It can be observed that there is an increase in the overlapping ratio after the initial position alignment is complete. Figure 13(a) is a graph showing the transition of the overlapping ratio from the end of the initial alignment to the end of the movement. A decrease in the overlapping ratio is observed for each movement, and the overlapping ratio decreased by approximately 20%. However, after the movement, the overlapping ratio showed a higher coincidence ratio when compared with the coincidence ratio after the completion of the initial position adjustment. From the beginning of the experiment, it showed a considerably high concordance rate.

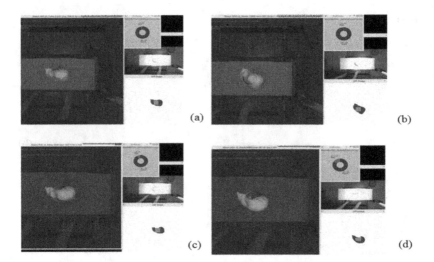

Fig. 11. A real red liver obstructed by a box with a circle window, is followed by its virtual blue liver formed by STL polyhedron in a surgical operation room with two shadow less lamps. (a), (b) The liver is rotated before and after a surgical operation, respectively. (c), (d) The liver is translationally moved before and after a surgical operation, respectively (Color figure online).

In succession, a human controls a real liver model translationally, and then its virtual liver model follows the real liver model. As shown in Fig. 11(c), the overlapping ratio is 90.3% before moving, which is considerably high. However, it showed a slightly lower overlapping ratio when compared to when no shadow light was used or when one shadow light was used. When moved (Fig. 11(d)), the overlapping ratio fluctuated, and after the movement, it was reduced to 82.9%, as shown in Fig. 13(b). Although the decrease in the overlapping ratio is seen in comparison with the ratio before the movement, the result shows a high overlapping ratio exceeding 80%. Figure 13(b) is a graph showing the transition of the overlapping ratio from the end of the initial alignment to the end of the movement. The result shows that the overlapping ratio is low on an average as compared with when the shadow-less light is not used.

3.4 Surgical Translational Observation with Two Lamps Covered by an Invisible Light Filter SL999 Constructed by Nexfil Co.

The rotational movement is observed by following a real liver model by its virtual liver model. Figure 12(a) shows the real 3D liver before the movement. In the first stage, the real and virtual livers coincide with each other as 99.9% overlapping ratio is observed. Thereafter, when a human controls the real liver translationally, the overlapping rate fluctuated. If the movement is finished as illustrated in Fig. 12(b), the overlapping ratio decreased to 98.8%, as shown in Fig. 13(c). The overlapping ratio did not decrease even after the completion of the initial position adjustment. Figure 13(c) is a graph showing the transition of the overlapping ratio from the end of the initial alignment to the end of the movement. A decrease in the overlapping ratio was observed every time the model was moved, and at times, it reduced to less than 90%. After the movement, the result showed a high coincidence ratio after the completion of the initial position adjustment. The overlapping ratio was high even during the movement.

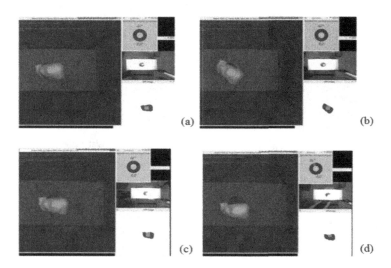

Fig. 12. A real red liver obstructed by a box with a circle window, is followed by its virtual blue liver formed by STL polyhedron in a surgical operation room with two shadow less lamps covered by an infrared shielding filter SL999. (a), (b) The liver is rotated before and after a surgical operation, respectively. (c), (d) The liver is translationally moved before and after a surgical operation, respectively (Color figure online).

Similar to the previous experiments, a human controls the real liver translationally. Thereafter, by using our motion transcription algorithm, its virtual liver model follows the real liver model stably. Prior to the movement, as shown in Fig. 12(c), the overlapping ratio was 98.9%, which was considerably high. It showed an overlapping ratio of approximately 8% higher as compared with the case when two shadow-less lights were used. When moved (Fig. 12(d)), a variation in the overlapping ratio was observed, and after the movement, it became 89.3%, as shown in Fig. 13(d). Although a decrease in the overlapping ratio is seen when compared with the same ratio before the movement, the result showed a high overlapping ratio, which exceeded 80%, after the movement. Figure 13(d) is a graph showing the transition of the overlapping ratio from the end of the initial alignment to the end of the movement. Although a sharp decrease in the overlapping ratio was observed before the end of the movement, the overlapping ratio increased to nearly 90% when the movement was over.

2 lamps

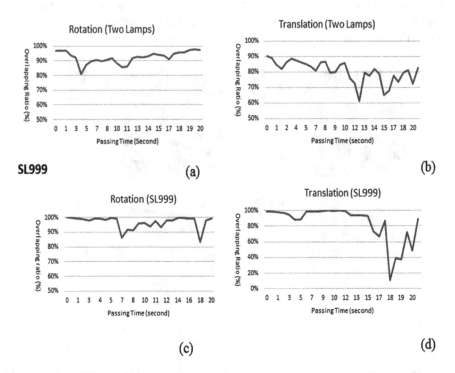

SL999   (a)   (b)

                                         (c)   (d)

Fig. 13. (a), (b) The overlapping ratio is changed during a surgical operation if a human moves a 3D liver rotationally and translationally, in a surgical room with two shadow less lamps. (c), (d) The overlapping ratio is changed during a surgical operation if a human moves a 3D liver rotationally and translationally, in a surgical room with two shadow less lamps covered by an invisible light filter SL999 developed by Nexfil Co.

3.5 Surgical Rotational Observation with Two Lamps Covered by an Infrared Shielding Filter TS6080 Made in SyberLeps Co

A real liver model is rotationally manipulated by a human, to study the rotational movement. In succession, our algorithm always leads its virtual liver model so that the virtual liver follows the real liver. Prior to the rotational movement (when the initial state is described in Fig. 14(a), the overlapping ratio was 98.8%, which was very high. When moved, the overlapping ratio changes. After the movement (Fig. 14(b)), the ratio decreased to 94.4%, as shown in Fig. 15(c). The variation in the overlapping ratio is considerably small, since the initial alignment was completed. Figure 15(c) is a graph showing the transition of the overlapping ratio from the end of the initial alignment to the end of the movement. A decrease in the overlapping ratio was observed each time the model was moved. However, it did not fall below 90%, indicating an overall high overlapping ratio. This result showed a high overlapping ratio after the initial position is adjusted.

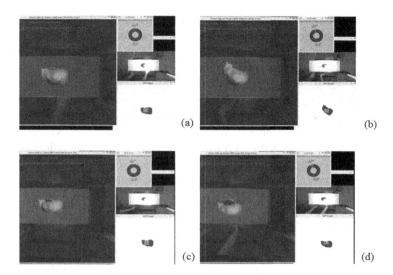

Fig. 14. A real red liver obstructed by a box with a circle window, is followed by its virtual blue liver formed by STL polyhedron in a surgical operation room with two shadow-less lamps covered by an infrared shielding filter TS6080. (a), (b) The liver is rotated before and after a surgical operation, respectively. (c), (d) The liver is translationally moved before and after a surgical operation, respectively (Color figure online).

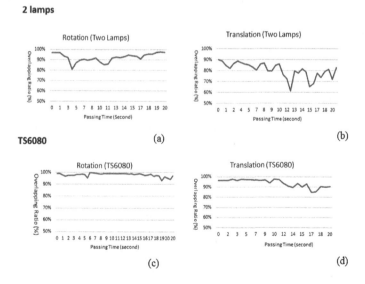

Fig. 15. (a), (b) The overlapping ratio is changed during a surgical operation if a human moves a 3D liver rotationally and translationally, respectively, in a surgical room with two shadow less lamps. (c), (d) The overlapping ratio is changed during a surgical operation if a human moves a 3D liver rotationally and translationally, respectively, in a surgical room with two shadow less lamps covered by an infrared shielding filter TS6080 made in SyberLeps Co.

During the translational movement of a real liver model, its virtual liver model, which is supported by our algorithm, follows the real liver model precisely. As illustrated in Fig. 14(c), it is as high as 97.8% before moving. When moved (Fig. 14(d)), a variation in the overlapping ratio is observed, and after the movement, it is reduced to 90.5%, as shown in Fig. 15(d). Although a decrease in the overlapping ratio is observed as compared with the same ratio before the movement, the result showed a high overlapping ratio, which exceeded 90%, even after the movement. Figure 15(d) is a graph showing the transition of the overlapping ratio during the movement. The overlapping ratio decreased to 80%, but when the movement finished, the overlapping ratio increased to approximately 90%. The fluctuation in the overlapping ratio during movement is less than when SL999 was used, but the fluctuation is consistent.

4   Conclusions

In this paper, we carefully evaluate our liver following algorithm during a liver surgery with some artificial occlusion in a surgical room with at most two shadow-less lamps covered by two types of infrared shielding filters, SL999 and TS6080. Our motion transcription algorithm uses a sequence of depth images captured practically within a circle obstructed by a cardboard box. Here, the real depth images are strongly affected by the shadow-less lamps. In general, the light spectrum of shadow-less lamp should be between 350 and 1000 nm. Therefore, in this research, we locate an infrared shielding-type filter in the front of the shadow-less lamps to cut the infrared radiation (invisible light) over 900 ns. Thereafter, the following performance of our depth-depth matching algorithm is evaluated by using only the visible radiation. As a result, the performance of experimental following a real liver by its virtual liver with some occlusion is aggressively improved by using two types of infrared shielding filters SL999 and TS6080S.

Acknowledgments. This study was supported partly by the 2014 Grants-in-Aid for Scientific Research (No. 26289069) from the Ministry of Education, Culture, Sports, Science and Technology, Japan. The study was also supported by the 2014 Cooperation Research Fund from the Graduate School at Osaka Electro-Communication University.

References

1. Besl, P.J., McKay, N.D.: A method for registration of 3-D shapes. IEEE Trans. Pattern Anal. Mach. Intell. **14**(2), 239–256 (1992)
2. Zhang, Z.: Iterative point matching for registration of free-form surfaces. J. Comput. Vis. **13**(2), 119–152 (1994)
3. Granger, S., Pennec, X.: Multi-scale EM-ICP: A fast and robust approach for surface registration. In: 7th European Conference on Computer Vision, pp. 69–73 (2002)
4. Liu, Y.: Automatic registration of overlapping 3D point clouds using closest points. J. Image Vis. Comput. **24**(7), 762–778 (2006)
5. Salvi, J., Matabosch, C., Fofi, D., Forest, J.: A review of recent range image registration methods with accuracy evaluation. J. Image Vis. Comput. **25**, 578–596 (2007)

6. Rusu, R.B., Cousins, S.: 3D is here: Point cloud library (PCL). In: IEEE International Conference on Robotics and Automation, pp. 1–4 (2011)
7. Wu, Y.F., Wang, W., Lu, K.Q., Wei, Y.D., Chen, Z.C.: A new method for registration of 3D point sets with low overlapping ratios. In: 13th CIRP Conference on Computer Aided Tolerancing, pp. 202–206 (2015)
8. Noborio, H., et al.: Tracking a real liver using a virtual liver and an experimental evaluation with kinect v2. In: Ortuño, F., Rojas, I. (eds.) IWBBIO 2016. LNCS, vol. 9656, pp. 149–162. Springer, Cham (2016). doi:10.1007/978-3-319-31744-1_14
9. Noborio, H., Watanabe, K., Yagi, M., Ida, Y., Nankaku, S., Onishi, K., Koeda, M., Kon, M., Matsui, K., Kaibori, M.: Experimental results of 2D depth-depth matching algorithm based on depth camera kinect v1. J. Bioinform. Neurosci. **1**(1), 38–44 (2015). ISSN: 2188-8116
10. Noborio, H., Watanabe, K., Yagi, M., Ida, Y., Onishi, K., Koeda, M., Nankaku, S., Matsui, K., Kon, M., Kaibori, M.: Image-based initial position/orientation adjustment system between real and virtual livers. Jurnal Teknologi, Med. Eng. 77(6), 41–45 (2015). Penerbit UTM Press, doi:10.11113/jt.v77.6225, E-ISSN 2180-3722

Capturing a Surgical Area Using Multiple Depth Cameras Mounted on a Robotic Mechanical System

Masahiro Nonaka[1], Kaoru Watanabe[2], Hiroshi Noborio[2(✉)],
Masatoshi Kayaki[3], and Kiminori Mizushino[3]

[1] Department of Computer Science, Osaka Electro-Communication University, Neyagawa, Japan
[2] Department of Neurosurgery, Kansai Medical University, Hirakata, Japan
{Kaoru,nobori}@oecu.jp
[3] Embedded Wings Cooperation, Osaka, Japan
{m_kayaki,k_mizushino}@ewings.biz

Abstract. In our surgical navigation study, we construct a mechanical system for steadily capturing several surgical scenes by using two parallel robotic sliders and multiple vision cameras. In this paper, we first determine how to select an adequate time interval during which each camera projects a pattern to calculate depth against an organ. If multiple cameras project and receive patterns simultaneously, pattern interferences occur around the organ and, consequently, the cameras cannot capture depth images. Second, we investigate whether few or no occlusions occur in several surgical scenarios for an organ operation. Finally, we check experimentally whether distance precision in depth images is exactly maintained when a surgeon raises the camera to insert a microscope during a microsurgery. If the above functions are performed correctly, our proposed transcription algorithms for position, orientation, and shape from a real organ to its virtual polyhedron's organ with STL-format play an active part during an actual surgery.

Keywords: Robotic system · Depth cameras · Capturing a surgical area

1   Introduction

There are many methods for capturing a surgical area that includes multiple kinds of organs and/or several medical tools in an abdominal or laparoscopic surgery using different types of surgical operative procedures [1–3]. In the last year, we designed and constructed a prototype including one robot and one camera to capture a wider visible surgical area. The unique characteristic of this prototype is that the camera and robotic slider are connected to a surgical bed. By this connection, even though a surgeon controls the surgical bed rotationally or translationally, the relative position and orientation between the camera and surgical area are completely fixed, and therefore our proposed position, orientation, and shape transcription algorithms [4–6] can be directly used in real surgeries.

In this study, we extend the robotic mechanical system to eliminate many types of occlusion in a surgical area by a surgeon's hand, head, and/or microscope. We use three

© Springer International Publishing AG 2017
A. Marcus and W. Wang (Eds.): DUXU 2017, Part II, LNCS 10289, pp. 540–555, 2017.
DOI: 10.1007/978-3-319-58637-3_42

types of depth image cameras: Kinect v1, Kinect v2, which were provided by Microsoft Co., and RealSense SR300 made by Intel Co. In this navigation study, we use multiple cameras numbering three or more. For this reason, we select the RealSense camera made by Intel Co. because of its small size. Multiple RealSense cameras can easily be placed at the top of the surgical area.

The Intel RealSense SR300 is based on the same principles as the PrimeSense technology used in the Microsoft Kinect v1. PrimeSense was recently purchased by Apple. The infrared structured light projector emits a structured pattern of infrared light, which is reflected back from the scene and detected by the infrared image sensor. The position of the reflected light pattern depends on the distance to the reflecting surface, determined through simple geometry. Hence, with bit of trigonometry, it is possible to reconstruct a three-dimensional (3D) scene. As shown in the explanation, a structured pattern of infrared light is projected to a target object (in our study, this is a human organ). If two or more cameras project structured patterns of infrared light simultaneously, corresponding confusion can occur, and thus, no depth images can be obtained by any of the cameras. To overcome this obstacle, we use multiple cameras whose depth images are controlled by time shearing to avoid any interference.

Subsequently, we check whether three cameras with different positions and view axes are enough to exactly capture the operations of a doctor's hand and head in several surgical scenes (in reality, a microscope during a brain microsurgery should be added). The RealSense is formed using three components: a conventional color CMOS image sensor camera, an infrared images sensor, and an infrared light projector (the main focus of this article). There is also an image processor. If the RealSense camera and surgical area are too close, our target organ becomes too wide in the RGB color image, IR image, and depth image. As a result, our target organ is frequently obstructed by a human hand or head during a normal surgery, and/or a microscope during a microsurgery. In these cases, translation and rotation movement, deformation, and incisions in the affected surgical parts during this period are overlooked. Consequently, they cannot be copied into the virtual liver using our motion and shape transcription algorithms [7–9]. To overcome this problem, we use two parallel robotic sliders—single axis robot RS 1 (straight type) made by MISUMI Co.—to climb up a ring of three RealSense cameras. The precise movement of the robotic slider has a repeat positioning accuracy of 0.01 mm. The other specifications are as follows: the maximum payload mass is 6 kg / 4 kg, the vertical stroke is 50–400 mm, the maximum speed is 600 mm/s, stepping motor specifications. Because two robotic sliders are simultaneously controlled in parallel by our computer program, if the camera is returned to previous positions, the same image is obtained at that position. In addition, the SR300 has a very effective object tracking software SDK (Software Development Kit) [11]. By using this SDK, the color, infrared, and depth images always automatically focus on a target organ, even though the cameras are moved by the robotic sliders. Therefore, in this paper, we evaluate whether or not the precision of the depth image is maintained without affecting the robot movements in several types of experiments, when we use this automatic object tracking software (Fig. 1).

In this paper, we explain our robotic capturing mechanism in Sect. 2. In Sect. 3, we investigate cases where there were few to no instances of damage to depth images due to interference between three cameras used simultaneously by several experiments. Furthermore, in Sect. 4, we examine cases with few to no instances of occlusion of a surgical area by surgeon's hand or head in several experiments. In Sect. 5, we carefully evaluate which distance variation in depth images is precisely linked with the robot movement. Finally, we conclude our research in Sect. 6.

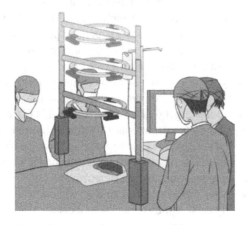

Fig. 1. Our surgical measurement system with two robot sliders and three cameras.

2   Experimental System

In this section, we explain our visual system for steadily capturing a surgical area. As shown in Figs. 2 and 3, even though a surgeon slides or rotates a surgical bed to maintain

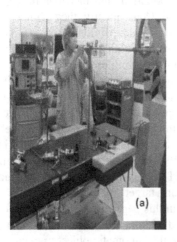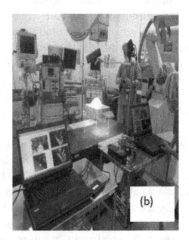

Fig. 2. (a) Many kinds of attachments for a surgical bed, and a mechanical frame is built by some of attachments and metal poles, (b) Two cameras are located over a 3D liver printed by our 3D printer based on a patient's practical liver with DICOM data. In addition, RGB color, infrared, and depth images are simultaneously and adequately captured by the two cameras.

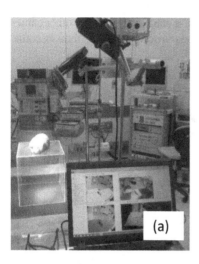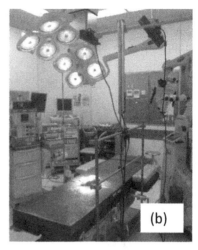

Fig. 3. (a) One location of two cameras, metal poles, robotic slider, and computer monitor, (b) the other two cameras, metal poles, and robotic slider.

a wider, more comfortable view over the surgical field, the relative position and orientation between the camera and surgical field should be completely fixed. Therefore, in our navigation study, the camera and bed are directly connected (Fig. 2(a), (b)) [4–6]. Using a 3D liver printed by our 3D printer based on a patient's practical liver with DICOM data, we investigate whether Microsoft Kinect v1, v2, and Intel RealSence SR300 can successfully capture three kinds of images: RGB color image, infrared image, and depth image. Appropriately, the former two cameras include a special SDK for capturing human body motions while the latter camera includes a special SDK for tracking a target object visually. For this reason, we have recently begun using the latter camera, Intel RealSence SR300.

Furthermore, since there are many types of surgical operations, engineers and doctors should discuss with each other how to place the mechanical measurement system around the surgical bed. Otherwise, the mechanical measurement system might get in the way of medical work. In such a case, a surgeon, surgical assistant, anesthetist, nurse, and other medical technologists do not work well and support a surgery adequately during an operation. For this purpose, we are investigating a suitable location for the poles, robotic sliders, and computer monitor when there are several people working together around the surgical bed (Fig. 3(a), (b)). Furthermore around a surgical area, there are many kinds of organs and/or medical tools in an abdominal surgery escape from the laparoscopic and robot surgery surgeries. Therefore, different types of surgical operative procedures are interfered by multiple methods for capturing the surgical area. For this reason, the camera is moved up and down using a one-degree-of-freedom robot slider when a surgeon needs to insert the microscope between the surgical area and his head. Because one camera is vertically located along the gravity, the images always includes the surgical area through the up and down movements (Fig. 4(a), (b)). In this research, we will extend our previous mechanism and therefore capture an affected part using multiple cameras (Fig. 5(a), (b)). Using this type of multiple camera system, if a diseased part cannot be caught by initial camera images, it can be captured by other cameras. As a result, our proposed position/orientation/shape transcription algorithms become active with the support of the captured data.

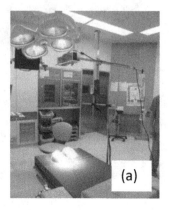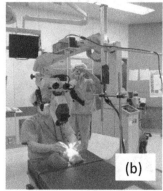

Fig. 4. (a) One camera is controlled by one robotic slider by the up and down manner, (b) camera moves up for inserting the microscope.

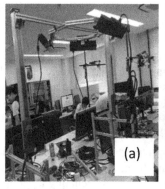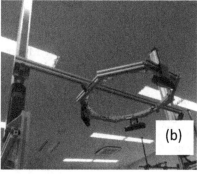

Fig. 5. (a) Three cameras are steadily controlled by two robotic sliders in an up and down manner, (b) Three smaller cameras are located on a ring between two robotic sliders.

3   Few or No Instances of Interference Damage to Depth Images Between Three Cameras Used Simultaneously

The RealSense SR300 essentially calculates a depth image (the depth distance at each pixel) by triangular calculation via a structured pattern of infrared light that is projected by a projector and simultaneously received by an infrared image sensor. Therefore, if two or more structured patterns of infrared light overlap around the surface of a target organ, the reflected data are quite confusing and, consequently, none of the cameras can receive a depth image (a set of distances from each camera to the target organ).

To overcome the pattern interferences between multiple cameras, we develop software to maintain skipping frames between pattern projections of two cameras as illustrated in Fig. 6. In our research, we change the number of capturing frames (Nc) and the number of skipping frames (Ns) as follows: the pair of Nc = 4, Ns = 1–3, and the pair of Nc = 10, Ns = 3 (Fig. 6).

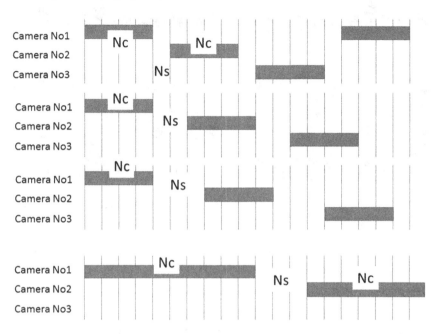

Fig. 6. In our software used to control three RealSence RS300 cameras, we use time shearing with the number of capturing frames (Nc) and the number of skipping frames (Ns).

If we decrease the number of capturing frames, the response of depth image calculation by projecting and receiving the pattern increases. Therefore, an obstacle situation of a color image and its shape situation of a depth image are almost the same. Otherwise, if we increase the number of capturing frames, the response becomes slower and the obstacle situation (i.e., hand movement) in the color image and its shape situation of depth image differ from each other. Moreover, if the number of skipping frames is reduced, a degree of interference frequently occurs and, as a result, the present camera cannot capture the depth image.

- Nc = 4 and Ns = 1: pattern projecting and receiving frequently interfere with each other, and, consequently, a depth image frequently cannot be obtained (Fig. 8).
- Nc = 4 and Ns = 2: pattern projecting and receiving rarely interfere with each other, and, consequently, a depth image rarely cannot be obtained (Fig. 7).

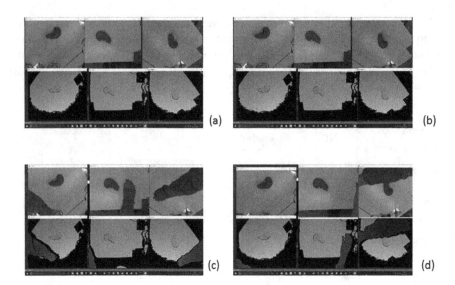

Fig. 7. If we set Nc = 4 and Ns = 2, a depth image rarely cannot be obtained as in (a) and (b), but the depth image cannot quickly follow the color image as in (c) and (d).

- Nc = 4 and Ns = 3: pattern projecting and receiving do not interfere with each other, and consequently depth image can always be obtained (Fig. 9).

    It is important to note that this may change depending on the distance to the camera.

4   Few or No Instances of Occlusion of a Surgical Area by a Surgeon's Hand or Head

In this section, using our system during several surgical operations, which are simulated with typical participants, we meticulously check if at least one of the three cameras captures a surgical area. As shown in Figs. 7, 8, and 9, if a typical person watches and simultaneously operates a 3D liver while capturing with three RealSense cameras, at least one camera always captures the 3D liver and thus precisely provides color and depth images.

One in a million, if all cameras cannot capture any 3D liver, a human controls two robotic sliders in order to climb up the ring of three RealSense cameras. By this movement, each camera has a wider view and, consequently, at least one of the three cameras can capture the 3D liver (Fig. 10).

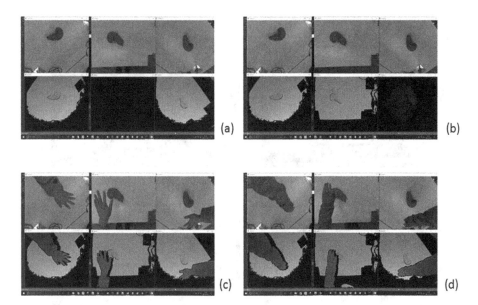

Fig. 8. If we set Nc = 4 and Ns = 1, a depth image frequently cannot be obtained as in (a) and (b), but the depth image quickly follows the movement of the hand in the color image as in (c) and (d).

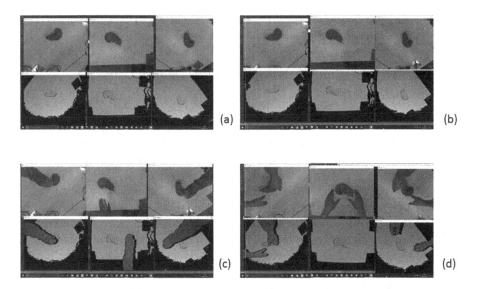

Fig. 9. If we set Nc = 4 and Ns = 3, a depth image can always be obtained as in (a) and (b), but the delay (difference) between the depth image and the color image becomes larger as in (c) and (d).

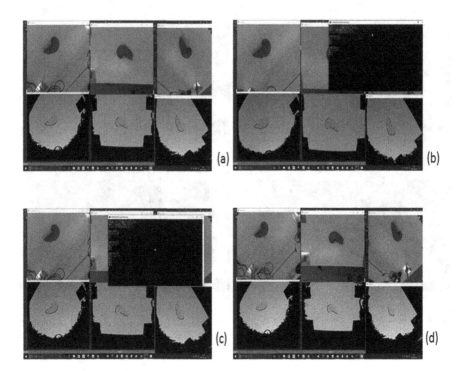

Fig. 10. If we climb up the ring of three RealSense cameras at (b) and (c) through an automatic program, the camera view with color and depth images becomes wider from (a) to (d).

5   Distance Precision Variation of Depth Images Using Robotic Sliders

In our navigation study, we use the RealSense SR300 and its Tracking SDK [10]. The SDK is explained as follows: The Metaio 3D-object-tracking module provides optical-based tracking techniques that can detect and track known or unknown objects in a video sequence or scene. The Metaio Toolbox is provided to train, create, and edit 3D models that can be passed to various object detection and tracking algorithms.

Table 1 provides an overview of various tracking techniques and how they can be configured [10]. First and foremost, the following steps explain the operation concretely. 1. Detect feature points on the screen. 2. Register feature points instead of markers. 3. Compute the movement of the screen based on the center coordinates of the feature points. In our navigation study, we use Marker Tracking provided by the RealSense SDK for tracking. The provided Marker Tracking occurs as follows:

In order to scan objects that have a simple symmetric shape, such as cylinders or spheres, enable the optional marker-based tracking system and use the marker according to the following instructions.

1. Print the marker in color (not black and white), making sure that you turn off any scaling (e.g., Fit to Page) in print options; print at actual size.

Table 1. The tracking techniques [10].

Tracking method	Configuration/Input
2D objects tracking (planar objects)	Input a reference image
Feature based 3D tracking	Use the toolbox to create a point cloud. Save the configuration in a .slam file
Edge based 3D tracking from CAD models	Provide a CAD model (.obj) and use the Edge Creation tool to extract prominent edges and then save the configuration in a .xml file
Instant 3D tracking	Track the camera ego motion in an unknown configuration

2. Place the printed marker on a flat surface, like a tabletop or floor. It might be helpful to tape the marker down.

3. Place your object on the marker, centering it as best as you can within the dashed circle.

   The object must not cover too much of the marker; the camera should be able to see at least three of the four long red and blue edges at all times. The majority of the object should lie within the dashed circle.

4. Start scanning, making sure object stays in place on marker. Move camera around the object and marker, making sure the marker stays in view the whole time.

   It is possible to leave the camera stationary and rotate the marker by hand (like a turntable), as long as your hand stays near the edges so as not to be visible to the camera, and the object does not move relative to the marker during the scan process. In this case, it might be helpful to attach the marker to a rigid board and also attach the object to the marker.

5. If tracking gets lost, go back to a previously scanned area and hold still for a few seconds; if tracking does not resume, then restart the scan.

Even though the ring of three cameras is moving up or down, the object tracking always keeps the 3D liver at the center of the images. Further, robot movement can be precisely cancelled at each distance of the depth image. In other words, several types of depth images obtained by the robot control are precisely normalized in relation to depth distance. These properties are experimentally investigated for capturing 30 points around a 3D liver (Fig. 11).

As shown in Fig. 12(a), we describe experimental results captured by camera No. 1 without object tracking for 30 points around a 3D liver. Subsequently, we calculate their average and indicate the variances by red colored bars while the camera ring is moved up or down by the robotic sliders, whose invariable distances are colored green, blue, red, light green, and orange. In Fig. 12(a), the difference in robot movement deviates significantly from the difference in depth change.

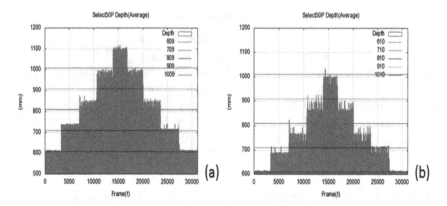

Fig. 11. (a) Camera No.1 without object tracking captures depths at 30 points as shown in Fig. 9. Then, we calculate their average and indicate the variances by red colored bars while the ring of three cameras is moved up or down by the robotic slider's movement, which are colored green, blue, red, light green, and orange. The difference in robot movement deviates significantly from the difference in depth change. (b) Camera No. 1 with the object tracking captures depths at 30 points. Then, we calculate their average and indicate the variances by red colored bars while the ring of three cameras is moved up or down by the robotic slider's movement, which are colored green, blue, red, light green, and orange. The difference in robot movement slightly differs from the difference in depth change (Color figure online).

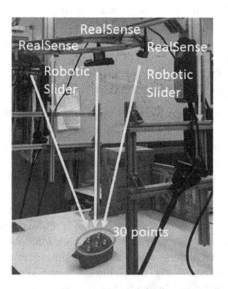

Fig. 12. We move up or down the ring of three RealSense RS300 cameras by using two robotic sliders in parallel, and then capture 30 depths at 30 points around a 3D liver. Then, by evaluating these variations of depths, we check whether the robot movements are adequately cancelled in the sequence of 30 depths.

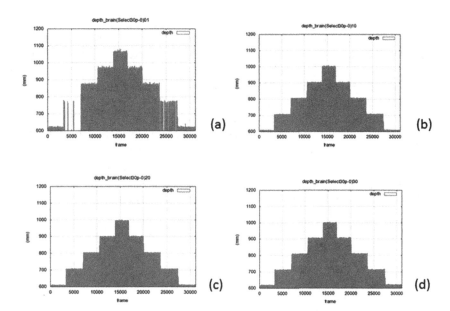

Fig. 13. (a), (b), (c), (d) Depth variance at points 1, 10, 20, 30 captured by camera No. 1 with the object tracking are explained. Point 1's data is quite bad and this leads to the difference in robot movement slightly differing from the difference in depth change, as shown in Fig. 12(b).

As illustrated in Fig. 12(b), camera No. 1 with object tracking captures depths at 30 points. We then calculate their average and indicate the variances by red colored bars while the ring of three cameras is moved up or down by the robotic slider's movement, colored green, blue, red, light green, and orange. The difference in robot movement slightly differs from the difference in depth change. The reason for this result is that the data captured at point 1 is not good data, as shown in Fig. 13(a).

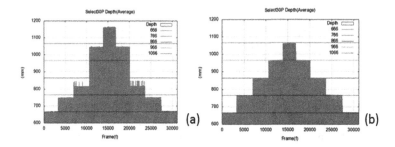

Fig. 14. (a) Camera No.2 without object tracking captures depths at 30 points. Then, we calculate their average and indicate the variances while the ring of three cameras is climbed up or down by the robotic slider's movement. The difference of robot movement extremely differs from the difference of depth change. (b) Camera No.2 with object tracking captures depths at 30 points. Then, we calculate their average and indicate the variances while the ring of three cameras is climbed up or down by the robot movement. The difference of robot movement is coincident with the difference of depth change.

In addition, as shown in Fig. 14(a), we describe experimental results captured by camera No. 2 without object tracking for 30 points around a 3D liver. After that, we calculate their average and indicate the variances by red colored bars while the camera ring is moved up or down by the robotic sliders whose depth distances are colored green, blue, red, light green, and orange. The difference of robot movement extremely differs from the difference of depth change.

Moreover, in Figs. 14(b), camera No.2 with the object tracking captures depths at 30 points. Then, we calculate their average and indicate the variances by red colored bars while the ring of three cameras is climbed up or down by the movements of robotic slider, which are colored green, blue, red, light green, and orange. The difference in robot movement is equivalent to the difference in depth change. The reason for this result is that all data captured at all points are quite good, as shown in Fig. 15.

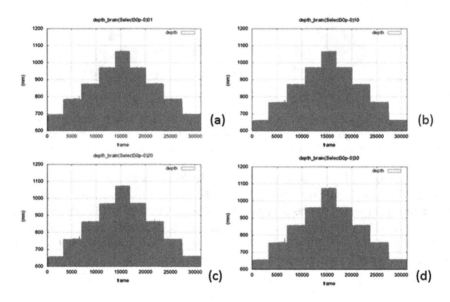

Fig. 15. (a),(b),(c),(d) Depth variance at the points 1, 10, 20, 30 captured by the camera No.1 with the object tracking are explained, respectively. All point data are very good, and, consequently, the difference of robot movement coincides with the difference of depth change as shown in Fig. 14(b).

Furthermore, in Fig. 16(a), we describe the experimental result captured by camera No. 3 without object tracking for 30 points around a 3D liver. We then calculate their average and indicate the variances while the camera ring is moved up or down by the robotic sliders. The difference in robot movement deviates from the difference in depth change.

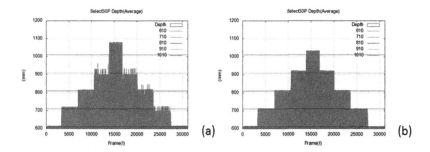

Fig. 16. (a) Camera No. 3 without object tracking captures depths at 30 points. Then, we calculate their average and indicate the variances while the ring of three cameras is moved up or down by the robotic slider's movement. The difference in robot movement varies significantly from the difference in depth change. (b) Camera No. 3 with object tracking captures depths at 30 points. Then, we calculate their average and indicate the variances while the ring of three cameras is moved up or down by the robot movement. The difference in robot movement concurs with the difference in depth change.

Further, in Figs. 16(b), camera No. 3 with object tracking captures depths at 30 points. We then calculate their average and indicate the variances while the ring of three cameras is moved up or down by the robotic slider's movement. The difference in robot movement concurs with the difference of depth change. The reason for this result is that there is no bad data captured at any point, as shown in Fig. 17.

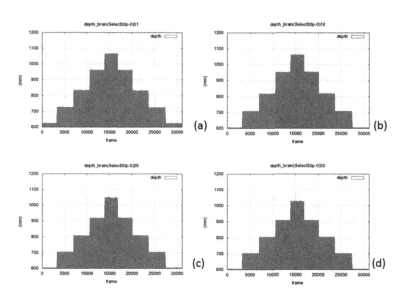

Fig. 17. (a), (b), (c), (d) Depth variances at points 1, 10, 20, and 30 captured by camera No. 1 with object tracking are explained. All the point data are very good and, consequently, the difference in robot movement coincides with the difference in depth change, as shown in Fig. 16(b).

6   Conclusions

In this research, we focus on two functions: (1) At least one of three cameras can capture a surgical area by using three cameras placed at different positions and pointing in different directions. (2) When a doctor inserts a microscope between multiple cameras and a surgery area for microsurgery, the camera set climbs up and down using our robotic sliders. In this case, even though the distance from each camera to a 3D liver is changed by the robot movement, depth distance captured by the camera is synchronously changed. Since the two functions are firmly maintained, our position/orientation/shape following algorithms are always available in our navigation study.

Acknowledgments. This study was supported in part by 2014 Grants-in-Aid for Scientific Research (No. JP26289069) from the Ministry of Education, Culture, Sports, Science, and Technology, Japan. Further support was provided by the 2014 Cooperation Research Fund from the Graduate School at Osaka Electro- Communication University.

References

1. Logan, W.C., Prashanth, D., William, C.C., Benoit, M.D., Robert, L.G., Michael, I.M.: Organ surface deformation measurement and analysis in open hepatic surgery: Method and preliminary results from 12 clinical cases. IEEE Trans. Biomed. Eng. **58**(8), 2280–2289 (2011). doi:10.1109/TBME.2011.2146782
2. Xu, A., Zhu, J.F., Zhang, D.: Development of a measurement system for laparoendoscopic single-site surgery: Reliability and repeatability of digital image correlation for measurement of surface deformations in SILS port. JSLS 18(3) (2014). doi:10.4293/JSLS.2014.00267, PMCID: PMC4154418
3. Kang, N., Lee, M.W., Rhee, T.: Simulating liver deformation during respiration using sparse local features. IEEE Comput. Graph. Appl. **32**(5), 29–38 (2012). doi:10.1109/MCG.2012.65
4. Watanabe, K., Kayaki, M., Mizushino, K., Nonaka, M., Noborio, H.: A mechanical system directly attaching beside a surgical bed for measuring surgical area precisely by depth camera. In: Proceedings of the 10th MedViz Conference and the 6th Eurographics Workshop on Visual Computing for Biology and Medicine (EG VCBM), Bergen, Norway, pp. 105–108, 7–9 September (2016). ISBN:978-82-998920-7-0 (Printed), ISBN:978-82-998920-8-7 (Electronic)
5. Watanabe, K., Kayaki, M., Mizushino, K., Nonaka, M., Noborio, H.: Brain shift simulation controlled by directly captured surface points. In: Proceedings of the 38th Annual International Conference of the IEEE Engineering in Medicine and Biology Society (EMBC 2016), Category: Late Breaking Research Posters, Theme: BioMedical Imaging and Image Processing, Sessions: Ignite_Theme 2_Fr2, Poster Session III, Orlando Florida USA, 16–20 August (2016)
6. Watanabe, K., Kayaki, M., Mizushino, K., Nonaka, M., Noborio, H.: Capturing a brain shift directly by the depth camera kinect v2. In: Proceedings of the 38th Annual International Conference of the IEEE Engineering in Medicine and Biology Society (EMBC 2016), Category: Late Breaking Research Posters, Theme: Computational Systems & Synthetic Biology; Multiscale Modeling, Sessions: Ignite_Theme 4_Fr1, Poster Session II, Orlando Florida USA, August 16–20 (2016)

7. Noborio, H., et al.: Tracking a real liver using a virtual liver and an experimental evaluation with kinect v2. In: Ortuño, F., Rojas, I. (eds.) IWBBIO 2016. LNCS, vol. 9656, pp. 149–162. Springer, Cham (2016). doi:10.1007/978-3-319-31744-1_14

8. Noborio, H., et al.: Depth image matching algorithm for deforming and cutting a virtual liver via its real liver image captured using kinect v2. In: Ortuño, F., Rojas, I. (eds.) IWBBIO 2016. LNCS, vol. 9656, pp. 196–205. Springer, Cham (2016). doi:10.1007/978-3-319-31744-1_18

9. Noborio, H., Watanabe, K., Yagi, M., Ida, Y., Nankaku, S., Onishi, K., Koeda, M., Kon, M., Matsui, K., Kaibori, M.: Experimental results of 2D depth-depth matching algorithm based on depth camera kinect v1. J. Bioinform. Neurosci. 1(1), 38–44 (2015)

10. Noborio, H., Watanabe, K., Yagi, M., Ida, Y., Onishi, K., Koeda, M., Nankaku, S., Matsui, K., Kon, M., Kaibori, M.: Image-based initial position/orientation adjustment system between real and virtual livers. Jurnal Teknologi, Med. Eng. 77(6), 41–45 (2015). doi:10.11113/jt.v77.6225, Penerbit UTM Press, E-ISSN: 2180-3722

11. Intel® RealSense™ SDK 2016 R2 Reference Manual: Object Tracking, API Version 10.0 (2016)

A Study of Guidance Method for AR Laparoscopic Surgery Navigation System

Katsuhiko Onishi[✉], Yohei Miki, Keishi Okuda, Masanao Koeda,
and Hiroshi Noborio

Osaka Electro-Communication University, Shijonawate, Japan
{onishi,ht14a081,ht14a013,koeda,noborio}@oecu.jp

Abstract. Laparoscopic surgery is becoming popular as a minimally invasive operation. It is widely used as a technique for various kinds of surgical operation. In this surgery, a surgeon uses an endoscopic camera, which is limited view volume, and forceps into the patient body. It has been needed to support system such as navigation system.

Therefore, we are studying about the AR laparoscopic surgery navigation system support the surgeon to find these organs by using semi-automatic registration method to make an overlay video image of virtual organs and real organs. In this paper, we focus on the guidance method by using the endoscopic view image and the endoscopic position. We introduce our study about registration method of the position and orientation of the endoscope camera. Our method tracks the tools position and orientation by using markers. Then, it uses the camera reference frame based on this position and orientation for generating the overlay image of virtual organs and real organs. The result of using our method can be showed a potential for efficient guidance method of AR surgical navigation system.

Keywords: Laparoscopic surgery · Marker tracking · Surgical navigation · Augmented reality

1 Introduction

Laparoscopic surgery is becoming popular as a minimally invasive operation. It is widely used as a technique for various kinds of surgical operation. It allows the surgeon to access the target organs in the patient body without making large incisions on the skin. It has been able to decrease post-procedure complications and the post-operative trauma of the patient. However, there is a higher risk of damaging the internal organs, nerves, and major blood vessels, which are like arteries and veins. Because the surgeon has to make surgical operation with the limitation of manipulation space and viewing angle which can be seen from the endoscope camera. Therefore, it has been needed to make the effective system the surgical operation training and support the surgeon during the preoperative period that is like navigation system.

© Springer International Publishing AG 2017
A. Marcus and W. Wang (Eds.): DUXU 2017, Part II, LNCS 10289, pp. 556–564, 2017.
DOI: 10.1007/978-3-319-58637-3_43

There are many kinds of research about laparoscopic surgery simulation and navigation system. some of them about surgical simulation focus on the very specific topic and beginning to appear it on the market [1–5]. Hence, the research about navigation system for laparoscopic surgery has been also many efficient results [6–8]. Some of them have appeared on the market. The best impact laparoscopic surgery navigation systems, like da Vinci [9], aims to focus on supporting total surgical operation. They are not capable of supporting the surgeon to find the affected part of the organ, nerves, and the blood vessels around the target organ. Some of them focus on supporting the surgeon to guide and find these organs by using VR/AR technology [7, 8]. However, most of them need to adjust registration between virtual organs and real organs by the operator from the endoscopic view image.

Therefore, we are aiming to develop the AR laparoscopic surgery navigation system that supports the surgeon to find these organs by using semi-automatic registration method to make an overlay video image of virtual organs and real organs. Particularly, we focus on the guidance method by using the endoscopic view image and the endoscope camera position. In this paper, we introduce our study about measuring method by using the endoscope camera position and orientation. Our method uses specific markers to track the position and orientation. Moreover, we introduce the prototype system. The system allows a user to operate the endoscope camera with showing the overlay image of virtual organs and real organs produced by our method.

2   Guidance Method

2.1   Overview

Our proposed method image is showed in Fig. 1. At first, the system measures position and orientation of the endoscope camera during laparoscopic surgery. After that, it generated the 3D virtual scene in which it includes 3D CG organ model. Finally, the system displays the 3D CG organ model in which it is overlaid on video image from the camera. In this situation, the endoscope camera is in patient body and it cannot be measured from outside the body directly. Therefore, our system has to measure the camera position and orientation through the opposite side of endoscope camera which is seen the outside body.

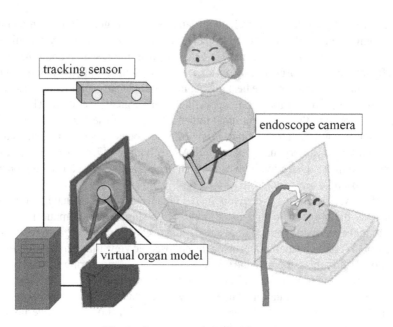

Fig. 1. Our proposed method overview.

2.2 Tracking Method

There are also two kinds of tracking method used in general. One of that use a unique marker and detect its position and orientation. Other do not use the marker, also use just image processing like future detection technique. It is useful for tracking object such as existing tools like an endoscopic camera. However, it needs more cost to detect the object precisely than marker-based tracking method. Therefore, our system use marker based tracking method for making our tracking method robustly.

Figure 2 shows the maker and a prototype endoscopic camera tool which is used in our system. The design of it is aiming for simple and robustness. It uses a hexagonal mount for attaching marker because it can detect at least any two markers for measuring the object position and rotation. This mount is made in advance precisely by using 3D CAD and 3D printer system. Figure 3 shows the mount used in our method.

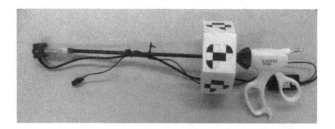

Fig. 2. Prototype endoscopic camera.

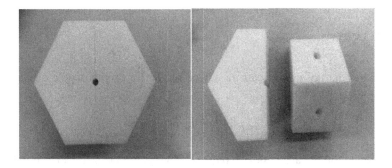

Fig. 3. Hexagonal maker mount.

To detect camera position and orientation precisely during the operation, our method defines the relative vector between markers and camera device, which is on the edge of an endoscope camera [10]. Figure 4 shows the coordinate system overview.

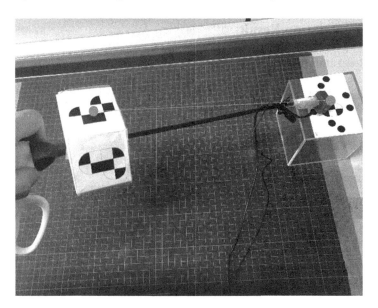

Fig. 4. Calculating relative vector.

Our method uses concrete registration method assuming a tracking device coordinate system Σ_d and an endoscopic camera coordinate system Σ_c. To acquire the relative vector, one must set the endoscopic camera to the origin point P^d_{table} of the fixed marker M_{table} on the flat table. The position P^d_{cam} and orientation R^d_{cam} of the marker attached to the camera M_{cam} are measured in Σ_d. The relative vector P^c_{rel} is calculated by

$$P^c_{rel} = P^d_{table} - P^d_{cam} \tag{1}$$

in Σ_c. To convert P^c_{rel} to P^d_{rel} in Σ_d,

$$P^d_{rel} = R^{d^{-1}}_{cam} \cdot P^c_{rel} \tag{2}$$

Therefore, the position of camera device on the tip of endoscopic camera P^d_{tip} is calculated by

$$P^d_{tip} = R^d_{cam} \cdot P^d_{rel} + P^d_{cam} \tag{3}$$

The orientation of camera device on the tip of endoscopic camera R^d_{tip} is calculated by

$$R^d_{tip} = R^c_n \cdot R^d_{cam} \tag{4}$$

where R^c_n means constant matrix determined for each markers.

3   Implementation Result

3.1   Implementation

We implemented a prototype system including our proposed method and conducted a preliminary experiment. Our prototype system configuration follows.

Computer.

CPU: Intel Core i7-4710MQ, 2.50 GHz
Memory: 32 GB
OS: Microsoft Windows 8.1 ×64

Tracking device.

Model: Claron Technology Micron Tracker 3 (H3-60)
Measurement rate: 16 Hz
Sensor resolution: 1280 × 960 pixel
Lens: 6 mm, 50 × 38 degree
Accuracy of single marker: 0.20 mm RMS
(20,000 averaged positions at depths of 40–100 cm)

Prototype endoscopic camera.

Camera model: AVC-301B1
Camera resolution: 2.5 Megapixel
Camera lens: 70 degree
Camera size: 12 mm × 12 mm
Video capture (VC) model: I-O Data Inc. GV-USB2
VC resolution: 720 × 480 pixel
VC capture frame rate: 30fps

The system overview shows in Fig. 5. It uses a training tool for laparoscopic surgery and 3D organ model designed from CT scan data. The tracking device is installed in such a way as to see the target object from above.

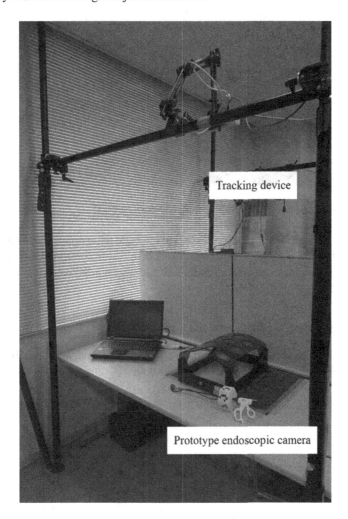

Fig. 5. System overview.

3.2 Experiment

The purpose of this experiment is to confirm the accuracy of alignment precision between actual and measuring position and orientation. Figure 6 shows the experimental environment.

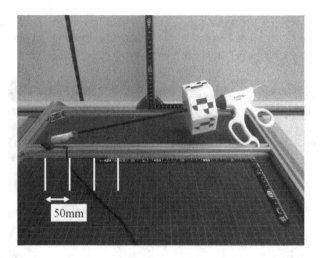

Fig. 6. Experimental environment.

The experimental task for the position is to measure the 4 points placed at the equal interval, 50 mm, on each orthogonal axis. As a result, it is confirmed that the average deviation of position is almost 0.81 mm, and the average deviation of orientation is almost 0.75°.

3.3 Pilot Operation for Laparoscopic Surgery Navigation

We confirmed the pilot operation for laparoscopic surgery navigation task by using our prototype system. Figure 7 shows an example of the operation scene. The system uses

Fig. 7. Pilot navigation system.

a kidney model produced on a 3D printer by using CT scanning data from an actual patient. The system generates overlay video image that is 3D kidney model on the video image from the endoscope camera, while the user operates the endoscopic camera. An example of the overlay image shows in Fig. 8.

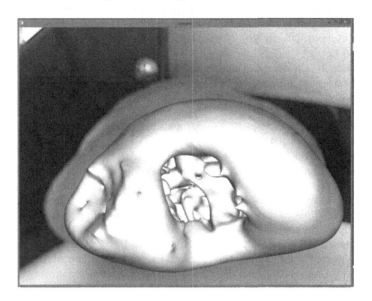

Fig. 8. Example of our system view image.

4   Conclusion

We introduced our study of guidance method for developing AR laparoscopic surgery navigation system. We proposed the measurement method of endoscope camera that is able to track the position and orientation of the camera during surgery operation. It uses specific markers that placed on the hexagonal mount attached endoscope camera. We developed a prototype navigation system provided with our measurement method and confirmed the accuracy of the method through conducting the experiment. Furthermore, it is confirmed the potential of efficiency by using the guidance method which generates the overlay video image which shows 3D virtual kidney model on the actual kidney model.

In the future, it needs to conduct the experiment that is even more detailed and improve the accuracy of the overlay video image, and plan to conduct the experiment in the case of an actual surgery operation.

Acknowledgement.   This work was supported by JSPS KAKENHI Grant Number JP15K00291.

References

1. Qian, K., Bai, J., Yang, X., Pan, J., Zhang, J.: Virtual reality based laparoscopic surgery simulation. In: Proceedings of the 21st ACM Symposium on Virtual Reality Software and Technology, pp. 69–78 (2015). http://doi.org/10.1145/2821592.2821599
2. Coles, T.R., Meglan, D., John, N.W.: The role of haptics in medical training simulators: A survey of the state of the art. IEEE Trans. Haptics **4**(1), 51–66 (2011). http://doi.org/10.1109/TOH.2010.19
3. Kalavakonda, N., Chandra, S., Thondiyath, A.: Development of virtual reality based robotic surgical trainer for patient-specific deformable anatomy. In: Proceedings of the 2015 Conference on Advances in Robotics - AIR 2015, pp. 1–5 (2015). http://doi.org/10.1145/2783449.2783465
4. Delingette, H., Ayache, N.: Hepatic surgery simulation. Commun. ACM **48**(2), 31–36 (2005). http://doi.org/10.1145/1042091.1042116
5. Nicolau, S.A., Goffin, L., Soler, L.: A low cost and accurate guidance system for laparoscopic surgery. In: Proceedings of the ACM Symposium on Virtual Reality Software and Technology - VRST 2005, pp. 124–133 (2005). http://doi.org/10.1145/1101616.1101642
6. Desai, J.P., Tholey, G., Kennedy, C.W.: Haptic feedback system for robot-assisted surgery. In: PerMIS 2007 - Workshop on Performance Metrics for Intelligent Systems, pp. 188–195 (2007). http://doi.org/10.1145/1660877.1660904
7. Hughes-Hallett, A., Mayer, E.K., Marcus, H.J., Cundy, T.P., Pratt, P.J., Darzi, A.W., Vale, J.A.: Augmented reality partial nephrectomy: Examining the current status and future perspectives. Urology **83**(2), 266–273 (2014). http://doi.org/10.1016/j.urology.2013.08.049
8. Su, L.M., Vagvolgyi, B.P., Agarwal, R., Reiley, C.E., Taylor, R.H., Hager, G.D.: Augmented reality during robot-assisted laparoscopic partial nephrectomy toward real-time 3D-CT to stereoscopic video registration. Urology **73**(4), 896–900 (2009). http://doi.org/10.1016/j.urology.2008.11.040
9. Intuitive Surgical - Products: http://www.intuitivesurgical.com/products/
10. Koeda, M., et al.: Depth camera calibration and knife tip position estimation for liver surgery support system. In: Stephanidis, C. (ed.) HCI 2015. CCIS, vol. 528, pp. 496–502. Springer, Cham (2015). doi:10.1007/978-3-319-21380-4_84

A Comparative Usability Analysis of Virtual Reality Goggles

Ana Carol Pontes de França(✉), Danilo Fernandes Vitorino, Aline de Oliveira Neves,
Cristiane Nunes de Lima, and Marcelo Márcio Soares

Department of Design, Federal University of Pernambuco, Recife, Brazil
acpsicologa@gmail.com, danilodmster@gmail.com,
linebelar@gmail.com, nuneslima.cris@gmail.com,
soaresmm@gmail.com

Abstract. The emergence of Virtual Reality goggles with low prices and higher technological simplicity contributed to a further spread of VR among smartphone users. Focused on this type of immersive device, this study consists in a comparative usability analysis of two virtual reality goggles. The adopted criteria to choose the devices was the compatibility with most smartphones and consequently their use by a wide range of users. For the study, we adopted the Leventhal and Barnes' usability model in order to investigate: the ease of learning, ease of use, ease of relearning, flexibility and task match. Finally, it sought to verify the positive and negative aspects in which concerns to the analyzed products in order to make recommendations to improve the quality of use of these devices.

Keywords: Virtual reality · VR goggles · Immersive devices · Usability

1 Introduction

Virtual Reality (VR) is a three-dimensional computer-generated environment, which simulates the physical world through interactive devices that send and receive information. [1] At this synthetic environment, the user takes the physical body as a reference with which he/she coordinates his/her actions on the virtual environment, so the user contextually undergo the experience that leads to the sensation of physical involvement [2].

Similar to a book or a picture, which transports the reader or the observer from the physical environment to that of the story or painting, VR transports the person from the physical world to an environment in which he/she is not physically present, although he/she feels like he/she was [3].

Even if it appeals to fiction, the simulation in this environment presents situations with a degree of realism that allows the user to make decisions and solve problems in the physical world.

Considering that the user presents him/herself as information, metaphorized in the virtual environment, on VR environments the biological and virtual bodies coexist and act in a coordinated way, so the user can present him/herself, interact and modify the virtual world [1].

© Springer International Publishing AG 2017
A. Marcus and W. Wang (Eds.): DUXU 2017, Part II, LNCS 10289, pp. 565–574, 2017.
DOI: 10.1007/978-3-319-58637-3_44

In other words, VR employs multimedia, computer graphics, image processing and other resources to create synthetic environments so the body acts both as a support for cultural prosthetics (user dressed with VR devices) and as a sign (user immersed, metaphorized, on the virtual environment) [1].

In this context, concepts such as immersion, presence, interaction and involvement, fundamental to the study of VR, are indispensable to the understanding of the users' physical and psychological experience in these systems [3, 4].

Taking these assumptions as a starting point, this study focuses on the immersion, which for Witmer and Singer [3] is related to the psychological state characterized by being involved in, included in and interacting with an environment that provides a continuous flow of stimuli.

Thus, this study aimed to evaluate the usability of two types of VR goggles for smartphone users, since the less the user can perceive the physical world (see, touch or hear), the greater the VR immersion is [5].

2   Immersive Technologies

These technologies integrate the physical world to a simulated, virtual world, creating in the user a sense of immersion.

The high degree of sophistication provides realistic, immersive and perceptual experiences through multiple technological components (interactional and perceptual devices, software and applications).

Generally, products developed for commercial use are focused on immersive visual, auditory and tactile solutions.

2.1   VR Goggles

VR goggles, many with an integrated audio system, stimulate visual and auditory perception to create realistic perceptual sensations for VR users.

Aware of these issues, the gaming industry and social media, especially Facebook[1], realized the great potential of these technologies and bet on the development of new devices that contributes to the users' interaction with other people and characters in simulated virtual environments[2].

In this context, the development of VR goggles with low prices and greater technological simplicity, contributed to the dissemination of VR among smartphone users.

This was possible due to the emergence of intelligent technology devices and sensors that use the force of gravity to locate a position of an object in space. Thus, VR use the smartphone device as a display, making VR goggles cheaper and not requiring specific configurations such as we can see in more sophisticated VR goggles.

---

[1] https://www.facebook.com/.

[2] For aditional information: https://www.cnet.com/news/facebook-mark-zuckerberg-shows-off-live-vr-virtual-reality-chat-with-oculus-rift/.

One of the best known versions of this type of goggles is the VR Gear (Fig. 1), from Samsung, which enables the use of applications and videos in virtual reality. However, these goggles are only compatible with some specific devices of the brand itself.

Fig. 1. Gear VR (Source: https://cdn0.vox-cdn.com/thumbor/LJsvpfKqmt3u0CFhAaKRU vuhe_A=/0x0:1100x619/1600x900/cdn0.vox-cdn.com/uploads/chorus_image/image/47262136/ gear_vr.0.0.jpg)

However, other devices on sale are compatible with a wider range of devices and are cheaper. The Google Cardboard (Fig. 2), one of the cheapest for sale, is designed to support most smartphones. It costs about $15 and is made out of cardboard[3].

Fig. 2. Google cardboard (Source: http://cdn2.hubspot.net/hubfs/307727/Stock_Photos/ Cardboard.jpg)

There are other devices that follow the same functional principle of the Google company goggles, being compatible with most appliances and at low cost, although made in plastic. Looking like the VR Gear, the VR Box 2.0 (Fig. 3) and VR Box 360 (Fig. 4) goggles are an example.

Fig. 3. VR BOX 2.0 (Source: http://www.buyvrguide.com/vr-headsets/vr-box-2-0/)

---

[3] http://www.eumed.net/rev/cccss/2016/03/realidade-virtual.html.

Fig. 4. VR BOX 360 (Source: https://vrbox360.com/products/vr-box-360?variant=148487 29543)

The VR Box 2.0 goggles are made of ABS plastic; Adjustable side and top handles (with velcro), made of elastic material; They have padded for comfort of the facial region (foam of PU and synthetic leather); Adjustment knobs for the lenses (eye distance and focus); Holes for sound output on the front; Removable (drawer-type) cover (Fig. 5) for attaching 3,5 to 6 inch smartphones with adjustable spring-loaded locking device; Side holes for earphone wiring, and front sliding cover for use by the rear camera of the smartphone in Augmented Reality (AR) applications.

Fig. 5. Removable drawer-type cover - VR BOX 2.0 goggles (Source: http://www.shoptime.com.br/produto/16470981/oculos-realidade-virtual-3d-com-controle-vr-box-2.0?condition=NEW&cor=BRANCO&tamanho=UNICO)

The VR Box 360 goggles have practically the same characteristics in regard to the material (ABS plastic); Lens adjustment knobs (however, with different texture); Side holes for wired headphones and padding for facial comfort (PU foam and elastic synthetic fabric). However, the coupling of the smartphones is different, with articulated axle system for the opening of the cover (Fig. 6), through lower hinge, and an attachment of the device by an adhesive contained inside (compatible with smartphones from 4 to 6 inches); The adjustment of the lateral and superior handles is made through a plastic buckle extension system; There is a magnet slider button on the side of the device, responsible for selecting menu options in some VR mobile applications but it does not have access to the back camera of the smartphone in applications.

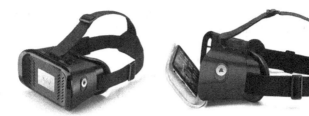

Fig. 6. Cover with articulated axle system - VR BOX 360 goggles (Source: https://vrbox360.com/products/vr-box-360?variant=14848729543)

Despite the similarity of the products in many aspects, the changes in some characteristics like: opening and fastening system for the coupling of the smartphone; adjustment system of the head loops; absence of sliding magnet button on one of the devices; and the difference of material and texture in some parts of the products, among other factors, may cause different results in the usability of the product.

In this study, we evaluated the usability of these devices, through a comparative analysis, performed from the test with users, in order to identify usability problems and propose recommendations for their solution.

3   Usability Analysis

There are several definitions for usability. According to Tullis and Albert [6] they are all related to the involvement of a user developing an activity and using an interface.

For Krug [7], usability is the guarantee that something works correctly regardless of the user's degree of knowledge. Jordan [8] follows the same line of reasoning, stating that the term usability is directly related to the friendly use of products. He underscores the importance of user satisfaction when using the product to achieve his/her purposes that is related to the degree of comfort provided.

ISO 9241-11 [9] defines usability as "the extent to which a product can be used by certain users to achieve specific goals with effectiveness, efficiency, and satisfaction in a certain context of use." Leventhal and Barnes [10] consider the definition of ISO insufficient to evaluate whether a product is usable or not, although they point out what a product should present to be satisfactory in this matter.

Some authors have defined usability models which are composed by features of an usable interface, how they fit together, what they mean and their contribution to usability from common points, although these models remain unique. In this sense, Leventhal and Barnes [10] rely on three different usability models - Shackel, Nielsen and Eason - to construct their own, bringing together the most relevant points of each.

Shackel [11] defines usability as the capability of a product being effectively and easily used by a wide number of users, to acquire the knowledge and conditions necessary for an exercise of an activity at a specified time and environment.

For Nielsen [12], the goal of usability is to construct transparent interfaces that would be capable to provide ease of use, effectiveness and efficiency in user experience, allowing the activity to be controlled by the user in a freer interaction.

Eason [13] considers usability resulting from the relationship between the user interface and a set of situational variables: characteristics of the task, user, system and user reactions.

In these terms, the Leventhal and Barnes [10] usability model is more complete because it assumes that several variables considered together define whether an interface is usable or not, since the different variables levels may generate different demands on interface.

4   Method

This study is the result of a usability evaluation of two VR goggles, held in a room of the Design Department at Federal University of Pernambuco, Brazil.

It was adopted the 'Think Aloud Protocol', in which the user him/herself narrates about the actions taken, the decisions made, as well as speaks about his/her own opinions and feelings about the evaluated product.

This method had two phases: (1) systematic users' statements collecting; and (2) statements analysis, in order to obtain a model of the user's cognitive processes when faced with a problem.

The pilot study was carried out with 02 users to verify the procedures and make adjustments in the experiment.

The convenience sample [6] consisted of 10 smartphone users, of both genders and aged between 18 and 29 years (due to the higher acceptance of VR among young people). Participants were recruited at UFPE Design Department through classroom disclosure, spontaneously attending the study.

During the usability test, the products were randomly delivered to users who had 10 min to perform the task. The devices evaluated were two VR goggles for smartphone users: (1) VR BOX 2.0; and (2) VR BOX 360.

Considering the crescent production of VR goggles over the years and the constant search to novelty by smartphone users, the criteria of choice of the evaluated devices was the compatibility with several smartphone models and the consequent use by a large number of users.

The experiment was performed in an air-conditioned room where the user positioned him/herself in front of a table, where were two VR goggles, its respective guides and an iPhone 5.

Before the usability test has started the user was informed about the test, about the task being performed and asked to speak loudly about what he/she was thinking while performing the task.

After receiving the smartphone with the app 'Sites in VR' with the main screen opened, the participants were asked to: (1) insert the smartphone in the VR goggles; (2) set the straps to fit the user head diameter; (3) adjust the lenses; (4) choose the 'Tower' option through eyetracking; (5) choose the 'Eiffel Tower' option; (6) choose the 'Garden I' immersion scenario; (7) explore the interface; (8) remove smartphone from VR goggles; and (9) remove the goggles.

As the participant had already used the smartphone app in the 'Garden I' immersion scenario, the following steps were requested: (1) to insert the smartphone in the VR goggles; (2) set the straps to fit the diameter of the head; (3) adjust the lenses; (4) explore the interface; (5) remove smartphone from VR goggles; and (6) remove the goggles.

Users were asked to speak loudly whatever came to their mind during the use of the product. The records were filmed for later qualitative and quantitative data analysis.

After the test with the product, the participants were asked to respond to a post-test questionnaire from which users' opinions were obtained.

The frequency and the situational constraints of the task as well as the users' level of expertise were evaluated.

The problems were identified and categorized according to the variables: ease of learning, ease of use, ease of relearning, flexibility, satisfaction and task match.

By the problems identification were discussed the main aspects of the product and were suggested improvement recommendations for the evaluated devices.

5   Results

Considered by Nielsen [12, 14] the most valuable usability test, the 'Thinking Aloud Protocol' corresponds to the users' narrative about the actions performed, the decisions made, their opinions and their feelings while interacting with the product (or prototype) under evaluation. According to Jasper [14, 15], this method consists of two phases: (1) systematic users' statements collecting; and (2) statements analysis, in order to obtain a model of the user's cognitive processes when faced with a problem.

According to Nielsen [12, 14], the method can be performed both individually and in groups, with two variations: the critical response and the periodic report. In the critical response, the user reports their actions during its execution.

The usability test and the users' statements were filmed to data analysis. The problems identified were categorized from the variables: ease of learning, ease of use, ease of relearning, flexibility and task match according to Leventhal and Barnes' usability model [10].

This model was chosen because VR goggles alone does not guarantee users' immersion, since the goggles integrates a human-computer interface that only allows the user experience if the user connects the device to a smartphone and an app.

Regarding the results obtained in the usability test, 80% of the participants (n = 8) had never used any evaluated goggles. About the first variable, **ease of learning**, when questioned, the participants reported difficulty in handling the devices (60%, n = 6), assessing the level of difficulty for beginners as very high. At the time, the participants classified themselves as non-dominant in the use of VR goggles (60%, n = 6), although they recognized the importance of this type of device (100%, n = 10).

On the second variable, **ease of use**, 50% of the participants (n = 5) experienced difficulty handling VR BOX 2.0 and suggested changes such as: better fit for the smartphone; leave buttons more visible facilitating handling and instinct; improve the cushioning and drawer where smartphone is located. Regarding VR BOX 360, 70% of the participants (n = 7) reported feeling easier to perform the task, because they found the goggles more practical, comfortable, with better smartphone positioning and better image visualization. Regarding the cover opening the VR goggles, the best evaluated was the hinged axle system, through the lower hinge of the VR BOX 360. However, the participants warned about the possibility of wear of the fixing sticker of the smartphone, which would make it impossible to use the product.

When asked about the third variable, **easy to relearning**, 60% of the participants (n = 6) reported to be very difficult undo an action in VR BOX 2.0. During filming, on several occasions the participants had to remove their goggles, resort to the manual or even to the experimenter to try to complete the task.

Regarding the item **flexibility and task match**, 50% (n = 5) expressed and reported discomfort during the task with both goggles. In VR BOX 2.0 the participants reported: nuisance at the nose support, difficulty adjusting the lenses, dizziness and overlapping images. To VR BOX 360 goggles, the complaints were: dizziness, visualization of goggles edges and overlapping images.

During the test it was also possible to obtain informations about the user satisfaction. Regarding this item, 50% of the participants (n = 5) said they were satisfied and 10% (n = 1) was very satisfied with the VR BOX 360. When questioned about which goggles they would choose to buy, 80% (n = 8) choosed the VR BOX 360 goggles, although they find their looks less appealing. The users' criteria were: the ease of use, the best image visualization and the fact that it was more practical to insert the smartphone.

In conclusion, the post-test questionnaire ratifies the results found in the usability test and allows an even more detailed analysis about the users interactions with the product.

6   Discussion

The interaction with VR goggles for smartphones users presents certain peculiarities that distinguish this type of device from the VR goggles to conventional computers.

In this sense, the main aspects to be considered in the design and redesign of this type of device were listed in order to provide the users a better product usability and, consequently, better quality of immersion.

1. The first aspect identified was the need to insert a smartphone into the VR goggles. This seemingly simple procedure needs to be so intuitive that the user could easily identify where the smartphone should be stored.
2. It is necessary that the handling to open the smartphone compartment be adapted to the size of users hands and to different handles, especially to those who have some type of motor disability.
3. The smartphone attachment to the storage compartment should not offer resistance for the user, facilitating the device insertion and removal.
4. In addition to intuitiveness, the location for adjusting the lenses should be well signaled so that even a person with little schooling or vision problems can use the device.

5. It is important that the focus of the image be adjusted based on the physical characteristics of the user. The device could make use of swingable spherical knobs for this purpose.
6. It is essential that VR goggles, with an inserted smartphone, present a maximum weight compatible with the body proportions (consider anthropometric metrics) of the users, avoiding to generate muscle, cervical and postural discomforts.

Regarding the fact that VR goggles depend on the smartphone's settings to provide an immersion experience, it is recommended that the user, after adjusting the device to his/her own head, can configure the gyroscope and accelerometer only with head movements, avoiding interferences in the experience of immersion and the smartphone removal.

7   Recommendations

To integrate the goggles to a smartphone, we suggest that when the user purchases the product, it comes with an app. Once installed, the app identifies the user's smartphone version and configures the needs of VR (like a "Virtual Reality mode"). In this way, the phone remains connected to the internet, but does not ring, vibrate or receive calls during the immersion.

Another recommendation for a better interaction with the interface would be to redesign the goggles by integrating the eye tracking feature. With eye tracking the user could select the command and configuration options on the smartphone screen. This feature would also allow the user to interact with the interface from any VR app, without the need to acquire a bluetooth remote control or remove the goggles.

Finally, it is recommended that the graphic information which indicates the functions (e.g. lens adjustment, cover opening and holes for the passage of the headphone plugs) should be printed in high relief and in contrasting colors with the surface of the product.

8   Conclusion

Despite the widespread acceptance of VR goggles for smartphone users, much still needs to be improved in order to ensure a better immersion experience.

In this sense, eye tracking feature contributes for greater user autonomy while interacting with the product and it is a small investment compared with its benefits.

We also recommend attention to informational and handling aspects of the product, as improper use can cause serious users discomfort.

In a few words, we can conclude that ergonomics brings important contributions to the design, analysis and development of VR products, in order to provide a better adaptation of the product to the user.

This adaptation, in addition to providing a better performance for the users, also contributes to funnier, safer, and more challenging experiences.

References

1. França, A.C.P., Pereira Neto, J., Soares, M.M.: We are all cyborgs: Body-machine and body-information in virtual reality systems. In: Marcus, A. (ed.) DUXU 2016. LNCS, vol. 9748, pp. 287–293. Springer, Cham (2016). doi:10.1007/978-3-319-40406-6_27
2. França, A.C.P., Soares, M.M.: Metaphors and embodiment in virtual reality systems. In: Marcus, A. (ed.) DUXU 2016. LNCS, vol. 9748, pp. 278–286. Springer, Cham (2016). doi: 10.1007/978-3-319-40406-6_26
3. Soares, M., et. al.: Virtual reality in consumer product design: Methods and applications. In: Human Factors and Ergonomics in Consumer Product Design: Methods and Techniques. CRC Press (2011)
4. França, A.C.P., Soares, M.: Dialogical self on virtual reality systems: Presence and embodiment in human situated interaction. In: 6th International Conference on Applied Human Factors and Ergonomics (AHFE) and the Affiliated Conferences, AHFE (2015)a
5. França, A.C.P., Soares, M.: Realidade Virtual Aplicada à Educação: a era Matrix do processo de ensino e aprendizagem. XIII Congresso Internacional de Tecnologias na Educação (2015)b
6. Tullis, T., Albert, B.: Measuring the user experience: Collecting, analyzing and presenting usability metrics. Elsevier, New York (2008)
7. Krug, S.: Don't Make Me Think! A common sense approach to web usability. New Riders Press, IndianaPolis (2000)
8. Jordan, P.: An Introduction to Usability. Taylor & Francis, London (1998)
9. ISO/IEC 9241-11. Ergonomic Requirements for Office Work with Visual Display Terminals (VDT)s - Part II Guidance on Usability (1998)
10. Leventhal, L., Barnes, J.: Usability Engineering: Process, Products and Examples. Pearson Education Inc., New Jersey (2008)
11. Shackel, B.: The concept of usability. In: Bennett, J., Case, D., Sandelin, J., Smith, M. (eds.) Visual Display Terminals: Usability Issues and Health Concerns. Englewood Cliffs, NJ (1984)
12. Nielsen, J.: Usability Engineering. Academic Press, San Diego (1993)
13. Eason, K.D.: Towards the experimental study of usability. Behav. Inf. Technol. 3(2), 133–143 (1984)
14. Catecati, T., et al.: Métodos Para a Avaliação da Usabilidade no Design de Produtos. DAPesquisa: Revista de Investigação em Artes, Florianópolis 8(8), 564–581 (2010). Jul. 2011 Disponível   em: <http://www.ceart.udesc.br/dapesquisa/edicoes_anteriores/8/files/04DESIGN_Fernanda_Gomes_Faust.pdf>
15. Jasper, M.W.M.: A comparison of usability methods for testing interactive health technologies: Methodological aspects and empirical evidence. Int. J. Med. Informatics 78(5), 340–353 (2009)

Augmented Reality Navigation System for Robot-Assisted Laparoscopic Partial Nephrectomy

Atsushi Sengiku[1], Masanao Koeda[2], Atsuro Sawada[1], Jin Kono[1], Naoki Terada[1], Toshinari Yamasaki[1], Kiminori Mizushino[3], Takahiro Kunii[4], Katsuhiko Onishi[2], Hiroshi Noborio[2], and Osamu Ogawa[1(✉)]

[1] Department of Urology, Graduate School of Medicine, Kyoto University, Kyoto, Japan
ogawao@kuhp.kyoto-u.ac.jp
[2] Osaka Electro-Communication University, Neyagawa, Japan
[3] Embedded Wings Co. Ltd., Osaka, Japan
[4] Kashina System Co. Ltd., Shiga, Japan

Abstract. We have developed a surgical navigation system for robot-assisted laparoscopic partial nephrectomy (RALPN). In this system, a three-dimensional computer graphics (3DCG) model generated from each patient's computed tomography image is overlaid on the endoscopic image, and we control it manually to navigate the vascular structure and tumor location in real time. The position and orientation of the 3DCG model is calculated from the optical flow of the endoscopic camera images, which enables the model to move semi-automatically. We conducted 20 navigations for RALPN from April 2014 to December 2016. Our support system worked appropriately and was helpful to localize the tumor and determine the resection line.

Keywords: Robotic surgery · Navigation system · Partial nephrectomy

1 Introduction

In recent years, progress in diagnostic radiographic imaging technology and a heightened awareness of early detection of cancer have facilitated incidental discovery of small renal tumors. Therefore, while radical nephrectomy, which was conventionally the gold standard treatment for localized renal cell carcinoma, is decreasing as the treatment of choice, partial nephrectomy has become the standard therapy for small renal cell carcinoma. In addition, laparoscopic surgery has become more widespread because of the progression in surgical techniques and medical engineering as well as the requirement for minimally invasive surgery [1]. Robot-assisted laparoscopic partial nephrectomy (RALPN) is an excellent minimally invasive treatment that can achieve both cancer control and renal function preservation. RALPN has been conducted in several hospitals to realize higher-precision surgery.

A limitation of RALPN is the impairment of haptic feedback. This problem has not yet been resolved; therefore, surgeons should discern the border between the tumor and normal kidney only from visual information. Conventionally, we have used ultrasonography during partial nephrectomy to identify the location and margin of tumors.

© Springer International Publishing AG 2017
A. Marcus and W. Wang (Eds.): DUXU 2017, Part II, LNCS 10289, pp. 575–584, 2017.
DOI: 10.1007/978-3-319-58637-3_45

However, ultrasonography is not always sufficient for discerning the precise border when the tumor is totally endophytic or appears relatively isoechoic. Thus, proper image guidance can offer a potential clinical advantage with respect to accurate anatomic identification and unambiguous dissection of a tumor, contributing to a safe and rapid surgical operation [2, 3]. Additionally, the number of RALPNs are sharply increasing because RALPN became covered by the national health insurance system of Japan in April 2016. We herein describe our development of a surgery support system for RALPN in April 2014.

2   Overview of Navigation System

We developed a RALPN navigation system with augmented reality technology using the following three steps. First, we generated a three-dimensional computer graphics (3DCG) model that includes a kidney, arteries, veins, tumors, and urinary tract from DICOM images of computed tomography (CT) scans with SYNAPSE VINCENT (FUJIFILM Holdings Corporation, Tokyo, Japan), and each generated part was saved separately. Second, we projected the 3DCG model on the operator's console monitor and operating room monitor. Third, one medical doctor manually controlled the projected 3DCG model to overlay it on the visceral structure in real time (Fig. 1).

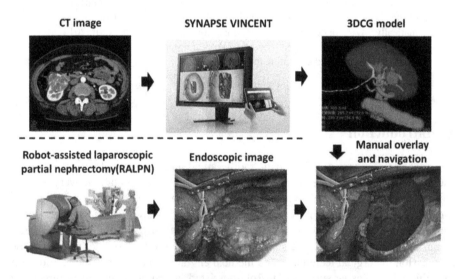

Fig. 1. Overview of navigation system

3   3DCG Generation with SYNAPSE VINCENT

We originally generated the 3DCG model by using 3D Slicer [4]; however, we began generating the 3DCG model with SYNAPSE VINCENT (Fig. 2a) beginning in March 2016. It takes about 30 min to make one 3DCG model semi-automatically, but the accuracy of the 3DCG model depends on the quality of the CT images. Enhanced CT images should be taken in multiple phases, including the early phase for arteries, late phase for veins and tumors, and excretory phase for the urinary tract. Furthermore, enhanced CT images should be taken in thin slices to achieve a high-quality 3DCG model. As shown below, a 3DCG model generated from enhanced CT images taken in 1-mm slices (Fig. 2b) is more accurate than that taken in 5-mm slices (Fig. 2c).

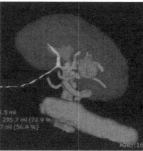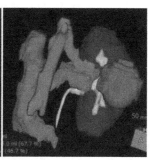

(a) SYNAPSE VINCENT   (b) 3DCG from 1mm slice CT   (c) 3DCG from 5mm slice CT

Fig. 2. 3DCG model generated by SYNAPSE VINCENT

4   System Overview

Our support system was improved and upgraded in April 2014. The following configuration is the latest version of our system (Fig. 3).

Computer and Developing Environment
Model: MouseComputer, NEXTGEAR-NOTE i420BA3-SP-W7
OS: Windows 8.1 Professional 64 [bit]
CPU: Core i7-4710 MQ
RAM: 8 [GB]
GPU: NVIDIA GeForce GTX 860M
Tools: Visual Studio 2013, OpenCV 3.1.0, freeglut 2.8.1
Video Capturing Device
Model: Epiphan, AV.io HD
I/O: HDMI to USB3.0
Resolution and Frame Rate: 1980 × 1080 [px], 60 [fps]
Rotary Controller
Model: Griffin Technology, PowerMate
Interface: USB2.0

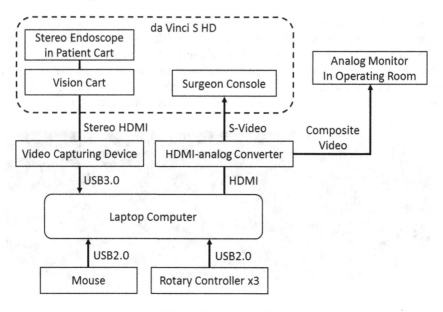

Fig. 3. System overview

5   Image Processing

The image for navigation is generated as described in our previous report [5]:

1. Capture the stereo endoscope video image to the laptop computer and separate the left and right video images (Fig. 4a).
2. Convert to hue, saturation, and value images and create a mask for surgical tools based on the saturation value (Fig. 4b).
3. Calculate optical flows and delete the noisy flows using the mask (Fig. 4c).
4. Overlay the 3DCG model on the video image and move it with the averaged optical flow to x, y, and z translation and vertical axis rotation (Fig. 4d).
5. Move the 3DCG manually using a mouse and control the transparency of each part of the 3DCG using rotary controllers (Fig. 6b).
6. Output the overlaid image to the surgeon console monitor and operating room.

For accurate navigation, it is important to present necessary information to the navigation monitor in each phase of the operation because the vascular structures and organ shapes vary as the surgery progresses. Each part of the 3DCG model, including the kidney, arteries, vessels, tumors, and urinary tract, is saved separately, enabling us to control the display condition of each part independently. The status of the 3DCG model changes with respect to whether it is displaying, hiding, or making one or all parts transparent (Fig. 5).

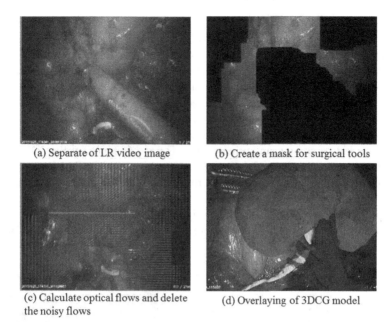

(a) Separate of LR video image   (b) Create a mask for surgical tools

(c) Calculate optical flows and delete
the noisy flows

(d) Overlaying of 3DCG model

Fig. 4. Image processing

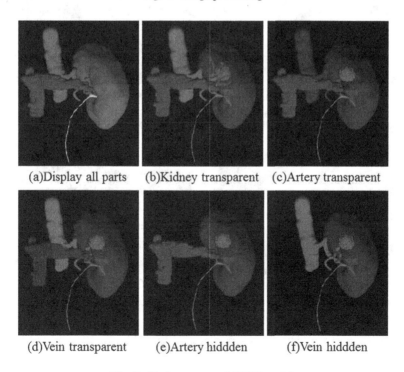

(a)Display all parts   (b)Kidney transparent   (c)Artery transparent

(d)Vein transparent   (e)Artery hiddden   (f)Vein hiddden

Fig. 5. Various status of 3DCG model

6 Navigation Procedure

We conducted 20 navigations for RALPN from November 2014 to December 2016. The position and orientation of the 3DCG model was calculated through the optical flow of the endoscopic camera images, which enabled the 3DCG model to move semi-automatically. To match the overlaid 3DCG model to organs and vessels intuitively in real time, we used three rotary and one mouse controller simultaneously (Fig. 6b). The three rotary controllers were configured for three parts: red for arteries, blue for veins, and black for the kidney, tumor, and urinary tract. The requirements of the 3DCG model appearance sequentially changed during the various phases of the RALPN surgery. To respond to these changes, we used the three rotary controllers to quickly alter the permeability of the kidney, arteries, and veins in real time.

The projected images were simultaneously confirmed in both the surgeon's console and the operating room monitor, which helped surgeons, nurses, and medical students to understand the surgical situation (Fig. 6c, d).

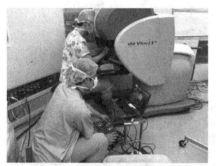

(a) Surgeon console (behind) and operator of our system (front)

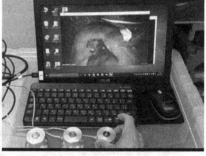

(b) Navigation system controller

(c) 3DCG navigation image in surgeon console view (lower left)

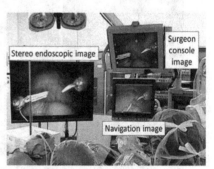

(d) 3DCG navigation image in operating room

Fig. 6. Display of our navigation system

7   Case Presentation

Our support system was especially helpful in patients with small endophytic tumors or complicated vascular structures. When the tumor was small or totally endophytic, localization of the tumor and determination of its resection margin was time-consuming and laborious.

We herein present three cases in which our navigation system contributed to safe and smooth progression of RALPN.

Case 1. The patient was a 62-year-old man with a stage 1 right renal cell carcinoma. The tumor was small and half endophytic in the renal parenchyma (Fig. 7a, b). During the surgery, the tumor could not be localized on the endoscopic image before removing the fat around the kidney (Fig. 7c), but the 3DCG navigation image appropriately showed the location and size of the tumor (Fig. 7d). This navigation image assisted the surgeons in accurately approaching the tumor.

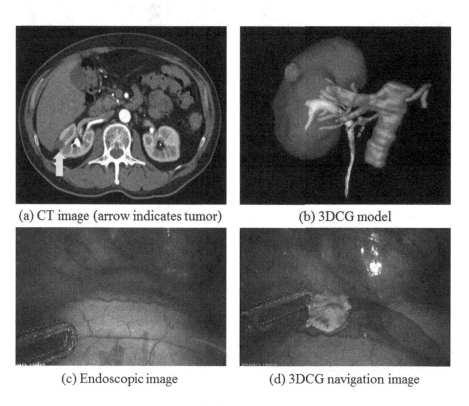

(a) CT image (arrow indicates tumor)   (b) 3DCG model

(c) Endoscopic image   (d) 3DCG navigation image

Fig. 7. Case 1

Case 2. The patient was a 68-year-old man with a stage 1 left renal cell carcinoma. The tumor was small and almost totally endophytic in the renal parenchyma (Fig. 8a, b). In addition, the tumor was located on the dorsal side of the kidney, which made tumor localization difficult. The tumor could not be identified on the endoscopic image even after removing the surrounding fat (Fig. 8c), but the 3DCG navigation image appropriately showed the location, size, and depth of the tumor.

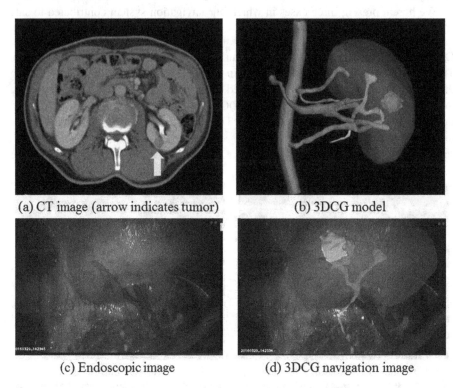

(a) CT image (arrow indicates tumor)   (b) 3DCG model

(c) Endoscopic image   (d) 3DCG navigation image

Fig. 8. Case 2

Case 3. The patient was a 44-year-old man with a stage 1 left renal cell carcinoma. The tumor was also totally endophytic in the renal parenchyma (Fig. 9a, b) and could not be identified on the endoscopic image even after removing the surrounding fat (Fig. 9c). Our navigation image appropriately showed the location, size, and depth of the tumor and indicated that the tumor was in contact with the urinary tract. This navigation image helped the surgeons to determine the resection line and to realize the possibility of opening the urinary tract.

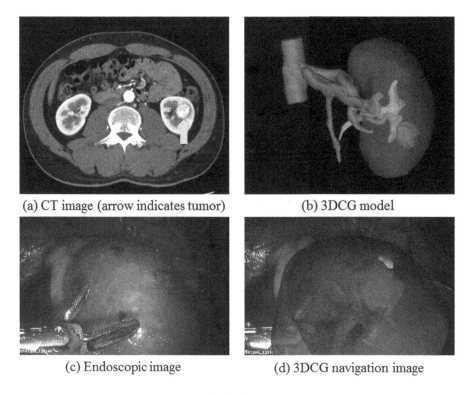

(a) CT image (arrow indicates tumor)   (b) 3DCG model

(c) Endoscopic image   (d) 3DCG navigation image

Fig. 9. Case 3

8   Conclusion

We have developed an augmented reality navigation system for RALPN. Our support system worked appropriately and was helpful to localize the tumor and determine its resection lines. Our navigation system is used under two-dimensional image registration and mainly manual control by an experienced medical doctor at present, but 3D-CT stereoscopic image registration and an automatic tracking system are currently in development. We are convinced that our system will bring significant benefits to both surgeons and patients.

References

1. Sengiku, A., et al.: A multi-institutional questionnaire survey on surgical treatment for a small renal mass: factors related with decision-making in indications for partial nephrectomy. Hinyokika Kiyo. **58**, 665–669 (2012)
2. Hughes-Hallett, A., et al.: Augmented reality partial nephrectomy: examining the current status and future perspectives. Urology **83**, 266–273 (2014)

3. Su, L.M., et al.: Augmented reality during robot-assisted laparoscopic partial nephrectomy: toward real-time 3D-CT to stereoscopic video registration. Urology **73**, 896–900 (2009)
4. 3D Slicer: http://www.slicer.org/
5. Koeda, M., et al.: Image overlay support with 3DCG organ model for robot-assisted laparoscopic partial nephrectomy. In: Stephanidis, C. (ed.) HCI 2016. CCIS, vol. 617, pp. 508–513. Springer, Cham (2016). doi:10.1007/978-3-319-40548-3_84

Laser Intensity Data Visualization for Laser Physics

Jee Ho Song[1], Han Sol Shin[1], Tae Jun Yu[2], and Kun Lee[3(✉)]

[1] Department of Information and Communication, Handong Global University,
Pohang, Republic of Korea
[2] Department of Advanced Green Energy & Environment,
Handong Global University, Pohang, Republic of Korea
[3] School of Computer Science & Electronic Engineering,
Handong Global University, Pohang, Republic of Korea
kunlee@handong.edu

Abstract. In the field of laser simulation, Visualization of intensity data is a very important work. The laser intensity data is characterized by scattered volumetric data and does not have relation information between each data. We used an iso-surface, a representative indirect volume rendering method, as a method to analyze the geometric characteristics of the intensity data. However, iso-surface visualization requires the proper choice of an iso-value. If you determine the iso-value in a fully interactive manner without any guidance, then the value will not be what you want most. Hence, most visualization tools involve preprocessing that analyzes the values and calculates the appropriate iso-value, but this method is not suitable for laser intensity data, which is the scattered volume data. To solve this problem, we divide the whole grid, and calculate the weights for the specific areas to derive the appropriate iso-value that the user wants.

Keywords: Laser physics · Laser intensity · Data visualization

1 Introduction

Laser technology is very important in generating plasma waves. Plasma generated by passing a laser through a gas or a screen is utilized in various applications such as energy, new materials, semiconductor device manufacturing, and environmental fields required in the 21st century. The generation of high-efficiency plasmas is closely related to the development of high-intensity lasers. Therefore, in the study of high intensity plasma generation, visualization of intensity data is a very meaningful task [1–4].

In general, volume visualization is performed using two approaches: direct volume rendering and surface rendering. Direct volume rendering algorithms render every voxel in the volume raster directly, without conversion to geometric primitives or first converting to a different domain and then rendering from that domain. On the other hand, surface rendering algorithms first fit geometric primitives to values in the data, and then render these primitives. Therefore, we have visualized the intensity data through iso-surface methods, one of the surface rendering methods that is easy to analyze the geometric characteristics (Fig. 1).

© Springer International Publishing AG 2017
A. Marcus and W. Wang (Eds.): DUXU 2017, Part II, LNCS 10289, pp. 585–593, 2017.
DOI: 10.1007/978-3-319-58637-3_46

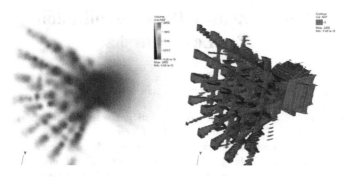

Fig. 1. Direct volume rendering (left) vs surface rendering (right)

2 Problem Description

The iso-surface is a method of generating surface by connecting values having certain value, called iso-value, in volume data. The iso-value may be chosen in a purely interactive manner without any guidance. And the selected value may be inappropriate. The previous way to assist in determining iso-value is to use the histogram and previews. As a first level of support, the histogram of the dataset is displayed and labeled to enable the user to select a certain value. Previews, as a further supporting method, may be provided by rendering a down-sampled images and enable the user to select from them (Table 1).

Table 1. Data properties

Type	HDF5 scalar dataset
No. of dimensions	3
Resolution	$800 \times 800 \times 41$
Data type	32-bit floating point

The laser intensity data is characterized by scattered volumetric data. Figure 2 shows that the distribution of laser data is too broad (min: 9.0e−15, max: 2.5e + 03) to be represented through the histogram. In addition, there is a problem that big data requires a lot of time to process the preview each time. Therefore, programs such as MatLab take a built-in algorithm to compute and provide the appropriate iso-value. However, this is an advantageous method if the volume data has a clear surface, and is not a suitable method for scattered data with unclear surfaces such as laser intensity data. In addition, significant iso-values for users studying through visualization of laser intensity data may be different each time. Therefore, we propose an improved method to propose a moderate iso-value to the user [5–7].

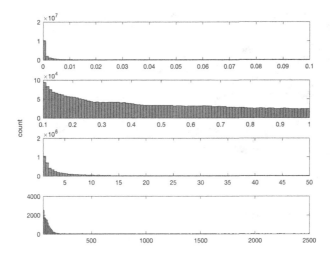

Fig. 2. Distribution of laser intensity values

3 Camera Metering System

There is a metering system in the camera that we can see easily around us. The metering system measures and calculates the amount of light that can be confirmed by the viewfinder and sets the appropriate exposure value. Considering that the laser intensity data is light intensity, we are adopting the concept of metering system in that it is the same as iso-value selection and camera exposure value selection. In Fig. 3, each camera is slightly different, but the basic metering system is spot, center-weighted, and matrix. We analyze these three methods and consider appropriate methods for analyzing laser intensity data [8, 9].

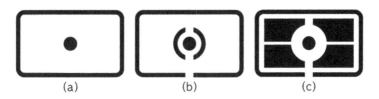

Fig. 3. Three kinds of metering systems on nikon camera: (a) spot, (b) center-weighted, and (c) matrix

3.1 Spot Metering

Spot metering is a method of measuring the center of the area corresponding to about 3.5% of the area in the viewfinder (Fig. 4). This method is suitable for cases where the illumination difference between the background and the subject is large because only a specific portion is precisely measured irrespective of the overall brightness.

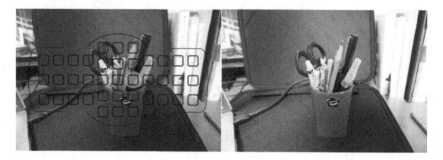

Fig. 4. Spot metering in the viewfinder (left) and output (right)

3.2   Center-Weighted Metering

Center-weighted metering focuses on the center of the viewfinder and then measures the overall average brightness. As shown in Fig. 5, the measured value of the central area corresponding to $20 \sim 30\%$ of the viewfinder is weighted by $60 \sim 80\%$, and the measured value of the other area is weighted by $20 \sim 40\%$. Therefore, it is the most suitable measurement method when the subject is in the middle.

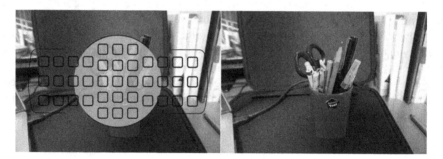

Fig. 5. Center-weighted metering in the viewfinder (left) and output (right)

3.3   Matrix Metering

Matrix metering divides the entire screen into zones and then analyzes the exposure patterns of each zone through the built-in algorithm of each manufacturer. It then determines the exposure value of the average of all the zones. Different manufacturers have different exposure patterns, and Nikon has a database that contains more than 30,000 referenceable exposure information (Fig. 6).

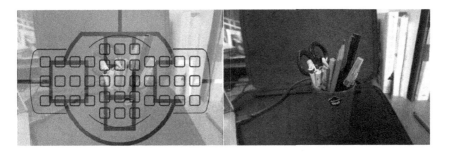

Fig. 6. Matrix metering in the viewfinder (left) and output (right)

4 Laser Intensity Metering System

The algorithm used in our proposed laser intensity metering system is based on algorithm embedded in MatLab. First, we convert the volume data to a histogram of N-bins, the range of values. Next, we average the remaining bins by removing mode value lower than the median, which are most likely to be a garbage. We used this filtering algorithm to determine the iso-values of the following measurement methods; entire volume metering, spot metering, center-weighted metering [10, 11].

4.1 Entire Volume Metering

Figure 7 shows the selected region in the entire volume data and the histogram of its region. As can be seen from Fig. 7, the bin count to the minimum value occupies the largest portion. Figure 8 shows the average values before and after removing the mode value. By eliminating the bin that is close to zero and occupies the most amount, we can see that the result is a more meaningful average.

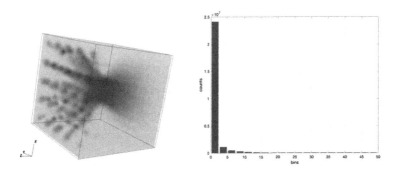

Fig. 7. Histogram of the entire volume data

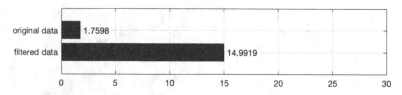

Fig. 8. Comparison of iso-value before and after removal of mode data

4.2 Spot Metering

Figure 9 shows histograms in three randomly selected spots, which are 3.5% of the total volume. As you can see from the obvious difference between Spot 2 and the other two spots, the distribution of the values depends on the selected area. Furthermore, the distribution of the values of spots 1 and 3 is similar at first glance, but the magnitude of the maximum intensity value present in the area is different. Thus, the filtered iso-value is also different for each zone (Fig. 10).

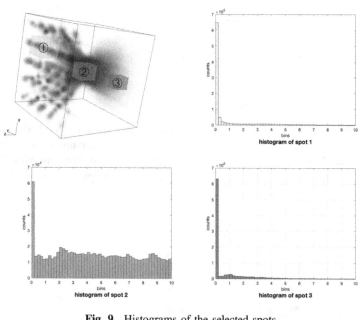

Fig. 9. Histograms of the selected spots

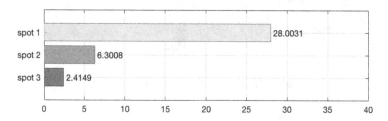

Fig. 10. Comparison of iso-value in each spot

4.3 Center-Weighted Metering

Figure 11 depicts about 25% of the entire volume and the histogram of selected area. The unweighted central area is equivalent to widening the area of spot 2 in Fig. 9. The central area has a relatively stable form of the distribution value as compared to the remaining area, but has relatively low intensity values.

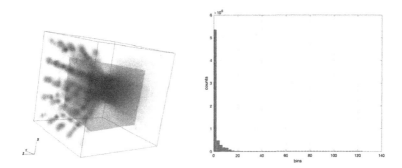

Fig. 11. Histogram of the selected central data

In the center-weighted metering method, which is a mixed method of entire metering and spot metering, we use weighting method to reduce the difference in results depending on the selected position. The weighted average equation we used is:

$$i_{avg} = \frac{\sum_{i=1}^{n} w_i \times i_i}{\sum_{i=1}^{n} w_i}$$

In this equation w_i is the weight given in each area, and i_i is the iso-value of each area. We used this equation to assign a weight of 75% to the central area and 25% to the other areas. The result is shown in Fig. 12.

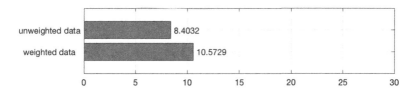

Fig. 12. Comparison of iso-value before and after weighting

5   Visualization

In an experiment to visualize the iso-surface of the laser intensity data, we used VisIt. VisIt was developed by LLNL (Lawrence Livermore National Laboratory) and is an open source visualization tool for effectively representing science and engineering data by BSD licensing. In addition, VisIt is capable of visualizing data from over 120 different scientific data formats including HDF5 [12].

Table 2 shows the iso-values used in the experiment. The iso-values required to perform iso-surface were obtained through the methods described above; entire volume metering, spot metering and center-weighted metering; and those obtained through the built-in algorithm in MatLab.

Table 2. Iso-value of each algorithm

	Algorithm		Iso-value
(a)	Built-in ALGO in MatLab		7.6105
(b)	Entire volume metering		14.9919
(c)	Center-weighted metering		10.5729
(d)	Spot metering	(1)	28.0031
(e)		(2)	6.3008
(f)		(3)	2.4149

Figure 13 is the result of surface rendering the laser intensity data through the iso-surface. Figure 13(e) and (f) show larger surfaces because they have lower iso-values than Fig. 13(a). In addition, the results of Fig. 13(b), (c), and (d) show that the surfaces of the laser intensity data are broken away in the form of islands.

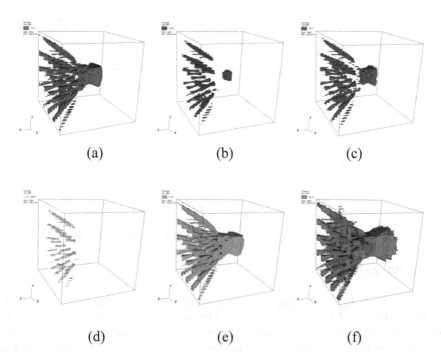

(a)   (b)   (c)

(d)   (e)   (f)

Fig. 13. The result of surface rendering by iso-values of Table 2

6   Conclusions

In this paper, we used iso-surface as a representative surface visualization method for geometric analysis to visualize laser intensity data. However, due to the properties of the scattered volumetric data of the laser intensity data, it is difficult to select appropriate iso-values for the iso-surface. Therefore, we adopted the camera metering system; A method of providing an average value by removing a value close to garbage in the entire region or selected spot, and a method of providing center-weighted average value. Through these methods, it is possible to suggest a more meaningful iso-value to the user. For further research, we are trying to provide a more appropriate iso-value by matrix pattern metering that reflects the user's interest through machine learning.

Acknowledgments. This work was supported by the Industrial Strategic technology development program, 10048964, Development of 125 J·Hz laser system for laser peering funded by Ministry of Trade, Industry & Energy (MI, Republic of Korea).

References

1. Rübel, O., Geddes, C.G.R., Chen, M., Cormier-Michel, E., Bethel, E.W.: Feature-based analysis of plasma-based particle acceleration data. IEEE Trans. Vis. Comput. Graph. **20**(2), 196–210 (2014)
2. Shin, H.S., Yu, T.J., Lee, K.: Visualization of scattered plasma-based particle acceleration data. J. Korea Multimedia Soc. **18**(1), 65–70 (2015)
3. Lücke, P.: Volume Rendering Techniques for Medical Imaging. Technische Universität München (2005)
4. Preim, B., Botha, C.: Visual Computing for Medicine: Theory, Algorithms, and Applications, 2nd edn. Morgan Kaufmann, Burlington (2013)
5. Abbas, M.Z., Prasad, P.: Query-Based Visualization of Iso-Surfaces for Tetrahedral Meshes (2008)
6. Sanderson, A.R. Whitlock, B., Rübel, O., Childs, H., Weber, G., Wu, K.: A system for query based analysis and visualization. In: International Symposium Visual Analytics Science and Technology (2012)
7. Battiato, S., Messina, G., Castorina, A.: Exposure correction for imaging devices: an overview. In: Single-Sensor Imaging Methods Applications for Digital Cameras, pp. 323–349 (2008)
8. Nourani-Vatani, N., Roberts, J.M.: Automatic camera exposure control. In: Proceedings Australasian Conference on Robotics and Automation, pp. 1–6 (2007)
9. Metering *Nikon.* http://imaging.nikon.com/lineup/dslr/basics/18/01.htm
10. Visit *LLNL.* https://wci.llnl.gov/simulation/computer-codes/visit
11. Peterson, D.: Which is best? spot, center weight, or matrix metering? Digital Photo Secrets. http://www.digital-photo-secrets.com/tip/2879/which-is-best-spot-center-weight-or-matrix-metering
12. Shin, H.S., Song, J.H., Yu, T.J., Lee, K.: Creative interaction for plasma physics. In: Marcus, A. (ed.) DUXU 2016. LNCS, vol. 9748, pp. 214–222. Springer, Cham (2016). doi:10.1007/978-3-319-40406-6_20

A New Organ-Following Algorithm Based on Depth-Depth Matching and Simulated Annealing, and Its Experimental Evaluation

Kaoru Watanabe[✉], Shogo Yoshida, Daiki Yano, Masanao Koeda, and Hiroshi Noborio

Department of Computer Science,
Osaka Electro-Communication University, Neyagawa, Japan
{kaoru,ht12a101,mt16a009,koeda,noborio}@oecu.jp

Abstract. Medical simulation technology has been rapidly developing, owing to the production of cheap high-performance computers and depth cameras. We are developing a surgery navigation system. In such a system, it is important to track a virtual organ model based on a real organ model. For this purpose, we should examine the coincidence of positions/orientations between two organs at any time. In order to achieve this, we compare depth images of virtual or real organ model. The former is calculated by the z-buffer on a graphics processing unit (GPU) board, while the latter is captured by a depth camera. Then, we search for the same position/orientation between real and virtual organ models by comparing the differences between two depth images. In this paper, we use simulated annealing (SA) to search for the same position/orientation.

Keywords: Simulated annealing · Organ-following algorithm · Depth-depth matching

1 Introduction

In a surgery navigation system, it is necessary to track a virtual organ model (which is displayed to users) against a real organ model, and to match the positions of the two organ models at any time (Fig. 1). Several papers [1–4] proposed typical matching methods. Independently, we are developing a navigation system for liver surgery [5–7].

Our system captures the surface depth image of an organ by using a depth camera such as the Kinect v2, and loads depth-image data on a z-buffer on the PC. Graphics processing unit (GPU) board on the PC generates the surface image of the 3D virtual organ model, which is displayed to users, on another z-buffer on the GPU board. Figure 2 shows the two z-buffers in our system. To match the positions and orientations of the virtual and real organ (liver) models, we denote the position/orientation of a 3D virtual organ object by p = (x, y, z, φ, θ, ψ), where x, y, z are the coordinates in Euclidean 3D space, φ is the roll angle, θ is the pitch, and ψ is the yaw. We also denote p = (p1, p2, p3, p4, p5, p6). In this system, the position/orientation p is searched to decrease the differences between the depth images of the virtual and real liver models in order to match the depth images.

© Springer International Publishing AG 2017
A. Marcus and W. Wang (Eds.): DUXU 2017, Part II, LNCS 10289, pp. 594–607, 2017.
DOI: 10.1007/978-3-319-58637-3_47

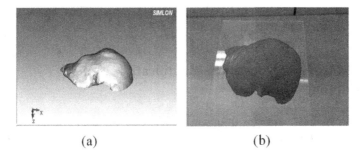

Fig. 1. (a) Polyhedral liver in STL format, and (b) 3D-printed plastic liver.

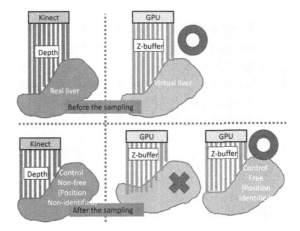

Fig. 2. Position/orientation of virtual liver model is searched to decrease the difference of depth images of virtual and real liver models.

In this paper, we propose a new depth-depth matching algorithm based on the simulated annealing algorithm, which replaces the steepest descendent algorithm. The steepest descendent algorithm sometimes cannot escape from local minima in a search space with six degrees of freedom. Consequently, during surgery, the system fails to track the virtual organ model to the position/orientation of a real liver model.

Simulated annealing (SA) is a type of randomized search algorithm that was first proposed by S. Kirkpatrick, C. D. Gelatt, M. P. Vecchi et al. in 1983 [8]. This was fortunately rediscovered by V. Cerny in 1985 [9]. SA is a metaheuristic that finds global optimization in a large search space. Steepest descent is a simple search method. At each step, it selects the best neighbor of the current point that is stuck at a local optimum and often cannot find a global optimum. SA selects a neighbor probabilistically and finds the global optimum for a long enough time.

To overcome the drawbacks in our system, we use SA for matching two depth images. In Sect. 2, we describe our simulated annealing algorithm. Then, in Sect. 3, we evaluate the simulated annealing algorithm by changing several parameters, and consequently obtain some significant properties following a real 3D liver, using its virtual

3D liver model expressed by a polyhedron in an STL format. Then, in Sect. 4, we give some concluding remarks.

2   Initial Position/Orientation Identification Under Overlapping Ratio

In this study, we use two kinds of depth images. One is a depth image calculated by z-buffering of the GPU for a virtual model expressed as a polyhedron in STL format. The other is separate depth image captured by the Kinect v2 camera. By overlapping two kinds of depth images, a user can identify the degree of overlapping in real and virtual 3D livers (Fig. 3).

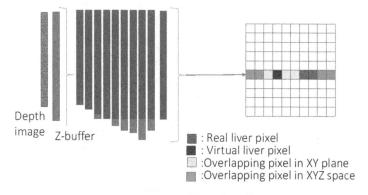

Fig. 3. In our experiment, we evaluated our motion transcription algorithm by calculating the overlapping ratio (number of green pixels)/(number of blue pixels) × 100. This is how much a virtual 3D liver overlaps its corresponding real 3D liver during surgical navigation. (Color figure online)

By observing the colors on a PC monitor, the user can select several parameters related to the 3D CG (Computer Graphics) virtual environment according to the consistency between the real liver in the camera coordinate system and the virtual liver in the graphics coordinate system. In the image, blue and red pixels are expressed as pixels projected from virtual and real 3D livers along the vertical (Z) axis, respectively. In addition, yellow and green pixels are represented as pixels overlapping the virtual and real 3D livers in the XY plane and XYZ space, respectively. If depth differences between the real and virtual images are less than 1 cm at a pixel, the pixel color is changed from yellow to green. The reason is that many liver surgeons indicated that general liver surgery is not so precise, and that a 1 cm clearance is allowed in a real liver surgery.

In this image-based position/orientation adjustment system, the CG virtual world, captured artificially by the z-buffer of the GPU, should agree with the real world captured by a real depth camera [7]. Furthermore, we always calculate (the number of green pixels)/(the number of blue pixels) × 100 during a surgical operation. Using this ratio, we can understand how much a virtual 3D liver overlaps its corresponding 3D real liver (Fig. 3).

In the next section, we calculate the overlapping ratio during an experimental operation in a surgical room with shadow-less lamps. As a result, we can evaluate our motion transcription algorithm with zero, one, or two shadow-less lamps. The evaluation area is defined as a circle by which we can see the 3D liver through an occluding object. By changing the size of the circle, we can flexibly simulate many types of real liver surgeries.

3   Simulated Annealing Algorithm

During surgery, our system continues to capture depth images of a liver at fixed sampling intervals of Δt. Let t0, t1, t2, ... be the capture times. Then, $ti + 1 - ti = \Delta t$. The surgery system must finish matching two depth images within a sampling interval of Δt.

We denote the position/orientation of a 3D virtual organ object by $p = (x, y, z, \varphi, \theta, \psi)$, where x, y, z are the coordinates in Euclidean 3D space, φ is the roll angle, θ is the pitch, and ψ is the yaw. We denote also $p = (p1, p2, p3, p4, p5, p6)$. In this system, the position/orientation p is searched to decrease the difference between two depth images of virtual and real liver models to match the depth images. Below is the SA search algorithm used in our system.

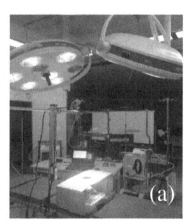

Fig. 4. In our navigation study, we evaluated our motion transcription algorithm in a real surgical room with zero, one, and two shadow-less lamps. In our navigation, a 3D liver is always obstructed by a cardboard box with a circle. Through the circle, the camera can capture a part of the 3D liver. In another experiment, we evaluated the motion transcription algorithm by changing the size of the circle.

SA_search(ti)

t ← ti

p ← position/orientation of the virtual liver model at time ti

f ←fitness (p)

f_best ← f

pbest ← p

while (t i+1 − t > 0)

>**randomly select a neighbor p' of p such that |p'i − pi | ≦ D**

for all i

>**f ' ← fitness(p')**

>**if f' < f_best then**

>>**f_best ← f '**

>>**pbest ← p'**

>**if f' < f or random(0,1) ≧ (t − ti) / Δt then**

>>**f_best ← f '**

>>**pbest ← p'**

t ← t+1

The function random(0,1) returns a random value from zero to one, and the function fitness(p) is the difference between the two depth images in this algorithm. The parameter D is half the width of the area, which is a six-dimensional hypercube with width 2D, in which a new position/orientation p' is randomly generated. If D increases, the algorithm can choose a more distant neighbor to avoid falling into a local minimum.

4   Experimental Results Obtained by the Proposed Algorithm

Using our new algorithm, we conducted several experiments with/without shadow-less lamps. In this section, we consider cases in which a surgeon rotationally or translationally operates a real 3D lever printed by our 3D printer. This lever is based on an STL polyhedron converted from a segmented DICOM (Digital Imaging and Communication in Medicine) of a patient by a CT (Computed Tomography) scanner. Using our simulated annealing algorithm (explained in the previous section), the virtual liver formatted by the STL polyhedral model automatically follows the real liver perfectly.

In this study, compared with our previous studies [5–7], many realistic experiments are conducted not in a laboratory but in a medical surgical operation room. The overall layout of the experimental equipment is shown in Figs. 4 and 5. In order to move the liver, an acrylic plate of 25 cm in length, 25 cm in width, and 2 cm in thickness was placed on the surgical bed, and a real object liver model was placed on the top. The printed 3D liver was created by moving the acrylic plate rotationally or translationally instead of moving the actual liver model. In succession, in order to consider several types of occlusions by the human body against a 3D liver, the liver is covered by a cardboard with a hole of 10 cm in diameter. The surface of this corrugated board was colored in light orange using a coloring spray to make it look like normal human skin. Meanwhile, our Kinect v2 camera can change the distance from the 3D real liver. The Kinect is placed horizontally with respect to the operating table at a height of 84 cm from the bottom of the actual liver model. The Kinect is fixed by attaching metal fittings to a metal rod.

By using the matching algorithm based on real and virtual depth images against real and virtual livers (explained in the next section), initial positions/orientations between the real and virtual livers are coincident with each other. Then, a real liver model placed on an acrylic board was covered with corrugated cardboard and subjected to parallel movement and rotational movement within a corrugated cardboard box. Before the movement, the actual liver model was installed so that it could be seen through the entire hole of the cardboard. Thus, the range visible from the hole of the cardboard remained at least half after the translation movement. The offset value was 10 mm for the real and virtual depth images against the 3D real liver and its polyhedron in STL format in our surgical navigator. The amount of movement was 5 cm along the Y-axis during parallel movement, and the rotation movement was 45° around the Z-axis. Each coordinate axis is shown in Fig. 4.

First, we explain several differences between our current and previous experiments [5–7]. The main difference is that we used a real surgical room with one or two shadow-less lamps (Figs. 4 and 5). A minor difference is that a 3D real liver is occluded by a cardboard with a hole of 10 cm in diameter. All previous experimental results were obtained in our research room using daylight and/or fluorescent lamps for a 3D liver which is not covered by any another object. In the following paragraphs, for pairs of translation and rotation movements of the 3D liver with some occlusion, we introduce experiments without a lamp, with one lamp, and with two lamps.

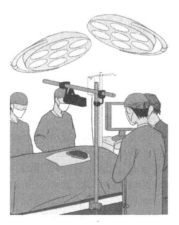

Fig. 5. Our surgical navigation is used in the actual operation room of a hospital. Capturing an organ such as a liver is stable because the camera is completely fixed to the surgical bed.

4.1 Surgical Experience Without a Lamp

In the surgical operation room without any shadow-less light, several experiments were carried out. These are shown in Fig. 6. Rotating and translating a 3D real liver is recorded using Kinect Studio in several types of windows. As shown in Fig. 6, the black window indicates a real liver in the real world, and the white window is the virtual liver in the virtual world. The bottom-right window is an RGB color image that corresponds to the depth image. All experiments were performed using our simulated annealing algorithm based on data taken in the black and white windows. The accuracy of the algorithm is evaluated by the overlapping ratio from the initial position/orientation to the target orientation (Fig. 7).

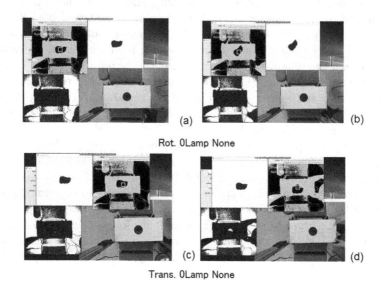

Fig. 6. Actual red liver obstructed by a box with a circle window, followed by its virtual blue liver formed by STL polyhedron in surgical operation room without a shadow-less lamp. In each figure, the black window indicates a real liver in the real world, and the white window is its virtual liver in the virtual world. The bottom-right window is the RGB color image that corresponds to the depth image. (a), (b) Liver is rotationally moved before and after surgical operation, respectively. (c), (d) Liver is translationally moved before and after surgical operation, respectively.

After the real and virtual livers were initially overlapped using our software (explained in the previous section), a human operated the real 3D liver rotationally. Before rotating (Fig. 6(a)), the overlapping ratio was 99% in Fig. 7(a). When moving rotationally (Fig. 6(b)), the overlapping ratio was always maintained at least 96%. Then, after movement, the ratio became 100% in Fig. 7(a). The graph shows the transition of the overlapping ratio from the start to the end during a surgical operation. With regard to the simulated annealing method liver navigator during traveling, there was no significant decrease in the overlapping ratio.

Δt=500, D=1

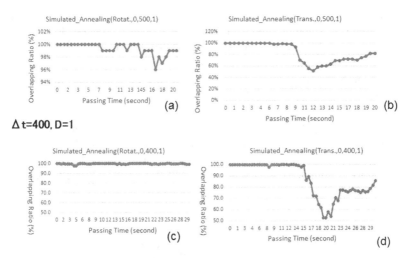

Fig. 7. Our simulated annealing algorithm. Overlapping ratio is changed during surgical operation if a human moves a 3D liver rotationally and translationally. In a surgical room, there is no shadow-less lamp. (a), (b) Δt = 500 and D = 1. (c), (d) Δt = 400 and D = 1.

After the real and virtual livers initially overlapped each other using our software explained in the previous section, a human operator controlled the real 3D liver translationally (Fig. 6(c), (d)). Unfortunately, compared with the rotational movement, the overlapping ratio from the start to the end was not as effective, especially in a middle of the interval (Fig. 7(b)). The main reason is that a real 3D liver moves out of the circle that the Kinect camera can capture. However in a real surgery, such a situation is rare. Even in such a difficult situation, the ratio finally becomes over 80% after the operation.

As mentioned in the previous section, our simulated annealing algorithm has several parameters in which search space and speed can be flexibly changed. In this study, we add two parameters: Δt and D. In our algorithm, Δt leads the size of the search space in the while loop, and D leads the size of the movement within the search space. If Δt becomes larger, the search space becomes wider. If D becomes larger, the density of the search decreases. As illustrated in Fig. 7(c) and (d), we describe the overlapping ratio during a surgical operation rotationally and translationally, respectively, when Δt is changed from 500 to 400 in our algorithm. Furthermore, in Fig. 9 (c) and (d), we describe the overlapping ratio during a surgical operation rotationally and translationally, respectively, when D is changed from 1 to 2 in our algorithm. The difference in the overlapping ratio is quite small, even though two parameters are changed. As a result, we can see that our simulated annealing algorithm achieves stable motion when tracking a real 3D liver to its virtual 3D liver.

4.2   Surgical Experience with One Lamp

In a surgical room with one shadow-less light, we conducted several experiments, as illustrated in Fig. 8. The translating and rotating movements of the real liver were taken with Kinect Studio. The accuracy as evaluated by using the overlapping ratio from the start to the end of the rotation and translation movements (Fig. 10). After the real and virtual livers initially overlapped each other in our software (explained in the previous section), a human operator controlled the real 3D liver rotationally. Before rotating (Fig. 8(a)), the overlapping ratio was 100%, as shown in Fig. 10(a). When moved (Fig. 8(b)), the overlapping ratio was always higher than 95%; and after movement, it became 98%, as shown in Fig. 10(a). The figure is a graph showing the transition of the overlapping ratio from the end of the initial alignment to the end of the movement. With regard to the simulated annealing method liver navigator during traveling, there was no significant decrease in the overlapping ratio.

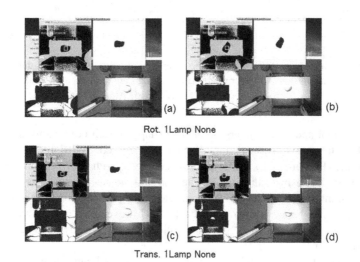

Rot. 1Lamp None

Trans. 1Lamp None

Fig. 8. A real red liver obstructed by a box with a circle window, followed by its virtual blue liver formed by STL polyhedron in a surgical operation room with one shadow-less lamp. In each figure, the black window indicates a real liver in the real world, and the white window is its virtual liver in the virtual world. Bottom-right window is the RGB color image that corresponds to the depth image (a), (b) Liver is rotationally moved before and after a surgical operation, respectively. (c), (d) Liver is translationally moved before and after a surgical operation, respectively.

After the real and virtual livers initially overlapped each other in our software (explained in the previous section), a human operator controlled the real 3D liver translationally (Fig. 8(c), (d)). Unfortunately, compared with the rotational movement, the overlapping ratio from the start to the end is not as effective (Fig. 10(b)). However, compared with the case that did not use a lamp, even in a middle of an interval, the damage was quite

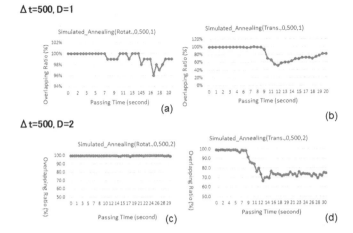

Fig. 9. Our simulated annealing algorithm. Overlapping ratio is changed during surgical operation if a human moves a 3D liver rotationally and translationally. In the surgical room, there is no shadowless lamp. (a), (b) $\Delta t = 500$ and $D = 1$. (c), (d) $\Delta t = 500$ and $D = 2$.

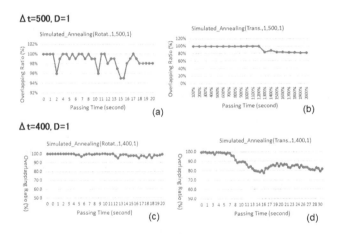

Fig. 10. Our simulated annealing algorithm. Overlapping ratio is changed during surgical operation if a human moves a 3D liver rotationally and translationally. In the surgical room, we used one shadow-less lamp. (a), (b) $\Delta t = 500$ and $D = 1$. (c), (d) $\Delta t = 400$ and $D = 1$.

Moreover, as illustrated in Fig. 10(c) and (d), the overlapping ratio changed during a human operation when Δt was changed from 500 to 400 in our algorithm.

In this case, a human operator moved the real 3D liver rotationally and translationally. However, the difference between the two parameters with regard to the overlapping ratio is quite small (Fig. 11(c) and (d)). Meanwhile, using our algorithm, we described how the overlapping ratio changed during a human operation if D was changed from 1 to 2. The difference between the two parameters with regard to the overlapping ratio is also small (Fig. 10(c), (d) and Fig. 11(c), (d)). As a result, our simulated annealing algorithm achieves stable motion when tracking a real 3D liver to its virtual 3D liver.

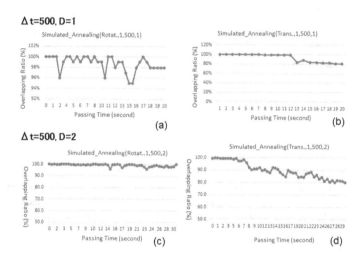

Fig. 11. Our simulated annealing algorithm. Overlapping ratio is changed during surgical operation if a human moves a 3D liver rotationally and translationally. In the surgical room, we used one shadow-less lamp. (a), (b) $\Delta t = 500$ and $D = 1$. (c), (d) $\Delta t = 400$ and $D = 1$.

4.3   Surgical Experience with Two Lamps

In this section, we first evaluate our simulated annealing algorithm for a 3D real liver rotated by a human. With the help of the algorithm, the motion of the real liver is coincident with that of its virtual liver. Before moving rotationally, the overlapping ratio is 100%, as shown in Fig. 12(a). When moved (Fig. 12(b)), the overlapping ratio is always maintained by high scores and also the variation is quite small. Then, after movement, the ratio became 100%, as shown in Fig. 13(a). This resulted in an increase in the overlapping ratio after the initial position alignment was complete.

Figure 13(a) is a graph showing the transition of the overlapping ratio from the end of the initial alignment to the end of the movement. A decrease in the overlapping ratio is observed for each movement, and the overlapping ratio decreased by approximately 10% in the middle, but after the movement, the overlapping ratio showed a higher coincidence ratio than after the completion of the initial position adjustment. From the beginning, it showed a considerably high concordance rate.

A human controlled a real liver model translationally, and then its virtual liver followed the real liver model. As shown in Fig. 13(b), the ratio is as high as 100% before moving (Fig. 12(c)). When moved translationally (Fig. 12(d)), the overlapping ratio fluctuated over 80%; and after the movement, it became 90%, as shown in Fig. 13 (b). Although the overlapping ratio decreases, the result always shows a high

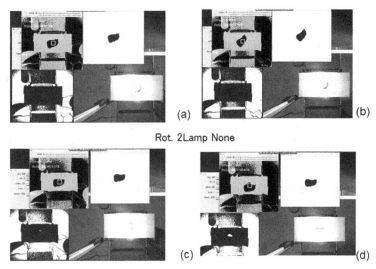

Rot. 2Lamp None

Trans. 2Lamp None

Fig. 12. A real red liver obstructed by a box with a circle window, followed by its virtual blue liver formed by STL polyhedron in a surgical operation room with two shadow-less lamps. (a), (b) Liver is rotationally moved before and after a surgical operation, respectively. (c), (d) Liver is translationally moved before and after a surgical operation, respectively. (Color figure online)

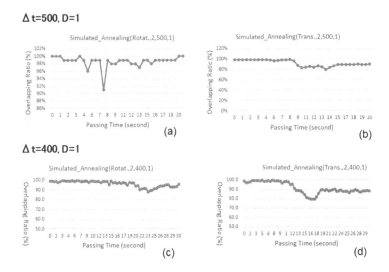

Fig. 13. Our simulated annealing algorithm. Overlapping ratio is changed during surgical operation if a human moves a 3D liver rotationally and translationally. In the surgical room, we used two shadow-less lamps. (a), (b) $\Delta t = 500$ and $D = 1$. (c), (d) $\Delta t = 400$ and $D = 1$.

overlapping ratio that exceeds 80%. Figure 13(b) is a graph showing the transition of the overlapping ratio from the end of the initial alignment to the end of the movement. The result shows that the overlapping ratio is low on average compared with when the shadow-less light is not lit.

Moreover, as illustrated in Fig. 13(c) and (d), the overlapping ratio changed during human operation if Δt was changed from 500 to 400 in our algorithm. In this case, a human operator controlled the real 3D liver rotationally and translationally. The difference concerning the overlapping ratio is quite small (Fig. 13(c) and (d)). On the other hand, the overlapping ratio is changed during human operation if D is changed from 1 to 2 in our algorithm. The difference in the overlapping ratio is also small (Fig. 14(c) and (d)). As a result, our simulated annealing algorithm achieves stable motion when tracking a real 3D liver to its virtual 3D liver.

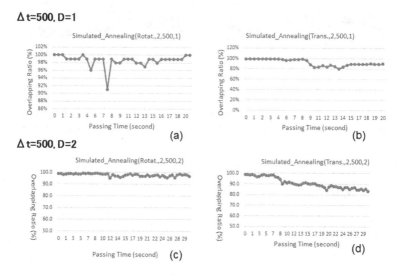

Fig. 14. Our simulated annealing algorithm. Overlapping ratio is changed during surgical operation if a human moves a 3D liver rotationally and translationally. In the surgical room, we used two shadow-less lamps. (a), (b) Δ*t* = 500 and *D* = 1. (c), (d) Δ*t* = 400 and *D* = 1.

5   Conclusions

In this study, we proposed a simulated annealing algorithm and checked its usefulness by conducting several kinds of experiments in a real surgical room with shadow-less lamps. In addition, to simulate a practical surgery operation, we printed a 3D liver using a 3D printer based on segmented DICOM data captured for a patient by a CT scanner. Then, we put the 3D liver on an acrylic board of a surgical bed, which was covered with corrugated cardboard and subjected to translational movement and rotational movement within a corrugated cardboard box. By changing the circle size, we could create many types of occlusions. According to many experimental results of the simulated annealing algorithm, whose parameters were flexibly changed, the algorithm was stable for the motion transcription method from a real 3D liver to its virtual 3D liver. Therefore, this algorithm can be used in our liver surgical navigation.

Acknowledgments. This study was partly supported by the 2014 Grants-in-Aid for Scientific Research (No. 26289069) from the Ministry of Education, Culture, Sports, Science, and Technology, Japan. Further support was provided by the 2014 Cooperation Research Fund from the Graduate School at Osaka Electro-Communication University.

References

1. Liu, Y.: Automatic registration of overlapping 3D point clouds using closest points. J. Image Vis. Comput. **24**(7), 762–781 (2006)
2. Salvi, J., Matabosch, C., Fofi, D., Forest, J.: A review of recent range image registration methods with accuracy evaluation. J. Image Vis. Comput. **25**, 578–596 (2007)
3. Rusu, R.B., Cousins, S.: 3D is here: Point Cloud Library (PCL). In: IEEE International Conference on Robotics and Automation, pp. 1–4 (2011)
4. Wu, Y.F., Wang, W., Lu, K.Q., Wei, Y.D., Chen, Z.C.: A new method for registration of 3D point sets with low overlapping ratios. In: 13th CIRP Conference on Computer Aided Tolerancing, pp. 202–206 (2015)
5. Noborio, H., Watanabe, K., Yagi, M., Ida, Y., Nankaku, S., Onishi, K., Koeda, M., Kon, M., Matsui, K., Kaibori, M.: Tracking a real liver using a virtual liver and an experimental evaluation with kinect v2. In: Ortuño, F., Rojas, I. (eds.) IWBBIO 2016. LNBI, vol. 9656, pp. 149–162. Springer, Cham (2016). doi:10.1007/978-3-319-31744-1_14
6. Noborio, H., Watanabe, K., Yagi, M., Ida, Y., Nankaku, S., Onishi, K., Koeda, M., Kon, M., Matsui, K., Kaibori, M.: Experimental results of 2D depth-depth matching algorithm based on depth camera Kinect v1. J. Bioinform. Neurosci. **1**(1), 38–44 (2015). ISSN: 2188-8116
7. Noborio, H., Watanabe, K., Yagi, M., Ida, Y., Onishi, K., Koeda, M., Nankaku, S., Matsui, K., Kon, M., Kaibori, M.: Image-based initial position/orientation adjustment system between real and virtual livers. Jurnal Teknologi, Medical Engineering **77**(6), 41–45 (2015). doi:10.11113/jt.v77.6225. Penerbit UTM Press, E-ISSN 2180-3722
8. Kirkpatrick, S, Gelatt Jr., C.D., Vecchi, M.P.: Optimization by simulated annealing. Science **220** (4598): 671–680. Bibcode 1983Sci...220..671 K. doi:10.1126/science.220.4598.671. JSTOR 1690046. PMID 17813860 (1983)
9. Černý, V.: Thermodynamical approach to the traveling salesman problem: an efficient simulation algorithm. J. Optim. Theory Appl. **45**, 41–51 (1985). doi:10.1007/BF00940812

Development of a Surgical Knife Attachment with Proximity Indicators

Daiki Yano, Masanao Koeda(✉), Katsuhiko Onishi, and Hiroshi Noborio

Osaka Electro-Communication University, Shijonawate, Osaka, Japan
koeda@osakac.ac.jp

Abstract. To prevent liver surgical accidents, we have been developing a surgery navigation system with two depth cameras with different characteristics. In this paper, we describe our developed surgical knife attachment which indicates the proximity of the blood vessels in the liver by light and sound. The method to calibrate the tip position of the knife in our camera system is also mentioned. Using this attachment, some experiments to navigate operator were conducted and the results indicated that the navigation worked correctly within the target range.

Keywords: Liver surgery support · Navigation · Proximity · Alert · Calibration

1 Introduction

The liver is a large and soft organ. Several blood vessels (arteries, veins, portals, etc.) present in the liver are not externally visible. Surgeons use X-ray imaging, computed tomography (CT) or magnetic resonance imaging (MRI) to preoperatively determine the position of these vessels in the liver. During surgery, incision points are located by touching the targeted incision site using fingers and feeling for a pulse-beat. The accuracy of this method is poor and can result in bleeding and injury to the blood vessels.

Several surgical support and navigation systems are commercially available [1–3]. These systems determine the position of the surgical tools, synchronize with the tomographic images captured prior to surgery, and navigate the tool to the target position. These systems are mainly used for orthopedic, dental, or brain surgery. The body parts targeted in orthopedic or dental surgery are rigid and exhibit negligible deformation. The tissue targeted during brain surgery is soft and is subject to deformation. During surgery, the hard skull bone, which shields the brain, is fixed to the operating table, which results in minimal deformation. These surgery support and navigation systems are successfully implemented in practice owing to the negligible level of deformation achieved before and during the surgery.

The liver is soft and continuously deforms during an operation due to the patient's breathing, organ pulsation, the incision process, and the manual operation of the surgeon. The shape of the liver must be constantly measured during surgery. Existing support systems are insufficient and cannot be reliably applied to liver surgery. Research on liver surgery support systems has been limited, and no effective system have been developed yet. We have been developing a liver surgery support system with Kansai Medical

© Springer International Publishing AG 2017
A. Marcus and W. Wang (Eds.): DUXU 2017, Part II, LNCS 10289, pp. 608–618, 2017.
DOI: 10.1007/978-3-319-58637-3_48

University Hospital. The proposed system aims to remove the cancer tissue completely and save the liver without causing injury to the inner vessels. In this paper, our developed knife attachment is described. It indicates the proximity of the blood vessels by illuminating light emitting diodes (LEDs) and by generating audible beeping sounds to prevent blood vessel injury (Fig. 1).

2 Liver Surgical Support System

The proposed system consists of two depth cameras with different characteristics. The first camera is lower precision but a wide measurement range used for determining the shape of the liver during surgery. We preoperatively prepare a three-dimensional (3D) model using CT or MRI data. The model contains the shape of the liver, inner blood vessels, and tumors. By matching the low precision depth image with the 3D model during surgery, the position of the invisible blood vessels and tumors is estimated. The details are given in [4–7]. The second camera is higher precision and performs single point measurements using single markers [8] to determine the tip position of the surgical knife. By merging the camera and 3D model information, the distance between the knife tip and the vessels or tumors is calculated and the proximity of the knife to the arteries or portals is determined. The distance between the knife tip and tumor can be calculated [9] and the navigation to remove cancers preformed.

To indicate the proximity to the vessels or tumors, we have developed a surgical knife attachment with LEDs and an audible alarm. We chose a versatile attachment device, which uses a clamp for easy attachment of a knife or other surgical tools.

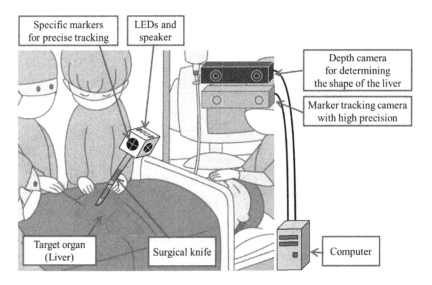

Fig. 1. Overview of our liver surgical support system

3   Surgical Knife Attachment with Proximity Indicators

Multiple markers (Fig. 2) are attached to the top of the knife to estimate the tip position during surgery. The attachment is connected to a clamp (GoPro Sportsman Mount), which is easily clipped to the end of a surgical tool (Fig. 3). When the knife approaches a liver part that must not be cut, such as an artery or a portal, the attachment generates an alarm by gradually turning on lighting LEDs and producing a beeping sound. The attachment contains a micro-computer (Arduino Nano), a LED bar module (OSX10201-GYR1) [10], and a piezoelectric speaker (Figs. 4 and 5). The LED module has 10 LEDs arranged in the order of five green, three yellow and two red. The cubic case is fabricated from plastic by using a 3D printer, and measures approximately 70 × 70 × 70 [mm]. The micro-computer is connected to a primary PC through a USB 2.0 interface. This interface is used to supply power and transmit the proximity data indicated by the number of illuminated LEDs. The micro-computer controls the LEDs and the frequency of the beeping sound (Fig. 6). For simplicity, the connection between the PC and micro-computer is currently hardwired. It is not difficult, however, to convert to a wireless interface for future implementations.

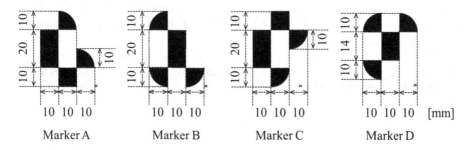

Fig. 2. Design and size of markers on the surgical knife attachment

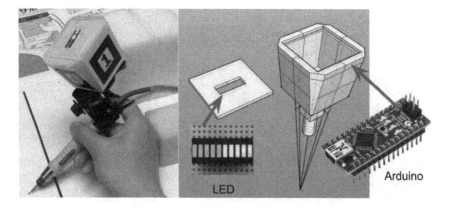

Fig. 3. Surgical knife attachment with proximity indicators (The markers in the left image are for demonstration.)

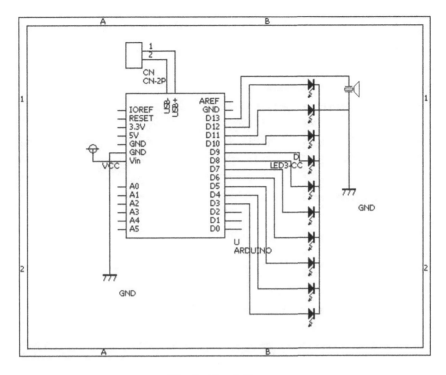

Fig. 4. Circuit diagram

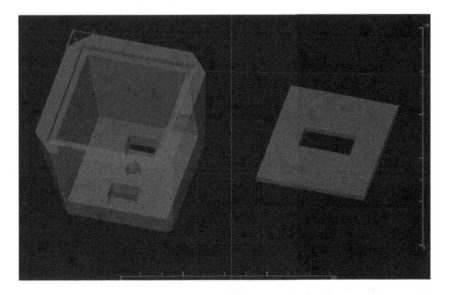

Fig. 5. Inner structure of the attachment (left: main case, right: top lid)

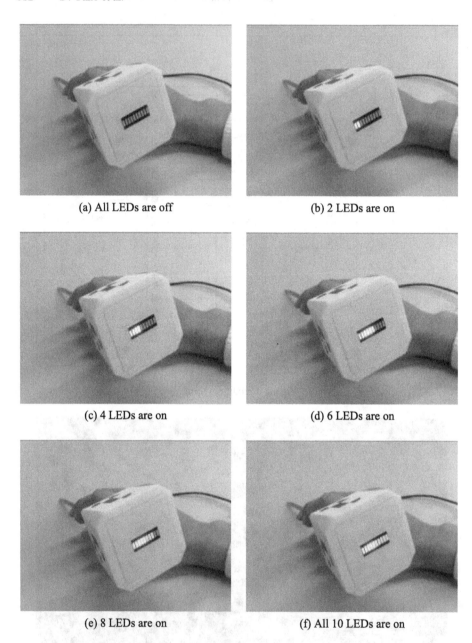

(a) All LEDs are off   (b) 2 LEDs are on

(c) 4 LEDs are on   (d) 6 LEDs are on

(e) 8 LEDs are on   (f) All 10 LEDs are on

Fig. 6. Experimental results of trajectory of each subject

4   Knife Tip Position Calibration

The knife tip position is estimated from the markers on the surface of the cubic attachment. Prior to surgery, the relative vectors from each marker to the tip of the knife are

calibrated. The calibration procedure is simple and recalibration can be performed as required.

Camera and knife coordinate systems are defined as $\sum_c$ and $\sum_k$ respectively. One of the markers attached to the knife is designated as M_{knife}, and the fixed marker on the table is designated as M_{table}. To acquire a relative vector from M_{knife} to the knife tip, the knife tip is placed at the origin point p^c_{table} of M_{table}, and the position and posture of each marker are measured in $\sum_c$. The position P^c_{knife} and orientation R^c_{knife} of the marker attached to the knife M_{knife} are measured in $\sum_c$. The relative vector P^c_{rel} is calculated by the following equation P^k_{rel}.

$$P^c_{rel} = P^c_{table} - P^c_{knife}$$

To convert P^c_{rel} to $\sum_k$ coordinates, the following is used.

$$P^k_{rel} = (R^c_{knife})^{-1} \cdot P^c_{rel}$$

Finally, the knife tip position P^c_{tip} in $\sum_c$ is estimated as follows.

$$P^c_{tip} = R^c_{knife} \cdot P^k_{rel} + P^c_{knife}$$

If multiple markers are detected and multiple tip positions are estimated at the same time, the positions are averaged. The estimation error in the knife tip position is less than 1 [mm]. The details of the error evaluation are given in [11].

5   Navigation Experiment and Result

We conducted experiments to validate operator navigation using the attachment. The task is to trace an invisible target circle with the tip of the knife based on the LED information. The beeping sound was not used for this experiment. The target circle is set on a flat horizontal table in front of the subject (Fig. 7). The diameter of the circle is 100 [mm]. To measure the navigation error precisely, the attachment cube was fixed to a hard steel rod (130 [mm] in length, 6 [mm] in diameter) using a strong adhesive (Fig. 8). The LED array is illuminated incrementally in 1 [mm] step as the distance to the target circle is reduced. All LEDs are illuminated when the tip touches the target circle. The six subjects (A to F) are not surgeons, they are undergraduate or postgraduate students, in their twenties, from the Osaka Electro-Communication University.

Fig. 7. Experiment environment

Fig. 8. Tool for navigation experiment

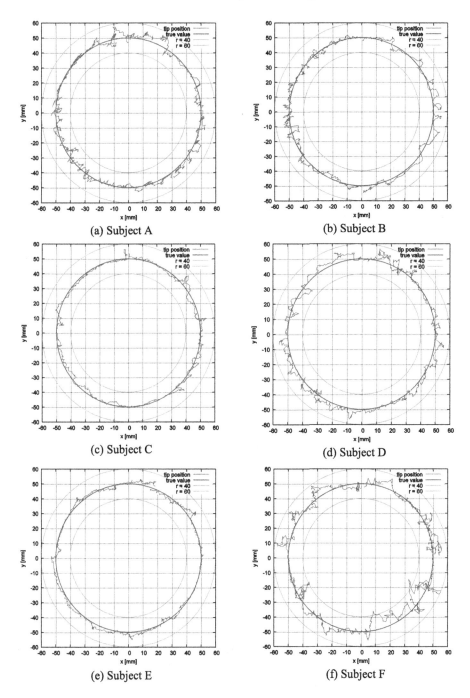

(a) Subject A

(b) Subject B

(c) Subject C

(d) Subject D

(e) Subject E

(f) Subject F

Fig. 9. Experimental results of trajectory of each subject

With (x_{tip}, y_{tip}) as the knife tip position, (x_c, y_c) as the center of the circle, and r as the radius of the circle, a distance L between the knife tip and the circle is calculated from the following equation.

$$L = \left| r - \sqrt{(x_c - x_{tip})^2 + (y_c - y_{tip})^2} \right|$$

The LED's are gradually illuminated between $1 \le L \le 10$ [mm]. The LED array contains 10 LEDs; therefore, we can navigate over a range in ± 10 [mm] of the circle.

The experimental results of the trajectory of the tip position are shown in Fig. 9. The red circle is the target circle and the purple dots show the trajectory. The LEDs turn on within the range between the blue and yellow circles. The average navigation errors and standard deviation for each subject are shown in Fig. 10. The results show that the maximum error is 14 [mm], and the error remained within a LED illumination range of 20 [mm]. These results confirm that the LED based navigation works correctly.

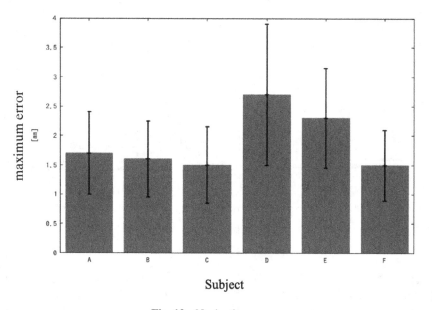

Fig. 10. Navigation errors

6 Preliminary Experiment for Sterilization

A sterile surgical environment is important. We conducted a preliminary experiment to determine if the marker can be measured while covered with a transparent sterile sheet. The initial results showed that when the marker was loosely covered, there were measurement failures due to light reflection or refraction. However, by ensuring that the marker was tightly covered with no wrinkling (Fig. 11), no problems were encountered and stable measurements were achieved. The transparent sterile sheet used in this experiment was for medical use and was provided by Kyoto University Hospital.

Fig. 11. Marker block covered by transparent sterile sheet

7   Conclusion

We developed a surgical knife attachment that indicates the proximity of the blood vessels by illuminating LEDs and generating beeping sounds to prevent blood vessel injury. To validate operator navigation using this device, navigation experiments using six subject were conducted. Based on the results we conclude that the navigation of this device works well. The maximum navigation error is limited to 14 [mm]. In the future, we will improve the accuracy of navigation, downsize the device, and conduct experiments in an actual surgery support setting.

Acknowledgement. This research was supported by Grants-in-Aid for Scientific Research (No. 26289069) from the Ministry of Education, Culture, Sports, Science and Technology (MEXT), Japan.

References

1. Knee Navigation Application - Brainlab. https://www.brainlab.com/en/surgery-products/orthopedic-surgery-products/knee-navigation/
2. ClaroNav - Dental and ENT Navigation Solutions. http://www.claronav.com/
3. Surgical Theater - Surgical Navigation Advanced Platform (SNAP). http://www.surgicaltheater.net/site/products-services/surgical-navigation-advanced-platform-snap
4. Noborio, H., Onishi, K., Koeda, M., Mizushino, K., Kunii, T., Kaibori, M., Kon, M., Chen, Y.: A fast surgical algorithm operating polyhedrons using Z-Buffer in GPU. In: Proceedings of the 9th Asian Conference on Computer Aided Surgery (ACCAS 2013), pp. 110–111 (2013)
5. Watanabe, K., Yagi, M., Shintani, A., Nankaku, S., Onishi, K., Koeda, M., Noborio, H., Kon, M., Matsui, K., Kaibori, M.: A new 2D depth-depth matching algorithm whose translation and rotation freedoms are separated. In: Proceedings of the International Conference on Intelligent Informatics and Biomedical Sciences (ICIIBMS 2015), Track 3: Bioinformatics, Medical Imaging and Neuroscience, pp. 271–278 (2015)

6. Noborio, H., Watanabe, K., Yagi, M., Ida, Y., Nankaku, S., Onishi, K., Koeda, M., Kon, M., Matsui, K., Kaibori, M.: Experimental results of 2D depth-depth matching algorithm based on depth camera Kinect v1. In: Proceedings of the International Conference on Intelligent Informatics and Biomedical Sciences (ICIIBMS 2015), Track 3: Bioinformatics, Medical Imaging and Neuroscience, pp. 284–289 (2015)
7. Onishi, K., et al.: Virtual liver surgical simulator by using Z-Buffer for object deformation. In: Antona, M., Stephanidis, C. (eds.) UAHCI 2015. LNCS, vol. 9177, pp. 345–351. Springer, Cham (2015). doi:10.1007/978-3-319-20684-4_34
8. MicronTracker. http://www.claronav.com/microntracker/
9. Noborio, H., Kunii, T., Mizushino, K.: GPU-based shortest distance algorithm for liver surgery navigation. In: Proceedings of the 10th Anniversary Asian Conference on Computer Aided Surgery, pp. 42–43 (2014)
10. OSX10201-GYR1 data sheet. http://akizukidenshi.com/download/ds/optosupply/OSX10201-XXXX.PDF
11. Doi, M., Yano, D., Koeda, M., Noborio, H., Onishi, K., Mizushino, K., Kayaki, M., Matsui, K., Kaibori, M.: Knife tip position estimation for liver surgery support system. In: Proceedings of Japanese Society for Medical Virtual Reality (JSMVR 2016), pp. 46–47 (2016). (in Japanese)

Wearables and Fashion Technology

TEA Band: An Interactive System to Aid Students with Autism Improve Their Social Interactions

Fernanda Bonnin[✉] and Victor M. Gonzalez[✉]

Computer Engineering Department, ITAM, Mexico City, Mexico
ferbonnin@gmail.com, victor.gonzalez@itam.mx

Abstract. Our research aims to aid children with autism improve social interactions through discrete messages received in a waist smart band. In this paper, we describe the design and development of an interactive system in a Microsoft Band 2 and present results of an evaluation with three students that gives us positive evidence that using this form of support can increase the quantity and quality of the social interactions.

Keywords: Autism · Social interactions · Interactive technologies · Smart-bands

1 Introduction

Advances in wearable, mobile and tactile computation are defining a new generation of interactive systems where the quality of the user experience and the creation of applications immersed in the day-to-day activities is transforming the life of many people. In particular, the use of those interactive systems to support physiologic, physical, or mental disorders such Autism Spectrum Disorder (ASD), has awakened the interest of the Human-Computer Interaction (HCI) research community and drives efforts to provide novel and affordable solutions as technology evolves. Moreover, the publishing of the newest edition of the Statistical Manual of Mental Disorders (DSM-5) [1] has changed the way we see autism and thus, we must design supporting technologies that respond properly to that development.

Acknowledging the importance of social interactions and building upon the work developed in MOSOCO [2], that showed that an interactive system in a smartphone can be a tool to enable social interactions, our research seeks to create an assistive application to aid students with autism improve their social interaction. Following a user-centered design approach, we developed a solution that generates low sensory stimuli and an interactive method that integrates the therapy used with the participants of the study. Our approach explores the opportunity of supporting social interactions in a more natural way by working on a smartwatch that is a less intrusive and more personal device compared with a laptop, a tablet or a phone.

© Springer International Publishing AG 2017
A. Marcus and W. Wang (Eds.): DUXU 2017, Part II, LNCS 10289, pp. 621–635, 2017.
DOI: 10.1007/978-3-319-58637-3_49

The application, called TEA Band (*Trastorno del Espectro Autista* is Autism Spectrum Disorder in Spanish[1]) is conceptualized as a support tool to learn, not a substitute of therapy nor a permanent assistive technology.

2 Background

2.1 Autism Spectrum Disorder

The Autism Spectrum Disorder is described in the Statistical Manual of Mental Disorders (DSM-5) as a mental disorder characterized by persistent deficits in social communication and social interactions and restricted, repetitive patterns of behavior, interest, or activities [1]. The DSM-5 defines three levels of autism, which indicate the level of support necessary for a person with autism with diagnostic criteria in the areas of social communications and atypical behavior.

The prevalence of autism about 1%–2% in the world [3] with 5 more boys with ASD than girls. In Mexico, although it does not exist any statistics or epidemiological data, a study to generate an estimate of the prevalence of ASD in the country, surveying children in Leon, Guanajuato, indicated that the numbers are consistent with the world prevalence rate [4]. Only in USA and England the cost of maintaining an individual with ASD during his life span is estimated in 1.4 million dollars if the person does not have an intellectual disability [5]. This sum is the result of medical, scholar and therapy expenses, plus the loss of productivity of the parents and the residential and support personal needed when the person reaches adultness; besides, 80% of the adults with autism are unemployed [6].

Typically, individuals with ASD display certain social difficulties such as: difficulties to communicate, with trouble to interpret non-verbal interactions and following conversation rules, difficulties to create friendships appropriate for their age, low sustained attention, lack of visual contact, and stereotyped behavior patterns like motor movements, mutism and echolalia. Furthermore, persons with ASD are also extremely dependent to routines and sensible to changes in their environment.

The fifth edition of the DSM-5, published in 2013, changed the way we understand autism when two of the basic triad problems were joined into one: social interaction and social communication impairments are now described as one conjoined problem. Almost 20 years of separate therapy for language and social interaction have now been deemed unsuitable and new strategies to design assistive technologies are required.

2.2 Inclusive Education

The 26th article in the Universal Declaration of Human Rights declares that "everyone has the right to education [...] and it shall be directed to the full development of the

---

[1] *Trastorno del espectro autista, autismo* and *persona con autismo* are the correct terms to refer to somebody with autism, with the former being the correct medical term. In Mexico, it is considered pejorative to say *autista* (autistic) since you are removing any other qualities of the individual with this label.

human personality and to the strengthening of respect for human rights and fundamental freedoms" [7], this article and the Salamanca Statement, a UNESCO statement which calls on all governments to give priority to inclusive school, support the necessity of education for everybody in an integrated environment that celebrates the differences and support learning by responding to the different needs of every individual [8]. However, the probability of a child with a disability attending school is much lower than a child without a disability [9]. In Mexico, 23.6% of people with disabilities between 15 and 24 years of age are analphabets and children with a disability have 17% to 25% less possibilities to have access to education in comparison of children without a disability [10].

In 2011, the Mexican government created the general law for the inclusion of the people with disability in Mexico [11]. This law defines inclusive education as education that facilitates integration of people with disabilities into regular basic education through the application of specific methods, techniques and materials; however, this definition only talks about integration and there have been barriers to include children with ASD, such as: lack of resources, inflexibility to adapt the curriculum, and teachers that are not sufficiently qualified to support children with autism [12].

Due in part to the difficulties in the social communication, many children with autism in inclusive schools around the world suffer from bullying by their peers. Just in the USA and England, 63% [13, 14] of students with autism have suffered from bullying from their peers. In Mexico, there is not sufficient data but there is evidence that children with autism suffer from bullying from their classmates and rejection from the teachers [15, 16].

Although schools provide an excellent opportunity for the students to interact, the difficulties in social interactions is one of the elements that define the Autism Spectrum Disorder; the lack of successful interactions impacts their concept of identity and belonging, does not allows them to learn what others expect from them, or see appropriate behaviors, and it does not permit incrementing the flexibility in thinking as the consequence of multiple opinions in an interaction. These difficulties to have successful interactions persist and impact all their life and has motivated multiple efforts to increase and improve social interactions in children with autism [17–19].

2.3 Technology for Supporting Children with ASD

In certain neurodevelopmental disorders, particularly, in ASD, the use of an interactive system has the potential to be a tool that allows focusing the attention of the individual, avoiding the stress that provokes their environment and, at the same time, to be a support tool to interact with said environment. Taking this in consideration, diverse investigations in the Human-Computer Interaction (HCI) area are focused on the creation of technologies that allow persons with autism, particularly children, to create or improve their social interactions.

Tentori and Hayes created the concept of interaction immediacy: "a set of guidelines help children maintain appropriate spatial boundaries, reply to conversation initiators, disengage appropriately at the end of an interaction, and identify potential communication partners" [20] and established design principles to apply those elements in assistive technologies. Escobedo used that information to create MOSOCO [2], a mobile application that allows the students to remember the lessons of the Social Compass Curriculum [21], a curriculum that helps train social abilities, outside the classroom in real time situations. The study was developed in seven weeks with three students with autism and nine neurotypical between the ages of 8 and 11 years old.

Hourcade et al. [22] conducted a research to analyze the impact of tactile applications in tablets and their impact in social interactions by allowing collaboration, creativity, compromise of interests and a better understanding of emotions. The study analyzes three of the candidates in thirteen sessions of two hours. Similarly, McEwen [23] demonstrated that the use of the *iPod Touch* in the classroom can motivate the start of a social interaction between classmates in a longer study with 12 students in a 6 months' period.

The use of smartwatches or smart bands and their sensors in TEA are a relatively new field that opens multiple research opportunities. Multiple sensors in controlled environments have been studied [24–26] but the plausibility to use them in a real-world situation is inoperative. Within the framework of affective technology, Picard developed *Empatica*: a watch with sensors that allow the detection of emotions using sensors. She and her team at the MIT Media Lab are also the creators of *Affectiva Q Sensor*, a wearable with sensors that was initially created to measure emotions like stress, excitation or calm in children with autism [27]. Similarly, *Reveal*, developed by Palmer, can help predict crisis alerting the parents or even preventing them since it gives time to react appropriately [28].

3   Designing TEA Band

3.1   Selection of the Smartwatch

To select an appropriate hardware, we considered various aspects to prompt an easy adoption of the device and characteristics that allowed us to exploit all the capabilities of the smartwatch such as weight, fragility, battery life, sensors in the smartwatch and the possibility to develop an application on the device that worked in real time, the outcome of an analysis of 8 smartwatches supported the decision to choose the Microsoft Band 2[2].

The Microsoft Band 2 fulfilled all the requirements with developer tools to design applications and obtain data of the sensors; the selected smartwatch has Gorilla Glass 3 in the screen, a highly resistant material, the band is made with medical level steel and Thermal plastic elastomer silicone vulcanite, a resistant and comfortable material. The Microsoft Band 2 allowed personalization of colors, icons, vibrations, reading speed and messages. Although we choose this device for the study, the software can be developed for any other device that has the appropriate sensors and developer tools, but the adoption of another smartwatch might be different.

---

[2] This study was developed between September 2015 – May 2016. At that moment, Microsoft Band 2 was a recent device and it did not seem like it was going to be discontinued.

3.2 Interface and Behavior

Our senses enable us to perceive and capture the world, but many people with autism have a problem modulating all the sensory input they receive, resulting in stereotyped behavior and abstraction of the individual from the outside world [29]. The DSM-5 includes again the hyper- or hypo-reactivity to sensory input (this was not included in the DSM-IV) as criteria under the "Restricted, repetitive patterns of behavior, interests or activities". When we analyzed which elements must be considered in the design, we recognize this sensory sensibility and we seek to develop an assistive technology with low sensory stimuli in two senses: touch and sight.

The color of the application was a very important sensory element, a 2005 study reported that 85% of the people with autism see colors with much more intensity [30]; a simple design with neutral colors that can be modified for each user's needs, was key. The iconography is another element key for the adoption, the National Autistic Society in England mentions that many people with ASD are visual learners [31], and the icons are an instinctive way to understand TEA Band.

We seek to understand the difficulties the students have communicating and the strategies used by the psychologist and parents to deliver messages on the device in a clear and comprehensive way. The guidelines for language, instructions, and feedback methods are derived from the methodology used in Domus[3].

Domus institute uses the Relationship Development Intervention (RDI), as their principal behavioral treatment; this program is based on families and searches to remedy autism attacking the primary symptom: the social interaction. RDI is based in the belief that the development of a dynamic intelligence, using neural connectivity, is the key to improve the life quality of a person with autism. The program causes parent to return to their role as guides and, therefore, children become learners again - a role that is lost when parents adjust to the child and their static thinking - and proposes to give information in a multimodal way: body language, verbal, sounds, facial expressions and gestures with the hands, prioritizing the social relation over an activity and eliminating the static process of giving instructions and orders as part of a therapy [32].

We used declarative communication, a language that allows sharing of experiences, ideas, perspectives and thoughts [31]. This type of communication allows a self-regulation of thoughts and actions with cortically integrated and dynamic answers, in contrast of an imperative communication that only has predetermined answers. Also, following the RDI approach, the therapy used delivered immediate feedback to reassure the student and reduce the stress in the moment while the attention of the user is still in the activity.

To deliver the messages we decided to use the haptic sensor to send a small vibration in the wrist, like most smartwatches, but with the possibility of modulating the intensity of it, to control the sensory stimuli created to draw the attention of the user. All the messages were preloaded and unique for each user. The messages were defined with

---

[3] Domus A.C was founded in 1980 and it was the first institution for attention and autism support in Mexico. In 1991 they contributed to the foundation of the Mexican Society of Autism. Domus has as general objectives to provide comprehensive services for people with ASD and their families, to raise awareness, train and contribute to the construction of a culture of respect through their unique model of attention.

feedback of the users and validated via proxy with the psychologist and the inclusive education monitors. We followed all the recommendations, maintaining a declarative language and the briefness of the messages as the only immovable elements.

The interface color, the background image on the front tile, the haptic sensor, the reading speed and the position of the Microsoft Band 2 (in which wrist and inside or outside of the wrist) were chosen by each participant to involve them in the design of TEA Band and motivate a sense of appropriation.

3.3   Application Design

Following the guidelines of design and experience of the Microsoft Band 2 [33] we created a band application with three tiles, alongside with an iPhone application for setting control and data visualization in real time. We also deleted all the other tiles the device had, leaving only the start screen -named Me tile- that indicates the hour, steps walked, stairs climbed, calories and heart rate, and the Configuration tile, since they could not be deleted.

The application, called TEA Band, has three tiles as shown in Fig. 1.: Stress, Hints and Topics, each one of them has a different purpose and interact different with the user, as a response of the sensors, predefined, and through a user request, respectively.

Fig. 1.   TEA band interface: Stress, Hints and Topics tiles

The Stress tile's objective is tranquilizing the student sending a message when there is an increment in the stress level of the user. To measure the stress level, we used the formula developed by Garcia and Gonzalez [34] that detects stress using the values of the heart rate, galvanic skin response and temperature sensors. The formula was initially developed to detect stress posteriori and with data that had one-minute granularity, so we worked with Jesus Garcia to modify it so it would work in real time and with data granularity of one second.

The Hints tile helps the students to improve their social interactions with short messages that remind them appropriate social behaviors such as saying hello and goodbye and keeping a proper distance and voice volume. This tile was initially going to be automatic, sending the messages with time constraints or as a response of the sensors, but since the Bluetooth of the device had a very limited range, sometimes the Microsoft Band 2 would disconnect so we opted to send each message manually, but making the user think they were automatic.

Finally, the Topics tile gives the student various conversation topics to improve the quality and length of an interaction. This tile responds to a touch of the user; it does not send messages unless the user asks for them.

4   Study Description

We worked with Domus, an autism institute, because of their trajectory and the opportunities they offer to do research with them. Since 1994, Domus has had a program of inclusive education, with students in all education levels up to high school. The idea of this project was presented to the director of the institute and later, to the whole team for its approval. We followed their ethical guidelines for the project and both the Domus team and the ITAM's University Board approved the study.

The access to the students with autism was a long and complex process due to the impact on them and their therapy that implied clear changes such as involving meeting a new person and conducting an experiment with their help. Also, since autism is a spectrum, finding suitable candidates willing to perform the experiment implies an additional limitation. Finally, the authorization to enter the schools and perform the study had other limitations and lengthy bureaucratic protocols that were managed by the Domus team; we made the request to do the study to Domus on September 2015 and seven months later we received permission to access two different inclusive schools.

Domus selected four participants with autism between the ages of 11 and 18 years old. The requirements we made were that the candidates knew how to read, were verbal, had difficulties to interact and, preferably, assisted to an inclusive school; although we did not have any preference with male or female candidates, all the candidates were male; this is consistent with reports indicating that autism is more prevalent in boys than girls. Due to some agenda complications, the first candidate had to retire from the study and we proceeded with the other three students. The study was made with three male candidates (Tadeo, Sergio and Adrian[4]) with ASD, ages 17, 15 and 18, each one with different challenges and abilities.

Tadeo is a student with autism who had his 17th birthday while we developed the study and was in the 1st grade of high school in an inclusive school. At the school breaks he does not interact because he does not have too many common interests with his classmates and he uses this time to switch off for a while. He likes to interact verbally presenting few stereotyped movements, and his social abilities are adequate with his mentor and professors who are patient with him but he struggles to find the same sympathetic behavior from his classmates; his social errors are usually that he forgets to say "excuse me" "please" and "thank you".

Sergio was in 3rd grade of middle school and had 15 years at the moment of the study. He is very shy and has a lot of difficulties to interact. During his breaks, he does not interact unless someone approaches him, and even then, sometimes he just ignores the interaction attempts. He does not move at all from the place he chooses to eat his lunch. Sergio presents few stereotyped movements and low social abilities, in part because of his shyness.

Adrian is a young man with autism that had 18 years when we developed the study and he was not in an inclusive school anymore. Adrian enjoys verbal interactions but he has very restrained interests and not always responds to another person's intentions to start an interaction. He has very poor social abilities, with difficulties to respect

---

[4] Not their real names.

personal space and modulate his voice volume, and presents echolalia and multiple stereotyped behaviors. The echolalia affects all his interactions since this language perturbation does not allows his interactions to flow naturally and keeps him in a loop for quite a long time.

We would like to remark that although we are describing three candidates with autism spectrum disorder with similar ages and characteristics (i.e. ASD level 1, difficulty to interact, verbal, assisted at some point to an inclusive school) we could observe different challenges and abilities in each one of them. These are expected differences because autism is a spectrum and they present an excellent opportunity to test all the capabilities TEA band has to impact in different scenarios.

4.1 Development of the Study

We programmed fifteen sessions of twenty minutes for each participant, giving priority to the school breaks or activities where we could observe the candidate interact in uncontrolled activities and ensure that these sessions were continuous for up to three weeks. The number of sessions and the duration were suggested considering other studies involving students with autism and the use of technology [2, 35–37] and, more important, the availability of the schools we visited. The time used for the student to adjust to the device and the observer as well as the time necessary for a closing with the candidates, were not considered as sessions.

To avoid stressing the participants, the fact that the device was going to measure their stress was hidden and we emphasized that they were helping us to understand how they interacted with their peers. Also, the neurotypical students were not made aware of the purpose of this study to avoid a bias in their behavior.

The functionality of the device was introduced gradually. The first five sessions we observed the individual using the device without TEA Band interacting with them, while we measured their stress, and observed their social interactions. Over the next five sessions, we gradually introduced the tiles and, from the eighth session, we motivated the student to start social interactions using TEA Band. Finally, in the last five sessions the student had all the functionalities of TEA Band working and used them to interact with their classmates while we sent messages and observed the interactions.

4.2 Data Recollection

Using the criteria elements in the DSM-5 and the ADOS-G, the Autism Diagnostic Observation Schedule-Generic [38], as well as the First-Grade Unstructured Peer Interaction Observation System [39] an observation instrument developed by the ORCE based in the Classroom Observation system: COS-1 we constructed an instrument with key elements to observe during the interactions. This instrument included data about the interaction, the device, the conversation and the social errors. We also sent messages when the individual was stressed using the stress formula [34] and the information from three sensors: galvanic skin response, heart rate and skin temperature.

5   Results

5.1   Device Adoption

The device was easily adopted; none of the students expressed any concerning about using it or its functionality. The Microsoft Band 2 resisted perfectly to the use and although it was not thrown, it was bended, beaten and scratched (although not on purpose) without suffering any damage.

An important activity to make the students feel comfortable with the observer and the device was showing them that you could change the screen color and the image for the MeTile and allowing them to choose those; also, as another way to make them participate in the process, they chose how to use the device: in which hand and position, the reading speed and the haptic level for the alerts allowing them to feel comfortable while using the Microsoft Band 2. The interaction with TEA Band was very intuitive and did not require an extra training.

5.2   Interaction with the Device

TEA Band had the objective of being a very discreet support device during the interactions, and we paid particular attention to every time when the users saw or touched the device during an interaction. The messages suggesting them to start an interaction or congratulating them after a successful interaction, were not considered in the observation since they were not intruding an interaction.

Before sending the messages, we prepared the candidate, explaining that they were going to receive messages and, with Tadeo and Adrian (since both like superhero movies) we compared it with the fictional A.I. J.A.R.V.I.S. writing messages to help them instead of talking to them. We introduced the messages gradually during the second phase with positive reactions from the users (*"It say Hi!"*, *"My favorite part was that it sent me messages"*, Reading the message *"Good job. I did a good job!"*) and their inclusive educator monitors (*"He gets very stressed [trying to talk with his classmates] because he did not know if he is doing a good job"*).

The adoption of the messages was diverse. Tadeo read them all, following the recommendations and commenting them with the observer, while Sergio ignored them the first day and then started following the guidance, and Adrian needed extra reinforcement with the psychologist to start reading the messages on his own. It is important to mention that this behavior was not an intuition problem, he simply did not have any motivation to read the messages.

The Topic tile required a request from the student but it was mostly used before an interaction, trying to find a conversation starter. While Adrian read the ideas sometimes but he decided not to use them and Sergio used it as a relaxation method just reading them, Tadeo actually suggested this functionality in the first phase when the device did not have the TEA Band tiles: (*"[the Microsoft Band 2] could remind me that I can talk with my classmates about this movie I just saw"*) and he was the one that used it the most during the second and third phase.

5.3 Impact on the Interactions

The analysis of the results and observations allowed us to conclude that the device impacted positively in the quantity of the interactions for two of the participants, Tadeo and Sergio as we can observe in Fig. 2; in this figure, we only report the number of interactions that got an initial response from the other party.

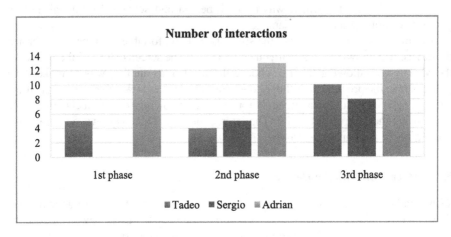

Fig. 2. Number of interactions in each phase.

Both Tadeo (*1ˢᵗ phase:* 5 interactions; *2ⁿᵈ phase:* 4 interactions; *3ʳᵈ phase:* 10 interactions) and Sergio (*1ˢᵗ phase:* 0 interactions; *2ⁿᵈ phase:* 5 interactions; *3ʳᵈ phase:* 8 interactions) incremented their interactions from the first phase to the third phase. Even when Tadeo was in exams week during the second phase, a stressful moment for him, and some of the observation spaces changed to more uncontrolled scenarios in the last two phases, from theater class in a classroom to theater class in the schoolyard, he incremented his interactions and the change of scenario only impacted slightly the average length of every conversation (*1ˢᵗ phase:* 2 min; *2ⁿᵈ phase:* 1.2 min; *3ʳᵈ phase:* 1.2 min). Sergio did not talk with anybody during the first phase. The device encouraged him to speak with his classmates and allowed to gradually increment the average length of his conversations when he started feeling more comfortable (*1ˢᵗ phase:* 0 min; *2ⁿᵈ phase:* 1.3 min; *3ʳᵈ phase:* 1.6 min). Since Adrian presented constant echolalia and neither the psychologist nor the messages on TEA Band, were able to withdraw him from a constant loop of repetition, he did not use the device during the interactions, only between them. The changes in his interactions and the length of them (*1ˢᵗ phase:* 5.2 min; *2ⁿᵈ phase:* 1.9 min; *3ʳᵈ phase:* 1.9 min). cannot be considered an impact of TEA Band.

TEA Band motivated two of the participants, Tadeo and Sergio, not only to interact more, it also gave them the confidence to be the ones that initiated the interactions as we can observe in Fig. 3. Tadeo did not respond on time to an intent to start a conversation on the 1ˢᵗ phase, later, he was ignored once both on the 2ⁿᵈ and 3ʳᵈ phase by another student when he tried to start a conversation. Sergio ignored two intents to start a conversation, one on the 2nd phase and one on the 3rd phase, however his classmates continued trying to talk with him in other occasions.

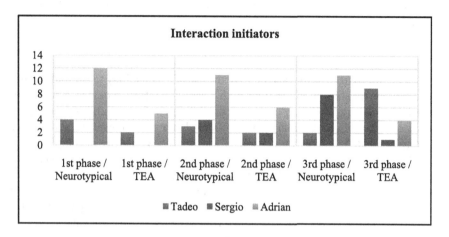

Fig. 3. Interactions initiators in each phase.

The use of TEA Band allowed the students to feel comfortable talking with more than one person at the same time and helped to increment the exchanges (commentaries made during the conversation) and questions (questions or commentaries that require feedback for the other part) during the interactions. Tadeo needed more time to gradually increment his participation during the interactions (*1st phase:* 6 exchanges, 2 questions; *2nd phase:* 9 exchanges, 5 questions; *3rd phase:* 14 exchanges, 17 questions), while Sergio was very involved during the second and third phase (*1st phase:* 0 exchanges, 0 questions; *2nd phase:* 11 exchanges, 12 questions; *3rd phase:* 10 exchanges, 10 questions). Once again, the echolalia loops make the results not conclusive for Adrian.

Since Adrian only read the messages after the interactions, the quantity and quality of the interactions was not impacted by TEA Band; however, his social errors were impacted because he read all the messages at the end of the interaction and remembered them, using the corrections for his next interaction; consequently, he reduced his social errors considerably specially lowering his voice volume and respecting the other party personal space (*1st phase:* 27 errors; *2nd phase:* 16 errors; *3rd phase:* 20 errors). TEA Band also helped Tadeo to reduce his social errors to zero but since Sergio was starting to have interactions (he did not interact at all in the first phase), his social errors augmented slightly, with his voice volume too low and walking out of the conversation without disengaging himself properly (*1st phase:* 0 errors; *2nd phase:* 2 errors; *3rd phase:* 4 errors).

Observing the results, we can note that the use of TEA Band impacted positively the three candidates, even if the impact to Adrian was marginal compared to the impact on the other two candidates. It is notable the increment in the social interactions that had both Tadeo and Sergio, specially the effort they made to be them the ones who started a conversation and the increment in the exchanges and questions they made in the inter-actions, augmenting their participation in them. Additionally, it is important to remark that TEA Band did not impacted negatively in the therapy of any of the students.

6 Conclusion

This study allowed us to design and analyze the use of a technology to aid students with autism improve their social interactions with a very low intrusive device, a design that considers the sensory sensibility of the users and different functionalities to support an interaction. From the very beginning, we considered the profile of the students – without forgetting to create an inclusive technology for everybody- and we developed an app that was easy to adopt and intuitive in its use, keeping in mind the requirements and needs of our users with autism. The adoption of the device and its intuitive use show how relevant was the design, with clear iconography, adequate messages written specif-ically for each user with the aid of the psychologists at Domus and the participation of the candidate designing his own experience with the interface and the device.

The three tiles worked as expected, although the Topic tile, that required a request of the user was used before and after an interaction, not during it. This indicates a possible improvement for this tile; the users decided not to request a conversation topic during an interaction because it implied a distraction of several seconds: moving the wrist, pressing a button, searching for the Tile and request a Topic (again by pressing a button) and waiting 1–3 s. The use of the formula developed by Garcia and Gonzalez to detect stress worked as expected, sending messages to the students to reassure them when needed, indicating that the sensors worked well and introduced very little noise to the data. However, it is important to remember that the Hints tile worked manually and not automatically, which means that we cannot depend completely on the device to detect or suggest appropriate social behaviors automatically, but we can use it as a non-intru-sive support method, controlled by a parent, psychologist or inclusive education monitor to aid students learn appropriate social behaviors while giving them confidence and reassurance to interact with their peers.

The data collected during the interactions with the aid of the observation scheme provided enough qualitative data to back up the analysis made of the use and adoption of TEA Band. It is also important to mention that the use of the device did not impact the interactions nor the behavior of the neurotypical students during them. The Microsoft Band 2 was a very discrete device and the messages could be read fast to continue with the interaction, but this same fact also made that the students did not always made a conscious effort to interact, ignoring sometimes the attempts to start a conversation of a student with TEA.

Finally, we would like to point out, once again, that each student participating in the study had different challenges and thus, had different results as well. Although the impossibility to withdraw Adrian from the echolalia with TEA Band provides a new limitation for our candidates' profile and a new challenge to create an application that can distract an individual during an echolalia episode or a crisis, we saw improvements in our three candidates: Sergio and Tadeo incremented the number of interactions they had, feeling confident to start a conversation and started to participate more in them, making commentaries and asking questions while Adrian reduced his social errors.

Acknowledgments. This study was conducted with the support of Domus: Institute of Autism, we thank for the help and feedback while working on this study, granting us access to the students and we gratefully acknowledge the three students that allowed us to work with them. We thank Lizbeth Escobedo for sharing her expertise and colleagues at ITAM for their observations and advice. We thank the Mexican Association of Culture A.C. for all their support. Finally, we also want to thank all the people that provided feedback in previous versions of this paper.

References

1. American Psychiatric Association, Diagnostic and statistical manual of mental disorders, 5th edn. Washington, D.C. (2013)
2. Escobedo, L., Nguyen, D., Boyd, L., Hirano, S.H., Rangel, A., Garcia-Rosas, D., Tentori, M., Hayes, G.: MOSOCO: a mobile assistive tool to support children with autism practicing social skills in real-life situations (2012)
3. Centers for Disease Control and Prevention: Autism Spectrum Disorder (ASD) (2016)
4. Fombonne, E., Marcin, C., Manero, A.C., Bruno, R., Diaz, C., Villalobos, M., Ramsay, K., Nealy, B.: Prevalence of autism spectrum disorders in Guanajuato, Mexico: the Leon survey. J. Autism Dev. Disord. **46**, 1669–1685 (2016)
5. Buescher, A., Cidav, Z., Knapp, M., Mandell, D.: Costs of autism spectrum disorders in the United Kingdom and the United States (2014)
6. Naciones Unidas: El empleo: la ventaja del autismo (2015)
7. General Assembly of the United Nations: Universal Declaration of Human Rights, Paris (1948)
8. World conference on special needs education: access and quality: The Salamanca Statement and Framework for Action on Special Needs Education. Salamanca (1994)
9. UNESCO: Disabilities, 2 December 2015
10. Solano, L.: Prácticamente sin crecimiento, el gasto para educación: INEE. La Jornada, p. 34, 22 Agosto 2015
11. Congreso General de los Estados Unidos Mexicanos: Ley General para la inclusion de las personas con discapacidad (2011)
12. Universidad de Manchester: La inclusión de Niños y Niñas con Trastorno Del Espectro Autista en las Escuelas en la Ciudad de México, p. 52 (2012)
13. Anderson, C.: IAN research report: bullying and children with ASD. Interactive Autism Network (2014)
14. Bancroft, K., Batten, A., Lambert, S., Madders, T.: The Way We are: Autism in 2012. National Autism Society, London (2012)
15. Excelsior. http://www.excelsior.com.mx/topico/bullying
16. Todos somos uno: todos somos uno, 05 septiembre 2014. http://todossomosuno.com.mx/portal/index.php/madres-de-ninos-con-autismo-piden-inclusion-en-escuelas-publicas/
17. Kamps, D.M., Leonard, B.R., Vernon, S., Dugan, E.P., Delquadri, J.C., Gershon, B., Linda, W., Flok, L.: Teaching social skills to students with autism to increase peer interactions in an integrated first-grade classroom. J. Appl. Behav. Anal. **25**, 281–288 (1992)
18. Gaylord-Ross, R.J., Haring, T.G., Breen, C., Pitts-Conway, V.: The training and generalization of social interaction skills with autistic youth. J. Appl. Behav. Anal. **17**, 229–247 (1984)

19. Owen-DeSchryver, J.S., Carr, E.G., Cale, S.I., Blakeley-Smith, A.: Promoting social interactions between students with autism spectrum disorders and their peers in inclusive school settings. Peer Reviewed Articles, p. Paper 18 (2008)
20. Tentori, M., Hayes, G.R.: Designing for interaction immediacy to enhance social skills of children with autism. In: Ubicomp 2010 Proceedings of the 12th ACM International Conference on Ubiquitous Computing, Copenhagen, Denmark (2010)
21. Boyd, L., McReynolds, C., Chanin, K.: The Social Compass Curriculum: A Story-Based Intervention Package for Students with Autism Spectrum Disorders. Brookes Pub, Baltimore (2013)
22. Hourcade, J.P., Bullock-Rest, N.E., Hansen, T.E.: Multitouch tablet applications and activities to enhance the social skills of children with autism spectrum disorders. Pers. Ubiquit. Comput. **16**, 157–168 (2012)
23. McEwen, R.: Mediating sociality: the use of iPod Touch™ devices in the classrooms of students with autism in Canada. Inf. Commun. Soc. **17**(10), 1264–1279 (2014)
24. Albinali, F., Goodwin, M.S., Intille, S.S.: Recognizing stereotypical motor movements in the laboratory and classroom: a case study with children on the autism spectrum (2009)
25. Gay, V., Leijdekkers, P., Agcanas, J., Wong, F., Wu, Q.: CaptureMyEmotion: helping autistic children understand their emotions using facial expression recognition and mobile technologies. In: eInnovations: Challenges and Impacts for Individuals, Organizations and Society, Bled (2013)
26. Spectrum News: Sensors measure social interactions during autism diagnosis. Spectrum News, 20 October 2015
27. Picard, R.W.: Measuring affect in the wild. In: D'Mello, S., Graesser, A., Schuller, B., Martin, J.-C. (eds.) ACII 2011. LNCS, vol. 6974, p. 3. Springer, Heidelberg (2011). doi: 10.1007/978-3-642-24600-5_3
28. Palmer, A.: Reveal (2015). http://www.awakelabs.com/index#reveal
29. Baranek, G.T.: Autism during infancy: a retrospective video analysis of sensory-motor and social behaviors at 9–12 months of age. J. Autism Dev. Disord. **29**, 213–224 (1999)
30. Paron-Wildes, A.J.: Sensory Stimulation and Autistic Children. University of Minnesota, Minnesota (2005)
31. The National Autism Society: Visual Supports. Inglaterra (2014)
32. Reza, D.: Curso: intervencion basada en la relación social. Curso impartido por Domus (2015)
33. Microsoft: Microsoft Band Experience Design Guidelines 2 (2015)
34. Garcia-Mancilla, J., Gonzalez, V.M.: Stress quantification using a wearable device for daily feedback to improve stress management. In: Zheng, X., Zeng, D.D., Chen, H., Leischow, S.J. (eds.) ICSH 2015. LNCS, vol. 9545, pp. 204–209. Springer, Cham (2016). doi: 10.1007/978-3-319-29175-8_19
35. Bossavit, B., Parsons, S.: "This is how I want to learn": high functioning autistic teens co-designing a serious game. In: CHI 2016 (2016)
36. Carter, E., Hyde, J., Williams, D., Hodgins, J.: Investigating the influence of avatar facial characteristics on the social behaviors of children with autism. In: CHI 2016 (2016)
37. Suzuki, K., Hachisu, T., Iida, K.: EnhancedTouch: a smart bracelet for enhancing human-human physical touch (2016)
38. Lord, C., Risi, S., Lambrecht, L., Cook, E.H., Leventhal, J.B., DiLavore, P.C., Pickes, A., Rutter, M.: The autism diagnostic observation schedule. J. Autism Dev. Disord. (2014)
39. Observational Record Caregiving Environment: First Grade Unstructured Peer Interaction Observation System (2000)
40. O'Neill, M., Jones, R.S.P.: Sensory-perceptual abnormalities in autism: a case for more research. J. Autism Dev. Disord. **27**, 283–293 (1997)

41. Asamblea General de las Naciones Unidas: Declaración Universal de los Derechos Humanos, París (1948)
42. Riedl, M., Arriaga, R., Boujarwah, F., Hong, H., Isbell, J., Heflin, L.J.: Graphical social scenarios: toward intervention and authoring for adolescents with high functioning autism. In: AAAI Fall Symposium on Virtual Healthcare Interaction (2009)
43. Bernard-Opitz, V., Sriram, N., Nakhoda-Sapuan, S.: Enhancing social problem solving in children with autism and normal children through computer-assisted instruction. J. Autism Dev. Disord. 31(4), 377–384 (2001)

User Oriented Design Speculation and Implications for an Arm-Worn Wearable Device for Table-Top Role-Playing Games

Oğuz Turan Buruk[✉] and Oğuzhan Özcan

Koç University – Arçelik Research Center for Creative Industries (KUAR), İstanbul, Turkey
{oburuk,oozcan}@ku.edu.tr

Abstract. Augmenting table-top role-playing games (TTRPG) with computers is an extensive research area. Nevertheless, wearable devices were not considered a part of TTRPG before. Previous studies speculate that wearables may be valuable additions for games by altering many aspects some of which can address TTRPG such as character identification. Still, we did not encounter a player oriented exploratory study which suggests possible utilization ways for these devices. Therefore, we organized a participatory design workshop with 25 participants aiming at eliciting ideas from users to produce design knowledge about the interaction techniques, actions, visual properties and the GM's role. We also wanted to understand users' overall reactions to the idea of wearables in TTRPG. The workshop resulted in 5 conceptual device designs which led to design implications that can guide designers in this unexplored area. Moreover, we proposed a speculative arm-worn device drawing upon these implications.

Keywords: Wearables · Role-playing · Games · Game research · Game design · Movement-based game-play · Participatory design · Design workshop · User centered design · Design speculation

1 Introduction

Table-top Role Playing Games (TTRPG) are games in which players assume the role of their fictional characters. Game consists two types of actors which are players and the game master (GM). Players role-play their characters in an imaginary world written and moderated by the GM. TTRPG can have ancillary objects such as dice, character sheets, boards or figures. Conventional setting of TTRPG (Fig. 1), however, does not include digital artifacts. Nevertheless, recent studies integrate computer assisted devices such as notebook computers, interactive boards or surrounding systems like interactive rooms into role-playing games for altering especially narrative, ludic and functional properties [6, 14, 21]. However, previous studies did not consider wearable devices as a part of TTRPG. Thus, design knowledge regarding to user preferences for wearable devices do not exist in the field.

There are many studies aiming at augmenting the table-top games. [5, 14, 21, 23]. These studies aimed to enhance the table-top gaming experience by speeding up the

© Springer International Publishing AG 2017
A. Marcus and W. Wang (Eds.): DUXU 2017, Part II, LNCS 10289, pp. 636–655, 2017.
DOI: 10.1007/978-3-319-58637-3_50

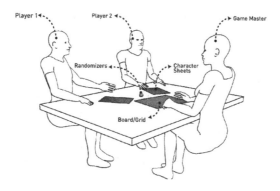

Fig. 1. Setting of conventional PnPRPG

calculation processes, improving communication abilities, bolstering sensory experiences and adding novel mechanics. In case of TTRPG, these additions left more space for role-playing by debilitating the conditions interfering with acting process. Drawing upon the previous studies, we believe that exploration of these devices in TTRPG context is valuable since wearable devices are claimed to enhance game experience with introduction of new interfaces and modalities [1], utilization of body as a controller [1, 2] and strengthen the feeling of character identification [3]. Still, we did not encounter a player oriented exploratory study which suggests possible utilization ways for these devices.

In the direction of these arguments, we believe that an arm-worn device may enhance the TTRPG experience. However, providing the ideal experience to players can only be possible with a ready-to hand device and such device can be designed with user-oriented design knowledge which was not covered by previous studies. In order produce this design knowledge, we organized a participatory design workshop with 25 participants including TTRPG players, game masters, cosplayers, jewelry designers and interaction designers. In this workshop, we asked participants to design non-working arm-worn device prototypes and "role-play" using them in a game scenario. Our expectations from the workshop were to (1) see users' reactions on positive and hindering parts of the wearable idea, (2) learn their preferences about the game actions to perform with this device, (3) understand their desires about the interaction techniques which refers to input and output methods (4) see their visual design decisions and (5) understand GM's role in controlling these devices. We especially focus on arm-worn devices, since they are easy to reach and control, attached to the upper part of the body which is visible in a table-top setting. Moreover, we wanted to narrow down to scope to have a more fertile workshop process. Upon the workshop, we discussed the design implications and proposed a speculative design with the design knowledge gained from the workshop.

2   Related Work

Augmenting table-top games with computers is a well-adopted practice in game design field [4–8]. However, we did not encounter any example which specifically proposes augmenting the TTRPG with arm-worn devices. Nevertheless, utilization of wearable devices is common in games which have similar characteristics [9–14]. Pervasive games, physical games and live-action role playing games (LARP) were considered suitable environments for the integration of the wearable devices.

Before referring to wearables, we should examine the work on computer augmented games (CAG). STARS Platform [7] is a remarkable example which was designed to be adaptable for different kinds of games with a room-sized interactive environment. This is one of the first and noteworthy examples of a working CAG system. Other than implemented systems, a recent work by Bergström and Björk pointed out 6 different CAG cases and extracted 8 dimensions which define the game design space for CAG [4]. These dimensions form constructive insights and define the design space of CAG in a convenient way. A similar study puts the primary aim of the CAG to decrease uncaptivating game processes, integrate game mechanics which can only work with computational power and maintain the social interaction level [6]. Another project, Undercurrents is a software which will remove undesired gaming processes like complex calculations and add enhanced properties like private communication by also emphasizing the importance of calm technology [5].

Another domain which is more related with TTRPG is Live-Action Role Playing Games (LARP). Lindley and Eladhari coined the Trans-Reality RPG concept which combines LARP, TTRPG and computer RPG (CRPG) using the advantages of each game modalities [15]. Proposed design does not include wearables, yet the concept of bringing together CRPG, TTRPG and LARP also corroborates with our concept of creating sensory experiences and costuming properties which is essential for LARP [16]. We may exemplify usage of wearables in LARP with the projects of Thumin Glove [13] and Gauntlet [12]. Both of these devices were developed for enhancing the game experience with new game mechanics generated by the computational power. Both studies draw conclusions from the user remarks.

Previous studies also suggest that wearables can strengthen the bond between player and the imaginary world which is an essential quality for TTRPG. Lightning Bug [3] examines wearables as costumes and question how they can foster the connectedness to imaginary worlds. Tanenbaum et al. also claimed that wearable devices can mediate one to feel as another character [2]. Supported by these projects we believe that connectedness to fictional world and characters in TTRPG can be bolstered by wearables.

The studies are indicators of how computers may be sources that can foster the table-top games by shortening undesired processes, introducing new game mechanics and fostering the sensory aspects. Moreover, previous studies indicate that wearable devices can bolster the game experience by increasing the connectedness to imaginary worlds. Wearables also were speculated to support calm technology which has been coined as an important aspect for CAG [5]. However, these projects did not investigate wearable devices for TTRPG. Moreover, they do not focus on presenting user-oriented design knowledge which can inspire designers. Therefore, in our study we aimed at exploring this unvisited field by involving users in the design process, understanding their reactions and eliciting ideas.

3   Method

For examining the use of wearables in TTRPG, we integrated users in the design process from the very beginning with a participatory design (PD) workshop. PD is a widely adopted method for eliciting design ideas from the users, understanding them and producing design knowledge which will serve to the broad-range of fields [17–19].

3.1   Participants

25 participants which are *TTRPG players, game masters, cosplayers, interaction designers and jewelry designers* took part in the workshop. TTRPG players and GMs were our main users. We included cosplayers due to their knowledge in making costumes of fictional characters. Interaction designers were to assist projects in terms of interaction techniques while the jewelry designers helped in the visual design. We included jewelry designers since the wearable device design were mostly related also with smart jewelry. Table 1 demonstrates users' backgrounds, experiences and relation with the field. For acquiring participants, we posted a call to social media pages and e-mail groups related to RPG, cosplay, games and design. This call included a brief explanation of the workshop and a visual prepared by us to attract attention. We chose participants among 143 applicants according to their backgrounds and experience in related fields. We provided breakfast, lunch and transportation for the participants, yet we did not offer a payment. We believe that the TTRPG players, GMs and cosplayers wanted to participated in the workshop since they are usually enthusiastic for alternative culture events. Jewelry and interaction designers may also be motivated by the novel topic (wearable devices) of the workshop.

3.2   Procedure

We motivated the workshop by stating that we investigate the usage of wearable devices in TTRPG and did not disclose the arguments of previous work about costume properties, embodiment of characters and unobstructed interaction in order not to direct participants towards our opinions and to elicit objective ideas which are not affected by a certain point of view. The workshop lasted two consecutive days, in total 16 h.

The first day of the workshop focused on creating use case scenarios for devices. It started with a brief presentation about the utilization of wearables in HCI, in role-playing games and the schedule of the workshop. After the presentation, participants were divided into five groups. Each group incorporated one participant from all audiences. Then, in a brainstorming session which lasted about two hours, each group generated several ideas about the employment of the arm-worn device in the game. Jewelry and interaction designers led this brainstorming process. Each group presented their ideas with sketches, notes and mind-maps after the brainstorming session. All the participants watched the presentations and made their comments on the ideas. After presentations, we wanted each group to choose one of the alternatives and prepare detailed use case scenarios for the wearables. First day of the workshop concluded with final PowerPoint presentations which explains the preliminary use cases.

Table 1. Breakdown of participants (CP: Cosplayer, IxD: Interaction Designer, JD: Jewelry Designer, RP: RPG Player, GM: Game Master, XP: Experience in Years)

Part.	Age	Sex	XP	Notes
CP1	28	F	5–10	Masqueraded more than 10 characters
CP2	24	F	2–5	Masqueraded more than 10 characters
CP3	21	F	2–5	Masqueraded more than 10 characters
CP4	31	F	2–5	Masqueraded more than 10 characters
CP5	20	M	0–2	Masqueraded 3 characters
IxD1	24	F	3	Designer in a web-design company
IxD2	30	M	2	Musician working on wearable devices
IxD3	22	M	2–5	IxD student worked in prof. projects
IxD4	25	M	2–5	Industrial designer working on electronic devices and interfaces
IxD4	26	F	5–10	IxD in a game studio
JD1	27	F	0–2	Industrial designer with the fashion accessories master degree
JD2	29	F	>10	Jewelry designer and seller
JD3	34	F	5–10	Fashion design researcher with a master degree in fashion in game design
JD4	25	F	2–5	Industrial designer who designs and sells jewelry
JD5	24	F	0–2	Industrial designer with a jewelry design related work background
RP1	23	F	4–6	Knowledgeable D&D and custom RPG systems
RP2	24	M	4–6	More than 5 different RPG systems
RP3	21	F	4–6	More than 5 different RPG systems
RP4	21	M	>6	4 different RPG systems
RP5	21	M	0–2	More than 5 different RPG systems
GM1	27	M	>6	Knowledgeable in moderating 5 different RPG systems
GM2	33	M	>6	3 different RPG systems
GM3	25	M	>6	More than 5 different RPG systems
GM4	26	M	4–6	3 different RPG systems
GM5	25	M	>6	More than 5 different RPG systems and the co-founder of a RPG community

The second day of the workshop aimed at defining the form factor, visual properties, making the visual (non-working) prototypes and "role-playing" the use cases, which were designed in the first day, in a real game scenario. First, participants designed and produced visual prototypes with the materials we provided such as leather strips, beads, jewelry accessories, model clay, cardboard and cloth pieces. Groups also used the materials which the cosplayers and jewelry designers brought along to the workshop. After the visual prototypes were created, they wore them and played a short (about an hour and half) session of TTRPG by "role-playing" as if the devices were working (Fig. 2). Forming user scenarios with role playing and making users explore the design space by creating prototypes was claimed to be effective also by previous research [20]. The game systems and the scenarios in these sessions were decided by GMs in each group. We also wanted participants to document this process with photos. These photos were turned into video sketches [21] to be presented at the end of the second day. We specifically facilitated video sketches, as they are useful expressing the ideas quickly and finding hindering parts of the use cases. After the presentations, we made a semi-structured group interview to understand participants' opinions on the possible contribution of the device. Questions were about the main contribution of the device, effects on the game, visual properties, ways of integration, GM's Role and the possible interaction techniques.

Fig. 2. Gameplay session in the second part of the workshop

We analyzed the workshop results drawing upon the visual prototypes, video sketches, video records of presentations and voice record of the group interview.

4   Device Concepts

In this section, we explained all projects in detail by commentating the concepts, interaction techniques, game actions, visual factors and GM's Role since a product is comprised of form, material, function, cultural aspects, interaction and environmental design dealing with the mental models of users [22]. We encapsulate the form (visual aspects), function (actions), interaction (interaction technique). We also examine the

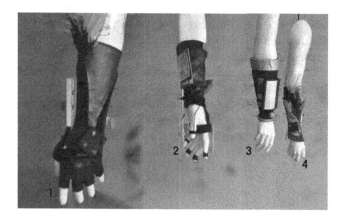

Fig. 3. Some of the visual non-working prototypes from the workshop

GM's role as a separate entity, since it is a special case for TTRPG. Material, cultural aspects and mental models of players can only be examined in production level and upon long-term engagement with the product. Figure 3 shows visual non-working prototypes and Table 2 demonstrates the main properties of designs.

Table 2. The properties of the device concepts – C (Combat), NC (Non-Combat), PC (Private Communication), DR (Dice-Rolling), MF (Move Figure), FC (Fully Customizable), PDC (Pre-designed Customizable)

	Interaction techniques		Game actions		Visual styles		GM Control
	Input	Output	In-game	Out-of-game	Feature	Appearance	
Group1	Tangible, auxiliary	Visual, haptic	C, NC, PC	–	FC	–	Separate console
Group2	Gestures, body sensors, touch	Visual	C, NC, PC	–	FC	–	Separate console
Group3	Gestures, voice, touch	Audial, visual, haptic	PC	DR, MF	PDC	Daily Use	Enhanced wearable
Group4	Tangible, touch	Visual, haptic	C, PC	DR	PDC	Character	Enhanced wearable
Group5	Voice, auxiliary, tangible	Audial	C, NC, PC	DR	PDC	Character	Enhanced wearable

4.1 Group 1 – RPGear (Fig. 4)

RPGear is focused on increasing the spatial awareness of the player about the fictional world. The concept adapts a gameplay similar to role-playing games which includes boards and figures. RPGear has auxiliary parts, called "beacons", which are used for defining the game area/map as if there is a board. Moreover, beacons are also used for defining the character figures, their locations and their connection with the wearable device. As the game progress, the information about the environment is transferred to the device and the players can react to the events according to their skills. For examples, if a player come across with a cliff, she/he can use Climb command if she/he has the ability. Similarly, during the combat, players can select the skills they had when the turn is theirs. The success of the moves is shown with LEDs which are visible to all players. Private information like private messages, character properties, intractable objects or available skills are demonstrated with a private display which remains under the front-arm.

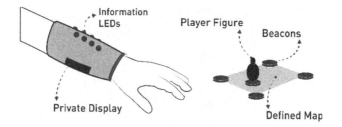

Fig. 4. Group 1 - RPGear device instructions

4.2   Group 2 – Nameless One (Fig. 5)

Nameless one focused on encouraging players enact their characters by making use of gestures and body conditions. Mid-air arm gestures and player's body conditions detected by body sensors like galvanic skin sensors are the primary inputs. Instead of expressing the command verbally and rolling the dice for calculating the outcome, players perform mid-air gestures. For example, when encountered to foes, on should swing her/his arm for performing a sword attack. After the gesture is performed, body conditions detected by sensors also affect the outcome.

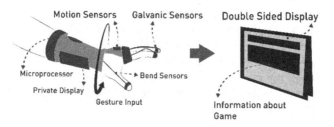

Fig. 5. Group 2 - the nameless one device instructions

Different than other projects, primary output is provided via a separate double sided display one side of which is visible to all players. Game events are to be monitored from this display. Information which should not be available to public is shown by small displays on wearables. The group also added a small device which emits scents to the environment in order to increase sensory experiences.

Other side of the double-sided display was faced to GM and functions as GM console. GM can manipulate the environment, alter the difficulty of the game and decide the outcomes of the moves.

4.3   Group 3 – RProp (Fig. 6)

The primary goal of the RProp is to provide private communication capability to players by using directional speakers. The device is consisted of two parts. One part includes

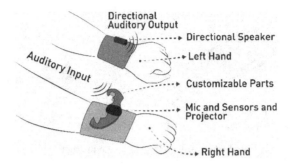

Fig. 6. Group 3 – RProp device instructions

the main module comprised of a projector and a microphone. Other part hosts the directional speaker. Players speak the messages directly to microphone and point their arms to the player who should hear the message.

As a secondary function, RProp simulates dice-rolling when a player performs the dice-rolling gesture. When the dice is rolled, device calculates the outcome by the virtue of character information loaded in its memory. The outcome can be seen from the projected display which is formed via the projector embedded the main module. This display can also be used as an alternative for getting private messages. Moreover, figures on the grid can be controlled through this display.

RProp provides a playful engagement for GM. GM device can be linked with the objects in the gaming environment. For example, when GM says "It's getting dark" while telling the story, the lights of the room dim.

Both parts of RProp are customizable and players can customize them with pre-designed parts. Group 3 expressed that, they aimed at designing a minimal device which can be worn also in their daily life.

4.4   Group 4 – RPGear (Fig. 7)

RPGear aims at speeding up the dice rolling process and encouraging players to express their character's progress with visual cues. Group 4's prototype stores the character information and lets players attach badges to device which shows their character achievements and history.

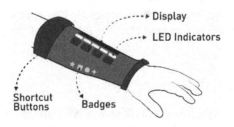

Fig. 7. Group 4 – RPGear device instructions

RPGear has buttons, a display, LED indicators and badge sockets. Buttons are for performing various dice-rolls and specific attacks. The LED indicators show the mana or health level of the players. When the move type is chosen and the dice are rolled by the device, the display shows a solid color depending on the success of this move. Although device can manage all kind of dice-rolling, Group 4 decided to keep dice in the game. They are not functional but they expressed that dice should not be removed completely as they were a symbolic part of TTRPG.

GM device differentiates from other players by its size and look. Its design is more flamboyant compared to the player devices. RPGear adds physical interaction to game. GM should touch other players' devices to make the outcome affect them when s/he performs a move.

Players can add badges to the device which reflects the characters' properties and achievements. These badges also activate the achievements in an online platform which functions as a social network between players who has a RPGear.

4.5   Group 5 – Gauntlet of Fate (Fig. 8)

The main purpose of Gauntlet of Fate (GoF) is reflecting the fictional character by using nano-technological clothes which can morph into different shapes. Therefore, every player may turn their devices into something which is related to their character properties.

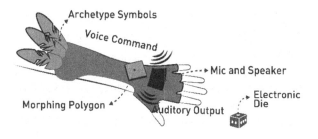

Fig. 8. Group 5 - gauntlet of fate device instructions

As a primary input, Group 5 used voice commands. For example, when a player says "Fireball", the device executes that move. Dice is also a part of the input system. When the dice is rolled, the outcome is transferred to the device for calculating the value of the move. The output of the move is also announced by device via speech. Group 5 indicated that this interaction technique provides non-distracting gameplay. Additionally, device has a part which has a shape of a polygon. The edge number of the polygon is determined according to the number of players. If there are 4 players, this polygon-shaped part morphs into a square and each corner represents a player. GM can select specific players by touching the specific corners.

GM device, different from the players' devices, is two part and worn to both arms. Therefore, it is more radiant than others. The device of the GM has several enhanced properties. For example, GM can attach some figures to the devices which show the number of the fictional characters who passed away during the games that he moderated.

Moreover, GM can send a "whisper of GM" which includes private information by talking towards his palm. Players can listen these messages via speakers of the device. Furthermore, device is able to change the voice of the GM during the storytelling according to characters she/he enacted.

GoF can also be upgraded with new parts as the fictional character levels up. Therefore, players can represent their fictional characters with their device's appearance.

5 Discussion

We evaluated the visual prototypes, presentation videos, workshop notes and the voice record of the semi-structured group interview for analyzing the outcomes of the workshop. According to the evaluation, players' opinions indicate that arm-worn devices may contribute to the RPG environment by (1) adding new game play styles, (2) automatizing the undesired game process, (3) enhancing the sensory experiences. Apart from these positive additions, participants expressed their concerns about the distraction possibility which may be caused by the interaction with the device. In this section, we commented on how the results corroborate with previous studies and how our implications may hint to design of wearables for TTRPG. We believe that these implications are important since they provide the design knowledge which is open to interpretation [23] that can lead to many different designs.

5.1 New Gameplay Styles

Previous research on CAG indicates that integration of new game play styles as a result of the computational power is an expected result [6]. Our study also shows that this also reflects the TTRPG players' mind as four of the groups proposed changing the game play style slightly or radically.

The most radical change was proposed by Group 2 with the introduction of movement-based play and the effects of body conditions. Previous research in games indicates that movement is a phenomenon which may result in an increased engagement [24–26]. Yet, movement-based play was not investigated in the context of long-term games with rich narrative. As RPGs may have limitless in-game actions, assigning different movement patterns to each action can be mentally or physically fatiguing. Substantiated with this statement, Group2 assigned gestures only to main actions like attack, defense or spell-casting instead of all actions. This way, players do not have to memorize different gestures, for different spells. To exemplify, they can use the same gesture for all ranged attack spells, yet imagine different results. In this way, the system becomes more scalable and usable for players. This new addition to game, turned the game into a real-time game where players need to react events in real time instead of the turn-based structure of conventional RPGs. For instance, players may have to attack to a certain enemy by swinging their arms for attacking with a sword. In the conventional structure, dice should be rolled for the player and for the enemy to conclude this encounter. However, new structure proposes players to swing their arms in a right timing and reduces the process into just one move. If player can have a good timing, than she/he can take out the enemy successfully. Still, each player performs their moves in the turn-based system and rest until the turn is theirs which bypasses the physical fatigue.

Group1 also radically changed game play style by removing dice and the board completely. They used beacons for digitally defining the map and instead of using dice, implemented CRPG-like system in which players can choose skills to perform on the wearable device's display. Moreover, device can provide sensory feedback like visual and haptic easing the spatial comprehension for the imaginary environment. The approach of this group put the game into a space between CRPG and TTRPG by adopting sensory and scripted nature of CRPG and social, limitless and imaginary environment of TTRPG. Other groups also made slight additions to gameplay like tangible inventory system (Group5), global achievement system (Group4).

Although changes in game-mechanics were acceptable, players expressed that RPG elements like character properties should not be overwhelmed by new additions. For example, during our discussion in the group interview, challenge-based game mechanics were taken skeptically. One of the players said that "I am a tiny person, however I always role-play a barbarian character. How will I overcome the physical challenges which will be faced by my character with my tiny body?" This indicates that imaginary characters' properties and similar role playing elements always should be the primary concern and their emphasis should not be reduced by new additions.

Players preferences and opinions indicate that wearable devices can conceive new game play styles, interactions and mechanics which may bring the TTRPG closer to CRPG and LARP. Still, new game mechanics should be implemented carefully by not overwhelming the RPG elements like character skills.

5.2   Transforming the Undesired Game Properties

RPGs are based on impersonating a character and acting it. However, most of the RPG systems have game rules which require long and complex calculation processes. These calculation processes can be considered uncaptivating [6]. Participants showed an inevitable consensus on automatizing these processes. Similar features also were introduced in previous CAG [5].

First, the common point for all groups was assigning character information and dice calculation to devices. However, they followed different approaches. Group1 and Group2 replaced the conventional dice rolling system with new game mechanics, whereas other groups decided to keep the conventional game play. Group4 and Group5 kept the dice physically in the game while the Group3 replaced it with a dice-rolling gesture. Moreover except for Group2, all groups kept the tangible props like figures or a game board in the game. Previous research also suggests that the tangible props, and especially dice [27], have an important effect in table-top gaming experience. The moment when the dice is rolled, the excitement occurred until the result is revealed and the materiality [28] of it stand as important properties of TTRPG experience. Even, one of the players said "Dice is like the treasure for role playing gamers and I am attentive not to lose any of them".

Another common point was the private communication feature. In a conventional TTRPG setting, private communication is only possible with note papers or whispering to the ear of players. However, this process does not create the ideal experience since all the players are aware that a secret message is delivered to a specific player. With wearable devices, participants emphasized the opportunity which improves transmitting secret and private messages.

Our observations showed that removing and automatizing the processes which intervenes with role-playing process and entertainment such as calculating dice outcomes should be done by devices. Still, we saw that, as also previous work suggests [27, 28], player may keep the dices or other tangible props in the game system even if their functionality are replaced by devices. Therefore, how these kinds of props will be integrated to the game system supported by wearable devices should be scrutinized by designers. Other than this, wearables can transform and enhance the communication between players by providing features such as secret or private messaging.

5.3 Sensory Experiences and Character Identification

TTRPG is built on the imagination of players and visual support is usually provided by miniature figures and boards. However, players took the opportunity of using more dynamic visual, audial and haptic feedback to foster the sensory aspects of the TTRPG with wearables. Previous studies also remark the advantages of computers in enhancing the sensory experiences [29]. Group1 used LED and Haptic indicators, Group2 coined the idea of a scent emitter, Group3 gave the proposal of GM's ability to manipulate environmental conditions, Group4 and Group5 came up with visually customizable devices enhancing the identification experience with fictional characters.

Still, participants also expressed the worry for the distraction that can be caused by the excessive visual feedback. Therefore, peripheral interaction methods were proposed which are not visually distracting and captivating like gestures, voice commands, tangible buttons, haptic and audial feedback. Moreover, visual feedback is mostly used as sole colors, simplified information and mostly for calculation results and character information. At group interview, one of the participants also said "If we are stuck to the device, this may break our concentration to game."

Designers should acknowledge that although players consider that an arm-worn device may enhance the game, the interaction techniques should not be distracting and prevent social communication. Wearables can more advantageous then other types of devices in that sense, since they are speculated to support "calm technology" by remaining at the periphery of users [30]. The maintenance of social aspects was also asserted as an important property by previous research [6]. Moreover, especially haptic feedback come forward as specific to wearables as they are attached to the body. Similarly, identification with characters through customization, as also indicated by previous research [2, 3, 14], is wearable specific.

5.4 GM's Role

Previous studies in augmenting TTRPG explored the possible functions for GM's in CAG which also corroborates with many of the features proposed by participants like immediate control availability, map and story preparation [5]. However, different from the previous work, our study put forth interaction, game-play, visual style and feature preferences of GMs for arm-worn devices in TTRPG.

First of all, while two groups proposed a separate console, other groups preferred a wearable device for GM. A separate console is advantageous in administering a detailed interface which may let GM control the players' wearables and the game with much force. On the other hand, a wearable for GM can be more desirable as it can include GM in the game not only as a moderator but a player. One of the GMs expressed that "Game Masters should also be considered as a "player", as moderation and story-telling get boring if you cannot participate in the game."

The enhanced features for GMs were environment control, voice changing, private communication, manipulating game environment, creating NPCs and controlling other devices. Moreover, wearable GM consoles were visually different than the player devices. Group3 preferred a different color, Group4 expressed that GM has a more flamboyant device and Group5 proposed devices which can be worn to both arms different from the single-arm devices of players.

Participants preferences in the workshop showed that GM's can either have a separate console or a wearable device for controlling the game. Independent from the version they have, GMs should be able to manipulate many aspects of the game. Some of the abilities they have even may make them feel as if they are super-powered players of the game. Corroborating with this, in case they have wearable devices, these devices should be different and even more flamboyant and superior than player devices.

6   Design Implications

User reactions and device concepts lead us to extract design implications which may guide the designers of such devices. Moreover, we believe that these implications will also be constructive for other kinds of wearable and personal gadgets which may be used in computer games, pervasive games, serious games or gamification projects.

Non-Distracting Interaction Techniques.   All groups preferred interaction techniques which remains in the perceptual area of the players. For example, haptic or audial feedback which does not require a direct attention to be perceived preferred more than other techniques. Visual feedbacks were mostly solid colors or LED lights at which can be perceived without directly looking. Likewise, gestural, voice or tangible inputs preferred which does not require a direct look, browsing and such. This is important for maintaining the social interaction and satisfies our motivation about the calm interaction [28].

Designing devices in interaction with the auxiliary objects.   Four of the groups decided to keep the supportive objects like dice, grids, and figures. Therefore, instead of assigning the roles of these objects to wearable by removing them from the game, designers should scrutinize to form an interaction between this objects and the wearable. This finding is also supported by previous research suggests that use tangible objects like dice increase the table top gaming experience [5].

Automatization of Uncaptivating Processes. By design, out of game moments like calculation after dice rolling occur repeatedly during the gameplay of TTRPG. All of the groups assigned processes like dice-rolling or storing character information to device. Thus, device has to speed up all of the out-of-game processes. Previous research on CAG role-playing games also suggest the advantage of electronic devices in this manner [18, 19].

Different information levels. As explained in the descriptions of "Device Concepts", the information needed by players were classified into two as public and private information. Therefore, designers should consider how to place information which is relevant to other players and which is private to the wearer. Private displays or audial feedback were preferable for private information while LED's or public displays were used for public information.

Enhancing the communication between players. Another function used by all groups was private communication between players via auditory output or via displays. GM or other players need to communicate with each other secretly time to time. This property also was reported preferable by users in a previous study [3]. Therefore, easing the communication between players should be considered as an important property of the device.

Assigned in-game actions should be adaptable to narrative. All actions assigned to the devices have to be simple actions like attacks, or skills which are liable to success check, details of which can be expressed by game master according to the narrative. Otherwise assigning commands to each action is not scalable. Therefore, no action should be precluded because the device does not support them.

Exploring new gameplay styles. All the groups proposed new interaction techniques both for players and GMs via use of embedded sensors or electronic auxiliary objects. Moreover, Group1 transferred mechanics from CRPG while Group2 introduce a whole new approach with movement-based gameplay. Therefore, designers should not ignore that novel interaction techniques and gameplay mechanics are welcome by players in an integration of such device.

Customization of the device can serve as an upgrade to character properties. As Group 4 and Group 5 suggested devices may be a part of an environment where the fictional characters' skills are developing as the device is visually upgraded with different parts in real life. This also supported the claim of Isbister suggesting that costumes may increase the connectedness to imaginary world [11] as players consider them as a part of their fictional characters.

Participatory customization space. While three of the groups proposed a customization space with pre-designed parts, two of them proposed customizing the device from the scratch. We believe that a customization space for such device should form an environment which guides players to design their devices easily with pre-designed parts while letting them to modify it with outer parts.

GM as a player. Game masters can be considered as god-like beings in the fictional world of the game while granted with improved skills for their devices. One of the participants expressed that "Game Masters should also be considered as a "player", as moderation and story-telling get boring if you cannot participate in the game." Therefore, while designing a wearable device for PnPRPG, game masters should not be considered referees or moderators only as they also devote themselves to the game voluntarily and for enjoyment.

Enhanced visual appearance for GM Device. Visual properties of the devices also showed differences from the players' devices. Group 3 favored a color change in modules, Group 4 and Group 5 designed a bigger, more flamboyant and multiple-module device. Therefore, GM device should be different than the other players' devices and its visual properties should express the GM's superior status.

Immediate control ability of GM. As in the GM consoles of Group 1 and Group 2, game master should be able to step in the decision mechanism of devices whenever she/ he wants and manipulate the outcomes according to the story. For example, if a dice calculation or a result of a challenge based attack is more than what is meant to be according to story, GM should be able to change the output.

7   Design Speculation

Upon our analysis and design implications extracted from the user preferences, we designed a speculative arm-worn device which may satisfy the TTRPG Players (Fig. 9). Design speculations contribute to the field by informing the community about the possible future designs about a specific topic [31–33]. Still, this is only a one type of interpretation of the design knowledge we presented and it may lead to many more different proposals. Among our many implications we extracted following design motivations for our speculative design. We only focus on player device, thereby our implications about GM device are not in the scope of the following speculation. Our motivation for this speculative design is based on (Design Motivation 1) automatization for uncaptivating process, (DM2) introduction of new game mechanics with movement-based play, (DM3) support by auxiliary objects, (DM4) customization depending on the

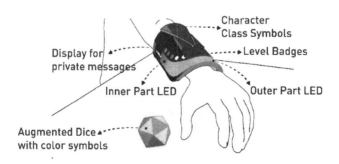

Fig. 9. Speculative arm-worn device design for TTRPG

fictional character, (DM5) non-distracting interaction techniques, (DM6) introducing actions adaptable to narrative. We also conducted a preliminary user test with an experience prototype which encapsulates some of these design motivations as a successor of this project [34].

Concept. This device aims at encouraging the players to act their characters by performing the actions with body movements and visually customizing the device for reflecting the fictional character. Moreover, the device works for automatizing the dice calculations and private communication between players.

Interaction Technique. WeaRPG is mainly operated with gestures (DM2, DM5). Gestures are only assigned for actions which may define the essence of the movement like power, concentration, reflex and precision (DM6). In this way, these actions can be adapted to many different scenarios in the narrative of the game. For example, an attack with sword requires power gesture which needs swinging the arm as strong as possible while dodging requires rapid movements of arm in the right timing. However, gestures do not affect the outcome directly, yet affect the augmented dice. If the gesture is successful, the green sides of the dice increase compared to red sides (DM3). Output is provided with a LED stripe inner part of which reflects the private information like a secret notification from GM while the outer part demonstrates the public information like a success of the move performed (DM5). There is also a small display which only shows private messages from the GM (DM5).

Actions. Combat and Non-combat actions can be performed with WeaRPG thanks to the global gesture system which may be adapted to a wide range of actions in the game. Moreover, it also calculates dice-rolls and provides private communication (DM1). In an example scenario, a player encounters with an enemy and performs concentration and power gestures for activating a fireball spell. The gesture performance is fairly good, so the green parts of the dice increase. When the dice is rolled, luckily, green side comes which result in the elimination of the foe.

Visual Factors. The device includes a component which allows magnetic parts to be attached. As seen in Fig. 9, players can attach different figures which can reflect their factions, races or classes depending on the different game systems (DM4). Moreover, badges define the levels of the character (DM4). Other than the customization properties, a LED strip surrounds the device. Moreover, a display is embedded to the inner part of the device enabling only the player who wears it see.

8 Conclusion

As a result of our study we presented detailed explanation of all projects in our participatory design workshop with 25 participants. We also reflected our designerly comments on the devices, extracted design implications drawing upon the proposed designs, participants' comments, ideas, presentations and made a design speculation for a wearable device which can be used in TTRPG. Our findings demonstrated that an arm-worn device may contribute to augmentation of table-top games in terms of adding new gameplay styles, removing the undesired game processes and fostering the sensory experiences which lacks in conventional table top setting. Moreover, we conclude that non-distracting interaction techniques like gestures, tangible buttons, voice commands, simple visuals and audial feedback should be preferred in order to maintain the social environment without capturing players' attention to devices.

The speculative design we proposed should be tested with further user tests to understand its effect on player experience. However, a product which would works towards enhancing the gameplay experience with a better character identification can only be possible with a ready-to-hand product. Our study proposes the detailed explanation of conceptual projects, design implications and a speculative concept which adds to the field with user-oriented design knowledge on wearable device design for TTRPG and forms the path which goes to such ready-to-hand design.

Acknowledgements. We thank all volunteer participants of our workshop. We also thank our colleagues at KUAR for their detailed review in this paper.

References

1. Tanenbaum, J., Tanenbaum, K.: Envisioning the future of wearable play: conceptual models for props and costumes as game controllers. In: Proceedings of the 2015 International Conference on the Foundations of Digital Games - FDG 2015 (2015)
2. Tanenbaum, J., Tanenbaum, K., Isbister, K., Abe, K., Sullivan, A., Anzivino, L.: Costumes and wearables as game controllers. In: Proceedings of the 9th International Conference on Tangible, Embedded, and Embodied Interaction - TEI 2015, pp. 477–480 (2015)
3. Isbister, K., Abe, K.: Costumes as game controllers: an exploration of wearables to suit social play. In: Proceedings of the 9th International Conference on Tangible, Embedded, and Embodied Interaction - TEI 2015, pp. 691–696 (2015)
4. Bergström, K., Björk, S.: The case for computer-augmented games. Trans. Digital Games Res. Assoc. - ToDiGRA. **1** (2014)
5. Berkström, K., Jonsson, S., Björk, S.: Undercurrents a computer-based gameplay tool to support tabletop roleplaying. In: DiGRA 2010, p. 439 (2010)
6. Peitz, J., Eriksson, D., Björk, S.: Augmented board games - enhancing board games with electronics. DiGRA 2005 (2005)
7. Magerkurth, C., Memisoglu, M., Engelke, T., Streitz, N.: Towards the next generation of tabletop gaming experiences. In: Proceedings of Graphics Interface 2004 - GI 2004, pp. 73–80 (2004)
8. Mandryk, R.L., Maranan, D.S., Science, C., Inkpen, K.M.: False prophets: exploring hybrid board/video games. In: Extended Abstracts on Human Factors in Computing Systems - CHI EA 2002, pp. 640–641 (2002)
9. Antifakos, S., Schiele, B.: Bridging the gap between virtual and physical games using wearable sensors. In: Proceedings of the 6th International Symposium on Wearable Computers - ISWC 2002, pp. 139–140 (2002)
10. Cheok, A.D., Fong, S.W., Goh, K.H., Yang, X., Liu, W.: Human Pacman: a mobile entertainment system with ubiquitous computing and tangible interaction over a wide outdoor area. In: Proceedings of the 2nd Workshop on Network and System Support for Games - NETGAMES 2003, vol. 8, pp. 209–224 (2003)
11. Pagliarini, L., Lund, H.H.: Wearing the playware. Artif. Life Robot. **15**, 381–384 (2011)

12. Martins, T., Romão, T., Sommerer, C., Mignonneau, L., Correia, N., Torre, Q.: Towards an interface for untethered ubiquitous gaming. In: Proceedings of the 2008 Advances in Computer Entertainment Technology - ACE 2008, pp. 26–33 (2008)

13. Waern, A., Montola, M., Stenros, J.: The three-sixty illusion: designing for immersion in pervasive games. In: Proceedings of the 2009 CHI Conference on Human Factors in Computing Systems - CHI 2009, pp. 1549–1558 (2009)

14. Abe, K., Isbister, K.: Hotaru: the lightning bug game. In: Proceedings of the 2016 CHI Conference on Human Factors in Computing Systems - CHI 2016, pp. 277–280 (2016)

15. Lindley, C.A., Eladhari, M.: Narrative structure in transreality role-playing games: integrating story construction from live action, table top and computer-based role-playing games. In: DiGRA 2005, pp. 1–9 (2005)

16. Falk, J., Davenport, G.: Live role-playing games: implications for pervasive games. IFIP International Federation for Information Processing, pp. 127–138 (2004)

17. Foster, D., Linehan, C., Schoonheyt, M., Lawson, S.W.: Cool and the gang. In: Extended Abstracts on Human Factors in Computing Systems - CHI EA 2013, p. 1479 (2013)

18. Knudsen, S., Jakobsen, M.R., Hornbæk, K.: An exploratory study of how abundant display space may support data analysis. In: Proceedings of the 7th Nordic Conference on Human-Computer Interaction Making Sense Through Design - NordiCHI 2012, p. 558, New York, USA (2012)

19. Lindberg, S.: Participatory design workshops with children with cancer: lessons learned. In: Proceedings of the 12th International Conference on Interaction Design and Children - IDC 2013, pp. 332–335 (2013)

20. Svanaes, D., Seland, G.: Putting the users center stage: role playing and low-fi prototyping enable end users to design mobile systems. In: Proceedings of the 2004 SIGCHI Conference on Human Factors in Computing Systems - CHI 2004, pp. 479–486 (2004)

21. Zimmerman, J.: Video sketches: exploring pervasive computing interaction designs. Pervasive Comput. **4**, 91–94 (2005)

22. Tuuli Mattelmäki: Design Probes (2006)

23. Sengers, P., Gaver, B.: Staying open to interpretation: engaging multiple meanings in design and evaluation. In: Proceedings of the 6th Conference on Designing Interactive Systems - DIS 2006, pp. 99–108 (2006)

24. Bianchi-Berthouze, N., Whan, W., Patel, D.: Does body movement engage you more in digital game play? And why? In: Affective Computing and Intelligent Interaction - ACII 2007, pp. 31–32 (2007)

25. Isbister, K., Rao, R., Schwekendiek, U., Hayward, E., Lidasan, J.: Is more movement better? a controlled comparison of movement-based games. In: Proceedings of the 6th International Conference on Foundations of Digital Games - FDG 2011, pp. 331–333 (2011)

26. Calleja, G.: In-game: From Immersion to Incorporation. MIT Press, Cambridge, Mass (2011)

27. Carter, M., Harrop, M., Gibbs, M.: The roll of the dice in Warhammer 40,000. Trans. Digital Games Res. Assoc. - ToDiGRA. **1** (2014)

28. Rogerson, M.J., Gibbs, M., Smith, W.: "I love all the bits": the materiality of boardgames. In: Proceedings of the 2016 CHI Conference on Human Factors in Computing Systems - CHI 2016, pp. 3956–3969 (2016)

29. Magerkurth, C., Stenzel, R., Prante, T.: STARS – a ubiquitous computing platform for computer augmented tabletop games. In: Video Track and Adjunct Proceedings of the Fifth International Conference on Ubiquitous Computing – UBICOMP 2003 (2003)

30. Berzowska, J.: Electronic textiles: wearable computers, reactive fashion, and soft computation. Textile **3**, 58–74 (2005)

31. Aipperspach, R., Hooker, B., Woodruff, A.: The heterogeneous home. Interactions **16**, 35–38 (2009)
32. Helmes, J., Taylor, A.S., Cao, X., Höök, K., Schmitt, P., Villar, N.: Rudiments 1, 2 & 3: design speculations on autonomy. In: Proceedings of the International Conference on Tangible, Embedded, and Embodied Interaction - TEI 2011, pp. 145–152 (2011)
33. Auger, J.: Speculative design: crafting the speculation. Digit. Creativity **24**, 11–35 (2013)
34. Buruk, O.T., Özcan, O.: WEARPG: game design implications for movement-based play in table-top role-playing games with arm-worn devices. In: Proceedings of the 20th International Academic Mindtrek Conference - MindTrek 2016 (2016)

Critical and Speculative Wearables: Boundary Objects

Patricia Flanagan[(⊠)] [ID]

University of New South Wales, Sydney, Australia
patricia.flanagan@unsw.edu.au

Abstract. The emergence of a critical and speculative design philosophy is evident across a multitude of disciplines and practices and as such is articulated through various methodologies and terminology. Wearable technology is evolving into non-traditional devises, permeating forms from data clouds to implants, breaking down traditional borders of the body, of inside and outside. Our relationship with wearable artefacts poses questions that challenge the notion of who we are and how we understand ourselves. This paper takes a humanities approach to the future-self, exploring how the role of Human Computer Interaction (HCI) mediates experience through wearables. Examples are discussed from the author's practice as ARTographer (artist, researcher, teacher) as well as experience with skin psychology, machine assisted living and organ transplant. Wearables and smart textile prototypes created by the author's tertiary students are analyzed as: speculative following Stuart Candy's futurology methodology (2010); critically designed following Anthony Dunne's approach (2006); and critically made following Matt Ratto, Sara Ann Wylie & Kirk Jalbert's approach (2014). The article first describes and contextualizes the methodological and philosophical position of this approach, describing how it pertains to art and design practice, then elucidates potential directions for wearable HCI extending Star and Griesemer's notion of boundary objects (1989).

Keywords: Wearables · Boundary objects · Cyborganic · Prototyping · Diagetic prototypes · Critical design · Speculative design · Critical making

1 Humanistic HCI

The last twenty years has seen the growth of a humanistic approach to Human-Computer Interaction (HCI) that has profoundly influenced theories and methodologies of design, user experience, and usability. This evolution has involved a merger of two seemingly disparate disciplinary methods, whose differences are largely based on relationships. The relationship of scientific theory, methods and data; in contrast to the humanities relation to researcher and theory, methods and data. The end goals of the disciplines have unique characteristics – where science sees theories, methods and data as distinct and validity is legitimated by fact and reproducibility of results by different researchers; a humanities approach attributes uniqueness to every situation as it is always considered in relation to context. A 'text' is a term used in humanities to encompass almost any

© Springer International Publishing AG 2017
A. Marcus and W. Wang (Eds.): DUXU 2017, Part II, LNCS 10289, pp. 656–672, 2017.
DOI: 10.1007/978-3-319-58637-3_51

human-made work for example: novels, paintings, sculptures, wearables, designed artefacts. There are theorists within humanities who attribute a mental resources model to knowledge and would argue that each act of reading or encountering a work is a unique experience, that can be understood differently in different contexts. This view contrasts with the scientific notion of replication. "The reason for the difference between the science's objective research and the humanities' expert subject has to do with the nature of the object of enquiry. Whereas science seeks to discover laws and patterns that are hidden from everyday observation, humanistic "theories concern *what human beings already know and do*" [1]. Science aims to eliminate subjectivity, whereas humanities cannot discount it. Bruce Mau views the formation of each memory as a new experience, a mental construction unique from its source, and in this way memory is a process with potential for growth [2], "experience transforms how we think and who we are" [3]. User experience is an area of HCI that has grown from the overlaying of alternative philosophies onto more traditional scientific approaches to HCI. For example, Thecla Schiphorst's and Kristina Andersen's performative wearables based on Richard Schusterman's system of somaethetics [4] or Lian Loke's wearables drawing on Eugene Gendlin's focus-oriented psychotherapy [5] open new areas of enquiry. Critical approaches to HCI go beyond functionality and take aesthetics as a core value of design. The rise in interest is evident in Anderson and Pold's writing urging designers to consider a scaffold to support interface criticism that attend to:

- stylistic references;
- standards and conformance to tradition;
- materiality and remediation;
- genre;
- functional vs cultural dimensions of an interface;
- representational techniques;
- challengers to user expectations; and
- capacity for unanticipated use [6].

2 Defining a Critical and Speculative Approach to Wearables

2.1 Science Fiction Prototyping/Futurecasting

The ongoing speed of change in the technological environments of human-computer interaction and design makes it appealing as a focus for ongoing study by the humanities. Artists and designers offer insight as they adopt new materials and tools and use creativity to speculate design futures. Bardzell uses the term Technological Imaginaries, "that is, our capacity to look beyond individual technologies, which come and go, and improve our capacity to imagine futures, and specifically futures that can be made possible through technologies and technological imagination" [7]. Tech industry giants like Intel use prototyping to test future scenarios before they invest time and energy in mass production. Brian David Johnson from Intel promulgates Science Fiction Prototyping, through Future Vision(ing) also known as Future Vision Video. His scenarios are based on a version of strategic forecasting he calls Futurecasting – a combination of trend analysis with technology development and ethnography [8]. Johnson uses techniques from the movie and gamming industries, techniques we also see appropriated in crowd funding strategies. A less commercial approach is taken by Joanna Berzowska who believes the pervasive clothing and electronics industries "exclusive focus on health monitoring and surveillance technologies clearly reflects the (military and pharmaceutical industries) funding structures and fail to deliver appealing product ideas that respond to personal, social, and cultural needs" [9]. A decade after she made this claim there has been much work developing "wearable technologies that challenge social structures and assumptions in relation to embodied interaction (or concepts of knowledge)" but much of this research is documented only by grey material and is still somewhat invisible to mainstream HCI. Although a canon of literature is emerging, "current wearable technology design practices [still] represent a reductionist view of human capacity" [10].

Flanagan is one of a small group of early innovators in critical speculative wearables. This group of artists and designers are apt at using video techniques as a way to capture and document interaction or performative actions that often may be context specific, for example reactive to environmental conditions or biodata. Video documentation is a logical way to disseminate research, a way to leverage a project's reach when the fragility and instability of interactive prototypes may be difficult to transport. Future visioning adopt filmic and storytelling techniques and leverage social media platforms to engage far reaching audiences, and although not superior to first hand interaction with the pervasive apparel, negate other challenges of performative electronic artefacts such as freighting batteries or uncertified tech configurations, that often raise eyebrows and need negotiation to cross international borders and meet customs regulations. A sign that this grey material is merging into a canon of academic research in the field can be seen by the inclusion of an Interactivity Supplement focusing on the role of video as mediator of wearable concepts in the ACM SIGCHI 2013 conference on Human Factors in Computing Systems for Computer Human Interaction. The emergence of this session evidences the rise of techniques such as Future Visioning in design research that fall outside the commercial imperatives that form the focus of Johnsons approach – that of staying ahead of the market and predicting or designing future consumer needs and desires.

2.2   Designed Fiction

Designed fiction is another term that appears in academic literature – generally pertaining to science fiction and technological futures, it can be perceived as a subset of Future Vision Video. Anthony Dunne suggests Designed Fictions are rarely critical but tend to celebrate rather than question technology [11]. Designed fictions "are assemblages of various sorts, part story, part material, part idea-articulating prop, part functional software. []... A kind of object that has lots to say, but it is up to us to consider their meanings. []... Like artefacts from someplace else, telling stories about other worlds. []...Design fiction is about creative provocation, raising questions, innovation and exploration. ... It is a way of probing, sketching and exploring ideas" [12].

2.3   Diagetic Prototypes

David Kirkby coined the term Diagetic Prototypes, as an extension of his earlier research on Performative Artefacts. Drawing from the use of the term diegesis in film. "Cinematic depictions of future technologies demonstrate to large public audiences a technology's need, viability and benevolence … The performative aspects of proto-types are especially evident in diegetic prototypes because a film's narrative structure contextualizes technologies within the social sphere" [13]. A narrative is set up in which fictive prototypes appear to exist as everyday objects in the real world scenarios depicted. This is a speculative approach to design through methods of prototyping and storytelling as a means to design possible futures in the present that engage with the material ethics of new technologies (Figs. 1 and 2).

Fig. 1. HIF Cloud pop-up exhibition 2015, visitors at the opening function.

Fig. 2. HIF Cloud pop-up exhibition 2015, Dr. Rafael Gomez congratulating the participating artists, designers and scientists.

The following projects "Emotional" and "Instinct [In-stinkt]" were created in the HIF Cloud workshop 2015. They were developed working collaboratively across cultures, disciplines and international borders between undergraduate students from

Australia and Hong Kong to prototype future wearables[1]. Short video clips document production and use diagetic prototyping to convey narrative and human computer interaction. Two examples of prototypes created at HIF Cloud workshop are described by the artists/designers in the following statements:

"Emotional: Texting has become second nature to a generation that delights in connecting with each other through mobile devices. However, humans communicate on many levels simultaneously. In our technologically savvy world, people are finding it difficult to interpret the true meaning and emotional context of a text message deprived of the myriad of more-subtle signals given face-to-face. The aim of Emotional is to eliminate the interpersonal barriers that messages have created, in order to enrich communication through texting and other means of distant communication. The acrylic shoulder piece houses neo pixel (lights) and communicates emotion through a visual display of colour. The brass necklace houses vibration motors and communicates emotion according to different sequences of vibration. Studies have shown vibration is an effective silent method of communication that humans can train themselves to understand, as we learn to understand any language. ... Emotional communicates the emotional state of the person at the time they write the text message to the wearer ensuring the wearer can interpret the message accurately. Emotional uses Bluetooth technology to connect the garment to the user's phone. When a message is received, a signal is sent to the garment, which then reacts using varying degrees of vibration and light according to the sender's emotion. The person sending a text message will also wear the device as it has the ability to read emotion through a sensor"* [14] (Fig. 3).[2]

Fig. 3. Emotional 2015, Steve Buhagiar, Anna Kalma, Lauren Richardson, Liv Tsim, Ryan Ustinoff and Kosa Law Wing Yi. Materials: Laser cut acrylic, brass, neopixles, Arduino and vibration motors.

"Instinct [in-stinkt] is an illustrative sensory concept designed to amplify emotional experience, transcending boundaries and connecting people in new ways. Instinct [in-stinkt] acts as an emotional translator for vision, hearing and socially impaired users. To enable this, the user wears a discrete camera and microphone sensor that acts as their eyes and ears by deploying expression and voice inflection recognition sensors. The two actuators (mechanisms that convert energy into motion) were created in two separate countries and instinctually facilitate technologically improved emotional connection. The ... actuator exhibits emotion - these are expressed via the headpiece - creating an

---

[1] HIF Cloud workshop 2015 involved participants from Hong Kong Baptist University, Queensland University of Technology and Griffith University led by Dr. Flanagan, Dr. Gomez and Dr. Davis. Video documentary of the workshop is available at http://triciaflanagan.com/event/hif-cloud-workshop-2015/ Accessed Mar 6 2017.

[2] Emotion video documentary at https://youtu.be/3RBb0y76YJo Accessed Mar 6 2017.

interesting platform for discussion. The various shapes of the headpiece individually moving up and down in relation to the areas of the brain that specific emotion stimulates, creating a dramatic show of emotion that is not often acknowledged. The geometric shapes symbolize the organic shapes of the brain as a visual emotional structure. The actuator notifies the user by enriching and enhancing the emotional connection. The actuator sends tingles up their spine via the enclosed 3D printed actuator. Through natural instinct, the user will be conditioned to interpret the positive or negative feelings that have been projected. Neopixels simultaneously light up under the surface of the 3D printed component (placed along the spine) in a visual display to stimulate the other senses. Instinct [In-stinkt] is a product that stimulates an emotional response, an aspect of the human experience sometimes taken for granted" [15] (Fig. 4).[3]

Fig. 4. Instinct In-Stinkt 2015, David Chapman, Stella Franks, Holy Hutson, Chan Hong Wing and SiuYing Lam. Mixed media – cloth, servo motors, camera and microphone sensors, vibration motors, LEDs, 3D printed ABS plastic housing, Rasberry Pi and Arduino microprocessors.

2.4   Futurology

The futurist Stuart Candy [16] describes what he calls the 'cone of possibility space', which is a useful model for our purposes to illustrate the space of critical and speculative design. The model maps possible, probable, and preferable futures as subsets of possibility space. Candy developed this model from Norman Henchey's (1987) description published in Making Sense of Future Studies. Bezold and Hancock define the 4 P's of Henchey's model as: 1. "Possible, i.e. what might happen; 2. Plausible, i.e. what could happen; 3. Probable, i.e. what will likely happen; and 4. Preferable, i.e. what we want to have happen" [17]. The visual map depicts today as the starting point of the future, the closer to this point the more similar futures appear. The further away from the starting point the harder it is to predict as futures diverge, but clearly the choices made today or in the near future can have dramatic impact over time [18]. The tip of the cone starts at the present and as the cone radiates out it represents distance into the future. The cone is filled with the space of what is possible, a smaller cone in the center represents what is probable. Mainstream design usually takes place in the bounds of the probable, but critical and speculative work takes place in another conical section. In Candy's model it intersects the probable and breaks outside its border. Voros offers another version of the model [19] in which the space of preferable future is mapped to slightly overlap probable, encompass plausible, and reach across into possible futures [20].

---

[3] Instinkt video documentary at https://youtu.be/7Dx6iaHPntg Accessed Mar 6 2017.

2.5   Critical Design

Anthony Dunne adopts Candy's model with the addition of Hencheys 'plausible' to define the space of critical design. Critical design works by engaging people, and to do this successfully it must stay partially within the realm of the plausible so that a dialogue with reality can take place. In Dunne's 5 'P' diagram Present (now), Probable Futures, Plausible Futures, Possible Futures and Preferable Futures, the space of preferable takes a trajectory from the present across probable and plausible. However, what lies outside the space of the plausible is science fiction, it is fantasy, or magic, beyond what we understand as the laws of science. In Dunne's opinion a design that posits anything is possible, lacks the credentials for critical contemplation or dialogue that Dunne's products seek to engage. Dunne's projects look like products, familiar but strange, their ambiguity is a strategic attempt to engage thought. Within the space of the plausible are a range of alternative future scenarios that seem to make sense based on our knowledge of the present.

Probable futures can also be described as Descriptive Forecasting, usually based on a continuation of the present and short term trend developments. A reliance on probable

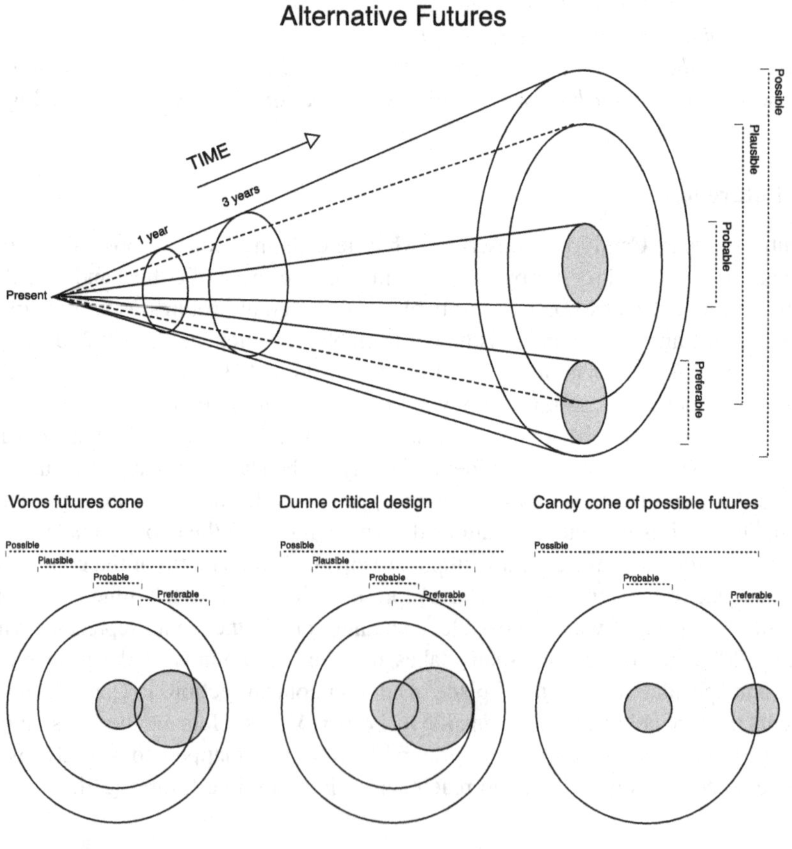

Alternative Futures

Fig. 5. Modelling futures. Source: adapted from diagrams by Henchy (1978), Berzold (1993), Voros [19], Dunne [23], Candy [16]

futures leaves us unprepared for wildcard events. Preferable futures offer alternative visions that may be very different to what presently exists, also known as Normative Forecasting or Prescriptive Futurism (Fig. 5).

The important point made by Candy, Dunne and Raby, Kirkby and in line with the authors view is that critical and speculative design are kinds of discursive interventions.

Susan-Elizabeth Ryan proposes that Speculative wearables are a subset of wearables that have grown out of academic institutions, due to their lack of engagement with the demands of consumer culture. They have trouble sustaining themselves in a commercial sense but are rather the physical articulation of experimental research ideas [21]. This is a new kind of 'cognitive speculation' [22] to borrow a term from literary theory, or we could borrow Rich Gold's term Evocative Knowledge Objects to describe an object which is designed to provoke conversations. Works such as those illustrated above can be seen as elaborate Cultural Probes, this is a term that views artefacts like litmus paper, they are put into a situation as catalysts to provoke responses and gauge conditions. In Dunne's view the 'use' of an object generates narrative spaces where users understanding or experience is changed or enlarged. This is a space between desire and determinism, a world he describes as the "infra-ordinary" [23].

2.6 Critical Making

Critical Making is a term used by Matt Ratto to describe forms of material-conceptual critique as an expansion of information systems, and science and technology studies (STS) that he feels have emerged due to increased engagement between design research and social studies. This approach has gained momentum driven by civic engagement in do-it-yourself movements, open source technologies, community commons licensing, hacker communities and events such as "maker" fairs. Ratto posits an alternative mode to the dominant deconstructive method to knowledge acquisition replaced by the notion of assemblage. Deconstructive modes that "reduce all of science and technology to semiotics seem to lack the power to provide substantive critique" [24].

2.7 Speculative Design

Speculative design is a term promulgated largely by Anthony Dunne and Fiona Raby in their book "Speculative everything" (2013). In the forward to Dunne's earlier publication "Herzian Tales," Crampton Smith draws parallels between fine-arts methodologies of – provocation, making ambitious, making strange – imported into product designer's vocabulary as "a speculative arena to imagine possible and impossible futures" [25]. Dunne reiterates that sentiment stating that speculative design portrays fictions that are "glitchy, strange, disruptive, and hint at other places, times and values" [11]. The relationship between creativity and critical thinking was a key question that Flanagan posed as the theme of the International Conference on Research Creativity – Praxis 2012. Across the presentations a common creative tactic evident, although different speakers identified it by different names, involved creating a sense of estrangement, a dislocation, a reframing of perspective. In 2013 in a talk at the MCA as part of Sydney Vivid festival Flanagan articulated this in terms of embracing mutation.

Creativity, inclusive of its experiments and failures is, in fact, something that is key to our evolution. Critical to maintaining art and designs relevance to the world it inhabits. All the terminology used to describe these practices clearly overlap a great deal, their difference often is rooted in their epistemology from different disciplines or cultural origins or the emphasis that the choice of literary term alludes. For example, 'critical' connotes a negative investigatory perspective, 'fiction' takes away any connection to reality. Speculative Design draws parallels with the continental philosophers of Speculative realism. The influence of Quentin Meillassoux [26] led to contemporary notions of *object-oriented ontology* [27] and *intra-action* as proposed by Karen Barad [28]. While this paper does not have the space to go into philosophy in any depth, (for more detail read Flanagan 2016 [52]) "Visceral design: Sites of Intra-action at the Interstices of waves and particles") these ideas underline an interest in breaking down traditional cognitive borders between human and non-human entities, bodies and things.

2.8   Displacement, Estrangement and Cognitive Dissonance

The hardware of computers and the soft materials of textiles are combining. Undermining the "cold hard metal of digital technology" Ebru Kurbak and Irene Posch of Stitching Worlds explore textiles technologies as a means to create electronic and high-tech objects from textiles. For example, they created a knitted sweater that appears ordinary, but with the addition of a battery becomes a transistor radio. "Wool, insulated copper wires and silk yarn spun with stainless steel can be used to knit resistors, capacitors and coils necessary to form a simple FM radio transmitter (http://www.translocal.jp/radio/micro/howtosimplestTX.html)" [29]. Maggie Otto's Earbeds are soft felt headphones designed for comfort to wear while relaxing and falling asleep. Earbeds feature couching with coils of stainless steel conductive thread. The only hard component is a flat round neodymium magnet. Although neither of these projects represents technical innovation, they exemplify a disruption in our assumptions about how such devises should look. This slippage between our expectation of an object's aesthetic and functional properties, is a kind of creative mutation that can be encountered as cognitive dissonance. Evelyn Fox Keller highlights the underlying controversy in this proposition, "namely that concerning the relationship between form and matter, where form is generally construed as active and matter as passive" [30]. By acknowledging the material properties of both the physical and ephemeral Kurbak, Posh and Otto attribute agency to what was formally considered dormant matter (Fig. 6).

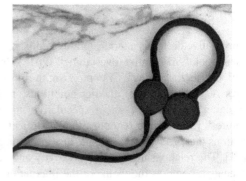

Fig. 6. Maggie Otto, Earbeds 2016

3 A Materials Approach

The industrial revolution spawned the machine age. The materials of this generation were iron and then steel, the proliferation of the latter, increased in viability through the innovation of the Bessemer steel-making process and steam engines. The increase in quality and decrease in cost was rapid, dropping from 170 US dollars per ton in 1867 to 15 US dollars by 1900 [31]. The second machine age was electronic, its expediential growth was due to the innovation of the transistor and its miniaturization to microchip, increased capacity and lowering price attributed the material of this generation – silicone. Graphene may hold the secrets of the next wave of innovation. Nano-chips with further miniaturization, increased capacity and lower price extend Moore's law beyond what we believed was possible. At nano-scales, mechanics change, quantum physics come into play and material properties undergo state changes as they are reconfigured. The only truly sustainable systems are natural ones and we are rapidly advancing our understanding of them. Innovation by integration with natural systems and the life sciences is moving beyond biomimicry, design with biology will integrate mechanics, electronics and chemistry to bio-design our future. The architecture of these systems is at the level of DNA, the sequencing and synthesizing of base pairs are becoming more financially viable following the Carlson Curve [32]. The tools of the industrial age were like mechanical extensions of our musculature. "Electronic machines can extend our minds, our subjective relationship with the world, our active relationship with other people" [33]. The machines of the future will extend the biology of our bodies and redefine our perception of our bodies and the world. But as Crampton Smith reminds us "Objects of use, in short, seldom have solely practical significance, but also carry ritual and symbolic meaning" [33]. This is more than evident in our long cultural history's intertwinement with clothing and bodily adornment, it is these artefacts integration with technologies which are the focus of wearables in this paper.

Art and design converge with material, biological and computer science, to design future wearable artefacts. In Sydney Australia, students of Dr. Flanagan and Dr. Knothe-Tate at the University of New South Wales created prototypes inspired by biomimicry. Collaboration at the intersection of courses in Smart Textiles and New Technologies and Mechanical Properties of Bio Materials produced creative results presented in a public exhibition as part of Sydney's Spark festival. For example, Nicholas Bentley's Zero Waste Regenerative Textiles proposes a fibrous compound that can be woven into textiles that will mimic natural regenerative processes of lizards, worms and starfish effectively healing rips or tears. In nature, incurring a wound triggers an influx of chemicals below the surface of the wound to form a fresh 'epidermis'. Bentley explains that "mature muscle and tissue cells revert to their immature state rendering them 'indifferent'. These indifferent cells are then programmed by 'macrophage cells' (similar to stem cells in utero) dividing into muscle tissue, skin, spinal cord and cartilage cells, although these cells are brand new they have an exact memory of the limb that was lost, allowing them to seamlessly regenerate an exact copy" [34]. Jasper Moy prototyped a synthetic fur that is antimicrobial, fire resistant, impact resistant and stain and water resistant made from aramid Kevlar fibers and Nomex yarns that he called Furture [35]. Tobie Kerridge and Nikki Stott are jewellery designers who collaborated with the bioengineer Ian Thompson to create a new breed of wedding ring [36]. They harvested the dental tissue of engaged couples, and grew it over a scaffold to create bone tissue rings that were effectively an amalgam of the couple's DNA. Similarly designer Sofie Boons collaborated with scientist Jodie Melbourne in the creation of nanoparticle infused, scented jewellery [36].

3.1   Nano Scale - Beyond the Visible

Advances in technology have enabled faster speeds, greater capacity and smaller scale to a point where technology is wearable. Moore's Law of computing where technology doubles in capacity and halves in scale every year, has gone beyond what was believed to be physically possible, beyond the point at which silicone, cut so small and packed so close, that it loses the functional property of conducting electrons and rather they begin to jump across them – a problem known as tunneling. Silicone coats naturally with oxide, a natural occurrence that grows on the silicone surface and acts as an insulator to create a conductive pathway. The oxide layer has enabled vertical scaling by stacking layers of silicone, it is possible to stack layers of silicone vertically in columns, extending the capacity and extending the validity of Moore's Law. To make the stacking as thin as possible that material science and nano-technology has opened-up the next generation of speed and scale by creating micron thick layers of material that are used as insulator sheets on top of thin layers of silicone. Vertical transistors known as Nano wires and Nano meter films are created through Atomic Layer Deposition with materials such as hafniem oxide. A new paradigm is evident by changing the architecture of the transistor completely. It appears that graphene can enable electrons to travel 1000 times faster than silicone. Sheets of Graphene, one atom thick, rolled into carbon nanotubes, use almost no energy and remain cool. Depending on the direction that the tubes are roles they can have different properties, from a

Fig. 7. Jasper Moy: Furture 2015

conductor to a metal. The architecture of computers themselves are set to be re-envisioned, to embrace the variability, and harness the properties of materials at the nano scale. Electrons behave in new ways in the field above a micron thick layer of graphene, electrons skim across the surface with almost no friction. This property indicates that some of the thermal limitations of silicon can be overcome with graphene. The new properties of the nano environment involve quantum mechanics that, will be harnessed to design and evolve computing electronics into machines beyond our current imagination (Fig. 7).

K. Eric Drexler's 1986 book *Engines of Creation* [37] enthusiastically paints a picture of Nano-systems of molecular machines, gears, pulleys, conveyor belts conjuring mechanical metaphors that are common in our descriptions of the body. R.D. Astumian's 2001 book *Making Molecules into Motors* [38] includes description of a molecular forklift and a ratchet and pawl created from triptycene and helicene. Drexler's speculative designs imagine nanoassemblers, teams of nanobot construction crews, in order to mass produce his machines [39]. This work has influenced future design of microbots which are largely still experimental or being tested. As we gain greater understanding of the Nano-world the implications appear boundless. For example, Flagelbots were inspired by biomimicry, they were an early generation nanobot, approximately thirty microns long, designed with a corkscrew mechanism to propel themselves along like naturally occurring e-coli bacterium which has a rotating cork screw tail. The difficulty of mobility in the human body is the viscosity of the environment so although Flagelabots swam well in water their application in the body was a challenge. One way to overcome issues of mobility associated with environments at a nanoscale is by using "swarms of swimming bacteria to serve as drug mules" [40]. Brad Nelson from ETH Zurich discovered a way to propel nanobots with ultrasonic waves and steer them magnetically [41]. The Eyebot fits into the needle of a syringe and carries a small dose of medicine. It is being used in eye surgery where it is navigated along blood vessels to deliver its payload. The nanobot is created from a magnetic material and receives direction from an array of powerful electro magnets that surround the patients head. Magnetic microbots are being developed to target cancer cells [42]. Microbots already in production include the Robo bee – a three centimeter bot that flies like a bee; Festo Ant that has jaws to grip and move things around; Water Striderbot that walks on water and jumps; Micro Tugbots that drag things around much larger than themselves; SRI Bots; Origami bots that self-assemble; Starfishbots that can be smaller than 1 mm and are used for biopsies; Micro Scallop Bots that can move through fluids like clams; Micro Motor Bots that are self-propelled nanobots; Pillcam is a one inch capsule that passes through the body in approximately eight hours. It can be swallowed and takes 360° pictures inside as it travels around the body. Pictures are sent wirelessly to a wearable computer.

Fabrics of nanofibers and buckytubes are very strong. Buckytube fibers are about 150 times stronger than silk. That implies that a nanosuit made of this material could be so fine, just five microns thick, that it would weigh as little as two teaspoons full of water. Like a layer of skin covering the body a nanosuit would be completely reconfigurable. Over a decade ago Hall described the vision for this material, constructed from two or more layers of scales, that could slide past one another. Each scale hollow and filled with a vacuum, and reflective to deflect transfer of heat through radiation.

The system he proposed operates as a Nano-scale reversible heat pump, pumping heat away from the body if it is too hot and if it is too cold acting as heat engines harnessing energy from heat flow from your body to outside. Hall's hypothesis includes Nano-suits configured to provide oxygen as in a molecular sieve oxygen concentrator enabling human habitation in extreme environments such as mountaintops or under the ocean [43].

3.2 Boundary Objects

What is the effect of future wearables on the self? If we imagine the city as a body, within this ecosystem our individual bodies are like floating wetland islands. We know that our bodies harbor vast ecologies of micro-organisms. It is estimated that foreign microbial cells outnumber human cells by a ratio of ten to one. This is a symbiotic relationship essential to our survival and key to our digestion and which helps us to resist infection. We conceptualize the body as an autonomous organism separated from the external world by a defined boundary, yet, in reality no biological integument exists that divides the interior from the exterior. "Biology recognized many bodies, corresponding to many skins: in higher organisms, there is the multicellular organism contained within an outer integument; in all organisms, cellular bodies are contained by nuclear membranes" [44].

Neri Oxman has been designing wearables at the intersection of materials science, synthetic biology and computer aided additive manufacturing processes. Her projects take direction in relation to the properties of the various media she is working with, in combination with templates developed around digital or physical growth. Her designs are inspired by morphological, biochemical and biological as well as synthetic-biological systems. Her methodology involves "technical challenges of templating bits, genes and atoms to inform design with biological principles on the one hand, and augment{ation of} these designs with biological functionality on the other" [45] ({...} inserted by Flanagan).

Zbigniew Oksiuta believes growing the biological materials for the products we make must be an integral part of the design process. Rather he proposes a future which will "one day allow us to create objects, machines or architectural structures not only from dead materials such as metal, concrete or plastic, but also through growing them in biological ways. Soon we will be able to create a new 'replicator' that will open the way for a new evolution – a hybrid between nature and culture occurring at speeds previously unheard of" [46].

An expanding definition of wearable artifacts includes wearables transplanted deep inside the body, circulated in our blood stream, beneath or on the surface of the skin, worn as body coverings, peripherally active in data clouds, locally active around the body, and distributed through the world wide web. Design thinking takes place across these fields integrally with that of their surfaces. Just as "the skin (the surface of the body) and the brain (the surface of the nervous system) derive from the same embryonic structure, the ecoderm" [47], wearable haptic interfaces are intra-related, dissolving the traditional corporeal borders of inside and outside the body. Extending this line of thinking further, augmented and virtual realities immerse our bodies in imaginary spaces. Pervasive apparel extends our senses and perception beyond the current limitations of our understanding of physics and human scale. The expanded notion of materiality in the creation of the wearables described above, lend to this approach, and so does the collaborative nature of the work typically involved in the creation of wearables – in the multiple stakeholders that engage with the artifact, the designer, the engineer, the scientist, the wearer and the viewer etc., – this leads to a definition of wearables as inhabiting a kind of translational space, where the art of good design is to "craft objects containing elements which are different in different worlds" - objects that hover on the periphery, "marginal to those worlds" [48], they are, to borrow a term from Susan Leigh Star, 'boundary objects' [49].

Wearables viewed as boundary objects are in some ways analogous to the skin itself. Didier Anzieu describes skin-ego as a state of progressive permeability. The notion of wearables as 'boundary objects' draws on the idea of skin-ego as one of permeable layers wrapping our sense of corporeality. A historical precedence can be found in the wet-wrapping techniques used in the treatment of psychotics in nineteenth century French psychiatry. The treatment involved wrapping patients in cold wet cloth and them warming them, whilst also keeping them physically surrounded by medical staff. Another precedence can be seen in the therapeutic burial rituals found in African culture or the practice of emersion in ice-baths by Tibetan Monks. Anzieu posits that "the Skin-ego has a dual anaclisis– a biological one based on the surface of the body and a social one based on the support of a united group of people attentive to what the person is going through at that moment" [50].

Beyond enhancing functionality, what is the experience of a foreign object in the body? In medical organ transplants the focus has naturally been on survival of the patient, but now that many transplants are viewed as routine operations, research into the psychological experience of transplants can help improve quality of life and indicate potential issues surrounding future wearables as they enter the body. From the dialysis ward Flanagan observed patients who depended on machines for daily survival. Mandy (Bebe) Taylor (1969–2003) was one such patient who spent a large portion of her later life seated in an armchair, one arm rendered useless connected by tubes to a dialysis machine filtering her blood. A transplant appeared to offer her freedom for a new life, but the psychological trauma proved otherwise. Anti-rejection drugs changed her hormones dramatically, her face changed shape, she grew facial hair, her smell was different, in fact she described the experience of not being able to recognize herself in the mirror. The dislocation was so severe that she stopped taking her medication and the kidney went into rejection. Whereas most people would affiliate their bodies with nature, left to nature Mandy faced death, her relationship to the machine was complete dependence. The natural world, away from a hospital was a dangerous world that was uninhabitable for her for any length of time. Para-olympian and model Amy Mulins' reflections on human machine relationships, was heavily tainted by the third party viewer. Born with fibular hemimelia, both her lower legs were amputated at the age of one. As a child she was teased for her disability, but as she grew older the younger generation, who had been raised on 'Transformers' and 'Manga' culture had a different perspective. Rather than a disability Amy Mulins now was viewed as having enhanced capabilities, not unlike super powers. Evelyn Fox Keller highlights the underlying controversy in this proposition, "namely that concerning the relationship between form and matter. Where form is generally construed as active and matter as passive" [51].

Our evolution has always been one of techno geneses, and this continues today as we design systems, artefacts, implantables and wearables, that integrate seamlessly with the body, where DNA itself becomes one of the designer's materials, new realms of possibility open at the Nano-scale. Designing wearables call for a renewed interest in materiality and the creation of tangible social artefacts where membranes between media are conceived as active rather than passive. Rather than separating inside from outside, membranes are permeable and constantly negotiated. In this way dialogical praxis extends to be inclusive of all entities: human to human, human to non-human, non-human to human, non-human to non-human as well as dissolving these binary notions to be inclusive of entities that are in varying degrees cyborganic.

Acknowledgements. This research was supported by the University of New South Wales, Art and Design PS41525 COFAS OP001. HIF Cloud Workshop would not have been possible without the generous support of Seeed Studios China and The Woolmark Company Australia. HKBU students received funding support from Hong Kong Baptist University Academy of Visual Arts to travel to Australia for the HIF Cloud exhibition. Thank you to Griffith University's Dr. Beck Davis, and Queensland University of Technology Dr. Rafael Gomez for hosting the HIF Cloud Australian event.

References

1. Bardzell, J.: Humanistic HCI: San Rafael, p. 36. Morgan & Claypool, California (2015)
2. Mau, B.: An incomplete manifesto for growth. http://www.manifestoproject.it/bruce-mau/. Accessed 25 Feb 2017
3. Bardzell, J.: Humanistic HCI: San Rafael, p. 37. Morgan & Claypool, California (2015)
4. Shusterman, R.: Thinking through the body, educating for the humanities: A plea for somaesthetics. J. Aesthet. Educ. **40**(1), 1–21 (2006)
5. Gendlin, E.: Palpable existentialism: A focusing-oriented therapy. Psychother. Aust. **20**(2), 36–42 (2014)
6. Andersen, C.U., Pold, S.E.: Interface Criticism: Aesthetics Beyond the Buttons, p. 41. Aarhus University Press, Aarhus (2010)
7. Bardzell, J.: Humanistic HCI: San Rafael, p. 59. Morgan & Claypool, California (2015)
8. Johnson, B.D.: Science Fiction Prototyping: Designing the Future with Science Fiction. Morgan & Claypool, San Rafael (2011)
9. Berzowska, J.: Personal technologies: memory and intimacy through physical computing. AI Soc. **20**(4), 446–461 (2006). doi:10.1007/s00146-006-0033-x. p. 447
10. Flanagan, P., Papadopoulos, D., Voss, G.: Ethics, power and potential of wearable technologies. In: Barfield, W., Ebrary, I. (eds.) Fundamentals of Wearable Computers and Augmented Reality, 2nd edn., pp. 31–56. Taylor & Francis, Boca Raton (2015). p. 32
11. Dunne, A.: Speculative Everything Design, Fiction, and Social Dreaming, p. 100. The MIT Press, Cambridge (2013)
12. Bleecker, J.: Design Fiction: a short essay on design fact and fiction. Near-Future Laboratory, pp. 6–8, 17 March 2009. http://www.nearfuturelaboratory.com/2009/03/17/design-fiction-a-short-essay-on-design-science-fact-and-fiction/. Accessed 25 Feb 2017

13. Kirby, D.: The future is now: diegetic prototypes and the role of popular films in generating real-world technological development. Soc. Stud. Sci. **40**(1), 41 (2010)
14. Hung, H.Y., Man, H.Y., Flanagan, T. (eds.): Wear next - an exploration into the future of wearables technology. In: Wear Next, p. 13. Hong Kong Baptist University, Griffiths University, Queensland University of Technology, Hong Kong (2016)
15. Hung, H.Y., Man, H.Y., Flanagan, T. (eds.): Wear next - an exploration into the future of wearables technology. In: Wear Next, p. 14. Hong Kong Baptist University, Griffiths University, Queensland University of Technology, Hong Kong (2016)
16. Candy, S.: The futures of everyday life: politics and the design of experiential scenarios. In: Dator, J. (ed.) ProQuest Dissertations Publishing (2010)
17. Bezold, C., Hancock, T.: An Overview of the Health Futures Field for the WHO Heath Futures Consultation. Retrieved from Geneva, IN: Ann Taket, Heath Futures in support of health for all, report of an international consultation convened by the World Heath Organisation, p. 72 (1993)
18. Bezold, C., Hancock, T.: An Overview of the Health Futures Field for the WHO Heath Futures Consultation. Retrieved from Geneva, IN: Ann Taket, Heath Futures in support of health for all, report of an international consultation convened by the World Heath Organisation, p. 73 (1993)
19. Voros, J.: A generic foresight process framework. Foresight **5**(3), 10–21 (2003). doi:10. 1108/14636680310698379. p. 16
20. Bezold, C., Hancock, T.: An Overview of the Health Futures Field for the WHO Heath Futures Consultation. Retrieved from Geneva, IN: Ann Taket, Heath Futures in support of health for all, report of an international consultation convened by the World Heath Organisation, pp. 69–91 (1993)
21. Ryan, S.E., Publishing, E.: Garments of Paradise: Wearable Discourse in the Digital Age. The MIT Press, Cambridge (2014)
22. Suvin, D.: The cognitive commodity: fictional discourse as novelty and circulation. Mosaic **19**(3), 85 (1986)
23. Dunne, A.: Hertzian Tales: Electronic Products, Aesthetic Experience, and Critical Design, p. 71 (2006)
24. Ratto, M., Hockema, S., Dekker, A., Wolfsberger, A.: Walled garden, p. 86 (2009)
25. Crampton Smith, G.: Forward to the 1999 edition. In: Dunne, A. (eds.) Hertzian Tales: Electronic Products, Aesthetic Experience, and Critical Design, p. ix. The MIT Press, Cambridge (2006)
26. Meillassoux, Q.: After Finitude an Essay on the Necessity of Contingency. Continuum, London (2009)
27. Bryant, L.R., Srnicek, N., Harman, G. (eds.): The Speculative Turn: Continental Materialism and Realism. Re.Press, Melbourne (2011)
28. Barad, K.: Posthumanist performativity: toward an understanding of how matter comes to matter. Signs **28**(3), 801–831 (2003)
29. Posch, I.: The knitted Radio (2017). http://www.ireneposch.net/the-knitted-radio/. Accessed 25 Feb 2017
30. Keller, E.F.: Beyond the gene but beneath the skin. In: Griffiths, P.E., Oyama, S., Gray, R.D. (eds.) Cycles of Contingency: Developmental Systems and Evolution, p. 31. MIT Press, Cambridge (2001)
31. Myers, W.: Bio Design - Nature, Science, Creativity, p. 11. Thames and Hudson, London (2012)
32. Carlson, R.: Biology is Technology: The Promise, Peril, and New Business of the Engineering Life, pp. 63–79. Harvard University Press, Cambridge (2010)

33. Crampton Smith, G.: Forward. In: Dunne, A. (ed.) Hertzian Tales: Electronic Products, Aesthetic Experience, and Critical Design, p. viii (2006)
34. Bentley, N.: Zero Waste Regenerative Textiles (2016). Unpublished
35. Moy, J.: Furture (2016). Unpublished
36. Miodownik, M.: The case for teaching the arts. Mater. Today **6**(12), 36–42 (2003). doi:10. 1016/S1369-7021(03)01224-0
37. Drexler, K.E.: Engines of Creation, 1st edn. Anchor Press/Doubleday, Garden City (1986)
38. Astumian, R.D.: Making molecules into motors. Sci. Am. **285**(1), 56 (2001)
39. Hayles, N.K.: Conecting the quantum dots: nanotechscience and culture. In: Hayles, N.K., Foushee, D., Los Angeles County Museum of Art (eds.) Nanoculture: Implications of the New Technoscience, Bristol, UK, pp. 12–13 (2004)
40. Guizzo, E.: Computer-controlled swarm of bacteria builds tiny pyramid. IEEE Spectrum (2010). http://spectrum.ieee.org/automaton/robotics/medical-robots/032510-swarm-of-bacteria-builds-tiny-pyramid. Accessed 25 Mar 2010
41. Chautems, C., et al.: Magnetically powered microrobots: a medical revolution underway? Eur. J. Cardiothorac. Surg. **51**, 405–407 (2017)
42. Martel, S.: Magnetic microbots to fight cancer. IEEE Spectrum (2012). http://spectrum.ieee. org/robotics/medical-robots/magnetic-microbots-to-fight-cancer. Accessed 25 Sep 2012
43. Storrs Hall, J.: Nanocomputers - The Transhumanist Reader, pp. 134–136. Wiley (2013)
44. Keller, E.F.: Beyond the gene but beneath the skin. In: Griffiths, P.E., Oyama, S., Gray, R.D. (eds.) Cycles of Contingenc: Developmental Systems and Evolution, P300-1. MIT Press, Cambridge (2001)
45. Oxman, N.: Templating design for biology and biology for design. Architectural Des. **85**(5), 100–107 (2015). doi:10.1002/ad.1961
46. Oksiuta, Z.: Breeding the future. Architectural Des. **79**(3), 48–53 (2009). doi:10.1002/ad.887
47. Anzieu, D.: The skin-ego: translated by Naomi Segal. In: Corporation Ebooks, pp. 103–104. Karnac Books Ltd., London (2016)
48. Star, S.L., Griesemer, J.R.: Institutional Ecology, translations and boundary objects - amateurs and professionals in Berkleys Museum of Vertebrate Zoology, 1937–1939. Soc. Stud. Sci. **19**(3), 412 (1989)
49. Star, S.L.: The structure of ill-structured solutions: boundary objects and heterogeneous distributed problem solving. In: Bond, A.H., Gasser, L.G. (eds.) Readings in Distributed Artificial Intelligence, p. 62. Morgan Kaufmann, San Mateo (1988)
50. Anzieu, D.: The skin-ego: translated by Naomi Segal. In: Corporation Ebooks, p. 121. Karnac Books Ltd., London (2016)
51. Keller, E.F.: Beyond the gene but beneath the skin. In: Paul, E., Griffiths, S.O., Gray, R.D. (eds.), Cycles of Contingency: Developmental Systems and Evolution, p. 300. MIT Press, Cambridge (2001)
52. Flanagan, P.: Visceral design: sites of intra-action at the interstices of waves and particles. In: Marcus, A. (ed.) DUXU 2016. LNCS, vol. 9747, pp. 3–15. Springer, Cham (2016). doi:10.1007/978-3-319-40355-7_1

Melissa's Concept Store: Physical Environment for Experience

Stella Hermida[1(✉)] and Adriano Bernardo Renzi[2]

[1] Universidade Federal do Rio de Janeiro, Rio de Janeiro, Brazil
stella.s.hermida@gmail.com
[2] Serviço Nacional de Aprendizagem Comercial/Senac-Rio, Rio de Janeiro, Brazil
adrianorenzi@gmail.com

Abstract. This research analyses the Melissa's concept store and its role in building users connection with the brand through users' experiences in the planned physical environment in comparison with the whole experience through physical and digital branches. For this purpose, it is used the flow-task observation technique to map users' routes and interactions within the concept store to understand the planned experience and its relation in building the brand's values. From the task-flow observation collected data, an analisys through all other interaction channels is conducted with the purpose of reckoning if the physical environment experience is construed as part of a full pervasive user experience based on the narrative journey concept.

Keywords: User experience · Concept store · Branding

1 Introduction: Experiences Built by Digital and Physical

This research aims to understand the projection of physical spaces to build experiences with a brand, approximating Interior Design and UX Design concepts. The experience with products goes beyond the product itself to build relations with any particular brand, as Nielsen and Norman [1] emphasize: "user experience includes all aspects of interaction of the final user with a company, its services and products".

Under and Chandler [2] are more specific when explaining about user experience and add physical interactions through all five human senses as part of the experience: it is the synchronization of elements that affect the experience of users with a company, with the intent of influencing their perceptions and behaviors regarding the process. Beyond the use of isolated systems, these elements include things to be touched, listened and smelled. It includes things that users can interact digitally and physically. The authors [2] also append that to create a true and memorable experience, the UX designer has to build a logical and viable structure for experience, as well as understand the important elements for an emotional connection of users with products, services and brands. A system built without acknowledging the needs and processes of users, it probably will miss opportunities to create fluid and integrated experiences.

As experiences with digital systems do not occur in a vacuum, systems are also integrated to experiences that take place outside it, in the physical world. The authors suggest

© Springer International Publishing AG 2017
A. Marcus and W. Wang (Eds.): DUXU 2017, Part II, LNCS 10289, pp. 673–682, 2017.
DOI: 10.1007/978-3-319-58637-3_52

concern with the effects of the tangible experience, since the ambience of use, as well as the devices part of the process, are important and can influence the experience process.

The experience process has to be acknowledged as a narrative journey [3], put together by the integration of short scenes (single interactions) to build one whole story. And for this, the integration of systems into an experience journey has to embrace the ambiance and contexts of use, as each part of it contribute and influence the users' relation with products and brands.

2 Melissa

As a case study for this research we used Melissa showroom store located at Oscar Freire Street, in São Paulo, Brazil. Melissa is a contemporary brand of shoes (Fig. 1), the principal branch of the company Grandene. The company started in 1971 as a plastic bottle producer for wines. In 1979, inspired by fashion tendencies in Paris and New York launches its first collection of plastic sandals under the name Melissa and in the same year becomes the first Brazilian brand to use branded entertainment in a Brazilian famous soup opera (Dancing Days) for national audience. In 1982, Melissa begins its international positioning and two commercials are released in Los Angeles and Las Vegas, and one year later, following the international new grounds intent, the brand launchs new models signed by famous stylists, such as, Jean Paul Gaultier, Thierry Mugler, Jacqueline Jacobson and Elisabeth De Seneville. Each one of them using Melissa shoes as part of their new collection shows. The Melissa Dorothée Bis sells more than 4 million pairs the next year. In 1988, the brand is a world success and the shoes are present in all the coolest girls' feet around the world.

Fig. 1. Sample of Melissa's shoes based on plastic materials.

In 1993 the brand takes a break in order to re-structure the company and re-think its position and stand in the fashion industry. From this break, Melissa re-launchs itself and partner with the Canadian designer Patrick Cox the following year. And soon after, the international model Claudia Schiffer, uses the brand in promotional campaigns in magazines, TVs and fashion shows.

In 1998, Melissa starts a repositioning campaign to transform the brand into fashion accessory and in 1999 the company creates the Mellissa division, focused only on the fashion shoes brand.

With the turn of the century, the company is ready for a new fashion moment and, on its backstage, a new campaign is developed for a success repositioning of the brand. The following years were marked by successful sequence of new releases and experiences approaching even more their new collections to fashion events, strengthening the brand among consumers.

The company believes in the direct participation of consumers (users) in building the company's image, and therefore, has been cultivating throughout the years the delineation of communication elements that relate to their consumers. In their manifest, attitude is their concept and message, transmitted through objects around us, the places we are and what we consume. The company preaches a conscious decision to make a stand in the verge of new ideas and to open possibilities throughout the world and our diversity of cultures. Melissa intends to position itself as beyond simple shoes, but a design object that transcend form and concept to transmit the message of the new, the transformation, the modern, the creativity, the technology, the sustainability and the alternative way. From its bottle production business model, it chose to be a fashion accessory and create new fashion tendencies, from research and creative partnerships, and build a fashion experience.

This reflects, from the architecture point of view, in a store with a different purpose of just selling shoes. Characteristics of the showroom (Figs. 2 and 3) suggests an intent to build experiences of users with the brand, resulting in small dimension shop window displays, visual displays with constant transformations, themed spaces to create an atmosphere, a front facade retreat opposing the urban integration and ambience structures that help build value to their products and brand.

Fig. 2. Concept store in São Paulo

The physical space becomes an important part of the narrative experience and can influence consumers' decisions of acquisition and help complete the digital-physical relation. The idea of physical and digital stores being branches of the same company gets strength from Chris Anderson's first discussions regarding the long tail [4] business in 2004 and

Fig. 3. Concept store in São Paulo.

Brysjolfsson et al. [5] (2006) articles about mixed business (with both physical and digital stores as selling ramifications) and the relation between the online store and the brick and mortar stores as a mean to reach a larger group of consumers. As presented in Renzi's research [6] comparing bookstores' digital and physical ramifications, both ramifications of the store must complete each other in building a narrative in order to expand its possibilities of full potential (Fig. 4).

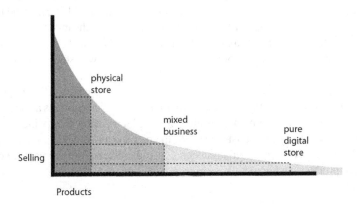

Fig. 4. Selling possibilities comparison between physical stores, mixed business and pure digital stores – from Renzi's research, 2010.

Unlike Renzi's digital-physical comparison to understand the reach of selling possibilities, this research on Melissa's stores intends to go beyond and perceive the experience of users as a journey through a cross-channel interaction, what is the role of Melissa's concept store, the relation to their brand experience and the links through different channels.

3   Concept Stores

When considering commercial spaces as places to communicate the brand through experiences with products and the space itself, it is important that users help build this relation in scenes, parts of the whole narrative. These spaces, such as the observed Melissa store, are known as concept stores. The physical store is composed by architecture and graphical elements, its volumetric composition, its insertion in urban landscape and representation of a brand [7].

The brand experience environment provides the experience of the brand to users, transmitting its values and meanings in contextual meanings. According to Peirce's creation scheme, a planned environment can establish a consumption incentive intent through its set of elements in relation to a brand. The spatial distribution of components, the flow of trajectories, the disposition of products and interactions transmit to users meanings and significances of the brand in semiotic processes.

The environment highlights representational meanings and values of the brand in every moment of interaction with users. Its symbolic meanings show multiple possibilities and discoveries in the communication process with consumers to set up a connection of experience with the brand.

The principal intent of the Melissa concept store is to create emotional relations with consumers through experiences. The store presents shoes with no price tags, simulating an art exhibit where each shoe concept is exposed individually as a piece of art. The planned trajectory expects to bring an art gallery felling to empower the experience, the brand and its products.

4   Flow-Task Observation in Concept Store – São Paulo

The execution of the technique had the objective of analyzing consumers' flow, behavior and interaction with the planned ambiance. Precedent to the observation, the researcher visited the location for permission to use the technique, for determination of points of observation and for a first sketch of the environment in order to map the store in a visual matrix and facilitate the observation of consumers (users) in real time (Fig. 5).

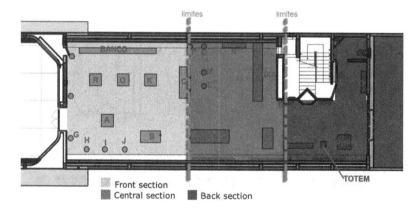

Fig. 5. Map of the concept store to help the task-flow observation with costumers.

For the execution of the technique, the researcher positioned at a chosen spot to visualize all and every corner of the store. From there, it was possible to follow consumers (users) throughout their experience. Every user who entered the store could be randomly selected for observation, whenever possible.

While observed, users were categorized by gender, approximate age and purchase decisions inside the store. Each user's route was observed and drawn in the store's map for comparison. A total of eighty-seven users were observed in 3 days.

With the help of the flow-task observation, it was possible to understand the most common route of users, their interactions with brand experience points, products exhibition, colors, forms, textures, light and its relation to Melissa's elements of communication and values. It was objectified through the observation of users interactions in the ambiance and their route to see if the pre-definition of brand experience points were effective and contributed to the experience, acquisition and empowerment of the brand through users.

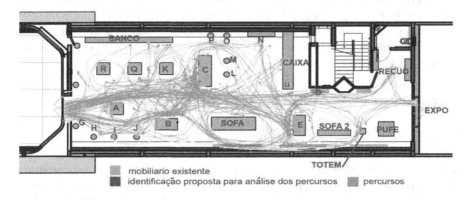

Fig. 6. Store map showing consumers' routes in green, furniture and structures in gray and red letters for identification during the flow-task observation (Color figure online)

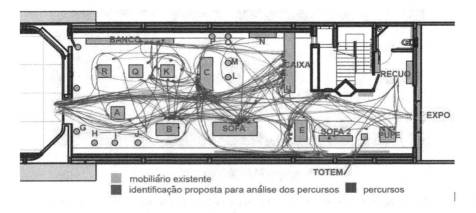

Fig. 7. Store map showing consumers' routes in purple, furniture and structures in gray and red letters for identification during the flow-task observation. (Color figure online)

As predicted by the purpose of the concept store, most part of users observed during the research did not purchase any product inside the store. The sixty-nine users conducted a similar pattern (green lines) of flow, as shown in Fig. 6, instigated to follow a trajectory similar of an art gallery. The map evinces the central space of the store as common path to users observe the exhibit of new concept shoes, but theses users showed a deeper interaction with the store, reaching a broader space for browsing and experiencing the environment to its totality.

Just a small portion of consumers observed while visiting the store, bought on site, totalizing only 18 people. The Fig. 7 shows a purple pattern that could misguide into similarities with the green paths, specially regarding the interactions in central space of the store. But the buying users were more objective on their visit, focusing principally on the first part of the store, using sofas or any other sitting furniture to try shoes (points B, C, sofa, E, D and the cashier to purchase), in what seems to result in shallow

Fig. 8. Melissa's homepage with featured content simulating fashion magazines' organization.

interaction with the planned ambience. All 18 observed users, executed routes focused only on the frontal and central areas of the store. And only half of this category visited the back part of the store. As a result, a new perfume release, located in the back of the store was hardly approached by these users (Fig. 8).

5   Online Store

Visiting Melissa's website (www.melissa.com.br) the visual feeling and organization of topics is very different from other e-business. From the starting point at Melissa's home-page, informational and visual characteristics differ from the usual online store with sales ads, featured products, new releases, product names and prices. At first impact, the website presents itself more focused in the experience with fashion and with art. Visual-written contents are visually separated in animated blocks with mouse-over interactions. These are not organized by aligned sections, but are spread in disorganized canvas (on purpose) that takes its reference on fashion magazines. The topics are majorly focused on style, art, fashion "happenings", and have indirect relation to shoes wearing. Each of these contents offers a link to an associated content (that has a direct connection with shoes), to fashion magazine games and to storytelling actions, where users can see videos with artists involved in an specific exhibit, sponsored by Melissa, and their impressions exposed like Instagram's short videos. All these possibilities of interaction end up in shoes, but with a fashion magazine feeling. For instance, when playing the Party persona game, the users' answers lead to a new year's eve perfect shoes suggestion. Finding your perfect color for 2017 (a tradition in Brazil) has content presented as a teenage blog with tips associating personal characteristics to shoes.

However, when interacting through the main top navigation, the magazine feeling sometimes escapes from the proposed experience, as internal pages can be very different visually and organizationally from each other, leaving only the top section as a common pattern. The information architecture can be confusing as users go deeper into the struc-ture, resulting in difficulties to find their way back to the beginning or to cross horizontal-linked contents in their architecture structure. When going to the online store (lojame-lissa.com.br) from the magazine feeling site, it is impossible to go back. Users have to open a new browser window to start over. Even the storytelling idea to increase the experience has its flow broken, since the video has its source from Youtube and the end of it brings video options related to the viewer's Youtube preferences, instead of related videos to the exposed content by Melissa. Some articles with poetic-fashion intent, such the example "teu espaço te transpassa" (your ambiance runs through you), take users to written poetic content that ends with a link to the outside: a visual blog from Melissa makers, a complete different website that presents itself as a project to connect the brand to writers, artists, designer etc., that are reference throughout the country. But the link takes users to a page so different that loses the connection between the two points, breaking the flow.

6   Conclusion: Concept with Broken Experience

The physical concept store in São Paulo (Melissa has concept stores also in New York and London), called "Galeria Melissa", clearly does not intent to sell shoes within its facilities. The structure and ambience concepts showing the company's new tendencies and fashion features are focused in constructing a bond with users through their brand experience. The experience hardly urge consumption action from users while integrated in their brand experience, as seen from the users' flow observation, but it strengthen the values of Melissa's brand with their consumers, creating a fashion reference that can result in future acquisition in stores focused in selling shoes. Symbolic meanings sticks with users while experiencing the planned ambiance, creating brand awareness and building new relations consumers-product-brand, as Norman and Nielsen emphasized in their conception about user experience: "user experience includes all aspects of inter-action of the final user with a company, its services and products". The company has been able to spread the Melissa brand awareness around the word to the point of creating an unique smell, injected on every plastic shoe they produce, that soon became known as the "Melissa smell". Their branding actions created a product-consumer relation built on ambiance, experiences and situations of symbolic significances that is absorbed through visual, material, colors and smell.

In this sense, a brand experience is built by a mash up of sensations that strengthen the brand through users. However, thinking of user experience as a narrative composed by short scenes [3], these sensations does not work in a flow motion, as the experience is not pervasive and show break points, especially and thinking of the digital "scenes" of the journey.

The physical concept stores (São Paulo, New york and London), for instance, provide an ambience experience that is fulfilled within it. While users are in the planned ambiance, users are filled with symbolic sensations related to the brand, and the bond with the brand may be strengthen when users leave the store. But there is a break in the narrative of experience, as the online part of the company doesn't relate to the physical concept.

When users have a strong relation with the brand, and its products, it is natural that they stretch the experience through other channels of media, going from physical concept ambiances to selling stores, short videos, ad campaigns, social media, website etc. Companies such as Disney and Lego, use different medias to build a full experience and complete users' story.

Melissa uses their website as a base for new features and releases, with graphics and contents that resemble fashion magazines, and within it, integrate short videos to help compose the experience. Outside the website, its Facebook page shows synchronicity and presents content that matches the website's features, with posts that continue the fashion magazine experience. But this experience doesn't follow on other company's networks such as Instagram or Twitter. Different Melissa Stores have independent Instagram profiles (club melissa poços, club melissa recife, club melissa palmeira etc.) and post irrespective contents with no link to the website's features. Each part of the interaction shows a broken link to the whole, as if users did not intent to jump from one channel to the next. These breaks may not affect the relation consumer-brand too hard, as Melissa's fashion strategies show to feed constantly the connection, but creates a noise on the back.

Today, Melissa's multi-channel integration, analyzed from users' journey perspective, lacks the cross-channel user experience. The concept stores create isolated experiences that do not match the whole. Even if compared to each other, the galleries in São Paulo, London and New York also function with no relation between them. They are "unique" experiences that strengthen users bond with the brand, but miss the opportunity to bring the experience to another level. With all technological possibilities advancing and multiplying around us, Melissa could upgrade the physical concept stores to digital interaction possibilities, unifying physical and digital into interactive space environments and continue users stories through other channels, each part contributing with short scenes to help build a full experience narrative. With innovation and interactions evolving to new levels in the next few years [8], new expectations surface in users and a more integrated experience may be needed.

References

1. Norman, D.: Systems thinking: a product is more than the product. Interactions 16(5), 52–54 (2009). http://interactions.acm.org/content/?p=1286
2. Unger, R., Chandler, C.: A Project Guide to UX Design – for User Experience Designers in the Field or in the Making. Peachpit Press, Berkeley (2009). 288f
3. Renzi, A.B.: Experiência do ususário: a jornada de Designers nos processos de gestão de suas empresas de pequeno porte utilizando sistema fantasiado em ecossistema de interação cross-channel. Doctorate thesis. 239p. Escola Superior de Desenho Industrial. Rio de Janeiro, Brazil (2016)
4. Anderson, C.: The Long tail. Wired magazine, October 2004. http://www.wired.com/wired/archive/12.10/tail.html
5. Brynjolfsson, E., Hu, Y.J., Smith, M.D.: From Niches to riches: anatomy of the long tail. MIT Sloan Manage. Rev. 47(4), 67–71 (2006). Massachusetts, summer
6. Renzi, A.B.: Usabilidade na procura e compra de livros em livrarias online. Dissertation (Master of Science). Esdi – UERJ, Rio de Janeiro (2010)
7. Kothler, P., Keller, K.L.: Administração de marketing, 12th edn., pp. 101–750. Pearson Prentice Hall, São Paulo (2006)
8. Renzi, A.B., Freitas, S.F.: Delphi method to explore future scenario possibilities on technology and HCI. In: Marcus, A. (ed.) DUXU 2015. LNCS, vol. 9186, pp. 644–653. Springer, Cham (2015). doi:10.1007/978-3-319-20886-2_60

Wearables Design: Epistemic Cultures and Laboratory Performances

Valérie Lamontagne(✉)

Design and Computation Arts, Concordia University,
1515 St. Catherine Street West, Montréal, QC H3G 2W1, Canada
valerie@3lectromode.com

Abstract. This paper investigates four case studies of wearables laboratory production and their relationship to performativity. By investigating the epistemic cultures of technological innovation and design within the field of techno fashion, the paper aims to prove that performance is a seminal driving force in the creation and use of wearable devices and fashion-tech designs.

Keywords: Wearables · Performance · Laboratory culture · Design · Embodiment · Interface culture · Textiles · Prototyping

1 Introduction

This paper investigates how laboratory performativity and epistemic cultures of technology and research influence and seed the design outcomes of techno-fashion and wearables. The sites investigated reflect how the complex intersection of materials, technologies and situated practices of research influence and shape techno-fashion development. This paper seeks to argue that the events produced within the context of the wearables atelier/laboratory are aligned with the notion of "performativity" as explored in other disciplines such as performance, theatre, sociology more specifically Science Technology and Society (STS). STS theories argue that fundamental scientific research is developed on the basis on performative amalgams of machines and humans [1–6]. The usefulness of STS literature is in examining scientific research occurring within laboratory contexts within a frame that encompasses the myriad elements at play in a lab from: people, machines, the weather, methodologies, modes of inscription and the passing of time. For this reason STS describes events taking place in the laboratory—such as material testing, prototype development, fabrication of new materials, note taking and technology testing—as "performative." I believe it is useful to bring this type of large scope analysis to the production analysis of wearables because of its complex nature. Wearables bring together a multitude of expertise along with many use outcomes that include the human body, fashion, technology, and public perceptions. The nature of my desire to use "performative" as a lens through which to better understand wearables is because it permits a leveling of influences, where human and non-human contributions can be compared and valued with equally stakes and impacts.

© Springer International Publishing AG 2017
A. Marcus and W. Wang (Eds.): DUXU 2017, Part II, LNCS 10289, pp. 683–703, 2017.
DOI: 10.1007/978-3-319-58637-3_53

2   Epistemic Cultures of Wearables Laboratories

STS theories of performativity owe much to mid-twentieth century sociological and anthropological theories of performance, which directed research towards performance as a mode of analysis and a methodology for understanding various social and organizational structures [7–14]. However, today's STS theories on performativity—expanding into the unheralded territory of combining scientific, material and social research—question the core assumption that material research is objective, consistent or even reproducible. Instead, STS theories of performativity argue for a nuanced, unique and situated (location-based) analysis of laboratory cultures that includes the many converging actants (machines, material, practices, tools, people etc.) participating in research on a "performative" scale. STS theories of performativity applied to wearables sites of production—such as university laboratories; media arts centers; design studios; and DIY ateliers—offer unique ways of understanding this emergent form of techno-artistic research from within.

An STS/performative lens gives due consideration to the many complex narratives, dynamic agendas and focuses at play in the wearables laboratory ranging from: the material, social, technological and economic. In my opinion an STS model sheds important light onto numerous intersecting events taking place during the course of developing a prototype and design for wearables. This focus is scalable from the material manipulation and knowhow of the specific laboratory; to the community and audience around the building of objects from researchers, curators to consumers; the access and expertise around new technologies from the digital to the analogue; and finally the economic structures built around these testing and production sites that range from private to public sector.

It is my argument and belief that without a framework to compare the specific range of events that unfold in these unique (and often hybrid) laboratories engaged in wearables and fashion-tech innovation, it is difficult to compare, understand or even critique current wearables innovations. For obvious reasons, not all designs studios are structured around the same material resources, goals, technological leverages, or economic structures. While some laboratories focus on fundamental research intended for wearable technologies that have yet to be invented; other ateliers engage in the iteration process of creating an irresistible consumer product based on existing components and production practices; while other labs are principally concerned with putting on a good show for their arts audience; and finally an open-design community will be focused on sharing knowhow and making the process as transparent as possible. Because wearables are being innovated in varied contexts from university laboratories to media arts organizations, product design studios or small DIY communities, it is important to speak about what happens behind the scenes of production before comparing the results.

STS theories of performativity are engaged in looking at the events unfolding in the laboratory wherein weighted consideration is given to the human and non-human contributors within the developmental process of researching, testing, designing and iterating to a final wearables invention. I believe that this exciting post-humanist perspective wherein machines and materials drive and shape human behaviors as much as humans shape machine and material outcomes opens up to a series of possibilities for considering the co-creation of wearables from a wider scope than ever attempted. Herein I propose to take the time to look at the unique practices of four wearables design laboratories with a lens to value and consider four specific contributing factors: the material, the social, the technological and the economic.

3 Wearables: Four Case Studies

The four specific case studies pertaining to wearable technology ateliers/laboratories that I have chosen to expand on and explain through the lens of STS theories of performativity feature: Joanna Berzowska's XS Labs at Hexagram Institute of Concordia University, Montréal, Canada; Anouk Wipprecht's works executed at V2_ Institute for the Unstable Media, Rotterdam, Netherlands; Diffus Design's Copenhagen techno atelier; and finally my own DIY production platform, 3lectromode, situated at the intersection of fashion, art, and technology.

3.1 XS Labs

The first case study explores XS Labs, situated within the Milieux Institute (formerly Hexagram Institute) at Concordia University and directed by Joanna Berzowska, associate professor of design and computation arts. Joanna and I have been colleagues in the same department for over a decade, and by virtue of intersecting interests, I have had the privilege of witnessing the evolution of her studio, and even curating some of its works in international exhibitions, such as *Sartorial Flux* (A+D Gallery, Columbia College, Chicago, 2006) and *Electromode* (2010 Vancouver Olympics). With XS Labs nearby in the same institution where I teach, I have benefited from its proximity by intersecting with and learning from the research conducted in its laboratory, and in sharing resources and information. Furthermore, being embedded at Concordia, XS Labs has provided a research focus on wearables engineering and crafting, thus attracting researchers and collaborators both locally and internationally, to the benefit of the local academic milieux, as well as the wider professional wearables community.

Background. Berzowska's background combines degrees in design and mathematics in an era before computation arts, interaction design, or digital-arts education. As an academic researcher, her lab is focused on innovation, knowledge building, education, publishing, and lecturing in the field of e-textiles, new materials for wearables, and interaction design. Important research grants from the Fonds de Recherche du Québec—Société et culture (FRQSC) and the Social Sciences and Humanities Research Council of Canada (SSHRC) have guided the lab's focus toward a combination of fundamental research, design concerns, and the training of what Berzowska calls "highly qualified people" (HQP). XS Labs seeks to innovate in design via new technologies, while responding to such designs' impact and poetic resonance on the body's actions. In this way, how interactive garments script the body is a central question for the lab. Having studied at MIT's Tangible Media Lab, the founding institution for wearables technologies, Berzowska is well versed in the challenges and aims of creating meaningful design that can inspire both industry and art.

Laboratory Culture. XS Labs, a design research studio founded in 2002, focuses on innovating in electronic textiles and responsive garments. Says Berzowska, "A core component involves the development of enabling methods, materials, and technologies—in the form of soft electronic circuits and composite fibres—as well as the exploration of the expressive potential of soft reactive structures" [15]. XS Labs works at the intersection of two communities: researchers and students. In this way, the laboratory's epistemic culture combines material and design innovation via the continuing education of her student researchers. Berzowska describes her lab as a playful and experimental space where students are encouraged to try new ideas and materials, thus creating a collaborative, collegial approach to research-creation.

Technology. Core research at XS Labs is focused around the creation of design platforms for emergent technologies. The studio approaches new technologies with a concern and sensibility to make design "softer," and hence more wearable. Motivated by the lack of e-textiles and poor wearability in traditional HCI applications, XS Labs has cultivated a palette of techniques and materials better suited to embodied and worn-interaction platforms. Berzowska explains that XS Labs is:

> particularly concerned with the exploration of interactive forms that emphasize the natural expressive qualities of transitive materials. We focus on the aesthetics of interaction, which compels us to interrogate and to re-contextualize the materials themselves. The interaction narratives function as entry points to question some of the fundamental assumptions we make about the technologies and the materials that drive our designs [16].

From a technical standpoint, the studio works with materials including conductive fibers, reactive inks, photoelectrics, shape-memory alloys, conductive inks, LEDs, thermochromic inks, motors, and more. While cutting-edge material inventions propel the studio's designs forward, the cultural history of textile fabrication processes (weaving, stitching, embroidery, knitting, beading, quilting) also inform how this innovation will take shape. These experiments allow the construction of "complex textile-based surfaces, substrates, and structures with transitive properties" [16]. Examples of this high-tech craft approach include the *Karma Chameleon* research project, carried out in collaboration with Dr. Maksim Skorobogatiy, Canada Research Chair in Photonics at the École Polytechnique de Montréal, which involved a mixture of nanotechnology and traditional weaving.

Body/Interaction. XS Labs' designs reconsider how interaction through soft and textile networks can foster novel, and at times ludic or even dark-humored forms of physical and body-based interaction. As Berzowska notes, new materialities "promise to shape new design forms and new experiences that will redefine our relationship with colour, texture, silhouette, materiality, and with digital technology in general" [17]. This body-material-focused design approach has influenced many of the studio's early designs, like the *Memory Rich Clothing* series, featuring dresses that invited strangers to touch the wearer in order to activate the material transformation of thermochromic inks (*Spotty Dress*, 2004); or garments that beckoned you to whisper into them so as to activate a series of lights and thus tangibly display the act of intimacy (*Intimate Memory Shirt & Skirt*, 2003). In this way, the technology arrives at its logical (or illogical, in the case of self-described absurdist or transgressive projects) placement and interaction, focused on creating meaning as opposed to efficiency, productivity, or other more mainstream Wearable Tech strategies.

This visceral and whimsical approach to designing new modes of interaction with emergent materialities is succinctly illustrated in the *Captain Electric and Battery Boy* (CEBB) research project (2007–2010). Initiated on the occasion of a class titled "Second Skin and Softwear," which Berzowska taught at Concordia in the winter of 2008, the project took off with a student brief to create "Human Powered Illumination." The results propelled further investigations (and a 2008 summer workshop) into haptic platforms for power generation and storage via wearables. Exploring the potential for garments to harness the body for electricity, the project produced three designs, which playfully highlight our co-dependent relationship with electricity. Inspired by conceptual frameworks of co-dependence, parasitic systems, or even extreme power relations between users and their need for or use of electricity, the designs stage a series of physical interactions that both amplify and visualize this exchange, or power dynamic.

The results of CEBB showcase erratic, intransigent garments that provoke the user to pull, scratch, and wrestle comically with its materiality, in the aim of generating future available wattage. Fittingly named *Itchy*, *Sticky*, and *Stiff*, the garments stage body-generated energy systems, capitalizing on various strategic, gestural platforms of activation. Building on intuitive actions, such as pulling, pushing, and rubbing, the garments activate both the collection of energy, as well as its visualization through a variable output (sound or light). For example, *Itchy* invites the wearer (or others) to rub the concentric circles of its wool collar, thus creating static energy that powers a series of LEDs. *Stiff*, meanwhile, projects a parasitically passive platform for energy creation that necessitates the participation of an external player, who must push its attractive little back hump in order to activate a recoding only available to the wearable's wearer. Alternately, like a cat trying to scratch its own back, the wearer can also seek to collide with objects so as to activate the awkwardly placed bump. Finally, *Sticky* features a waist-activated lever system that both restricts and benefits from the wearer's natural arm/hand actions to feed its need for energy. Admittedly, these are at once awkward and provocatively thoughtful systems that force us to consider the human-energy relationship in a new light, as well as the concept of "natural" forms of wearable interaction scenarios.

These three CEBB wearables force the wearer to "work" in order to have access to energy. Each fashion-tech garment forces the wearer to negotiate not only awkward or uncomfortable textiles and sartorial shapes, but also to engage in unnatural movements in order to create electricity friction. In the case of *Itchy*, the wearer must rub the collars together, or invite others to do so in a way that is "normal," or socially condoned. We all know that static is the enemy of good fashion; yet here, fashion invites the creation of static friction through robust movement. In the case of *Stiff*, the garment is literally stiff—the antithesis of textile garment comfort. The hump-like protrusion embedded into the garment is not only anti-fashion in shape, but also rather inaccessible, as an interactive platform for the wearer. In this way, the garment becomes a parasitic system, in search of participants to activate it, or proposing unconventional ways of interacting with the environment, such as repeatedly bumping into walls or other objects in order to charge it. The final design, *Sticky*, is a bully system that requires the wearer to pull the device in order to be charged. However, the device also influences normative movements such as picking things up, because any movement using the hands must interact with the pulley. In this way, any movement of the hand has no choice but to participate in the kinetic ecosystem of energy gathering, whether the wearer wishes to do so or not. An inverse way of looking at the interaction is to think of the wearables as hosts who make use of the body to power themselves, thus inverting the power dynamic of wearable and wearer.

Furthermore, such projects exacerbate the limits of "smart" design by highlighting both the very real, as well as absurdist nature of our present-day technological demands. This work highlights current concerns over energy, environment, and climate issues, which are at once distant and day-to-day concerns. Perhaps it could even be argued that, as transitional objects of an absurdist nature, CEBB designs demonstrate a "liminoid" quality, as they neither fully adhere to the expectations of an HCI system, nor are they purely art. Not quite functional, and not quite purely playful, the CEBB designs reside at the limit of what we might expect or be willing to engage in when using a wearable. Berzowska reminds us that we "need wearable computing that is irrational, poetic, musical, and theatrical. We need wearable computing that stimulates magical and literary experiences in our everyday life rather than just trying to improve productivity or our efficiency" [1. In this way, XS Labs' designs question the form and meaning of the wearable through their choreography of distinctly "off" interactions.

3.2   V2_ Institute for the Unstable Media

The next case study begins in 2011 at V2_ Lab for the Unstable Media in Rotterdam, where I met Anouk Wipprecht, fashion-tech designer-in-residence at the time. While at V2_ for a three-month PhD residency stay, I participated in the E-Textile Workspace research cluster, which conducted monthly meetings on the themes of craft, DIY, and wearables. I also organized a Test_Lab event (single-evening events dedicated to showcasing new works) entitled "Clothing without Cloth," which featured members of the European wearables community (Italy, Holland, England, France) involved in active material experimentation that pushes the limits of "clothing" and textiles.[1] Since this research stay, Wipprecht and I worked on organizing the *TechnoSensual* exhibition,

---

[1] Participants in "Clothing without Cloth" included: Emily Crane, a recent MA graduate from Kingston University, London, working with edible textiles (UK); Christien Meindertsma, a materials designer from Rotterdam (Netherlands); Carole Collet, then director of the Textile Futures MA program at Central Saint Martins, London (France/UK); Giada Dammacco, lead designer at Grado Zero Espace, a technology and design company in Florence (Italy); Pauline van Dongen, an independent fashion-tech designer (Netherlands); and Brian Garret, a 3D designer at Freedom of Creation (Netherlands).

which took place at the MuseumsQuartier in Vienna (2013), and for which I curated the symposium. We have also sat on panels together, including a recent one on "Embracing Fashion + Technology" at the Atelier Néerlandais in Paris (2016), and we have collaborated on an upcoming fashion-tech festival to be held in Montreal in 2017.

Background. Wipprecht, trained as a fashion designer and later in engineering for design, is one of the few mavericks in the field of wearables to straddle skill sets in aesthetics and engineering with equal virtuosity. With the mindset of an inventor and the ambition of a fashion star, she has built an impressive collection of works, collaborators, and followers, influencing the field of fashion tech. Capitalizing on the growing maker movement, multimedia entertainment events, and opportunities for fashion tech to tell its story and be at center-stage, she has developed a style that combines robotics and techno-aesthetics. As a researcher, she is keenly invested in wearables' interactive and inter-relational dimensions, and in the potential for wearables to offer the body new capacities for expression that traditional fashion cannot. In short, Wipprecht has crafted a fine creative balance, in which her designs—combining fashion, technology, and the body—permit us to visualize, experience, and dream how we may wish to perform with the fashion tech of the future.

Laboratory Culture. To begin with the laboratory, or studio context in which Wipprecht works, one should first mention her nomadic and collaborative praxis approach to fashion-tech design. Unlike other designers, who may have set places and spaces of production, Wipprecht prefers to embed herself within R&D work settings such as Intel, Autodesk, or Microsoft. Once on site, she builds partnerships with internal teams to develop new designs that respond to technical needs, embark on explorations, or undertake media showcasing of new fashion-tech technologies. The majority of Wipprecht's work of the last fours years has been the result of client-based commissions and sponsorships from some of the biggest tech industries in America, allowing her unheralded access to new technologies, materials, and processes, not to mention high-profile platforms for the presentation of her completed designs. As an epistemic culture, it is one that is often times predicated on a client's needs to create a better aesthetics and/or stories around emergent technologies in the form of desirable fashion-tech displays. In this way, one of the biggest challenges is balancing the need to showcase a clients' technology with maintaining a consistent signature design. Keeping this goal in mind, Wipprecht's fashion tech has been structured around a techno-futurist aesthetic that (to date) consistently features 3D printing, robotics, sensors, exoskeletons, and leather.

Wipprecht's works often result from opportunities to forge into new materials and technical or expressive explorations with both clients and collaborators, in what she calls a "collision of practices." As notes Wipprecht: "The best context for collaborating is when someone wants to get into fashion" [18]. For example, the *Smoke Dress*, developed for a 2013 Volkswagen car show, resulted in a collaboration with Italian architect Niccolo Casas. Harnessing the opportunity to fund a new series of works, Wipprecht invited Casas to participate in developing the new pieces for VW. Their collaboration provided an opportunity for Casas to experiment in the field of fashion (he has since become one of Iris Van Herpen's main collaborators in the fabrication of her 3D-printed fashions), while Wipprecht benefited from the hands-on tutelage of Casas to master the 3D software Maya for fashion-design use. In this way, both designers could benefit by expanding their skill sets while creating new work, a common strategy for Wipprecht.

Technology. In fact, the *Smoke Dress* had an earlier iteration, presented at the *TechnoSensual* exhibition (prototyped with Dutch fashion technologist Aduen Darriba), prior to its VW redesign. In explaining the initial prototyping process for the *Smoke Dress*, Wipprecht describes how she (and Darriba) first experimented with the use of smoke machines to visualize the effects on the body. Wipprecht often begins with ideas, images, or concepts that later spur and feed technical experimentation. Examples of this process include: the visual effect of ink floating in water, as s starting point for the *Pseudomorphs* dress (developed at V2_ in 2009); the idea of a "disappearing" garment, which informed the *Intimacy 2* dress (also developed at V2_ in 2009); and finally the notion of social invisibility, propelling the idea of the *Smoke Dress*. Once the concept is established, Wipprecht engages in a process of visualization—both through tangible mock-ups and collage/moodboards—in order to map the placement of technologies, as well as the interactive system's architecture, on the body, thus defining the garment's shape. As Wipprecht cautions, "You can visualize through photos or drawing, but with interaction you need to physically see it in action" [18].

Early in the design process, accommodation for technical needs and limitations is at the forefront of the design parameters. For example, questions around battery and wire placement can dictate the shape and style of the garment, as in the case of Fergie (of the Black Eyed Peas, performers at the Super Bowl 2011 halftime show), where the batteries were located on the shoulders as epaulettes, instead of around the waist, in order to preserve the pop star's silhouette. In the case of the *Smoke Dress*, the overall shape of the garment was structured in an hourglass shape as a consequence of accommodating the smoke machine in the lower-torso section; while the *Spider Dress* features black spheres (that look like eyes) integrated into the design in order to conceal the proximity sensors. Notes Wipprecht, "my style is created out of the spaces that I create around the body in order to place the electronics." Hence, as a design process, it is one that is predicated on action and tacit experiments that oscillate between the concepts and technical possibilities. This performative model of discovery—which engages in a process of virtual-to-tangible modelling—dictates the final garment's shape, style, and materiality.

The idea for *Spider Dress* stemmed from a short, experimental stop-motion video featuring an analog puppet mechanism placed on the body, which was produced in collaboration with Viennese programmer/technologist Daniel Schatzmayr. After posting the video online and receiving an enthusiastic number of "likes" literally overnight, the duo proceeded to create the piece in earnest. In this way, the Internet could even be considered as a collaborator/performer, as it instigated the development of the piece.

Spider Dress is based on the idea of creating personal space for its wearer. Conceived as an "aggressive" and perhaps even anti-social wearable, it features animatronic arachnid limbs that are activated by the presence and approach of others. Protecting its human "prey," this exoskeleton can enact twelve different behavioural states, depending on the type of approach (fast/slow, back/front, etc.), featuring different speeds and combinations of activations for the spider legs. *Spider Dress* was developed in two iterative processes (Wipprecht often reworks previous designs): the first version was created with Schatzmayr; the second, in collaboration with Intel. The principal difference, other than the showcasing and embedding—and the Intel Edison chip in the second design—is the color. In our interview, Wipprecht emphasizes the importance of aesthetic choices in choreographing wearables' interactions, and notes how the first version, fabricated in black, was too menacing, and thus antithetical to interaction [18].

Fashion Tech. *Spider Dress* was manufactured using PA-12 material via 3D printing using SLS (selective laser sintering) techniques at Materialise in Belgium. Meanwhile, the upper dress bodice was developed in collaboration with Studio Palermo in Austria. Wipprecht describes the inner workings of the *Spider Dress* as follows:

> The Edison module runs embedded Linux, the design is programmed in Python. The dress inter-actions are defined in *"twelve states of behavior"* through two Mini Maestro twelve-channel USB servo controllers from Pololu, and uses inverse kinematics. I am working with twenty small 939 MG metal gear servos (0.14 s.60°/0.13 s.60°—stall torque 2.5 kg.cm/2.7 kg.cm). All servos run back to the system. I am also working with Dynamixels (XL-320 series) of Robotis, which are super-nice to work with, as they are smart, strong, and very accurate [19].

Spider Dress works via a series of embedded sensors that react intelligently to the ambient interactions it encounters. The 3D-printed robotic shell is enabled with proximity and breath sensors that trigger the carapace's movements. Wipprecht explains: "Using wireless biometric signals, the system makes inferences based on the stress level in your body. It can differentiate between twelve states of behavior." The behavior of the legs modulates depending on the speed at which one approaches the devices, as well the wearer's physiological reaction as measured by her breath. The technology powering these effects are a combination of an Intel Edison bluetooth controller and a Maxbotix proximity sensor encased in the dark globe at the front of the wearable. Wipprecht's arachnid wearable thus operates as a collaborative visualization of events both within the wearer (breath and proximity) and through the actions and reactions of those surrounding the wearer (speed of approach, distance to fashion-tech garment, length of stay, and sequence of movements). Hence, the movements of the legs are an amalgam of the performance of fashion, body, and technology as encountered both on the wearer's body and through the public's interactions. In this way, the *Spider Dress* is a co-created performance involving wearer, device, and public.

Collaboration. While Wipprecht is hired by companies and sponsors to create fashion-tech designs that promote and showcase their technologies (software, hardware, auto-mobiles), the element of social interaction, relatability, or "readability" is paramount in her design choices, both from an aesthetic and an interaction standpoint. For the designer, a wearable piece has several layers of interaction, of which approachability is the first. The white, Intel version (or albino, as she calls it) of the *Spider Dress* was altered in order to enhance this first layer of interaction. Wipprecht had felt that the first (black) design was too ominous, and hence did not invite the public/user to approach it. Second, the shape of the design itself, explains Wipprecht, should reveal, or announce, its nature/character from afar [18]. Thus, the 3D-printed, spider-like legs and overall dress structure announce early on that the garment will feature animalistic qualities. Furthermore, for the designer, fashion tech should speak to all audiences, including (perhaps most of all) those uninitiated to wearables, fashion tech, or this type of technology. With the *Spider Dress*, because of the strong visual spider theme, the behavioral dimension of the design is easily relatable to almost anyone, as a spider is both recognizable and behaviorally predictable. This known, or "readable," motif makes the garment that much more successful, according to Wipprecht, because it can be immediately accepted and understood, and does not require initiation or special knowledge. Like fashion, which at all ends of the design spectrum must be socially recognizable (e.g., what is the value of a luxury item that cannot be recognized as such?), the wearable, too, must fit into an ecology of fashion.

Considering Wipprecht's design process, we may surmise that her epistemic culture is one of demand, availability, and co-design: the *demand* of the client/market to create something for a specific context (a spectacular Super Bowl halftime-show garment; an Audi/VW brigade of tech-dressed car presenters; or an Intel/Edison intelligent dress); *availability* because through tech-industry partnerships like Intel, Autodesk, and Materialise, Wipprecht secures access to special resources, which she engineers toward fashion-tech outcomes. And, finally, *co-design*, as the internal workings of this nomadic studio practice is primarily choreographed around friendships, the sharing of skills, and the collective pursuit of developing new technologies for the body. Thus, Wipprecht's pieces are rarely a solo process—or a solo vision, for that matter—and the public is often invited to witness, provide aid (crowdsourcing via social media for help and tips), and weigh in on the evolution of the designs as she posts process images online and via social media platforms (Instagram, Facebook).

Bodies/Interaction. When planning the body's actions and the "attitude" of the wearable, Wipprecht works through a number of different scenarios. The piece's attitude comes together in the final stages, often in the context of the photoshoot, which is also often the first time all the parts are seen together and on a body. The styling and choice of model further influences the feeling of the piece, together with choices over how to perform for the camera, all the while emphasizing certain parts of the wearable above others. Wipprecht describes the process:

> For example, in the Spider Dress photo the model is looking down, the system gets more attention this way. It depends what you want to highlight. Do you want to take away a little bit of the face and the information through that? And, what kind of attitude do you want to create with it. That is what you mostly do with the photo shoot. This is the place where you figure out the piece's identity and the DNA [18].

The performance and presentation contexts of the *Spider Dress* were guided by Intel's need to promote a new product—the Intel Edison chip. Hence, presentations of this iteration of the *Spider Dress* took place principally at tech events, such as the Consumer Electronic Show (CES), held in Las Vegas every January. As trade fairs are focused on "demo-ing" new technologies to industry and media audiences, the *Spider Dress* was presented in a format Wipprecht calls a "walking act," wherein the model walks amongst the attendees and demonstrates the work. In the case of CES, the *Spider*

Dress was additionally accompanied by a small flock of 3D-printed robotic spiders, mirroring the wearable via an ambulatory cluster creatures of similar design.

Beyond the need to promote industrial clients is Wipprecht's overarching aim to craft new forms of intimacy via wearables. Inspired by the social challenges faced by many in their efforts to connect, assimilate, and build appropriate social "fronts," Wipprecht's designs speak for the socially awkward, resistive, and ambivalent [20]. For Wipprecht, social malaise is a universal concern, which is perhaps most directly tackled in her recent project *Agent Unicorn*. Developed in collaboration with the Ars Electronica Center in Linz, Austria, *Agent Unicorn* is a wearable adapted for ADHD kids. Playfully designed to look like a unicorn horn, and fabricated via 3D printing, it monitors moments of concentration (when the wearer is still and focused) and communicates this information back to the child/wearer. In this way, affected children can better identify and understand their own patterns of attention/inattention, and thus act on them in a more deliberate fashion.

However, Wipprecht is adamant that the interactions and experiences offered by wearables go well beyond the panacea of health, fitness, and happiness too often marketed via consumer wearables [18]. Rather, Wipprecht pushes her wearables into uncomfortable emotional terrains of anger, shyness, indecency, or misfire. As Wipprecht notes, she is interested in how "these systems around our bodies intuitively might both behave and misbehave ... wearables should not behave, because we are misbehaving most of the time, or at least I do. Wearables should provoke the idea of making us better, by calling us out." Hence, in the choreography of her fashion-tech wearables, Wipprecht aims at the co-structuring of experience *with* the garment. She is chiefly interested in how we perform with the wearable, as well as the potential for it to perform for us, and even solicit better, or more authentic performances from us. As notes the designer, "If you wear a design that you partly control and it partly extends your agency through its autonomous actions, you start to question where you end and my system begins."

This symbiotic performance proposes new ways of thinking about how wearables can extend performatively around and with our bodies, as well as through our mental and emotional states. In a way, one could argue that Wipprecht is interested in breaking the artificiality of the "front" and other social constructions proposed by sociologists like Austin and Goffman more than half a century ago [7, 20]. Her work expresses a dimension of social breakage and re-invention that both resembles König's concept of sartorial deviance and elucidates the states of non-closure and transition as described in Turner's theory of "liminoid" states [12–14, 21]. Given this line of thought, is it possible to imagine a future in which it will be acceptable for our garments to push people away, or obliterate us in a cloud of smoke when we grow tired of someone or are uncomfortable speaking to them? To be sure, these scenarios, in being more complex and contradictory, are also richer than many of the socially interactive platforms that we engage with today.

3.3 Diffus

The next case study considers the work of Danish design studio Diffus. In the fall of 2011, invited by Diffus, I participated in the Copenhagen Artist in Residency program (CPH AIR), and, later that fall, in the Danish International Visiting Artist (DIVA) program via an invitation from Aarhus University. The CPH AIR provided me with an atelier space at the Fabrikken: Factory of Art and Design, where artists have access to traditional fine-arts workshops for wood, metal, and painting. During this residency, I worked with Diffus' co-directors, Hanne-Louise Johannesen and Michel Guglielmi, at their research office/atelier. While at Diffus, I familiarized myself with their various wearables and interactive textile designs, as well as their material libraries, and collaborated on brainstorming sessions with local and international partners: Alexandra Instituttet (Denmark), Forster Rohner (Switzerland), and Cetemmsa (Spain).

Background. Diffus design is a multidisciplinary, materials-focused studio working at the intersection of theory and application in art, industrial design, architecture, smart fabrics, and wearables. In existence since 2004, they have developed a number of client-based works and projects that highlight material innovation with design excellence. Wearables have comprised a part of their research focus, though not exclusively. Johannesen has a master's degree in art history and has worked as assistant professor in visual culture at the University of Copenhagen, and now teaches at the IT University of Copenhagen, while Guglielmi is an architect working with tangible media and interaction design, who teaches at the Royal Danish Academy of Fine Art in the schools of architecture and design.

Laboratory Culture. Diffus describes its approach as both practical and theoretical, wherein which art, culture, aesthetics, and technology all play equal parts in informing design decisions. Particularly, they are interested in experimenting at the intersection of traditional know-how (and craft) combined with new materials in order to create both "soft" and complex technologies. Recognized for their attention to detail in design, Diffus is increasingly sought out by international companies and universities to contribute to the conceptualization of new "smart" designs. Their added value, they assert, is in creating aesthetic objects from technological and innovative materials from various textile and research industries [22]. In their quest to create designs (and meaning) out of brute materiality, Guglielmi and Johannesen often approach their task from a philosophical point of view, wherein feelings and concepts about materials, bodies, and interaction guide the decision process and feed into the final design. In this way, the firm seeks to innovate designs that "appeal to our emotional self and open up to the sensibility of a large public."

The Diffus studio is a small, intimate space located in Copenhagen's central Vesterbrø neighbourhood and situated in a former residential building with other creative studios. The Diffus workspace, however, also extends to remoter spaces, including: their personal and teaching settings, and the laboratories of collaborators and service industries—all depending on material needs or convenience of work flow. Many collaborators intersect in their design development process, including seamstresses, engineers, 3D printers, and other textile/material professionals. Because of Diffus' location in the EU, many of their clients, partners, and collaborators come from government-funded research grants (such as Horizon 20/20), putting them in direct contact with small and medium enterprises, notably in the field of industrial design—Pilotfish (Germany), VanBerlo (Netherlands), Fuelfor (Spain), and Zaha Hadid Architects and Base

Structures (UK)—as well as research universities—Delft University (Netherlands), Southampton University (UK), Polytechnic Milano (Italy)—and graduate students. In this way, Diffus is able to benefit from a large network of materials and research resources that both inspire and feed the direction of their projects. As Johannesen mentions in the course of our interview, these collaborations open up the studio to new and not-yet-distributed (or published) processes and materials, which guides the design concept phases and tangible possibilities. Furthermore, says Guglielmi, the EU grants also offer precious time for reflection and discussion—key to developing aesthetic and material concepts and ideas.

Technology. Materials are the essence, or core, of Diffus. As explains Guglielmi, "We always try to remember where we come from, which is, exploring the possibilities of creating reactive materials from a design standpoint. Sometimes we try to go back to those roots, as a way of remembering" [22]. A key way in which this materiality is concretized, from a research point of view, is through an ever-expanding "sample book." Functioning much like a materials library, this sample book permits Diffus to archive and collect materials (which they may have encountered or tested during research), as well as to communicate their skill set to potential clients or collaborators. Explains Johannesen, "the sample library acts as a very active communicator" [22]. In these sample books are contained various kinds of conductive materials (yarns, textiles, metal components) and processes (inks, embroidery), through which they highlight their past projects, breakthroughs, and expertise. While these tests are often the result of contracts and requests on the part of collaborators, Guglielmi notes that the process is not always systematic, but consists more of "making associations from materials that you use in one field and looking at the possibilities of translating them through small adaptations that you find interesting as a designer" [22]. In either case, experimentation and research are "more or less equal" for the design process at Diffus [22].

Through their EU and client networks, and via their extensive experience and expertise, much of the work at Diffus is client-oriented. In this way, the epistemic culture of the lab is driven by external needs and opportunities (both financial and materials-based). It is in part through such a process that the *Climate Dress* was developed in 2009. The dress was conceived as a proof-of-concept collaboration with the Swiss textile company Forster Rohner, funded in part by the Alexandra Instituttet, a Danish technology think tank. Seeing a need to diversify their core business of *haute couture* embroidery and lace manufacturing, Forster Rohner has embarked upon engineering embroidery for smart fabrics. Led by Dr. Jan Zimmermann, head of textile innovations at Forster Rohner, the company has been developing smart fabrics for various textile and design uses (from fashion to architecture to auto industries) adapted to the integration of hardware, such as LEDs, sensors, and batteries. The partnership with Diffus emerged from mutual needs: that of Forster Rohner, to showcase their new expertise in smart embroidery fabrication; and of Diffus, to secure access to emergent processes and industry techniques for smart textiles. The *Climate Dress* features a combination of conductive embroidery parts, embroidered LEDs, a CO_2 sensor, and an Arduino to compute and manage the data inputs and outputs. The dress is designed to be wearable as a visible air-quality sensor, which can navigate various geolocated spaces and assess environmental air quality. The dress alerts the wearer and those near the dress to distressing levels of CO_2, both to warn the public over air quality and to sensitize them to the dangers of pollution.

Fashion. The partnership between Diffus and Forster Rohner was initiated through an invitation to showcase a design within the context of the COP15 Climate Summit in Copenhagen in 2009. Some of the parameters that the design duo took into consideration when developing this piece included: creating a garment using traditional craft; revealing information through aesthetics; and creating a new relationship with embroidery that featured technology. Hence, the *Climate Dress* was born from a desire to fuse craft and tech in such a manner that would aesthetically reveal its functionality. Inspired by the methods of turn-of-the-century French architect Gustav Eiffel and his decorative use of metal structures, Diffus set out to create a garment that could build on the concept via embroidery rather than steel. Created in under two months, the process saw meetings between students from the Danish Design School, technicians from the Alexandra Instituttet, and the technical team at Forster Rohner. Diffus describes their primary work as mediating between the various participants and collaborators in order to arrive at the results they aimed for. Along the way, considerations had to be made for the capacity of the conductive thread and LEDs to adequately illustrate CO_2 levels in a visually cohesive and pleasing manner. Guglielmi describes the process of negotiating needs with aesthetics:

> The interaction played a major role in the design of the embroidery and indirectly in the design of the garment on which the embroidery would be applied. More LEDs with more processing abilities could have been added but we needed to constrain ourselves to clear interaction rules between CO_2 levels and the LED patterns as pulse. Those clear rules influenced the design of the circuit layout as well as the design of the required algorithm [17].

Because the departure point for research at Diffus is materials exploration, it makes sense that the fashion (and aesthetic) frameworks are built around technical and interaction needs. Instead of seeing this as a limitation, the Diffus team is inspired to make "form follow function," as coined by American architect Louis Sullivan. Interestingly, Johannesen refers to Adolf Loos, also a proponent of functional architecture, as an inspiration for their design ethos. She explains: "I think that because of someone like Loos, I was scared to go into something to do with embroidery, because embroidery is just ornament. I think it is really interesting, then, to give this ornament a functionality. Trying to respect Loos, and at the same time subvert him, or being subversive towards him" [22]. Another concrete example of this philosophy in action is the *Solar Handbag*, created in collaboration with Forster Rohner, the Alexandra Instituttet, and the Hochschule für Technik Rapperswil, in Switzerland—and also the outcome of an EU-funded research grant. The bag uses solar cells to power portable devices; instead of concealing the solar cells, Diffus approached the problem similarly to the *Climate Dress*, making the square cells an integral part of the exterior fabric and design.

In this way, the Diffus studio is closely guided by the quest to discover appropriate form and function through materiality. In describing his action- and time-based performative laboratory, Pickering outlines how human agency's intentionality must be mediated through the nonhuman agencies of matter, machines, and things. Because Pickering's "dance of agency" proceeds across this human-nonhuman negotiation, which unfolds via *temporal emergence*, outcomes can neither be forced nor predicted. Diffus' philosophical approach to integrating new technologies into design in a holistic and self-evident way is, in my opinion, indicative of a performative laboratory approach. Rather than force ideas about interaction, use, or aesthetics onto a material or a technology, the studio embraces the process of discovering these things, of seeing them revealed *through* the process. In this way, their studio often arrives at results that fittingly display and propose a logic (and aesthetic) of use that may have not been readily apparent at the start, but which springs from the nature of the initial material. For these reasons, it is not unreasonable to see their process—focused primarily as it is on creating interaction and design out of technology—as inherently performative.

Body/Interaction. The designs of Diffus—wearables or otherwise—are always informed with the body in mind, in consideration both of how the body will react to the design and how it will interact with it. Concern over touch, texture, manipulation, and interaction feeds many of their form and material design decisions. In this way, the emphasis on materiality subscribes to the project of the re-embodiment and re-materialization of the technical object, as opposed to screen and data streams. Johannesen explains their position on materiality: "When you work with technology and you work with human beings using the technology, it has to somehow occur within an experience. I think that we are working with technology that wants to be noticed, and thereby, it enters the fashion area" [22]. For Diffus, interaction, aesthetics, and technology are inextricably intertwined.

One could also argue that Diffus' performative design matrix builds on new-media concepts of embodiment and experience. Foregrounding the body (touch, sight, movement, etc.), they bring a phenomenological dimension to the experience of their wearables. Diffus' work thus focuses on how design objects can, through good design and style, enter into the world of body-centric, sensuous, and interactively rewarding experiences, which reposition the body at the center of the technological question. Not surprisingly, as Diffus works for clients seeking new forms of expression for materials that have yet to find a use, meaning, or shape, their work often consists in unlocking (and scripting) the interactive and poetical dimensions of matter. More than orchestrating new functionalities for technologies and smart materials, the Diffus team believes their design objects should also offer a respite and meditation for the future user, opening a door to deeper experiences. However, as they are well aware, designing for technology, as Guglielmi notes, is "a polarity, really. On the one side, the need to do things simpler, and on the other side, exploring the complexity of structures, materials, and so on. It is about finding the balance between those things" [22]. As a performative platform, their designs invite the sensing, sensitive, living, touching body back into the technology, both through attention to detail and a sensibility toward form that follows function.

3.4   3lectromode

The last case study concerns my own DIY artistic wearables practices through my company 3lectromode. For several years, while researching this topic for my PhD, I have been active in creating accessible DIY wearable platforms that borrow equally from the culture of at-home garment sewing (i.e., *Vogue* and *McCall's* patterns) and hobbyist electronics. These platforms and communication devices have been produced at my label's atelier, as well as at various collaborative institutions—Hexagram Institute (Montreal), V2_ Lab for the Unstable Media (Rotterdam), Fabrikken for Kunst & Design (Copenhagen), Oboro (Montreal), and InterAccess (Toronto)—and been funded primarily through grants from the Canada Council for the Arts, the Conseil des arts et des lettres du Québec, and the Concordia University Part-Time Faculty Association. During this time, I have also partici-pated in a number of residencies, conferences, and other events to trace the limits and poten-tials of this emerging field. Residencies have included the Danish International Visiting Artist program (DIVA), hosted by the Department of Information and Media (IMV) Studies at Aarhus University, where I delivered a conference presentation titled "Kitchen Table Wearables," together with a series of workshops with design students titled "How to Knit Your Own Computer." Other conferences on the subjects of DIY and performance include an "Open Wearables" panel and workshop, which I led at ISEA 2011 in Istanbul, Turkey; an "Open Hardware Summit," held at Eyebeam Art + Technology Center in New York City in 2012; MEDEA's "Prototyping Futures" conference in Malmö, Sweden, also in 2012, which examined emergent DIY technologies; and the MODE@MOTI symposium in Breda, Netherlands, in 2013, as part of a master class in fashion and technology where I tested my ideas on the link between fashion tech and Modern-era innovation.

Background. In short, I have been active in researching and testing the limits of e-textiles and DIY culture in informing wearables aesthetics and production methods. The field of e-textiles, while lacking the finesse and resources of more industrial or academic research projects, offers a rich platform of collaborative and self-directed explorations for embedding electronics in garments. In this sense, my atelier is more like an artist studio than a design company or service-oriented studio. Due to the nature of the funding—arts exploration grants—the projects are, for the most part, self-directed and independently developed. That said, the techno-arts atelier of today relies on a number of external industries and resources that directly impact on the design. As I argued in my talk "Open Design Practices + Wearables + 3lectromode" (ISEA 2011), there is a growing body of research describing the shift in production paradigms taking place as a result of the proliferation of new technologies, machines, and shared expertise, as seen in the "Maker" movement. Examples of this increased access range from the multipli-cation of shared physical spaces offering access to rapid-prototyping technologies (fab labs and hacker spaces) to the expanding networked possibilities of "print-on-demand" services for remote 3D printing, as well as textile and circuit printing. Increasingly, the arts and design "laboratory" has much in common with the cottage industries that existed before the Industrial Revolution, with small artist/artisan spaces playing critical roles in fabrication processes and choices, all the while retaining control over the end-product or design—an element that Modern production chains had all but erased [23–25]. Hence, for a field such as wearables design, access to machines, technicians, and materials can make all the difference. This dimension of DIY wearables has been explored in a number of how-to and instructional publications [17, 26–28]. Much like fashion designers who began their careers with a collection of accessible equipment, like home sewing machines and sergers housed in basement studios, the wearables designer and techno-crafter of today has access to a fast-growing palette of technologies and tools—from LilyPad Arduinos, conductive threads, and inks, to remote technical resources like laser cutters, textiles, and 3D printers—to create her/his creations.

Laboratory Culture. 3lectromode is a small design atelier run by myself as designer/owner, together with a variety of other experts from textiles, fashion, and engineering and media arts who work on an ad-hoc basis on various aspects of designing, developing, making, and disseminating or marketing fashion-tech designs. Our designs range from material explorations, fashion-tech design, and workshops that straddle the communities of high-tech, craft, arts, product design, and speculative design. Key to 3lectromode's design ethos is the desire to create a library of executable open-source fashion designs that may be assembled as kits by anyone with an interest in wearables, electronics, or fashion.

Performativity in the 3lectromode laboratory occurs among the individuals on site in the atelier, together with the extended community of users and collaborators, from pattern makers to textile specialists, graphic designers, and engineers. The team works toward a functional wearable aimed at satisfying a number of parameters, from the aesthetic and technical standpoints, a central one being the ability to be built by anyone. For this reason, all steps for producing (and reproducing) an 3lectromode wearable are integrated and communicated via the design itself. This is done by means of graphically illustrating the placement of all necessary parts—from electronics, batteries, sensors, circuit layout, to buttons and garment sewing—needed to assemble a functional wearable. Hence, many of the design parameters depend on the construction of a product that can be translated into a functioning wearable design. In this way, DIY culture expands the possibilities for anyone and everyone wishing to participate in it. By making the design and electronics open-source and accessible, 3lectromode, like many electronics companies that publish instructional videos, blogs, and schematics, including Arduino and Adafruit, allows the general public access to various toolkits for the construction of wearables, thus contributing to the collective effervescence and activity in the field.

Technology. As a case in point, *Strokes&Dots* was designed with the intention of communicating the fabrication process of wearables to a general audience. Part of a micro-collection of sixteen garments, *Strokes&Dots* was inspired by early Modernist representations of speed, graphic design, abstract art, and technology—as well as the print work of Russian/French textile visionary Sonia Delaunay. We began the design process by looking at early Modernist textile pattern and fabrication processes, which flourished during the early twentieth century. To begin with, a series of watercolor graphics inspired by Delaunay were created as design explorations. Next, we created four different garment patterns around which to build the collection: a top, a shirt, a skirt, and a dress. Then we digitized the watercolor graphics and made them into textile patterns that could later be integrated into the (also) digitized garment patterns, created on a 1:1 scale in large Adobe Illustrator files. Finally, we integrated the layout guidelines for the placement of the electronics, which could later be machine- or hand-sewn with conductive threads onto the wearable. The digital document, now containing schematics of the transformed watercolor graphics, the garment pattern layout for sewing, and the electronics placement guides, was printed on Japanese Hobotai silk with a Mimaki digital textile printer at the Hexagram Institute at Concordia University. While the electronics guides were printed on a "bottom" layer along with the textile graphics, the "top" layer, a slightly thinner fabric, acted as light diffuser for the integrated LEDs. From a material standpoint, the *Strokes&Dots* kit contains: a textile printout featuring the outline of the garment pattern and the layout placement for the electronics, which include: a LilyPad Arduino, an accelerometer or light sensor, and five to twelve (depending on the design) embroidered, responsive LEDs. The garments are reactive depending on the types of movements made by the individual wearing them. Three states of LED light displays were embedded into the design to communicate with the wearer and those nearby. The first state is when the wearer is at rest, and the lights cycle through lighting each LED to display its presence. When the wearer moves more dynamically, the LEDs respond by lighting up more actively and randomly, as though they had be "woken up" or charged. Inversely, when the wearer stops moving for a long period of time, the LEDs display a warning sequence, in which all the lights light up at once and flash, indicating that the person should perhaps move. This playful communication between the wearer and the garment expresses the interactions taking place, and having taken place, for all to see. In this way, they become a second layer of communication for all to "read".

As kits, which can be sold, constructed at home or in DIY wearables ateliers, or sewed in workshops or educational contexts, they are design objects that reveal their fabrication process and thus transform the user into a maker (or at the very least, a "learner"). This method takes some of the initial guesswork out of electronics assembly, while allowing the user to create a customized and fashionable design. As each piece is uniquely designed and comes with customizable options for different print patterns, colors, and sizes, the designs aim to give the user/designer agency in fabricating his/her own iteration. Computational variations are also included to modify the LilyPad Arduino program, with the aim of simplifying the programming one step further. So far, 3lectromode designs have focused on integration of LEDs with various sensors, using the LilyPad Arduino platform for electronic components and programming. However, this is but a starting point for later iterations, which may integrate other emerging DIY technologies, as well as customizable options, thus adding to the landscape of maker-directed wearables. The 3lectromode label's next goal is to develop a maker/meeting space to foster community exchange and building around DIY wearables, as seen internationally in events such as Fashion Hack Day (Berlin) and the E-Textiles Summer Camp (Loire Valley, France).

Fashion. Beyond the mission to create a kit that can visually communicate how they can be built, a second important driver in the *Strokes&Dots* project is the creation of a collection of interactive objects that can stand on their own in the world of fashion. Being as many fashion-tech projects are one-off designs, this element of reproducibility in the studio was ever important to create a large collection, as opposed to a singular prototype. In this way, the sixteen stylistically connected garments could be deployed as a micro-collection on the runway, or in other live events. Furthermore, the wearability—the ability for the garments to be worn in the everyday, on a variety of bodies, of varied ages, and for a prolonged periods of time, like at a cocktail party, art opening, or fashion show—further reaffirmed their viability as fashion objects. Aesthetically, the *Strokes&Dots* garments had to "pass" as fashion first and electronics second in order to make headway into the universe of fashion. With this goal in mind, the wearables were fabricated with silk and followed the shape of prêt-à-porter fashion; in other words, the garments are meant for "everyone" and for "anytime" contexts. These stylistic and functional factors meant that the studio was able to mount traditional fashion shows (*D-Moment*, 2014; *Academos*, 2015) with the interactive garments, as well as participate in a number of public events (Augmented World Expo 2014; Boston Consulting Group 2014; CES Las Vegas and New York 2012, 2013, 2014, 2015). Having the garments stylistically echo fashion trends was important, enhancing visibility and in this way providing ample testing grounds to engage in live presentations, as well as encounters with a diverse public.

Body/Interaction. Finally, as a performative object, what does the wearable communicate? In the case of *Strokes&Dots*, a few elements can be identified. First, as they are disseminated as kits, the garments are often worn by their makers, and hence are tangible testimony of their maker's process and skill, as expressed in the wearing. A close collaboration with the technology is enacted, as the wearable's "performance" runs parallel to that of the lived—and creative—body that wears it. As the technology (the accelerometer or light sensors that give information on the body's movements or environment) is set into motion, the effects (LEDs, in the case of the DIY Social Skin) have an expressive dimension not fully controllable by the actual and situated body. At times, one might have the impression that the technology speaks with, for, or even on top of the body. This duplicitous relationship between a self-unfolding technology, a garment as fashion expression (what says "technophile" more than embedded technologies in your clothing?), and a body in action reflects the complex, negotiated performativity that is the wearable.

Two strong messages arise out of the culture of DIY wearables, as exemplified in 3lectromode's design strategy. The first concerns the individual's participation in the construction of technology, or otherwise getting dirty, beyond the smooth surfaces of the Web 2.0 culture of input apps and content interface screens. The second touches on the political act of wearing your technology as a craft movement. As a performative object, the DIY wearable is not a consumer item, but rather an object of technological affirmation for the masses. More than putting on a wearable gadget, DIY electronics and interfaces are about the storytelling and the individual's David-versus-Goliath struggle to have a voice in an increasingly technologized environment. One could even argue that it is a creative form of performative resistance to popular consumer tech culture, which forces the wearer and others to position themselves vis-à-vis the greater landscape and politics of an increasingly technocratic society.

4   Conclusion

The above four wearables case studies invite us to reflect on how performance informs wearables and fashion tech's epistemic cultures of production and internal systems of performance occurring in the studio/atelier/laboratory. By following key works produced within each studio, we see how performative potentials are seeded though the course of their conceptualization and developmental processes. Furthermore, we can see how contemporary wearables are pushing the boundaries of performance through design, style, interaction, and use of technology by infusing their works with questions of social interaction, emotions, poetry, agency, bodies, and politics. In each case study we encounter the processes, agendas, tools, materials, dreams, and struggles at play within the theater of wearables creation. Furthermore, each case study proposes a new angle on the kind of performance unfolding in the studio, from those of collaborative industry research in fashion tech (Wipprecht); to smart-fabrics innovation via fashion and design (Diffus); and from DIY e-textile production (3lectromode); to the rethinking of HCI scenarios via wearable design (XS Labs). Most importantly, however, we become aware of performance's role as central to the *raison d'être* of the wearable, as it is present its logic of use. In other words, wearables need bodies, fashion, and technology, and each of these facets contributes to how a wearable is experienced. The performance of robotics mixed with emotion, as seen in the world of Wipprecht, or the acrobatic interaction scenarios proposed by Berzowska through CEBB, both point to the body performing *with* technology. Furthermore, these examples confirm how the wearable would be devoid of meaning without a body to push up against it (sometimes literally), and without the shapes and materials that inform/comprise them. The same can be said of how matter performs over the course of its process toward becoming an "intelligent" design, as seen in the Diffus studio; or the proposition that DIY wearables can offer appreciation and knowledge through their hands-on production and deployment. In the contemporary wearables atelier, we encounter a positioning vis-à-vis wearables' capacity to offer new experiences for the body, as well as new relationships to fashion and technology.

References

1. Barad, K.: Posthumanist performativity: toward an understanding of how matter comes to matter. Signs J. Women Cult. Soc. **28**(3), 801–831 (2003)
2. Barad, K.: Meeting the Universe Halfway: Quantum Physics & the Entanglement of Matter & Meaning. Duke University Press, Durham (2007)
3. Herzig, R.: Performance, productivity, and vocabularies of motive in recent studies of science. Feminist Theory **5**, 127–147 (2004)
4. KnorrCetina, K.: Epistemic Cultures: How the Science Make Knowledge. Harvard University Press, Cambridge (1999)
5. Pickering, A.: The Mangle of Practice: Time, Agency, and Science. University of Chicago Press, London, Chicago (1995)
6. Pickering, A.: The Cybernetic Brain. University of Chicago Press, London, Chicago (2010)
7. Austin, J.L.: How to Do Things with Words. Harvard University Press, Cambridge (1975)
8. Carlson, M.: Performance: A Critical Introduction. Routledge, London, New York (1996)
9. Conquergood, D.: Poetics, play, process and power: the performative turn in anthropology. Text Perform. Q. **9**(1), 82–95 (1989)
10. Schechner, R.: Performance Studies: An Introduction. Routledge, London, New Yok (2002)
11. Schechner, R.: Performance Theory. Routledge, London, New York (1988/2008)
12. Turner, V.: The Ritual Process: Structure and Anti-Structure. Aldine, Chicago (1969/1995)

13. Turner, V.: Dramas, Fields and Metaphors: Symbolic Action in Human Society. Cornell University Press, Ithaca (1975)
14. Turner, V.: From Ritual to Theatre: The Human Seriousness of Play. PAJ Publications, New York (1982)
15. Berzowska, J.: Programming materiality. In: 5th International Conference on Tangible, Embedded, and Embodied Interaction, pp. 23–24 (2012)
16. Berzowska, J.: XS Labs: Seven Years of Design Research and Experimentation in Electronic Textiles and Reactive Garments. XS Labs, Montréal (2010)
17. Genova, A., Katherine, M.: Fashion and Technology: A Guide to Materials and Applications. Fairchild Books, New York, London (2016)
18. Interview with Anouk Wipprecht (2016)
19. MakeZine, 19 December 2014. http://makezine.com/
20. Goffman, E.: The Presentation of Self in Everyday Life. Anchor Books, New York (1959)
21. König, R.: À la mode: On the Social Psychology of Fashion, trans. F. Bradley. Seabury Press, New York (1974)
22. Interview with Diffus (2016)
23. Anderson, C.: Makers: The New Industrial Revolution. Signal, Toronto (2012)
24. Gershenfeld, N.: FAB: The Coming Revolution on Your Desktop: From Personal Computers to Personal Fabrication. Basic Books, New York (2005)
25. Openshaw, J.: Postdigital Artisans: Craftmanship with a New Aesthetic in Fashion, Art, Design and Architecture. Frame Publishers, Amsterdam (2015)
26. Buechley, L., Peppler, K., Eisenberg, M., Kafai, Y.: Textile Messages: Dispatches from the World of E-Textiles and Education. Peter Lang, New York (2013)
27. Hartman, K.: Wearable Electronics: Design, Prototype and Make Your Own Interactive Garments. Maker Media, Sebastopol (2014)
28. Pakhchyan, S.: Fashioning Technology: A DIY Intro to Smart Crafting. O'Reilly Media, Sebastopol (2008)

The Grayman Project

Darien H. Lovell[✉]

School of Art and Design, The University of New South Wales,
Corner of Oxford and Greens Rd, Paddington, NSW 2021, Australia
darien.lovell@protonmail.ch

Abstract. *The Grayman Project* is an adaptive, biomimetic, defensive, camouflage wearable technology. Designed utilizing 3D photogrammetry, 3D modeling and digital fabrication for on-demand rapid prototyping of a customized photorealistic composite prosthesis and illusion technology. *The Grayman Project* draws upon *bian lian* or *face changing*; the ancient Chinese magic art of the Sichuan Opera and one of world's most guarded secrets of magic; recognized as a class-2 national secret of The People's Republic of China. The device sees the weaponizing of magic as a military strategy and tactic of deception to counteract physical surveillance and military grade facial recognition enabled with artificial intelligence (AI) present in CCTV, mobiles and drones.

Keywords: Human Computer Interaction · Wearables · Facial recognition · CCTV · 3D photogrammetry · 3D visualization · 3D modeling · Surveillance · Sousveillance · Cyber security · Hacking · Generative design · Uncanny valley · Military intelligence · Military strategy · Perception management · Espionage · Performance magic · Magic history · Bian lian · Face changing · Camouflage

1 Introduction

"Any sufficiently advanced technology is indistinguishable from magic" [7]. Magic is a house with many rooms. Historically, there are two 'magic' traditions, that of magic as *performance* art, the other *ceremonial*: a collection of diverse ritualistic, esoteric, philosophical and socio-cultural practices [20, 48]. The 'perceived' division of performance and ceremonial magic is largely a modern phenomenon [30, 46]. Magicians in ancient cultures developed wearable, body-focused, interactive designs; which speak to Shusterman's [51] somaesthetics where, "…use of one's body (is) a locus of sensory-aesthetic appreciation (aesthesis) and creative self-fashioning". Shusterman [52] acknowledges, "…art originally emerged from 'magic' and religious ritual…". Aristotle reinforces this perspective in 335BC; in *Poetics* he describes the origin of Ancient Greek theatre; a core foundation of modern Western performance and interaction art; originating from the cult of Dionysus [3]. Ammitzboll et al. [2] and Kapsali [26] describe early paleo-lithic shamanic cultures embracing animal skins not only for their somaesthetic value but their technological: biomimetic properties of camouflage and deception [62]. Modern human-computer interaction (HCI) and media artists often collaborate with neuroscientists; however, "Neuroscientists are novices at deception. Magicians

© Springer International Publishing AG 2017
A. Marcus and W. Wang (Eds.): DUXU 2017, Part II, LNCS 10289, pp. 704–718, 2017.
DOI: 10.1007/978-3-319-58637-3_54

have done controlled testing in human perception for thousands of years" [47, 57]. Scientists at the *Stanford Research Institute* used sophisticated, military specification, video/audio surveillance; a variety of bio-sensing technologies and infrared; under controlled conditions studying magician and 'psychic' Uri Geller yet they were deceived [12]. Geller's deception of world-class scientists (trained observers) and surveillance technologies; was repeated at *Washington University* by skeptic, magicians James Randi and Steve Shaw pka. *Banachek* as part of the Project Alpha hoax, they successfully maintained the deception for (4) years, under extreme, controlled surveillance conditions before self-disclosure [45, 55]. Macknik et al. [33] used human-computer interaction; to understand the neuroscience of magic; they discovered humans have a neurological 'blind spot' that allows magicians to camouflage their actions [56].

Historical Wearables. The philosophical goal of *ceremonial* magic is to transcend the body; to become perfected; this tradition manifests in many ways today through the transhumanist movement [29]. Macknik et al. [33] state historically, "...magicians (are) at the forefront of technology and innovation...". Media arts' origin in film and theatre began with magician's theatrical séances called: *Phantasmagoria*, today interaction designers and media artists continue to use an illusion technology called *Pepper's Ghost* [43]. Prior to Steve Mann, 'the father of wearable computing' was Edward Thorp; credited as the inventor of the first wearable computer [39]. Thorp [14, 58] created a wearable computer utilized to cheat casinos; his device was used covertly, in secret, averting the casino's CCTV and physical surveillance; his apparatus is similar to wearable devices used by modern magicians and mentalists. Keynote *Wearables 2013* speaker Kirkland [27] describes, 'the father of modern magic', Robert-Houdin as a technologist and magician who worked with automata (robotics/interaction design) and watchmaking (wearable technology); he was utilizing, "...the nanotechnology of (his) day". Robert-Houdin is cited as the figurehead who stripped performance magic of its ceremonial traditions; in addition, for the adoption of clothing fashioned with 'hidden-in-plain-sight' integrated and wearable technology. This disruptive innovation embraced a form of semiotic, social camouflage by using the familiarity of day-to-day fashion whilst simultaneously exploiting, visual salience, psychologically and visually concealing the magician's skills, identity and apparatus [46]. Kirkland [27] is convinced Robert-Houdin, if he were alive today would continue his pioneering body-focused and interactive designs, "...he would be very interested in the biohacking movement".

Weaponized Magic. We are driven by our *perception* of reality not reality itself; and in magic and discourses of power and by extension military strategy- *power perceived, power achieved*. Machiavelli [32] states, "Never attempt to win by force what can be won by deception" and Tzu [61] reinforces, "All warfare is based on deception". Sun Tzu [61] the genius military strategist of ancient China; emphasizes the critical importance of deception as a concept, tactic and strategic framework in warfare. Ting [59, 60] recounts ancient China's '*vagabonds*' (military assassins) precursors of feudal Japan's ninja; utilized *performance* magic and wearable technology for psychological warfare and camouflage; strategically invoking the fears and superstitions of their enemies. '*Smoke and mirrors*' coexists in the world of '*cloak and dagger*'; interaction design and wearable technology are essential to both. In 1856, a French colony in Algeria was in mortal conflict with local Arabian Tribal Chiefs and was upon the precipice of a violent rebellion, Colonel de Neveu enlisted Robert-Houdin who recalls, "…the government was, therefore, anxious to destroy their pernicious influence and reckoned on me to do so" [46]. Kirkland [27] says, "…he stopped a rebellion in Algeria by doing magic". Robert-Houdin utilized one of the world's first electro-magnets for an interaction design. Combining it with wearable technology; he convinced the Arabian Tribal Chiefs, "… we are their superiors in everything, and, as for sorcerers; there are none like the French" [46]. As a technologist, Robert-Houdin anticipated modern surveillance and security technology by inventing the first electric house security alarm; in addition his home was automated; security and automation are key domains of wearable interaction and the *Internet of Things* (IoT) [46]. Beyond Robert-Houdin, magician Jasper Maskelyne was enlisted by British Military Intelligence in WW2 to create large-scale interaction designs and wearable technology for: misdirections, deceptions and camouflage [17, 38]. Houdini inspired military intelligence techniques using wearable technology [33]. During the Cold War, the US: *Central Intelligence Agency* (CIA) enlisted magician John Mulholland to design wearable technology and, "…to teach magic (illusion) methods to field personnel" [40, 53]. Pilkington's [44] *Mirage Men* historically documents to current day; ongoing global engagement by governments, military and intelligence agencies in campaigns of deception, camouflage, misdirection and disinformation. These psychological warfare campaigns are used during and between wartime on enemies of state and domestic citizens for 'herd management'; the science of population management. Magic, deception, perception management, intelligence, information, interaction design, wearable technology and privacy are all inter-related concepts. *Power perceived, power achieved*; few philosophers understand discourses of power like Foucault [19].

Foucault's Panopticon. Foucault's [19] concept of the: *Panopticon*; is of major importance in understanding the theories, issues and frameworks underscoring emerging surveillance technologies and it's impact and response form the field of human-computer interaction and media arts. Foucault's *Panopticon* echoes Machiavelli [32]; the idea is that modern governments enforce authority *psychologically* rather than *physically*. Surveillance technologies lead to self-governance of the population by winning their *perceptions*, conjuring conformity and banishing free will; setting the stage for what Foucault describes as '*dynamic normalization*' [19, 34, 36].

Brignall [6] anticipated the rise of the *Internet of Things* (IoT) as a potential network enabling Foucault's [19] *Panopticon*. Revelations of whistleblowers, Julian Assange's *Wikileaks*, Edward Snowden, the NSA *Trapwire Program* (facial scanning CCTV surveillance on domestic populations) and masked hacktivists group *Anonymous* confirm the reality of surveillance permeating our lives [9]. On the fringes of the deep web, corporations and organized *black hat* hacker groups have taken control of home CCTV security systems and spime devices connected to the Internet of Things (IoT) for criminal purposes [23]. Steve Mann, pioneer of wearable computing describes the current environment as, "…the DEMOCRATIZATION OF VOYEURISM on a planetary scale, (that) has overexposed even our most private activities" [36].

Sousveillance. Mann et al. [36] disclose their perspective that the art of *deception, camouflage* or *magic* is informing a *Panopticon* design that is, "...invisible through its disappearance into the fabric of buildings, objects and bodies" [31, 35, 37]. Mann argues the design-solution to the problem of surveillance is to embrace a personal counter-surveillance technology; in Mann's case it's his wearable computers; he calls this response, "Sousveillance: Surveilling the Surveillers" [15, 36]. As a form of passive resistance, alerting our awareness to the power dynamics of the various forms of surveil-lance and for personal protective documentation, *sousveillance* is great in theory; however, individuals are suspicious of cameras or anything visually unfamiliar; provoking violent reactions, Mann experienced this when he, "...was physically assaulted by McDonald's employees who were acting in a vigilante capacity to enforce laws that do not even exist" [34].

Privacy Enhancing Technology. Mann's pioneering work is thought to have directly inspired *Google Glass*; yet, "Portable and wearable imaging devices such as mobile phones and *Google Glass* are a privacy threat of the current decade"; particularly when CCTV or bystander video/photography include facial-recognition of social media networks and meta-data of: time, date and geocaching location [10]. Dabrowski et al. [10] and Echizen [16] detail their work developing a wearable technology they call a *Privacy Enhancing Technology* (PET); the device is a visor that houses an array of mounted infrared LEDs. The infrared light obscures the wearers face to cameras; disrupting facial-recognition CCTV surveillance whilst exploiting the fact infrared light, whilst perceivable to computers and CCTV; is outside the visible spectrum of human sight [10, 16]. Although disrupting facial-recognition; this technology fails on (2) counts: (1) according to Goldstein [21], within *camouflage theory* the goal is, "... blending, disruption (and) mimicry"; the *PET* infrared visor on camera is like a flashlight in the dark; directing not misdirecting attention. (2) Dabrowski et al. [10] and Echizen [16] failed to consider Robert-Houdin's [46] advocacy of the importance of: perform-ance over dependence on apparatus and design for concealment of the apparatus. Although hidden from *physical* surveillance the device announces itself in *digital* surveillance space. This *concealment* is akin to *animal camouflage* and *biomimicry*. Surveillance *algorithms* or *bots* could easily receive a software patch to focus attention on unusual instances of infrared light.

Adaptive Camouflage – Invisibility Cloak. Magic is a *science* and an *art*; so too is camouflage. In this context, when evaluating body-focused designs to counteract CCTV facial-recognition surveillance technology, according to Goldstein [21] first we must defer to *camouflage theory* as informed by *animal camouflage* and then *biomimetics* in wearable camouflage technologies. Contextually, camouflage in animals and wearables; is a *performance* that is dependent on *blending* and *mimicry* of the environment and disruption of the observers critical, scanning salience and supporting senses [21]. Furthermore, the human-computer interaction of surveillance CCTV technology; requires us to adopt a hacker's insight when fashioning a design-solution for a wearable body-focused design that engages *blending, mimicry* and *disruption* to deceive *facial recognition algorithms* and *bots* [9]. Philip K. Dick's *A Scanner Darkly* [13] offered a vision of future wearable technology in the "scramble suit"; that uses a continuous projection map of holographic generated identities. According to *CNN* [8] and other major media outlets; the most advanced military wearable camouflage technology renders the wearer *virtually invisible*; often this technology is referred to as *adaptive camouflage* or *quantum camouflage*. Inami et al. [25] developed a retro-reflective projection technology that has been cited since the mid-2000 s as an example of futuristic, military high tech dubbed by the media as the *invisibility cloak*. Upon researching their original patents I identified the fact their *optical camouflage* technology was actually a modern form of an old stage magic illusion called: *Pepper's Ghost* [43]. Further investigation uncovered the nanotechnology-based textile to be a variant of common 3 M safety reflective material. What Inami et al. [25] have invented is not a camouflage technology but rather an in-camera illusion that relies on the principles of *Pepper's Ghost* [43] and Marlon Brando's reflective 3 M costume from the 1978 film *Superman* [24]. Unfortunately news coverage of the Inami et al. [25] *invisibility cloak* appears to be a military propaganda narrative with a reality more akin to Hans Christian Anderson's (1837) *The Emperor's New Clothes*.

URME Device. Famed magician, Teller [57] explains the secret of magic is to, "exploit pattern recognition". Selvaggio [49, 50] employed this tactic using a 3D printed, "… wearable, photorealistic prosthetic" called the *URME* device; he utilized *deception*, *biomimicry* and principles of *camouflage theory* [49, 50]. However, the device lacks ergonomics, is expensive to fabricate in stereolithic 3D printed resin and is rigid *physically* and *conceptually* locked by one alternate identity; missing possibilities presented by *fungibility*. Ahearn and Horan [1] describe the *'Grayman'* concept; which stresses the importance of blending into a crowd and misdirecting attention. They describe the *Internet of Things* (IoT) and CCTV as accumulating a cross-referenced, digital footprint and they suggest utilising *burner* or *decoy* identities. Unfortunately, the *URME* carries a traceable digital footprint. Although the device may deceive CCTV; it simultaneously broadcasts its digital footprint; and in terms of physical surveillance the *URME* is victim to the *uncanny valley effect*; drawing attention and compelling repulsion from observers [41, 42]. The *URME* is a compelling piece of surveillance art but not a practical camouflage wearable technology.

2   Case Study - Prototype

Background. *The Grayman Device* (prototype) (see Fig. 1) was designed utilizing 3D photogrammetry (see Fig. 2) by the author. 3D photogrammetry utilizes data from 2D photographs and laser scanning to accurately retrieve information of 1:1 scale, shape, texture, pattern and measurement to translate and reconstruct the physical object as a mathematically accurate, proportional 3D asset and digital material- complete with a photorealistic texture. The exported photorealistic texture can then be unwrapped providing a 2D stencil; much like a tailor's clothing pattern. A 3D model is built using a polygonal structure; within the 3D modeling environment a designer may reduce the level of sculptural detail (reducing the polygons). Upon the creation of a low-polygon model (adjustable to the level of detail required); the 3D model's photorealistic texture may be exported as a stencil and reassembled in 3D paper form using techniques of Japanese Pepakura (3D origami); this technique was adopted for initial rapid prototypes. I used a variety of high-end, photographic and laser based 3D photogrammetric devices used for the creation of 3D assets for: *Virtual Reality* (VR), *Augmented Reality* (AR), *Volumetric Holography* and 3D *Visualization*; in addition, I utilized *High Dynamic Range* (HDR) smart phone cameras due to recent advances in smart phone, open source photogrammetric applications. The advent of photogrammetric smart phone and portable device applications not only democratizes access to this technology at low cost; it enables an opportunity for the intended user of the *Grayman Device* to dispose of the burner phone (an anonymously registered prepaid disposable mobile phone) best practice for privacy or anonymity of digital footprint. The scanning process generally takes multiple passes and the scanner must adopt the simultaneous focus of a 3D modeler, photographer and sculptor. In my design process, I scanned each subject (facial profile); however, it may be possible with some development that a cost effective rig may enable the subject (facial profile) to self-scan. It is a goal for future development to further close the design and fabrication pipeline for autonomy, privacy and anonymity; this is also in keeping with the secretive traditions of magic; this secrecy becomes a source of literal power.

Fig. 1. Prototype of *The Grayman Device* demonstrated by the author.

After photogrammetry, the 3D asset (facial profile) is edited in a 3D modeling environment; I primarily utilized: *Autodesk Maya*, however, there are open source alternatives. The 3D modeling environment has many advantages especially: previsualization, scalability, 3D modeling, generation/manipulation of photorealistic UV texture maps and opportunities for myopic control of model polygonal topology: controlling the concave and convex features of a facial profile (mask) to custom fit, flush to the surface of the intended user making it blend visually upon observation but also embodying ergonomic design. This strong sense of ergonomics is a critical feature for the eyes; as each profile must align perfectly and as close as possible to the user's eyes; not only is this for comfort but it's to maintain a clear field of vision and eye line without any

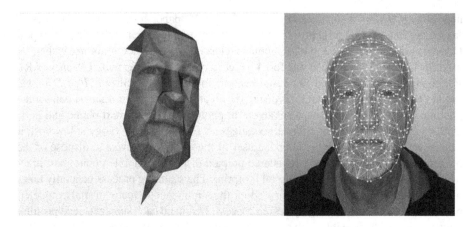

Fig. 2. 3D Photogrammetry mapping biometric facial profile.

obstruction. Before detailing the 3D design pipeline it is important to understand it in contrast to the traditional silicon-based prosthetic design process.

Uncanny Valley. Historically, silicon-based makeup prosthetics, are used as a persuasive disguise for: *magic* and *theatric* purpose but in a modern context also for strategic deception within: law enforcement, military intelligence and spy craft. The technology behind silicon-based photorealistic prosthetics are also used extensively for medical facial prosthetics to mediate facial disfiguration and also in realistic android robotic morphology in the field of social robotics as seen in the android designs of David Hanson of *Hanson Robotics* and Hiroshi Ishiguro's *Geminoid F*. There are multiple issues with silicon-based designs as a solution to deceive *physical* and *digital* surveillance. The design process of silicon molds, on both a technical and creative level toward final application is resource intensive. It requires prosthetic workshop resources: plaster bandages, clay, fiberglass, molding and casting materials; and the physical presence of a team of professionals; which further compromises the privacy loop and anonymity of the user. The cost and time of manufacture is also resource intensive. The application of prosthetics is dependent on the cooperation of others but so too is the prosthetic's removal, so as a wearable it rarely allows for autonomy in the field or rapid deployment-as a consequence the user is mostly constricted to one alternate identity. Highly realistic prosthetic makeup can convincingly dilute, augment or exaggerate a person's features; however, the process of skin texturing and airbrushing may create a compelling result on camera but fall short of physical realism- even the best prosthetics require blending makeup for concealment, the goal of silicon prosthetics is to create a convincing *illusion*; in instances of makeup apparatus the illusion in best cases can be realized, however, this becomes increasingly difficult in the area of: masks, medical prosthesis, bionics and in particular android robotics design as they're subject to Mori's [41] *Uncanny Valley Effect*. Mori [41] theorized that the closer we get to achieving a human-like, photorealistic visage the observer initially experiences a connection or empathy that is quickly followed by an overwhelming sense of eeriness or repulsion. I speculate and it requires further research; but I propose that as aspect of the uncanny valley effect relates to our subconscious, primal survival instinct and hyper vigilance to potential biomimetic, camouflaged predators. Silicon molding and casting reproduces the scale and size of the source face or object; however, 3D design enables an extremely detailed level of virtual scaling and surface sculptural manipulation allowing for a customized fit of a (biometric facial profile) to another face (user) with a minimum material profile and without the need for an extensive workshop. This aspect created a design opportunity to create a series of composite, rapidly interchangeable, highly realistic facial profiles that collectively, seamlessly fit to the user's face and nest together, like a metaphoric matryoshka doll. Upon adopting this design I pursued inspiration from the ancient Chinese magic art of *bian lian* or *face changing*.

Manipulation of the 3D polygonal topology and scaling are essential to creating a series of composite facial profiles (masks) for an effective *Grayman Device*. The author found the preparatory use of 2D photographic manipulation and editing software (*Adobe Photoshop* was utilized) served as a useful diagnostic tool to better match the facial profiles to one another for the nesting process (see Fig. 3). By layering upon a split screen, a designer may easily align facial profiles that are complimentary for nesting; front and most importantly the side facial profile may be tested with transparencies and scaling tools. 2D photographic editing tools are also essential for altering the exported photorealistic texture map and provides the opportunity to color grade the skin tone to the user's own skin tone. I found as with blending makeup on silicon prosthetic pieces; the *illusion* of blending is more convincingly camouflaged by gradually blending the skin tones to the eye lids; this also subtly mitigated the uncanny valley effect placing the *Grayman Device* more in the domain of prosthetic makeup despite being functionally an adaptive, composite mask with a fixed expression. However, a tight, flush shadow and depth-free positioning to the eyes is essential for a user. Key facial features are: the setting of the eyes and nose from the front perspective and the nose and jaw from the side perspective. 3D facial models may be tested in the 3D environment before proceeding with digital fabrication. 3D modeling and animation platforms enable real world, virtual simulations of: light, shadows, movement and angles that may be customized for testing the performance aspect and the target environment (as this environmental awareness is key to camouflage theory as too successful magical illusion) and predicting topology requirements (level of detail) and the predictive distance and angles for defensive camouflage (see Fig. 4). Generally, the *Grayman Device* provides defensive camouflage at a 140-degree angle and at a minimum of 2 m. The initial *Grayman Device* prototypes could retain a loading of (3–5) alternative biometric facial profiles; however with further research and development this is likely to increase. From the perspective of *magic*, the set up time for the device is minimal; however, the focus of this paper is the design of wearable technology not a magic performance instruction or an expose of *bian lian*; one of magic's most guarded secrets and an important part of China's cultural heritage. With any tool of camouflage or defensive technology: training, rehearsal and performance are critical to success; this is especially the case for *bian lian*; the *Grayman Device* for this reason is not a 'magic bullet'; however, camouflage is situational, mission specific and designed for environmental conditions- for example, arctic camouflage is not appropriate for the desert. Although our focus is on counter-surveillance, wearable technology to deceive the biometrics of military grade facial recognition; we must acknowledge that 'weaponized' *magic* is routinely employed in law enforcement, military intelligence and spy craft through the use of disguise and quick-change magic techniques. *Bian Lian* masters often not only change their faces, they instantly change their clothing, head to toe with lighting speed when surrounded by spectators at a short distance.

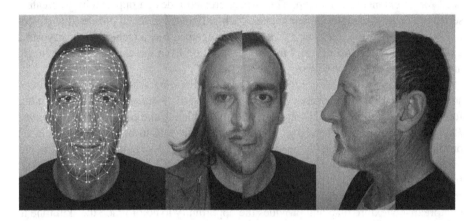

Fig. 3. Split-screen 2D facial profiles utilized as a tool to select nesting facial profiles.

Fig. 4. 3D virtual environment simulation informs digital fabrication whilst isolating requirements to counteract artificial intelligence and facial recognition.

Inspired by modern magic wearable apparatus and medical facial prosthesis design-each subsequent facial profile (mask) adheres using a concealed, low profile neodymium magnet; in extreme instances the entire armature of the *Grayman Device* may be adhered to the face using concealed subdermal neodymium magnetic implants or a simple concealed wearable disposable elastic attachment (as per prototype). Incorporated into the design is a tactile, concealed tab system to the side of the face allowing for decisive selection and instant *attachment* or *detachment* of the device's: *individual* or *collective* biometric facial profiles by the user. Utilizing one of the many mechanical, wearable techniques of *bian lian*, physics and in general misdirection psychology and performance of modern magic, each facial profile is built to accommodate a magician's *pull* (a manual, retractable hidden pulley system) evading physical and digital surveillance (including higher frame rates); as in magic, 'the hand is quicker than the eye', which is essentially the skilled magician's manipulation of an exploitable neurological 'blind spot'. As each biometric facial profile (mask) retracts; they retreat into a concealed tailored pocket; a wearable utility feature commonly employed by magician's referred to as a magician's *Topit*. Although, initial *Grayman Device* rapid prototypes were constructed utilizing cardstock; working the concept closer to traditional *bian lian*; it is possible to use heat transferable printer ready photographic sheets which transfer the 3D asset's exported photographic texture map as a stencil which may be adhered to matte silk material; maintaining the thin profile of paper but conforming to *bian lian* master's traditional use of silk. The silk may be hardened and molded into the facial form of the user using starch or other textile hardening formulas.

Further Development - Grayman Project. As the creator and designer of the *Grayman Device*; the author, at the initial stage of creation of the first rapid prototypes, in realization of the concept; utilized 3D photogrammetric scans of (3) voluntary subjects; whose biometric facial profiles as physically manifest 3D assets were incorporated in the nested device- utilizing the concept of multiple decoy identities. Clearly, there are ethical implications for using another's biometric facial profile to deceive physical and digital surveillance. However, the *Grayman Device* is the foundation for what the author proposes as an ethical design solution to this problem in the companion: *Grayman Project*. The *Grayman Device* to completely realize its potential as an adaptive, biomimetic, defensive camouflage device must be designed as a physical wearable but also toward a digital footprint of anonymity and privacy that incorporates on-demand generative design. Through social network visualization mapping, triangulation of the various digital footprints, facial biometric databases and the increasing sophistication of surveillance technologies occupying physical and digital materiality, it is critical to employ a: strategic and tactical, defensive, adaptive, encrypted information architecture that is cyber security conscious to more effectively combat future advances in human-computer interaction and artificial intelligence. Currently, each successive *Grayman Device*, like many wearable technologies of *magic* are custom made according to the profile template for the end user; as tailor made precision is essential in convincing, repeatable illusion performance. It is the goal of the *Grayman Project* to establish a biometric facial profile database of its own 3D assets. These facial profiles will be procured from as wide a range of age, gender, ethnicity, geo-location and nationality as possible. One possibility may see individual 3D facial assets anonymously uploaded utilizing *Tor* browser with end-to-end military grade encryption to a cloud based server in Iceland with a mirror in Switzerland- selected for their strong privacy laws and jurisdictional advantages of anonymity. The host server subscriptions would utilize crypto currencies; dispersed through a utility like *Dark Wallet*. The database of 3D assets would be used for generative design to create original non-existent facial profiles for use with a *Grayman Device*; rather than reproducing a doppelganger of another's facial profile. As seen in the historical use of political decoys and decoys used in intelligence circles for tactical illusions; it is more than likely that each individual has a lookalike or 'twin'; this is currently being explored by the online community: *Twin Strangers* which provides a platform for users to locate and socially connect with their real world doppelganger. To counteract this possibility, the 3D assets, could be subdivided into their respective features: nose, eyes (left and right)... then drawing upon a compatible pool of 3D facial profile faces; a composite new, purpose specific face may be created through generative design; in effect it's similar to a forensic artist's composite sketch only in 3D space using photogrammetric data. For example, if there were a database of (1000) 3D profiles and (8) component sections the mathematic potential combinations would be vast and with each successive composite nesting facial profile that potentially would be exponential. To illustrate the point, the 3D classic designer combination puzzle: the $(3 \times 3 \times 3)$*Rubik's Cube* has: (43) quintillion possible combinations. The *Grayman Device* combined with the potential combinations of the *Grayman Project's* 3D composite generative designs may provide a wearable, 'cryptographic', camouflage to defend against not only current but *future* advances in digital surveillance, biometric facial recognition and artificial intelligence.

Bian Lian - Illusion Technology. One of the most guarded secrets of *magic* is the ancient Chinese magic art of: *bian lian* or *face changing* [11]. Among China's population of *1.375 Billion* people it is estimated *200* magicians guard the secret of *bian lian*. Originally from *Sichuan Opera*, today *bian lian* is a Chinese, "...second-class national secret"; that is, "...registered with the State Secrets Bureau" [22, 54]. I can disclose the principles for my device are based upon traditional *bian lian*; however, the realization of the device has drawn upon wide influence from other forms of mask magic; one modern example of the art is seen in famed magician Jeff McBride. I utilized *Autodesk Reality Computing* [5] for 3D photogrammetry; then textured the acquired photorealistic, UV texture map and facial topology to a Japanese Pepakura (paper craft) inspired prosthetic. In designing my device I will utilize multiple 3D scanned photorealistic faces (*biomimicry*); these faces will be deployed in reproducible, digitally distributable stencil format for reasons of *fungibility*; the data may also be repurposed to generate random faces; these faces may realize *fungibility* and be, "...materialized in different ways" [18]. A modern 3D photorealistic *bian lian* device to deceive CCTV achieves *fungibility* and as a body-focused, biomimetic, defensive camouflage technology it is companion to Mann's *sousveillance* [36]; as a mask it resides in Shusterman's [51] *somaesthetics* to counter human-computer interaction and facial scanning it achieves what Flanagan and Vega [18] states as, "...(engaging) with flows of information and integrates seamlessly with the physical world – blurring the boundaries between body, clothing and the physical environment, between the real and the artificial" [18]. As a *deception, camouflage* and *decoy*; as its paper based it is what Ahearn and Horan [1] describe as "*burnable*", counteracting digital footprints.

Grayman Device as Bio-digital Artifact of (HCI). In the context of Human Computer Interaction (HCI), *the Grayman* Device is clearly an *input device*, although as itself it is free of onboard computing it is purpose designed to extend human-computer interactive/communicative functionality and designed (or one could say programmed) for a specific outcome from the interaction. Upon the *Grayman Device's* introduction into the human-computer *loop of interaction* it not only mediates and disrupts that interaction; as 3D modeled physible bio-data the sensors of the surveilling computer system's application detect and authenticate physiological biometric identifiers-the computer identifies a 'human'. Furthermore, the computer records the exchange of data visually in the form of video; convincingly enough that a human observer may also recognize a 'human' upon investigation of the recorded video data. In this exchange of information, the device enables the user to conceal their identity but it also allows for the deliberate programing of *biometric data* into an adaptive wearable *input device*. Facial recognition systems utilize multiple algorithms and there are numerous competing applications, however, the technology remains imperfect, in an effort to evolve, research and design in the field is moving toward *three-dimensional facial recognition*. The emerging technology sees the advent of a wider net of biometric identifiers; the *Grayman Device* anticipates this move toward facial recognition focused (HCI) moving toward three-dimensional physiological interactions. Security focused (HCI) and authentication relies on preemptive programming of recognition or validation data; in this sense, similar wearable technologies that extend and are part of this loop of interaction include implantable or wearable devices that utilize: Near Field Communication (NFC), Radio-frequency Identification (RFID) or a QR code; each of these technologies are only realized upon interacting with a computer. In this respect as an *input device*, the *Grayman Device* similarly stores programmed data and communicates it upon interaction and becomes a disruptive/ mediating technology in the *loop of interaction*. 3D photogrammetry itself begins with a process involving sensors and (HCI) in the recording, recognition and controlled design of *biometric data based designs* but like steganography, 3D photogrammetry has further potential applications as a receptacle of data that can inspire innovation in the design and technology that informs wearables and the field of Human Computer Interaction (HCI). The potentiality for 3D based designs as smart objects and expressions of data infused objects that may be digital and material give rise to Mixed Reality (MR) applications, which can lead to the design of our own ubiquitous computer interactions.

3   Conclusions

Inami et al. [25], Dabrowski et al. [10] and Echizen [16] all attempted to use additive light in various frequencies for camouflage; the issue with this is humans exist on the *subtractive color space model* whereas light generating electronics or LEDs exist on the *additive color space model* [28]. In time I foresee my 3D photogrammetry textured, modern, *bian lian* concept evolving and utilizing projection mapping or spatial augmented reality; the *masks* will become a projected surface and appear to a human observer akin to Asai's [4] *OMOTE Project*. Before this occurs, from the perspective of human-computer interaction; the difference in *color space models* (subtractive and additive) must be resolved; I speculate; possibly through the creation of what I would call a nano-based textile that is a: *synthetic biological, biophotonic cell*.

No doubt this advanced technology would be *indistinguishable from magic*.

References

1. Ahearn, F., Horan, E.: How to Disappear: Erase your Digital Footprint, Leave False Trails and Vanish Without a Trace. Lyons Press, Guildford (2010)
2. Amimitzboll, T., Bencard, M., et al.: Clothing. British Museum Publications, London (1991)
3. Aristotle: The Poetics of Aristotle. (trans: Epps PH). The University of North Carolina Press, Chapel Hill (1970)
4. Asai, N.: Omote/ real-time face tracking & projection mapping. Available via VIMEO (2014). http://vimeo.com/103425574. Accessed 5 Sept 2016
5. Autodesk Reality Computing: Autodesk remake- how to take photos for photogrammetry. Available via YOUTUBE (2016). https://www.youtube.com/watch?v=D7Torjkfec4. Accessed 24 May 2016
6. Brignall, T.: The new panopticon: the internet viewed as a structure of social control. Theory Sci. **3**(1), 1527–1558 (2002)
7. Clarke, A.C.: Profiles of the Future. Macmillan, Hampshire (1973)
8. CNN: New technology makes troops invisible. Available via YOUTUBE (2012). https://www.youtube.com/watch?v=Rqi3jpBSyCc. Accessed 5 Sept 2016
9. Coleman, G.: Hacker, Hoaxer, Whistleblower, Spy: The Many Faces of Anonymous. Verso Books, New York (2014)
10. Dabrowski, A., Krombholz, K., Weippl, Edgar R., Echizen, I.: Smart privacy visor: bridging the privacy gap. In: Abramowicz, W. (ed.) BIS 2015. LNBIP, vol. 228, pp. 235–247. Springer, Cham (2015). doi:10.1007/978-3-319-26762-3_21
11. Daimei, F.: Bian lian: a unique art of the sichuan opera. Available via CSS TODAY: China (2013). http://www.csstoday.net/ywpd/Features/69873.html. Accessed 3 Sept 2016
12. Diaconis, P.: statistical problems in ESP research. Science **201**(4351), 131–136 (1978). doi: 10.1126/science.663642
13. Dick, P.K.: A Scanner Darkly. Houghton Mifflin Harcourt, Boston (2011)
14. Dresher, M., Thorp, E.O.: Beat the dealer: a winning strategy for the game of 21. Math. Comput. **18**(86), 331 (1964). doi:10.2307/2003323
15. Dwyer, T.: Convergent Media and Privacy. Palgrave Macmillan, London (2015)
16. Echizen, I.: Privacy protection techniques using differences in human and device sensitivity (2016). http://www.nii.ac.jp/userimg/press_details_20121212.pdf. Accessed 8 Sept 2016
17. Fisher, D.: The War Magician. Berkley Books, New York (1983)
18. Flanagan, Patricia J., Vega, K.F.C.: Future fashion – at the interface. In: Marcus, A. (ed.) DUXU 2013. LNCS, vol. 8012, pp. 48–57. Springer, Heidelberg (2013). doi: 10.1007/978-3-642-39229-0_6
19. Foucault, M.: Discipline and Punish. Pantheon Books, New York (1975)
20. Frazer, J.G.: The Golden Bough, pp. 701–711. Palgrave Macmillan, London (1990)
21. Goldstein, E.B.: Encyclopedia of Perception. SAGE Publications, Thousand Oaks (2009)
22. Guo, X.: Andy lau clears his name in bian lian controversy. Available via CHINA DAILY: China (2006). http://chinadaily.com.cn/china/2006-06/06/contect_610035.htm. Accessed 12 Sept 2016
23. Hall, J.: A New Breed: Satellite Terrorism. Strategic Book Publishing & Rights Agency, Houston (2009)
24. Hughes, D.: Comic Book Movies, pp. 5–23. Virgin Books, London (2003)
25. Inami, M., Kawakami, N., Tachi, S.: Optical camouflage using retro-reflective projection technology. In: Proceedings of the 2nd IEEE/ACM International Symposium on Mixed and Augmented Reality, p. 348. IEEE Computer Society, Washington, DC (2003)

26. Kapsali, V.: Biomimetics and the design of outdoor clothing. In: Williams, J.T. (ed.) Textiles for Cold Weather Apparel, 1st edn., pp. 113–121. Woodhead Publishing, Sawston (2009)
27. Kirkland, K.: Make magic and influence people – kieron kirkland – TEDxExeter. Available via YOUTUBE (2015). https://www.youtube.com/watch?v=kmlPL66vWZk. Accessed 8 Sept 2016
28. Krause, J.: Color for Designers: Ninety-Five Things you Meed to Know When Choosing and Colors for Layouts and Illustrations. Peachpit/New Riders, San Francisco (2014)
29. Kurzweil, R.: The Singularity is Near: When Humans Transcend Biology. Penguin Books, London (2006)
30. Lamont, P.: The First Psychic: The Peculiar Mystery of a Victorian Wizard. Little, Brown & Company, Boston (2005)
31. Lefebvre, H.: La production de l'espace. Editions Anthropos, Paris (1974) (English edition: Lefebvre, H.: The Production of Space (trans: Nicholson-Smith D). Wiley-Blackwell, Hoboken (1991))
32. Machiavelli, N.: The Prince (trans: Bondanella P). Oxford University Press, Oxford (2005)
33. Macknik, S.L., Martinez-Conde, S., Blakesee, S.: Sleights of Mind: What the Neuroscience of Magic Reveals About Our Everyday Deceptions. Picador, London (2011)
34. Mann, S., Ferenbok, J.: New media and the power politics of sousveillance in a surveillance-dominated world. Surveill. Soc. **11**(1/2), 18 (2013)
35. Mann, S., Niedzviecki, H.: Cyborg: Digital Destiny and Human Possibility in the Age of the Wearable Computer. Doubleday Canada, Toronto (2001)
36. Mann, S., Nolan, J., Wellman, B.: Sousveillance: inventing and using wearable computing devices for data collection in surveillance environments. Surveill. Soc. **1**(3), 331–355 (2002)
37. Marx, G.T.: The engineering of social control: the search for the silver bullet. In: Hagan, J., Peterson, R.D. (eds.) Crime and Inequality. Stanford University Press, Stanford, California (1995)
38. Maskelyne, J., Groom, A., Dawes, E.A.: Maskelyne's Book of Magic. Dover Publications, New York (2013)
39. Melanson, D.: Gaming the system: edward thorp and the wearable computer that beat vegas. Available via ENGADGET (2013). https://www.engadget.com/2013/09/18/edward-thorp-father-of-wearable-computing. Accessed 12 Sept 2016
40. Melton, K.H., Wallace, R.: The Official CIA Manual of Trickery and Deception. HarperCollins, New York (2010)
41. Mori, M.: Bukimi no tani (The uncanny valley). Energy **7**, 33–35 (1970)
42. Mori, M., MacDorman, K.F., Kageki, N.: The uncanny valley (from the field). IEEE Robot. Autom. Mag. **19**(2), 98–100 (2012). doi:10.1109/mra.2012.2192811
43. Pepper, J.H.: True History of the Ghost: and All About Metempsychosis (Cambridge Library Collection- Spiritualism and Esoteric Knowledge). Cambridge University Press, Cambridge (2012)
44. Pilkington, M.: Mirage Men: A Journey into Disinformation, Paranoia and UFOs. Constable, London (2010)
45. Randi, J.: The Truth About Uri Geller. Prometheus Books, New York (1982)
46. Robert-Houdin, J.-E.: Confidences d'un prestigitateur. Librarie Nouvelle, Paris (1859). (English edition: Robert-Houdin, J.-E.: King of the Conjurers: Memoirs of Robert-houdin (trans: Mackenzie RS). Porter & Coates, Philadelphia (1859))
47. Sanchez, J.C.: Neuroprosthetics: Principles and Applications. CRC Press, Florida (2015)
48. Scot, R.: The Discoverie of Witchcraft. Dover Publications, New York (1972)
49. Selvaggio, L.: URME surveillance: indiegogo campaign. Available via VIMEO (2014). http://vimeo.com/90828804. Accessed 8 Sept 2016

50. Selvaggio, L.: URME surveillance: analyzing viral face-crime. In: ISEA 2015, Proceedings of the 21st International Symposium on Electronic Art, Simon Fraser University, Vancouver, 14–19 August 2015 (2014)
51. Shusterman, R.: Body Consciousness: A Philosophy of Mindfulness and Somaesthetics. Cambridge University Press, Cambridge (2008)
52. Shusterman, R.: Thinking Through the Body: Essays in Somaesthetics. Cambridge University Press, Cambridge (2012)
53. Siljander, R.P., Fredrickson, D.D.: Fundamentals of Physical Surveillance: A Guide for Uniformed and Plainclothes Personnel. Charles C Thomas Publisher, Springfield (2016)
54. Smith, C.: Chengdu journal: man of a thousand faces planning to share a few. Available via NEW YORK TIMES (2001). http://nytimes.com/2001/02/07/world/Chengdu-journal-man-of-a-thousand-faces-planning-to-share-a-few.html. Accessed 12 Sept 2016
55. Stein, G.: The Encyclopedia of the Paranormal. Prometheus Books, New York (1996)
56. Stone, A.: Fooling Houdini: Magicians, Mentalists, Math Geeks, and the Hidden Powers of the Mind. Harper Paperbacks, New York (2013)
57. Teller: Teller reveals his secrets. Available via SMITHSONIAN (2012). http://www.smithsonianmag.com/arts-culture/teller-reveals-his-secrets-100744801/?no-ist. Accessed 9 Sept 2016
58. Thorp, E.O.: The invention of the first wearable computer. In: Wearable Computers, Digest of Papers. Second International Symposium on Wearable Computers (Cat. No. 98EX215). IEEE Computer Society, Washington, DC (1998). doi:10.1109/iswc.1998.729523
59. Ting, L.: Behind the Incredibles: Skills of the Vagabonds II. Leung Ting Co, Hong Kong (1991)
60. Ting, L.: Skills of the Vagabonds. Leung Ting Co, Hong Kong (1998)
61. Tzu, S.: The Art of War (trans: Giles L). Tuttle Publishing, North Clarendon (2015)
62. Vincent, J.F., Bogatyreva, O.A., Bogatyrev, N.R., Bowyer, A., Pahl, A.K.: Biomimetics: its practice and theory. J. R. Soc. Interface **3**(9), 471–482 (2006). doi:10.1098/rsif.2006.0127

Digital Humanities and Techno-Animism in Wearables: A Case-Study-Based Collaborative Design Framework for Digitally-Ensouled Jewellery

Doros Polydorou[1], Kening Zhu[2(✉)], and Alexis Karkotis[3]

[1] University of Hertfordshire, Hatfield, UK
d.polydorou@herts.ac.uk
[2] City University of Hong Kong, Kowloon Tong, Hong Kong
keninzhu@cityu.edu.hk
[3] Independent Researcher, Lefkosia, Cyprus
Alexis.Karkotis@gmail.com

Abstract. Technology-enhanced jewelleries capable of collecting bio-data are rapidly establishing a presence in the market. Yet there is limited focus on applying core values of traditional jewellery in the making process. In this research, we were inspired by the theory of animism, and investigated the concepts of techno-animism and digital ensoulment of jewellery. By going back to the roots of jewellery design, we investigate the cultural and social importance of the jewellery components and making techniques and propose a set of guidelines that consider data collection as a fundamental component of the creation process. Our findings are based on two research based jewellery-making workshops, along with a technology review and our guidelines aim to provide a set of accessible and actionable suggestions for the design of future technology-enhanced jewellery.

Keywords: Animism · Wearable · Jewellery · Digital ensoulment · Design

1 Introduction

What is observed in the latest wave of technological tools to appear in the global market, is an exponential rise in the number of wearable accessories which can gather and analyse bio-data from the user. As these technological accessories attempt to digitally "ensoul" information – store bio-data inside the physical object – we form an analogy with animistic practices in the sense of attributing a spirit (anima) to inanimate objects and categorize the process as a form of techno-animism. Even though the idea that we are living in a techno-animist world is not something new – theorists from a number of disciplines such as Laurel, Erik Davis, Alfred Gell, Betti Marenko- have discussed variations of this concept extensively in their work [3, 9, 10, 17, 18] there was never a correlation, to our knowledge, between design methodologies and creation techniques rooted in animist principles – and our contemporary designers and makers working on the current generation of techno-animist wearable accessories.

© Springer International Publishing AG 2017
A. Marcus and W. Wang (Eds.): DUXU 2017, Part II, LNCS 10289, pp. 719–736, 2017.
DOI: 10.1007/978-3-319-58637-3_55

Our contribution is in the field of jewellery making and animism, particularly in the practices itself of 'ensoulement.' Whereas 'ensoulement' of things and objects in animist societies is often carried out ceremonially, underlying cultural etiquettes and cosmological worldviews, the process of "data ensoulment" by technological tools such as digital jewellery is approached from a perspective reflecting consumerist principles. It is not so much cultural narrative and design process of the tech tool itself in its entirety which is given special significance but its internal memory card and the information saved within it: photos, videos, documents, notes and passwords. Emerging technologies currently available in the market that gather bio-data such as the 'Fitbit' fitness products and 'Jawbone' bracelets are indicative of this trend [16, 30]. These digital wearables, as with most products that follow technological break-throughs, place emphasis primarily on product design intended for mass production – and not on their perennial use. They are designed to be functional only for very short period of time, perhaps a few years. Moreover they show little concern to core values of traditional jewellery design, which is the focus of our investigation.

In this research, we attempted to re-ground the field by firstly investigating the roots of "data ensoulment" in jewellery and to create a methodology of creating technology enhanced wearable accessories, based on the knowledge of the past. We believe that our research can positively contribute towards the maturity of the practice and to the much needed shift towards a greater balance between core values of craftsmanship from one end, and cutting edge technology on the other, so that they integrate and inform each other in a unified practice. This paper delineates the results of the first part of our research, a dialogue and a workshop with traditional craft jewellery designers, to produce a set of guidelines to drive further our research. 22 designers, ranging from undergraduate students to experienced designers, were invited to create jewellery that "evolve" over the course of time, depending on the data collected from the wearer. The designers were interviewed and invited to talk about their design methodology and thinking process. The results were then used to produce a set of guidelines, which were subsequently contextualized by findings taken from public research.

This research builds further on the work of pioneers in the field such as Jayne Wallace and her collaborators who conducted extensive work on over the years on the concept of "digital jewellery" [34–36] and how they can be used as a communication device. We also acknowledge the work done by Yulia Silina and Hamed Haddadi who created a very detailed and comprehensive survey of current "ensouled jewellery" that are currently in the market [29]. This work differentiates itself by concentrating specifically on shape changing, evolving jewellery. The aim of research is twofold. Firstly, to invite the disciplines working in this field to start re-thinking their approach on the process of ensoulment of technological tools which collect bio-data and secondly to produce a set of easily accessible and actionable guidelines for designers and engineers currently working towards shape-shifting wearable accessories.

In the next section, we will shortly discuss our theoretical grounding, exploring the theories of animism within the discipline of social anthropology. Following up, an outline of existing products and research on digital jewellery will be presented. We will then introduce our workshop process and data collection method. The following section is our main contribution, the presentation of our 10 guidelines supported by the empirical evidences from the workshops. We will further discussed the current wearable technologies and their future usage in digital ensouled jewellery. Finally, the paper concludes by an overview of the author's future plans and the technologies they are currently investigating.

2 Digital Humanities

Tracing the historical evolution of the field Digital Humanities, Schnapp and Presner explained in an article entitled 'Digital Humanities Manifesto 2.0' [33] that there have been two waves. During the first wave the field was known as "Computational Humanities" or "Humanities Computing" and it was expected to provide support to "real" humanists who treated the machineries efficiency as a "servant" in humanities research projects rather than as "its participant enabling of criticism" [25]. We argue that we are experiencing the onset of the second wave. As the outreach of research projects have expanded and the computationally efficiencies are rapidly advancing it has become clear in academic circles that "Computational Humanities", though by nature a hybrid domain, has reached a point where it constitutes a disciplinary field in its own right, with its own orthodoxies, particular professional practices, standards and theories. As Hayles noted [14], renaming the field to "Digital Humanities" was done to acknowledge that computational analysis was part and parcel of research projects ranging from STEM to Social Sciences and Humanities. Thus if the first wave of Digital Humanities is quantitative, focusing on archiving, taxonomizing data, text encoding, markup, scholarly editing and establishing a technological infrastructure, the second wave, quoting Schnapp and Presner, is "qualitative, interpretive, experiential, emotive [and] generative in character." In this wave Digital Humanities are employed in the service of "humanities core methodological strengths" such as "attention to complexity, medium specificity, historical context, analytical depth, critique and interpretation." Digital Humanities 2.0 introduced new disciplinary paradigms, convergent fields, hybrid methodologies, and publications models that are not limited to print culture.

Berry [2] proposes and invites scholars to ride a third wave. In this shift he explains we should explore how knowledge is transformed in the 21st century by assuming a philosophical approach to the subject of computer coding and software and connect these are "to the materiality of this growing digital world." Rather than focus exclusively on digital practices that tend to be conceptualized in terms of ICT skills and competences, in Digital Humanities 3.0 we should reflect upon "the epistemic changes produced by the digital component in the digital humanities in the light of its medium specificity" and explore how the various possibilities that can be presented as computational forms mediate our experience of contemporary culture and society. Therefore, "If code and software are to become objects of research for the humanities and social sciences, including philosophy, we will need to grasp both the ontic and ontological dimensions of computer code." "[We] could say" Berry writes "that third-wave digital humanities points the way in which digital technology highlights the anomalies generated in a humanities research project and which leads to the questioning of the assumptions implicit in such research, e.g. close reading, canon formation, periodization, liberal humanism, etc. Moreover, no matter (pun intended) how immaterial and wireless digital information may be appear or critically argued to be abstracted from matter, it is never independent from material processes, nor abstracted from infrastructural constraints. Bits are both logical and material entities. Blanchette [4] argued that "the historical dialectic between abstraction and implementation is absent from computer scientists' own accounts of their discipline" and cautions that without a mode of analysis addressing the "stuff of computing" we run the risk of resorting to theories addressing embodied subjects interacting "in environments curiously lacking specific material constraints."

In this paper, we contribute to the debate by setting up an experiment which brings together stakeholders from different disciplines and ask them to work together in order to produce a coherent methodology of action. The chosen stakeholders – anthropologists, jewellery designers and engineers - have limited experience working across the disciplines and through this case study our aim is to identify any issues and propose a working methodology of collaboration.

3 Theories of Animism

Encountered in societies around the world animism is the worldview whereby non-human entities, non-organic objects, cultural artefacts and natural formations are embedded with a spiritual essence or soul, as well as a sense of 'secondary agency,' often retaining the capacity to assume personhood and engage in direct dialogue with humans. The process itself of ensoulment can be spontaneous or performed ceremonially. Amongst Amerindian people for example objects are believed to be endowed with the capacity to attract individuals with whom they come into casual contact, while other objects can only become animated through intimate association. Some objects in-turn may be perceived as a source of sorcery or to be endowed with important fertilising powers which increase with the passage of time and with their transmission from generation to generation [26].

Animism is not absent from 'modern societies, nor the West, despite positivist and objectivist discourses – a characteristic of the modern world and Western thought– which insists on the interior differences between humans and non-humans (as well as natural objects) in that only humans possess a meaningful sense of selfhood, whether individual (mind, language, capacity of symbolism) or collective [12]. In a recent article Santos Granero offers several examples of objects treated as if ensouled within the west, from Paganinis violin, to wedding dresses passed down from mothers to their daughters, to cell phones with important data [26]. Objects, artefacts or tools with significance that goes beyond the metaphorical, but touches upon the spiritual. Santos Granero presents the case of Barack Obama who was sworn in as US president using not one but two bibles. The one was the bible used by Abraham Lincoln and the other was the bible used by Martin Luther King because, as Barack Obama explained there was a "connection" between "the sacrifices of these two men" and himself getting elected.

Anthropologist writing on animism since the postmodern turn in the 1980's have considered animism as a relational notion regarding human-environmental relationships [2] with things and objects in a landscape retaining capacity for 'secondary agency'. Strathern proposes the concept of the 'dividual' as opposed to "individual" to describe members in animists societies, which denotes 'a person constituted by relationships [19], material objects included." In her work Strathern draws from Gibsons's Ecological Approach to Visual Perception and his affordance theory where the landscape is not only perceived as spatial and morphological relationships, but filled with latent possibilities for action (*affordance*). "The perceiving of an affordance is" wrote Gibson "a process of perceiving a value-rich ecological object. Any substance, any surface, any layout has some affordance for benefit or injury to someone. Physics may be value-free, but ecology is not" [15]. A stone affords to be sited upon, to be used as a table, as a door holder, to be thrown against a wall. If it's small enough it can be used as a bead on a jewellery, and in recent years, embedded with technologies collecting bio-data.

In recent theories on animism, led by Viveiros de Castro [32], authors call for an ontological reorientation of our theoretical framework that resonates with the natives' point of view. Producing animist accounts premised on non-animist assumptions, these authors argue, will only produce contradictory results. Cartesian metaphysics and concepts such as Nature Vs Culture –characterising the Western Intellectual Tradition– are not capable of analysing the relational ontology of animism or grasp an animist universe where such distinctions are absent [4, 12, 25, 26, 31, 32] "This approach "writes Holdbraad" gives logical priority to the task of conceptualization: what kind of thing must 'things' and 'spirits' be if statements such as 'things are spirits' are to make sense as more than just bizarre oxymorons?" [12].

Whereas symbolism and cultural metaphor are implicit in the relational approach which advances the ideas of multiculturalism, inter-subjectivity and one nature, an animist worldview from an ontological framework is multinatural, perspectival and uni-cultural. Spirits, entities in dreams, rivers, trees, insects, cultural artefacts, animals and humans co-exist symmetrically in one experiential reality as 'persons' clothed with a particular form (nature) and who act according to the perspective accorded by that form in a cosmological performance of alliances amidst warfare [31, 32]. Engaging with animism thus becomes an existential ontology which, following Tim Ingold, sets to "recover that original openness to the world in which the people whom we (that is, western-trained ethnologists) call animist find the meaning of life" [12]. Tim Ingold fuses together ecology and phenomenology to argue that societal culture is in many respects the weaving together of material objects in a process of "emerging involvement" within the "lifeworld" and that life itself is woven together by a web of movements [13].

It is within this theoretical narrative of animism where we place our research for digital jewellery identifying the creative as well as ritual process that needs to be followed in order to induce meaning and the sentiments of craftsmanship to the maker and the wearer.

4   Wearables and Fashion

During the last twenty years, research into technology enhanced jewellery was primarily conducted by technology companies like IBM and Nokia [28]. Most of the commercial available wearables currently fall under the *Wellness and Sports & Fitness* market sectors [6] and these objects focus around the idea of telling the wearer something about their bodily state. Researchers, such as Wallace and Seymour, argue towards the potential computational jewellery however they stress the importance to move away from products that look too much like gadgets [19, 27]. Jayne Wallace did extensive research in the field of "digital jewellery" and she describes her work as an exploration of the potential of jewellery, digital technologies and design artefacts within meaningful spaces in people's lives [5]. In her work, which is both physical and conceptual has laid out the foundation for both design and theory of technology embedded jewellery, primarily investigating the development of digital artefacts and design methods that explore intimate contexts of human experience [36]. Building on the hypothesis that *"If an object embodies elements of personal significance for an individual, attachment with that object may occur. Attachment through form and function will lead to an enduring relationship between individual and object"* [35] Wallace developed three research strands: The exploration of significance and attachment of a jewellery piece through (a) personal use (b) personal symbolism and (c) through the unique communication afforded by the digital function of the jewellery. Both the hypothesis and the research directions exemplify the commonalities between the literature and the principles of Animism.

Yulia Silina, in her paper "New Directions in Jewellery" has done an extensive survey, examining 187 jewellery-like devices that are either already available on the market or at various stages of development and research [28]. In their discussion, they state that "although jewellers understand the market, consumers and historical context of adornment and jewellery use, until recently they were able to create simple on/off devices, missing out on the potential of computational technology. On the other hand engineers and to some extend product designers, often misunderstood the core requirements surrounding fashionable technology" (ibid). Recently however, they are happy to notice an increase in collaboration between engineers and jewellers and they has been an increase in aesthetical and technological pieces evident in pieces such as *Misfit Swarosky Shine*, *Cuff* [29] and *FibBit Tory Burch* [30]. Unlike traditional jewellery pieces, Yulia noted that the majority of the current jewellery-like devices use material which are "but a poor shadow" of precious metals, gemstones, woods and shells. They then continue to identify products such as *Purple* [23] and *Looksee* [17] that clearly demonstrate that it's well worth looking at producing pieces through the eyes of a jeweller (ibid). It is also very interesting to note that they identify the immerse potential of color/odor/temperature and shape shifting material to the new dimension and communication they can offer to technology enhanced jewellery.

A final related discussion point, raised by Yulia, is the one regarding interaction modalities. In order to move away from what we call "gadgets", makers are now attempting to conceal screens and LEDs. This opens up unexplored avenues of novel modalities and this is exactly where our research falls under.

5   Our Approach Towards the Guidelines

The investigation began with an extensive literature review on technologically enhanced jewellery design methodologies (presented in the previous section) and technological trends (presented in a subsequent section) in both the academic and the commercial sectors, followed by two design workshops.

In the beginning, we compiled a questionnaire, which was sent to 22 designers (12 undergraduate students and 10 experienced designers, averagely aging 33.5 years-old, and 19 are females), aimed to get an insight into their background and skills, current work methodologies, past experience with technology and their interest to experiment with new methods and techniques. These questions were partially shaped by the three research strands identified by Wallace and discussed in the previous section. In order to enhance creative spontaneity and freshness we intentionally looked for designers with no extensive experience with technology, as we wanted to avoid bringing in their past methodologies in the creative process.

Subsequently, the designers were asked to attend a full day workshop where they would have to complete a brief by creating prototype designs. As there were a large number of participants, two workshops were organized at two university labs in two days. The designers were introduced to current trends in digital jewellery design and subsequently presented with the workshop brief. The designers had one full day to complete the work and present their prototypes by the end of the day. They had the creative freedom to use any kind of materials they wished. At the end of each workshop, there was a presentation session and a discussion and the whole day was documented through video recordings.

Here we present an outline of the brief:

This research envisions the creation of jewellery that evolve (change characteristics such as shape and color) over the course of time, depending on the data it collects from its wearer. Our aim is to create pieces of jewellery that become personalized over a period of time thus creating a deeper emotional connection with its owner.

The speculative material you are meant to use, will be infused with a technology that will be able to "en-soul" the bio data of its wearer. It will be able to understand a persons' mood, attributes and emotional state (happiness, sadness, excitement, fear, anger) and gradually evolve to reflect the person's life.

As each piece will be slowly changing, no two pieces will be the same. At its final form, the jewellery will by a visualization of certain character traits of an individual and because of this we hope the jewellery will acquire an even greater emotional value and be able to transcend generations.

6   Guidelines for Digitally "Ensouled" Jewellery

The following guidelines were prepared by drawing from the literature review, our grounding theory on Animism, and the 2 workshops. The guidelines are separated into two types – Type A Guidelines which should apply to all types of "ensouled" jewellery and Type B Guidelines – Which offer possibilities of different variations.

Reviewing core Animism principles, we can see that objects: act as a representation of past events (addressed in our guidelines 2, 3, 9, 10), carry social status (addressed in guideline 9 and 10) and that the manner which with they are worn (address in guideline 4). We can also see that there is a great importance in the act of making them (address in guideline 6) and at the moment where they are passed over from one generation to the next (address in guidelines 5 and 6). Furthermore, Tim Ingold, talking about the "lifeworld" it's almost as he is predicting the fusion of the real and the virtual worlds in our contemporary society and the importance it will play in the development of emotions and the self (guideline 7). Finally, by looking at the work of Wallace and Yulia, it is clear to say that the most common pitfall of technology enhanced jewellery is their look and feel. Most of the guidelines are pushing towards traditional jewellery design but this is addressed directly in guidelines 1, 6, 8, 9 and 10.

6.1   Type A: *General* Guidelines

1. Aesthetic Qualities
   "Current technology jewellery forgets the importance of tradition and nostalgia, and even though I usually stay away from traditional designs, in this case I think it's important to go back to the basics."
   Jewellery pieces should adhere to classic jewellery design principles.
   Strategies for designers:

   - Consider attractiveness and aesthetics of traditional jewellery pieces. Designers should pay special attention to craftsmanship and quality of materials.
   - Aesthetic values should be considered by designing for different user groups and offering a choice of diverse material qualities – for example precious or non-precious materials to meet customer satisfaction.

2. Reflecting feelings (or data) on the Jewellery piece
   Create a *code* that translates the data into different configurations, adhering to aesthetic qualities of your target market.
   Figure 1 (a) and (b) show two examples where happiness creates more elongated shape, sadness creates compress, confidence creates smooth surface, and shy for rough surface, and anxiety for ripple.

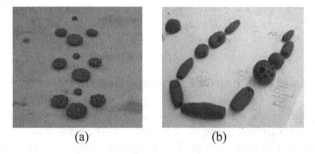

(a)   (b)

Fig. 1. (a) Clay Prototype, 2015, Kelly Santer. (b) Clay Prototype, 2015, Lukas Grewenig

Fig. 2. Clay Prototype, 2015, Kristina Sutcliffee

Fig. 3. Sketch Prototype, 2015, Annette Holmgaard Laugesen

Strategies for Designers:

– Consider a variety of shapes and/or colours that are distinguishable by different types of emotions (or data).
– Distinguish individual emotions derived from different occurrences through a variety of shapes and/or colours so that they can be identified.

3. Transparency of Feelings to the outside world
It is evident from the research that not all designers want to create jewellery that make the feelings of the wearers transparent to everyone. A method needs to be identified that "protects" the wearer from feeling over exposed.
Strategies for Designers:

– Consider finding ways to personalize the meaning to the owner. One way to do this could be to have a modular design that allows different configurations.
Consider a form that allows you to conceal and reveal personal qualities within individual jewellery pieces, like a pendant, bracelet or ring. Not only to think about the placement, but also take into account colour and texture as a means to conceal and reveal. As shown in Fig. 2, Krsitna stated "Outside is pretty and beautiful, inside it has green spikes, reflecting the real emotion."

4. Contact with the Skin
Jewellery should have direct contact with the skin, as this creates a much more intimate relationship with the object.
Strategies for designers:

– Consider bangles, necklaces and rings.
– Biodata can be more easily connected when there is contact with the skin.

5. Pass down generations
With the sketch illustrated in Fig. 3, Annette said "the family is like rings in tree junk, in different colors to represent period in life".
Ancestral knowledge can be accumulated and then re-mapped when passed down a generation.
Strategies for Designers:

– Clearly differentiate where one generation begins and where it ends.

- Differentiating between generations could be one way to build up layers of evolution of the piece.
- Slow down the shape shifting process.
- Changes should occur over a number of years.

6. Involve the owner in the making process
The owner should feel part of the making process of the piece. This offers greatest personalization and expresses individuality. Figure 4 shows an example of the rings breaking apart based on the wearer's life event.
Strategies for Designers:

- Single jewellery breaks and into more pieces, creating multiple individual heirlooms.
- Single jewellery breaks/fractures and re-assembles in different configurations.

7. Collect information from the virtual self
Emotions are expressed in more than one realm with the virtual self – realized through online interactions and social networks – being equally important as physical interactions.
Strategies for designers:

- Consider the possibility to also collect emotional data from social networks.
- Use online data as a way to filter bio data (e.g. identify what caused spikes in emotions).

6.2 Type B - Guidelines for Variations

8. Modular Designs
Through the use of a modular system (pieces of jewellery made to allow user customization) wearers have the flexibility to choose from a range of custom-generated components.
Strategies for designers:

- Offer pieces which be worn alone or as part of a set.
- Each piece should evolve in a different manner to allow differentiation.
Joanna sketched a set of bracelets where each represents wearer's emotion in each day, as shown in Fig. 5. She says, "You could choose which ones you want to wear depending on your mood – You can choose to wear the ones that were generated in a happy day of your life or a sad one."

9. Social Status
By demonstrating a literal depiction of emotions or circumstances, the designer creates pieces that elevate the social status of the wearer, as shown in Fig. 6.
Strategies for Designers:

Fig. 4. Clay Prototype, 2015, Philip Palmen

Fig. 5. Sketch Prototype, 2015, Joanna Garner

- Consider the use of demonstrating emotions in a literal (1 to 1 mapping) to create pieces that demonstrate pure characteristics – i.e. honesty, courage.

"A piece of jewellery can be viewed like a diary of your life." Says Mirka

10. Negative Emotions

Research reveals that in some occurrences, people would like to disclose attributes, which are perceived as not being positive (such as fear, pain and frustration). Figure 7 shows one example sculpture that reflects the anger.

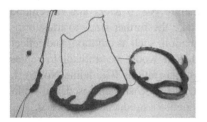

Fig. 6. Clay Prototype, 2015, Mirka Janeckova

Fig. 7. Wood Prototype, 2015, Annette Holmgaard Laugesen

Strategies for Designers:

- Turn negative emotions into powerful shapes.
- Consider the use of segmental structures, which can grow freely in a variety of different directions to create spectacular forms.

Annette states, "What if the jewellery turns beautiful when negative emotions happen?"

7 Further Case-Study

In this section we will analyse two existing digital jewellery (i.e. Fitbit Charge[1] and Ringly Ring[2]), in the context of Animistic Jewellery, by applying the ten guidelines described in the previous sections.

7.1 Fitbit Charge

Fitbit Charge, released in October 2014, is a device that user wears on his/her wrist and tracks a number of statistics in real-time, including steps taken, distance travelled, calories burned, stairs climbed and active minutes throughout the day, while the Charge in the night, tracks sleep. As shown in Fig. 8, the Fitbit Charge is made of a flexible, durable elastomer material similar to that used in many sports watches, and it shows the real-time data on its OLED display, to notify the wearer with light flashing and tactile vibration. In addition, the wearer's information will be shown with more visualization in the online dashboard or the mobile application which synchronize with the wearable Fitbit Charge in real time.

Although the Fitbit Charge could be closely attached to the wearer's skin (Guideline No. 4), we can see that its form did not follow the aesthetics of the traditional jewellery (Guideline No.1), but present a type of industrial product design. With its unified (i.e. non-personalized) shape (Guideline No. 6 & 7) and dis-embodied information, the Fitbit Charge system doesn't take the further steps to transform the bio-data into more personally meaningful information, such as emotion, and reflect on the accessory itself (Guideline No. 2 & 3), thus it would be difficult to represent personal meanings and be passed down through generations (Guideline No. 5). Like most of today's digital gadget, Fitbit Charge could be easily disposed and replaced while newer generations or more advanced competitive products are released.

7.2 Ringly Ring

The Ringly Ring (Fig. 9) is a Bluetooth-enabled notification ring that connects to the wearer's smartphone and keeps them updated with incoming texts, calls, and emails via dimming LEDs and vibrating patterns. The Ringly Ring hides the technologies under the normal form of a ring, keeping the traditional aesthetics of the ring-type jewellery (Guideline No. 1). Compared to the Fitbit Charge which is to be worn on the wrist, the Ringly Ring presents a more closed contact to the wearer with the finger as the tightly wearing position (Guideline No. 4). In addition, the company provides a customization service that allows their customers to design their own shapes and sizes, to create a more personalized accessory (Guideline No. 6). However, falling into the same dilemma as the Fitbit Charge, the Ringly Ring does not elaborate the digital information into a more personalized representation, further limiting its capability of

---

[1] https://www.fitbit.com/hk/charge.

[2] https://ringly.com/.

reflecting emotions and social status, and being passed down through generations (Guideline No. 2, 3, 5, and 9).

Fig. 8. Fitbit Charge. Website: https:// www.fitbit.com/hk/charge

Fig. 9. Rignly Ring. Website: https:// ringly.com/

In summary, we observed the upcoming trend of bringing back and personalizing the aesthetics of traditional jewellery in the design of wearable accessories. However, there is still a long way to achieve the animistic jewellery that could reflect the wearers' personal feelings, both positive and negative, through the intrinsic properties (i.e. color and shape) of the accessories, and further be transferred through generations, partly due to the limitation in the current technologies. In the next section, we will provide our insights and visions on how science and technology could support the design of animistic jewellery.

8   Insights on Technology

While most of emerging wearable technologies have been overlooking rich emotional associations of jewellery [36], we envision that, underlining animist, or rather techno-animist principle the future of digital jewellery, "ensouled" though technologies, will re-emphasize core values such as reflecting social and emotional states. In this section, we will review and discuss the existing wearable technologies, and provide our vision on how the future technology could support the design and manufacturing of digital jewellery as transgenerational life reflection, i.e. ensoulment.

8.1   Viewing Past Experiences

As animism revealed that inanimate objects were often painted in various colors as the reflection of ensoulment, existing digital garment and jewellery have widely adapted color as their main output channel, and this was also reflected in our workshops that colors were used to indicate emotions.

LED is the most popular visual components embedded in fashion items and controlled by digital personal information [1, 7, 30]. Although LED lights were currently common due to its low cost, its emissive nature leads to the reduction of ubiquity [37].

On the other hand, non-emissive display technologies that have recently emerged, such as *e-ink* [8] and *thermochromic paint* [20], are currently being applied in digital garment design. Although the thermochromics ink is currently limited by the size of the controlling system and the variety of the colors, it is predictable that this technology can be embedded into tiny jewellery with future manufacturing technology that could minimize the size of the system. E-ink is one more mature technology has been applied in tablets and current research explores its application in wearables, such as bracelet [6] and shoes [33].

In summary, non-emissive display technology would be more preferred for the digitally-ensouled jewellery in the future, as the surface could be dyed or painted with e-ink or thermochromic ink, and controlled by the minimized technology inside.

8.2 Shaping Past Experiences

While color has been widely adapted in digital fashion design, our workshops revealed that the colors in one piece of jewellery were rarely designed to evolve through generations, but rather being utilized as indicators and associated with particular emotions/activities (guideline 2). Instead, similar to the ancient ensouled statues which were often either manually crafted or naturally weathered into various shapes, the 3D information of the jewellery (e.g. shape, layout, and surface texture) were preferred by our workshop participants for reflecting the accumulated information of the wearer. A few participants commented that when the wearer touches it, he/she can feel the shape and the surface, and empathize the past (guideline 4).

The shape evolvement of the digital jewellery is highly related to the research in shape-changing interface. Hiroshi Ishii envisioned Radical Atoms [14], which "takes a leap beyond tangible interfaces by assuming a hypothetical generation of materials that can change form and appearance dynamically" based on digital information. Under this vision, Yao et al. [39] invented bioLogic, a new shape-changing interface using bacillus subtilis cells that can be actuated by different humidity. The demonstrated application in wearables suggested the possible adoption by the digital ensouled jewellery in our vision. What's more, thin pieces of shape-memory alloy (SMA) have been well adapted in flexible materials, such as fabric and paper, to trigger shape-changing effects in handicraft [40]. Yang et al. [38] invented the 3D printing technique with shape memory polymer, which can be used in wider usage of personal fabrication for digitally-ensouled jewellery in the future.

8.3 Collecting Past Experiences

While the traditional ensouled objects were often crafted manually in the beginning and naturally worn through generations, we envision that the digital "ensouled" jewellery could update itself automatically through sensing the daily life of the wearer. Two types of the input channels were observed in our workshops: actively accumulating the wearer's physiological information; and passively receiving life events from the wearer's digital profile, such as social media.

The most obvious signs of emotional arousal involve changes in the activity of the visceral motor (autonomic) system [24]. As jewellery, such as ring, necklace, bangle, and bracelet, are directly contacted to the human skin (guideline 4), the galvanic skin response (GSR) [11] and the heart/pulse rate [22] can be used to reflect the emotional states of the wearer. The optical-reflection-based pulse sensor has been widely available, and can be integrated into various wearables, such as bracelet and bangle, necklace, and earring.

While emotional states could be directly retrieved from the on-body physiological sensor, more specific life events can inserted by the wearer, e.g. through social network. One common comment from the workshop is that "the wearer would like the privilege to decide which emotion/life event to be reflected from the worn jewellery". Thus, manual input of emotions/events provides a controllable method for digital "ensouled" jewellery. This design suggestion can be supported by a recent development from Google "Project Jacquard" [21], which created a woven material that contains integrated conductive threads that enables the wearer to interact with cloth through touching.

In addition, although most participants proposed real-time update on the digital-ensouled jewellery, a few designers stated the importance of "updating"/"ensouling" the jewellery offline, concerning the issue of privacy leaking. We envision that in the future, there would be a charging station for the wearer to update his/her jewellery which would be made of advanced smart materials.

9 Discussion and Conclusion

In general our workshops revealed that designers desired the technology to be an integral part of the jewellery though not the dominant aspect. The challenge is to create a common platform and language that enables a fluid and clear communication between artists and engineers. This case study presents the working process of a cross discipline collaborative project between a group of designers, anthropologists, craft makers and engineers. The case study produced a set of guidelines for "digitally ensouled" jewellery that have emerged from our workshops. The aim of this study was to a) produce a set of guidelines which can be made available to jewellery designers and engineers working in the field and b) to study and evaluate the work process of multi-disciplinary collaboration. During our workshops we identified the following issues:

- Jewellery makers did not always identify the need of embedding technology in their crafts, nor did they recognise outright the potential applications of tech-jewellery. Many makers expressed the feeling that their hand made crafts are "better" and more "authentic" without technological capabilities.
- Jewellery makers and designers sometimes asked for technologically impossible solutions.
- Engineers often prioritised functional and high level concepts whereas designers could spend a considerable amount on details which contributed on aesthetic qualities rather than functionality. In general designers placed more attention to

aesthetics, placing attention to detail, a feature which was not considered important by engineers.

- Engineers were over-eager to include technical solutions or technological capabilities to all pieces as well as to explore functional purpose in the crafts.
- Designers desired to work along a design concept. Engineers were more fluid with experimenting with technological possibilities often deviating from design briefs and concepts laid out by designers.

The specificity of our workshop was that it explored how "techno-animistic" principles can be applied in traditional jewellery making. Underlining the capacity of technological tools and accessories to digitally store intimate information we formed an analogy with animistic practices observed worldwide of attributing a spirit (anima) to inanimate objects. We highlighted two central aspects of animism that physical objects that are considered ensouled have a cross genealogical life span and that process itself of its production and consumption is, depending on the particular culture at hand, often performed ceremonially. Our workshop examined the process of production of jewellery which have the capacity to be digitally 'ensouled' throughout the users life and which could be passed down generations. We envisioned the creation of jewellery that evolve or change characteristics such as shape and color– over the course of time, depending on the data collected from its wearer. Our aim was to create pieces of jewellery that become personalized, both in form and content- over a period of time thus creating a deeper emotional connection with its owner.

In today's fast paced society we have become accustomed to receive immediate feedback in our communication interactions associating technological progress with faster results. Jewellery pieces, however, can be symbols of status, knowledge and worldviews. Elements might take a lifetime to develop. Our workshop findings suggested that there is a need to dis-associate digitally "ensouled" jewellery from the notion of immediate feedback and instead install to the users who wear them that its production and use is conducted rather ceremonially and that the accumulation of digital information within it will evolve organically and over a large period of time, similar to the way a sacred armband is passed down generations.

Based on these workshop findings, we derived 10 design guidelines for designing digital ensouled jewellery that could reflect the wearer's life and be passed through generations. Our future plan is to develop a prototype of the technology and we invite jewellery designers to apply our guidelines in their work. This will help us better understand how the guidelines work in practice, and provide insights about how they need to be developed further. We anticipate the need to occasionally revisit the guidelines, especially as material technologies continue to evolve.

References

1. Ahde, P., Mikkonen, J.: Hello: bracelets communicating nearby presence of friends. In: Proceedings of PDC 2008. ACM (2008)
2. Berry, D.: The computational turn: thinking about the digital humanities. Cult. Mach. **12**, 1–22 (2011)

3. Bird-David, N.: 'Animism' revisited: personhood, environment, and relational epistemology. Curr. Anthropol. **40**(Supplement), 67–92 (1999)
4. Blanchette, J.-F.: A material history of bits. J. Am. Soc. Inform. Sci. Technol. **62**(6), 1042–1057 (2011)
5. Davis, E.: Techgnosis: Myth, Magic, and Mysticism in the Age of Information. Harmony Books, New York (1998)
6. Descola, P.: Beyond Nature and Culture. University of Chicago Press, Chicago (2013)
7. Digital Jewellery (2016). http://www.digitaljewellery.com/jaynewallace/home.html
8. Eyecatcher: The Smart, Large-Display, Super-Charged Wearable. www.kickstarter.com/projects/eyecatcher-smartband/eyecatcher-the-smart-large-display-super-charged-w
9. Fortmann, J., et al.: Illumee: aesthetic light bracelet as a wearable information display for everyday life. In: Proceedings of UbiComp 2013 Adjunct Publication. ACM (2013)
10. Gelinck, G.H., et al.: Flexible active-matrix displays and shift registers based on solution-processed organic transistors. Nat. Mater. **3**(2), 106–110 (2004)
11. Gell, A.: Technology and magic. Anthropol. Today **4**(2), 6–9 (1988)
12. Gell, A.: The technology of enchantment and enchantment of techonology. In: Coote, J., Shelton, A. (eds.) Anthropology, Art, and Aesthetics, pp. 40–66. Clarendon Press, Oxford (1992)
13. Gruber, M., Moore, P.: Galvanic skin response. Sci. Teach. **64**(9), 52 (1997)
14. Hayles, N.K.: How we think: transforming power and digital technologies. In: Berry, D.M. (ed.) Understanding Digital Humanities, pp. 42–66. Palgrave Macmillan, London (2012)
15. http://store.misfit.com/collections/swarovski-shine
16. https://www.artefactgroup.com/content/work/purple-a-wearable-locket-for-the-21st-century/
17. Ingold, T.: Rethinking the animate, re-animating thought. Ethnos **71**(1), 9–20 (2006)
18. Ishii, H., et al.: Radical atoms: beyond tangible bits, toward transformable materials. Interactions **19**(1), 38–51 (2012)
19. Boddy, J., Lambek, M.: A Companion to the Anthropology of Religion G ….underpinnings of social life Trigger 2003; Whitehouse and Hodder (2010)
20. Jawbon. https://jawbone.com/
21. Kohn, E.: How Forests Think: Toward an Anthropology Beyond the Human. University of California Press, Berkeley (2013)
22. Looksee. http://www.lookseelabs.com/infinitepossibilities
23. Strathern, M.: The Gender of the Gift. University California Press, Berkeley (1988)
24. McCarthy, J., Wright, P., Wallace, J., Dearden, A.: The experience of enchantment in human–computer interaction. Pers. Ubiquit. Comput. **10**(6), 369–378 (2006). Springer
25. McCarty, W.: Attending from and to the machine. Inaugural lecture. Kings College London 2 (2010)
26. Project Jacquard. https://www.google.com/atap/project-jacquard/
27. Pulse sensor. http://pulsesensor.com/
28. Purple: A Locket for the 21st Century
29. Purves, D., Augustine, G.J., Fitzpatrick, D., Katz, L.C., LaMantia, A.S., McNamara, J.O., Williams, S.M.: hysiological Changes Associated with Emotion (2001)
30. Santos-Granero, F. (ed.): The Occult Life of Things: Native Amazonian Theories of Materiality and Personhood. University of Arizona Press, Tucson (2009)
31. Santos-Granero, F.: Introduction: Amerindian constructional views of the world. In: Santos-Granero, F. (ed.) The Occult Life of Things: Native Amazonian Theories of Materiality and Personhood, pp. 1–29. University of Arizona Press, Tucson (2009)
32. Santos-Granero, F.: Ensoulment as social agency: Life and affect at the interface between people and objects. In: Paper Presented at the 112th Annual Meeting of the American Anthropological Association, Chicago (2013)

33. Schnapp, J., Presner, T., Lunenfeld, P.: The digital humanities manifesto 2.0 (2009). Accessed 23 Sep 2012
34. Seymour, S.: Fashionable Technology: The Intersection of Design, Fashion, Science, and Technology. Walter de Gruyter & Co, Berlin (2008)
35. Silina, Y., Haddadi, H.: New directions in jewelry: a close look at emerging trends & developments in jewelry-like wearable devices. In: Proceedings of the 2015 ACM International Symposium on Wearable Computers
36. Swarovski Shine Collection
37. Tory Burch for Fitbit: Tory Burch for Fitbit (2016). http://www.fitbit.com/uk/toryburch
38. de Castro, E.V.: Cosmological deixis and Amerindian perspectivism. J. R. Anthropol. Inst. (N.S.) 4(3), 469–488 (1998)
39. de Castro, E.V.: The transformation of objects into subjects in Amerindian ontologies. In: Presented at the 98th Annual Meeting of the American Anthropological Association, Chicago (1999)
40. Volvorii Timeless. https://www.indiegogo.com/projects/volvorii-timeless/

Wearable Rhythms: Materials in Play

Amy Winters[✉]

Royal College of Art, Kensington Gore, London, SW7 2EU, UK
amy.winters@network.rca.ac.uk
http://www.rainbowwinters.com

Abstract. This paper will consider a future of wearable fluidic materials through a frame of embodied making and imagination. It will be presented through the design, construction, and reflection of a design case study: 'Wearable Rhythms.' This exploration is undertaken by drawing upon the rhythm of natural, elemental materials such as water and air. The aim of the study is to develop material-led design thinking to support soft, haptic, palpable, affective, tactual and computational experimentation. We conclude by considering how the experiment can provide new capabilities, both embodied and speculative, for design researchers to explore the invention of emerging technologies for Wearables.

Keywords: Rhythm · Play · Elemental · Material imagination · Soft robotics · Human-material interaction · Speculative design · Temporal · Currents · Ephemeral

1 Introduction

1.1 Background

The fast-emerging soft robotics movement is shaping a whole set of meta-materials, which are ripe for development in exploring the affective, aesthetic, imaginative and critical dimensions of wearable technology. These morphable machines are uniquely appropriate to the pliable and adaptable nature of textiles; appearing as a soft skin ready to interface with the human body.

Lewis Lab [1] and Whitesides Research Group Whitesides [2] (both at Harvard University), MIT's Soft Active Materials Lab [3], Bristol SoftLab (BRL) [4], AMOLF, Amsterdam [5] and the Faboratory at Purdue, University, Indiana [6] are formulating sensor-triggered artificial muscles, shape-changing fabrics, self-healing materials, and micro-fluidic systems. However, having gained traction across the field of HCI, [7] these developments stay under-explored for the creative, material and practice-led disciplines of fashion, textiles, and jewelry. Thus, fresh opportunities are evolving for material designers to propose alternative approaches and scenarios beyond the classical wearable application of soft exoskeletons. [8] Second Skin, [9] an emergent bio-system for the body is one such example; it is crafted as a synthetic bio-textile, actuated by sweat, and driven by living bacteria. While not a commercially available product, the prototype invites us to reconsider a creation, or even production process, whereby actuators are positioned as 'grown rather than manufactured' [9].

© Springer International Publishing AG 2017
A. Marcus and W. Wang (Eds.): DUXU 2017, Part II, LNCS 10289, pp. 737–746, 2017.
DOI: 10.1007/978-3-319-58637-3_56

This paper, therefore, extends and builds on our previous methodology of an embodied approach [10] to the design of a 'soft machine' - but seen through the lens of speculative design. Shaped through the developing 'material turn' in HCI, [11] this paper will discuss how an embodied engagement with these materials offers the possibility to re-imagine the experiential characteristics of dynamic matter [12].

2   Related Work

2.1   Bodily Dreamscape

Through a bodily 'dreamscape,' we can now consider the relationship between reflective, [13] embodied [10] and tacit [14] knowledge with the conceptual, fictional and speculative.

Previously, we have used an embodied relationship with material to build an inter-active composite textile using tacit textiles knowledge; exploring a visceral engagement with material through a series of small-scale experiments using fluidic and pneumatic actuators to develop expressive textile surfaces [15].

Within HCI literature, scholars place emphasis on the value of an embodied approach to developing novel forms of interaction. Klemmer et al. [16] advocate 'thinking through prototyping' as a more nuanced method of developing the digital-physical blur in tangible computing. Similarly, Wilde et al. advocate the importance of our 'sensory motor skills.' [17] Meanwhile, fashion and textiles theorist Pajaczkowska reflects on our tactile relationship with the imagination; [18] whereby the act of physical making can activate subliminal tendencies, in which, 'neural pathways of kinaesthetic memory serve as pathways for unconscious thought, fantasy and meaning' [18].

Speculative Design can be thought of as adding a complementary dimension to an embodiment approach. Wakkary et al. introduce the term 'Material Speculation' whereby 'Material speculation utilizes physical design artifacts to generate possibilities to reason upon' [19].

In this paper, the design process of 'Wearable Rhythms' is presented to articulate a subjective and reflexive approach towards the process of emerging technology-development. The prototypes are composed of programmable pneumatic and hydraulic channels. It is proposed that through devising this on-body system, a design space is offered for the practitioner to imagine fluidic interaction through a material system – reflecting on flows, blurs, and rhythms.

2.2   Temporal Expressions

Soft programmable materials possess the ability to reframe textiles from a position of static expressions to one of temporal expressions. As these materials grow from stationary to dynamic soft systems, designers translate concepts from the disciplines of animation, music, dance, theatre, and film, into a new context of computational materials. [20] Worbin, for example, argues for textiles to connect with the 'time arts.' [21] This is closely connected with Berzowska's analogy of 'stage production' [22] and Robles and Wiberg's emergent vocabulary for novel interaction approaches, such as 'elements scale, datum, rhythm, transformation, circulation, approach and entrance' [11].

Winkler et al. present 'MetaSolid,' an 'imaginary material' built on the concept of programmable phase-change properties. Oscillating at whim between hard and soft, the concept of MetaSolid suggests fresh user interactions with material such as 'crumbling' or 'tickling' as opposed to purely conventional interactions such as 'folding'. [23] Using a similar example, Rozendaal et al. question how, in the context of domestic products, human interaction could shift for shape-changing materials.

Passive materials are archetypically triggered active through human agency. Kinetic interaction qualities offer a life-like character to passive materials. As these products become actants, our relationship to the product is altered. Rozendaal et al. thus asks us how we might consider, '*collaborating* with these products, as opposed to *using* them.' [24].

Building on the exploration of future flexible interfaces, the design process, and experiments in this paper aim to transform air and water into a form of wearable programmable matter. Can we imagine affective terms to express sensorial and affective material interactions such as seeping, oozing, soaking - The Crying Dress?

These descriptions can offer an enhanced mode of reflecting on and about a wearable interface, thus evoking new experiences, feelings, and interactions. Arguing that rather than compartmentalizing and engineering a wearable experience through pre-scripted procedures, we align with Sengers et al. in using physical computing to design for 'open-ended engagement' [25].

Consequently, how can embodied making inspire new speculative materialities? If reflecting with and through materials, as posed by Schön, [26] and Sennett, [27] can stimulate a distinctive type of thinking, this paper questions what type of bodily experiences and material interactions are open for discovery? How can a fluidic materiality extend the capacity of HCI? Here we take Merleau Ponty's theories on embodiment [25] as viewed through Bachelard's phenomenological approach whereby 'imagination' flourishes in matter [28] and the tools of the designer transform into extensions of imagination.

2.3   Elemental Materials

Drawing insight from elemental matter, we can acknowledge that our experience of the natural elements such as rain, sun, wind and fog is sensual and multisensory. Bachelard conveys the unconscious attraction to water as being due to its 'viscosity' and organic associations [29].

Designers have experimented with these natural materials through performance landscapes. Theatre-designer, Shearing's 'The Weather Machine' [30] devises an immersive environment embedded with light-breezes and sprinkling rain, aiming to create 'gentle, reflective immersive spaces.' [30] While, architects Diller Scofidio + Renfro's Blur Building is formed in its entirety out of mist, as a pure water vapour construction, the architects identify this transient set-up as an atmosphere rather than a building. [31] It is these specific atmospheric qualities which have the potential to evoke sensory and emotional engagement.

Organic materials have been employed within HCI interfaces to offer novel and sensory forms of interaction. Rudomin et al. expand on this notion of incorporating water and air as an interface, with an interactive art installation, 'Fluids' - asserting that this type of 'tactile reference expands the imagination of the user.' [32] Further, Döring et al. introduce their design space of the Ephemeral User Interface (EUI) which captures fleeting moments, for example, soap bubbles as an interaction element. The inherent materiality of translating transient phenomena found in nature such as ice, bubbles, water, fog and air into a user interface is presented as offering playful interaction qualities [33].

3 Wearable Rhythms

3.1 Tactile Experiments

To translate fluid and invisible phenomena such as water, air, and sound into a visible, tactile wearable; early material experiments were devised built on soft robotic structures. These soft elastomer channels and chambers (Pneu-Nets) [34] actuate in response to air pressure. The molds are fabricated through a 3D printer, and then soft silicon (EcoFlex 30) is poured into the cast. Air is pumped through the chambers, directing the soft bodies to bend and twist. This air can be further controlled and programmed through a microcontroller and sensors.

The designed elastomer structures were embedded with various color and texture variations. The internal pattern of the chambers then creep and squirm along giving the suggestion of anthropomorphism. This led us to imagine a wearable prototype with crawling textures. From this it can be proposed that a material surface can seem to be crawling, creeping, sliding, slithering or even wriggling (Fig. 1).

3.2 Prototype: Water Dress

The Water Dress Wearable is based on a similar principle of the soft elastomer channels and chambers from our tactile experiments. This time, however, we have fabricated interconnected macro-fluidic channels, which are programmable and interact with the environment by sensing sound frequency.

Developing soft-material based fluidics enables a shift away from the traditional focus of microfluidics as purely a medical diagnostic application. 'Unconventional' micro-fluidics, as defined by Nawaz et al. [35] locate microfluidics into new contexts such as robotics and electronics and assert that expanding this discipline will inspire creative approaches. The following case-study reflects on the development of our experiment.

Design Development
Microfluidics are traditionally fabricated in rigid materials. A soft fluidic layer was tested not only for potential tactile and wearable properties but also perceptual values; soft materials, as opposed to hard materials, own, according to Karana et al., a quality of 'being *alive*' [12].

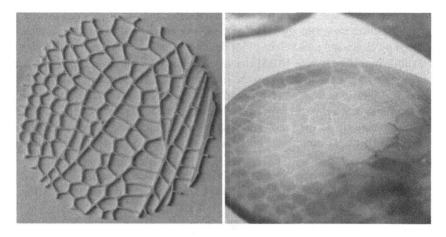

Fig. 2. Initial tests on silicon microfluidic sample. Left: 3D printed ABS channels. Right: red dye liquid flushed through dissolved channels in silicon material. (Color figure online)

Fig. 1. Soft robot design process. Tactile rhythm is discovered through pneumatic actuation.

The following design process is extracted from the analysis of personal experience, using a first-person methodology. Based on a fabrication approach towards microfluidics introduced by Saggiomo and Velders, [36] the microfluidic is fabricated by 3D printing Acrylonitrile butadiene styrene [ABS] channels as a scaffold. Encapsulating the channels within a single layer Polydimethylsiloxane silicone (PDMS) and subsequently dissolving the ABS scaffolds in acetone to reveal hollow channels. This method offered scope for creative development as no specialist laboratory facilities are required. It is also adaptable and quick to fabricate. In the following experiment, EcoFlex silicon replaced PDMS to offer extra elasticity. 3D printing and laser cutting methods were used to fabricate the ABS scaffold (Fig. 2).

For the wearable prototype experiment, we employed water imbued with blue dye; the liquid medium was pumped throughout the dress filling the channels and chambers (Fig. 3).

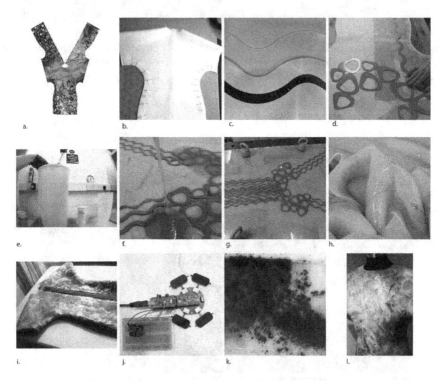

Fig. 3. Making process of the water dress. (a) digital print. (b) toile (c) laser cut ABS (d) constructing ABS pattern (e) silicon mixture (f) casting the mould. (g) cure for four hours. (h) Soak in acetone. (i) final construction of dress. (j) electronics prototyping. (k) blue dye solution. (l) flushing coloured liquid through the dress.

We see this approach as a method to enhance expressivity, colors can be interchanged, and various states of opacity and iridescence can be achieved. By blending these pigments together, the designer can adopt the role of the painter, alchemist or cook rather than the programmer or engineer.

Technical Development

To assemble the macro-fluidic material, channels were laser-cut in ABS and hand-constructed together. The dress was cast in a laser-cut mold with a soft polymer (Eco-flex 00-50), and the ABS channels were dissolved in acetone. The prototype hardware is driven by a micro controller (Arduino Nano) and four controlled micro-pumps and a pump driver (mp6-QuadKEY Bartels). [37] Liquids are pumped through the macro-fluidics using 1.3 mm Tygon tubing (Fig. 3).

Sound is detected via a microphone, specifically a sound frequency sensor detecting bass, mid range, and treble levels. We used the 'audio-shades' development board by MaceTech [38] which is built on the MSGEQ7 chip and an amplified micro-phone. The MSGEQ7 chip splits the signal into seven frequency bands; 63 Hz, 160 Hz, 400 Hz, 1 kHz, 2.5 kHz, 6.25 kHz, and 16 kHz. These bands offer a direct current representation of the amplitude of each band. [39] The bass sounds are low frequency (63–140 Hz), and the higher trebles are (1 kHz–6.25 Hz). Software to power the development board was sourced and adapted from the Rheingold Heavy online tutorial [40] (Fig. 3).

The Water Dress is programmed to detect high-pitched frequencies which subsequently trigger the pigmented ink to flush through the macro-fluidic wearable.

The making of the prototype began to address another notable set of questions. Can we conceive a space of design-led scenarios for technology development? (Fig. 4) Using the concept of wearable macro-fluidics, new types of material interaction start to emerge. Stimuli-responsive hydrogels, [41] for example, have the potential to be embedded into channels, resulting in shape-shifting adaptive surfaces and rendering the garment tunable in shape. Hybrid recipes could extend to other types of pigments experiments such as nano flakes for iridescence, UV sensitive photochromic pigment for chromatic change, or hydrophobic sand for texture transformations.

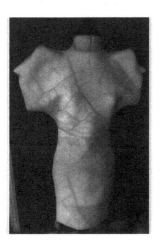

Fig. 4. Left: speculative macro-fluidic dress with pigmented crimson veins. Right: microfluidic vein pattern sample.

4   Future

In the next phase of this project, we wish to develop a soft programmable material platform, using a multi-material 3D printer to fabricate soft material fluidic systems, testing novel material concoctions, which can be programmed inside the elastomer chambers.

A framework to evaluate on the speculative and rich possibilities of Wearable Fluidics will be employed. In devising the evaluation structure, we draw on Döring et al. proposed areas for future research, namely 'Ephemeral Smart Materials' [33]. Using a sensory ethnography approach [42] a workshop of material-led design participants will engage in their own, embodied design of a wearable fluidic system, testing out a set range of programmable elemental materials. Participants within this framework might focus on as Döring et al. states, 'the design and invention of a new material instead of selecting an existing one.' [33] In this fashion, the fabrication and speculative development of novel wearable interfaces, interactions and materials recipes are led through design and user-experience rather than focusing on purely technical constraints.

5   Conclusion

In this paper, we have discussed the opportunities for wearable and imaginative material alchemy. We have presented Wearable Rhythms, a design experiment which has explored the potential use of elemental materials such as water and air to open up design opportunities for Wearables as expressive interactions. To conclude, within an R&D model of soft materials, there are benefits to an embodied and speculative approach. The material designer can be equipped and re-wired with an expanding material imagination 'tool-box.' Rather than calling themselves 'Digital Hackers,' such designers could rebrand themselves as 'Material Hackers.'

Acknowledgments. The author would like to thank Laurence Symonds for support with electronics prototyping and coding.

References

1. Lewis Research Group. http://lewisgroup.seas.harvard.edu
2. Whitesides Research Group: Research > Soft Robotics. http://gmwgroup.harvard.edu/research/
3. MIT SAMs Lab. http://web.mit.edu/zhaox/www/
4. Soft robotics. http://www.brl.ac.uk/researchthemes/softrobotics.aspx
5. Overvelde, B., Albert, D., Oliveri, G., Commandeur, N., Li, Y., Platform, S.: Soft Robotic Matter – AMOLF. https://amolf.nl/research-groups/soft-robotic-matter
6. The Faboratory at Purdue University. https://engineering.purdue.edu/Faboratory/
7. Coelho, M., Zigelbaum, J.: Shape-changing interfaces. Pers. Ubiquit. Comput. **15**, 161–173 (2010)
8. Case Study 2: Bending SPA Design for Hand Rehabilitation Glove. http://softroboticstoolkit.com/book/modeling-soft-pneumatic-actuators/case-studies/study-2

9. Yao, L., Steiner, H., Wang, W., Wang, G., Cheng, C., Ou, J., Ishii, H.: Second skin. In: Proceedings of the 2016 CHI Conference Extended Abstracts on Human Factors in Computing Systems - CHI EA 2016 (2016)
10. Merleau-Ponty, M.: Phenomenology of perception, p. 144. Routledge, London (2002)
11. Robles, E., Wiberg, M.: Texturing the "material turn" in interaction design. In: Proceedings of the Fourth International Conference on Tangible, Embedded, and Embodied Interaction - TEI 2010 (2010)
12. Hekkert, P., Karana, E.: Designing material experience. In: Karana, E., Pedgley, O., Rognoli, V. (eds.) Materials Experience: Fundamentals of Materials and Design, pp. 3–13. Butterworth-Heinemann, Amsterdam (2014)
13. Schön, D.: The Reflective Practitioner, p. 49. Basic Books, New York (1983)
14. Polanyi, M., Sen, A.: The Tacit Dimension, p. 4. University of Chicago Press, Chicago (2009)
15. Winters, A.: Building a soft machine: new modes of expressive surfaces. In: Design, User Experience, and Usability: Technological Contexts, pp. 401–413 (2016)
16. Klemmer, S., Hartmann, B., Takayama, L.: How bodies matter. In: Proceedings of the 6th ACM Conference on Designing Interactive Systems - DIS 2006 (2006)
17. Wilde, D., Tomico, O., Lucero, A., Höök, K., Buur, J.: Embodying embodied design research techniques. Aarhus Ser. Hum. Centered Comput. 1, 4 (2015)
18. Pajaczkowska, C: Making known, the textiles toolbox- psychoanalysis of nine types of textile thinking. In: Jefferies, J., Wood Conroy, D., Clark, H. (eds.) The Handbook of Textile Culture, p. 79. Bloomsbury Academic, London (2015)
19. Wakkary, R., Odom, W., Hauser, S., Hertz, G., Lin, H.: Material Speculation: Actual Artifacts for Critical Inquiry. http://dx.doi.org/10.7146/aahcc.v1i1.21299
20. Vallgårda, A., Winther, M., Mørch, N., Vizer, E.: Temporal form in interaction design. Int. J. Design 9, 1–15 (2015)
21. Worbin, L.: Designing dynamic textile patterns, Göteborg: Chalmers University of Technology, p. 258 (2010)
22. Berzowska, J.: Programming materiality. In: Proceedings of the Sixth International Conference on Tangible, Embedded and Embodied Interaction - TEI 2012 (2012)
23. Winkler, C., Steimle, J., Maes, P.: MetaSolid. In: CHI 2013 Extended Abstracts on Human Factors in Computing Systems on - CHI EA 2013 (2013)
24. Rozendaal, M., Heidingsfelder, M., Kupper, F.: Exploring embodied speculation in participatory design and innovation. In: Proceedings of the 14th Participatory Design Conference on Short Papers, Interactive Exhibitions, Workshops - PDC 2016 (2016)
25. Sengers, P., Boehner, K., Mateas, M., Gay, G.: The disenchantment of affect. Pers. Ubiquit. Comput. 12, 347–358 (2007)
26. Schön, D.: The Reflective Practitioner, p. 79. Basic Books, New York (1983)
27. Sennett, R.: The Craftsman, p. 149. Penguin Books, London (2009)
28. Bachelard, G.: Air and dreams, p. 7. Dallas Institute Publications, Dallas Institute of Humanities and Culture, Dallas (1988)
29. Bachelard, G.: Water and Dreams, p. 105. Pegasus Foundation, Dallas (1983)
30. The Weather Machine. http://www.davidshearing.com/works/the-weather-machine/
31. Blur Building, diller scofidio + renfro. http://www.dsrny.com/projects/blur-building
32. Rudomin, I., Diaz, M., Hernández, B., Rivera, D.: Water, temperature and proximity sensing for a mixed reality art installation. In: Maybury, M., Stock, O., Wahlster, W. (eds.) INTETAIN 2005. LNCS, vol. 3814, pp. 155–163. Springer, Heidelberg (2005). doi:10.1007/11590323_16
33. Döring, T., Sylvester, A., Schmidt, A.: A design space for ephemeral user interfaces. In: Proceedings of the 7th International Conference on Tangible, Embedded and Embodied Interaction - TEI 2013 (2013)

34. Soft Robotics Toolkit. http://softroboticstoolkit.com
35. Nawaz, A., Mao, X., Stratton, Z., Huang, T.: Unconventional microfluidics: expanding the discipline. Lab Chip **13**, 1457 (2013)
36. Saggiomo, V., Velders, A.: Simple 3D printed scaffold-removal method for the fabrication of intricate microfluidic devices. Adv. Sci. **2**, 1500125 (2015)
37. Bartels Mikrotechnik GmbH - Flow Controlled Micropump. http://www.bartels-mikrotechnik.de/content/view/60/102/lang,english/
38. shades_audio_sensor. http://docs.macetech.com/doku.php/shades_audio_sensor
39. Graphic Equalizer Display Filter - MSGEQ7 - COM-10468 - SparkFun Electronics. https://www.sparkfun.com/products/10468
40. MSGEQ7 Arduino Tutorial 01: Getting Started. https://rheingoldheavy.com/msgeq7-arduino-tutorial-01-getting-started/
41. Yoshida, R., Okano, T.: Stimuli-responsive hydrogels and their application to functional materials. In: Ottenbrite, R.M., Park, K., Okano, T. (eds.) Biomedical Applications of Hydrogels Handbook, pp. 19–43. Springer, New York (2010)
42. Pink, S.: Situating sensory ethnography: from academia to intervention. In: Doing Sensory Ethnography, pp. 7–22 (2009)

Author Index

Printed in the United States
By Bookmasters